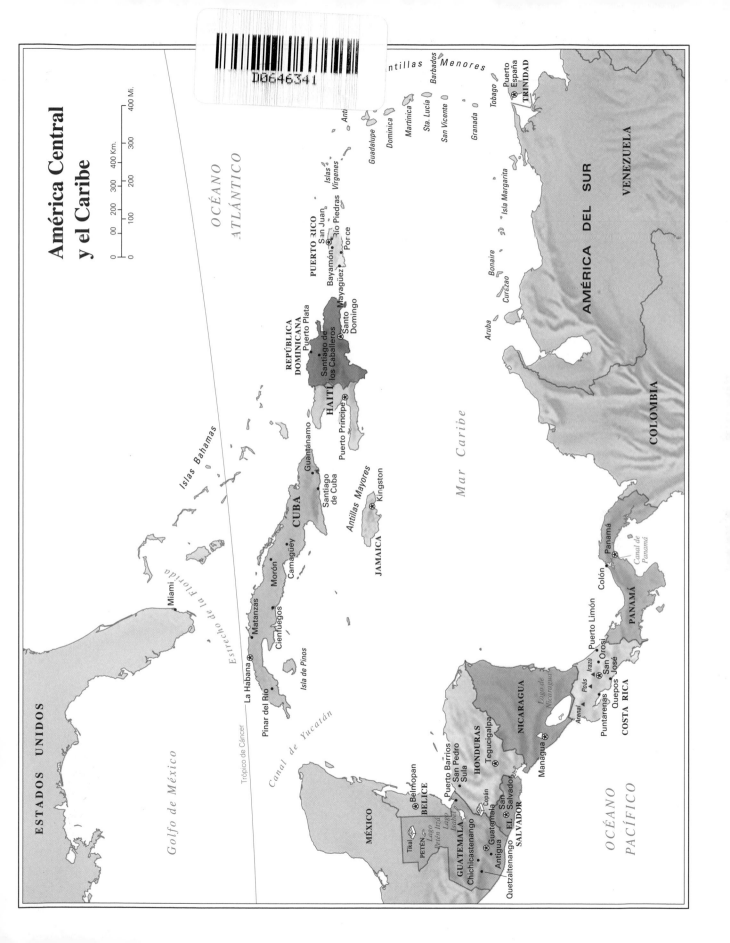

América Central y el Caribe

OCÉANO ATLÁNTICO

OCÉANO PACÍFICO

Golfo de México

Mar Caribe

ESTADOS UNIDOS

MÉXICO

Miami

Islas Bahamas

Trópico de Cáncer

Estrecho de la Florida

Canal de Yucatán

CUBA

La Habana
Pinar del Río
Matanzas
Cienfuegos
Isla de Pinos
Morón
Camagüey
Santiago de Cuba
Guantánamo

Antillas Mayores

JAMAICA
Kingston

HAITÍ
Puerto Príncipe

REPÚBLICA DOMINICANA
Puerto Plata
Santiago de los Caballeros
Santo Domingo

PUERTO RICO
San Juan
Bayamón
Río Piedras
Mayagüez
Ponce

Islas Vírgenes

Anti

Antillas Menores
Barbados
Guadalupe
Dominica
Martinica
Sta. Lucía
San Vicente
Granada
Tobago
Puerto España
TRINIDAD

Aruba
Curazao
Bonaire
Isla Margarita

VENEZUELA

COLOMBIA

AMÉRICA DEL SUR

BELICE
Belmopán
GUATEMALA
Tikal
PETÉN
Lago Petén Itzá
Lago Izabal
Guatemala
Antigua
Chichicastenango
Quetzaltenango
Copán
San
EL SALVADOR
SALVADOR

Puerto Barrios
San Pedro Sula
HONDURAS
Tegucigalpa

NICARAGUA
Managua
Lago de Nicaragua

COSTA RICA
Arenal
Poás
Irazú
San Orosi
San José
Puntarenas
Quepos

PANAMÁ
Puerto Limón
Colón
Panamá
Canal de Panamá

400 Mi.
400 Km.
0 100 200 300 400
0 100 200 300

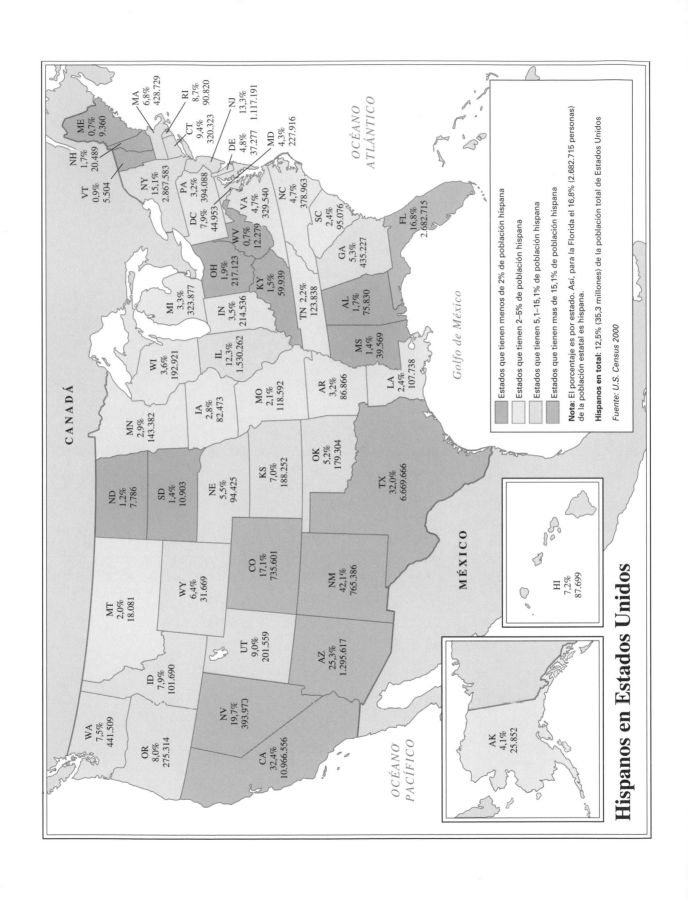

Hispanos en Estados Unidos

Estados que tienen menos de 2% de población hispana

Estados que tienen 2–5% de población hispana

Estados que tienen 5,1–15,1% de población hispana

Estados que tienen más de 15,1% de población hispana

Nota: El porcentaje es por estado. Así, para la Florida el 16,8% (2.682.715 personas) de la población estatal es hispana.

Hispanos en total: 12,5% (35,3 millones) de la población total de Estados Unidos

Fuente: U.S. Census 2000

CANADÁ

MÉXICO

OCÉANO ATLÁNTICO

OCÉANO PACÍFICO

Golfo de México

ME
0,7%
9.360

NH
1,7%
20.489

VT
0,9%
5.504

MA
6,8%
428.729

RI
8,7%
90.820

CT
9,4%
320.323

NJ
13,3%
1.117.191

NY
15,1%
2.867.583

PA
3,2%
394.088

DE
4,8%
37.277

MD
4,3%
227.916

DC
7,9%
44.953

VA
4,7%
329.540

WV
0,7%
12.279

NC
4,7%
378.963

SC
2,4%
95.076

FL
16,8%
2.682.715

GA
5,3%
435.227

OH
1,9%
217.123

MI
3,3%
323.877

IN
3,5%
214.536

KY
1,5%
59.939

TN 2,2%
123.838

AL
1,7%
75.830

MS
1,4%
39.569

LA
2,4%
107.738

WI
3,6%
192.921

IL
12,3%
1.530.262

IA
2,8%
82.473

MO
2,1%
118.592

AR
3,2%
86.866

MN
2,9%
143.382

ND
1,2%
7.786

SD
1,4%
10.903

NE
5,5%
94.425

KS
7,0%
188.252

OK
5,2%
179.304

TX
32,0%
6.669.666

MT
2,0%
18.081

WY
6,4%
31.669

CO
17,1%
735.601

NM
42,1%
765.386

ID
7,9%
101.690

UT
9,0%
201.559

AZ
25,3%
1.295.617

NV
19,7%
393.970

WA
7,5%
441.509

OR
8,0%
275.314

CA
32,4%
10.966.556

HI
7,2%
87.699

AK
4,1%
25.852

NEXOS

INSTRUCTOR'S ANNOTATED EDITION

NEXOS

Sheri Spaine Long
University of Alabama at Birmingham

María Carreira
California State University at Long Beach

Sylvia Madrigal Velasco

Kristin Swanson

HOUGHTON MIFFLIN COMPANY

Boston New York

Publisher: Roland Hernández
Sponsoring Editor: Van Strength
Development Manager: Sharla Zwirek
Senior Development Editor: Sandra Guadano
Editorial Assistant: Erin Kern
Senior Project Editor: Florence Kilgo
Senior Production/Design Coordinator: Sarah Ambrose
Senior Manufacturing Manager: Florence Cadran
Senior Marketing Manager: Tina Crowley Desprez
Associate Marketing Manager: Claudia Martínez

Cover image credit: Joseph Maruska, "La Calavera de Hoy," oil on masonite, 48" × 48", 1994. Courtesy of Patricia Correia Gallery, www.correiagallery.com

Text, photo, and art credits appear on pages 502–504, which constitute an extension of the copyright page.

Printed in the U.S.A.

Library of Congress Catalog Card Number: 2001133303

Student Text ISBN: 0-618-06797-3

Instructor Annotated Edition: 0-618-06798-1

1 2 3 4 5 6 7 8 9—DOW—08 07 06 05 04

INSTRUCTOR'S GUIDE

Program Approach and Philosophy

Nexos is a multi-faceted, multi-skills approach to teaching Spanish. It is a results-oriented program—*Nexos* draws its contextual and communicative theory and practice from the *National Standards for Foreign Language Learning* and then focuses on implementing and achieving these goals within the Spanish classroom. The program carefully integrates the 5Cs of Communication, Culture, Connections, Community, and Comparisons, offering many organized presentational activities and a variety of opportunities to connect, compare, and communicate with local and virtual Spanish-speaking communities.

The *Nexos* program is strongly committed to reminding students and teachers alike that the United States has the third largest Spanish-speaking population in the world. Spanish is truly a second language in the U.S., with extensive commercial, educational, and media applications. In the global world of the 21st century, students will have the opportunity to communicate with Spanish speakers from many different regions and backgrounds, using various types of technology. The *Nexos* program, with its emphasis on linguistic know-how and technical literacy in Spanish, helps prepare students to participate fully in that new environment.

The rich content of *Nexos* is presented succinctly and accessibly, and focuses on topics that are particularly appealing to college students. From a cultural perspective, *Nexos* presents strong coverage of the contributions and influences of the U.S. Latino population and also exposes students to global Hispanic communities rarely covered in other books, such as Equatorial Guinea, Morocco, and the Canary Islands.

In short, *Nexos* provides a realistic and graduated pacing of interesting content, while implementing the National Standards and highlighting the achievements of Spanish-speakers across the United States. The *Nexos* program prepares first-year students to communicate meaningfully in Spanish and to become fully participating members of the global community.

THE *NEXOS* PROGRAM...

◆ **promotes culturally focused, content-based language learning, concentrating on technological themes and content with strong student appeal.**
Nexos explores key subject matter in an analytical and engaging way, such as technology as content (e.g., netiquette), up-to-date core vocabulary for basic proficiency, and diverse cultural content from the Spanish-speaking world in a global context.

◆ **weaves all five goals of the Standards for Foreign Language Learning throughout the program.**
The *Nexos* program is carefully structured around the National Standards, and includes specific *Student Textbook* features to help students achieve these goals. The emphasis on the Standards motivates students through community and interdisciplinary connections, as well as through interesting content and humor. Additionally, instructor annotations point out connections to the National Standards and ways to implement them in the classroom.

◆ **explores Spanish as a second language in the United States.**
The United States is home to the third largest and the wealthiest Spanish-speaking population in the world. Spanish is also the most widely studied language in the United States, and after English, the world over. The *Nexos* program strives to encourage students to reach out to the Spanish that surrounds them and to see the ways in which Spanish and Spanish speakers are helping to shape the society of the 21st century.

◆ **profiles successful U.S. Hispanics in different fields and regions.**
Hispanics are the largest minority in the United States, with a population of more than 38 million. Spanish speakers are a vital part of the American workforce and key players in the worlds of arts, politics, and sports. *Nexos* features the contributions of leading Hispanics from these and other fields. In so doing, the program aims to reinforce cultural pride in Hispanic students, acquaint all students with the work of highly successful U.S. Hispanics, and point students to sources of information on the use of Spanish in the professional fields.

◆ **promotes a positive, real-world and diverse view of the Spanish language and its speakers.**
The *Nexos* program strives to present cultures within the context of a global community, focusing on the shared histories and cultures that interweave through the history of the world's Spanish-speaking countries. *Nexos* also provides unique perspectives and coverage of little-studied areas such as Morocco, Equatorial Guinea, and the Canary Islands.

◆ **references and compares linguistic structures.**
The United States is a microcosm of the entire Spanish-speaking world. At the same time, it is like no other Spanish-speaking country in the world, in that Spanish speakers in the U.S. negotiate meaning in two languages, English and Spanish. Using Spanish appropriately in this context requires not only linguistic and cultural competence, but also a contrastive understanding and analysis of the grammar and linguistics of the two languages. The **¡Fíjate!** notes in *Nexos* take an in-depth look at the linguistic aspects of Spanish, while preparing students for more advanced coursework in Spanish linguistics and pedagogy. Additionally, the **Cómo usarlo** and **Cómo for-**

marlo sections of the grammar explanations guide students to recognize and understand the similarities and differences between the two languages.

◆ **contains a complete grammatical infrastructure.**
The *Nexos* program includes complete and succinct grammar explanations divided into manageable presentations that are immediately followed by real-life, form-based and communicative practice. The program emphasizes teaching language via content, and this includes grammatical explanations in English for those students who prefer a more deductive approach to language learning.

◆ **presents contextualized vocabulary through video focused on student life to enhance student appeal.**
The *Nexos Video* provides language input through an engaging and humorous story line that involves the adventures of six Spanish-speaking students who are studying in Costa Rica. The textbook vocabulary presentations include still photos from the video as well as excerpts from the video dialogue to present new vocabulary items in context. Additionally, grammatical examples drawn from the video are used to enhance the textbook's grammar presentations.

◆ **contains opportunities for language practice and creation in the pre-sentational mode.**
The *Nexos* program's emphasis on rich cultural content and technology provides students with many opportunities to conduct research on a number of chapter-related topics. At least once per chapter, students are encouraged to find information via the Internet or the library and to prepare presentations in order to share their findings with the rest of the class.

◆ **encourages communicative oral exchange in class about a wide variety of subjects.**
The emphasis on content-based learning in *Nexos* means that students are exposed to many topics for discussion. All practice of vocabulary, grammar, and culture moves from structured to open-ended, allowing students many opportunities for personal expression in pairs and small groups.

◆ **promotes life-long language learning through humor in each chapter's cartoon.**
The **Sonrisas** cartoon, found in one of the chapter's grammar sections, is an opportunity for students to relax and enjoy the progress they have made in their knowledge of Spanish. The cartoon humorously recycles chapter grammatical and lexical topics in a way that is both entertaining and thought provoking, and then provides students with the opportunity to discuss the content and expand upon it. The **Sonrisas** sections lead students toward the goal of lifelong learning by encouraging them to enjoy the Spanish language through humor.

◆ **systematically develops reading strategies and process-based writing through progressive practice.**
Students are encouraged to approach the authentic content of the reading selections armed with a variety of reading strategies that are presented in the text chapters. The reading sections guide students through tasks that do not require them to understand every word of the reading passages, and encourage them to focus on getting the main ideas and understanding words from context. The writing sections teach writing through a process approach

and develop writing strategies systematically across the textbook and workbook chapters.

♦ **addresses the intellectual needs of novice language learners by offering analytical activities.**

The *Nexos* program provides students with abundant content that requires them to think—comparing and contrasting information, analyzing structures and content, predicting information and outcomes, and so on. This focus on higher-order thinking skills guides students toward thinking about language and content together, rather than presenting each in isolation. Novice language learners become interested in continued language study because they are engaged in working with thought-provoking content from the very beginning.

♦ **addresses the needs of heritage learners through annotations that provide specific pedagogical and content-related tips at various points throughout the chapter.**

Because heritage language students sometimes lack formal training in Spanish, they benefit from a curriculum that focuses on the development of literacy skills, the expansion of vocabulary, and the acquisition of linguistic forms from the formal registers of Spanish. The *Nexos* program includes instructor annotations aimed at helping instructors meet these goals and engage heritage learners more fully in the introductory Spanish program.

Components of the *Nexos* Program

The *Nexos* program provides a wide array of both student and instructor materials in order to facilitate various learning styles and approaches.

STUDENT COMPONENTS

♦ **Student Textbook**

The *Student Textbook* contains all the information and activities students need for in-class use. It is divided into fourteen chapters that contain vocabulary presentations and activities, grammar presentations and activities, video-related practice, cultural information, reading selections, and writing practice. There are also valuable reference sections at the back of the book, including Spanish-English and English-Spanish glossaries, and verb charts showing the conjugations of different categories of verbs.

♦ **In-Text Audio CD**

The *In-Text Audio CD* contains the listening material for the listening-based grammar activities in the *Student Textbook* that are marked with a listening icon. This Audio CD is packaged with the *Student Textbook*. Instructors may play this in the classroom during class time, or can assign students to do the listening activities outside of class.

♦ **Workbook / Lab Manual**

The *Workbook / Lab Manual* includes out-of-class practice of the material presented in the *Student Textbook*. It is divided into a *Workbook* **(Cuaderno de práctica)**, which focuses on written vocabulary and grammar practice, reading, and writing, and a *Lab Manual* (**Manual de laboratorio**), which focuses on pronunciation and listening comprehension. The *Workbook* contains extra reading practice and additional writing instruction and practice. Every even-numbered *Workbook* chapter presents a new writing strategy and implements it with a writing task. The odd-numbered *Workbook* chapters practice the writing strategy presented in the *Student Textbook*. In addition, each *Workbook* chapter includes a reminder for students about the SMARTHINKING online tutoring available to them.

◆ **Workbook Answer Key**

The answers to all single-response or partially single-response activities in the *Workbook* are provided in the *Workbook Answer Key*. This answer key may be packaged with the *Workbook / Lab Manual* at the instructor's request so that students can check their own work.

◆ **Online Workbook / Lab Manual**

The *Online Workbook / Lab Manual* is an electronic version of the printed *Workbook / Lab Manual*. It allows students to complete the same practice as presented in the print version, but in a computerized format with immediate feedback for many exercises. The audio corresponding to the lab exercises and a direct link to SMARTHINKING online tutoring are also included.

◆ **Audio CD Program**

The *Audio CD Program* contains the pronunciation and listening practice that corresponds to the *Lab Manual* portion of the *Workbook / Lab Manual*. The listening passages on the *Audio CD Program* progress in level of difficulty from simple words and sentences through longer conversations and narratives. The material on the *Audio CD Program* is meant to be used by students outside of class at the language lab or communications center.

◆ *Nexos* **Video**

The *Nexos Video* follows the humorous adventures of six university students in Costa Rica as they cross paths, meet, and (in some cases) fail to meet. Carefully structured to integrate chapter vocabulary and grammar, these segments progress in level of difficulty across the fourteen episodes. Additional cultural material is included after every even-numbered chapter. All activities related to the video segments are included in the *Student Textbook*. Instructors may play the video in class or provide it to students for out-of-class use at the language lab or communications center.

◆ *Nexos* **Multimedia CD-ROM 1.0**

The dual-platform multimedia CD-ROM that accompanies *Nexos* helps students practice each chapter's vocabulary and grammar, and provides immediate feedback so that they can monitor their progress in Spanish. Each chapter includes games, art- and listening-based activities, and the opportunity to record selected responses to help students develop their reading, writing, listening, and speaking skills. As students work, they can access a grammar reference and a Spanish-English glossary and also link directly to SMARTHINKING online tutoring. Students can use the program for extra practice as they study a chapter and for review before quizzes and exams. The CD-ROM also contains clips from the *Nexos Video* with related activities and the corresponding video script. Students can do these activities before or after watching the complete video episodes, which are also included on the CD-ROM.

◆ *Nexos* **Student Website**

The *Student Website* written to accompany *Nexos* has six components:

- **Search Activities:** These activities are designed to give students further practice with chapter vocabulary and grammar while exploring existing Spanish-language websites.
- **ACE Practice Tests:** Each chapter contains a series of chapter-specific exercises designed to help students assess their progress and practice chapter vocabulary and grammar. Feedback on students' answers includes hints to help them understand errors and pinpoint areas in need of review. Students may do some or all of the language activities as they study the chapter or as a review for quizzes and exams.
- **ACE Video Activities:** Included for reinforcement or extra practice are video exercises based on clips from the *Nexos Video*.
- **Cultural Links:** The extra chapter cultural links list additional sites related to the chapter content, and to the **Voces de la comunidad** and **¡Conéctate!** activities.
- **Flashcards:** Flashcards help students learn the chapter's new vocabulary.
- **MP3 Files:** Downloadable MP3 files of the text listening activities allow students to review the activities or prepare them as homework.

◆ **SMARTHINKING™ Online Tutoring for Spanish**

Houghton Mifflin offers students free real-time online tutorial support via state-of-the-art chat technology, feedback tools, and virtual whiteboards. Students interact one-on-one with specially trained Spanish tutors in live sessions during specified times that correspond with peak homework hours. SMARTHINKING also enables students to submit questions to a tutor and receive a reply within 24 hours, or access around-the-clock independent study resources. You can learn more about SMARTHINKING at *http://college.hmco.com/languages/spanish/instructors*.

INSTRUCTOR COMPONENTS

◆ **Instructor's Annotated Edition**

The *Nexos Instructor's Annotated Edition* (*IAE*) provides marginal annotations with classroom tips, ideas for additional activities, and answers to *Student Textbook* activities. It also includes annotations that highlight particular Standards and goal areas and that provide ideas for working with heritage learners in the classroom. The *Instructor's Guide* material at the beginning of the *Instructor's Annotated Edition* provides information about the program, ideas for teaching with *Nexos*, and possible course configurations across varying numbers of semesters or quarters. It also includes the audioscript of the *In-Text Audio CD*, which contains the listening practice for the two listening-based grammar practice activities in each chapter.

◆ **Instructor Website**

The *Instructor Website* includes the audioscript that coordinates with the *Audio CD Program*, the *Videoscript*, PowerPoint slides of grammar charts from the text, overheads, and an integration guide that provides tips for integrating technology in your course.

◆ **Instructor Class Prep / HM Testing CD-ROM**

This CD-ROM contains a variety of instructor resources, including:
- the *Audioscript* for the *Audio CD Program*
- the *Audioscript* for the *In-Text Audio CD*
- the *Lab Manual Answer Key*
- the *Videoscript*
- the complete *Testing Program* (PDFs for printing tests as is and in Word so that instructors can modify the tests, as well as a test generator) and *Testing Program Answer Key*
- sample syllabi
- a lesson plan
- PowerPoint slides of grammar charts from the text
- overhead transparencies

◆ **Instructor's Test Cassette**

This cassette contains the recorded material corresponding to the listening portions of the *Testing Progam*.

◆ **Online Workbook / Lab Manual**

This electronic version of the *Workbook / Lab Manual* includes automatic grading of discrete-answer exercises, and the capability for instructors to review and revise grading decisions, give feedback to students, and grade open exercises individually. Instructors can also customize exercises, as well as create their own exercises and quizzes. Audio files for the lab program and a direct link to SMARTHINKING online tutoring are also included.

Chapter Organization

Nexos is organized into easily recognizable sections that present and practice the new chapter content.

BASIC CHAPTER SECTIONS AND ORDER

◆ The chapter opening spread offers students communicative and cultural objectives for the chapter. It provides cultural information and asks students to test their comprehension, while guiding them to access prior knowledge of the Spanish-speaking countries that will be presented in the chapter.

◆ The **¡Imagínate!** vocabulary sections present vocabulary in context through photos and dialogue taken from the chapter's video segment. Sections of dialogue showing part of the new vocabulary in use provide an instant context for vocabulary acquisition. New thematic vocabulary is immediately practiced through activities that progress from structured to more open-ended. Each chapter has two to three cycles of vocabulary presentation and practice.

◆ The **A ver** video viewing section presents a new video viewing strategy with each chapter. The pre-viewing activities encourage students to activate background knowledge and anticipate content. The viewing activities allow them to practice the new video viewing strategy presented in the chapter, while the post-viewing activities allow them to test their comprehension and move beyond that to oral and written extension activities. Each chapter focuses on a new episode of an ongoing story line featuring six characters, yet each episode is completely self-contained. Even-numbered chapters include an extra cultural presentation that is tied to the cultural content of one of the two previous chapters. Extra practice of this cultural material is included as a final activity in the **A ver** section of even-numbered chapters.

◆ **Voces de la comunidad** features a prominent Hispanic living in the United States and guides students to recognize the diversity and contributions of the U.S. Hispanic community. By recognizing outstanding Hispanics, the *Nexos* program reinforces cultural pride in heritage learners and introduces all students to the accomplishments of highly successful U.S. Hispanics. The **Voces de la comunidad** sections also guide students to explore other sources of information on the use of Spanish in the professional fields. A link to a website containing more information about the featured person is provided, along with a question that pushes students to think more about that person's work and contributions.

◆ **¡Prepárate!** grammar sections include both grammar presentations and practice. Each chapter contains three to four cycles of presentation and practice. The grammar presentations are designed to be functional and succinct, yet complete. They are divided into two sections: **Cómo usarlo**, which focuses more on usage and a conceptual understanding of the grammatical topic, and **Cómo formarlo**, which presents the grammatical forms along with rules about formation and structure. **Lo básico** boxes explain grammatical terms with examples to ensure comprehension of concepts. Additionally, one of the chapter presentations includes a piece of realia from the Spanish-speaking world that allows students to identify the structure as it is used in "the real world." The remaining presentations each feature a video photo and example of the grammatical topic taken from the video. In this way, students view grammar in a real-life context, in addition to learning how to form it and how it is used. The activities that practice each grammar presentation progress from controlled through communicative practice. There are two listening-based grammar activities in each chapter. The audio portion of these activities is contained on the *In-Text Audio CD* that is packaged with the *Student Textbook* and *Instructor's Annotated Edition*.

◆ **Sonrisas** is a cartoon feature that subtly but comically practices a chapter grammatical or lexical topic and encourages students in the goal of lifelong learning of Spanish through humor. **Sonrisas** is intended for students' enjoyment—a lighthearted look at the chapter theme and grammar that is followed by a short activity. In the first four chapters of the book, a **Comprensión** activity tests students' comprehension of the cartoon. Starting with Chapter 5, the activity becomes an extension activity **(Expresión)** that encourages students to express their reactions and to go beyond the basic content of the cartoon.

◆ **Exploraciones culturales** is a cultural section that focuses on the chapter's featured country or countries. It is designed to give students cultural information while challenging them to work with texts that are at a higher level of difficulty. The tasks the students perform have been modified so that they do not need to understand every word of the cultural information in order to complete them. The tasks are both analytical and organizational; often students are asked to complete a Venn diagram, match photos and captions, or match the main idea with a number of texts. A student anno in this section provides the answers to the **¡Adivina!** activity on the chapter opener, which guides students to assessing background knowledge about the featured countries.

◆ The **¡Conéctate!** section refers students to the *Nexos Student Website*, where links are given for students to follow in order to research additional information about the chapter's country or countries. It provides themes for students to explore and encourages them to prepare presentations on their findings to share with their classmates.

◆ The **A leer** reading sections are divided into pre-reading, reading, and post-reading practice. Each section introduces a new reading strategy and guides students to practice it when reading the chapter selection. Starting with Chapter 2, all the readings are authentic texts, and, as with the **Exploraciones culturales**, questions and tasks are simplified so that students do not need to understand every word or sentence of the reading in order to complete them. The reading selections relate to modern topics with the goal of keeping students interested and engaged. Two of the chapters (Chapter 10 and Chapter 14) include literary selections to help begin to prepare students for higher-level courses.

◆ The **A escribir** writing sections appear in the odd-numbered chapters of the *Student Textbook*. (In addition, writing sections in the even-numbered chapters of the *Workbook* introduce new writing strategies. The odd-numbered *Workbook* chapters provide extra practice of the *Student Textbook* writing strategies.) All the writing sections focus on writing as a process, and have students implement specific writing strategies. The tasks build sequentially across the chapters, moving from audience and topic selection, through writing a topic sentence, adding supporting detail, writing paragraphs, and creating transitions between paragraphs. Students progress through pre-writing, writing, and revision activities in each writing section, and create a variety of written pieces, including e-mails, reviews, descriptions, letters, journal entries, and anecdotes.

◆ The end-of-chapter **Vocabulario** is a complete list (with translations) of the chapter active vocabulary. This vocabulary list is included in the end-of-book glossaries, with numbers that refer to the chapter where the item was introduced.

SPECIAL FEATURES

These sections may appear in different places in the chapter, depending upon their content.

◆ The **¡Fíjate!** linguistic notes are designed to raise awareness of issues that are vital to navigating the complex linguistic waters of Spanish, especially as spoken in the U.S. This unique and innovative feature of *Nexos* also aims to provide a foundation for more advanced coursework in Spanish linguistics and pedagogy. **¡Fíjate!** notes include topics such as dialectal variation in the Spanish-speaking world, Spanish-English contact phenomena, and past and present evolutionary developments in the language. The notes are followed by a short **Práctica** that guides students to explore the topic a little further. The **¡Fíjate!** sections often appear in the **¡Imagínate!** vocabulary presentations, but may also be found in the **¡Prepárate!** grammar sections or with the **Exploraciones culturales**.

◆ **¡Compárate!** is a cultural note that focuses on cross-cultural comparisons. It addresses a cultural aspect related to one or more of the featured chapter countries and often provides similar information about the United States. The **¡Compárate!** information is followed by a **Práctica** that guides students to making cross-cultural comparisons and widening their cultural perspectives. The **¡Compárate!** notes are located either in the **¡Imagínate!** section or with the **Exploraciones culturales.**

◆ Student annotations appear in the margin throughout the text, pointing out specific details to students or providing them with extra information related to the topic or content they accompany.

Nexos and the National Standards

Integrating the *Standards for Foreign Language Learning in the 21st Century*, developed by foreign and second language professionals in the late 1990s, is at the core of the *Nexos* philosophy. The Standards advocate an interconnected approach to language learning through five goal areas (Communication, Cultures, Connections, Comparisons, Communities). The "5Cs" serve as the foundation for the *Nexos* program, with the aim of producing culturally and linguistically intelligent students of the Spanish language who are able to:

◆ **Communicate** in the language

◆ Make **cultural and linguistic comparisons**

◆ Achieve a high level of **cultural appreciation**

◆ **Connect** information in *Nexos* with other disciplines and interests beyond the text

◆ Reach out and experience Spanish-speaking **communities** both locally and virtually

As language instructors know, teaching is at its *best* when it weaves the 5Cs simultaneously into classroom presentations, activities, tasks and options beyond the classroom. In other words, rarely does the instructor teach one "C" at a time. Activities throughout the textbook provide opportunities for interpersonal and presentational communication. In addition, the following textbook sections explicitly focus on specific standards:

◆ **¡Compárate!** (Cultures, Comparisons)

◆ **¡Conéctate!** (Connections, Communities)

◆ **Exploraciones culturales** (Cultures, Communication)

- ◆ **¡Fíjate!** (Cultures, Comparisons)
- ◆ **Sonrisas** (Communication, Communities)
- ◆ **Voces de la comunidad** (Communities, Cultures)
- ◆ **Conexión cultural** in **A ver** (Cultures, Comparisons)
- ◆ Chapter opener (Cultures, Connections)

Icons in the IAE margins accompany the annotations that make reference to the Standards and identify by number the particular Standard or Standards practiced.

- ◆ Communication ①
- ◆ Culture ②
- ◆ Connections ③
- ◆ Comparisons ④
- ◆ Communities ⑤

Nexos and Heritage Learners

The *Nexos* program makes an extra effort to help teachers incorporate heritage learners into the first-year Spanish classroom by providing a number of heritage learner annotations in each chapter. These annotations provide specific ideas on how to work with heritage learners to engage them and to develop further the areas where they need more guidance. The *Nexos* heritage learner annotations were written with the following guidelines in mind.

- ◆ Good heritage language instruction is grounded in a solid understanding of the learner's background, abilities, needs, and goals. The designation "heritage language speaker" generally refers to individuals who grew up in a Spanish-speaking home and have some degree of proficiency in Spanish.

- ◆ There are some important differences between heritage language students and traditional students who come to the Spanish classroom with little to no knowledge of the language. Traditional students need to develop basic communicative skills in Spanish through the acquisition of general vocabulary and grammar. By contrast, heritage language students usually possess some degree of fluency in Spanish and have implicit knowledge of Spanish morphosyntax, phonology, and vocabulary.

- ◆ Because heritage language students may have no formal training in Spanish, they benefit from a curriculum that focuses on the development of literacy skills, the expansion of vocabulary, and the acquisition of linguistic forms from the formal registers of Spanish.

- ◆ It is important to bear in mind that heritage language speakers are by no means a homogeneous group. They study Spanish for a variety of reasons: to explore their cultural roots, to communicate with family members, to pursue career interests, to fulfill a language requirement, and so on. They exhibit levels of linguistic proficiency that range from only receptive abilities in a nonstandard variety of Spanish to well-developed literacy skills in formal varieties of the language. Hispanics have their roots in many different parts of the Spanish-speaking world and some are foreign-born, while others may be third or even fourth generation.

◆ Because they may have had limited exposure to formal Spanish and because they may speak a nonstandard dialect of this language, heritage language students tend to feel insecure about their linguistic abilities. Teachers should make every effort to validate students' linguistic and cultural know-how and to foment a classroom environment that respects regional variation, particularly in the areas of vocabulary and pronunciation.

◆ Above all, teachers should exercise patience with students' pace of progress. Years of research and teaching amply demonstrate that it takes a great deal of time and practice to master the rules of standard Spanish.

Sample Syllabi and Teaching with *Nexos*

Nexos is a flexible program that allows you to teach the way you want to teach by providing a complete four-skills presentation of introductory Spanish. Although everyone's class time and teaching styles vary, here are some possible configurations for courses of different lengths and with different meeting times. Following the sample syllabi are tips for assigning material and what to cover in class, depending on the number of contact hours.

TWO-SEMESTER SYLLABUS (3-5 class periods per week)

FIRST SEMESTER		SECOND SEMESTER	
Week 1	Opening spreads / Capítulo 1	Week 1	Capítulo 8
Week 2	Capítulo 1	Week 2	Capítulo 8
Week 3	Capítulo 2	Week 3	Capítulo 9
Week 4	Capítulo 2	Week 4	Capítulo 9
Week 5	Capítulo 3	Week 5	Capítulo 10
Week 6	Capítulo 3 / Midterm Exam	Week 6	Capítulo 10 / Midterm Exam
Week 7	Capítulo 4	Week 7	Capítulo 11
Week 8	Capítulo 4	Week 8	Capítulo 11
Week 9	Capítulo 5	Week 9	Capítulo 12
Week 10	Capítulo 5	Week 10	Capítulo 12
Week 11	Capítulo 6	Week 11	Capítulo 13
Week 12	Capítulo 6	Week 12	Capítulo 13
Week 13	Capítulo 7	Week 13	Capítulo 14
Week 14	Capítulo 7	Week 14	Capítulo 14
Week 15	Review / Final Exam	Week 15	Review / Final Exam

THREE-SEMESTER SYLLABUS (3 class periods per week)

FIRST SEMESTER		SECOND SEMESTER		THIRD SEMESTER	
Week 1	Opening spreads / Capítulo 1	Week 1	Review 1–4	Week 1	Review 5–9
Week 2	Capítulo 1	Week 2	Capítulo 5	Week 2	Capítulo 10
Week 3	Capítulo 1	Week 3	Capítulo 5	Week 3	Capítulo 10
Week 4	Capítulos 1 / 2	Week 4	Capítulos 5 / 6	Week 4	Capítulos 10 / 11
Week 5	Capítulo 2	Week 5	Capítulo 6	Week 5	Capítulo 11
Week 6	Capítulo 2	Week 6	Capítulo 6	Week 6	Capítulo 11
Week 7	Capítulo 2	Week 7	Capítulo 7	Week 7	Capítulo 12
Week 8	Capítulo 3	Week 8	Capítulo 7	Week 8	Capítulo 12
Week 9	Capítulo 3	Week 9	Capítulos 7 / 8	Week 9	Capítulos 12 / 13
Week 10	Capítulo 3	Week 10	Capítulo 8	Week 10	Capítulo 13
Week 11	Capítulos 3 / 4	Week 11	Capítulo 8	Week 11	Capítulo 13
Week 12	Capítulo 4	Week 12	Capítulo 9	Week 12	Capítulo 14
Week 13	Capítulo 4	Week 13	Capítulo 9	Week 13	Capítulo 14
Week 14	Capítulo 4	Week 14	Capítulo 9 / Review	Week 14	Capítulo 14 / Review
Week 15	Review / Final Exam	Week 15	Review / Final Exam	Week 15	Review / Final Exam

THREE-QUARTER SYLLABUS (3 class periods per week)

FIRST QUARTER		SECOND QUARTER		THIRD QUARTER	
Week 1	Opening spreads / Capítulo 1	Week 1	Review 1–4	Week 1	Review 5–9
Week 2	Capítulo 1	Week 2	Capítulo 5	Week 2	Capítulo 10
Week 3	Capítulo 1	Week 3	Capítulos 5 / 6	Week 3	Capítulos 10 / 11
Week 4	Capítulo 2	Week 4	Capítulo 6	Week 4	Capítulo 11
Week 5	Capítulo 2	Week 5	Capítulo 7	Week 5	Capítulo 12
Week 6	Capítulo 3	Week 6	Capítulos 7 / 8	Week 6	Capítulos 12 / 13
Week 7	Capítulo 3	Week 7	Capítulo 8	Week 7	Capítulo 13
Week 8	Capítulo 4	Week 8	Capítulo 9	Week 8	Capítulo 14
Week 9	Capítulo 4	Week 9	Capítulo 9 / Review	Week 9	Capítulo 14 / Review
Week 10	Review / Final Exam	Week 10	Review / Final Exam	Week 10	Review / Final Exam

General Guidelines for Lesson Planning with *Nexos*

Most teachers know what works best in their classroom and what they have time to do in class, given the number of hours and weeks in their semester or quarter. In general, here are some ideas about using the different components of the *Nexos* program in and outside the classroom.

◆ Chapter opener: Have students read the opener and complete the two activities. Review them in class the next day. If preferred, save the ¡**Adivina!** activity until the end of the chapter when you cover the **Exploraciones culturales**.

◆ ¡**Imagínate!** vocabulary sections: Have students review the vocabulary and read the video excerpts before coming to class. Focus class time on vocabulary activities and clarification of vocabulary presentation as needed. Remind students that there is additional vocabulary practice on the website and flashcards. You can also assign the written vocabulary practice in the *Workbook* at this point.

◆ **A ver** video sections: If possible, start the course by showing the video segments in class for the first several chapters. Allow students time to do the pre- and post-viewing activities in class. Help them work with the video episode as needed. Once students become familiar with the video viewing process, continue in class or assign as homework as syllabus permits.

◆ **Voces de la comunidad:** Have students read as homework. Assign follow-up written work as necessary or discuss in class the next day. Have students pursue the featured website as time permits.

◆ ¡**Compárate!** and ¡**Fíjate!** sections: If time permits, allow students to read in pairs or as a group and then do the follow-up activities together. If time is tight, assign as homework and have students do the **Práctica** activity in class the next day.

◆ ¡**Prepárate!** grammar sections: Have students read the grammar explanations as homework. As preferred, assign any listening or written grammar activities as homework or do in class. Do the rest of the activities in class. Focus class time on the grammar activities and discussion of any difficult content. Have students follow up with the additional practice on the website and the CD-ROM. After all the grammar presentations have been introduced, students may also complete the web search activities on the website. You can also assign the written grammar activities in the *Workbook*, along with the chapter listening activities in the *Lab Manual*.

◆ **Sonrisas:** If possible, try to do in class if time permits, so that students can share the humor as a group. If time is tight, assign as homework and have students do the **Comprensión** or **Expresión** activity in class the next day.

◆ **Exploraciones culturales:** Many of these sections are designed to be done in pairs and groups. If necessary, have students review the material before class, but have them complete the reading and task in class the next day. If you did not previously discuss the answers to the ¡**Adivina!** activity on the chapter opener, do so now. The accompanying ¡**Conéctate!** activity is meant to be done outside of class as a research and report assignment.

- **A leer:** Again, this is designed to be done in pairs and groups, but if time is tight, assign as homework the day before. Cover the activities and provide clarification as needed in class the next day. Assign the **A leer** section in the *Workbook* for additional reading practice outside of class. (For even-numbered chapters, assign the **A escribir** section in the *Workbook* as well.)

- **A escribir** (odd-numbered chapters only): In most cases, the pre-writing work in this section should be done, if possible, in class with partners or groups. The actual writing and revision may be done in or out of class as time permits. For odd-numbered chapters, follow up by assigning the **A escribir** section in the *Workbook*.

- **Vocabulario:** Have students review this list as preparation for the chapter test. Only words in this list are considered active vocabulary.

TEACHING TIPS

- Activities are presented in an order that moves from more structured to more open-ended. Once you gain knowledge of your students' backgrounds and linguistic levels, you can choose to focus more on one part of the sequence, as the situation demands.

- When time permits, extend activities or provide follow-up practice where students close the book and focus on the input you provide. In other cases, when possible write cues on the board to focus students away from the book and into the classroom.

- Instructor annotations provide answers to activities as well as ideas for activity follow-up or extension. They suggest ways to present explanations in the classroom and extend explanations in classes where students are ready for more content.

- When possible, call students' attention to the material in student annotations and make sure they are aware of the information contained there.

- When time permits, do some of the listening, video viewing, reading, and writing activities in the classroom so that students gain greater insight into the process approach for accomplishing these tasks. In particular, completing the listening and video activities as a group can help bolster student confidence and comprehension.

In-Text CD Audioscript

This audioscript corresponds to the listening activities in the grammar practice sections of the *Nexos Student Textbook*. The material in this audioscript is contained on the *In-Text Audio CD*.

CAPÍTULO 1

ACTIVIDAD 1 **¿Femenino o masculino?** Listen to the speaker name a series of items and people. First, write down if the item or person is masculine or feminine. Then write the singular noun with its correct definite article. Lastly, write the plural noun with its correct definite article.

MODELO: libro

1. bolígrafo
2. pizarra
3. mesa
4. escritorio
5. amigo
6. estudiante
7. artista
8. ventana

ACTIVIDAD 14 **La fiesta.** Listen to the conversation between Marta and Juan. They are talking about the birthdays and ages of various friends. Write down the age and the birthdate of each person.

[Marta]:	Es una gran fiesta. Celebramos el cumpleaños de varias personas.
[Juan]:	¿Ah, sí? ¿De quién?
[Marta]:	Pues, Miguel tiene veintidós años.
[Juan]:	¿Cuándo es su cumpleaños?
[Marta]:	El 30 de julio.
[Juan]:	Y ¿cuándo es el cumpleaños de Arturo?
[Marta]:	El cumpleaños de Arturo es el 27 de julio.
[Juan]:	¿Ah, sí? Y ¿cuántos años tiene?
[Marta]:	¡Uy! Arturo es viejo. Tiene veinticinco años.
[Juan]:	¿Celebran otros cumpleaños?
[Marta]:	Sí, el cumpleaños de Enrique es el primero de agosto. Cumple veinticuatro años. Y el cumpleaños de Isabel es el cinco de agosto y ella cumple veintiséis años.
[Juan]:	¡Qué maravilla! Nos vamos a divertir.

CAPÍTULO 2

ACTIVIDAD 6 **¿Quién?** You work at a dating service and you have to decide who to introduce to whom. You have some descriptions in writing and some on audio. First read the following descriptions. Then listen to the audio descriptions. For each description you hear, write the person's name next to the description below that is most compatible with that person.

1. Me llamo Andrés. Me gusta mirar televisión. No soy muy activo.
2. Me llamo Marta. Soy muy trabajadora. Estudio todos los días.
3. Yo soy Jorge. Me gusta bailar y cantar. Soy extrovertido.
4. Yo soy Ángela. Visito a mis amigos por las tardes. Me gusta tomar refrescos con ellos y conversar.
5. Me llamo Rudy. Me gusta navegar por Internet. Soy un poco tímido.
6. Me llamo Sara. Me gusta practicar deportes. Soy muy activa.

ACTIVIDAD 8 **Les gusta.** Susana and Alberto like to participate in certain activities together, but prefer to do other things alone. First listen to what they say and decide who likes to do the activity mentioned. After you listen, use the verbs indicated to create a sentence saying who likes to do what. Follow the models.

MODELOS:

Los fines de semana, nos gusta ir a una discoteca a bailar. También bailamos en casa. Camino en el parque los domingos. Me gusta mucho.

1. ¡Susana habla por teléfono todos los días! Habla con los amigos y con la familia.
2. Nos gusta mucho la comida mexicana. Los fines de semana cocinamos comida mexicana en mi casa.
3. ¡Susana saca muchas fotos! Saca fotos muy buenas.
4. A nosotros nos gusta navegar por Internet. ¡Es muy divertido!
5. Alberto toca la guitarra en un café todos los fines de semana. Toca muy bien.

CAPÍTULO 3

ACTIVIDAD 1 **Las preguntas.** What question would you have to ask to produce the response shown? You will hear three questions. Choose the correct one.

1. a. ¿Dónde es la clase de informática?
   b. ¿A qué hora es la clase de informática?
   c. ¿Cuál es la clase de informática?
2. a. ¿A qué hora tienes que ir al centro de computación?
   b. ¿Cuándo tienes que ir al centro de computación?
   c. ¿Adónde tienes que ir para la clase de informática?
3. a. ¿De quién es la computadora portátil?
   b. ¿Quién es tu compañero de cuarto?
   c. ¿De dónde es la computadora portátil?
4. a. ¿Dónde hay que comprar los libros para la clase de informática?
   b. ¿Cuántos libros hay que comprar para la clase de informática?
   c. ¿Cuándo hay que comprar los libros para la clase de informática?
5. a. ¿Por qué estudias informática?
   b. ¿Qué estudias?
   c. ¿Cuándo estudias informática?
6. a. ¿De dónde es la profesora de informática?
   b. ¿Cómo es la profesora de informática?
   c. ¿Quién es la profesora de informática?

ACTIVIDAD 14 **¡Pobre Miguel!** Listen as Miguel describes his schedule to his best friend Cristina. As you listen, write down where he goes on each day of the week. Then use **ir + a** to create seven complete sentences that describe his schedule.

[Miguel]:	Tengo un horario muy difícil este semestre.
[Cristina]:	¿Ah, sí? A ver, cuéntame.
[Miguel]:	Pues, los lunes y los miércoles tengo tres clases: español, biología y química.
[Cristina]:	Uy, biología y química. ¡Qué difícil!
[Miguel]:	Sí, entonces, los martes y los jueves tengo clase de música por la mañana y clase de psicología por la tarde.
[Cristina]:	Ay, ¡hombre! Me canso sólo escuchándote.
[Miguel]:	Espera, todavía no termino. Luego, los jueves por la noche tengo que ir al laboratorio de lenguas para practicar francés.
[Cristina]:	¿Tienes los viernes libres?

[Miguel]:	Uy, no, ¿estás loca? Los viernes y los sábados trabajo en la biblioteca por la tarde. Necesito el dinero para comprar mis libros y cubrir mis otros gastos.
[Cristina]:	Dios mío, hombre, ¿cuándo descansas?
[Miguel]:	Bueno, descanso un poco los domingos. Voy al parque a leer el periódico y a tomar un refresco.
[Cristina]:	No sé cómo vas a sobrevivir este semestre.

CAPÍTULO 4

ACTIVIDAD 10 **¿A qué hora vuelves?** Un amigo te pregunta cuándo vuelven a casa tú, tus amigos y varios miembros de tu familia. Escucha la pregunta y escribe la respuesta correcta en una oración completa. Estudia el modelo.

MODELO: ¿A qué hora vuelves de la clase de computación?

1. ¿A qué hora vuelven tus amigos Mario y Marcos del colegio?
2. ¿A qué hora vuelven ustedes de la fiesta?
3. ¿A qué hora vuelve tu mamá del trabajo?
4. ¿A qué hora vuelven tú y tus compañeros de la universidad?
5. ¿A qué hora vuelve tu papá de la oficina?
6. ¿A qué hora vuelves del gimnasio los sábados?

ACTIVIDAD 15 **¿Cómo?** Escucha a Miriam mientras describe su vida a una amiga. Completa sus oraciones. Escoge el adjetivo más lógico del grupo y conviértelo en un adverbio añadiendo el sufijo **-mente.**

1. Es fácil instalar el programa antivirus.
2. Me gusta chatear por Internet con frecuencia.
3. Ese sitio web es muy lento.
4. Para mí es normal navegar por Internet dos o tres horas por día.
5. Con este módem interno, es rápido hacer una conexión a Internet.
6. Soy muy cuidadosa cuando instalo los programas de software en mi computadora.
7. Tengo tarea todos los días. Es constante.
8. Los domingos descanso, bebo un cafecito, escucho música… todo muy tranquilo.

CAPÍTULO 5

ACTIVIDAD 6 **Necesito…** Para vernos y sentirnos bien, todos tenemos que hacer ciertas cosas antes o después de participar en ciertas actividades. Escucha las descripciones y escoge el dibujo que le corresponde a cada descripción.

MODELO: Necesito peinarme antes de fotografiarme.

a. Necesito ponerme desodorante después de ducharme.
b. Necesito cepillarme los dientes después de comer.
c. Necesito ducharme después de jugar tenis.
d. Necesito afeitarme antes de salir para el trabajo.
e. Necesito lavarme el pelo después de hacer ejercicio.
f. Necesito ponerme maquillaje antes de salir para la fiesta.

ACTIVIDAD 11 **Preparaciones.** La familia González va a una boda y todos están preparándose. Escucha la conversación telefónica de un miembro de la familia y escribe qué está haciendo cada persona mencionada. Usa la forma del modelo.

¡Qué maravilla! ¡Hoy se va a casar mi prima Olga! Todos en la familia están preparándose. Yo ya estoy lista. A ver, ¿qué están haciendo? Pues, mi prima Raquel se está peinando. Ya sabes que pasa horas peinándose. Creo que papá se está afeitando. Se afeita todos los días, no sé por qué. Mamá se está bañando. A ella le falta mucho todavía para estar lista. Mi hermanito se está lavando los dientes. Ese chico tarda mucho en el baño. Mi hermanita se está secando el pelo en su dormitorio. Creo que no le falta mucho para estar lista. ¿Y los abuelos? Los abuelos están en su cuarto. Se están vistiendo. No sé si saben qué hora es. Mis tías se están maquillando. Quiero que todos se apuren. ¡No puedo esperar más! ¡Va a ser muy divertido!

CAPÍTULO 6

ACTIVIDAD 9 **La oficina de correos.** Escucha la conversación entre un señor y una señorita. La primera vez que escuches la conversación, apunta la información que vas a necesitar. Luego, escribe las instrucciones que le da la señorita al señor para llegar a la oficina de correos. Usa los siguientes verbos en tus oraciones.

[Señor]:	Perdone, ¿me puede decir cómo llegar a la oficina de correos?
[Señorita]:	Sí, por supuesto. Mire, primero camine dos cuadras. Luego doble a la derecha.
[Señor]:	Dos cuadras y doblo a la derecha.
[Señorita]:	Sí, precisamente. Luego, siga derecho por una cuadra.
[Señor]:	Derecho por una cuadra.
[Señorita]:	Así es. Después de una cuadra, va a llegar a la calle Central. Entonces, cruce la calle Central.
[Señor]:	Cruzo la calle Central.
[Señorita]:	Sí. Doble a la izquierda, camine otra cuadra y allí va a ver la oficina de correos. Es un edificio pequeño. Está entre una farmacia y una tienda de videos.
[Señor]:	Muchas gracias, señorita.
[Señorita]:	De nada.

ACTIVIDAD 11 **El visitante.** Un visitante pasa el fin de semana en tu casa. Te hace preguntas sobre tu barrio. Contesta sus preguntas en el negativo. Sigue el modelo.

MODELO: ¿Hay alguna estación de trenes en el barrio?

1. ¿Hay algún supermercado en el barrio?
2. ¿Alguien puede decirme cómo llegar al centro comercial?
3. ¿Siempre compras la carne en la Carnicería La Villita?
4. ¿Tienes alguna tienda de ropa preferida?
5. ¿Hay alguna cancha de tenis en el barrio?
6. ¿Hay algo bueno en el cine?

CAPÍTULO 7

ACTIVIDAD 1 **¿Presente o pasado?** Escucha las oraciones e indica si las actividades que se describen ocurren en el presente o el pasado.

1. Javier y Lidia esquían frecuentemente.
2. Susana se entrena todos los días.
3. Yo navegué en rápidos durante las vacaciones.
4. Mi padre pescó casi todos los días el verano pasado.
5. Tú remas muy bien.
6. ¿Jugaste golf esta mañana?
7. Patino sobre hielo en el lago en el invierno.
8. Nadé en el océano el verano pasado.

La reunión. Escucha mientras Cecilia describe qué pasó la semana pasada en la reunión de ex alumnos de su colegio. Primero, completa la tabla con la información necesaria. Luego, escribe oraciones completas según el modelo.

Cecilia y su mejor amiga Rosa Carmen hablan por teléfono sobre la reunión de ex alumnos de su colegio.

[Cecilia]:	¿Y qué pensaste de Marcos?
[Rosa Carmen]:	Ay, me pareció muy contento. Es periodista, ¿verdad?
[Cecilia]:	Sí. Dijo que trabaja para *El Nuevo Herald de Miami*.
[Rosa Carmen]:	¿Y qué le dijiste de tu vida?
[Cecilia]:	Le dije que estoy casada y que tengo tres hijos. ¿Qué le dijiste tú?
[Rosa Carmen]:	Que trabajo como enfermera y que me gusta mucho.
[Cecilia]:	¿Hablaste con José María?
[Rosa Carmen]:	Sí. Dijo que es profesor de matemáticas.
[Cecilia]:	Claro. Siempre fue muy inteligente. ¿Qué tal Laura y Sebastián?
[Rosa Carmen]:	Dijeron que son profesores de lenguas en la misma universidad.
[Cecilia]:	Ay, ¡tantos profesores!
[Rosa Carmen]:	Es raro, ¿verdad? ¿Qué más... ? ¿Hablaste con Leticia?
[Cecilia]:	Sí, un poco. Dijo que ahora vive en Seattle.
[Rosa Carmen]:	Está muy lejos, ¿no?
[Cecilia]:	Sí, pero le gusta. También hablé con Pilar y Antonio.
[Rosa Carmen]:	¿Y qué tal ellos? Siempre fueron muy inteligentes también.
[Cecilia]:	Bueno, dijeron que se casaron en 1998. Ahora los dos son médicos en el mismo hospital.
[Rosa Carmen]:	¿Te dijeron el nombre del hospital? ¿Es el mismo donde trabajo yo?
[Cecilia]:	Ay, no sé. No me dijeron el nombre.

CAPÍTULO 8

ACTIVIDAD 8 **De compras.** Marisela les compra varias prendas de ropa y accesorios a diferentes miembros de su familia y a varias amistades. Escucha mientras ella describe sus compras. Luego, escribe oraciones que expliquen qué le compró a cada quién. Primero estudia el modelo.

MODELO: Escuchas: A mi tía le encantan las blusas bordadas. Cuando estaba de vacaciones en Ecuador, le compré una blusa bordada muy bonita.

1. Busqué un cinturón para mi padre pero por fin le compré una cartera que vi en la tienda de hombres.
2. A mis abuelos les gusta llevar las mismas camisetas. Les compré dos camisetas de la universidad.
3. Fui a la joyería a buscarle unos aretes a mi madre, pero al final decidí que le gustaría más una pulsera de oro.
4. Sé que te gustan los guantes de piel, por eso te compré unos negros muy bonitos que vi en oferta.
5. Fui a la tienda de ropa para comprarles un regalo a los niños. Por fin les compré unos pantalones cortos para el verano.
6. Como necesitan unos zapatos de tenis, les compré a ustedes unos que vi en la tienda de deportes.

ACTIVIDAD 11 **El almacén Toneti.** Escucha el anuncio sobre Toneti, un almacén grande. Pon una X al lado de cada objeto que se menciona. ¡Ojo! Asegúrate de que la descripción de cada objeto es la correcta.

Este fin de semana, ¡todo está en oferta en Toneti! ¡Ya tenemos todo lo que necesitas para volver a la escuela! Para los niños, ¡las mochilas más grandes por los precios más bajos! Para toda la familia, ¡los zapatos de tenis en una variedad de colores! ¡Y en los estilos más populares! ¿Los pantalones? ¡Los tenemos para toda la familia! ¡Y son menos caros que en cualquier otra tienda del centro! ¿Necesitas camisetas? ¡Las tenemos todas en oferta! Y son camisetas de la más alta calidad, todas de puro algodón. Todo rebajado, todo en oferta. ¡No te lo pierdas! En Toneti, ¡la tienda de las grandes rebajas!

CAPÍTULO 9

ACTIVIDAD 6 **Los veranos de Chela.** Escucha mientras Chela describe cómo pasaba los veranos cuando era niña. En un papel aparte, haz dos columnas como las siguientes. Mientras escuchas, escribe los verbos en el pretérito en la primera columna y los verbos en el imperfecto en la segunda columna.

Cuando yo era chiquita, visitaba a mis abuelos todos los veranos. Me encantaba visitarlos porque vivían en un pueblito lindo en las montañas. Un verano fuimos a visitarlos mi hermana y yo. Mi hermana llevó su computadora. Mis abuelos se sorprendieron porque pensaban que ella no necesitaba una computadora en las montañas. Ese verano, mis abuelos y yo nos levantábamos muy temprano, desayunábamos e íbamos a dar una vuelta por el centro. Pero mi hermana se quedaba en casa, jugando en la computadora. Un día llegamos a casa después de hacer las compras y vimos que mi hermana estaba muy triste. ¡Su computadora no funcionaba! Al siguiente día, todos salimos juntos a disfrutar de la vida en el pueblo. Mi hermana nos acompañó por primera vez. Le gustó tanto que jamás usó la computadora el resto del verano.

ACTIVIDAD 10 **A la hora de comer.** Es la hora de comer en casa de Emilia Gutiérrez. La señora Gutiérrez le da instrucciones a Emilia. Escucha lo que le dice y escoge la frase que mejor complete sus instrucciones.

1. Tu abuela quiere una taza de café.
2. Necesito el azúcar.
3. La sal y la pimienta están en la cocina y tu padre las necesita.
4. Tu hermano necesita un cuchillo para la mantequilla.
5. Tus hermanas quieren un vaso de leche.
6. Tu abuelo quiere un té caliente.
7. Todos queremos unas tortillas.
8. No puedo abrir este paquete.

CAPÍTULO 10

ACTIVIDAD 1 **Abuelita quiere que…** Miguelín, Andrea y Arturo son hermanos. Están de visita en casa de su abuelita. Ella quiere que ellos la ayuden con algunos de los quehaceres. Escucha los mandatos que les da a los niños. Completa las siguientes oraciones según el modelo.

Buenos días, niños. Vamos a tener un día estupendo. Vamos a hacer un picnic al lado del río, pero primero tenemos que hacer un poco de limpieza. Miguelín, por favor, dale de comer al gato. Arturo y Andrea, no quiero decírselo dos veces, ¿eh? ¡Tienen que poner todos los juguetes en su lugar! A ver, ¿qué más hay que hacer? Ah, sí, alguien tiene que sacar la basura. No les tengo que recordar que deben hacer las camas, ¿verdad? Además, les voy a hacer una sugerencia: hay que limpiar los baños regularmente. Creo que es todo. Ay, ¡el almuerzo! Andrea, ¿puedes tú preparar el almuerzo? Vamos a salir pronto. ¡Quiero que todos nos divirtamos!

ACTIVIDAD 6 **María, Elena y yo.** Un amigo quiere saber de quién son ciertos muebles y decoraciones. Contesta sus preguntas según el modelo.

MODELO: ¿De quién es esta lámpara?

1. ¿De quién es este espejo?
2. ¿De quién son las cortinas?
3. ¿De quién es esta silla?
4. ¿De quién son estos cuadros?
5. ¿De quién es esta alfombra?
6. ¿De quién es este sillón?

CAPÍTULO 11

ACTIVIDAD 2 **Felipe.** Felipe lleva dos años en Hollywood buscando trabajo como actor. Escucha la descripción de la vida de Felipe. Usando la frase indicada, expresa tu opinión sobre la situación de Felipe.

MODELO: Felipe piensa que quiere ser estrella de cine.

1. Felipe no sabe si debe quedarse en Los Ángeles.
2. Felipe cree que debe trabajar en el teatro.
3. Felipe piensa que tiene que buscar un agente.
4. Felipe no puede conseguir trabajo como actor.
5. Felipe no conoce a nadie en Hollywood.
6. Felipe está perdiendo esperanza.

ACTIVIDAD 8 **El productor ejecutivo.** Escucha al productor ejecutivo de un musical. Él describe lo que va a necesitar para poder montar un musical. Escucha su descripción y escribe lo que él dice que necesita en cada persona que busca.

MODELO: Primero, vamos a necesitar un director. El director tiene que tener mucha experiencia en el teatro.

¡Qué dicha! Recibimos los fondos que necesitamos para montar el musical. Ahora tengo que organizar una lista de todas las personas que voy a necesitar. Primero, vamos a necesitar un director. El director tiene que tener mucha experiencia en el teatro. También voy a necesitar a varios actores. La primera pregunta que les voy a hacer a los actores es: "¿Pueden cantar?" Porque si no pueden cantar, no pueden salir en el musical. Un conductor. Necesitamos un conductor. La música es muy complicada, así que el conductor tiene que saber conducir piezas largas. El set va a ser enorme y el diseñador tiene que ser experto en la historia de la Revolución francesa. El productor va a tener que manejar muchos detalles y muchas personas. El productor es la persona más importante del show. Tiene que ser muy organizado y eficiente.

CAPÍTULO 12

ACTIVIDAD 4 **En el consultorio.** Estás en la sala de espera del consultorio y escuchas a varias personas comentar sobre diferentes personas. Según lo que dicen, ¿conocen o no conocen a las personas que mencionan? Escucha los comentarios y luego marca la respuesta apropiada.

MODELO: ¿Me puedes recomendar un médico que me ayude con mis alergias?

1. No hay ningún paciente que no se queje del dolor.
2. Necesitamos una enfermera que sepa tratar a la gente.
3. Voy a llamar al médico que se especializa en las enfermedades geriátricas.
4. Busco un médico que se especialice en las enfermedades pediátricas.
5. Contrata a una recepcionista que tiene años de experiencia en consultorios.
6. No tengo el teléfono del paciente que necesita un análisis de sangre.

ACTIVIDAD 7 **El Año Nuevo.** Todos resolvemos cambiar de hábitos para el Año Nuevo. Vas a escuchar dos veces unas preguntas sobre tus resoluciones. Di si harás o no harás lo que se pregunta. Escribe las respuestas en oraciones completas. Primero estudia el modelo.

MODELO: ¿Vas a hacer una cita para un chequeo médico?

1. ¿Vas a perder peso este año?
2. ¿Vas a hacer ejercicio cinco veces por semana?
3. ¿Vas a poner más atención en lo que comes?
4. ¿Vas a tener más tiempo para descansar?
5. ¿Vas a salir menos en días de entresemana?
6. ¿Vas a seguir las recomendaciones del médico?
7. ¿Vas a dormir ocho horas al día?
8. ¿Vas a llevar una vida sana desde hoy en adelante?

CAPÍTULO 13

ACTIVIDAD 1 **Antes de la entrevista.** Es el día antes de la entrevista de Anilú y su mamá quiere saber si Anilú se ha preparado bien. Escucha la conversación entre Anilú y su madre. Marca con una X las cosas que Anilú sí ha hecho para prepararse para la entrevista. Luego, escribe una oración para cada cosa que sí ha hecho y una oración para cada cosa que no ha hecho.

[Mamá]:	Hija, ¿ya estás lista para tu entrevista? Ya sabes que es muy importante prepararse antes de ir a una entrevista. Todo está en la preparación.
[Anilú]:	Pues, sí, mamá, he hecho algunas cosas pero no otras.
[Mamá]:	¿Qué has hecho?
[Anilú]:	Pues, he preparado mi currículum vitae y lo he revisado varias veces. Parece estar perfecto.
[Mamá]:	Muy bien, hija. Y ¿la solicitud que te mandaron?
[Anilú]:	Sí, la he completado. Pero no he tenido tiempo para hacer una lista de mis habilidades. Y tampoco he averiguado muy bien cuáles son los requisitos del puesto.
[Mamá]:	Pues, te queda tiempo, no te preocupes. Vas a tener que hacer una presentación, ¿verdad? ¿Has tenido tiempo para practicarla frente al espejo? Eso sí que es muy importante.
[Anilú]:	Sí, mamá, la he practicado varias veces. Me la sé de memoria.
[Mamá]:	Muy bien, hija. Sé que quieres que te ayude a escoger el traje que te vas a poner. Todavía no lo hemos escogido. ¿Por qué no vamos a tu cuarto para hacer una selección?
[Anilú]:	Está bien, mamá, pero primero voy a confirmar la hora de la entrevista.
[Mamá]:	Muy bien, hija. Llámame cuando estés lista y vengo a tu cuarto para ayudarte.

ACTIVIDAD 6 **La clase de ciencias políticas.** Soledad describe su primer año en la universidad. Antes de llegar a la U, no había entendido la importancia de participar en la política del país y del mundo. La clase de ciencias políticas le despertó la conciencia y por eso ella y varios amigos hicieron muchas cosas que nunca habían hecho antes. Escucha a Soledad mientras ella describe su primer año en la U. Escribe una oración que describa lo que ella y sus amigos nunca habían hecho antes. Primero, estudia el modelo.

Cuando llegué a la universidad, tenía dieciocho años y no sabía mucho de la política. Ese año había elecciones presidenciales. Por primera vez voté en elecciones nacionales. No sólo voté, sino que mi compañera de cuarto y yo también contribuimos con dinero y tiempo a la campaña de un candidato político. Tomé una clase de ciencias políticas que me despertó la conciencia. Por primera vez en mi vida, me interesé en la política y la economía global. Para mí en ese momento, las manifestaciones eran cosa de la tele, pero ese primer año en la U, participé en varias manifestaciones contra la globalización y la desigualdad en los países del tercer mundo. Yo y varios amigos que nunca lo habían hecho fuimos voluntarios en el Centro para Mejorar la Economía del Tercer Mundo. Escribí varios ensayos sobre el problema para el periódico universitario. La universidad nos abrió los ojos sobre los problemas globales y la importancia de ser ciudadanos del mundo.

CAPÍTULO 14

ACTIVIDAD 1 **Las recomendaciones.** Quieres viajar a Buenos Aires. Hablas con una agente de viajes de la Agencia Paraíso. Escucha sus recomendaciones y escribe una oración que explique qué te recomendó. Sigue el modelo.

[Agente]:	Muy buenos días, señor. ¿En qué puedo servirle?
[Cliente]:	Sí, pues quiero hacer un viaje a Buenos Aires.
[Agente]:	Muy bien. Sugiero que compre un boleto de ida y vuelta, así le sale más barato.
[Cliente]:	Está bien.
[Agente]:	Estoy seguro de que ya sabe que… es muy importante que llegue al aeropuerto con tres horas de anticipación. Con todo eso de la seguridad, ¿me entiende?
[Cliente]:	Sí, señora.
[Agente]:	Y también les sugiero a todos mis clientes que no lleven más de una maleta. Si lleva más de una, tardan mucho en revisarlas.
[Cliente]:	Gracias por el consejo.
[Agente]:	Es mucho más fácil si factura el equipaje en vez de cargarlo, ¿no cree? Así no tiene que abrir su maleta en el control de seguridad.
[Cliente]:	Me voy a quedar dos semanas. No sé si voy a poder llevar todo lo que necesito en una maleta, pero lo intentaré.
[Agente]:	¿Dos semanas? Entonces va a necesitar un hotel bueno pero barato, ¿no es así? Le recomiendo que se quede en el Hotel Rioplatense. Es uno de los mejores hoteles en todo Buenos Aires. También le sugiero que le reservemos una habitación doble con baño. Le dan muy buen precio para la doble.
[Cliente]:	Gracias, resérvemela, por favor.
[Agente]:	En fin. La reservación está garantizada hasta cierta hora nada más, así que le sugiero que se registre en el Hotel inmediatamente al llegar a la ciudad.
[Cliente]:	Muchas gracias. Así lo haré.

ACTIVIDAD 6 **Las situaciones.** Escucha las siguientes situaciones y decide cuál de las explicaciones de la segunda columna es la más lógica para cada situación.

1. Juan no fue a clases toda la semana. Nadie sabe nada de él.
2. Fuimos al hotel de Alicia y Ana para buscarlas, pero ya no estaban registradas.
3. Mis hermanos dijeron que me iban a llamar en cuanto llegaran al aeropuerto, pero todavía no he sabido nada de ellos.
4. No sé por qué Arturo me llamó en el celular en vez de la casa.
5. Miguel y Eva quedaron en vernos en el restaurante a las ocho, pero ya son las nueve y no han llegado.
6. Mi papá es doctor y quedamos en cenar juntos esta noche, pero todavía no llega a casa.

NEXOS

NEXOS

Sheri Spaine Long
University of Alabama at Birmingham

María Carreira
California State University at Long Beach

Sylvia Madrigal Velasco

Kristin Swanson

HOUGHTON MIFFLIN COMPANY

Boston   New York

Publisher: Roland Hernández
Sponsoring Editor: Van Strength
Development Manager: Sharla Zwirek
Senior Development Editor: Sandra Guadano
Editorial Assistant: Erin Kern
Senior Project Editor: Florence Kilgo
Senior Production/Design Coordinator: Sarah Ambrose
Senior Manufacturing Manager: Florence Cadran
Senior Marketing Manager: Tina Crowley Desprez
Associate Marketing Manager: Claudia Martínez

Cover image credit: Joseph Maruska, "La Calavera de Hoy," oil on masonite, 48" × 48", 1994. Courtesy of Patricia Correia Gallery, www.correiagallery.com

Text, photo, and art credits appear on pages 502–504, which constitute an extension of the copyright page.

Printed in the U.S.A.

Library of Congress Catalog Card Number: 2001133303

Student Text ISBN: 0-618-06797-3

Instructor Annotated Edition: 0-618-06798-1

1 2 3 4 5 6 7 8 9—DOW—08 07 06 05 04

¡Bienvenidos! Welcome to the *Nexos* introductory Spanish program. Spanish is one of the most useful languages you can learn; it is spoken by more than 360 million people across the globe, including more than 38 million Hispanics in the United States alone. It is the most spoken language in the world after Mandarin Chinese and English. As you undertake your study of the Spanish language with *Nexos*, keep in mind the following:

♦ We strive to present the Spanish-speaking world in all its diversity, with particular attention to indigenous and African-Hispanic populations, as well as European and Latin American immigrant populations. We include a chapter on Morocco, the Canary Islands, and Equatorial Guinea as a reminder that not all Spanish-speaking countries are located in Europe or the Americas.

♦ We guide you to make cross-cultural comparisons between the cultures you learn about and your own. Too often in the past the emphasis has been on the differences among cultures, when what may be surprising is the number of things we have in common with Spanish speakers around the world.

♦ We encourage you to look at your own community and to meet and interact with the Spanish speakers you encounter there. Spanish is all around you— just keep your eyes and ears open for it!

♦ The *Nexos* program is designed to enrich your language-learning experience— while you are learning another language, you are also gathering information *about* the people who speak it and the countries where it is spoken. At first, you may think that you are unable to read or understand much Spanish, but in *Nexos*, the focus is on getting the main ideas, and the tasks expected of you are limited to what you have already learned or what you can safely deduce from context. You will be surprised to see that you can comprehend more than you think you can!

♦ Learning a language is easier if you relax and have fun. Keeping this in mind, we've included humorous and contemporary content with the goal of making language learning enjoyable and interesting.

We hope you enjoy your introduction to the Spanish language and its many peoples and cultures. Learning a language is one of the most valuable and exciting things you can do to prepare yourself to be a global citizen of the twenty-first century.

—The Authors

An Overview of Your Textbook's Main Features

With seamless integration of the National Standards for Foreign Language Learning, *Nexos* presents a complete grammatical infrastructure in fourteen easy-to-navigate chapters. Each chapter guides learners to think about the connections between language and content as they build their interpersonal, interpretive, and presentational communication skills in Spanish.

Chapter Opener emphasizes links between language and culture.

Each chapter opens with communication and cultural goals that establish clear learning objectives.

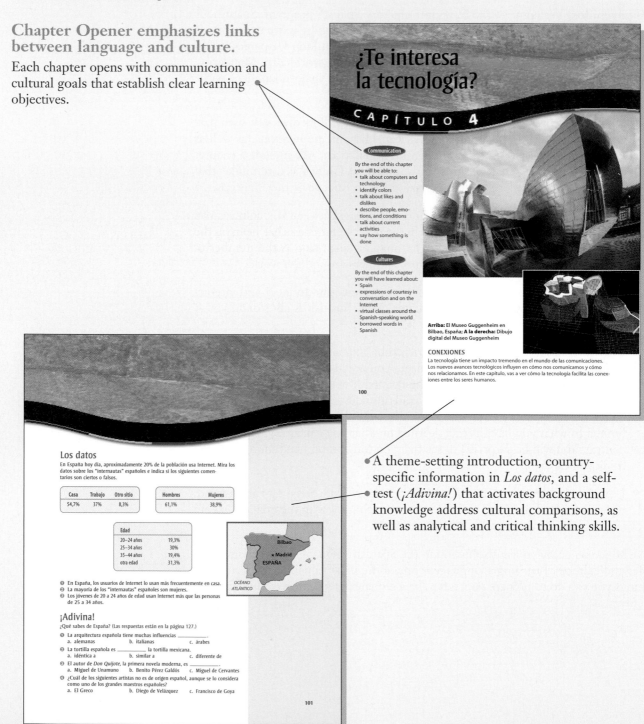

¿Te interesa la tecnología?

CAPÍTULO 4

Communication

By the end of this chapter you will be able to:
- talk about computers and technology
- identify colors
- talk about likes and dislikes
- describe people, emotions, and conditions
- talk about current activities
- say how something is done

Cultures

By the end of this chapter you will have learned about:
- Spain
- expressions of courtesy in conversation and on the Internet
- virtual classes around the Spanish-speaking world
- borrowed words in Spanish

Arriba: El Museo Guggenheim en Bilbao, España; **A la derecha:** Dibujo digital del Museo Guggenheim

CONEXIONES

La tecnología tiene un impacto tremendo en el mundo de las comunicaciones. Los nuevos avances tecnológicos influyen en cómo nos comunicamos y cómo nos relacionamos. En este capítulo, vas a ver cómo la tecnología facilita las conexiones entre los seres humanos.

100

Los datos

En España hoy día, aproximadamente 20% de la población usa Internet. Mira los datos sobre los "internautas" españoles e indica si los siguientes comentarios son ciertos o falsos.

Casa	Trabajo	Otro sitio
54,7%	37%	8,3%

Hombres	Mujeres
61,1%	38,9%

Edad	
20–24 años	19,3%
25–34 años	30%
35–44 años	19,4%
otra edad	31,3%

Bilbao
★ Madrid
ESPAÑA
OCÉANO ATLÁNTICO

① En España, los usuarios de Internet lo usan más frecuentemente en casa.
② La mayoría de los "internautas" españoles son mujeres.
③ Los jóvenes de 20 a 24 años de edad usan Internet más que las personas de 25 a 34 años.

¡Adivina!

¿Qué sabes de España? (Las respuestas están en la página 127.)

① La arquitectura española tiene muchas influencias _____.
   a. alemanas   b. italianas   c. árabes
② La tortilla española es _____ la tortilla mexicana.
   a. idéntica a   b. similar a   c. diferente de
③ El autor de *Don Quijote*, la primera novela moderna, es _____.
   a. Miguel de Unamuno   b. Benito Pérez Galdós   c. Miguel de Cervantes
④ ¿Cuál de los siguientes artistas no es de origen español, aunque se le considera como uno de los grandes maestros españoles?
   a. El Greco   b. Diego de Velázquez   c. Francisco de Goya

101

A theme-setting introduction, country-specific information in *Los datos*, and a self-test (*¡Adivina!*) that activates background knowledge address cultural comparisons, as well as analytical and critical thinking skills.

Focus on contemporary themes engages learners and promotes communication.

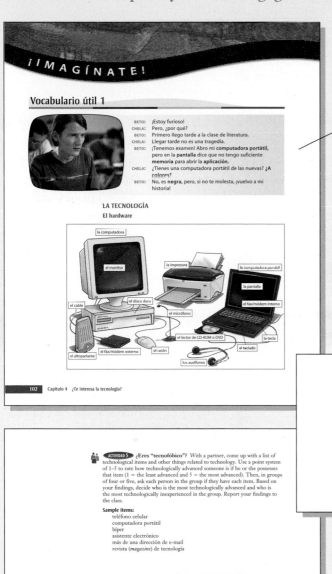

Relevant themes—such as technology, sports and leisure, and entertainment—colorful illustrations, and video narratives portraying everyday situations provide a context for presenting vocabulary.

A range of supporting practice, from controlled exercises to communicative activities, encourages learners to build vocabulary and communicate interpersonally in Spanish.

Actividades

ACTIVIDAD 4 **Las emociones.** Imagínate que conoces a las siguientes personas. Están en ciertas situaciones. ¿Cómo crees que están?

1. A Raúl le gusta navegar por Internet y jugar videojuegos. Hay una tormenta y por eso no hay electricidad en su casa. No tiene nada (*nothing*) que hacer.
2. Blanca acaba de comprar una computadora portátil pero cuando llega a casa, no funciona.
3. Julio tiene que escribir una composición de diez páginas para su clase de historia mañana y todavía no ha empezado (*hasn't begun*).
4. Mañana Luis tiene que ir al trabajo por tres horas, estudiar para un examen y hacer una investigación en Internet para la clase de filosofía.
5. Sabrina trabaja diez horas en la biblioteca, va a su clase de aeróbicos y camina a casa del gimnasio.
6. Marcos y Marina toman un refresco, escuchan música y conversan en un café en la Plaza Mayor.

ACTIVIDAD 5 **¿Eres "tecnofóbico"?** With a partner, come up with a list of technological items and other things related to technology. Use a point system of 1–5 to rate how technologically advanced someone is if he or she possesses that item (1 = the least advanced and 5 = the most advanced). Then, in groups of four or five, ask each person in the group if they have each item. Based on your findings, decide who is the most technologically advanced and who is the most technologically inexperienced in the group. Report your findings to the class.

Sample items:
teléfono celular
computadora portátil
bíper
asistente electrónico
más de una dirección de e-mail
revista (*magazine*) de tecnología

¡FÍJATE!

Los préstamos: Palabras inmigrantes

Todas las lenguas del mundo tienen **préstamos** (*borrowings*). Los préstamos son palabras que tienen su origen en otras lenguas. El español tiene muchos préstamos árabes que se originaron durante los siete siglos (*centuries*) de dominación musulmana de la Península Ibérica (711–1492 d. C.). Muchas palabras de las ciencias, el arte, las matemáticas, la agricultura y la arquitectura son de origen árabe: **álgebra, ajedrez** (*chess*)**, alfalfa, algoritmo**.

El español también tiene préstamos griegos, franceses, italianos, germánicos y amerindios. Los préstamos más recientes son del inglés y representan innovaciones tecnológicas o vienen del (*come from the*) mundo de los negocios, por ejemplo **bíper, fax, hacer clic** y **cheque**. Otros como **rock and roll, club** y **jazz** se originan en la cultura popular americana.

PRÁCTICA. El inglés tiene muchos préstamos de otras lenguas. En grupos, traten de identificar la lengua de origen de estas palabras: francés, italiano, español, alemán, indio o hebreo.

piano	al dente
rouge	veranda
bandana	tobacco
guru	presto
gesundheit	kibbutz
rendezvous	gestalt
patio	

To give students a broader context for understanding language, *¡Fíjate!* linguistic notes highlight topics such as dialectal variations, linguistic borrowings, and indigenous languages.

Chapter-ending *Vocabulario* summaries serve as a quick reference of active vocabulary to help learners review or prepare for quizzes and exams.

Diverse cultural perspectives connect students to the Spanish-speaking world while exploring the U.S. as a Spanish-speaking country.

Students are introduced to and asked to assess their previous knowledge of, as well as think critically about, the cultures of all 21 Spanish-speaking countries. A special focus on U.S. Hispanics and their contributions to society draws students into the Spanish-speaking culture that surrounds them.

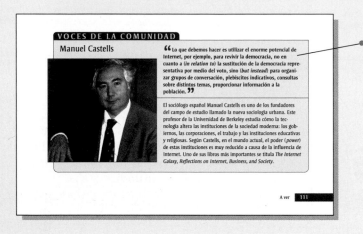

Voces de la comunidad connects students to the U.S. Hispanic community through profiles of successful U.S. Hispanics.

¡Compárate! notes encourage cross-cultural comparisons between the learners' culture and the rest of the Spanish-speaking world.

Exploraciones culturales readings highlight varied aspects of the chapter's country or region and include little-studied areas such as Morocco, Equatorial Guinea, and the Canary Islands.

EXPLORACIONES CULTURALES

España

Las riquezas culturales de España. Look at the photos, then read the paragraphs and titles on page 128. Can you match the photos and the correct title to each paragraph? Try to read quickly to catch the gist of each paragraph. Once you have identified the correct title and photo for each paragraph, read the paragraphs again to see if you understood the basic content of each one.

¡Adivinaste? Answers to the questions on page 101: 1. c 2. c 3. c 4.

Fotos

Foto 1

Foto 2

Foto 3

Foto 4

Títulos

La literatura   La influencia árabe   El arte   La cocina española

Párrafo 1

Las tapas son raciones o porciones pequeñas de comida típicamente española que se sirven en los bares españoles, especialmente en Madrid. Salir a comer tapas con los amigos es mucho más que sólo comer: ¡es una actividad esencial en la vida social española!

Párrafo 2

El ingenioso hidalgo Don Quijote de la Mancha (1605), por el autor español Miguel de Cervantes, se considera la primera novela moderna. Los dos protagonistas, Don Quijote de la Mancha, el idealista sincero, y Sancho Panza, el realista cómico, son unos de los personajes más famosos de la literatura española, y aún de la literatura mundial.

Párrafo 3

En el siglo VIII, colonizadores musulmanes, comúnmente llamados "los moros", conquistan la Península Ibérica. Durante esta época, bajo su influencia, florecen las matemáticas, las ciencias, la arquitectura y las artes decorativas. Las influencias árabes en la arquitectura son muy evidentes por todo el sur de España, en particular en Granada, Córdoba y Sevilla.

Párrafo 4

Los grandes maestros de la pintura española incluyen a El Greco (1541–1614), Diego de Velázquez (1599–1660) y Francisco de Goya (1746–1828). Las obras de El Greco tratan temas religiosos, mientras que las de Velázquez frecuentemente representan mitos y leyendas. Goya es famoso por sus retratos de la familia real y también por sus protestas gráficas contra la violencia y la guerra (*war*).

¡CONÉCTATE!

Internet

Your class needs to plan a virtual vacation to Sevilla, Spain, in order to get away from all the stress of modern technological living! Divide into four groups. Each group will choose one of the following categories and research it by following links on the *Nexos* website (http://college.hmco.com/languages/spanish/students/) to see a list of suggested websites. Each group should come up with a list of three suggestions for their category. Then, based on the group's suggestions, the class will prepare an itinerary for a virtual vacation to Sevilla.

Group 1: Housing / Lodging
Group 2: Entertainment
Group 3: Museums and other cultural sites
Group 4: Where to eat

¡Conéctate! sections encourage learners to explore the Internet and report back to the class to present their findings.

Contextualized grammar instruction emphasizes form, function, and comparisons.

Succinct, easy-to-understand explanations in English—where form, *Cómo formarlo*, follows function, *Cómo usarlo*—are presented through a variety of contexts including usage examples, realia, charts, video excerpts and stills, and humorous, thought-provoking *Sonrisas* cartoons that reward learners for their growing proficiency in the language.

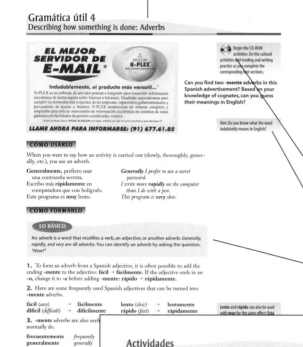

In-text icons correlate your textbook to practice in supporting program components.

Student annotations offer learning strategies, information, and study tips.

Lo básico notes provide useful tips and comparative English grammar terms with examples.

A range of thematic practice progresses from structured to transitional practice and features two listening-based activities per chapter.

A high-interest video adds a real-life dimension to learning.

The fourteen-episode video story line follows the humorous, tongue-in-cheek adventures of six university students in Costa Rica. Supporting activities in the *A ver* viewing section emphasize interpretive communication and practice of viewing strategies, as well as pre- and post-viewing practice. Even-numbered chapters conclude with a cultural comparison activity (*Conexión cultural*) related to a short cultural video segment.

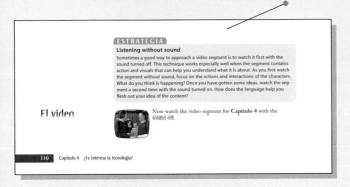

ESTRATEGIA

Listening without sound

Sometimes a good way to approach a video segment is to watch it first with the sound turned off. This technique works especially well when the segment contains action and visuals that can help you understand what it is about. As you first watch the segment without sound, focus on the actions and interactions of the characters. What do you think is happening? Once you have gotten some ideas, watch the segment a second time with the sound turned on. How does the language help you flesh out your idea of the content?

El video

Now watch the video segment for **Capítulo 4** with the sound off.

110 Capítulo 4 ¿Te interesa la tecnología?

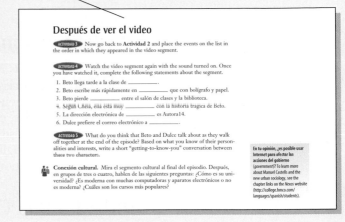

Después de ver el video

ACTIVIDAD 3 Now go back to **Actividad 2** and place the events on the list in the order in which they appeared in the video segment.

ACTIVIDAD 4 Watch the video segment again with the sound turned on. Once you have watched it, complete the following statements about the segment.

1. Beto llega tarde a la clase de _____.
2. Beto escribe más rápidamente en _____ que con bolígrafo y papel.
3. Beto pierde _____ entre el salón de clases y la biblioteca.
4. Según Chela, ella está muy _____ con la historia trágica de Beto.
5. La dirección electrónica de _____ es Autora14.
6. Dulce prefiere el correo electrónico a _____.

ACTIVIDAD 5 What do you think that Beto and Dulce talk about as they walk off together at the end of the episode? Based on what you know of their personalities and interests, write a short "getting-to-know-you" conversation between these two characters.

Conexión cultural. Mira el segmento cultural al final del episodio. Después, en grupos de tres o cuatro, hablen de las siguientes preguntas: ¿Cómo es su universidad? ¿Es moderna con muchas computadoras y aparatos electrónicos o no es moderna? ¿Cuáles son los cursos más populares?

En tu opinión, ¿es posible usar Internet para afectar las acciones del gobierno (*government*)? To learn more about Manuel Castells and the new urban sociology, see the chapter links on the *Nexos* website (http://college.hmco.com/languages/spanish/students).

A program of learning strategies supports skill development

A leer presents and practices specific techniques designed to help learners process authentic materials as they become more proficient readers. Readings include magazine and literary selections covering a range of contemporary topics.

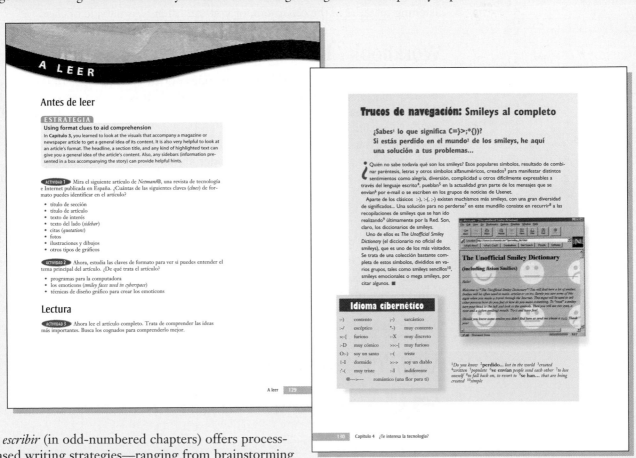

A LEER

Antes de leer

ESTRATEGIA

Using format clues to aid comprehension

In **Capítulo 3**, you learned to look at the visuals that accompany a magazine or newspaper article to get a general idea of its content. It is also very helpful to look at an article's format. The headline, a section title, and any kind of highlighted text can give you a general idea of the article's content. Also, any sidebars (information presented in a box accompanying the story) can provide helpful hints.

ACTIVIDAD 1 Mira el siguiente artículo de *Netmanía*, una revista de tecnología e Internet publicada en España. ¿Cuántas de las siguientes claves (*clues*) de formato puedes identificar en el artículo?

• título de sección
• título de artículo
• texto de interés
• texto del lado (*sidebar*)
• citas (*quotations*)
• fotos
• ilustraciones y dibujos
• otros tipos de gráficos

ACTIVIDAD 2 Ahora, estudia las claves de formato para ver si puedes entender el tema principal del artículo. ¿De qué trata el artículo?

• programas para la computadora
• los emoticons (*smiley faces used in cyberspace*)
• técnicas de diseño gráfico para crear los emoticons

Lectura

ACTIVIDAD 3 Ahora lee el artículo completo. Trata de comprender las ideas más importantes. Busca los cognados para comprenderlo mejor.

A leer 129

Trucos de navegación: Smileys al completo

¿Sabes[1] lo que significa C=}>;*{})?
Si estás perdido en el mundo[2] de los smileys, he aquí una solución a tus problemas...

¿Quién no sabe todavía qué son los smileys? Esos populares símbolos, resultado de combinar paréntesis, letras y otros símbolos alfanuméricos, creados[3] para manifestar distintos sentimientos como alegría, diversión, complicidad u otros difícilmente expresables a través del lenguaje escrito[4], pueblan[5] en la actualidad gran parte de los mensajes que se envían[6] por e-mail o se escriben en los grupos de noticias de Usenet.

Aparte de los clásicos :-), :-(, ;-) existen muchísimos más smileys, con una gran diversidad de significados... Una solución para no perderse[7] en este mundillo consiste en recurrir[8] a las recopilaciones de smileys que se han ido realizando[9] últimamente por la Red. Son, claro, los diccionarios de smileys.

Uno de ellos es *The Unofficial Smiley Dictionary* (el diccionario no oficial de smileys), que es uno de los más visitados. Se trata de una colección bastante completa de estos símbolos, divididos en varios grupos, tales como smileys sencillos[10], smileys emocionales o mega smileys, por citar algunos. ■

Idioma cibernético

:-)	contento	;-)	sarcástico
:-/	escéptico	*-)	muy contento
>:-[	furioso	:-X	muy discreto
:-D	muy cómico	>>:-[	muy furioso
O:-)	soy un santo	:-(	triste
l-I	dormido	>:->	soy un diablo
:'-(	muy triste	:-I	indiferente
@--->---	romántico (una flor para ti)		

[1]*Do you know* [2]*perdido... lost in the world* [3]*created* [4]*written* [5]*populate* [6]*se envían people send each other* [7]*to lose oneself* [8]*fin fall back on, to resort to* [9]*se han... that are being created* [10]*simple*

140 Capítulo 4 ¿Te interesa la tecnología?

A escribir (in odd-numbered chapters) offers process-based writing strategies—ranging from brainstorming to peer editing and revision—supported by pre- and post-writing activities, models of good writing, and guided writing practice.

ix

STUDENT COMPONENTS

Student Textbook

Your *Student Textbook* contains all the information and activities you need for in-class use. It is divided into fourteen chapters that contain vocabulary presentations and activities, grammar presentations and activities, video-related practice, cultural information, reading selections, and writing practice. There are also valuable reference sections at the back of the book, including Spanish-English and English-Spanish glossaries and verb charts showing the conjugations of different categories of verbs.

In-Text Audio CD

The *In-Text Audio CD* contains the listening material for the listening-based grammar activities in your *Student Textbook* that are marked with a listening icon. This Audio CD is packaged with your textbook. Instructors may play the listening material in the classroom, or you can listen to it outside of class.

Workbook / Lab Manual

The *Workbook / Lab Manual* includes out-of-class practice of the material presented in the *Student Textbook*. It is divided into a Workbook **(Cuaderno de práctica)**, which focuses on written vocabulary and grammar practice, reading, and writing, and a *Lab Manual* **(Manual de laboratorio)**, which focuses on pronunciation and listening comprehension. Each *Workbook* chapter includes a reminder about the SMARTHINKING online tutoring available to you. A *Workbook Answer Key* may be packaged with the *Workbook / Lab Manual* at the request of your instructor.

Online Workbook / Lab Manual

The *Online Workbook / Lab Manual* is an electronic version of the printed *Workbook / Lab Manual* described above. It allows you to complete the same practice presented in the print version, but in a computerized format with immediate feedback for many exercises. The audio corresponding to the lab exercises and a direct link to SMARTHINKING online tutoring are also included.

Audio CD Program

The *Audio CD Program* corresponds to the *Lab Manual* portion of the *Nexos Workbook / Lab Manual* and reinforces your pronunciation and listening skills.

Nexos Video

The *Nexos Video* follows the humorous adventures of six university students in Costa Rica as they cross paths, meet, and (in some cases) fail to meet. Carefully structured to integrate chapter vocabulary and grammar, each video episode has related practice in the corresponding chapter of your *Student Textbook*. The video is designed to help you learn about Spanish-speaking cultures, to practice your listening skills, and to reinforce chapter vocabulary and grammar. Additional cultural segments that expand upon the textbook themes are included after every even-numbered chapter.

Nexos Multimedia CD-ROM 1.0

The dual-platform multimedia CD-ROM that accompanies *Nexos* helps you practice each chapter's vocabulary and grammar, and provides immediate feedback so that you can check your progress in Spanish. Each chapter includes games, art- and listening-based activities, and the opportunity to record selected responses to help you develop your reading, writing, listening, and speaking skills. As you work, you can access a grammar reference and a Spanish-English glossary and also link directly to SMARTHINKING online tutoring. You can use the program for extra practice as you study a chapter and for review before quizzes and exams.

The CD-ROM also contains clips from the *Nexos* video program with related activities and the corresponding video script. You can do these activities before or after watching the complete video episodes, which are also included on the CD-ROM.

Nexos Student Website

You will find a variety of resources at the *Nexos Student Website* that provide additional language practice. Search activities give you practice with chapter vocabulary and grammar while exploring existing Spanish-language websites. ACE Practice Tests for each chapter help you assess your progress and practice chapter vocabulary and grammar. Feedback helps you understand errors and pinpoint areas you may need to review. You may do some or all of the ACE activities as you study the chapter or as a review for quizzes and exams. ACE Video Activities include extra practice based on short clips from the *Nexos Video*. Also included on the site are cultural links to sites related to the **Voces de la comunidad** and **¡Conéctate!** activities in your text, flash-cards for vocabulary practice, and MP3 files of the text listening activities. The website is accessible at *http://college.hmco.com/languages/spanish/students*.

SMARTHINKING™ Online Tutoring for Spanish

Access free online tutorial support—from the convenience of your dorm room, home, or lab—using chat technology, feedback tools, and virtual whiteboards. SMARTHINKING lets you work one-on-one with trained Spanish tutors in live sessions during your usual homework hours. If a question arises outside of a tutorial session, you can submit it to a tutor any time and receive a reply within 24 hours or access around-the-clock independent study resources. You can learn more about SMARTHINKING at *http://college.hmco.com/languages/spanish/students*.

ACKNOWLEDGMENTS

We would like to acknowledge the helpful suggestions and useful ideas of our reviewers, whose commentary was invaluable to us as we created the *Nexos* program.

Esther Aguilar, San Diego State University
Karen Brunschwig, St. Joseph's College
José R. Carrasquel, Northern Illinois University
Elizabeth Chamberlain, Dartmouth College
Carole A. Champagne, University of Maryland Eastern Shore
Stephen J. Clark, Northern Arizona University
Dorothy Diehl, Saint Mary's University of Minnesota
María de Lourdes Dorantes, University of Michigan
Joseph R. Farrell, California State Polytechnic University, Pomona
Charles Fleis, University of Arkansas–Monticello
Olgalucía G. González, Washington and Jefferson College
Hannelore Hahn, College of Saint Elizabeth
Ellen Haynes, University of Colorado
Polly J. Hodge, Chapman University
Carolina Ibanez-Murphy, Pima Community College
Luis E. Latoja, Columbus State Community College
Bro. Francisco Martin, Christian Brothers University
Timothy McGovern, University of California, Santa Barbara
Maureen Spillane McKenna, Centenary College of Louisiana
Lois Pontillo Mignone, Suffolk County Community College
Alice A. Miano, Stanford University
Peter Podol, Lock Haven University
Ronald Rapin, Oakland University
Gregory Rivera, Lorain County Community College
Regina F. Roebuck, University of Louisville
Beatriz Rosado, Virginia State University
Marcela Ruiz-Funes, East Carolina University
Marveta Ryan, Indiana University of Pennsylvania
Vanisa D. Sellers, Ohio University
George R. Shivers, Washington College
Louis Silvers, Monroe Community College
José A. Soler-Tossas, San Diego City College
Julie L. Stephens, Central Missouri State University
Kathleen Wheatley, University of Wisconsin–Milwaukee
Linda Zee, Utica College

A special word of appreciation for his careful review of the textbook, workbook / lab manual, and testing program manuscripts to help ensure accuracy of Spanish usage is due:

José R. Carrasquel, Northern Illinois University

Thank you also to the following focus group and survey participants for their constructive ideas and contributions in shaping the program.

Maria Amores, West Virginia University
Debra D. Andrist, University of St. Thomas, Houston, TX
Carole A. Champagne, University of Maryland Eastern Shore
Dorothy Diehl, Saint Mary's University of Minnesota
Charles Dietrick, Tufts University and University of Massachusetts at Boston
Robert E. Eckard, Lenoir-Rhyne College
Donald B. Gibbs, Creighton University
Lily Anne Goetz, Longwood University
Miguel González-Abellás, Washburn University
Curtis D. Goss, Southwest Baptist University
Monica Mendy Grigera, Penn State York
Hannelore Hahn, College of Saint Elizabeth
Margarita Esparza Hodge, Northern Virginia Community College, Alexandria Campus
Manel Lacorte, University of Maryland-College Park
Jeff Longwell, New Mexico State University
Esmeralda Martínez-Tapia, Oberlin College
Frank W. Medley, Jr. Professor Emeritus, West Virginia University
Maria M. Melendez, Albright College
Joyce Michaelis, Nebraska Wesleyan University
Luisa Piemontese, Southern CT State University
Barbara Place, Manchester Community College
Peter Podol, Lock Haven University
Harriet N. Poole, Lake City Community College
Orlando M. Reyes-Cairo, Owens Community College
Rita Ricaurte, Nebraska Wesleyan University
Lawrence Rich, Northern Virginia Community College
Gregory Rivera, Lorain County Community College
Esperanza Román Mendoza, George Mason University
Kimberley Sallee, University of Missouri–St. Louis
Jacquelyn Sandone, University of Missouri, Columbia
Julie Stephens de Jonge, Central Missouri State University
Joyce L. Szewczynski, Springfield College
Beatriz Teleki, Trinity College
Katalin A. Volker, Hagerstown Community College
Linda Zee, Utica College of Syracuse University

We would also like to thank the World Languages Group at Houghton Mifflin for making this project possible and for guiding us along the long and sometimes difficult path to its completion! Many thanks to Kris Clerkin and Roland Hernández for their professional guidance and support. Special thanks to Sandy Guadano, our developmental editor, for her careful, patient, and thorough comments on the manuscript at its various stages and for her hard work and persistence in seeing this program through to its conclusion. Thanks also to Florence Kilgo, our production editor, for her cheerful and good-humored tenacity in keeping the production side of things moving smoothly and quickly. We would like to acknowledge our copyeditor Steve Patterson, our proofreaders Priscila Baldovi and Grisel Lozano-Garcini, our illustrators Rick Morgan, Carlos Castellanos, Fian Arroyo, and Patrice Rossi, and the many design, art, production, and marketing staff and freelancers who contributed to the creation of this program.

We would also like to thank several people whose help was invaluable in initiating and shaping this project: Kristina Baer, Amy Baron, Beth Kramer, and Rafael Burgos-Mirabal. Many thanks for believing in us and helping us to get the ball rolling! Also, a special thank you to Yolanda Blanco at the website **dariana.com** for her kind help in locating and obtaining permission for the Nicaraguan poems, along with other editorial assistance and commentary. **¡Mil gracias a todos!**

A heartfelt thanks to *mi querida familia* John, Morgan and John R. Long and to my supportive colleagues in the Department of Foreign Languages and Literatures at University of Alabama at Birmingham.

—S.S.L.

I am particularly appreciative of the help and encouragement of my husband, Bartlett Mel, my father, Domingo Carreira, and my colleagues Ana Roca, Najib Redouane and Irene Marchegiani Jones.

—M.C.

I would like to thank my parents, Dulce and Óscar Madrigal, for bequeathing to me their language, their culture, their heritage, their passion for life and their *orgullo* in *México, lindo y querido*.

—S.M.V.

A special thanks to Mac Prichard and to Shirley and Bill Swanson for their constant support and encouragement, both personal and professional.

—K.S.

NEXOS

SCOPE AND SEQUENCE

NEXOS

Atrás Adelante Detener Actualizar Página principal Autorrelleno Imprimir Correo

Dirección: @ http://college/hmco.com/languages/spanish/students

¡Bienvenidos a la

The purpose of these pages is to introduce you to some of the "nuts and bolts" of Spanish you'll need right away. Familiarize yourself with these words and expressions and do the activities described. Don't worry about memorizing it all—you'll have many more opportunities to work with these words as you progress through *Nexos*. Optional: Play Hangman or Scrabble to provide spelling practice.

EL ALFABETO

The Spanish alphabet has 29 characters—the same as the English alphabet, plus the extra letters **ch**, **ll**, and **ñ**. When using a Spanish dictionary to look up words that begin with **ch** and **ll**, note that they do not have a separate listing, but are instead listed alphabetically under the letters **c** and **l**.

Go to your Lab Manual and practice the sounds of the alphabet.

a	*a*	**A**rgentin**a**		n	*ene*	**N**icaragua
b	*be*	**B**olivia		ñ	*eñe*	Espa**ñ**a
c	*ce*	**C**osta Ri**c**a		o	*o*	**O**taval**o**
ch	*che*	**Chich**én Itzá		p	*pe*	**P**araguay
d	*de*	República		q	*cu*	**Q**uito
		Dominicana		r	*ere*	Pe**r**ú
e	*e*	**E**cuador		s	*ese*	**S**antiago de
f	*efe*	las **F**ilipinas				Compo**s**tela
g	*ge*	**G**uatemala		t	*te*	**T**oledo
h	*hache*	**H**onduras		u	*u*	C**u**ba
i	*i*	**I**nglaterra		v	*ve*	**V**enezuela
j	*jota*	**J**alisco		w	*doble ve*	Bots**w**ana
k	*ka*	**K**enya		x	*equis*	Mé**x**ico
l	*ele*	**L**os Ángeles		y	*i griega*	**Y**ucatán
ll	*elle*	Va**ll**adolid		z	*zeta*	**Z**acatecas
m	*eme*	**M**arruecos				

Standards: Throughout *Nexos,* there are many activities based on the *Standards for Foreign Language Learning.* The *Instructor's Guide* at the beginning of the text contains helpful information about the standards and describes how they are implemented in *Nexos.* In addition icons and annotations are used to point out the standard or standards addressed in the various chapter sections and activities.

Suggestion: Model the pronunciation of vowels (**a, e, i, o, u**). Demonstrate the **g**, the silent **h**, **ñ** like *ny* (*canyon* from English), the trilled **rr**, and **v**. Point out that **p, t**, and **c** (with the "k" sound)

are aspirated or pronounced with a puff of air in English, unlike Spanish. Demonstrate this with **pan, tan, con.** Optional: In Castillian Spanish the **z** (**z, ci, ce**) is pronounced like the *th* in English.

Suggestion: For alphabet practice, model question and act out answer by writing letters on the blackboard: **¿Cómo se deletrea su/tu/mi nombre?** For example, **Mi nombre es J, u, a, n, a, B, e, n, í, t, e, z.** Ask students to spell their names. To review the alphabet, have students spell words letter by letter throughout the course.

clase de español!

LOS NÚMEROS 1–100

0	*cero*	**20**	*veinte*	**40**	*cuarenta*
1	*uno*	21	*veintiuno*	41	*cuarenta y uno*
2	*dos*	22	*veintidós*	42	*cuarenta y dos*
3	*tres*	23	*veintitrés*	43	*cuarenta y tres*
4	*cuatro*	24	*veinticuatro*	44	*cuarenta y cuatro*
5	*cinco*	25	*veinticinco*	45	*cuarenta y cinco*
6	*seis*	26	*veintiséis*	46	*cuarenta y seis*
7	*siete*	27	*veintisiete*	47	*cuarenta y siete*
8	*ocho*	28	*veintiocho*	48	*cuarenta y ocho*
9	*nueve*	29	*veintinueve*	49	*cuarenta y nueve*
10	*diez*	**30**	*treinta*	**50**	*cincuenta*
11	*once*	31	*treinta y uno*	51	*cincuenta y uno*
12	*doce*	32	*treinta y dos*	52	*cincuenta y dos*
13	*trece*	33	*treinta y tres*	53	*cincuenta y tres*
14	*catorce*	34	*treinta y cuatro*	54	*cincuenta y cuatro*
15	*quince*	35	*treinta y cinco*	55	*cincuenta y cinco*
16	*dieciséis*	36	*treinta y seis*	56	*cincuenta y seis*
17	*diecisiete*	37	*treinta y siete*	57	*cincuenta y siete*
18	*dieciocho*	38	*treinta y ocho*	58	*cincuenta y ocho*
19	*diecinueve*	39	*treinta y nueve*	59	*cincuenta y nueve*
				60	*sesenta*
				70	*setenta*
				80	*ochenta*
				90	*noventa*
				100	*cien*

Suggestion: Practice numbers with math problems. Teach these conventions:
+ **más,** − **menos,** × **por,** ÷ **dividido por,** = **es igual a.**

Standards/Optional: Have students create their own Bingo cards with paper. Playing Bingo practices listening comprehension in the interpretive mode (C 1.2) of both letters and numbers.

Memorize the numbers 1–10.

Notice the pattern for the numbers from 16 to 29: **diez** + **seis** = **dieciséis**; **veinte** + **uno** = **veintiuno**. Notice that 11–15 do not follow that pattern.

Notice the pattern for the numbers over 30: **treinta** + **uno** = **treinta y uno; cuarenta** + **dos** = **cuarenta y dos; cincuenta** + **tres** = **cincuenta y tres;** etc.

Do not confuse sixty and seventy. Notice that **sesenta** is formed from **sei<u>S</u>**, with an **s** and **setenta** is formed from **sie<u>T</u>e**, with a **t.**

With a partner, practice counting in Spanish by taking turns (Student 1: **uno;** Student 2: **dos,** etc.). Or, practice a sequence; for example, multiples of three (Student 1: **tres, seis, nueve;** Student 2: **doce, quince, dieciocho,** etc.).

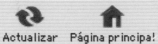
LAS PERSONAS

With a partner, name ten people you know. Take turns identifying them first by age and gender, and then by their relationship to you: **Marcos Martínez—hombre, amigo.**

el hombre   la mujer   el muchacho/ el chico   la muchacha/ la chica   el niño   la niña

el estudiante   el profesor   la instructora   el instructor   la estudiante   la profesora

Suggestion: Give classroom commands and have students act them out.

el compañero de cuarto   la compañera de cuarto   la amiga   el amigo

> **Ir**

EN EL SALÓN DE CLASE

EN EL LIBRO DE TEXTO

la actividad	*activity*
el capítulo	*chapter*
el dibujo	*drawing*
la foto	*photo*
la lección	*lesson*
la página	*page*

MANDATOS COMUNES

Abran los libros.	*Open your books.*
Adivina.	*Guess.*
Cierren los libros.	*Close your books.*
Contesten.	*Answer.*
Entreguen la tarea.	*Turn in your homework.*
Escriban en sus cuadernos.	*Write in your notebooks.*
Escuchen la cinta / el CD.	*Listen to the tape / CD.*
Estudien las páginas… a…	*Study pages . . . to . . .*
Hagan la tarea para mañana.	*Do the home- work for tomorrow.*
Lean el Capítulo 1.	*Read Chapter 1.*
Repitan.	*Repeat.*

LA PREGUNTA   *The question*

¿Cómo se dice… ?	*How do you say . . . ?*
¿Qué significa… ?	*What does . . . mean?*

LA RESPUESTA   *The answer*

Se dice…	*It's said . . .*
Significa…	*It means . . .*

Suggestion: Give classroom commands and have students act them out.

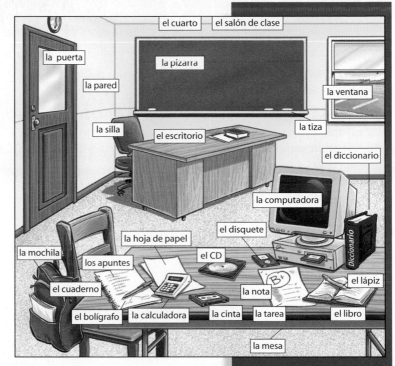

Suggestion: Point out as many classroom words as possible to introduce words in context. Bring supplies to show students the visual image of the written word. Classroom vocabulary: (1) Students can physically label items in the classroom. (2) Teach **¿Dónde está…?** by acting it out and writing it on the board. Ask questions and have students point at the item or object: **¿Dónde está la ventana?, ¿Dónde está el libro de Luis?**, etc. Then have them quiz a partner.

Suggestion: Emphasize the false cognate **nota** by writing A, A−, B, C+, C, etc., on the board. Also, you may want to give contrastive cultural information about grading systems in different Spanish-speaking countries: **sobresaliente, notable, suficiente, aprobado/no aprobado.**

With a partner, take turns pointing out objects shown in the illustration that you can see in your classroom.

Your professor will practice the most common classroom commands with the entire class and before you know it, you will know them by heart! Do not worry about memorizing them.

¿Cómo te llamas?

Communication

By the end of this chapter you will be able to:
- exchange addresses, phone numbers, and e-mail addresses
- introduce yourself and others, greet, and say good-bye
- make a phone call
- tell your and others' ages
- address friends informally and acquaintances politely
- write a personal letter

Cultures

By the end of this chapter you will have learned about:
- Spanish around the world
- Hispanics and Spanish in the United States
- Spanish-language telephone conventions
- formal and informal ways to address people

Standards: Examples of the other standards that will be met in Chapter 1 are: Communities (C 5.1) – contact Spanish-speaking communities on-line; and Communities (C 5.2) – interpret irony in cartoon strip based on experiential enrichment.

Los estudiantes conversan en la plaza.

LA IDENTIDAD PERSONAL

As individuals we value our uniqueness, while drawing strength from the similarities and experiences we share with others. How do we define ourselves, both as individuals and as members of various groups, in our daily interactions with other people?

¡Adivina!

How much do you know about the Spanish-speaking world? Match the information on the left with the correct country (**país**). Check your answers on page 28.

❶ el país con la mayor (+) área
❷ el país con la menor (−) área
❸ el país con la mayor población (*population*)
❹ el país con la menor población
❺ el país que produce más energía
❻ el país con la costa más larga
❼ dos países sin (*without*) costa

a. México
b. Chile
c. Venezuela
d. Argentina
e. Guinea Ecuatorial
f. Bolivia
g. Puerto Rico
h. Paraguay

¡Adivina! answers: 1. d 2. g 3. a 4. e 5. c 6. b 7. f, h

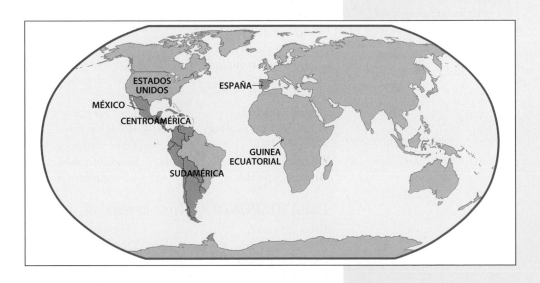

¡IMAGÍNATE!

Vocabulario útil 1

JAVIER: ¡Hola!

ANILÚ: Hola, Beto. ¿Cómo te va?

JAVIER: Bastante bien, pero… ¿Beto? Yo no soy Beto.

Notice: These conversational scenes from the *Nexos* video are designed to present the vocabulary in context. Video viewing activities appear later in the chapter.

Suggestion: One way to present this vocabulary is to model a two-way conversation. Greet a student, ask how he/she is, and sign off. If the student is *not* able to respond, ask the rest of the class for **ayuda** or **socorro**. Teach these words to your class. You will use them over and over again! Greet other students and carry on mini-conversations until they all catch on. Practice both informal and formal greetings. Finally, have students conduct mini-conversations with their neighbors.

Spanish has formal and informal means of address: singular formal (*s. form.*), singular familiar (*s. fam.*), and plural (*pl.*) for more than one person, formal or informal. You will learn more about how to address people on page 22.

PARA SALUDAR   *How to greet*

Hola.	*Hello.*
¿Qué tal?	*How are things going?*
¿Cómo estás (tú)?	*How are you? (s. fam.)*
¿Cómo está (usted)?	*How are you? (s. form.)*
¿Cómo están (ustedes)?	*How are you? (pl.)*
¿Cómo te va?	*How's it going with you? (s. fam.)*
¿Cómo le va?	*How's it going with you? (s. form.)*
¿Cómo les va?	*How's it going with you? (pl.)*
¿Qué hay de nuevo?	*What's new?*
Buenos días.	*Good morning.*
Buenas tardes.	*Good afternoon.*
Buenas noches.	*Good night. Good evening.*

PARA RESPONDER   *How to respond*

Bien, gracias.	*Fine, thank you.*
Bastante bien.	*Quite well.*
(No) Muy bien.	*(Not) Very well.*
Regular.	*So-so.*
¡Terrible! / ¡Fatal!	*Terrible! / Awful!*
No mucho.	*Not much.*
Nada.	*Nothing.*
¿Y tú?	*And you? (s. fam.)*
¿Y usted?	*And you? (s. form.)*

Actividades

ACTIVIDAD 1 **Conversaciones.** With a classmate, take turns greeting each other and responding. Either choose an appropriate response from those provided or provide your own response.

1. Hola, ¿qué tal?
   - a. Buenos días.
   - b. Muy bien, gracias.
   - c. ¿Y tú?
   - d. …

2. Buenas tardes. ¿Qué hay de nuevo?
   - a. No mucho.
   - b. Bastante bien.
   - c. Terrible.
   - d. …

3. Buenas noches. ¿Cómo le va?
   - a. Nada.
   - b. ¿Y usted?
   - c. Fatal.
   - d. …

4. Buenos días. ¿Cómo están?
   - a. Regular.
   - b. Buenas noches.
   - c. No mucho.
   - d. …

5. Hola, ¿cómo está?
   - a. ¿Cómo te va?
   - b. Bien, gracias, ¿y usted?
   - c. Nada.
   - d. …

6. Buenas tardes.
   - a. Terrible.
   - b. Buenas tardes. ¿Qué hay de nuevo?
   - c. No muy bien. ¿Y tú?
   - d. …

Standards: This activity, like many in *Nexos*, entails interpersonal communication (C 1.1 + C 1.2). Students ask, answer, and exchange information and opinions.

Answers: 1. b 2. a 3. c 4. a 5. b 6. b

¡FÍJATE!

Los celulares

Cellular phone technology has revolutionized telecommunications throughout the Spanish-speaking world. Cell phones are equally or more popular in Latin America and Spain than they are in the United States.

Although customs for speaking on the phone vary from one Spanish-speaking country to another, here are some useful phrases to get you started.

FAMILIAR CONVERSATION

—¡Hola!	*Hello?*
—¿Está…?	*Is . . . there?*
—Sí. Aquí está. / No, no está.	*Yes. Here he / she is. / No, he's / she's not here.*
—Soy… Mi número es el…	*I'm . . . My number is . . .*
—Muy bien. Hasta luego.	*OK. See you later.*
—Chau.	*Bye.*

FORMAL CONVERSATION

—¡Hola!	*Hello?*
—Hola. ¿Puedo hablar con…?	*Hi, may I speak with . . . ?*
—Sí. / Lo siento. No está.	*Yes. / I'm sorry. He's / She's not here.*
—Por favor, dígale que llamó (nombre). Mi número es el…	*Please tell him / her that (name) called. My number is . . .*
—Muy bien.	*OK.*
—Muchas gracias.	*Thank you very much.*
—De nada. Adiós.	*You're welcome. Good-bye.*
—Adiós.	*Good-bye.*

PRÁCTICA. With a partner, role-play two different phone calls, using the expressions provided. In the first call, you call a friend's apartment and speak to his roommate. In the second call, you call a friend's home and speak to his grandmother. In both cases, the person you are trying to reach is not in and you need to leave a message. Don't forget to use the correct level of address (familiar or formal).

Note that most Spanish speakers give their phone number by using pairs after the first digit. For example: **Mi número es el dos, treinta y seis, diez, dieciocho.**

Standards: The *¡Fíjate!* linguistic notes throughout *Nexos* encourage students to connect and compare information about languages, their history, and context. Topics usually relate to the chapter theme and vocabulary and help students understand the nature of language.

Suggestion: Point out that in-home phone service in the U.S. has been a way of life since the early to mid-20th century. This was not always the case in Latin America due, in many cases, to the extra expense or the difficulty of bringing phone lines into often rugged and isolated terrain.

10   Capítulo 1   ¿Cómo te llamas?

Vocabulario útil 2

ANILÚ: Pues, ¿cómo te llamas?

JAVIER: ¿Yo? **Soy** Javier de la Cruz. Y yo, ¿con quién hablo?

ANILÚ: **Me llamo** Anilú. Ana Luisa Guzmán. … Pero, ¿**cuál es tu número de teléfono?** Yo marqué el 3-39-71-94.

JAVIER: No, ése no es mi número de teléfono. **Mi número es el 3-71-28-12.**

PARA PEDIR Y DAR INFORMACIÓN PERSONAL
To ask for and give personal information

¿Cómo te llamas?	*What's your name? (s. fam.)*
¿Cómo se llama?	*What's your name? (s. form.)*
Me llamo…	*My name is . . .*
(Yo) soy…	*I am . . .*
¿Cuál es tu número de teléfono?	*What is your phone number? (s. fam.)*
¿Cuál es su número de teléfono?	*What is your phone number? (s. form.)*
Mi número de teléfono es el 3-71-28-12.	*My telephone number is 371-2812.*
Es el 3-71-28-12.	*It's 371-2812.*
¿Dónde vives?	*Where do you live? (s. fam.)*
¿Dónde vive?	*Where do you live? (s. form.)*
Vivo en…	*I live in / at / on . . .*
la avenida…	*avenue*
la calle…	*street*
la colonia…	*neighborhood*
¿Cuál es tu dirección?	*What is your address? (s. fam.)*
¿Cuál es su dirección?	*What is your address? (s. form.)*
Mi dirección es…	*My address is . . .*
¿Cuál es tu dirección electrónica?	*What's your e-mail address? (s. fam.)*
¿Cuál es su dirección electrónica?	*What's your e-mail address? (s. form.)*
Aquí tienes mi dirección electrónica.	*Here's my e-mail address. (s. fam.)*
Aquí tiene mi dirección electrónica.	*Here's my e-mail address. (s. form.)*

Optional: You may want to point out that abbreviations for **calle** and **avenida** are commonly seen in addresses: **C/Otero; Avda. Reina Mercedes.**

Actividades

Remind students to give their phone numbers by using pairs after the first digit: **Mi número es el ocho, veintidós, cuarenta y siete, treinta y cinco.**

Answers Act. 2: All items follow the pattern of the model.

Optional: Have students circulate and ask as many classmates as possible for their personal information.

ACTIVIDAD 2 **En la reunión.** You are at the first meeting of the Spanish Internet Group at your college. You have been elected secretary and must record the name, address, and phone number of every member. With a male and female classmate playing the parts of the members, ask for the information you need. Without looking at the book, listen to their responses and record their personal information on your computer or in writing. Then ask your partners for their real personal information and record that.

MODELO: Jorge Salinas, Avenida B 23, 2-91-66-45
　　　　　Tú: *¿Cómo te llamas?*
　　　　　Compañero: *Me llamo Jorge Salinas.*
　　　　　Tú: *¿Dónde vives?*
　　　　　Compañero: *Vivo en la Avenida B, veintitrés.*
　　　　　Tú: *¿Cuál es tu número de teléfono?*
　　　　　Compañero: *Es el dos, noventa y uno, sesenta y seis, cuarenta y cinco.*

1. Amanda Villarreal, Calle Montemayor 10, 8-13-02-55
2. Diego Ruiz, Colonia del Valle, Calle Iturbide 89, 7-94-71-30
3. Irma Santiago, Avenida Flores Verdes 12, 9-52-35-27
4. Baldemar Huerta, Calle Otero 39, 7-62-81-03
5. Ingrid Lehmann, Avenida Aguas Blancas 62, 4-56-72-93
6. ¿...?
7. ¿...?

Notice in the example how Spanish telephone numbers are given in pairs.

Notice that unlike English the street precedes the number in Spanish addresses: **Calle Iturbide 12** vs. *12 Iturbide Street.*

Heritage Learners: Here heritage learners and high beginners may want to review additional phone expressions: **Diga, Dígame, Aló, Mande, Sí, ¿Quién es?, Buenos días,** etc.

ACTIVIDAD 3 **¡Mucho gusto!** With a classmate, role-play a cell phone conversation in which one of you has dialed the wrong number. You are curious about the person you have accidentally reached. Try to get as much information from each other as possible.

MODELO: —Hola. ¿Marcos?
　　　　　—No, yo no soy Marcos.
　　　　　—Bueno, ¿cómo se llama Ud.?
　　　　　—...

Vocabulario útil 3

ANILÚ:	Beto, **quiero presentarte a** Javier de la Cruz.
BETO:	**Mucho gusto,** Javier.
JAVIER:	**Encantado,** Beto.
BETO:	Aquí está tu celular.
JAVIER:	Gracias, Beto. Y aquí está tu celular.
BETO:	**Bueno, ¡tengo que irme! Muchas gracias,** Javier. Y gracias a ti también, Anilú.
ANILÚ:	Pues, Javier, **mucho gusto en conocerte.**
JAVIER:	**El gusto es mío.**
ANILÚ:	Pues, entonces, **¡nos vemos!**
JAVIER:	**¡Hasta luego! Chau.**

Optional: You may want to point out that in Spain a cell phone is called a **móvil.**

Suggestion: Dramatize the scene with handshaking, kisses, and hugs. These sociolinguistic norms vary from country to country in the Spanish-speaking world. Give an example of differences in physical contact and spatial closeness compared with typical customs in the U.S.

PARA PRESENTAR A ALGUIEN   *To introduce someone*

Soy…	*I am . . .*
Me llamo… / Mi nombre es…	*My name is . . .*
Quiero presentarte a…	*I'd like to introduce you (s. fam.) to . . .*
Quiero presentarle a…	*I'd like to introduce you (s. form.) to . . .*
Quiero presentarles a…	*I'd like to introduce you (pl.) to . . .*

PARA RESPONDER   *To respond*

Mucho gusto.	*My pleasure.*
Mucho gusto en conocerte.	*A pleasure to meet you (s. fam.).*
Encantado(a).	*Delighted to meet you.*
Igualmente.	*Likewise.*
El gusto es mío.	*The pleasure is mine.*
Un placer.	*My pleasure.*

PARA DESPEDIRSE   *To say good-bye*

Adiós.	*Good-bye.*
Hasta luego.	*See you later.*
Hasta mañana.	*See you tomorrow.*
Hasta pronto.	*See you soon.*
Nos vemos.	*See you later.*
Chau.	*Bye.*
Bueno, tengo que irme.	*Well / OK, I have to go.*

Suggestion: Other common ways to end conversations are **Hasta la vista** and **Hasta ahora.**

The word **chau** comes from the Italian word **ciao,** which means *good-bye.* The spelling is changed to reflect Spanish pronunciation.

Actividades

Suggestion: After doing **Actividad 4** in groups or pairs, have several sets of students act out these dialogs in front of the class.

 ACTIVIDAD 4 **Quiero presentarte a…** Introductions are a normal part of everyday life. Study the drawing and, with a partner, create four short conversations in which one person introduces another person to a third party.

Optional: You may want to encourage students to create fictional names, phone numbers, and e-mail addresses to avoid having them reveal too much personal information on the Internet.

ACTIVIDAD 5 **E-mail.** You're on the Internet and you meet someone you really like in a chat room for Spanish speakers. Write out the conversation you might have with that person. Include the following.

greeting	exchange of phone numbers
response	exchange of addresses
introduction	good-byes

Standards: This e-mail activity allows students to meet the presentational standard (C 1.3) by identifying the audience to which the student will present specific information.

ACTIVIDAD 6 **Otro e-mail.** Write an e-mail to your Spanish professor introducing yourself. In it, give your name, address, e-mail address, phone number, and any other personal information you think it is important for your Spanish professor to have. Send it!

A VER

Antes de ver el video

Standards: Through video viewing students learn interpretative strategies for communication. Activities in this section regularly provide opportunities for students to interpret spoken language (C 1.2).

ACTIVIDAD 1 In this video segment, you will meet some of the main characters in the video. How many do you already know? Go back to pages 8, 11, and 13 in the **Vocabulario útil** sections and identify the people you see in the photos.

For additional practice, do the *Nexos* website and / or CD-ROM video exercises.

Answers Act. 1: Anilú, Javier, Beto

ACTIVIDAD 2 The following is a list of key new vocabulary used in the video. Quickly review this list and the video dialog segments on pages 8, 11, and 13 before watching the video segment.

Ha sido un placer.	*It's been a pleasure.*
marqué	*I dialed*
¡Tengo prisa!	*I'm in a hurry!*
voy a marcar	*I'm going to dial*

These words are to help you understand the video only. You will not be tested on them.

Based on the list of words above, which of the following topics do you think might play a role in this video segment?

- una conversación en clase
- una conversación por teléfono
- una conversación entre dos personas que no se conocen (*don't know each other*)
- una conversación entre amigos

ACTIVIDAD 3 Before you watch the video segment, look at the following pieces of information you'll need to identify as you watch. Then, as you watch the video, listen for this specific information.

1. Las personas que hablan por celular: ¿Cómo se llaman?
2. Las personas al final: ¿Cómo se llaman?
3. _____ tiene (*has*) el celular de _____ .

Answers Act. 3: 1. Javier, Anilú 2. Javier, Anilú, Beto 3. Javier, Beto

---

ESTRATEGIA

Viewing a segment several times

When you first hear authentic Spanish, it may sound very fast to you. Stay calm! Remember that you don't have to understand absolutely everything and that with video, unlike real life, you have the opportunity to replay it! The first time you view the segment, listen for a general idea of what it is about. The second time, listen for more details.

El video

Now watch the video segment for **Capítulo 1.** View it as many times as you need to in order to answer the questions in **Actividad 3.**

Suggestion: Use multiple viewing strategies (stop – start, show with no sound, chunk segments and rewind, etc.) when showing video. Throughout *Nexos,* students will be encouraged to view and review segments. If students will view most episodes outside class, demonstrate viewing strategies they can use to get the most from their viewing.

Después de ver el video

ACTIVIDAD 4 Now say whether the following statements about the video segment are true **(cierto)** or false **(falso).** Correct the false statements to provide correct information.

> Answers Act. 4: 1. falso; Javier tiene el celular de Beto. 2. falso; Anilú es una amiga de Beto. 3. cierto 4. cierto 5. cierto 6. cierto

You may not understand every word in the activities throughout the chapter, but focus on getting the main idea. You'll be surprised at how much you *do* understand!

1. Javier tiene el celular de Anilú.
2. Anilú es una amiga de Javier.
3. Beto es un amigo de Anilú.
4. El número del teléfono celular que tiene Javier es el 3-39-71-94.
5. El número de teléfono de Beto es el 3-39-71-94.
6. Anilú le presenta Javier a Beto.

VOCES DE LA COMUNIDAD

Dos cubanoamericanas de Miami, Florida

The U.S. is the fourth largest Spanish-speaking country in the world. The more than 38 million Hispanics (or Latinos) that make their home in this country represent the fastest-growing segment of the U.S. population. By 2005, U.S. Hispanics are projected to become the nation's largest minority group, comprising nearly 13% of the total population.

U.S. Hispanics are enjoying a period of unprecedented prosperity. They have an estimated buying power of $600 billion a year, a number which more than doubles the combined buying power of all other Spanish-speaking countries in the world. American companies have taken notice of the lucrative Hispanic market. From launching Spanish-language websites to creating new Spanish-language publications, they are striving to understand, entice, and better serve Latino consumers.

In this favorable social and economic climate, U.S. Hispanics are making their mark in all areas of American life, including the arts and entertainment, politics, the media, and the business sector. The **Voces de la comunidad** section of Chapters 2–14 of *Nexos* features an outstanding U.S. Hispanic from these and other areas, people whose contributions have direct relevance to the theme of the chapter.

Standards: Throughout **Voces de la comunidad,** students will read about successful Spanish speakers in the U.S. and acquire cultural information (C 2) that features distinctive viewpoints of Spanish-speaking people (C 3.2).

¡PREPÁRATE!

Gramática útil 1
Identifying people and objects: Nouns and articles

CÓMO USARLO

Nouns identify people, places, and things: **señora Velasco, calle,** and **teléfono** are all nouns. *Articles* supply additional information about the noun.

1. *Definite* articles refer to a specific person, place, or thing.

La Avenida Central es **la** calle más importante de **la** universidad. (*You already know which avenue and university you are talking about.*)

*Central Avenue is **the** most important street in **the** university.*

2. *Indefinite* articles refer to a noun without identifying a specific person, place, or thing.

Un amigo es **una** persona que te gusta mucho. (*You are making a generalized statement, true of any friend.*)

*A friend is **a** person you like a lot.*

How many plural nouns can you find in this advertisement from Ecuador? Can you find the definite article?

Answers: 6 plural nouns: *perros, gatos, pájaros, peces, accesorios, mascotas;* definite article: *las*

To check your progress as you complete each vocabulary and grammar topic, do the *Nexos* website (http://college. hmco.com/languages/spanish/ students) exercises. You can also use the flashcards and, after studying the chapter grammar, complete the search activities based on Spanish-language sites.

Suggestion: Dramatize this concept in the classroom. Hold up *Nexos* and say **Es el libro de español.** Then pick up any other book without identifying it and say **Es un libro.**

The idea of gender for non-person nouns and for articles does not exist in English, although it is a feature of Spanish and many other languages. When learning new Spanish words, try to memorize the article with the noun so that you can remember the gender.

Standards: Grammar explanations frequently compare similarities and differences between English and Spanish usage such as gender (C 4.1).

CÓMO FORMARLO

LO BÁSICO

- *Number* indicates whether a word is singular or plural:
  la calle (*sing.*), **las calles** (*pl.*), **un escritorio** (*sing.*), **unos escritorios** (*pl.*)

- *Gender* indicates whether a word is masculine or feminine:
  una avenida (*fem.*), **el teléfono** (*masc.*)

3. Noun number and gender

◆ Often you can tell the gender of a Spanish noun by looking at its ending. Here are some general guidelines.

Masculine	Feminine
1. Nouns ending in **-o:** el amigo, el muchacho	Exception to rule #1: **la mano** (*hand*)
Exceptions to rule #2: words ending in **-ma:** el sistema, el problema, el tema, el programa; also **el día, el mapa**	2. Nouns ending in **-a:** **la compañera de cuarto, una chica**
Exceptions to rule #3: **el avión, el camión**	3. Nouns ending in **-ión, -dad, -tad,** and **-umbre** are usually feminine: **la información, una universidad, la libertad, la costumbre**

When nouns ending in **-ión** become plural, they lose the accent on the **-o:** la corporación, but **las corporaciones.**

Optional: You may want to expose students to a variety of cognates that end in **-ción** and are all feminine: **acción, construcción, creación, destrucción, ficción, formación, función, información, imaginación, infección, operación, pronunciación, selección.**

Nouns referring to people often reflect gender by changing a final **-o** to **-a** (chico / chica, amigo / amiga) or adding **-a** to a final consonant **(profesor / profesora).** For nouns ending in **-e, -ista,** or **-a** that refer to people, the article or context indicates gender **(el estudiante / la estudiante, el guitarrista / la guitarrista, Juan / Juanita es atleta).**

◆ Spanish nouns form their plurals in several ways.

Singular	Plural
1. Ends in vowel: **calle**	1. Add **-s: calles**
2. Ends in consonant: **universidad**	2. Add **-es: universidades**
3. Ends in **-z: lápiz**	3. Change **z** to **c** and add **-es: lápices**

4. Definite and indefinite articles

◆ Here are the Spanish definite articles, which correspond to the English article *the*.

	Singular	Plural
masculine	**el** el amigo *the friend (male)*	**los** los amigos *the friends (male or mixed group)*
feminine	**la** la amiga *the friend (female)*	**las** las amigas *the friends (female)*

In the past, **los** and **unos**, rather than **las** and **unas**, were used to refer to groups containing one or more males. The **Real Academia de la Lengua Española** recently ruled that the feminine forms should be used for groups with more females than males, but usage is changing slowly.

◆ Here are the Spanish indefinite articles, which correspond to the English articles *a*, *an*, and *some*.

	Singular	Plural
masculine	**un** un amigo *a friend (male)*	**unos** unos amigos *some friends (male or mixed group)*
feminine	**una** una amiga *a friend (female)*	**unas** unas amigas *some friends (female)*

◆ Remember that you use masculine articles with masculine nouns and feminine articles with feminine nouns. When a noun is in the plural, the corresponding plural article (masculine or feminine) is used: **el hombre, los hombres.**

◆ When referring to a person's *profession*, the article is omitted: **Liana es profesora y Ricardo es dentista.**

◆ However, when you use a *title* to refer to someone, the article is used: **Es el profesor Gómez.** When you address that person directly, using their title, the article is not used: **Buenos días, profesor Gómez.**

The following titles are typically used with the article when referring to the person, and without the article when addressing the person directly.

Notice: The absence of the indefinite article before one's profession will need to be reinforced repeatedly. Model and practice: **Soy profesor/a. Soy estudiante. . . . es presidente,** etc.

Notice: When the noun is modified, the article is used: **Liana es una profesora excelente.**

señor (Sr.)	*Mr.*	**señorita (Srta.)**	*Miss / Ms.*
señora (Sra.)	*Mrs. / Ms.*	**profesor / profesora**	*professor*

Actividades

ACTIVIDAD 1 **¿Femenino o masculino?** Listen to the speaker name a series of items and people. First, write down if the item or person is masculine or feminine. Then write the singular noun with its correct definite article. Lastly, write the plural noun with its correct definite article.

MODELO: *masculino*
el libro
los libros

Standards: In this activity students must understand spoken language (C 1.2).

Answers Act. 1: 1. **m,** el bolígrafo, los bolígrafos 2. **f,** la pizarra, las pizarras 3. **f,** la mesa, las mesas 4. **m,** el escritorio, los escritorios 5. **m,** el amigo, los amigos 6. **m o f,** el o la estudiante, los o las estudiantes 7. **m o f,** el o la artista, los o las artistas 8. **f,** la ventana, las ventanas

ACTIVIDAD 2 **¿Definido o indefinido?** Work with a partner. Try to guess from the context whether it makes more sense to use the definite article, the indefinite article, or no article in each of the following pairs of sentences.

1. Es _____ calle en mi colonia.

   Es _____ calle central de mi colonia.

2. Es _____ profesor en mi universidad.

   Es _____ profesor de español.

3. Es _____ estudiante más (*most*) inteligente de mi clase.

   Es _____ estudiante en mi clase.

4. Es _____ avenida más importante de mi colonia.

   Es _____ avenida en mi colonia.

5. Es _____ universidad en mi estado (*state*).

   Es _____ universidad más importante de mi estado.

ACTIVIDAD 3 **Presentaciones.** With a partner, complete the following introductions with the correct definite or indefinite articles where needed.

1. —Sra. Oliveros, quiero presentarle a _____ Srta. Martínez.
   —Un placer. ¿Dónde vive usted?

   —Vivo en _____ calle Colón, en _____ colonia Robles.

2. —Oye, Ricardo, quiero presentarte a mi amiga Rebeca. Ella es
   _____ dentista.

   —¡Mucho gusto, Rebeca! Yo soy _____ profesor de matemáticas.

   —¿De veras? Yo tengo (*I have*) _____ amigo que es profesor también.

3. —Buenas tardes. Yo soy _____ Sr. Bustelo.
   —Sr. Bustelo, ¿cuál es su número de teléfono?

   —Es _____ 7-89-48-92. ¿Y cuál es su número?

   —Es _____ 8-21-98-32.

4. —¡Hola!

   —Buenos días. ¿Puedo hablar con _____ Sr. Lezama?
   —Lo siento. No está.

   —Por favor, dígale que llamó _____ Sra. Barlovento. Tenemos
   (*We have*) clase de administración mañana y necesito darle (*I need to give him*) _____ apuntes.

ACTIVIDAD 4 **Más presentaciones.** Introduce yourself to another classmate. Exchange information about where you live, phone numbers, and e-mail addresses. Then prepare to introduce your classmate to the entire class.

Gramática útil 2
Identifying and describing: Subject pronouns and the present indicative of the verb *ser*

The Spanish verb **ser** can be used to identify people and objects, to describe them, to make introductions, and to say when something will take place. It is one of two Spanish verbs that are the equivalents of the English verb *to be*.

Mi teléfono **es** el 2-39-71-49.	*My telephone number **is** 2-39-71-49.*
Yo **soy** Mariela y ella **es** Elena.	*I **am** Mariela and this **is** Elena.*
La fiesta **es** el miércoles.	*The party **is** on Wednesday.*

LO BÁSICO

- *Pronouns* are words used to replace nouns. (Some English pronouns are *it, she, you, him,* etc.)
- Verbs change form to reflect *number* and *person. Number* refers to singular versus plural. *Person* refers to different subjects.
- A verb's *tense* indicates the time frame in which an event takes place (for example, *talk, talked, will talk*). The *present indicative tense* refers to present-time events or conditions (*I talk, I am talking*).

Estar, which you have already used in the expression **¿Cómo estás?,** also means *to be.* You will learn other ways to use **estar** in Ch. 4.

Standards: In comparing English *to be* with the two verbs in Spanish, you may want to conjugate *to be:* I am, you are, he/she is, ... (C 4.1).

1. Subject pronouns

◆ Subject pronouns are pronouns that are used as the subject of a sentence. Here are the subject pronouns in Spanish.

Singular		Plural	
yo	*I*	nosotros / nosotras	*we*
tú	*you (fam.)*	vosotros / vosotras	*you (fam.)*
usted (Ud.)	*you (form.)*	ustedes (Uds.)	*you (fam., form.)*
él, ella	*he, she*	ellos, ellas	*they*

¿Tú eres Javier?

◆ The **vosotros / vosotras** forms are primarily used in Spain. They allow Spaniards to address more than one person informally. These forms are not generally used in the rest of the Spanish-speaking world. Instead, in most other places **ustedes** is used to address several people, regardless of the formality of the relationship. The **vosotros** forms of verbs are provided in *Nexos* so that you can recognize them, but they are not included for practice in activities.

In Spanish, it is not always necessary to use the subject pronoun with the verb, as long as the subject is understood. For example, it's usually not necessary to say **Yo soy Rafael,** since **Soy Rafael** is clear enough on its own.

In some countries, you will hear the form **vos** (Argentina and parts of Uruguay, Chile, and Central America). This is a variation of **tú** that is used only in these regions.

To show respect, you sometimes hear the titles **don** and **doña** used with people you address as **usted**. **Don** and **doña** are used with the person's first **name: don Roberto, doña Carmen.**

2. Formal vs. familiar

As you have already seen, Spanish has two basic forms of address: the **tú** form and the **usted** form. English has a single word—*you*—to address people directly, regardless of how well you know them.

◆ **Tú** is used to address a family member, a close friend, a child, or a pet.

◆ **Usted** (often abbreviated **Ud.**) is a more formal means of address used with older people, strangers, acquaintances, and sometimes with colleagues.

Levels of formality vary throughout the Spanish-speaking world, so it's important when traveling to listen to how **tú** and **usted** are used. Then follow the local practice.

3. The present tense of the verb **ser**

The present indicative forms of the verb **ser** are as follows. Note the subject pronouns associated with each form.

ser (*to be*)	
Singular	
yo soy	*I am*
tú eres	*you (s. fam.) are*
usted es	*you (s. form.) are*
él es	*he is*
ella es	*she is*
Plural	
nosotros / nosotras somos	*we are*
vosotros / vosotras sois	*you (pl. fam.) are*
ustedes son	*you (pl. form. or fam.) are*
ellos son	*they (masc. or mixed) are*
ellas son	*they (fem.) are*

Actividades

ACTIVIDAD 5 **Manuel.** Manuel writes an e-mail to a new Internet friend describing himself and his two best friends. Complete his e-mail with the correct forms of **ser.**

¡Hola! Yo (1) _____ Manuel Ybarra. (2) _____ estudiante en la Universidad Nacional Autónoma de México, que (3) _____ una de las universidades más importantes de las Américas. ¡La población estudiantil (4) _____ de más de 250.000 estudiantes!

　　Tengo dos amigos íntimos. Mi amiga Susana (5) _____ una persona muy sincera. Ella y yo (6) _____ inseparables. Mi amigo Hernán (7) _____ muy cómico. Hernán y yo (8) _____ compañeros de cuarto. Susana y Hernán (9) _____ buenos amigos también. Y tú, ¿cómo (10) _____?

ACTIVIDAD 6 **¿Quiénes son?** Use **ser** to say who the following people are.

Answers Act. 6: 1. es 2. es 3. es 4. somos 5. eres 6. es 7. son 8. son

1. [Nombre] _____ mi compañero(a) de clase.

2. [Nombre] _____ el profesor (la profesora) de español.

3. [Nombre] _____ el instructor (la instructora) en la clase de español.

4. Nosotros _____ estudiantes de español.

5. Tú…

6. Usted…

7. Ustedes…

8. Ellos…

 ACTIVIDAD 7 **Los saludos.** With a partner, match each of the following greetings with the correct group of individuals.

Answers Act 7: 1. d 2. b 3. a 4. c

1. two teens   a. —Buenos días. ¿Cómo está usted?
                              —Muy bien, gracias. ¿Y ustedes?

2. two professional acquaintances   b. —Buenos días, Sra. Sánchez.
                              —Y a Ud. también, Sr. Rivas.

3. an older man and two teens   c. —Buenas tardes. ¿Cómo están ustedes?
                              —Bien, Marcos, ¿y tú?

4. teen and two professors   d. —Hola, Carmen. ¿Cómo te va?
                              —Bien, Rosa. ¿Qué hay de nuevo?

ACTIVIDAD 8 **Le presento a…** In groups of three or four, act out an introduction in front of the class. Decide beforehand the ages and the social standing of the people you are role-playing, as well as how informal or formal the situation is. The class must guess whether the introduction is formal or informal. Follow the model.

MODELO: —*Buenos días, doña Esmeralda.*
              —*Buenos días, Susana.*
              —*Doña Esmeralda, le presento a mi amigo Paul. Es estudiante.*
              —*Encantada, Paul. ¿Cómo estás?*
              —*Muy bien. ¿Y usted?*

Gramática útil 3
Expressing quantity: *Hay* + nouns

CÓMO USARLO

1. Hay is the Spanish equivalent of *there is* or *there are* in English.

Hay una reunión en la cafetería.	**There is** a meeting in the cafeteria.
Hay tres estudiantes en la clase.	**There are** three students in the class.
Hay unos libros en la mesa.	**There are** some books on the table.
Hay una fiesta el viernes.	**There is** a party on Friday.

2. Hay is used with both singular and plural nouns, and in both affirmative and negative contexts.

Hay un bolígrafo, pero no hay lápices en la mesa.

Aquí **hay** un problema.

Suggestion: Reinforce examples by stating **Hay es una forma invariable.** Write the word **invariable** on the board. Then write **Hay un libro. Hay unos libros.** Model the question **¿Qué hay en el salón de clase?** Have students generate answers with **hay** + classroom vocabulary.

3. **Hay** can be used with numbers or with indefinite articles (**un, una, unos, unas**), but it is never used with definite articles (**el, la, los, las**).

¡**Hay** tres profesores en la clase, pero sólo **hay** una estudiante!	*There are three professors in the class, but there is only one student!*

4. With a plural noun or negative, typically no article is used with **hay** unless you are providing extra information: "some people" as opposed to just "people."

Hay papeles en la mesa.	*There are papers on the table.*
No hay libros en el escritorio.	*There aren't (any) books on the desk.*
Hay quince personas en la clase. BUT:	*There are fifteen people in the class.*
Hay unas personas en el cuarto.	*There are some people in the room.*

CÓMO FORMARLO

Hay is an *invariable verb form* because it never changes to reflect number or person. This means **hay** can be used with both singular and plural nouns.

Actividades

ACTIVIDAD 9 **Hay…** Say how many of the following things are in the places mentioned.

MODELO: ventana (5): salón de clase
Hay cinco ventanas en el salón de clase.

1. computadora (15): laboratorio
2. policía (2): calle
3. libro (5): escritorio
4. profesor (3): reunión
5. estudiante (40): cafetería
6. persona (20): fiesta
7. verbo (35): pizarra
8. celular (1): mochila

ACTIVIDAD 10 **¿Cuántos** (*How many*) **hay?** In groups of four or five, find out how many of the following objects there are in your group.

MODELO: *Hay tres teléfonos celulares en el grupo.*

1. teléfonos celulares
2. calculadoras
3. diccionarios
4. asistentes electrónicos
5. estéreos personales
6. ¿…?

ACTIVIDAD 11 **¿Hay o no hay…?** You are looking for something you need for class. Tell a classmate what you're looking for, and he or she will tell you if that item is or is not in the classroom. If what you ask for is there, he or she will tell you where to find it.

MODELO: Tú: *¿Hay un diccionario en la clase?*
Compañero(a): *Sí, hay un diccionario en la mesa.* (*No, no hay diccionario en la clase.*)
Tú: *¡Muchas gracias!*

Sonrisas

COMPRENSIÓN. Answer the following questions about the cartoon.

1. Según (*According to*) Dieguito, ¿qué hay en su cuarto?
2. En realidad, ¿qué hay en el cuarto de Dieguito?
3. Según la mamá de Dieguito, ¿qué hay en la cocina (*kitchen*)?
4. En realidad, ¿hay un elefante en la cocina?

Answers: 1. un elefante 2. un elefante
3. un elefante 4. no

 Standards: In **Sonrisas** cartoons, students will interpret written language (C 1.2) and examine language through humor, irony, and common sense. This technique guides students toward personal enjoyment and life-long uses of the language (C 5.2).

Gramática útil 4
Expressing possession, obligation, and age: *Tener, tener que, tener + años*

Begin the CD-ROM activities. Do the cultural activities and reading and writing practice as you complete the text sections.

Tienes el celular de mi amigo Beto.

Suggestion: Give the lesson on **tener** a personal dimension. Prepare a short biography of things that you own, or bring a bag of objects to class. Recycle vocabulary already presented or use cognates. Next, engage students in a group conversation about their possessions: **¿Qué tienes en la mochila? ¿Qué tienes en casa? ¿Qué tiene su compañero en casa?** etc.

You may want to expand with examples showing omission of the article: **¿Tienes computadora / mochila / amigos hispanos? Tengo (No tengo) calculadora / compañero de cuarto / fotos de la familia.**

In Spanish the word for birthday is **cumpleaños,** which literally means "completes **(cumple)** years **(años).**" Many Spanish speakers celebrate their saint's day **(el día de su santo),** which is the birthday of the saint whose name is the same as or similar to their own. For example: **El 16 de marzo es el día de San José.**

CÓMO USARLO

1. The verb **tener** means *to have.* It is used in Spanish to express possession and to give someone's age. You may also use it with **que** and another verb to say what you have to do: **Tengo que irme.** (*I have to go.*)

Ya **tienes** mi dirección.	*You already **have** my address.*
Tengo dos teléfonos en casa.	*I **have** two telephones in my house.*
Elena **tiene** veinte años. ¿Cuántos años **tienen** Sergio y Dulce?	*Elena **is** twenty years old. How old **are** Sergio and Dulce?*
Tengo que irme porque **tengo** clase.	*I **have to** go because I **have** class.*

2. When **tener** is used to express possession, the article is usually omitted, unless number is emphasized or you are referring to a specific object.

3. Note that while Spanish uses **tener… años** to express age, the English equivalent is *to be . . . years old.*

4. Remember, it's better to use the verb without a subject pronoun unless the subject is unclear or you want to emphasize it.

CÓMO FORMARLO

1. Here are the forms of the verb **tener** in the present indicative tense.

tener (*to have*)			
yo	**tengo**	nosotros / nosotras	**tenemos**
tú	**tienes**	vosotros / vosotras	**tenéis**
Ud., él, ella	**tiene**	Uds., ellos, ellas	**tienen**

2. When talking about age, it's helpful to know the months of the year so that you can say when people's birthdays are celebrated.

¿Cuándo es tu cumpleaños? (*When is your birthday?*)

enero	**julio**
febrero	**agosto**
marzo	**septiembre**
abril	**octubre**
mayo	**noviembre**
junio	**diciembre**

Notice: Reinforce that months are generally not capitalized in Spanish.

Suggestion: Have students sort themselves by birth month into different sectors of the room. After students return to their seats, see who can remember the most birth months of their classmates.

3. When giving dates in Spanish, the day of the month comes first: **el quince de abril** = *April 15th*. When writing the date with numbers, the day always comes before the month: 15/4/04 = **el quince de abril de 2004.**

Suggestion: For additional practice, write dates on the board (2/12, 5/6, etc.) and have students read them. Be sure they remember that the day precedes the month in Spanish.

Actividades

ACTIVIDAD 12 **¿Qué tienen?** Say what each person has. Mention a logical place that they would have it.

MODELO: un cuaderno (yo)
Tengo un cuaderno en el escritorio.

1. un celular (yo)
2. tres computadoras (nosotros)
3. unos apuntes (ellos)
4. dos libros (tú)
5. cinco lápices (el profesor)
6. dos calculadoras (ustedes)

Answers Act. 12: (*Answers may vary.*)
1. Tengo un celular en la mochila.
2. Tenemos tres computadoras en casa.
3. Tienen unos apuntes en el cuaderno.
4. Tienes dos libros en la mochila. 5. Tiene cinco lápices en el escritorio. 6. Tienen dos calculadoras en la mesa.

ACTIVIDAD 13 **¿Cuántos años tienen?** Tell a friend the birthdates and ages of the following people.

MODELO: Arturo (28/3; 25 años)
El cumpleaños de Arturo es el veintiocho de marzo. Tiene veinticinco años.

1. Martín (12/4; 21 años)
2. Sandra y Susana (14/7; 24 años)
3. mamá (16/6; 45 años)
4. papá (22/2; 47 años)
5. Gustavo (7/9; 23 años)
6. Irma y Daniel (19/1; 27 años)

The number **veintiuno** shortens to **veintiún** when it's used with a noun: **veintiún años.**

Answers Act. 13: El cumpleaños de...
1. ... Martín es el doce de abril. Tiene veintiún años. 2. ... Sandra y Susana es el catorce de julio. Tienen veinticuatro años.
3. ... mamá es el dieciséis de junio. Tiene cuarenta y cinco años. 4. ... papá es el veintidós de febrero. Tiene cuarenta y siete años. 5. ... Gustavo es el siete de septiembre. Tiene veintitrés años.
6. ... Irma y Daniel es el diecinueve de enero. Tienen veintisiete años.

ACTIVIDAD 14 **La fiesta.** Listen to the conversation between Marta and Juan. They are talking about the birthdays and ages of various friends. Write down the age and the birthdate of each person.

Standards: Here students interpret spoken language (C 1.2).

Answers Act. 14: 1. Miguel: 22 años; 30 de julio 2. Arturo: 25 años; 27 de julio 3. Enrique: 24 años; 1 de agosto 4. Isabel: 26 años; 5 de agosto

	EDAD	CUMPLEAÑOS
1. Miguel		
2. Arturo		
3. Enrique		
4. Isabel		

El español: tu conexión directa al siglo 21

¿Adivinaste? (*Did you guess correctly?*) Answers to the questions on page 7: 1. d; 2. g; 3. a; 4. e; 5. c; 6. b; 7. f, h

⊙ ② ③ Standards: Throughout *Nexos*, the **Exploraciones culturales** sections explore Spanish-speaking cultures (C 2) and reinforce and further knowledge of other disciplines—in this case geography (C 3).

Before beginning, model pronunciation of country names for repetition.

Answers: **Sudamérica:** Argentina, Bolivia, Chile, Colombia, Ecuador, Paraguay, Uruguay, Perú, Venezuela; **Centroamérica:** Costa Rica, El Salvador, Guatemala, Honduras, Nicaragua, Panamá; **El Caribe:** Cuba, Puerto Rico, República Dominicana; **Norteamérica:** Estados Unidos, México; **Europa:** España; **África:** Guinea Ecuatorial; **Asia:** las Filipinas

Optional: Have students study country capitals and then quiz each other: ¿Cuál es la capital de Chile?

⊙ ② ④ Standards: Throughout *Nexos*, the **¡Compárate!** section presents cultural information (C 2) that often can be compared to one's native culture (C 4).

El mundo hispanohablante. With a partner, look at the maps on the inside covers of your textbook. Take turns naming each country and pointing it out on the map. Make a list with the following headings: **Sudamérica, Centroamérica, El Caribe, Norteamérica, Europa, Asia,** and **África.** Put each of the following countries under its proper heading.

Países (*Countries*) de habla hispana

Argentina	Ecuador	Guinea Ecuatorial	Perú
Bolivia	El Salvador	Honduras	Puerto Rico
Chile	España	México	República Dominicana
Colombia	Estados Unidos*	Nicaragua	Uruguay
Costa Rica	las Filipinas*	Panamá	Venezuela
Cuba	Guatemala	Paraguay	

*Se habla español pero no es la lengua oficial.

¡COMPÁRATE!

With more than 360 million speakers the world over, Spanish is the third most spoken language in the world, after Mandarin and English. Here are some additional facts about the Spanish language.

- Spanish is the official language of 21 countries.
- In the U.S. it is spoken by more than 30 million people. More than half a million people also study Spanish in the U.S. at the college level every year.
- Like all languages, Spanish exhibits some regional variations which are mostly limited to vocabulary and pronunciation. In spite of these variations, Spanish speakers from all over the world communicate without difficulty.

PRÁCTICA. With a partner, discuss your reasons for studying Spanish. What professional or personal benefits do you expect to get out of your study of this language?

El mapa. In future chapters, you'll be studying these countries in greater detail. To help you learn about maps and geography, look at the map of South America with a partner and locate the following places.

1. cordillera: los Andes
2. volcán: Ojos del Salado
3. monte: Aconcagua
4. isla: Malvinas
5. río: Orinoco
6. lago: Maracaibo
7. catarata: Salto Ángel
8. cabo: Cabo de Hornos
9. océano: Atlántico
10. ciudad: Buenos Aires
11. país: Chile
12. mar: Caribe

Now use the terms above to identify each of the following as a **monte, volcán, río, mar, cordillera,** etc.

1. the Colorado
2. McKinley
3. Superior
4. Mediterranean
5. Oahu
6. Mount St. Helens
7. Niagara Falls
8. the Rockies

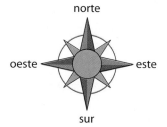

Answers: 1. río 2. monte 3. lago 4. mar
5. isla 6. monte 7. catarata 8. cordillera

¡CONÉCTATE!

Choose one of the 23 countries listed on the prior page. Find out the following information about it and prepare a brief country profile. Follow the links on the *Nexos* website (http://college.hmco.com/languages/spanish/students) to see a list of suggested websites.

1. population and area
2. capital and major cities
3. major indigenous groups
4. official language
5. major industries
6. major geographic features

Standards: Here students acquire information (C 3,2) and participate and learn about multilingual communities (C 5.1).

A LEER

Antes de leer

Standards: Throughout reading sections in *Nexos,* students learn to interpret language (C 1.2), as well as often acquire cultural information and gain insights into the nature of language.

¡Ojo! (literally, *eye*) is used in Spanish to direct a person's attention to something. It is similar to saying "Watch out!" or "Be careful!" in English.

Show students the gesture for **¡Ojo!**

ESTRATEGIA

Identifying cognates to aid comprehension

You have already learned a number of *cognates.* These are words that look similar in both Spanish and English, although they are pronounced differently. Some cognates you have already learned so far in this chapter are **regular, terrible, teléfono,** and **avenida.** Looking for cognates in a passage you are reading helps you get the general idea of the content, even if you don't know many of the other words and structures.

¡OJO! Occasionally you will come across *false cognates,* words that look similar in English and Spanish, but that mean two different things. For example, as you have learned, the Spanish word **dirección** means *address,* not *direction,* in English. If a word that looks like a cognate doesn't make sense in the context of what you are reading, it could be a false cognate, and you may need to look it up in a dictionary to discover its true meaning.

ACTIVIDAD 1 Look at the headline and the four sections of the following article. See if you can get the main idea of the article by relying on cognates and words you already know.

1. Put a check mark by the words that you already know in the title and the four bulleted sections.
2. Underline the cognates that appear in these sections. Can you guess their general meaning, based on context and where they appear in the sentence?

Answers Act. 2: 1. *Answer will vary.* 2. b
3. a 4. a 5. darthvader2@ciberglobal.com
6. *Answers will vary.*

ACTIVIDAD 2 Now choose the category in the reading that applies best to you and read it, concentrating on the cognates and words you already know. Then answer the following questions, based on what you have read.

1. ¿Qué tipo de dirección electrónica tienes?
2. Según (*According to*) el artículo, las personas que tienen una dirección electrónica con su nombre son…
   a. misteriosas   b. honestas   c. emocionales   d. introvertidas
3. Las personas que son lógicas y poco emocionales tienen una dirección electrónica…
   a. con números   b. con su nombre   c. de fantasía   d. descriptiva
4. Las personas que se describen con su dirección electrónica son…
   a. un poco inocentes   b. aventureras   c. agresivas   d. introvertidas
5. ¿Cuál es el nombre de fantasía que usan en el artículo?
6. En tu opinión, ¿es correcta o falsa la información sobre tu personalidad?

Lectura

¡Tu dirección electrónica revela tu personalidad!

¿Es simbólica la dirección electrónica que usas? Muchas personas creen[1] que no, pero en realidad, los "nombres de computadora" que usamos revelan información importante sobre nuestras características más secretas. ¿Es posible que tu dirección electrónica revela todo[2]? ¡Vamos a ver!

Escoge[3] el tipo de dirección electrónica más similar a la tuya[4]...

- **Nombre (ejemplo:** lucidíaz@internex.com)
  En este caso, la dirección electrónica puede[5] representar a una persona directa y honesta. Prefiere la realidad y es práctica y realista. No le interesa el misterio o la fantasía. Estas personas son muy aptas para los negocios[6] a causa de su estilo directo.

- **Números (ejemplo:** 1078892@compluservicio.com)
  Las personas con los números en las direcciones electrónicas no tienen mucho interés en las cortesías diarias o las interacciones sociales. ¡Prefieren el mundo[7] superracional de los números y las matemáticas puras! Otra explicación es que prefieren ser anónimos—quieren[8] mantener su misterio con un nombre que revela muy poco[9]!

- **Auto-descripción (ejemplo:** romántico29@mundored.com)
  Las personas que se describen con la dirección electrónica necesitan comprensión y cariño. Pueden ser amables, afectuosas y un poco ingenuas o inocentes. Pero, ¡cuidado[10]! ¡Estos nombres pueden ser totalmente falsos! Los nombres que indican que una persona es honesta o responsable pueden distorsionar la realidad completamente....

- **Fantasía (ejemplo:** darthvader2@ciberglobal.com)
  Por lo general, estas personas consideran al ciberespacio como una oportunidad para reinventarse. Prefieren identificarse como un personaje imaginario para participar en lo que es, para ellos, ¡un drama cibernético! Pueden ser aventurosas, emocionales y extrovertidas. Estos nombres también pueden atraer a las personas introvertidas que tienen la fantasía de presentarse completamente diferente de su realidad diaria.

[1]think [2]everything [3]Choose [4]yours [5]can [6]business [7]world [8]they want to [9]very little [10]careful

Después de leer

 ACTIVIDAD 3 With a partner, try to invent as many names in each of the last two categories (**auto-descripción** and **fantasía**) as you can. Try to use cognates from the reading when possible and be as creative as possible! You have five minutes.

 ACTIVIDAD 4 Now take the list of e-mail names you created in **Actividad 3** and add your own e-mail name to the list. (Or, if your e-mail name is simply your name or number, create one that you would like to use.) Then, you and your partner from **Actividad 3** should form a group with two other pairs. Share your lists and see if you can guess each other's e-mail addresses.

All of the reading passages in *Nexos* include translations of some words that you may not be able to guess from context. Try to get the gist of the passage before you look for the definitions. Saving them as a last resort allows you to read the passage more quickly and to concentrate on getting the main idea.

Optional: After students do **Actividad 3**, have them share their favorite creation with the class.

A ESCRIBIR

Antes de escribir

ESTRATEGIA

Prewriting—Identifying your target audience

Before you begin to write, or even to *think* about writing, you need to consider who will be reading your work. The identity of your intended reader is the crucial element that helps you establish the format, tone, and content of your written piece. Imagine you are writing two letters about the same event; for instance, how a computer you purchased turned out to be a lemon and you had to return it. How would the format, tone, and content of your letter vary if you were writing it (1) to a close friend, or (2) to the president of the company that manufactures the computer? Keeping in mind the intended audience for your writing is the first step toward creating an effective written piece.

 ACTIVIDAD 1 You are going to write a letter or e-mail message to your new roommate. This person has been assigned to you, but you have not yet met. With a partner, create a list of the information you should include in your message and identify its tone—how you want it to sound.

 ACTIVIDAD 2 Taking your list of information from **Actividad 1,** study the following partial model and see if you have included everything you need.

> Querido Roberto/Querida Susana,
>
> (*Greeting*) Me llamo... . Soy tu nuevo(a) compañero(a) de cuarto. Vivo en... . (*Ask about him/her.*)
>
> Aquí tienes mi dirección..., mi teléfono... y mi dirección electrónica... Mi cumpleaños es... . (*Ask for his/her personal information.*)
>
> Tengo un estéreo, un refrigerador y un televisor para el cuarto. ¿Qué tienes tú?
>
> Bueno, ya es todo por ahora. Nos vemos pronto. (*Say good-bye.*) Tu amigo(a),
> ...

Escritura

ACTIVIDAD 3 Using the previous model, write a rough draft of your letter to your roommate. Try to write freely without worrying too much about mistakes or misspellings. You will have an opportunity to revise your work later. Here are some additional phrases that may be useful.

tu nuevo(a) compañero(a) de cuarto	*your new roommate*
para el cuarto	*for the room*
un estéreo	*stereo*
un microondas	*microwave oven*
un refrigerador	*refrigerator*
un televisor	*television set*
una lámpara	*lamp*
una videocasetera	*VCR*
un DVD	*DVD player*
Eso es todo por ahora.	*That's all for now.*

Después de escribir

ACTIVIDAD 4 Exchange your rough draft with a partner. Read each others' work and comment on its content and structure. For example, put a check mark next to places where you would like more information. Put a star by your favorite sentence. Put a question mark where meaning is not clear. Underline errors in spelling and grammar.

ACTIVIDAD 5 Now go back over your letter and revise it. Incorporate your partner's comments. Use the following checklist to check your final copy. Did you . . .

- make sure you included all the necessary information?
- match the tone of your writing to your audience?
- follow the model provided in **Actividad 2**?
- look for misspellings?
- check to make sure you used the correct forms of **ser** and **tener**?
- watch to make sure articles and nouns agree?

Suggestion: For additional practice, have pairs revise one of their letters to make it more formal. Have them imagine it is addressed to the head of the residence hall instead of to their future roommate. Ask: How would you modify the language in the existing letter to make it more courteous and formal?

V O C A B U L A R I O

PARA SALUDAR   *How to greet*

Hola.	*Hello.*
¿Qué tal?	*How are things going?*
¿Cómo estás (tú)?	*How are you? (s. fam.)*
¿Cómo está (usted)?	*How are you? (s. form.)*
¿Cómo están (ustedes)?	*How are you? (pl.)*
¿Cómo te va?	*How's it going with you? (s. fam.)*
¿Cómo le va?	*How's it going with you? (s. form.)*
¿Cómo les va?	*How's it going with you? (pl.)*
¿Qué hay de nuevo?	*What's new?*
Buenos días.	*Good morning.*
Buenas tardes.	*Good afternoon.*
Buenas noches.	*Good night. Good evening.*

PARA RESPONDER   *How to respond*

Bien, gracias.	*Fine, thank you.*
Bastante bien.	*Quite well.*
(No) Muy bien.	*(Not) Very well.*
Regular.	*So-so.*
¡Terrible! / ¡Fatal!	*Terrible! / Awful!*
No mucho.	*Not much.*
Nada.	*Nothing.*
¿Y tú?	*And you? (s. fam.)*
¿Y usted?	*And you? (s. form.)*

PARA PEDIR Y DAR INFORMACIÓN PERSONAL   *To ask for and give personal information*

¿Cómo te llamas?	*What's your name? (s. fam.)*
¿Cómo se llama?	*What's your name? (s. form.)*
Me llamo…	*My name is . . .*
(Yo) soy…	*I am . . .*
¿Cuál es tu número de teléfono?	*What is your phone number? (s. fam.)*
¿Cuál es su número de teléfono?	*What is your phone number? (s. form.)*
Mi número de teléfono es el 3-71-28-12.	*My telephone number is 371-2812.*
Es el 3-71-28-12.	*It's 371-2812.*
¿Dónde vives?	*Where do you live? (s. fam.)*
¿Dónde vive?	*Where do you live? (s. form.)*
Vivo en…	*I live at . . .*
la avenida…	*avenue*
la calle…	*street*
la colonia…	*neighborhood*
¿Cuál es tu dirección?	*What is your address? (s. fam.)*
¿Cuál es su dirección?	*What is your address? (s. form.)*
Mi dirección es…	*My address is . . .*
¿Cuál es tu dirección electrónica?	*What's your e-mail address? (s. fam.)*
¿Cuál es su dirección electrónica?	*What's your e-mail address? (s. form.)*
Aquí tienes mi dirección electrónica.	*Here's my e-mail address. (s. fam.)*
Aquí tiene mi dirección electrónica.	*Here's my e-mail address. (s. form.)*

PARA PRESENTAR A ALGUIEN   *To introduce someone*

Soy…	*I am . . .*
Me llamo… / Mi nombre es…	*My name is . . .*
Quiero presentarte a…	*I'd like to introduce you (s. fam.) to . . .*
Quiero presentarle a…	*I'd like to introduce you (s. form.) to . . .*
Quiero presentarles a…	*I'd like to introduce you (pl.) to . . .*

PARA RESPONDER   *To respond*

Mucho gusto.	*My pleasure.*
Mucho gusto en conocerte.	*A pleasure to meet you.*
Encantado(a).	*Delighted to meet you.*
Igualmente.	*Likewise.*
El gusto es mío.	*The pleasure is mine.*
Un placer.	*My pleasure.*

PARA DESPEDIRSE   *To say good-bye*

Adiós.	*Good-bye.*
Hasta luego.	*See you later.*
Hasta mañana.	*See you tomorrow.*
Hasta pronto.	*See you soon.*
Nos vemos.	*See you later.*
Chau.	*Bye.*
Bueno, tengo que irme.	*Well / OK, I have to go.*

PARA HABLAR POR TELÉFONO
To talk on the telephone

Familiar

—¡Hola!	*Hello?*
—¿Está…?	*Is . . . there?*
—Sí. Aquí está. / No, no está.	*Yes. Here he / she is. / No, he's / she's not here.*
—Soy… Mi número es el…	*I'm . . . My number is . . .*
—Muy bien. Hasta luego.	*OK. See you later.*
—Chau.	*Bye.*

Formal

—¡Hola!	*Hello?*
—Hola. ¿Puedo hablar con…?	*Hi, may I speak with . . . ?*
—Sí. / Lo siento. No está.	*Yes. / I'm sorry. He's / She's not here.*
—Por favor, dígale que llamó (nombre). Mi número es el…	*Please tell him / her that (name) called. My number is . . .*
—Muy bien.	*OK.*
—Muchas gracias.	*Thank you very much.*
—De nada. Adiós.	*You're welcome. Good-bye.*
—Adiós.	*Good-bye.*

¿CUÁNDO ES TU CUMPLEAÑOS?
When is your birthday?

enero	*January*
febrero	*February*
marzo	*March*
abril	*April*
mayo	*May*
junio	*June*
julio	*July*
agosto	*August*
septiembre	*September*
octubre	*October*
noviembre	*November*
diciembre	*December*

PALABRAS ÚTILES *Useful words*

Títulos

don	*title of respect used with male first name*
doña	*title of respect used with female first name*
señor / Sr.	*Mr.*
señora / Sra.	*Mrs., Ms.*
señorita / Srta.	*Miss, Ms.*

Los artículos definidos

el, la, los, las	*the*

Los artículos indefinidos

una, una	*a*
unos, unas	*some*

Los pronombres personales

yo	*I*
tú	*you (fam.)*
usted (Ud.)	*you (form.)*
él	*he*
ella	*she*
nosotros / nosotras	*we*
vosotros / vosotras	*you (fam. pl.)*
ustedes (Uds.)	*you (fam. or form. pl.)*
ellos / ellas	*they*

Los verbos

estar	*to be*
hay	*there is, there are*
ser	*to be*
tener	*to have*
tener… años	*to be . . . years old*
tener que	*to have to (+ verb)*

Expresiones

Tengo prisa.	*I'm in a hurry.*

¿Qué te gusta hacer?

CAPÍTULO 2

Communication

By the end of this chapter you will be able to:
- express likes and dislikes
- compare yourself to other people and describe personality traits
- ask and answer questions
- talk about leisure-time activities
- indicate nationality

Cultures

By the end of this chapter you will have learned about:
- Hispanics in the United States
- world nationalities
- Mother's Day celebrations
- bilingual culture in the U.S.
- Spanish-language media in the U.S.

Standards: Examples of the other standards that will be met in Chapter 2 are: Connections – geography through nationalities; Comparisons – inviting in English- and Spanish-speaking cultures; Communities – Spanish-language media in the U.S.

A estos jóvenes les gusta el básquetbol.

GUSTOS Y PREFERENCIAS

We express aspects of our personalities through our likes and dislikes. In this chapter, we explore the relationship between personalities and preferences. How does what we like or dislike define us?

Los datos

Los resultados del censo de 2000 incluyen esta información. Analiza los gráficos y luego contesta las preguntas.

❶ ¿Qué grupo de hispanos es el más grande (+)?
❷ ¿Qué grupo de hispanos es el más pequeño (−)?

¡Adivina!

¿Qué sabes (*do you know*) sobre el español en Estados Unidos? (Las respuestas están en la página 60.)

❶ ¿Qué estados originalmente formaron (*formed*) parte de México?
   a. Texas, California, Nevada, Utah
   b. Oregon, Washington, Idaho, Montana
   c. Texas, Lousiana, Mississippi, Oklahoma

❷ ¿Qué ciudad estadounidense tiene una población de puertorriqueños más grande que San Juan, la capital de Puerto Rico?
   a. Los Angeles
   b. New York City
   c. Chicago

❸ ¿La Pequeña Habana es una sección de qué ciudad estadounidense?
   a. Washington, D.C.
   b. Miami, Florida
   c. New Orleans, Louisiana

Los datos Answers: 1. mexicanos 2. cubanos

¡Adivina! answers: 1. a 2. b 3. b

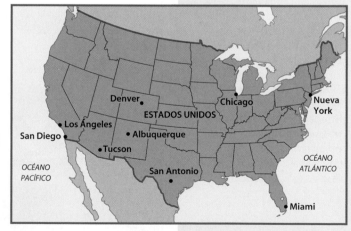

En Estados Unidos hay más de 38 millones de personas de ascendencia hispana.

otra nacionalidad 28%
mexicanos 58%
cubanos 3,5%
puertorriqueños 10%

Denver
Chicago
Nueva York
Los Ángeles
ESTADOS UNIDOS
San Diego
Albuquerque
Tucson
OCÉANO PACÍFICO
San Antonio
OCÉANO ATLÁNTICO
Miami

¡IMAGÍNATE!

Vocabulario útil 1

BETO:	Autora14, **¿qué te gusta hacer** los domingos? …
DULCE:	Los domingos generalmente **estudio** en la biblioteca.
ANILÚ:	¡Qué aburrida!
BETO:	**¡Estudias!**
ANILÚ:	Dile que **bailas** y **cantas** y **escuchas** música.
BETO:	¿No te gusta hacer otras cosas?
DULCE:	Pues sí. A veces mis amigos y yo **tomamos un refresco** en el Jazz Café o **alquilamos un video.**

Notice: In this section, **me gusta, te gusta, le gusta,** and **les gusta** are presented lexically followed by an infinitive. Students will learn this structure formally in the second grammar presentation of the chapter.

Point out that the days of the week are not capitalized in Spanish.

Suggestion: You may want to write the three cues for these scenes on the board as headings: **A mí me gusta…, A mi amiga le gusta…, A mis amigos les gusta…** Have students study the drawings with labeled vocabulary and generate both orally and in writing things that the characters in the drawings like to do. Write the activities on the board under the headings. This will serve as an introduction to the vocabulary in the chapter. Then personalize the activity by asking students what they like to do based on this vocabulary: **¿A ti te gusta…?**

LAS ACTIVIDADES   *Activities*

A ti, ¿qué te gusta hacer los fines de semana (los viernes, los sábados y los domingos)?

What do you like to do on the weekends (Fridays, Saturdays, and Sundays)?

A mí me gusta …

alquilar videos

estudiar en la biblioteca/ en casa

conversar

escuchar música

cocinar

bailar

caminar

cantar

Actividades

ACTIVIDAD 1 **Los verbos.** What Spanish verbs do you associate with the following? Choose from the list. (Some items can have more than one answer.)

1. _____ los murales
2. _____ la música
3. _____ los deportes
4. _____ una presentación oral
5. _____ un instrumento musical
6. _____ la familia

a. preparar
b. pintar
c. tocar
d. visitar
e. escuchar
f. practicar
g. conversar
h. estudiar
i. mirar

ACTIVIDAD 2 **Le gusta...** Your friends like to participate in certain activities. Say what they like to do, based on the information provided.

MODELOS: Ernestina: murales
Le gusta pintar.
Leo: orquesta de música clásica
Le gusta tocar un instrumento musical.

1. Neti: ballet
2. Antonio: himnos y ópera
3. Javier: paella y enchiladas
4. Clara: cámara
5. Ernesto: estéreo
6. Beti: programas de comedia, noticias
7. Susana: celular
8. Luis: páginas web

ACTIVIDAD 3 **Mis actividades favoritas.**

1. Make a list of five activities you like to do.

MODELO: *Me gusta patinar en el parque.*

2. Now ask three other students what their favorite activities are and record their responses.

MODELO: —*¿Qué te gusta hacer?*
—*Me gusta caminar.*
You write: *A Heather le gusta caminar.*

3. Compare responses to see who, if anyone, has similar favorite activities, and share this list with the class.

MODELO: *A Marta y a Juan les gusta sacar fotos.*

4. Make a list of the most frequent activities mentioned by your classmates. Write a short paragraph about what students like to do and what activities they don't like to do.

Vocabulario útil 2

ANILÚ:	Y tú, Experto10, ¿qué te gusta hacer los domingos?
SERGIO:	Autora14, soy un hombre **activo.** Bailo, canto, toco la guitarra, cocino…
BETO:	¡Sergio! **¡Mentiroso!** ¡No me gusta bailar, no me gusta cantar, no toco la guitarra y no cocino!
SERGIO:	¡Qué **aburrido** eres, hombre!

CARACTERÍSTICAS DE LA PERSONALIDAD   *Personality traits*

aburrido(a)	divertido(a); interesante	*boring / fun; interesting*
activo(a)	perezoso(a)	*active / lazy*
antipático(a)	simpático(a)	*unpleasant / pleasant*
extrovertido(a)	introvertido(a); tímido(a)	*extroverted / introverted; timid, shy*
generoso(a)	egoísta	*generous / selfish, egotistic*
impaciente	paciente	*impatient / patient*
impulsivo(a)	cuidadoso(a)	*impulsive / cautious*
inteligente	tonto(a)	*intelligent / silly, stupid*
mentiroso(a)	sincero(a)	*liar / sincere*
responsable	irresponsable	*responsible / irresponsible*
serio(a)	cómico(a)	*serious / funny*
trabajador(a)	perezoso(a)	*hard-working / lazy*

CARACTERÍSTICAS FÍSICAS   *Physical traits*

Dos personas y sus perros

Suggestion: Ask a variety of questions based on the art to recycle concepts of age, how many dogs, what elements in the drawing students can identify, etc. **¿Cuántos años tiene ella/él?, ¿Qué hay en el dibujo?**

Notice that you say **Tiene el pelo negro/rubio/moreno,** etc., but when someone is a redhead, you say **Es pelirrojo(a).** You can also say **Es rubio(a)** to indicate that someone is a blonde.

Heritage learners: Some of the vocabulary words in this chapter have variants that may be more commonly used by Heritage learners. Give or solicit examples: **rubio = güero; castaño = color café / oscuro; guapo = buen mozo / atractivo; perezoso = flojo, vago.**

Actividades

Answers Act. 4: 1. b 2. c 3. a 4. c 5. a 6. c

ACTIVIDAD 4 **¿Cómo son?** Benjamín describes himself and several of his friends and relatives. Which adjectives best describe each person?

1. No me gusta mirar televisión. Prefiero practicar deportes o levantar pesas.
   a. serio
   b. activo
   c. impulsivo

2. A mi amiga Marta le gusta ayudar (*to help*) a sus amigos.
   a. antipática
   b. mentirosa
   c. generosa

3. Mi profesora es una maestra muy buena. Explica la lección y repite todas las instrucciones.
   a. paciente
   b. impaciente
   c. interesante

4. Mi amigo Joaquín tiene una imaginación muy buena. Le gusta inventar historias falsas.
   a. tímido
   b. tonto
   c. mentiroso

5. Mi amigo Alberto habla y habla y habla... ¡pero no es muy interesante!
   a. aburrido
   b. serio
   c. divertido

6. Mi amiga Linda tiene muchas ideas buenas sobre qué hacer los fines de semana. Además es una persona muy cómica.
   a. inteligente
   b. tonta
   c. divertida

ACTIVIDAD 5 **Mis amigos.** Describe four people in the class to your partner. Provide both physical and personality traits in your descriptions. Your partner must guess which classmate you are describing.

MODELO: —*Es una persona alta y delgada. Tiene el pelo moreno. También (Also) es una persona cómica y divertida...*
—*¿Es Sean?*

> Notice that you use the **-a** form of all the adjectives in this activity. You will learn more about adjective endings later in this chapter.

ACTIVIDAD 6 **La clase de psicología.** What personality traits does it take to succeed in various professions? Choose characteristics on the right that you think best fit the professions on the left. Follow the model.

Standards: In Activities 5 and 6, students provide information and express opinions.

MODELO: *Los políticos tienen que ser honestos,...*

Profesiones	Características	
los políticos	sistemáticos	serios
los artistas	deshonestos	estudiosos
los criminales	honestos	sinceros
los actores	inteligentes	pacientes
los científicos	creativos	talentosos
los doctores	simpáticos	impulsivos
los policías	extrovertidos	egoístas
los estudiantes	trabajadores	mentirosos
	curiosos	cuidadosos
	temperamentales	¿...?
	responsables	

¡FÍJATE!

¡OJO! con los cognados falsos

In **Capítulo 1,** you learned how to use cognates to help you read in Spanish. But you also learned to beware of false cognates, words in English and in Spanish that look similar, but have different meanings. For example, the word **dirección** (*address*), which you learned in Chapter 1, is a false cognate with the English word *direction*.

Generally, false cognates derive from a common linguistic root. In the case of **librería** (*bookstore*) and *library,* the common ancestor is *liber,* the Latin word for the part of plants that the Romans used to make paper. In Spanish, the word became associated with the place where books are sold. In English, it became associated with the place where books are borrowed or loaned.

False cognates tell fascinating histories about the evolution of different languages. But be careful, because false cognates can cause confusion. When in doubt, look the word up!

PRÁCTICA. Look up the etymology of the English term *idiom* in an unabridged dictionary. What was the original meaning of its linguistic ancestor? Can you make an educated guess as to how *idiom* and **idioma** arrived at their current meaning?

Remember that **¡ojo!** (literally, *eye*) is used in Spanish to direct the reader's attention to something.

Standards: By looking at false cognates, students broaden their vocabularies and demonstrate understanding of the nature of language through comparisons of Spanish and English (C 4.2).

A VER

Antes de ver el video

 For additional practice, do the *Nexos* **website and / or CD-ROM video exercises.**

Again, notice that you use the **-a** form of all the adjectives in **Actividad 1.** You will learn more about adjective endings later in this chapter.

Notice: Activity 1 uses **una persona** in the model so that students do not have to change adjectives to agree with nouns.

ACTIVIDAD 1 Look back at the photos in the **Vocabulario útil** sections on pages 38 and 41. Give a short description of each person shown in the photos.

MODELO: *Anilú es una persona baja y guapa. Tiene el pelo negro.*

ACTIVIDAD 2 Before watching the video, quickly review the following list of unknown words that are used in the video. The video also uses many words you have already learned so far in this chapter.

apagar	*to turn off*
Dile que...	*Tell him / her that . . .*
No sé.	*I don't know.*

ESTRATEGIA

Using questions as an advance organizer

One way to prepare yourself for the content of the video segment you are about to view is to familiarize yourself thoroughly with the questions you will be expected to answer. Knowing what information to listen for helps you focus on the key sections of the video.

For example, look at the questions in **Actividades 3** and **4.** Before you watch the video, use these questions to create for yourself a short list of information you need to find.

Example: **la dirección electrónica de Beto, la dirección electrónica de Dulce, el amigo de Beto,** etc.

Once you have completed your list, make sure you have it at hand as you watch the video so that you can jot down the answers as you hear them.

El video

Standards: Here students interpret language, gestures, and expressions to help understand the spoken word (C 1.2).

 Now watch the video segment for **Capítulo 2.** As you watch, pay special attention to locating the information you need to complete **Actividades 3** and **4.**

Preparation: Show the video segment once, having students pick out cognates to help them relax and listen for similarities between Spanish and English. Let students call out the cognates in Spanish or English after the first showing. Then direct students to Activities 3 and 4 and have them focus on the information they need to look for in the second viewing. Follow up with a third showing of the segment, so that students can confirm their answers.

Después de ver el video

Answers Act. 3: 1. Experto10, Autora14 2. Sergio, Anilú 3. estudiar, tomar un refresco o alquilar un video con amigos 4. bailar, cantar, tocar la guitarra, cocinar

ACTIVIDAD 3 Answer in Spanish the following questions about the video.

1. ¿Cuál es la dirección electrónica de Beto? ¿Y la de Dulce?
2. ¿Cómo se llama el amigo de Beto? ¿Y la amiga de Dulce?
3. ¿Cuáles son las actividades preferidas de Dulce?
4. Según (*According to*) Sergio, ¿cuáles son las actividades preferidas de Experto10?

Answers Act. 4: 1. cierto 2. falso 3. falso 4. falso 5. cierto 6. falso

ACTIVIDAD 4 Now say whether the following statements about the video segment are true (**cierto**) or false (**falso**).

1. Según Anilú, Dulce es una persona muy aburrida.
2. Sergio es una persona muy sincera.
3. Dulce generalmente estudia en casa los domingos.
4. A Beto le gusta bailar, cantar y tocar la guitarra.
5. Según Anilú, un hombre que cocina y canta y baila es el hombre ideal.
6. Sergio apaga la computadora porque Anilú quiere (*wants*) su número de teléfono.

 Conexión cultural. Watch the cultural segment that concludes this chapter's video. Then in groups of three or four, answer the following questions: **¿Cómo saludas a tus amigos y a los miembros de tu familia? ¿Con un beso (*kiss*)? ¿Con un abrazo (*hug*)? Cuando te reúnes (*you get together*) con ellos, ¿qué les gusta hacer, generalmente?**

Optional: Have students work in pairs following these steps: 1. Choose one of the four characters you have just met. 2. Write a brief description of the character that includes personal and physical characteristics, based on what you learned about the characters in the video. 3. When you have finished, exchange your description with another pair of students, and see if they can guess who you described. **Modelo: Persona X es una persona... Le gusta...**

Try to get the main idea of these sentences from your knowledge of the basic vocabulary. Don't worry about understanding every single word.

¿Qué les gusta a los hispanos? To learn more about Isabel Valdés and her findings on Hispanics in the U.S., see the links on the *Nexos* website (http://college.hmco.com/languages/spanish/students).

VOCES DE LA COMUNIDAD

Isabel Valdés

❝Hispanics are becoming more and more entrenched in American society. Their participation is reflected in the growing number of Hispanic associations, libraries, research centers, and businesses throughout the United States. Furthermore, Hispanics are increasingly active in government at the federal, state, county, and city levels. They have also made significant contributions to American art, theater, literature, film, music, and sports. ❞

Isabel Valdés es la persona responsable por muchas campañas publicitarias en español en los Estados Unidos y Latinoamérica. Esta chilena-estadounidense es autora de *Marketing to American Latinos, A Guide to the In-Culture Approach*, un libro que presenta los gustos y preferencias de los hispanos en Estados Unidos. También es co-fundadora de una firma publicitaria especializada en los mercados (*markets*) de Estados Unidos, España y América Latina.

 Standards: Here students learn about Spanish-speaking communities in the U.S. (C 5.1).

¡PREPÁRATE!

Gramática útil 1
Describing what you do or are doing: The present indicative of -ar verbs

Internet For more practice of chapter topics, do the *Nexos* website exercises.

The use of the present tense to talk about future plans is used more in some regions of the Spanish-speaking world than others.

Suggestion: Reinforce the translations of the present tense on the board underlining options: **(Yo) estudio.** I study. I <u>do</u> study. I <u>am</u> studying. I <u>am going to</u> study. Students will learn other ways to talk about the future in Chapters 3 and 12.

Notice: Students will learn **-er/-ir** conjugations in Chapter 3.

Bailo, canto, toco la guitarra, **cocino...**

CÓMO USARLO

In English we use a variety of structures to express different present-tense concepts. In Spanish many of these are communicated with the same grammatical form. The present indicative tense in Spanish can be used . . .

◆ to describe routine actions:

¡**Estudias** mucho!	*You study a lot!*

◆ to say what you are doing now:

Estudias matemáticas hoy.	*You are studying mathematics today.*

◆ to ask questions about present events:

¿**Estudias** con Enrique todas las semanas?	*Do you study with Enrique every week?*

◆ to indicate plans in the immediate future:

Estudias con Enrique el viernes, ¿no?	*You're going to study with Enrique on Friday, right?*

Notice how the same form in Spanish, **estudias,** can be translated four different ways in English.

CÓMO FORMARLO

LO BÁSICO

- An *infinitive* is a verb before it has been conjugated to reflect person and tense. **Bailar** (*to dance*) is an infinitive.
- A *verb stem* is what is left after you remove the **-ar, -er,** or **-ir** ending from the infinitive. **Bail-** is the verb stem of **bailar.**
- A *conjugated verb* is a verb whose endings reflect person (*I, you, he/she, we, you, they*) and tense (*present, past, future,* etc.). **Bailas** (*You dance*) is a conjugated verb (person: *you familiar singular;* tense: *present*).

1. Spanish infinitives end in **-ar, -er,** or **-ir.** For now, you will learn to form the present indicative tense of verbs ending in **-ar.** To form the present indicative tense of a regular **-ar** verb, simply remove the **-ar** and add the following endings.

bailar *(to dance)*			
yo	bail**o**	nosotros / nosotras	bail**amos**
tú	bail**as**	vosotros / vosotras	bail**áis**
Ud., él, ella	bail**a**	Uds., ellos, ellas	bail**an**

2. Remember, as you learned in **Capítulo 1,** you do not need to use the subject pronouns (**yo, tú, él, ella,** etc.) unless the meaning is not clear from the context of the sentence, or you wish to clarify, add emphasis, or make a contrast.

Camino en el parque todos los días.	*I **walk** in the park every day.*
But:	
Yo camino en el parque, pero Lidia camina en el gimnasio.	*I **walk** in the park, but Lidia walks in the gymnasium.*

3. You may use certain conjugated present-tense verbs with infinitives. However, do not use two verbs conjugated in the present tense together unless they are separated by a comma or the words **y** (*and*) or **o** (*or*).

Necesitamos trabajar el viernes.	*We **have to work** on Friday.*
Los sábados, **trabajo, practico** deportes y **visito** a amigos.	*On Saturdays **I work, play** sports, and **visit** friends.*
Los domingos, **dejo de trabajar.** ¡**Bailo, canto** o **escucho** música!	*On Sundays **I stop working. I dance, sing,** or **listen** to music!*

*Optional: Students may ask about **dejo de** in the example. Explain that some verbs require a preposition after them and contrast **dejar de** + inf. with **necesitar** + inf. Recommend that students learn which verbs are followed by prepositions and memorize them.*

Notice that in this usage, Spanish infinitives are often translated into English as *-ing* forms: *I stop working.*

4. To say what you don't do or aren't planning to do, use **no** before the conjugated verb.

¡**No estudio** los fines de semana!	*I **don't study** on the weekends!*

5. Add question marks to turn a present-tense sentence into a *yes / no* question.

¿**No estudias** los fines de semana?	*Don't you study on the weekends?*
¿Tienes que estudiar este fin de semana?	*Do you have to study this weekend?*

6. Other regular **-ar** verbs:

apagar	*to turn off*	llegar	*to arrive*
buscar	*to look for*	necesitar	*to need (to do*
cenar	*to eat dinner*	(+ *infinitive*)	*something)*
comprar	*to buy*	pasar	*to pass (by), to*
dejar (de	*to leave, to stop*		*happen*
+ *infinitive*)	*(doing something)*	preparar	*to prepare*
descansar	*to rest*	regresar	*to return*
llamar	*to call*	usar	*to use*

*Suggestion: Here are some questions to help familiarize students with verbs and verb forms: ¿**Llamas** a tu mamá (a tus amigos) todos los días? ¿**Cenas** mucho o poco? ¿**Compras** muchos (o pocos) libros para la clase de español? ¿**Descansas** todos los días? ¿**Necesitas** comer mucho o poco? ¿**Usas** la computadora constantemente?*

Actividades

Answers Act. 1: 1. camino 2. Llego
3. estudio 4. necesito 5. Compro 6. ceno
7. paso 8. alquilo 9. Regreso 10. Hablo
11. navego 12. apago 13. descanso

Follow up and expand this activity into
an oral chat with your class to recycle
and integrate earlier structures. Ask
leading questions like ¿**Caminas a la
universidad? ¿Te gusta caminar?
¿Dónde cenas, en la cafetería o en
casa? ¿Alquilas videos? ¿De qué tipo
(de horror, románticos, de acción)?** etc.

ACTIVIDAD 1 **Beto.** Beto describes his day in an e-mail to a friend. Complete his description with the correct form of the appropriate verb from the list.

alquilar	navegar	necesitar	pasar	hablar
comprar	apagar	caminar	cenar	regresar
llegar	descansar	estudiar		

A las siete de la mañana, (1) _____ a la universidad. (2) _____ a las siete y media. Si tengo tiempo, (3) _____ un poco antes de las clases. A veces (4) _____ comprar unos libros. (5) _____ los libros en la librería. Generalmente (6) _____ en la cafetería. A veces (7) _____ por la tienda de videos y (8) _____ un video. (9) _____ al dormitorio a las siete de la noche. (10) _____ con mis amigos por teléfono o (11) _____ por Internet. Todas las noches, (12) _____ la computadora a las diez y (13) _____.

Answers Act. 2: 1. Anilú baila, pero Sergio
levanta pesas. 2. Anilú trabaja, pero
Sergio descansa. 3. Anilú toma un
refresco, pero Sergio toma café. 4. Anilú
estudia, pero Sergio navega por Internet.
5. Anilú alquila un video, pero Sergio
mira televisión. 6. Anilú escucha música
rap, pero Sergio toca la guitarra.

ACTIVIDAD 2 **Anilú y Sergio.** Anilú and Sergio do different things. Say what each of them does. Use **pero** (*but*) to contrast what they do. Follow the model.

MODELO: Anilú: cenar en un restaurante; Sergio: cocinar en casa
Anilú cena en un restaurante, pero Sergio cocina en casa.

1. Anilú: bailar; Sergio: levantar pesas
2. Anilú: trabajar; Sergio: descansar
3. Anilú: tomar un refresco; Sergio: tomar café
4. Anilú: estudiar; Sergio: navegar por Internet
5. Anilú: alquilar un video; Sergio: mirar televisión
6. Anilú: escuchar música rap; Sergio: tocar la guitarra

Answers Act. 3: *Answers may vary,
but all use the* **yo** *form.* 1. (No)
Camino... 2. (No) Toco... 3. (No) Visito...
4. (No) Trabajo... 5. (No) Ceno... 6. (No)
Necesito... 7. (No) Escucho...

ACTIVIDAD 3 **Tú.** Interview a partner about his or her activities.

MODELO: estudiar en la biblioteca o en casa
Tú: *¿Estudias en la biblioteca o en casa?*
Compañero(a): *Estudio en la biblioteca. / Estudio en casa.*

1. caminar a la universidad todos los días
2. tocar la guitarra
3. visitar a la familia los fines de semana
4. trabajar los fines de semana
5. cenar en la cafetería o en casa
6. necesitar una computadora
7. escuchar música clásica o música moderna

Answers Act. 4: *Verb forms:*
1. estudiamos, estudian 2. cenamos,
cenan 3. trabajamos, trabajan
4. visitamos, visitan 5. necesitamos,
necesitan 6. llegamos, llegan
7. navegamos, navegan 8. *Answers
will vary.*

ACTIVIDAD 4 **Ellos y nosotros.** Work in pairs to compare the activities of you and your friends (**nosotros**) and someone else's friends (**ellos**).

MODELO: estudiar
Nosotros estudiamos en la biblioteca. Ellos estudian en casa.

1. estudiar
2. cenar
3. trabajar
4. visitar a la familia
5. necesitar
6. llegar a la universidad
7. navegar por Internet
8. ¿...?

ACTIVIDAD 5 **Los fines de semana.** What do you generally do on the weekends? First, make a chart like the one below and fill in the **Yo** column. Compare your list with that of two classmates. Then write a paragraph comparing your typical weekend to theirs. (**¡OJO!: por la mañana / tarde / noche** = *in the morning / afternoon / night*)

¿Cuándo?	Yo	Amigo(a) #1	Amigo(a) #2
viernes por la noche:	*descansar en casa*		
sábado por la mañana:			
sábado por la tarde:			
sábado por la noche:			
domingo por la mañana:			
domingo por la tarde:			
domingo por la noche:			

MODELO: *Los viernes por la noche generalmente descanso en casa. Mi amigo Eduardo generalmente…*

ACTIVIDAD 6 **¿Quién?** You work at a dating service and you have to decide who to introduce to whom. You have some descriptions in writing and some on audio. First read the following descriptions. Then listen to the audio descriptions. For each description you hear, write the person's name next to the description below that is most compatible with that person.

Personas en el CD: Andrés, Marta, Jorge, Ángela, Rudy, Sara

Rosa: «Me gusta escuchar música de todo tipo. ¡Soy muy divertida!»
Sugerencia para Rosa: _____

Isidro: «Levanto pesas tres veces por semana. Soy muy atlético.»
Sugerencia para Isidro: _____

Roberta: «Me gusta alquilar videos. No practico deportes.»
Sugerencia para Roberta: _____

Carmen: «Uso Internet mucho en mis estudios. Soy introvertida.»
Sugerencia para Carmen: _____

José Luis: «Estudio mucho. Soy un poco serio.»
Sugerencia para José Luis: _____

Antonio: «Todos los días hablo por teléfono con mis amigos. Mis amigos son muy divertidos.»
Sugerencia para Antonio: _____

Now use the information above to find the best match for you and your classmates, based on the information you provided in **Actividad 5.**

MODELO: *Antonio es la persona más compatible con* (with) *Katie.*

Gramática útil 2
Saying what you and others like to do: *Gustar* + infinitive

Un hombre que cocina...
y también ¡le gusta
bailar y **cantar!**

Standards/Suggestion: Here *to like* in English is compared to **gustar** in Spanish. Capitalize on the English word *gusto* (*He lives his life with gusto.*) to connect these concepts.

CÓMO USARLO

The Spanish verb **gustar** can be used with an infinitive to say what you and your friends like to do. Note that **gustar**, although often translated as *to like*, is really more similar to the English *to please*. **Gustar** is always used with pronouns that indicate *who is pleased* by the activity mentioned.

—**Me gusta bailar** salsa.

*I like to dance salsa. (**Dancing** salsa **pleases me**.)*

—¿**Te gusta bailar** también?

*Do you like to dance, too? (**Does dancing please you**, too?)*

—No, pero a **Luis le gusta** mucho.

*No, but **Luis likes it** a lot. (No, but **it pleases Luis** a lot.)*

CÓMO FORMARLO

LO BÁSICO

The pronouns used with **gustar** are *indirect object pronouns.* They show the person who is being pleased or who likes something. You will learn more about them in **Capítulo 8.**

1. When **gustar** is used with one or more infinitives, it is always used in its third-person singular form **gusta.** Sentences with **gusta** + *infinitive* can take the form of statements or questions without a change in word order.

—**Nos gusta cocinar** y **cenar** en restaurantes.

We like to cook and to eat out in restaurants.

—¿**Te gusta cocinar** también?

Do you like to cook also?

2. Gusta + *infinitive* is used with the following pronouns.

gusta + *infinitive*	
Me gusta cantar. *I like to sing.*	**Nos** gusta cantar. *We like to sing.*
Te gusta cantar. *You like to sing.*	**Os** gusta cantar. *You (fam. pl.) like to sing.*
Le gusta cantar. *You (form.) / He / She like(s) to sing.*	**Les** gusta cantar. *You (pl.) / They like to sing.*

¡OJO! Do not confuse **me, te, le, nos, os,** and **les** with the subject pronouns **yo, tú, él, ella, Ud., nosotros, vosotros, ellos, ellas,** and **Uds.** that you have already learned.

3. When you use **gusta,** you can also use **a** + *person* to emphasize or clarify *who* it is who likes the activity mentioned. Clarification is particularly important with **le** and **les,** since they can refer to several people.

Le gusta navegar por Internet.	*He / She likes to surf the Internet.* (*Who does?*)
A Beto / A él le gusta navegar por Internet.	*Beto / He likes to surf the Internet.*
A ellos les gusta cantar.	*They like to sing.*
A nosotros nos gusta conversar.	*We like to talk.*
A Sergio y a Anilú les gusta bailar.	*Sergio and Anilú like to dance.*

4. If you want to emphasize or clarify what you or a close friend like, use **a mí** (with **me gusta**) and **a ti** (with **te gusta**).

A mí me gusta alquilar videos, pero **a ti te gusta** mirar televisión.	*I like to rent videos, but you like to watch television.*

5. To create negative sentences with **gusta** + *infinitive*, place **no** before the *pronoun* + **gusta.**

No nos gusta trabajar.	*We don't like to work.*
A Roberto **no le gusta cocinar.**	*Roberto doesn't like to cook.*

6. To express agreement with someone's opinion, use **también.** If you want to disagree, use **no** or **tampoco.** If you want to ask a friend if they like an activity you've already mentioned, ask **¿Y a ti?**

—¿Te gusta cocinar?	*Do you like to cook?*
—**A mí, no.** No me gusta. Me gusta cenar en restaurantes. **¿Y a ti?**	*No, not me. I don't like it. I like to eat in restaurants. And you?*
—**A mí también.** Pero no me gusta cenar en restaurantes elegantes.	*Me too. But I don't like to eat in fancy restaurants.*
—**¡A mí tampoco!**	*Me neither!*

Actividades

ACTIVIDAD 7 **Atleta23.** Can you tell what the following people like to do, based on their electronic names?

MODELO: Cantante29
A Cantante29 le gusta cantar.

1. Pianista18
2. Atleta23
3. Artista12
4. Estudiante31
5. Fotógrafo11
6. Cocinero13
7. Bailarina39

Answers Act. 7: 1. A Pianista18 le gusta tocar el piano. 2. A Atleta23 le gusta practicar deportes. 3. A Artista12 le gusta pintar. 4. A Estudiante31 le gusta estudiar. 5. A Fotógrafo11 le gusta sacar fotos. 6. A Cocinero13 le gusta cocinar. 7. A Bailarina39 le gusta bailar.

Suggestion: A graphic representation of **gustar** + *inf.* on the board may be helpful for students who prefer formulas. Arrange the following in 5 columns: A + [mí / ti / Ud. / él / ella / nosotros / vosotros / ellos / ellas / Uds.] + [me / te / le / nos / os / les] + gusta + [**bailar, estudiar, conversar,** etc.].

Notice that **mí** has an accent, but **ti** does not.

Suggestion: Practice **A mí también** and **A mí tampoco** by expressing likes and by asking students: **A mí me gusta mucho cocinar. ¿Y a ti? No me gusta estudiar. ¿Y a ti?**

ACTIVIDAD 8 **Les gusta.** Susana and Alberto like to participate in certain activities together, but prefer to do other things alone. First listen to what they say and decide who likes to do the activity mentioned. After you listen, use the verbs indicated to create a sentence saying who likes to do what. Follow the models.

MODELOS: (*A Susana y a Alberto*) *Les gusta bailar.*

	Susana	Alberto	Susana y Alberto
bailar			X

(*A Susana*) *Le gusta caminar en el parque.*

	Susana	Alberto	Susana y Alberto
caminar en el parque	X		

	Susana	Alberto	Susana y Alberto
1. hablar por teléfono			
2. cocinar comida mexicana			
3. sacar fotos			
4. navegar por Internet			
5. tocar la guitarra			

ACTIVIDAD 9 **En el parque.** With a partner, look at the drawing for five minutes, then close your books. From memory, try to describe what everyone in the illustration likes to do.

Las personas: Ana, Carlos, David, Elena y Francisco, Miguel y Natalia

ACTIVIDAD 10 **Mi amigo hispanohablante.** You have a Spanish-speaking friend who is coming to visit you today. You want to let him know what activities you and your friends like to do so he can think about which activities he'd like to do with you. Write a note to post on your door that tells your friend what you and your friends typically like to do and where, so that when he arrives, he can decide what he wants to do with you.

1. First fill out the following chart to help you organize the information. Here are some possible locations: **el parque, el gimnasio, el restaurante, la cafetería, la residencia estudiantil, la biblioteca, la discoteca.**

Me gusta...	Nos gusta...	¿Dónde?

2. Once you complete the chart, use the information to write a note to your friend, telling what you and your friends like to do and where, so that he can make plans to join you or not.

Gramática útil 3
Describing yourself and others: Adjective agreement

CÓMO USARLO

Find three adjectives in this advertisement from a Spanish magazine. What nouns do they modify?

Answers: *divertida, intolerable, ameno, divertido; divertida* and *intolerable* modify *revista; ameno, divertido* modify *contenido*

¿una revista sobre libros... y divertida?

intolerable

Un contenido aún más ameno y divertido

Begin the CD-ROM activities. Do the cultural activities and reading and writing practice as you complete the corresponding text sections.

As you learned in **Capítulo 1,** Spanish nouns must agree with definite and indefinite articles in both gender and number. This agreement is also necessary when using Spanish adjectives. Their endings change to reflect the number and gender of the nouns they modify.

Anilú es **delgada.**	*Anilú is **thin.***
Sergio y Beto son **inteligentes.**	*Sergio and Beto are **intelligent.***
Sergio es un hombre **alto.**	*Sergio is a **tall** man.*
Dulce y Anilú son mujeres **jóvenes.**	*Dulce and Anilú are **young** women.*

Notice that in these cases the adjectives go *after* the noun, rather than before, as in English.

CÓMO FORMARLO

LO BÁSICO

- A *descriptive adjective* is a word that describes a noun. It answers the question *What is . . . like?*
- *To modify* is to limit or qualify the meaning of another word. A descriptive adjective *modifies* a noun by specifying characteristics that apply to that noun: **un estudiante** vs. **un estudiante inteligente.**

1. If an adjective is used to modify a masculine noun, the adjective must have a masculine ending. If it is used to modify a feminine noun, it must have a feminine ending.

- ◆ The masculine ending for adjectives ending in **-o** is the **o** form.

- ◆ The feminine ending for adjectives ending in **-o** is the **a** form.

- ◆ Adjectives ending in **-e** or most consonants don't change to reflect gender.

- ◆ Adjectives ending in **-or** add **-a** to the ending for the feminine form.

Un profesor	Una profesora
simpátic**o**	simpátic**a**
interesant**e**	interesant**e**
trabajad**or**	trabajad**ora**

2. If an adjective is used to modify a plural noun or more than one noun, it must be used in its plural form.

- ◆ To create the plural of an adjective ending in a vowel, add **-s.**

- ◆ To create the plural of an adjective ending in a consonant, add **-es.**

- ◆ To create the plural of an adjective ending in **-or,** add **-es** to the masculine form and **-as** to the feminine form.

El profesor	Los profesores	Las profesoras
simpátic**o**	simpátic**os**	simpátic**as**
interesant**e**	interesant**es**	interesant**es**
trabajad**or**	trabajad**ores**	trabajad**oras**

3. As with articles and subject pronouns, adjectives that apply to mixed groups of males and females use the masculine form.

4. Adjectives of nationality follow slightly different rules. These adjectives add **-a / -as** feminine endings for nationalities whose names end in **-l**, **-s**, and **-n**. See the nationalities in the following group for examples.

Nacionalidades			
Argentina:	**argentino(a)**	Guatemala:	**guatemalteco(a)**
Bolivia:	**boliviano(a)**	Guinea Ecuatorial:	**guineano(a)**
Chile:	**chileno(a)**	México:	**mexicano(a)**
China:	**chino(a)**	Panamá:	**panameño(a)**
Colombia:	**colombiano(a)**	Paraguay:	**paraguayo(a)**
Cuba:	**cubano(a)**	Perú:	**peruano(a)**
Ecuador:	**ecuatoriano(a)**	Puerto Rico:	**puertorriqueño(a)**
El Salvador:	**salvadoreño(a)**	Rep. Dominicana:	**dominicano(a)**
Italia:	**italiano(a)**	Uruguay:	**uruguayo(a)**
Honduras:	**hondureño(a)**	Venezuela:	**venezolano(a)**
Canadá:	**canadiense(s)**	Estados Unidos:	**estadounidense(s)**
Costa Rica:	**costarricense(s)**	Nicaragua:	**nicaragüense(s)**

Alemania:	**alemán, alemana, alemanes, alemanas**
España:	**español, española, españoles, españolas**
Francia:	**francés, francesa, franceses, francesas**
Inglaterra:	**inglés, inglesa, ingleses, inglesas**
Japón:	**japonés, japonesa, japoneses, japonesas**

5. The descriptive adjectives you have learned so far in this chapter are almost always used *after the noun*, rather than before. Adjectives of nationality are always used after the noun.

6. Several adjectives in Spanish may be used *before* or *after* the noun they modify. Three common adjectives of this type are **bueno** (*good*), **malo** (*bad*), and **grande** (*big, large*). When **bueno** and **malo** are used before a singular masculine noun, they have a special shortened form. Whenever **grande** is used before any singular masculine or feminine noun, its shortened form **gran** is used.

un estudiante bueno	BUT:	un **buen** estudiante
una estudiante buena		una buena estudiante
un día malo	BUT:	un **mal** día
una semana mala		una mala semana
un hotel grande	BUT:	un **gran** hotel
una universidad grande	BUT:	una **gran** universidad

Remember that Puerto Ricans are U.S. citizens.

Estados Unidos is often abbreviated as **EEUU** or **EE.UU.** in Spanish. Some native speakers do not use the article **los** with **EEUU**: en Estados Unidos or en **EEUU.**

Notice: Nationalities should be used to allow students to choose the ones most applicable to their heritage when talking about origin. Add relevant nationalities as necessary, for example: **nigeriano, filipino, indio, sueco,** etc. Point out how to pluralize as necessary. You may want to designate which nationalities students are to learn for active use and which are for recognition only.

Suggestion: Give some examples of nationalities in a context: **Soy norteamericana. Mi madre es alemana. Mi padre es norteamericano. Mis amigos son chilenos, norteamericanos y cubanos.** This will reinforce not only agreement in number and gender, but also demonstrate that no article is necessary between the verb and the nationality as in some cases in English.

Point out that nationalities and languages are not capitalized in Spanish. Names of countries are always capitalized.

Grande has different meanings when used *before* the noun (*great, famous*) and *after* the noun (*big, large*).

Standards: Here students interpret the language and situation for enrichment and consider ethical behavior as a life-long issue.

COMPRENSIÓN. Answer the following questions about the cartoon.

1. Según el gato (*cat*), ¿cómo es?
2. Según el perro, ¿cómo es?
3. En realidad, ¿cómo es el gato? ¿Y el perro?
4. ¿Tienen consecuencias serias las mentiras del gato? En tu opinión, ¿son sinceras o mentirosas las personas cuando hablan por Internet?

Answers: 1. Es activo. 2. También es activo. 3. En realidad, el gato es perezoso y mentiroso. El perro es activo. 4. *Answers will vary.*

Actividades

 ACTIVIDAD 11 **Marcos y María.** Marcos and María are two of your best friends. They are not at all similar. Describe what they are like. Follow the model.

MODELO: Marcos es divertido.
María no es divertida. Es aburrida.

1. Marcos es paciente.
2. María es responsable.
3. Marcos es extrovertido.
4. María es perezosa.
5. Marcos es sincero.
6. María es antipática.
7. Marcos es rubio.
8. María es delgada.

Answers Act. 11: 1. María no es paciente. Es impaciente. 2. Marcos no es responsable. Es irresponsable. 3. María no es extrovertida. Es introvertida. 4. Marcos no es perezoso. Es trabajador. 5. María no es sincera. Es mentirosa. 6. Marcos no es antipático. Es simpático. 7. María no es rubia. Es morena. 8. Marcos no es delgado. Es gordo.

Suggestion: Expand Activity 11 by having students describe their own friends; for example: **Mi amigo John es divertido, pero no es trabajador.**

 ACTIVIDAD 12 **También.** Your partner tells you that a person you both know has a certain personality or physical trait. Say that two of your friends are just like that person.

Rocío

MODELO: Compañero(a): *Rocío es alta.*
Tú: *Tomás y Marcelo también son altos.*

1.
Gerardo

2.
Ángela

3.
Miguel

4.
Carmela

5.
Pablo

6.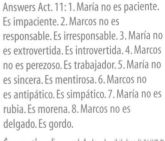
Jimena

 ACTIVIDAD 13 **Las nacionalidades.** With your partner, take turns asking the nationalities of the following people. Then mention another person of the same nationality.

MODELO: Ricky Martin (Puerto Rico)
Tú: *¿De qué nacionalidad es Ricky Martin?*
Compañero(a): *Es puertorriqueño.*
Tú: *¿De veras? Rosie Pérez es puertorriqueña también.*

1. Enrique y Julio Iglesias (España)
2. Venus y Serena Williams (Estados Unidos)
3. Sammy Sosa (República Dominicana)
4. Hugh Grant (Inglaterra)
5. Gabriel García Márquez (Colombia)
6. Rigoberta Menchú (Guatemala)
7. Steffi Graf y Boris Becker (Alemania)
8. Gloria y Emilio Estefan (Cuba)

Answers Act. 12: Answers will vary for second sentence. 1. Gerardo es atlético. 2. Ángela es pelirroja. 3. Miguel es cómico. 4. Carmela es perezosa. 5. Pablo es trabajador. 6. Jimena es impaciente.

Answers Act. 13: 1. Son españoles. 2. Son estadounidenses. 3. Es dominicano. 4. Es inglés. 5. Es colombiano. 6. Es guatemalteca. 7. Son alemanes. 8. Son cubanos (cubanoamericanos).

ACTIVIDAD 14 **Personas famosas.** In groups of four or five, each person takes a turn describing a famous person. The rest of the group tries to guess who is being described.

Palabras útiles: actor (actriz), atleta, cantante, músico(a), político(a)

MODELO: Tú: *Es actriz. Es estadounidense. Es alta, delgada y rubia. Es muy inteligente y simpática. Habla inglés, francés y español. ¿Quién es?*
Grupo: *Es Gwyneth Paltrow.*

ACTIVIDAD 15 **Los anuncios personales.**

1. Look at the personal ads on the next page from a Spanish-language magazine. Don't worry if you can't understand every word; just focus on getting the main idea.
2. Discuss the ads with a classmate. Play matchmaker. Who would you pair up? Why?

MODELO: (*Nombre 1*) *es bueno(a) para...* (*Nombre 2*), *porque* (because)...

Palabras útiles: soltero(a): *single;* **estatura:** *height;* **fines:** *intentions;* **cajón:** *mailbox;* **tez:** *skin, complexion;* **casarme:** *to get married;* **hogar:** *home;* **desear:** *to want;* **conocer:** *to meet;* **disfrutar la vida:** *to enjoy life*

Standards: Here students compare and develop insights into the culture studied and their own (C 4.2).

ACTIVIDAD 16 **Comparaciones.** With a partner, compare the ads you just looked at with the kinds of ads you would find in an English-language publication in your community. What differences and similarities do you see between the ads in Spanish and in English?

En inglés / En español las personas hablan de / no hablan de...
En inglés / En español los anuncios mencionan / no mencionan...

_____ los fines matrimoniales	_____ la personalidad
_____ la apariencia física	_____ los hijos
_____ las nacionalidades	_____ los intereses
_____ el estado civil	_____ las profesiones
_____ la edad	_____ el hogar
_____ los nombres completos	_____ ¿...?

Suggestion Act. 18: Have students edit and revise their ads from **Actividad 18** before they post them on the Internet. Suggest exchanging papers and reading for agreement, spelling, etc., or collect and make suggestions for revision. Return papers and have students revise their ads.

Optional: For additional practice, try this related activity. Instructions for **El novio o la novia ideal:** Write an ad describing the person of your dreams. Include as much detail as possible, including their physical and personality traits and their favorite leisure activities. In groups of three or four, exchange the ads of your ideal mate and see if you can guess whose ideal mate is being described in each ad.

ACTIVIDAD 17 **Tus cualidades.** You want to write your own personal ad for the Internet or for a newspaper or magazine. First, make a list of the qualities you wish to include. If you want to, include a physical description. Then make a list of all of your favorite activities. Exchange your lists with a classmate and suggest changes you think would be helpful.

ACTIVIDAD 18 **Tu anuncio personal.** Now, using the information you listed in **Actividad 17,** write your own personal ad. Present yourself as positively as possible. In groups of three or four, exchange your ads and see if you can guess whose ad is whose. If possible, as a follow-up, post your ad on the class website under a false name and see if others can guess who it is.

Encuentros

Las mujeres

- **Ana Lilla Flores Ramírez.** Educadora, soltera, 23 años, de estatura mediana, delgada, cubana, de tipo polinesio. Me gustan los hombres altos y delgados de los Estados Unidos, Canadá o Europa, con profesión estable y fines matrimoniales. **Cajón M2398-1.**
- **Marisa Ferdóndez.** Médica, divorciada, 26 años, guapa, de tez castaña. Soy una chica de sentimiento positivo. Me gusta el estudio y el trabajo, pero también me gusta hacer deportes. Camino en maratones. Busco hombre francés, canadiense, alemán o norteamericano para casarme y formar un hogar feliz. **Cajón M2258-0.**
- **Gladiz Torres.** Intérprete, soltera, 20 años, atractiva, sincera, deseo correspondencia con un hombre de buen carácter y de 20 a 40 años, atractivo, con fines serios y posición estable. **Cajón M2291-3.**

Encuentros

Los hombres

- **Guillermo Bustamante.** Soltero, 24 años, atractivo, sincero, busco mujer con fines matrimoniales. No importa si es divorciada o tiene hijos. No soy machista ni egoísta. Tengo una posición buena y muy económica. Me gusta sacar fotos, hacer deporte, caminar y conversar. **Cajón M3294-2.**
- **Selim Quintero.** Divorciado. Tengo dos hijos. 23 años. Deseo conocer a una mujer seria para casarme y formar un hogar. Soy serio y responsable, de nacionalidad hispano-árabe. Me gusta escuchar música y tocar la guitarra y el violín. **Cajón M3629-1.**
- **Efraín Ramos.** Soy un hombre español, residente en Estados Unidos. Tengo 21 años. Soy estudiante. Busco una mujer activa para hacer deportes, patinar, bailar y disfrutar la vida. Ella tiene que ser delgada, alta y muy atlética. **Cajón M2029-9.**

Hispanos en los EEUU

La identidad bilingüe. Look at the following article, divided into four paragraphs. Try to get the gist of each, and don't worry about understanding every word. Afterward, match each of the main ideas on the next page with the paragraph it summarizes. Focus on the *main* idea for each paragraph; two of the statements given, while they are true, relate to secondary details.

Doble identidad:
Los latinos en Estados Unidos

A. Los tres grupos de latinos en Estados Unidos de mayor número son los méxico-americanos (o los chicanos), los puertorriqueños y los cubanoamericanos. Cada grupo tiene una historia larga y distinta en relación a los Estados Unidos. Sin embargo, tienen en común la doble identidad del bilingüe.

B. Nueva York es el hogar de más de un millón de puertorriqueños. El Museo del Barrio en la Quinta Avenida, La Marqueta en el Este de Harlem, el Desfile Puertorriqueño de Nueva York y el "Nuyorican Poets Café" son testimonios de la vida bicultural de los "Nuyoricans".

Una tienda cubana en la pequeña Habana en Miami, Florida

Puertorriqueños en Nueva York celebran el Desfile Puertorriqueño.

Un mural chicano en California

C. En Miami, la pequeña Habana es el centro cultural de la vida cubanoamericana. Se escucha español en las tiendas, los restaurantes, los mercados y los cafés. En la pequeña Habana la vida tiene un ritmo especial gracias a la influencia cubanoamericana.

D. Los méxicoamericanos (o los chicanos) son una parte integral de la vida norte-americana en el suroeste. En las fronteras de Texas, en las ciudades de California y en las comunidades de Nuevo México, Arizona, Nevada y Colorado existe un ambiente bicultural y bilingüe en las áreas del arte, el teatro, la literatura, la televisión, la radio y la cocina, ¡por supuesto!

Ideas principales:

1. La existencia bicultural de los puertorriqueños es evidente por toda (*throughout*) la ciudad de Nueva York.
2. Los tres grupos más grandes de habla española en EEUU tienen en común la identidad del bilingüe, pero no la historia nacional.
3. Los nuyoricans son puertorriqueños que viven (*live*) en Nueva York.
4. Hay restaurantes cubanos en Miami.
5. En la sección de Miami que se llama la pequeña Habana, hay una atmósfera cubanoamericana muy distinta.
6. La cultura méxicoamericana tiene mucha influencia en la parte suroeste de EEUU.

Párrafo A: _____
Párrafo B: _____
Párrafo C: _____
Párrafo D: _____

Answers: Párrafo A: 2 / Párrafo B: 1 / Párrafo C: 5 / Párrafo D: 6

Optional: To expand this activity into a class discussion, survey students who may live, know, or be part of these cultures in the U.S. Ask students to share what they know about these heritage groups.

Standards: Here students gain knowledge of Spanish-speaking communities (C 5.1) and cultures (C 2.2). Students do this by considering the disciplines of mass communication and marketing (C 3.1).

Preparation: As a preview to this activity, bring some examples of print media published in Spanish to class. Ask students to bring examples as well. For a simple activity, bring copies of the subscription form from a Spanish magazine and fill out with students in class. This provides a review of names, numbers, streets, etc.

Optional: Remind students that the Latino population is roughly 38 million people total, so the interest in the Latino market does not come as a surprise. Ask students: Are there Spanish ads or classified ads in your local newspapers? Do you get a Spanish-language television station in your home? Encourage students to obtain ads and view Spanish programs and compare to English-language ads and TV programs.

Internet

¡CONÉCTATE!

In recent years, U.S. magazines and newspapers targeted at the Latino market have proliferated. Spanish has also become a major force in the television industry.

1. Divide into groups of three. Choose one of the following to investigate: U.S. Spanish-language magazines, newspapers, or television stations.
2. Follow the links on the *Nexos* website (http://college.hmco.com/languages/spanish/students) to see a list of suggested websites. Use the information there to answer the following questions about your chosen category.

• ¿Cuáles son los nombres de dos revistas (*magazines*), periódicos (*newspapers*) o canales de televisión?
• ¿Cuántas personas leen (*read*) o miran cada uno? ¿Cómo es la audiencia principal?
• ¿Qué secciones o programas principales tiene cada uno?

3. Put together your group's findings and prepare a short presentation to give to the class.

Antes de leer

For more on using a bilingual dictionary, see the **A escribir** section of the Workbook.

① ④ Standards: Here students will interpret the written word (C 1.2) and develop insight into the nature of language and culture (C 4.1, 4.2).

Suggestion: It may be helpful to bring several bilingual dictionaries to class so that students can see some titles and prices. There are many dictionaries on the market, and it can be overwhelming for a student to select one. Also don't forget to take this opportunity to familiarize students with the bilingual glossary at the back of *Nexos*. ·

ESTRATEGIA

Using a bilingual dictionary to aid in comprehension

When reading in Spanish, it is important to try to understand the general meaning of what you read and not spend time looking up every unknown word. If, however, there is a key word that you can't figure out another way, using a dictionary can save you time and lower your level of frustration.

Try to limit yourself to looking up only one or two words from each page of text. Focus on words that you cannot guess from context and that you absolutely must understand in order to get the reading's general meaning. When you do look up the word, don't settle on the first definition! Look at the different English translations provided. Which one seems to best fit with the overall content of the reading?

When looking up verbs, remember that you must look up the infinitive form (**-ar, -er,** or **-ir**) and not the conjugated form. (**Ser** instead of **soy, hablar** instead of **hablas,** etc.)

ACTIVIDAD 1 *People en español* is a monthly magazine that focuses on famous Latinos in the U.S., as well as Spanish-speakers from other countries. Its feature **"Dime la verdad"** (*"Tell me the truth"*) always poses a question to a number of well-known Spanish-speakers and asks them to answer it. This month's question is "How are you similar to your mother (**madre**)?"

1. Look at the quotes of the five people featured. Are there any words that you don't know? If so, what are they?
2. Can you guess from context any of the words you identified? For example, Chef Pepín has a television show called **"La cocina de Chef Pepín."** Based on the knowledge that he is a chef, and having learned the verb **cocinar,** what might the word **cocina** mean?
3. Of the remaining words, how many do you really need to know in order to understand the basic idea of what the person is saying—how he or she is like his or her mother? With a partner, decide if the words are necessary to get the main idea.

If **era** is one of the words you have left, it will be hard to find in the dictionary. It is a past-tense form of **ser** meaning *I was, he / she was, you (form.) were.*

ACTIVIDAD 2 Now that you have narrowed your list of unknown but key words down to one or two, look them up in the dictionary. Be sure to read all the English definitions. Which one(s) fit(s) best in the context of the article?

Lectura

Dime la verdad
¿En qué crees que te pareces a tu madre?

CHRIS ARMAS
futbolista, *Chicago Fire y Selección Nacional de Estados Unidos*
"Los dos somos personas reservadas y generosas".

CHEF PEPÍN
La cocina del chef Pepín
"De mi mamá aprendí a cocinar y también a cultivar el amor por la cocina".

DANIELA LUJÁN
actriz, *El diario de Daniela*
"Tenemos el mismo carácter. Como a ella, a mí me gusta mandar".

BOB VILA
Bob Vila's Home Again
"Soy muy franco como lo era ella".

LESLEY ANN MACHADO
presentadora, *Control*
"Yo soy super perfeccionista y ella también".

LUJÁN: LUZ MONTERO; ARMAS: ANDY LYONS/ALLSPORT; PEPÍN: CORTESÍA DEL CHEF PEPÍN; MACHADO: CORTESÍA DE UNIVISIÓN; VILA: BRIAN SMITH/OUTLINE

ACTIVIDAD 3 Now, as you read the entire article, complete the following chart with the information that says how each person is like his or her mother.

Chris Armas	Daniela Luján	Bob Vila	Chef Pepín	Lesley Ann Machado

Después de leer

ACTIVIDAD 4 Look at the drawing and, with a partner, describe how the mother and her children are similar and how they are different. Follow the model.

MODELO: *La madre es... y Mariela también es...*
La madre es..., pero Mario es...

Mario

La Sra. Gómez

Lucía

Mariela

 ACTIVIDAD 5 With a partner, discuss how you are similar to and different from your mother or other family members. Follow the models and use the list of family members as necessary.

MODELO: with **ser:**   *Mi madre y yo...*
Mi madre..., pero (but) yo...

with **gustar:**   *Nos...*
A mí..., pero a mi madre...

You will learn more names for family members in **Capítulo 5.**

Otros parientes: padre: *father;* **hermano:** *brother;* **hermana:** *sister;* **primo(a):** *cousin;* **tío:** *uncle;* **tía:** *aunt;* **abuelo:** *grandfather;* **abuela:** *grandmother*

¡COMPÁRATE!

In the United States, Mother's Day is usually a simple celebration marked by gifts and cards for Mom and perhaps breakfast in bed or dinner out. However, in many Spanish-speaking cultures, this holiday takes on a much greater importance. In Mexico, for example, **El Día de las Madres** is a much bigger celebration than the more internationally famous **Cinco de Mayo.**

Because Mexico has its religious origins in both indigenous religions and Catholicism, the idea of the Madonna or mother figure has particular resonance there.

In addition to giving cards and presents, many Mexican families also make pilgrimages to the Basilica of Guadalupe in Mexico City. Some hire **mariachi** bands to play mournful songs at their mother's graves or sing themselves. Traditional celebrations include closing offices and factories, presenting concerts and pageants in the schools, and enjoying lengthy lunch-time celebrations. Throughout Southern California, many immigrant families follow these traditions and even bring their mothers from Mexico for the occasion.

La Virgen de Guadalupe es la santa religiosa y figura de la madre más importante de todo México.

Some Mexican feminists and sociologists see a downside to the intensity of these celebrations: once the mother is put on a pedestal, she is no longer a real person with flaws, needs, and aspirations. The cult of motherhood places Mexican and Mexican-American women at a cultural crossroads, standing between the old-fashioned Mexican mother and the more liberated working woman who juggles motherhood and a career.

Regardless of one's viewpoint, as the Spanish saying goes: **Madre sólo hay una** and **El Día de las Madres** is the day to express your feelings, regardless of your nationality or the type of celebration you choose.

 PRÁCTICA. Discuss the following questions in groups of three or four.

1. ¿Qué diferencias hay entre las celebraciones de México y las de EEUU? Indica los aspectos de la celebración que se asocian con México (M), con EEUU (E) o con los dos (D).

   _____ más (+) importante
   _____ visita al cementerio
   _____ tarjetas (*cards*)
   _____ mariachis u otra música
   _____ espectáculos en las escuelas (*schools*)

   _____ menos (–) importante
   _____ regalos (*gifts*)
   _____ cenar en un restaurante
   _____ no hay trabajo
   _____ una celebración religiosa

2. Miren el artículo en la página 63 (**Dime la verdad**). Según ustedes, ¿es común que los hombres de los EEUU se comparen con sus madres?

3. Según ustedes, ¿tiene la religión alguna influencia en la representación de la madre en la sociedad estadounidense?

Standards: Here students gain insight into the Mexican culture (C 2.1, C 2.2) and compare insights with U.S. culture (C 4.2).

Optional: Have students go to the Internet, and locate information about Mother's Day in Spanish. A good way to begin is to use a Spanish-language search engine (such as yahoo.es) or to select Spanish as the target language on the browser you already use. Type in **Día + de + las + Madres** and see what kinds of sites there are. Have students report back on the information that they find.

Optional: Bring some Mother's Day cards in Spanish. Ask students to write a short comparison between them and English cards. Are they similar? Different? They should be prepared to report back to the class. **Modelo: La tarjeta en español es... La tarjeta en inglés es...**

Answer 1.:
M: más importante, visita al cementerio, mariachis u otra música, espectáculos en las escuelas, no hay trabajo, una celebración religiosa
E: menos importante
D: cenar en un restaurante, tarjetas, regalos

VOCABULARIO

PARA EXPRESAR PREFERENCIAS
To express preferences

¿Qué te gusta hacer?	*What do you like to do?*
A mí me gusta...	*I like . . .*
A ti te gusta...	*You like . . .*
A... le gusta...	*You / He / She like(s) . . .*
A... les gusta...	*You (pl.) / They like . . .*
¿Y a ti?	*And you?*

alquilar videos	*to rent videos*
bailar	*to dance*
caminar	*to walk*
cantar	*to sing*
cocinar	*to cook*
escuchar música	*to listen to music*
estudiar en la	*to study at the*
biblioteca /	*library /*
en casa	*at home*
hablar por teléfono	*to talk on the phone*
levantar pesas	*to lift weights*
mirar televisión	*to watch television*
navegar por Internet	*to surf the Internet*
patinar	*to skate*
pintar	*to paint*
practicar deportes	*to play sports*
sacar fotos	*to take photos*
tocar un instrumento	*to play a musical*
musical	*instrument*
la guitarra	*the guitar*
el piano	*the piano*
la trompeta	*the trumpet*
el violín	*the violin*
tomar un refresco	*to have a soft drink*
tomar el sol	*to sunbathe*
trabajar	*to work*
visitar a amigos	*to visit friends*

PARA DESCRIBIR *To describe*

¿Cómo es?	*What's he / she / it like?*
muy	*very*

Características de la personalidad
Personality traits

aburrido(a)	*boring*
activo(a)	*active*
antipático(a)	*unpleasant*
bueno(a)	*good*
cómico(a)	*funny*
cuidadoso(a)	*cautious*
divertido(a)	*fun, entertaining*
egoísta	*selfish, egotistic*
extrovertido(a)	*extroverted*
generoso(a)	*generous*
impaciente	*impatient*
impulsivo(a)	*impulsive*
inteligente	*intelligent*
interesante	*interesting*
introvertido(a)	*introverted*
irresponsable	*irresponsible*
malo(a)	*bad*
mentiroso(a)	*dishonest, lying*
paciente	*patient*
perezoso(a)	*lazy*
responsable	*responsible*
serio(a)	*serious*
simpático(a)	*nice*
sincero(a)	*sincere*
tímido(a)	*shy*
tonto(a)	*silly, stupid*
trabajador(a)	*hard-working*

Características físicas *Physical traits*

alto(a)	*tall*
bajo(a)	*short*
delgado(a)	*thin*
feo(a)	*ugly*
gordo(a)	*fat*
grande	*big, great*
guapo(a)	*handsome, attractive*
joven	*young*
lindo(a)	*pretty*
pequeño(a)	*small*
viejo(a)	*old*
Es pelirrojo(a) /	*He / She is redheaded /*
rubio(a).	*blond.*
Tiene el pelo negro /	*He / She has black /*
moreno / castaño /	*dark brown / brown /*
rubio.	*blond hair.*

Nacionalidades *Nationalities*

alemán (alemana)	*German*
argentino(a)	*Argentinian*
boliviano(a)	*Bolivian*
canadiense	*Canadian*
chileno(a)	*Chilean*
chino(a)	*Chinese*
colombiano(a)	*Colombian*
costarricense	*Costa Rican*
cubano(a)	*Cuban*
dominicano(a)	*Dominican*
ecuatoriano(a)	*Ecuadoran*
español (española)	*Spanish*
estadounidense	*U.S. citizen*
francés (francesa)	*French*
guatemalteco(a)	*Guatemalan*
hondureño(a)	*Honduran*
inglés (inglesa)	*English*
italiano(a)	*Italian*
japonés (japonesa)	*Japanese*
mexicano(a)	*Mexican*
nicaragüense	*Nicaraguan*
panameño(a)	*Panamanian*
paraguayo(a)	*Paraguayan*
peruano(a)	*Peruvian*
puertorriqueño(a)	*Puerto Rican*
salvadoreño(a)	*Salvadoran*
uruguayo(a)	*Uruguayan*
venezolano(a)	*Venezuelan*

PALABRAS ÚTILES

Los verbos

apagar	*to turn off*
buscar	*to look for*
cenar	*to eat dinner*
comprar	*to buy*
dejar	*to leave*
dejar de (+ *inf.*)	*to stop (doing something)*
descansar	*to rest*
llamar	*to call*
llegar	*to arrive*
necesitar	*to need*
pasar	*to pass (by)*
preparar	*to prepare*
regresar	*to return*
usar	*to use*

Otras palabras

los fines de semana	*weekends*
los viernes	*Fridays*
los sábados	*Saturdays*
los domingos	*Sundays*
el gato	*cat*
el perro	*dog*
pero	*but*
también	*also*
tampoco	*neither*

¿Cómo aprendemos?

Communication

By the end of this chapter you will be able to:
• talk about courses and schedules and tell time
• talk about present activities and future plans
• talk about possessions
• ask and answer questions

Cultures

By the end of this chapter you will have learned about:
• Puerto Rico, the Dominican Republic, and Cuba
• the 24-hour clock
• Afro-Caribbean rhythms

5·2·4 Standards: In this chapter students make connections and comparisons (C 4.2) with Caribbean communities via their exploration of authentic websites and readings (C 5.1) and gain insights into the Caribbean cultures (C 2.1).

Suggestion: To personalize, ask students who has visited or lived in the Caribbean, and invite them to share their experiences.

Unos estudiantes puertorriqueños hablan antes de ir a clase.

INVESTIGACIONES

Los seres humanos tenemos una capacidad tremenda para aprender. Pero, ¿cómo aprendemos? En este capítulo, vamos a explorar varias maneras de aprender.

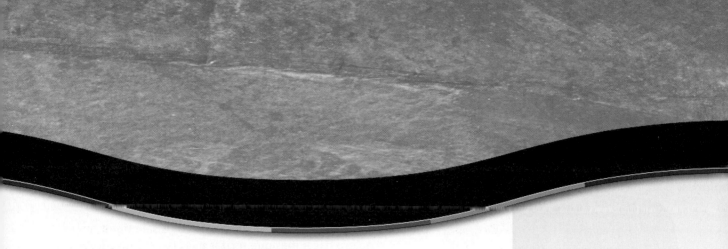

Los datos

Indica si los siguientes comentarios son ciertos o falsos, según la información de la tabla.

Campos de estudio	Cuba	República Dominicana	Estados Unidos / Puerto Rico
Educación	45,9%	11,6%	7,0%
Humanidades	1,7%	6,3%	13,0%
Ciencias sociales / Negocios	7,1%	31,1%	30,1%
Ciencias naturales	17,2%	10,0%	17,2%
Ciencias médicas	16,2%	6,0%	10,3%
Otros	11,9%	35%	22,4%

❶ La educación es el campo de estudio más popular en EEUU.
❷ El campo de estudio menos popular en Cuba es la educación.
❸ Las ciencias sociales y los negocios son los campos de estudio más populares en EEUU y la República Dominicana.

¡Adivina!

¿Qué sabes de Cuba, la República Dominicana y Puerto Rico? (Las respuestas están en la página 92.)

❶ ¿Cuál es el más pequeño? ¿y el más grande?
❷ ¿Cuáles tienen una influencia africana muy importante?
❸ ¿Dónde se originó (*originated*) la música merengue? ¿la rumba y el mambo? ¿la bomba y la plena?

Los datos Answers: 1. F 2. F 3. C

¡Adivina! answers: 1. Puerto Rico, Cuba 2. Puerto Rico, Cuba y República Dominicana 3. **el merengue:** República Dominicana; **la rumba y el mambo:** Cuba; **la bomba y la plena:** Puerto Rico

¡IMAGÍNATE!

Vocabulario útil 1

CHELA:	Para empezar, dime, ¿cuántas clases tienes?
ANILÚ:	Ay, ¡qué aburrido!, ¿no crees? Si voy a salir por Internet, quiero hacer más que recitar mis clases: **computación, diseño gráfico, psicología,** bla, bla, bla…
CHELA:	Comprendo que no son las preguntas más interesantes del mundo, pero…
ANILÚ:	Prefiero hablar de mi tiempo libre, los **sábados,** por ejemplo.

Suggestion: Point out to students Anilú's classes and ask: **¿Estudias computación, diseño gráfico o psicología?** Reinforce pronunciation as needed.

Suggestion: When presenting the vocabulary, ask students about their classes, majors, and minors to familiarize and create a personalized context for these words. Ask questions: **¿Es más fácil la ingeniería o la psicología? ¿Te gusta más la historia o la biología? ¿Qué estudias? ¿Cuál es tu especialidad? ¿Tienes otra concentración de estudios?** You may also want to ask about subjects they like to study using **gustar + estudiar: ¿Te gusta estudiar ciencias políticas?** Also survey students on **¿Cuál es tu clase favorita?**

Notice that many of the courses of study are cognates of their English equivalents. Be sure to notice the difference in spelling, accentuation, and pronunciation, for example: geografía = *geography.*

CAMPOS DE ESTUDIO

En el salón de clase

Los cursos básicos
la arquitectura
las ciencias políticas
la economía
la educación
la geografía
la historia
la ingeniería
la psicología

Las humanidades
la filosofía
las lenguas / los idiomas
la literatura

Las lenguas / Los idiomas
el alemán
el chino
el español
el francés
el inglés
el japonés

Las matemáticas
el cálculo
la computación / la informática
la estadística

Las ciencias
la biología
la física
la medicina
la química (*chemistry*)
la salud (*health*)

Los negocios
la administración de empresas
la contabilidad (*accounting*)
el mercadeo (*marketing*)

La comunicación pública
el periodismo (*journalism*)
la publicidad

En el estudio
el arte
el baile
el diseño gráfico
la música
la pintura

Heritage Learners: Use this vocabulary to review some basic rules of orthography and accentuation in Spanish. Point out to students that many names of disciplines end in **-ía**. However, not all words ending in **-ia** require an accent. Ask students to raise their hand if the word requires an accent: **geología, ecología, dislexia, primaria, historia, carpintería, secundaria, antropología, fotografía, astronomía, bacteria, librería, astrología, magia, enciclopedia, biología, hotelería, farmacia, secretaria, comedia.** Elicit spelling correspondences between English and Spanish: **farmacia** *pharmacy* (**f** v. **ph**); **antropología** *anthropology* (**t** v. **th**); **ciencias** *sciences* (**c** v. **sc**); **comercio** *commerce* (**m** v. **mm**); **administración** *administration* (**ción** v. **tion**); **química** *chemistry* (**qu** v. **ch**).

Otros lugares en la universidad

¿Dónde tienes la clase de...?   *Where does your . . . class meet?*
En el centro de computación.   *In the computer center.*
...el centro de comunicaciones.   *. . . the media center.*
...el gimnasio.   *. . . the gymnasium.*

la cafetería   *the cafeteria*
la librería   *the bookstore*
la residencia estudiantil   *the dorm*

Notice that the week begins on Monday in most Spanish-speaking countries. Also notice that the days of the week are not capitalized in Spanish as they are in English.

LOS DÍAS DE LA SEMANA

lunes	martes	miércoles	jueves	viernes	sábado	domingo
8	9	10	11	12	13	14

To say that something happens *on* a certain day, use the singular article with the day of the week: **La fiesta va a ser *el* sábado.**

To say that something happens on the same day every week, use the plural article with the day of the week: *Los* **sábados visito a mi madre.**

Actividades

ACTIVIDAD 1   **Las clases de Mariana.** With a partner, say on which days Mariana has each of her classes, based on her class schedule.

MODELO: economía
         Mariana tiene economía los lunes, los miércoles y los viernes.

	lunes	martes	miércoles	jueves	viernes
8:00	economía		economía		economía
10:00	psicología	literatura	psicología	literatura	
11:30	francés	francés	francés	francés	francés
3:00		contabilidad		contabilidad	
4:00	pintura		música	pintura	música

1. psicología
2. literatura
3. francés
4. contabilidad
5. pintura
6. música

Answers Act. 1: 1. Mariana tiene psicología los lunes y los miércoles. 2. Mariana tiene literatura los martes y los jueves. 3. Mariana tiene francés los lunes, los martes, los miércoles, los jueves y los viernes. 4. Mariana tiene contabilidad los martes y los jueves. 5. Mariana tiene pintura los lunes y los jueves. 6. Mariana tiene música los miércoles y los viernes.

ACTIVIDAD 2 **Mis clases.** Fill out a page from your agenda with your class schedule. Include days, times, and locations. Then, with a partner, ask each other questions about each day of the week. Be sure to save your schedule for later activities.

MODELO: Tú: *¿Qué clases tienes los lunes?*
Compañero(a): *Los lunes tengo psicología, arte y computación.*

ACTIVIDAD 3 **¿Dónde?** Ask your partner where he / she does certain activities.

MODELO: levantar pesas
Tú: *¿Dónde levantas pesas?*
Compañero(a): *En el gimnasio.*

1. visitar con tus amigos
2. navegar por Internet
3. escuchar los CDs de la clase de español
4. practicar deportes
5. comprar libros
6. vivir
7. tener clase de baile
8. estudiar

¡ F Í J A T E !

Las lenguas romances

Spanish evolved from Latin, the language of the Roman conquerors whose empire once included the Iberian Peninsula (known as Hispania), as well as part of Great Britain and most of Europe and northern Africa. Languages that evolved from Latin are known as the Romance languages. Major Romance languages include Spanish, French, Italian, Portuguese, and Romanian. This common origin often results in the cognates you learned about in **Capítulo 1**, as well as in the false cognates you learned about in **Capítulo 2.**

 PRÁCTICA. Work with a partner and see if you can match each word on the left with the correct language on the right.

1. _____ universitate   a. Latin
2. _____ universitas   b. Spanish
3. _____ université   c. Portuguese
4. _____ university   d. English
5. _____ universidad   e. Romanian
6. _____ università   f. Italian
7. _____ universidade   g. French

Vocabulario útil 2

CHELA:	¿Qué haces los sábados?
ANILÚ:	**Por la mañana,** corro por el parque. **A las dos de la tarde,** tengo clase de danza afrocaribeña.
CHELA:	¿Y **por la noche?**
ANILÚ:	Por la noche escucho música con mis amigos o vamos al cine o a un restaurante.
CAMARÓGRAFO:	Uy, **¿qué hora es?** ¡Tengo que irme!
CHELA:	Pero, ¿adónde vas? ¡Necesito otra entrevista!
CAMARÓGRAFO:	¡Tengo clase **a las once!**
CHELA:	**Son las once menos cuarto.** Espera un minuto, por favor.

PARA PEDIR Y DAR LA HORA   *To ask for and give the time*

¿Qué hora es?   *What time is it?*

Es la una.

Son las dos.

Son las cinco y cuarto.
Son las cinco y quince.

Son las cinco y media.

Son las cinco y diez.

Son las cinco menos cuarto.
Faltan quince para las cinco.

—**¿Tienes tiempo** para tomar un café?
—**Sí, es temprano.** / —¡Ay, no, **ya es muy tarde!**

Compare the following two questions and responses.

¿Qué hora es? (*What time is it?*)
Es la una. (*It's one o'clock.*)

¿A qué hora es la clase de español? (*[At] what time is Spanish class?*)
Es a la una. (*It's at one o'clock.*)

Point out: When you ask the time, use **¿qué?** and when asking what time something takes place, use **¿a qué?**

Preparation: Some students will prefer practicing with an old-fashioned clock face. Draw a large circle on the board, add numbers to clock and clock hands; you can quickly erase to change the time. To the right side of the clock write **y** (+) and to the left write **menos** (−), outside the clock face, label **cuarto** and **media** and draw a sun on the upper right and a moon to the upper left.

Notice: It takes a lot of practice for true beginners to be able to tell time efficiently. Practice random hours. Use a clock prop with movable arms or list times on a board and practice: 5:35, 2:15, 1:12, 10:45, 6:17, 7:07, 8:56, 3:32, 4:47, 9:25, 11:20, 12:05, 7:48, 10:10, 1:16, etc.

MAÑANA, TARDE O NOCHE *Morning, afternoon or night*

Mira **el reloj** para **decir la hora...** *Look at the clock to tell the time . . .*

Son las ocho de la mañana.

Son las tres de la tarde.

Son las nueve de la noche.

Es mediodía.	*It's noontime.*
Es medianoche.	*It's midnight.*
Es tarde.	*It's late.*
Es temprano.	*It's early.*

De la mañana is used for the morning hours between midnight and noon. **De la tarde** is used for daylight hours after noon. **De la noche** is used only for nighttime hours. These hours vary from country to country, given that in some countries it gets dark earlier or stays light later.

Compare the use of **de** and **por** in the following sentences.

> La clase es a las diez **de la mañana.**

> En general estudio **por la mañana.**

Note that you use **de la mañana / tarde / noche** to give a specific time of day. You use **por la mañana / tarde / noche** to give a more general time frame.

Suggestion: Point out to students when these expressions are preceded by **a**—**al mediodía / a la medianoche**—they mean *at noon* and *at midnight*.

Optional: To recycle these concepts, ask the day, date, and time at some point during every class meeting.

Actividades

Answers Act. 4: 1. Son las tres y cuarto de la tarde. / Son las tres y quince de la tarde. 2. Son las tres menos cuarto de la tarde. / Faltan quince para las tres de la tarde. 3. Son las diez y media de la mañana. 4. Es mediodía. / Son las doce de la tarde. 5. Son las seis y cincuenta cinco de la mañana. / Faltan cinco para las siete de la mañana. 6. Son las nueve y veinticinco de la noche.

ACTIVIDAD 4 **¿Qué hora es?** Ask your partner what time it is. He / She will tell you what time it is and add a comment about it. Take turns asking the time.

MODELO: 1:00 P.M.
Tú: *¿Qué hora es?*
Compañero(a): *Es la una de la tarde. ¡Uy, es tarde! Tengo que irme. Tengo clase a la una y cuarto.*

1. 3:15 P.M.	3. 10:30 A.M.	5. 6:55 A.M.
2. 2:45 P.M.	4. 12:00 noon	6. 9:25 P.M.

ACTIVIDAD 5 **Mi horario.** Get out the agenda page that you filled out for **Actividad 2.** Ask your partner about his / her class schedule. You name a day and a time, and your partner tells you what class he / she has at that time. Talk about all five days of the week.

MODELO: Tú: *Es lunes y son las diez de la mañana.*
Compañero(a): *Tengo clase de cálculo.*

ACTIVIDAD 6 **Tu horario.** Exchange your agenda page with your partner. Your partner names a day and a time, and you tell him / her where he / she is at that time. Take turns with each other's schedules.

MODELO: Compañero(a): *Es viernes y son las dos de la tarde. ¿Dónde estoy?*
             Tú: *Estás en la clase de danza afrocaribeña.*

Vocabulario útil 3

CHELA:	¿Así que te gustan más los fines de semana que los días de **entresemana**?
ANILÚ:	Pues sí, por supuesto. Los fines de semana son mucho más divertidos. Ay, **es tarde.** Yo también tengo clase a las once.
CHELA:	Gracias por la entrevista. …
ANILÚ:	Oye, ¿cuándo sale la entrevista en la red?
CHELA:	**Mañana.**

PARA HABLAR DE LA FECHA

¿Qué día es hoy?	*What day is today?*
Hoy es martes treinta.	*Today is Tuesday the 30th.*
¿A qué fecha estamos?	*What is today's date?*
Es el treinta de octubre.	*It's the 30th of October.*
Es el primero de noviembre.	*It's the first of November.*
¿Cuándo es el Día de las Madres?	*When is Mother's Day?*
Es el doce de mayo.	*It's May 12th.*
el día	*day*
la semana	*week*
el fin de semana	*weekend*
el mes	*month*
el año	*year*
todos los días	*every day*
entresemana	*during the week/on weekdays*
ayer	*yesterday*
hoy	*today*
mañana	*tomorrow*

Suggestion: For oral practice, have mini-conversations like **¿A qué fecha estamos?**, **¿Cuál es la fecha de tu cumpleaños?** **¿Te gusta más tu cumpleaños durante el fin de semana o entresemana?**, **¿Cuál es la fecha del cumpleaños de tu mamá?** Also ask students about their work or study habits. **¿Cuándo trabajas / estudias?**, **¿con quién(es)?**, **¿dónde?**, **¿qué días?**, **¿a qué hora?**

Optional: Expansion Activity. **La fiesta.** Charge your Spanish class with finding a common meeting time and date for a class party. Name a time and a day, and students will have to say whether they can come. The student with a conflict must suggest another time. The entire class must find a common meeting time, even if it means the party will be on Sunday at 3 A.M.!

Actividades

Preparation: Bring calendars to class to use as a visual aid. Also have students bring their planners or calendars to be able to record important dates in Spanish.

ACTIVIDAD 7 **Las fechas.** Form pairs. Bring out a yearly calendar or borrow one from your professor. Your professor will give each team five minutes to answer the following questions. Write out your answers in Spanish. There are some words that you might not know. Try to guess at their meaning, but don't let it hold you up!

1. ¿Qué día de la semana es Navidad (25 de diciembre) este año?
2. ¿Qué día de la semana es el Día de la Independencia (4 de julio) este año?
3. ¿Qué día de la semana es el Día de la Amistad (14 de febrero) este año?
4. ¿A qué fecha estamos? ¿Cuándo es el próximo (*next*) examen de español?
5. ¿Cuándo son las próximas vacaciones? ¿Qué día regresan los estudiantes de las próximas vacaciones?

ACTIVIDAD 8 **Fechas importantes.** Write down in Spanish ten to fifteen dates that are important for you. Then transfer them to your calendar. The following are some examples of the dates you might include.

los cumpleaños de los miembros de mi familia	el Día del Padre
los cumpleaños de mis amigos	las fechas de las vacaciones
el Día de las Madres	el aniversario de…
	las fechas de mis exámenes finales

Standards: Here students learn about the cultural differences (C 2.1, 2.2) and compare perspectives (C 4.2) on telling time.

Optional: Point out that one advantage of the 24-hour clock is that you don't have to add A.M. or P.M. after the time. In the U.S., the 24-hour clock is rarely used, except by the military and some government offices. Ask students: Why do you think that might be? Do you like the idea of using a 24-hour clock? Why or why not?

Suggestion: Have your class identify whether these times should be followed by **de la mañana, de la tarde,** or **de la noche:** 9:50h, 14:10h, 23:30h, 1:25h, 20:05h, 16:55h

¡COMPÁRATE!

Many Spanish-speaking countries use the 24-hour clock (**el reloj de veinticuatro horas**) in schedules or to give official times. The 24-hour clock is based on counting the hours from zero through twenty-four. The first twelve hours of the day (from midnight until noon) are represented with the numbers 0–12. Any time after noon is represented by that time + 12. The **h** after the time stands for **horas.** For example:

1:00 P.M. = 1:00 + 12 = 13:00h
2:30 P.M. = 2:30 + 12 = 14:30h
5:45 P.M. = 5:45 + 12 = 17:45h

The 24-hour clock is almost always used in written form. In conversation, Spanish speakers use the 12-hour format adding **de la mañana, de la tarde,** and **de la noche** for clarification.

PRÁCTICA. With a partner, look at the schedules that you used in **Actividad 2.** Convert the times on your schedules to hours on the twenty-four-hour clock. Follow the model.

MODELO: Tú: *Mi (My) clase de matemáticas es a las 3:00 de la tarde.*

Compañero(a): *Tu (Your) clase de matemáticas es a las 15:00 horas.*

A VER

Antes de ver el video

ACTIVIDAD 1 Look at the **Vocabulario útil** sections on pages 70, 73, and 75 and identify the three main characters you see in the photographs. Then match the person on the left with their concern on the right.

1. _____ Chela
2. _____ camarógrafo
3. _____ Anilú

a. Tiene que ir a clase.
b. Busca información sobre la vida universitaria.
c. Prefiere hablar sobre los fines de semana.

ACTIVIDAD 2 The following is a list of key words that are used in the video. Quickly review this list.

la entrevista   *the interview*
transmitir   *to transmit*
la red   *the Web, the Internet*

ACTIVIDAD 3 It is obvious from the list in **Actividad 2** that the video segment will probably include an interview. Write a list of five questions that you might ask a university student in an interview for your university's web page.

MODELO: *¿Cómo te llamas?*
            ¿Qué...?
            ¿Cuándo...?
            etc.

ESTRATEGIA

Using body language to aid in comprehension

In video, as in life, you can gain insight by observing the body language of the person speaking. Even if you don't understand every word that you hear, you can get clues to a person's meaning by watching facial expressions, gestures, hand movements, and overall body motion. If you ask a woman a question and she shrugs and walks away, her meaning is clear even if she hasn't uttered a single word.

The deciphering of body language is an automatic habit all people use in their daily interactions. This skill, which you have already developed through your day-to-day interactions with other people, will come in handy as you try to understand the characters in the video.

For additional practice, do the *Nexos* website and / or CD-ROM video exercises.

Answers Act. 1: 1. b 2. a 3. a, c

Suggestion: While watching the video without sound, have students jot down words to describe types of body language that they may observe. Words like **animado, indiferente, activo**, etc., or other descriptive words can be written on the board and students can choose from the list.

El video

As a previewing strategy to help guide your comprehension of the video segment, read the items in **Actividad 4** *before* you view the video.

Now watch the video segment for **Capítulo 3** without sound. Pay special attention to the body language of the actors as you watch.

1. What do you think Chela is asking the students that are walking by? Are they responding positively or negatively to her?
2. What do you think Anilú is like?
3. What does the cameraman's body language indicate?

Después de ver el video

Answers Act. 4: 1. cierto 2. cierto 3. falso 4. cierto 5. cierto

ACTIVIDAD 4 Say whether or not the following statements are true **(cierto)** or false **(falso),** based on your observation of the characters' body language in the segment.

1. Muchos estudiantes prefieren no participar en la entrevista con Chela.
2. Chela indica algo (*something*) al estudiante con la cámara.
3. El estudiante con la cámara no tiene prisa (*is not in a hurry*).
4. Chela es una persona muy responsable y trabajadora.
5. Anilú observa a Javier (el estudiante que aparece al final del segmento) con mucho interés.

Answers Act. 5: 1. aburrido 2. psicología 3. sábados 4. cine 5. once

ACTIVIDAD 5 Now, watch the video again with sound. Use the information you gathered from observing body language, along with what you understood from listening to the video, to complete the following statements.

1. En la opinión del estudiante con la cámara y de Anilú, el tema del programa de Chela es _____.
2. Anilú tiene clases de computación, diseño gráfico y _____.
3. Los _____, Anilú corre en el parque.
4. Los sábados por la noche, Anilú escucha música con amigos o va al _____ o a un restaurante.
5. El estudiante con la cámara tiene clase a las _____.

 ACTIVIDAD 6 Watch the video segment again. With a partner, make a list of the questions that Chela asks Anilú in her interview. Then interview two or three of your classmates, asking them those questions.

With a partner, dramatize one of the following situations.

- You are the reporter and you are attracted to the interviewee. Try to get the interviewee's phone number.

- You are the interviewee and you are attracted to the cameraman. Try to get the camerman's phone number.

- You are the interviewee and you don't like the reporter's attitude. Try to evade the reporter's questions.

VOCES DE LA COMUNIDAD

Erick Carreira

66 Though English is the international language of science, as a bilingual Hispanic, I take great pleasure and pride in my ability to communicate with my colleagues throughout Latin America and Spain, in my native language—Spanish. My Hispanic identity has enabled me to forge alliances with these colleagues that extend beyond the confines of science to encompass a long and rich array of shared cultural, social, and personal experiences. 99

66 Estudiar, aprender y explorar son actividades esenciales para mi felicidad y satisfacción personal. En mi opinión, estas actividades forman parte de un instinto exploratorio que define a los seres humanos. 99

Erick José Carreira es investigador y profesor de química en el Instituto ETH, un centro de investigaciones científicas en Zurich, Suiza. Este cubanoamericano recibe fama internacional por su trabajo relacionado con el colesterol. Tiene un doctorado en química de la Universidad de Harvard. Sus honores académicos incluyen el Premio Nobel Signature y el Premio Pecase de la Fundación Nacional de Ciencias (NSF).

Point out: As in the case of Erick Carreira, although much scientific research is published in English, many scientific research teams are composed of multilingual researchers from all over the world. Knowing multiple languages facilitates many professions.

¿A Erick Carreira qué le gusta hacer? To learn more about Erick Carreira and his scientific work, see the chapter links on the *Nexos* website (http://college.hmco.com/languages/spanish/students).

Gramática útil 1
Asking questions: Interrogative words

 For more practice of chapter topics, do the *Nexos* website exercises.

Suggestion: Clarify that interrogative words are question words, then ask, **¿Qué tienen todos los interrogativos?** (¡Acentos!) You may want to mention examples such as **que** = *that* and **como** = *like*, whose meanings change entirely with no accent.

Heritage Learners: Interrogatives always require an accent, but it is not always obvious to heritage learners where the accent is placed. For those students that have difficulty hearing the location of the written accent, have them practice saying interrogative words out loud in an exaggerated manner. This should make it easier to locate the stressed syllable.

You may want to point out that **cuál** + noun is also used, depending on region.

CÓMO USARLO

You have already seen, learned, and used a number of interrogative words to ask questions. **¿Cómo te llamas? ¿Cuál es tu dirección electrónica? ¿Dónde vives?** and **¿Qué tal?** are all questions that begin with interrogatives: **cómo, cuál, dónde, qué.**

As in English, we use interrogatives in Spanish to ask for specific information. Here are the Spanish interrogatives.

¿Cuál(es)?	*What? Which one(s)?*	**¿Dónde?**	*Where?*
¿Qué?	*What? Which?*	**¿Adónde?**	*To where?*
¿A qué hora?	*(At) What time?*	**¿De dónde?**	*From where?*
¿De qué?	*About what? Of what?*	**¿Quién(es)?**	*Who?*
¿Cuándo?	*When?*	**¿De quién(es)?**	*Whose?*
¿Cuánto(a)?	*How much?*	**¿Cómo?**	*How?*
¿Cuántos(as)?	*How many?*	**¿Por qué?**	*Why?*

1. **¿Qué?** and **¿cuál?** may appear interchangeable at first sight, but they are used in very specific ways.

¿Qué? is . . .

♦ used to ask for a definition: **¿Qué es el reloj de veinticuatro horas?**

♦ used to ask for an explanation or further information: **¿Qué vas a estudiar este semestre?**

♦ generally used when the next word is a noun: **¿Qué libros te gustan más? ¿Qué clase tienes a las ocho?**

¿Cuál? is . . .

♦ used to express a choice between specified items: **¿Cuál de los libros prefieres? ¿Cuál prefieres, las matemáticas o las ciencias?**

♦ used when the next word is a form of **ser** but the question is *not* asking for a definition: **¿Cuál es tu número de teléfono? ¿Cuáles son tus clases favoritas?**

2. **¿Dónde?** is used to ask where something is.

¿Dónde está la biblioteca?   ***Where** is the library?*

3. **¿Adónde?** is used to ask where someone is going.

¿**Adónde** vas ahora?   *Where are you going now?*

Notice that **dónde** and **adónde** are both translated the same way into English.

4. **¿De quién es?** and **¿De quiénes son?** are used to ask about possession. You answer using **de**.

—¿**De quién** es la computadora?   *Whose computer is this?*
—**Es de** Miguel.   *It's Miguel's.*

—¿**De quiénes** son los libros?   *Whose books are these?*
—**Son de** Anita y Manuel.   *They're Anita's and Manuel's.*

5. Questions using **¿por qué?** can be answered using **porque** (*because*).

—¿**Por qué** tienes que trabajar?   *Why do you have to work?*
—¡**Porque** necesito el dinero!   *Because I need the money!*

Note that the interrogative is two separate words with an accent on **qué**. **Porque** is one single word with no accent.

CÓMO FORMARLO

1. Interrogatives are always preceded by an inverted question mark (¿). The question requires a regular question mark (?) at the end.

2. Notice that in a typical question the subject *follows* the verb.

¿**Dónde estudia Marcos?**   *Where does Marcos study?*
¿**Qué instrumento tocan Uds.?**   *What instrument do you play?*

3. **¿Quién?** and **¿cuál?** change to reflect number.

¿**Quién** es el hombre alto? / ¿**Quiénes** son los hombres altos?
¿**Cuál** de los libros tienes? / ¿**Cuáles** son tus idiomas favoritos?

4. **¿Cuánto?** changes to reflect both number and gender.

¿**Cuánto** dinero tienes?   *How **much** money do you have?*
¿**Cuánta** comida compramos?   *How **much** food should we buy?*
¿**Cuántos** años tienes?   *How **many** years are you? / How old are you?*
¿**Cuántas** personas hay?   *How **many** people are there?*

5. When you want to ask "how much" in a general way, use **¿cuánto?**

¿**Cuánto es?** ¿**Cuánto necesitamos?**

6. Note that interrogatives always require an accent.

7. You have already learned how to form simple *yes/no* questions by adding **no** to a sentence.

¿**No escribes** e-mails hoy?   *Aren't you writings any e-mails today?*

8. You can also form simple *yes/no* questions by adding a tag question, such as **¿verdad?** (*Isn't that right?*) and **¿no?** to the end of a statement.

Cantas en el coro con Ana, **¿no?**   *You sing in the chorus with Ana, **right?***
Enrique baila salsa muy bien, **¿verdad?**   *Enrique dances salsa very well, **right?***

¿**Cuántas** entrevistas tenemos que hacer?

When a Spanish speaker adds **¿verdad?** or **¿no?** to a question, he or she is expecting an affirmative answer.

Actividades

 ACTIVIDAD 1 **Las preguntas.** What question would you have to ask to produce the response shown? You will hear three questions. Choose the correct one.

1. La clase de informática es a las once de la mañana.
2. Tengo que ir al centro de computación para la clase de informática.
3. La computadora portátil es de mi compañero de cuarto.
4. Hay que comprar tres libros para la clase de informática.
5. Porque me gustan mucho las computadoras y quiero aprender a programarlas.
6. La señora Delgado es la profesora de informática.

ACTIVIDAD 2 **En la cafetería.** You overhear a conversation between two students in the cafeteria. Fill in the correct form of the question words to complete their conversation.

—¿(1) _____ clases tienes este semestre?
—Tengo arte, literatura, cálculo, química y economía.

—¿(2) _____ son tus clases favoritas?
—El arte y la literatura.

—¿(3) _____ son tus autores favoritos?
—García Márquez, Borges y Allende.

—¿(4) _____ es tu profesor de literatura?
—El señor Banderas.

—¿(5) _____ libros necesitas para la clase de literatura?
—Diez, más o menos, pero son libros que puedo sacar de la biblioteca.

—¿A (6) _____ hora tienes la clase de literatura?
—A las diez de la mañana.

—¿(7) _____ vas ahora?
—Al centro de computación.

—¿(8) _____ vas allí?
—Porque necesito usar las computadoras para hacer mi tarea.

—Pero tienes computadora portátil. ¿(9) _____ es la computadora portátil?
—Es de mi compañero de cuarto. ¡Haces demasiadas (*You ask too many*) preguntas!

 ACTIVIDAD 3 **Encuesta #1.** In the chapter activities labeled **"Encuesta"** you will gather information from your fellow students in order to write a description of life at your college or university in the **A escribir** section at the end of the chapter.

1. First prepare a questionnaire by creating two questions for each category, using the cues provided, or coming up with your own.

El horario: clases por día / semana, lugar preferido para estudiar
El trabajo: lugar de trabajo, horas de trabajo
La computadora: tiempo que pasas en la computadora y por Internet, sitios interesantes en Internet
La universidad: clases difíciles y fáciles, las horas por semana que estudias, profesores buenos y malos

2. Now work with another group and ask the members to answer your questionnaire. Be sure to answer their questions as well. Keep track of your results. You will need them later in the chapter.

Gramática útil 2
Talking about daily activities: *-er* and *-ir* verbs in the present indicative

CÓMO USARLO

In **Capítulo 2,** you learned how to use the present indicative of regular **-ar** verbs to talk about daily activities. The present indicative of **-er** and **-ir** verbs are used in the same contexts.

Remember:

1. The present indicative, depending on how it is used, can correspond to the following English usages: *I read* (in general), *I am reading, I am going to read,* and, if used as a question, *Do you read?*

2. You can often omit the subject pronoun when the subject is clear from the verb ending used or from the context of the sentence.

Leo en la biblioteca todos los días.   *I read in the library every day.*
Lees en la residencia estudiantil, ¿no?   *You read in the dorm, right?*

3. You may use an infinitive after certain conjugated verbs.

¿Tienes que imprimir esto?   *Do you have to print this?*
¿Necesitas leer este libro?   *Do you need to read this book?*
¡Dejo de leer después de las nueve!   *I stop reading after 9:00!*

Por la mañana, **corro** en el parque.

4. However, do not use two verbs conjugated in the present tense together unless they are separated by a comma or the words **y** (*and*) or **o** (*or*).

Leo, estudio y escribo composiciones en la biblioteca.   *I read, study, and write compositions in the library.*

5. Remember that you can negate sentences in the present indicative tense to say what you don't do or aren't planning to do.

No comemos en la cafetería hoy.   *We're not eating in the cafeteria today.*
No leo todos los días.   *I don't read every day.*

CÓMO FORMARLO

To form the present indicative tense of **-er** and **-ir** verbs, simply remove the **-er** or **-ir** and add the following endings.

comer (*to eat*)			
yo	**como**	nosotros / nosotras	**comemos**
tú	**comes**	vosotros / vosotras	**coméis**
Ud. / él / ella	**come**	Uds. / ellos / ellas	**comen**

vivir (*to live*)			
yo	**vivo**	nosotros / nosotras	**vivimos**
tú	**vives**	vosotros / vosotras	**vivís**
Ud. / él / ella	**vive**	Uds. / ellos / ellas	**viven**

Here are some commonly used **-er** and **-ir** verbs.

-er verbs			
aprender a (+ *inf.*)	*to learn to (do something)*	**creer (en)**	*to believe (in)*
beber	*to drink*	**deber** (+ *inf.*)	*should, ought (to do something)*
comer	*to eat*	**leer**	*to read*
comprender	*to understand*	**vender**	*to sell*
correr	*to run*		

-ir verbs			
abrir	*to open*	**escribir**	*to write*
asistir a	*to attend*	**imprimir**	*to print*
compartir	*to share*	**recibir**	*to receive*
describir	*to describe*	**transmitir**	*to broadcast*
descubrir	*to discover*	**vivir**	*to live*

Actividades

ACTIVIDAD 4 **¿Qué hacen?** Based on the information provided, what do the people indicated do? Choose verbs from the list and work with a partner. Follow the model. There may be more than one verb possible for each item.

MODELOS: Carlos ya no necesita esa cámara digital.
Vende la cámara.

Tú y yo necesitamos hacer ejercicio.
Corremos en el parque.

Verbos posibles: vender / comer / compartir / asistir a / correr / aprender / leer / vivir

1. ¡Olivia tiene la clase de biología a las tres y ya son las tres y cinco!
2. A Susana no le gusta esa bicicleta.
3. Raúl y Enrique tienen que viajar a Puerto Rico en dos meses.
4. Elena y yo no comprendemos las lecturas del libro.
5. No me gustan los restaurantes aquí.
6. Susana vive con una compañera de cuarto.

ACTIVIDAD 5 **La vida estudiantil.** Say what the people indicated are doing today on campus. The numbers indicate how many actions are going on for each person.

1. Juan Carlos e Isabel (1)
2. Marcos (2)
3. Cecilia y Marta (2)

4. Radio WBRU (1)
5. Y tú, ¿qué haces (*are you doing*)?

ACTIVIDAD 6 **¿Qué hacemos?** Using an element from each of the three columns, create eight sentences describing what you and people you know do in and around campus.

MODELO: *Yo asisto a clases los lunes, los miércoles y los jueves.*

A	B	C
yo	aprender a hablar español	café por la mañana
tú		en el centro de comunicaciones
compañero(s) de cuarto	asistir a	clases (*número*) días de la semana
	beber	correspondencia electrónica todos los días
profesor(es)	comprender	en el estadio
estudiante(s)	correr	la importancia de Internet
amigo(s)	creer (en)	clases los (*día de la semana*)
	escribir	novelas latinoamericanas
	leer	en el parque
	recibir	poemas para la clase de literatura
		las lecturas del libro
		¿…?

ACTIVIDAD 7 **Encuesta #2.** Use the cues provided to create a questionnaire. Use the interrogatives you learned earlier in the chapter along with the cues provided. Once your group has completed the questionnaire, ask the questions to members of another group. Remember to save your responses for use later in the chapter.

1. leer libros / por semana
2. compartir cuarto / con compañero(a) de cuarto
3. asistir a clase / todos los días / todas las semanas
4. comer en la cafetería / por semana
5. vender / libros de texto

ACTIVIDAD 8 **La vida universitaria.** Write an e-mail to a friend describing your university life. Mention the following things or anything else you might want to talk about. Save your work for use later in the chapter.

- cuántas clases tienes y los días que asistes a clase
- dónde y cuándo comes
- dónde vives
- qué libros lees
- qué actividades te gustan (correr, levantar pesas, mirar televisión, navegar por Internet, leer, escribir, etc.)

Gramática útil 3
Talking about possessions: Simple possessive adjectives

What is the possessive adjective used in this Puerto Rican university's slogan? To whom does it refer?

Answer: **tu,** (potential) students

CÓMO USARLO

1. You already have learned to express possession using **de** + a noun or name.

Es la computadora portátil **de la profesora.**	*It's **the professor's** laptop computer.*

2. You can also use possessive adjectives to describe your possessions, other people's possessions, or items that are associated with you. You are already familiar with some possessive adjectives from the phrases **¿Cuál es *tu* dirección?** and **Aquí tienes *mi* número de teléfono.**

—¿Cuándo es **tu** clase de historia?	*When is **your** history class?*
—A las dos. Y **mi** clase de español es a las tres.	*At two. And **my** Spanish class is at three.*

3. When you use **su** (which can mean *your, his, her, its*), context will usually clarify who is meant. If not, you can follow up with **de** + name.

Es **su** libro. Es **de la profesora.**   *It's **her** book. It's **the professor's.***

Suggestion: Point out to students that **sus libros** can mean *his / her / their / your books* and must agree with the noun possessed—not the possessor.

CÓMO FORMARLO

LO BÁSICO

Possessive adjectives modify nouns in order to express possession. In other words, they tell who owns the item.

1. Here are the simple possessive adjectives in Spanish.

mi mis	*my*	nuestro / nuestra nuestros / nuestras	*our*
tu tus	*your (fam.)*	vuestro / vuestra vuestros / vuestras	*your (fam. pl.)*
su sus	*your (form.), his, her, its*	su sus	*your (pl.), their*

2. Notice that . . .

◆ all possessive adjectives change to reflect number: **mi clase, mis clases; nuestro compañero de cuarto, nuestros compañeros de cuarto.**

◆ **mi, tu,** and **su** do not change to reflect gender, but **nuestro** and **vuestro** do: **nuestro libro, nuestros amigos, nuestras clases,** but **mi libro, mi clase.**

◆ unlike other adjectives, which often go after the noun they modify, simple possessive adjectives always go before the noun: **su profesora, nuestras amigas.**

Notice that the subject pronoun **tú** (*you*) has an accent on it to differentiate it from the possessive adjective **tu** (*your*).

Tú trabajas los lunes, ¿verdad?

Tu libro está en mi casa.

Actividades

ACTIVIDAD 9 **¿De quién es?** Say who the following things belong to.

MODELO: computadora portátil (yo)
              Es mi computadora portátil.

1. apuntes, tarea, CDs, silla (yo)
2. bolígrafos, lápiz, celular, examen (María)
3. calculadoras, cuadernos, dibujos, cintas (nosotros)
4. diccionario, notas, escritorio, disquetes (tú)
5. libros, tiza, cuarto, papeles (la profesora Carrera)
6. computadora, fotos, salón de clase, apuntes (ustedes)

Answers Act. 9: 1. mis, mi, mis, mi 2. sus, su, su, su 3. nuestras, nuestros, nuestros, nuestras 4. tu, tus, tu, tus 5. sus, su, su, sus 6. su, sus, su, sus

Optional: Circulate around the classroom and look for items like the ones in **Actividad 9.** Pick up items and ask **¿De quién es?** Get student to answer **Es de...; es su libro.** You can line these items up in front of the class, and see who can remember all of the owners.

ACTIVIDAD 10 **Nuestros amigos.** Make two semantic maps like the one below—one each for two of your friends. Put your name at the bottom of each map. In groups of four, one map gets circulated to each person. The person whose map it is has to start the conversation. Then, each other person has to say something about the friend using a possessive adjective. Notice who you're talking to!

Mi amigo / a se llama _____.

¿Cómo es?

¿nacionalidad?   ¿características físicas?   ¿características de personalidad?

_____   _____   _____

¿nacionalidad de sus papás?

_____

MODELO:

Estudiante #1: Mi amigo es puertorriqueño.

Estudiante #2: Tu amigo puertorriqueño es alto. (*talking to Estudiante #1*)

Estudiante #3: Su amigo puertorriqueño es responsable. (*talking to others in group*)

Estudiante #4: Su amigo se llama Carlos y sus padres son puertorriqueños también.

ACTIVIDAD 11 **Conversaciones.** You just met someone from Cuba at the library. You want to learn more about that person. Write him or her an e-mail asking for more information. Use the following ideas for your e-mail if you want to, and if not, make up your own questions. Make sure to express possession correctly.

- dirección
- número de teléfono
- cumpleaños
- clases

- amigos / compañeros de cuarto
- actividades favoritas
- ¿...?

ACTIVIDAD 12 **Un juego.** In a group of five or six students, play the following word game. See which group is able to come up with the longest chain of sentences. One student should be the recorder and write down the number of correct sentences that are created. Try to use a possessive adjective in each sentence.

1. The first person makes a statement about one of his or her personal possessions: **Leo mi libro para la clase de historia.**
2. The second person then takes a word from that sentence **(libro)** and uses it in a new sentence: **Su libro es interesante.**
3. The third person takes a new word from that sentence **(interesante)** and uses it in a new sentence: **Mis clases son interesantes.**
4. The fourth person takes a new word from that sentence **(clases)** and uses it in a new sentence: **Nuestras clases de computación son difíciles.**
5. The fifth person takes a new word from that sentence **(difícil)** and uses it in a new sentence, and so on.

Sonrisas

Optional: In groups compile lists that reflect the items that most people are willing to share and those that they are least willing to share. Have students compare lists with rest of the class. **¿Cuáles son las cosas más típicas / no típicas?, ¿Quiénes son las personas más generosas de la clase?**

COMPRENSIÓN. In your opinion, how would you describe the characters in the cartoon?

1. En tu opinión, ¿es generoso y romántico o manipulador el hombre? ¿Por qué?
2. En tu opinión, ¿es inocente y romántica o manipuladora la mujer? ¿Por qué?
3. ¿Crees que los contratos prenupciales son una buena idea o una mala idea?

Answers: 1. manipulador 2. inocente y romántica 3. *Answers will vary.*

Gramática útil 4
Indicating destination and future plans: The verb *ir*

Quiero hacerle una entrevista para un programa que **vamos a transmitir** en la página web de la Universidad.

Begin the CD-ROM activities. Do the cultural activities and reading and writing practice as you complete the corresponding text sections.

CÓMO USARLO

You can use the Spanish verb **ir** to say where you and others are going. You can also use it to say what you and others are going to do in the near future.

Vamos a la biblioteca mañana.
Vamos a estudiar.

We're going to the library tomorrow.
We're going to study.

CÓMO FORMARLO

LO BÁSICO

- An *irregular verb* is one that does not follow the normal rules, such as **tener**, which you learned in **Capítulo 1.**
- A *preposition* links nouns, pronouns, or noun phrases to the rest of the sentence. Prepositions can express location, time sequence, purpose, or direction. *In, to, after, under,* and *for* are all English prepositions.

1. Here is the verb **ir** in the present indicative tense. **Ir,** like the verbs **ser** and **tener** that you have already learned, is an irregular verb.

ir (*to go*)			
yo	**voy**	nosotros / nosotras	**vamos**
tú	**vas**	vosotros / vosotras	**vais**
Ud. / él / ella	**va**	Uds. / ellos / ellas	**van**

2. Use the preposition **a** with the verb **ir** to say where you are going:

Voy *a* la cafetería.   *I'm going to the cafeteria.*

You have already used similar expressions: **necesitar** + infinitive (*to need to do something*), **tener que** + infinitive (*to have to do something*), and **dejar de** + infinitive (*to stop doing something*).

3. When you want to use the verb **ir** to say what you are going to do, use this formula: **ir** + **a** + *infinitive.*

Vamos a comer a las cinco hoy.
Después, **vamos a ir** al concierto.

We're going to eat at 5:00 today.
*Afterward, **we're going to go** to the concert.*

Suggestion: Emphasize that **él** (*he / him*) does not contract. Point out that contraction takes place only with the article **el** (*the*).

Suggestion: In pairs, have students interview each other to get as much information about a classmate's after-class plans as possible. First, model interview questions with a student: **Después de la clase de español, ¿adónde vas?, ¿con quién vas?, ¿quién es?, ¿por qué vas?, ¿a qué hora vas?...**

4. When you use **a** together with **el,** it contracts to **al.** The same holds true for **de** + **el: del.**

$$a + el = \mathbf{al} \qquad de + el = \mathbf{del}$$

Voy **a la** biblioteca y luego **al** gimnasio. Después, **al** mediodía, voy a estudiar en la biblioteca **del** centro de comunicaciones.

Actividades

ACTIVIDAD 13 **Vamos a...** Say what the people indicated plan to do and where they are going to do it.

MODELO: yo (estudiar)
Voy a estudiar. Voy a la biblioteca.

1. Pedro y Rafael (levantar pesas)
2. mi compañero de cuarto y yo (correr)
3. Fabiola (escuchar las cintas de español)
4. Tomás, Andrea y yo (tomar un refresco)
5. tú (comprar libros)
6. Lourdes (descansar)
7. tú (leer libros)
8. David y Patricia (comer)

ACTIVIDAD 14 **¡Pobre Miguel!** Listen as Miguel describes his schedule to his best friend Cristina. As you listen, write down where he goes on each day of the week. Then use **ir** + **a** to create seven complete sentences that describe his schedule.

1. los lunes: _____
2. los martes: _____
3. los miércoles: _____
4. los jueves: _____
5. los viernes: _____
6. los sábados: _____
7. los domingos: _____

ACTIVIDAD 15 **Encuesta #3.** You need to get more information about student life for the description you will be writing later this chapter. Find out as much as you can about your partner's leisure activities. Ask questions such as the following and take notes. Then, as a class, tally the information you found out.

El tiempo libre
1. ¿Adónde vas los viernes y sábados por la noche? ¿Con quién vas?
2. ¿Adónde vas los días de semana cuando no estudias? ¿Con quién vas?
3. ¿...?

Vocabulario útil: un club, una discoteca, el cine (*movie theater*), un restaurante, un centro comercial (*mall*), un partido (*game*) de fútbol americano / de básquetbol / etc.

Puerto Rico, Cuba, la República Dominicana

Standards: Here students gain knowledge and understanding of Caribbean culture (C 2.1) and explore cultural products such as dance (C 2.2).

Optional: The video *Buena Vista Social Club* can be rented at many commercial centers and will serve as an example of Afro-Cuban musical rhythms. Bring to class or students can be assigned to view it outside of class.

Suggestion: For more practice, have students read the descriptions and answer true-false questions on main ideas: **La rumba incorpora ritmos africanos y europeos. El Yunque es un parque nacional de los EEUU. Tiene poca flora y fauna porque es desértico,** etc.

Los países hispanohablantes del Caribe. Can you guess which text is about which country? Don't try to understand every word; simply skim rapidly through each passage to gather enough clues to indicate which country it's describing.

_____ el Estado Libre Asociado de Puerto Rico

_____ la República Dominicana

_____ la República de Cuba

Grupo de música rumba

1 ¡Aquí se oye (*you hear*) la música de la rumba día y noche! La rumba tiene su origen en los ritmos folclóricos africanos y europeos y ha afectado mucho el estilo y el espíritu de la música tan famosa y popular de este país. Además de las influencias culturales africanas y europeas, también hay una población china significante, resultado de la inmigración china a Norteamérica y al Caribe durante los años 1800.

2 Este país tiene una variedad de atracciones naturales. Tal vez la más importante es el Bosque Tropical El Yunque. El Yunque es el único en su clase dentro del sistema nacional de parques de Estados Unidos y exhibe una exótica e increíble variedad de flora y fauna. Esta isla pequeña también es famosa por sus playas tropicales, su arquitectura colonial y la bomba y la plena, formas musicales que reflejan las culturas africanas e indígenas del país.

Vista del bosque de El Yunque

3 Santo Domingo es el centro urbano más vital de este país. La ciudad, famosa por sus clubes de salsa y merengue, es alegre, hospitalaria, moderna y antigua a la vez. Es la primera ciudad del Nuevo Mundo (*New World*) y, a causa de los ataques constantes de piratas y corsarios, en 1503 se inicia la construcción de la Fortaleza de Santo Domingo. Como todos los países del Caribe, la influencia africana es evidente aquí, especialmente en la música y la cocina.

Fortaleza de Santo Domingo ▶

Standards / Preparation: If you plan ahead, this presents an opportunity to connect students with the music and dance community (C 5.1) in your area. Have students research local music and dance studios that offer classes in dances and music of the Spanish-speaking world. Arrange music and dance demonstrations.

¡CONÉCTATE!

Internet

👥 Divide into three groups. Each group should choose one country, find the answers to the questions about it, and then report back to the class with a brief summary. Follow links on the *Nexos* website (http://college.hmco.com/languages/spanish/students) to see a list of suggested websites.

Estado Libre Asociado de Puerto Rico (Group 1)
1. Why are Puerto Ricans U.S. citizens?
2. Do they have all of the same rights as the other citizens of this country?
3. How many Puerto Ricans live in the United States?

Cuba (Group 2)
1. How many Cuban Americans live in the United States? How does that number compare to the total population of Cuba?
2. When did Cuba gain its independence from Spain?
3. When did Fidel Castro rise to power?

La República Dominicana (Group 3)
1. How did Haiti and the Dominican Republic come to share the same island?
2. Who is the current head of state in the Dominican Republic?
3. How many Dominicans live in the United States? Do they live in a particular area?

Standards: In the ¡Conéctate! sections, students are encouraged to do independent web research on topics that will gradually require more Spanish to carry out the assignments by introducing more participation with Spanish-speaking communities on the web (C 5.1).

A LEER

Antes de leer

ESTRATEGIA

Using visuals to aid in comprehension

Depending on what you are reading, there are often visuals that accompany the text. Looking at the visuals first can often give you a good idea of what the text is about. When you approach a reading that seems difficult, it's a good idea to look first at the visuals and any captions that accompany them to see if you can figure out their content.

Answers Act. 1: 1. b 2. a 3. c

ACTIVIDAD 1 Look at the following newspaper article from *Diálogo*, the student newspaper of the **Universidad de Puerto Rico.** Focus on the photos, captions, and headlines, then match the general information on the right with the photo on the left.

1. _____ Foto A   a. Hay clases de la música bomba y plena para adultos.
2. _____ Foto B   b. La escuela ofrece clases de percusión.
3. _____ Foto C   c. Los niños con más talento tienen clases especiales.

Answers Act. 2: 1. d 2. f 3. h 4. c 5. g 6. a 7. e 8. b 9. i

ACTIVIDAD 2 The following are some unknown words you will encounter in the reading passage. Although not all the words are cognates, they are somewhat similar to their English counterparts. See if you can match the two.

1. _____ refleja   a. *unique, only*
2. _____ hoy día   b. *directs*
3. _____ mulato   c. *slave*
4. _____ esclavo   d. *reflects*
5. _____ mantener vivo   e. *beginner*
6. _____ único   f. *today, nowadays*
7. _____ principiante   g. *maintain alive, preserve*
8. _____ dirige   h. *mulatto (of Caucasian and African parentage)*
9. _____ negro   i. *black*

ACTIVIDAD 3 Now, using the information you gained from looking at the visuals, read the article and focus on getting the main idea. Don't forget to use cognates and active vocabulary to help you understand the content. Try not to worry about unknown words and just focus on getting the main information.

Lectura

Los ritmos afrocaribeños

En la Escuela de Bomba y Plena Rafael Cepeda los estudiantes aprenden los ritmos afrocaribeños tradicionales.

Escenas de las distintas clases que se ofrecen en la Escuela de Bomba y Plena Rafael Cepeda.

Este ritmo afrocaribeño, la bomba, representa la herencia africana de Puerto Rico. Pero hoy día la plena, otro estilo musical afrocaribeño, es más popular. ¿Por qué? Según don Modesto Cepeda, fundador y director de la Escuela de Bomba y Plena Rafael Cepeda, es una cuestión de racismo.

Cepeda opina que la plena hoy es más popular por no ser un baile tan "negro" como la bomba. La plena es de origen urbano, de la población pobre[1] y mulata de Ponce. Al contrario, la bomba se originó entre la población de esclavos negros de los sectores agrícolas rurales. Tiene un origen puramente africano.

En 1978 don Modesto instituye su escuela con la intención de renovar el interés en la bomba, y además en la plena. Su idea para la escuela es mantener vivas las tradiciones de las dos danzas y darle a la bomba la atención que merece[2]. Cada sábado a las diez de la mañana comienzan las clases en "la única escuela de bomba y plena del mundo", como asegura Modesto.

[1]*poor* [2]*it deserves*

> **La bomba, ay qué rica es, te sube el ritmo por los pies / mulato, saca tu trigueña / pa' que bailes bomba, bomba puertorriqueña.**

Notice: Clarify reduction of **para** to **pa'**.

Modesto, junto con sus hijas[3], dirige las lecciones, que incluyen la práctica de los bailes y la percusión, además de la historia de ambos[4]. Se dividen las lecciones en grupos: primero, los principiantes, que son niños entre los 5 y 12 años. La segunda sesión corresponde a los niños más talentosos, que participan en coreografías especiales. Luego es el turno de los jóvenes y adultos. El día termina con una clase de percusión. ■

[3]junto... *together with his daughters* [4]*both*

Después de leer

ACTIVIDAD 4 Answer the following questions about the reading to see how well you understood it.

1. ¿Cuál de los bailes es más popular hoy día, la bomba o la plena? Según don Modesto Cepeda, ¿por qué?
2. ¿Cuál es el origen de la plena? ¿de la bomba?
3. ¿De qué es director don Modesto Cepeda?
4. ¿Qué día de la semana son las clases?
5. ¿Qué otro tipo de clase hay, además de las clases de plena y bomba?
6. ¿Quiénes dirigen las lecciones?

ACTIVIDAD 5 With a partner, answer the following questions about the reading and about your own musical backgrounds.

1. ¿Les gusta la música caribeña como la bomba, la plena, la salsa, el merengue, el mambo, la rumba y la conga? ¿Conocen (*Are you familiar with*) algunos grupos que tocan este tipo de música?
2. ¿Saben (*Do you know how*) bailar uno de los bailes que se asocian con esta música?
3. ¿Saben los orígenes de los bailes típicos de EEUU? ¿Cuáles son?

A ESCRIBIR

Antes de escribir

ACTIVIDAD 1 Retrieve the information you gathered in the three **Encuesta** activities (**Actividad 3** on p. 82, **Actividad 7** on p. 86, and **Actividad 15** on p. 91). With a partner, study the results of your surveys and come up with ideas for a description of the life of a typical student at your university. You will write the description as a diary entry. Using the results of your surveys, brainstorm a list of ideas to include in the description.

Suggestion: If class time will not permit this series of activities, it may be modified and assigned to teams to do outside of class as a group project. Have students report on results of surveys in class.

 ACTIVIDAD 2 Once you and your partner have created a list of ideas for the description, go through your list and evaluate each one. Together decide which ideas you like the best and how much to include.

ACTIVIDAD 3 Look at the following partial model of a diary entry. Then organize your information into a similar format. If necessary, look up any words you don't know in a bilingual dictionary, but try to focus on using the words you've already learned.

> viernes, 10 de octubre
>
> ¡Tengo muchas actividades hoy! Por la mañana, a las ocho, tengo clase de química. Luego, voy a ir al café con mi amigo Luis para estudiar para el examen de historia a las diez...
> Por la tarde, tengo que...
> Por la noche, voy a...

Escritura

 ACTIVIDAD 4 Using the previous model, work with your partner to create a rough draft of your diary entry. Try to write freely without worrying too much about mistakes or misspellings. (You will have an opportunity to revise your work later.) Here are some additional words and phrases that may be useful as you write.

primero	*first*	**finalmente**	*finally*
luego	*later*	**mucho que hacer**	*a lot to do*
entonces	*then*	**un día (muy) ocupado**	*a (very) busy day*
después	*after that*	**con**	*with*

Después de escribir

 ACTIVIDAD 5 Now, with your partner, go back over your diary entry and revise it. Use the following checklist to guide you.

Did you . . .
- look for misspellings?
- check to make sure the verbs are conjugated correctly?
- watch to make sure articles, nouns, and adjectives agree?
- use possessive adjectives correctly?
- make sure you included all the necessary information?

Notice: Sharing writing in class is an important part of the process approach to writing that helps build class community and editing skills, while providing an audience for student writing.

CAMPOS DE ESTUDIO *Fields of study*

En el salón de clase *In the classroom*

Los cursos básicos *Basic courses*

la arquitectura	architecture
las ciencias políticas	political science
la economía	economy
la educación	education
la geografía	geography
la historia	history
la ingeniería	engineering
la psicología	psychology

Las humanidades *Humanities*

la filosofía	philosophy
las lenguas / los idiomas	languages
la literatura	literature

Las lenguas / Los idiomas

el alemán	German
el chino	Chinese
el español	Spanish
el francés	French
el inglés	English
el japonés	Japanese

Las matemáticas *Mathematics*

el cálculo	calculus
la computación	computer science
la estadística	statistics
la informática	computer science

Las ciencias *Sciences*

la biología	biology
la física	physics
la medicina	medicine
la química	chemistry
la salud	health

Los negocios *Business*

la administración de empresas	business administration
la contabilidad	accounting
el mercadeo	marketing

La comunicación pública *Public communications*

el periodismo	journalism
la publicidad	public relations

En el estudio *In the studio*

el arte	art
el baile	dance
el diseño gráfico	graphic design
la música	music
la pintura	painting

Otros lugares en la universidad *Other places in the university*

¿Dónde tienes la clase de...?	Where does your . . . class meet?
En el centro de computación.	In the computer center.
...el centro de comunicaciones.	. . . the media center.
...el gimnasio.	. . . the gymnasium.

la cafetería	the cafeteria
la librería	the bookstore
la residencia estudiantil	the dorm

LOS DÍAS DE LA SEMANA
The days of the week

lunes	Monday
martes	Tuesday
miércoles	Wednesday
jueves	Thursday
viernes	Friday
sábado	Saturday
domingo	Sunday

PARA PEDIR Y DAR LA HORA
To ask for and give the time

Mira el reloj para decir la hora...	Look at the clock to tell the time . . .
¿Qué hora es?	What time is it?
Es la una.	It's one o'clock.
Son las dos.	It's two o'clock.
Son las... y cuarto.	It's . . . fifteen.
Son las... y media.	It's . . . thirty.
Son las... menos cuarto.	It's a quarter to . . .
Faltan quince para las...	It's a quarter to . . .

tarde	late
temprano	early
¿A qué hora es la clase de español?	(At) what time is Spanish class?
Es a la / a las...	It's at . . .

MAÑANA, TARDE O NOCHE
Morning, afternoon, or night time

de la mañana	*in the morning* (with precise time)
de la tarde	*in the afternoon* (with precise time)
de la noche	*in the evening* (with precise time)
Es mediodía.	*It's noon.*
Es medianoche.	*It's midnight.*
por la mañana	*during the morning*
por la tarde	*during the afternoon*
por la noche	*during the evening*

PARA HABLAR DE LA FECHA
To talk about the date

¿Qué día es hoy?	*What day is today?*
Hoy es martes treinta.	*Today is Tuesday the 30th.*
¿A qué fecha estamos?	*What is today's date?*
Es el treinta de octubre.	*It's the 30th of October.*
Es el primero de noviembre.	*It's the first of November.*
¿Cuándo es el Día de las Madres?	*When is Mother's Day?*
Es el doce de mayo.	*It's May 12th.*
el día	*day*
la semana	*week*
el fin de semana	*weekend*
el mes	*month*
el año	*year*
todos los días	*every day*
entresemana	*during the week / on weekdays*
ayer	*yesterday*
hoy	*today*
mañana	*tomorrow*

PARA HACER PREGUNTAS   *To ask questions*

¿Cómo?	*How?*
¿Cuál(es)?	*What? Which one(s)?*
¿Cuándo?	*When?*
¿Cuánto(a)?	*How much?*
¿Cuántos(as)?	*How many?*
¿De quién es?	*Whose is this?*
¿De quiénes son?	*Whose are these?*
¿Dónde?	*Where?*
¿Por qué?	*Why?*
¿Qué?	*What? Which?*
¿Quién(es)?	*Who?*

VERBOS

abrir	*to open*
aprender	*to learn*
asistir a	*to attend*
beber	*to drink*
comer	*to eat*
compartir	*to share*
comprender	*to understand*
correr	*to run*
creer (en)	*to believe (in)*
deber	*should, ought*
dejar de	*to stop (doing something)*
describir	*to describe*
descubrir	*to discover*
escribir	*to write*
imprimir	*to print*
ir	*to go*
ir a	*to be going to (doing something)*
leer	*to read*
recibir	*to receive*
transmitir	*to broadcast*
vender	*to sell*
vivir	*to live*

ADJETIVOS POSESIVOS

mi(s)	*my*
tu(s)	*your (fam.)*
su(s)	*your (sing. form., pl.) his, her, their*
nuestro(a) / nuestros(as)	*our*
vuestro(a) / vuestros(as)	*your (pl. fam.)*

CONTRACCIONES

al (a + el)	*to the*
del (de + el)	*from the, of the*

OTRAS PALABRAS

porque	*because*

¿Te interesa la tecnología?

CAPÍTULO 4

Communication

By the end of this chapter you will be able to:
- talk about computers and technology
- identify colors
- talk about likes and dislikes
- describe people, emotions, and conditions
- talk about current activities
- say how something is done

Cultures

By the end of this chapter you will have learned about:
- Spain
- expressions of courtesy in conversation and on the Internet
- virtual classes around the Spanish-speaking world
- borrowed words in Spanish

Standards: Throughout this chapter, you will see examples (general chapter theme, technological vocabulary, *emoticon* reading, Internet use surveys, etc.) of making connections with technology (C 3.1, 3.2) in Spanish.

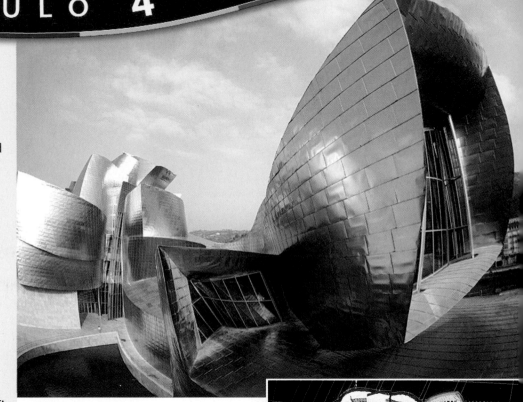

Suggestion: Point out Guggenheim photo and ask: **¿Cómo es el museo? ¿Cómo se llama el arquitecto?** (Frank O. Gehry) **¿De dónde es él?** (EEUU) **¿Dónde está Bilbao?** (Refer students to a map of Spain.)

Arriba: El Museo Guggenheim en Bilbao, España; **A la derecha:** Dibujo digital del Museo Guggenheim

CONEXIONES

La tecnología tiene un impacto tremendo en el mundo de las comunicaciones. Los nuevos avances tecnológicos influyen en cómo nos comunicamos y cómo nos relacionamos. En este capítulo, vas a ver cómo la tecnología facilita las conexiones entre los seres humanos.

Los datos

En España hoy día, aproximadamente 20% de la población usa Internet. Mira los datos sobre los "internautas" españoles e indica si los siguientes comentarios son ciertos o falsos.

Los datos Answers: 1. cierto 2. falso
3. falso

Casa	Trabajo	Otro sitio
54,7%	37%	8,3%

Hombres	Mujeres
61,1%	38,9%

Edad	
20–24 años	19,3%
25–34 años	30%
35–44 años	19,4%
otra edad	31,3%

❶ En España, los usuarios de Internet lo usan más frecuentemente en casa.
❷ La mayoría de los "internautas" españoles son mujeres.
❸ Los jóvenes de 20 a 24 años de edad usan Internet más que las personas de 25 a 34 años.

¡Adivina! answers: 1. c 2. c 3. c 4. a

¡Adivina!

¿Qué sabes de España? (Las respuestas están en la página 127.)

❶ La arquitectura española tiene muchas influencias _____.
   a. alemanas   b. italianas   c. árabes
❷ La tortilla española es _____ la tortilla mexicana.
   a. idéntica a   b. similar a   c. diferente de
❸ El autor de *Don Quijote,* la primera novela moderna, es _____.
   a. Miguel de Unamuno   b. Benito Pérez Galdós   c. Miguel de Cervantes
❹ ¿Cuál de los siguientes artistas no es de origen español, aunque se lo considera como uno de los grandes maestros españoles?
   a. El Greco   b. Diego de Velázquez   c. Francisco de Goya

¡IMAGÍNATE!

Vocabulario útil 1

BETO: ¡Estoy furioso!
CHELA: Pero, ¿por qué?
BETO: Primero llego tarde a la clase de literatura.
CHELA: Llegar tarde no es una tragedia.
BETO: ¡Tenemos examen! Abro mi **computadora portátil,** pero en la **pantalla** dice que no tengo suficiente **memoria** para abrir la **aplicación.**
CHELA: ¿Tienes una computadora portátil de las nuevas? **¿A colores?**
BETO: No, es **negra,** pero, si no te molesta, ¡vuelvo a mi historia!

LA TECNOLOGÍA

El hardware

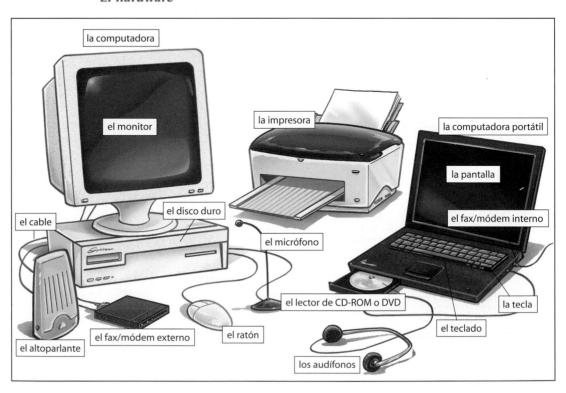

la computadora

el monitor

la impresora

la computadora portátil

la pantalla

el cable

el disco duro

el fax/módem interno

el micrófono

el lector de CD-ROM o DVD

la tecla

el fax/módem externo

el ratón

el teclado

el altoparlante

los audífonos

El software

la aplicación	*application*
los archivos	*files*
el ícono del programa	*program icon*
el juego interactivo	*interactive game*
el programa antivirus	*anti-virus program*
el programa de procesamiento de textos	*word-processing program*

Funciones de la computadora

archivar	*to file*
conectar	*to connect*
enviar	*to send*
funcionar	*to function*
grabar	*to record*
hacer clic / doble clic	*to click / double click*
instalar	*to install*
tener 512 MB de memoria	*to have 512 MB of memory*

LOS COLORES

azul amarillo anaranjado blanco café, marrón gris

morado negro rojo rosa, rosado verde

Suggestion: To make a transition from technological vocabulary to colors, begin a conversation with: **Mi impresora tiene cuatro colores: rojo, azul, amarillo**, etc. **Los otros colores son...** Always introduce colors with objects (**Mi libro es rojo**). Continue with simple, personalized questions: **¿De qué color es tu libro / tu bolígrafo / tu lápiz / la pizarra / la puerta, etc.? ¿Cuál es tu color preferido?**

When a color is used as an adjective, it comes after the noun it modifies.

- If it ends in **-o,** it changes to match the gender and number of that noun: **la silla negra, los cuadernos rojos.**

- If the color ends in **-e,** add an **-s** to the plural: **las pizarras verdes.**

- If the color ends in a consonant, add **-es** to the plural: **los libros azules.**

- **Marrón** in the plural changes to **marrones,** with no accent. Can you figure out why, for pronunciation reasons, it loses the accent?

- Note that **rosa** and **café** change to reflect number, but not gender.

Actividades

ACTIVIDAD 1 **La computadora.** Un amigo te dice que quiere hacer ciertas cosas en la computadora. ¿Qué parte de la computadora va a necesitar para hacer lo que quiere? Escoge de la segunda columna.

1. _____ Quiero imprimir el correo electrónico.
2. _____ Quiero enviar un fax.
3. _____ Quiero conectar el teclado al monitor.
4. _____ Quiero escuchar música mientras trabajo.
5. _____ Quiero abrir el programa de procesamiento de textos.
6. _____ Quiero archivar el documento.
7. _____ Quiero grabar un mensaje para enviar a mis amigos.
8. _____ Quiero instalar el progama antivirus.

a. audífonos
b. fax / módem
c. lector de CD-ROM
d. disco duro
e. impresora
f. cable
g. micrófono
h. ratón

Answers Act. 1: 1. e 2. b 3. f 4. a 5. h 6. d 7. g 8. c

Starting in this chapter, many of the activity direction lines will be presented in Spanish. Here are a few words that will help you understand Spanish direction lines: **di** (*say*), **haz** (*do*), **escoge** (*choose*), **luego** (*then, later*), **siguiente** (*following*), **oración** (*sentence*), **párrafo** (*paragraph*).

Notice: In Spain, the **computadora** is called an **ordenador. Pulsar** is also used for **hacer clic. El computador** is also used, mostly in Latin America.

In some countries, the Internet is referred to as **la Internet,** in others as **el Internet,** and in others still, it is referred to **simply** as **Internet** with no article to indicate gender.

ACTIVIDAD 2 **El sitio web.** Tu compañero(a) te dice que quiere buscar información sobre ciertos temas en el servicio ¡VIVA! Latino. Tú le dices en qué ícono debe hacer doble clic. Luego, él o ella te dirige a los íconos que corresponden a tus intereses.

¡VIVA! Latino

Directorio de sitios web

⭐ **Arte y cultura**
Literatura, Teatro, Museos, Guías

⭐ **Internet y computadoras**
WWW, Aplicaciones, Chat, Redes

⭐ **Educación**
Primaria, Secundaria, Universidades

⭐ **Medios de comunicación**
Radio, TV, Revistas, Periódicos

⭐ **Deportes y ocio**
Deportes, Fútbol, Juegos, Turismo

⭐ **Salud**
Medicina, Enfermedades, Ejercicio, Dietas

⭐ **Espectáculos y diversión**
Cine, Actores, Música, Humor

⭐ **Materias de consulta**
Bibliotecas, Diccionarios

MODELO: el Museo del Prado en Madrid
Tú: *Necesito más información sobre el Museo del Prado en Madrid.*
Compañero(a): *Haz doble clic en el ícono rojo.*

1. una dieta vegetariana
2. mi actor (actriz) favorito(a)
3. un diccionario español / inglés
4. la Copa Mundial de fútbol
5. un programa de procesamiento de textos
6. la Universidad Complutense de Madrid
7. el periódico *El País* de Madrid
8. ¿…?

ACTIVIDAD 3 **Mi computadora.** ¿Puedes describir tu computadora? Incluye en tu descripción todos los componentes de tu computadora y menciona el color de cada uno si es apropiado.

MODELO: *El monitor de mi computadora es azul y blanco. Los cables son grises. El ratón es blanco. Los altoparlantes son negros. Las teclas en el teclado son blancas…*

Vocabulario útil 2

BETO: Empiezo a salir del salón de clases. No sé en dónde, pero entre el salón y la biblioteca, pierdo mi **asistente electrónico.**

CHELA: Ya me voy. Estoy muy **aburrida** con tu cuento trágico.

LAS EMOCIONES

aburrido(a)	*bored*	**nervioso(a)**	*nervous*
cansado(a)	*tired*	**ocupado(a)**	*busy*
contento(a)	*happy*	**preocupado(a)**	*worried*
enfermo(a)	*sick*	**seguro(a)**	*sure*
enojado(a)	*angry*	**triste**	*sad*
furioso(a)	*furious*		

PRODUCTOS ELECTRÓNICOS

el asistente electrónico	*electronic notebook*	**el reproductor / grabador de discos compactos**	*CD player / burner*
el buscapersonas / el bíper	*beeper*		
la cámara digital	*digital camera*	**el reproductor / grabador de DVD**	*DVD player / burner*
la cámara web	*webcam*		
el CD portátil / MP3	*portable CD / MP3 player*	**la videocámara**	*videocamera*
el organizador electrónico	*electronic organizer*	**la videocasetera**	*VCR*

Actividades

ACTIVIDAD 4 **Las emociones.** Imagínate que conoces a las siguientes personas. Están en ciertas situaciones. ¿Cómo crees que están?

1. A Raúl le gusta navegar por Internet y jugar videojuegos. Hay una tormenta y por eso no hay electricidad en su casa. No tiene nada (*nothing*) que hacer.
2. Blanca acaba de comprar una computadora portátil pero cuando llega a casa, no funciona.
3. Julio tiene que escribir una composición de diez páginas para su clase de historia mañana y todavía no ha empezado (*hasn't begun*).
4. Mañana Luis tiene que ir al trabajo por tres horas, estudiar para un examen y hacer una investigación en Internet para la clase de filosofía.
5. Sabrina trabaja diez horas en la biblioteca, va a su clase de aeróbicos y camina a casa del gimnasio.
6. Marcos y Marina toman un refresco, escuchan música y conversan en un café en la Plaza Mayor.

Answers Act. 4: *Answers may vary.*
Sample responses: 1. Está aburrido.
2. Está furiosa / enojada. 3. Está nervioso.
4. Está preocupado. 5. Está cansada.
6. Están contentos.

ACTIVIDAD 5 **¿Eres "tecnofóbico"?** With a partner, come up with a list of technological items and other things related to technology. Use a point system of 1–5 to rate how technologically advanced someone is if he or she possesses that item (1 = the least advanced and 5 = the most advanced). Then, in groups of four or five, ask each person in the group if they have each item. Based on your findings, decide who is the most technologically advanced and who is the most technologically inexperienced in the group. Report your findings to the class.

Sample items:

teléfono celular
computadora portátil
bíper
asistente electrónico
más de una dirección de e-mail
revista (*magazine*) de tecnología

¡FÍJATE!

Los préstamos: Palabras inmigrantes

Todas las lenguas del mundo tienen **préstamos** (*borrowings*). Los préstamos son palabras que tienen su origen en otras lenguas. El español tiene muchos présta-mos árabes que se originaron durante los siete siglos (*centuries*) de dominación musulmana de la Península Ibérica (711–1492 d. C.). Muchas palabras de las ciencias, el arte, las matemáticas, la agricultura y la arquitectura son de origen árabe: **álgebra, ajedrez** (*chess*), **alfalfa, algoritmo.**

El español también tiene préstamos griegos, franceses, italianos, germánicos y amerindios. Los préstamos más recientes son del inglés y representan innova-ciones tecnológicas o vienen del (*come from the*) mundo de los negocios, por ejemplo **bíper, fax, hacer clic** y **cheque.** Otros como **rock and roll, club** y **jazz** se originan en la cultura popular americana.

PRÁCTICA. El inglés tiene muchos préstamos de otras lenguas. En gru-pos, traten de identificar la lengua de origen de estas palabras: francés, italiano, español, alemán, indio o hebreo.

piano	al dente
rouge	veranda
bandana	tobacco
guru	presto
gesundheit	kibbutz
rendezvous	gestalt
patio	

ACTIVIDAD 6 **El Corte Inglés.** El Corte Inglés es el almacén (*department store*) más grande en España. Con un(a) compañero(a), visiten el sitio web del Corte Inglés. (Hay un enlace en el sitio web de *Nexos*.) Entren en el Departamento de Electrónica y contesten las siguientes preguntas.

1. ¿Cuáles son las subcategorías en el Departmento de Electrónica?
2. Entren en la subcategoría DVD Reproductores. Nombren tres productos que hay allí y sus precios en euros (€).
3. Quieren comprarle un regalo (*gift*) a un amigo a quien le gusta la música. Busquen un regalo apropiado. ¿Qué es? ¿Cuánto cuesta?
4. Quieren comprarle un regalo a una amiga a quien le gusta grabar videos, pero no tienen mucho dinero (*money*). Busquen la videocámara con el precio más bajo (*lowest price*).
5. ¿Qué producto electrónico quieres comprar? ¿Cuánto cuesta?

Answers Act. 6: 1. Fotografía, DVD, Sonido, Teléfono móvil, TV y Video, y Videocámaras. 2.–5. *Answers will vary.*

Vocabulario útil 3

BETO:	¿Tú? ¿Tú eres Autora14?
DULCE:	Sí, yo soy Autora14. ¿Por qué preguntas?
BETO:	No, no, nada. ¿Te gustan los **grupos de conversación**?
DULCE:	No, en realidad, no. Prefiero el **correo electrónico**.

FUNCIONES DE INTERNET

el buscador	*search engine*
el buzón electrónico	*electronic mailbox*
chatear	*to chat*
el ciberespacio	*cyberspace*
la conexión	*the connection*
hacer una conexión	*to go online*
cortar la conexión	*to go offline, disconnect*
la contraseña	*password*
el correo electrónico / el e-mail	*e-mail*
en línea	*online*
el enlace	*link*
el grupo de conversación	*chat room*
el grupo de debate	*news group*
la página web	*web page*
el proveedor de acceso	*Internet provider*
la red mundial	*World Wide Web*
el sitio web	*web site*
el usuario	*user*

You are learning two words for e-mail: **correo electrónico** and **e-mail. Correo electrónico** refers more to the whole system of e-mail or a group of e-mails, while **el e-mail** refers to a specific e-mail message.

Optional: This vocabulary can be expanded with more specific questions about students' online habits and sites. For example: **¿Vas a las librerías electrónicas? ¿Cuáles? ¿Cómo se llaman? ¿Qué compras allí? (¿libros? ¿discos compactos? ¿películas?) ¿Tienes un sitio web favorito o personal?**

Actividades

 Standards: While working through the survey, students will interpret written language (C 1.2) and express opinions (C 1.1).

ACTIVIDAD 7 **¡Gran sorteo!** Completa el cuestionario para el concurso (*contest*) de *Newsweek en español*. Compara tus respuestas a las preguntas 1, 3, 8, 9 y 10 con las respuestas de diez compañeros de clase. Haz una gráfica que muestre (*shows*) los resultados de tu cuestionario. Llena los espacios en blanco (*Fill in the blanks*) con el número de estudiantes que marcaron (*marked*) esa respuesta.

Newsweek
EN ESPAÑOL

Participe en el sorteo de Canon y NEWSWEEK EN ESPAÑOL y gánese un Scanner Canon FB 630P

¡Gran sorteo!

El CanonScan FB 630P puede colocarse perfectamente sobre cualquier escritorio. Además, resulta fácil de usar y es perfecto para el escaneo personal. Este modelo puede ser conectado fácilmente a su PC, a través de un puerto paralelo.

1. ¿Tiene usted una computadora en su casa?
   Sí ❏   No ❏

2. ¿En su oficina?
   Sí ❏   No ❏

3. ¿Cuántas horas pasa diariamente en la computadora de su casa?
   ❏ menos de 2 horas
   ❏ 2 a 4 horas
   ❏ 4 horas o más

4. ¿Utiliza un software antivirus?
   Sí ❏   No ❏

5. ¿Tiene usted, o su compañía, un sistema de seguridad, contabilidad, inventario, administración etc.?
   Sí ❏   No ❏

6. ¿Cuántas horas pasa diariamente en la computadora de su oficina?
   ❏ menos de 2 horas
   ❏ 2 a 4 horas
   ❏ 4 horas o más

7. ¿Tiene acceso a la Internet?
   Sí ❏   No ❏

8. ¿Cuál es su razón primordial para utilizar la Internet?
   ❏ Compras
   ❏ Investigación

❏ Inversiones/Banca
❏ Correo electrónico
❏ Otro

9. ¿Tiene usted un teléfono celular?
   Sí ❏   No ❏

10. ¿Cuántas horas pasa por semana leyendo revistas?
   ❏ 1 a 2
   ❏ 3 a 4
   ❏ 5 horas o más

11. Edad:
   ❏ 25 a 35
   ❏ 36 a 45
   ❏ 46 a 65
   ❏ Otra _____

12. Sexo:
   M ❏   F ❏

13. Número de personas en su casa:
   1 2 3 4 5 6 ó más

14. Ingresos Anuales:
   ❏ Menos de $25,000
   ❏ $25,000 a $45,999
   ❏ $46,000 a $65,999
   ❏ $66,000 a $75,999
   ❏ $76,000 o más

Pregunta 1:	_____ Sí
	_____ No
Pregunta 3:	_____ menos de 2 horas
	_____ 2 a 4 horas
	_____ 4 horas o más
Pregunta 8:	_____ Compras
	_____ Investigación
	_____ Inversiones / Banca
	_____ Correo electrónico
	_____ Otro
Pregunta 9:	_____ Sí
	_____ No
Pregunta 10:	_____ 1 a 2 horas
	_____ 3 a 4 horas
	_____ 5 horas o más

ACTIVIDAD 8 **¿Cómo usas Internet?** ¿Qué más quieres saber sobre (*do you want to know about*) los hábitos de tus compañeros acerca de Internet? Escribe cinco preguntas más como las del cuestionario en la **Actividad 7.** Luego, hazle las preguntas a tu compañero(a) de clase y que él o ella te haga sus preguntas.

MODELO: *¿Te gusta chatear por Internet? ¿Cuántas horas por día pasas en los grupos de conversación?*
¿Tienes correo electrónico? ¿Cuántas veces por día lees tu correo electrónico?

ACTIVIDAD 9 **Los cursos virtuales.** Ahora es posible tomar cursos virtuales por Internet, pagar el costo del curso y luego leer las materias y participar en el curso por correo electrónico. Hay muchas universidades de habla española que ofrecen una gran variedad de cursos a distancia.

En grupos de cuatro, escojan (*choose*) un país de la lista de abajo. Visiten los sitios web que corresponden a este país, usando la lista de enlaces que está en el sitio web de *Nexos*.

Países: España, México, Argentina

1. ¿Qué cursos virtuales ofrece la universidad o escuela?
2. ¿En el sitio web es posible hacer una visita virtual? ¿Hay información sobre los profesores de los cursos? ¿Sobre los otros estudiantes?
3. Después de obtener toda la información sobre este sitio web, compárenla con la información de los otros grupos.

Standards: Students use Spanish through virtual educational communities beyond the school setting (C 5.1).

Optional: Have a discussion about online courses: **¿Hay ventajas de tomar un curso virtual en español? ¿Cuáles son? ¿Cuáles son las desventajas? ¿Te gusta más la idea de matricularse en un curso virtual de una universidad de habla española o la de visitar el país para tomar el curso en persona? ¿Por qué?**

A VER

Antes de ver el video

 For additional practice, do the *Nexos* website and / or CD-ROM video exercises.

Answers Act. 1: 1. preocupado, furioso, nervioso 2. memoria 3. computadora 4. computadora; negro 5. asistente electrónico

ACTIVIDAD 1 Based on the conversation and photos shown in the **Vocabulario útil** sections on pages 102, 105, and 107, complete these statements about the main characters.

1. Beto pasa por muchas emociones en este episodio. En varios puntos en el episodio, Beto está _____, _____ y _____.
2. La computadora de Beto no tiene suficiente _____ para abrir la aplicación.
3. Chela quiere saber (*wants to know*) si Beto tiene una _____ a colores.
4. El color de la _____ de Beto es _____.
5. Dulce tiene el _____ de Beto.

ACTIVIDAD 2 Before you watch the video segment, look at the following actions that occur in it. Take time to familiarize yourself with the list.

_____ Beto descubre que su computadora no tiene suficiente memoria.

_____ Dulce tiene el asistente electrónico de Beto.

_____ Beto está furioso porque tiene que escribir el examen con bolígrafo y papel.

_____ Beto llega tarde a clase.

_____ Beto ve una hoja de papel con el e-mail de Autora14.

_____ Beto deja su asistente electrónico en el salón de clase.

ESTRATEGIA

Listening without sound

Sometimes a good way to approach a video segment is to watch it first with the sound turned off. This technique works especially well when the segment contains action and visuals that can help you understand what it is about. As you first watch the segment without sound, focus on the actions and interactions of the characters. What do you think is happening? Once you have gotten some ideas, watch the segment a second time with the sound turned on. How does the language help you flesh out your idea of the content?

El video

Now watch the video segment for **Capítulo 4** with the sound off.

Después de ver el video

Answers Act. 3: 2, 5, 3, 1, 6, 4

ACTIVIDAD 3 Now go back to **Actividad 2** and place the events on the list in the order in which they appeared in the video segment.

Answers Act. 4: 1. literatura
2. computadora 3. el asistente
electrónico 4. aburrida 5. Dulce
6. los grupos de conversación

ACTIVIDAD 4 Watch the video segment again with the sound turned on. Once you have watched it, complete the following statements about the segment.

1. Beto llega tarde a la clase de _____.
2. Beto escribe más rápidamente en _____ que con bolígrafo y papel.
3. Beto pierde _____ entre el salón de clases y la biblioteca.
4. Según Chela, ella está muy _____ con la historia trágica de Beto.
5. La dirección electrónica de _____ es Autora14.
6. Dulce prefiere el correo electrónico a _____.

ACTIVIDAD 5 What do you think that Beto and Dulce talk about as they walk off together at the end of the episode? Based on what you know of their personalities and interests, write a short "getting-to-know-you" conversation between these two characters.

Standards: Students use Spanish while they make connections (C 3.1) with other disciplines (e.g., sociology, business).

Conexión cultural. Mira el segmento cultural al final del episodio. Después, en grupos de tres o cuatro, hablen de las siguientes preguntas: ¿Cómo es su universidad? ¿Es moderna con muchas computadoras y aparatos electrónicos o no es moderna? ¿Cuáles son los cursos más populares?

> **En tu opinión, ¿es posible usar Internet para afectar las acciones del gobierno (*government*)?** To learn more about Manuel Castells and the new urban sociology, see the chapter links on the *Nexos* website (http://college.hmco.com/ languages/spanish/students).

VOCES DE LA COMUNIDAD

Manuel Castells

❝ Lo que debemos hacer es utilizar el enorme potencial de Internet, por ejemplo, para revivir la democracia, no en cuanto a (*in relation to*) la sustitución de la democracia representativa por medio del voto, sino (*but instead*) para organizar grupos de conversación, plebiscitos indicativos, consultas sobre distintos temas, proporcionar información a la población. ❞

El sociólogo español Manuel Castells es uno de los fundadores del campo de estudio llamado la nueva sociología urbana. Este profesor de la Universidad de Berkeley estudia cómo la tecnología altera las instituciones de la sociedad moderna: los gobiernos, las corporaciones, el trabajo y las instituciones educativas y religiosas. Según Castells, en el mundo actual, el poder (*power*) de estas instituciones es muy reducido a causa de la influencia de Internet. Uno de sus libros más importantes se titula *The Internet Galaxy, Reflections on Internet, Business, and Society.*

¡PREPÁRATE!

Gramática útil 1
Expressing likes and dislikes: *Gustar* with nouns and other verbs like *gustar*

For more practice of chapter topics, do the *Nexos* website exercises.

Internet

¿**Te gustan** los grupos de conversación?

Remember that when you use **gustar** + infinitive you only use **gusta: Les gusta comer en la cafetería.**

CÓMO USARLO

As you learned in **Capítulo 2,** you can use **gustar** with an infinitive to say what activities you and other people like to do.

Me gusta estudiar en la biblioteca, pero a Vicente **le gusta estudiar** en la cafetería.	*I like to study in the library, but Vicente likes to study in the cafeteria.*

You can also use **gustar** with nouns, to say what thing or things you (and others) like or dislike. In this case, you use **gusta** with a single noun and **gustan** with plural nouns or a series of nouns.

—¿**Te gusta** esta **computadora**?	*Do you like this computer?*
—Sí, ¡pero **me gustan** más estas **computadoras portátiles**!	*Yes, but I like these laptop computers more!*

When you make negative sentences with **gusta** and **gustan,** you use **no** before the pronoun + **gusta / gustan.**

Nos gustan los programas de diseño gráfico, pero **no nos gustan** los programas de arte.	*We like the graphic design programs, but we don't like the art programs.*

CÓMO FORMARLO

LO BÁSICO

- In Spanish, an *indirect object pronoun* is used with **gustar** to say who likes something. Since **gustar** literally means *to please,* the indirect object answers the question: *Pleases whom?*
- A *prepositional pronoun* is a pronoun that is used after a preposition, such as **a** or **de.**

You will learn more about Spanish indirect object pronouns in **Capítulo 8.**

Standards: Emphasize that the person doing the liking is expressed by the indirect object in Spanish. Compare **me gusta** with the English construction "it is pleasing to me" (C 4.1).

Optional: Explain examples with the translation *to be pleasing* (i.e., it is pleasing to me, they are pleasing to me) emphasizing that the person (**me, te, le,** etc.) is receiving the action.

1. As you have already learned, you must use forms of **gustar** with the correct indirect object pronoun.

Me gusta	el video.	**Nos gusta**	el video.
Me gustan	los videos.	**Nos gustan**	los videos.
Te gusta	el video.	**Os gusta**	el video.
Te gustan	los videos.	**Os gustan**	los videos.
Le gusta	el video.	**Les gusta**	el video.
Les gustan	los videos.	**Les gustan**	los videos.

Notice: For true beginners, point out the **formas singulares y formas plurales** of **gustar** and pronouns for awareness and reinforcement.

Heritage Learners: Give a dictation with a series of statements with **gustar** to train heritage learners to notice pronouns, verb endings, and grammatical nuance.

2. As you have learned, if you want to *emphasize or clarify* who likes what, you can use **a** + name or noun, or **a** + prepositional pronoun. Note that when **a** + prepositional pronoun is used, there is often no direct translation in English. Notice that except for **mí** and **ti,** the prepositional pronouns are the same as the subject pronouns you already know.

Prepositional pronoun	Indirect object pronoun	Form of *gustar* + noun
A mí	me	gustan los videos.
A ti	te	gustan los videos.
A Ud. / a él / a ella	le	gustan los videos.
A nosotros / a nosotras	nos	gustan los videos.
A vosotros / a vosotras	os	gustan los videos.
A Uds. / a ellos / a ellas	les	gustan los videos.

Notice that while **mí** takes an accent, **ti** does not.

A mí me gustan los asistentes electrónicos, pero **a Elena** no le gustan.

*I like electronic notebooks, but **Elena** doesn't like them.*

A ella le gustan los organizadores electrónicos.

She likes electronic organizers.

3. A number of other Spanish verbs are used like **gustar.** These verbs are usually just used in two forms, as is **gustar.**

—**Me interesan** mucho estos celulares.

I'm interested in these cell phones.

—¿No **te molesta** hablar por teléfono todo el día?

*Doesn't **it bother you** to talk on the phone all day?*

Other verbs like gustar

- ◆ **encantar** *to like a lot*
- ◆ **fascinar** *to fascinate*
- ◆ **importar** *to be important to someone; to mind*
- ◆ **interesar** *to interest, to be interesting*
- ◆ **molestar** *to bother*

¡**Me encanta** la tecnología!

A Ana **le fascinan** Internet y los sitios web.

Nos importa tener acceso a Internet. ¿**Te importa** si usamos la computadora?

A ellos **les interesan** los grupos de noticias.

Nos molestan las computadoras viejas.

Suggestion: With heritage learners and high beginners, point out additional verbs like **gustar**: **doler** (*to hurt, pain, ache*), **faltar** (*to be missing, lack*), **hacer falta** (*to need*), **parecer** (*to seem, appear*), **quedar** (*to have left, remain*), **sorprender** (*to be surprising*).

Actividades

ACTIVIDAD 1 **¿Te gusta?** Di si te gustan o no las siguientes cosas.

MODELO: las computadoras portátiles
A mí me gustan las computadoras portátiles.

1. los juegos interactivos de tenis
2. el sitio web del Museo del Prado
3. la clase virtual de literatura en la Universidad Complutense
4. los productos electrónicos de El Corte Inglés
5. el nuevo CD de Shakira
6. los grupos de conversación sobre las playas más bellas de España

ACTIVIDAD 2 **Los gustos.** Pregúntale a varios compañeros de clase sobre sus gustos.

MODELO: AOL (Latino.net, Yahoo, ¿...?)
Tú: *¿Les gusta AOL?*
Compañero(a): *No, no nos gusta AOL, pero sí nos gusta Latino.net.*

1. el grupo de debate de profesores de español (de artistas chilenos, de actores de teatro, ¿...?)
2. la página web de Yahoo en español (de *Time* en español, de *Newsweek en español*, ¿...?)
3. el grupo de conversación de estudiantes de español (de profesores de español, de estudiantes de francés, ¿...?)
4. los juegos interactivos (de mesa, de niños, ¿...?)
5. las computadoras portátiles (PC, Mac, ¿...?)
6. el programa de arte (de diseño gráfico, de contabilidad, ¿...?)

ACTIVIDAD 3 **¿Te interesa?** Pregúntale a un(a) compañero(a) cómo se siente (*feels*) sobre varios aspectos de la tecnología.

1. molestar: recibir mucha correspondencia electrónica
2. interesar: grupos de debate sobre la política
3. gustar: juegos interactivos
4. molestar: buscadores muy lentos (*slow*)
5. interesar: sitios web comerciales
6. gustar: chatear con personas en otros países
7. importar: recibir e-mails de personas desconocidas (*unknown*)

ACTIVIDAD 4 **En resumen.** Pregúntale a seis compañeros qué les gusta de la tecnología y qué les molesta. Escribe un resumen sobre los resultados.

1. Nombra tres cosas que te gustan de la tecnología.
2. Nombra tres cosas que te molestan de la tecnología.

¡COMPÁRATE!

En las culturas de habla hispana, la cortesía es muy importante. Cuando dos personas se presentan, por ejemplo, se dan la mano (*they shake hands*) o se besan en la mejilla (*they kiss on the cheek*). La cortesía en la manera de hablar tiene una importancia igual.

Es muy común usar frases como **¿Le importa?** o **¿Le molesta?** para hacerle una pregunta a alguien (*to ask someone a question*): **¿Le importa si uso la computadora?**, en vez de **Voy a usar la computadora** o **¿Puedo usar la computadora?** También es común usar **por favor** antes de hacer una pregunta y decir (*to say*) **gracias** al recibir la información. Aquí hay otras palabras que se usan para hablar más cortésmente.

¡Perdón! / ¡Disculpe! / ¡Lo siento!
No hay de qué. / No se preocupe.

Pardon me! / Excuse me! /
I'm sorry!

No problem. / Not to worry.

Con permiso...
Cómo no.

Excuse me... /
With your permission...

Of course. / Certainly.

PRÁCTICA 1. En tu opinión, ¿tiene la cortesía mucha importancia en EEUU, bastante importancia o poca importancia? ¿Qué expresiones usas tú frecuentemente para expresar cortesía? ¿Cuáles de las expresiones presentadas usas?

PRÁCTICA 2. Con un(a) compañero(a) de clase, dramaticen las siguientes situaciones. Usen las expresiones de cortesía en su conversación.

Situación 1: Tu amigo(a) escribe una composición para su clase de inglés en tu computadora. Tú borras (*erase*) el archivo que contiene la composición.

Situación 2: Necesitas usar la impresora urgentemente antes de clase, pero hay un(a) estudiante que lleva mucho tiempo con un trabajo.

Optional: Have students get up out of their seats, pretend to bump into each other, and come up with an appropriate exchange. Model one exchange with a student before beginning the activity.

Standards: Here students have a creative presentational opportunity (C 1.3) that can be developed into a skit.

Gramática útil 2
Describing yourself and others and expressing conditions and locations: The verb *estar* and the uses of *ser* and *estar*

Estoy muy **aburrida** con tu cuento trágico.

Suggestion: Reinforce this with the statement: *Estar se usa para describir el estado y para decir dónde.* Write these terms on the board, and ask students to come up with 5–7 examples of each: **Estado = Estoy nerviosa. Dónde = Estoy en clase.**

Heritage Learners: The rules that govern the use of **ser** and **estar** in U.S. Spanish are not always the same as those of standard Spanish. In particular, the verb **estar** is sometimes used in cases where standard Spanish uses **ser.** For this reason, it is important go over the uses of **ser** and **estar** carefully with native speakers. U.S. Spanish: **El apartamento está pequeño.** Standard Spanish: **El apartamento es pequeño.**

Preparation: Bring a ball or other object(s) that can be tossed, moved, or passed around the classroom. Locate the object(s) with **¿Dónde está / están?**

Notice that expressing the location of people, places, and things (other than events) requires the use of **estar. Ser** is used only to indicate *where an event will take place.*

CÓMO USARLO

You already know that the verb **ser** is translated as *to be* in English. You have already used the verb **estar,** which is also translated as *to be*, in expressions such as **¿Cómo estás?** While both these Spanish verbs mean *to be*, they are used in different ways.

1. Use **estar** . . .

◆ to express location of people, places, or objects.

La profesora Suárez **está** en la biblioteca.	*Professor Suárez is in the library.*
Los libros **están** en la mesa.	*The books are on the table.*

◆ to talk about a physical condition.

—¿Cómo **está** Ud.?	*How are you?*
—**Estoy** muy bien, gracias.	*I'm well, thank you.*
—Yo **estoy** un poco cansada.	*I'm a little tired.*

◆ to talk about emotional conditions.

El señor Albrega **está** un poco nervioso hoy.	*Mr. Albrega is a little nervous today.*
Estoy muy ocupada esta semana.	*I'm very busy this week.*

2. Use **ser** . . .

◆ to identify yourself and others.

Soy Ana y ésta **es** mi hermana Luisa.	*I'm Ana and this is my sister Luisa.*

◆ to indicate profession.

Pablo Picasso **es** un artista famoso.	*Pablo Picasso is a famous artist.*

◆ to describe personality traits and physical features.

Somos altos y delgados.	*We are tall and thin.*
Somos estudiantes buenos.	*We are good students.*

◆ to give time and date.

Es la una. Hoy **es** miércoles.	*It is one o'clock. Today is Wednesday.*

◆ to indicate nationality and origin.

—**Eres** española, ¿no?	*You are Spanish, right?*
—Sí, **soy** de España.	*Yes, I am from Spain.*

◆ to express possession with **de.**

Este celular **es de Anita.**	*This is Anita's cell phone.*

◆ to give the location of an event.

La fiesta **es** en la residencia estudiantil.	*The party is in the dorm.*

CÓMO FORMARLO

1. Here are the forms of the verb **estar** in the present indicative tense.

estar (*to be*)			
yo	estoy	nosotros / nosotras	estamos
tú	estás	vosotros / vosotras	estáis
Ud. / él / ella	está	Uds. / ellos / ellas	están

2. In the **¡Imagínate!** section you learned some adjectives that are commonly used with **estar** to describe physical and emotional conditions.

aburrido(a)	nervioso(a)
cansado(a)	ocupado(a)
contento(a)	preocupado(a)
enfermo(a)	seguro(a)
enojado(a)	triste
furioso(a)	

Don't forget that when you use adjectives with **estar,** as with any other verb, they need to agree with the person or thing they are describing in both gender and number.

Los estudiantes están preocupados por Miguel.

The students are worried about Miguel.

Elena está nerviosa a causa del examen.

Elena is nervous because of the exam.

Actividades

ACTIVIDAD 5 **¿Dónde están?** Todos participan en diferentes actividades en diferentes lugares de la universidad. ¿Dónde están?

MODELO: Ricardo y Juana estudian.
           Están en la biblioteca.

1. Javier toma un refresco.
2. Mi compañero(a) de cuarto y yo descansamos.
3. Paula y Pedro navegan por Internet.
4. La profesora Martínez lee una novela.
5. Usted escribe en la pizarra.
6. Nosotros escuchamos las cintas de español.
7. El equipo de básquetbol practica para el partido.
8. Tú compras un libro para la clase de filosofía.

Preparation: Warm up for this activity by asking students: **Nombren algunos lugares de la universidad—por ejemplo, la biblioteca, la cafetería, el centro de computación, el salón de clase,** etc.

Answers Act. 5: *Answers may vary. Sample responses:* 1. Está en la cafetería. 2. Estamos en la residencia estudiantil. 3. Están en el centro de computación. 4. Está en el parque. 5. Está en el salón de clase. 6. Estamos en el centro de comunicaciones. 7. Está en el gimnasio. 8. Estás en la librería.

ACTIVIDAD 6 **¿Cómo están?** Tú y varias personas están en las siguientes situaciones. Usa **estar** + *adjetivo* para describir cómo están.

MODELO: Sales bien en el examen de francés, tomas el sol por la tarde, cenas con tu mejor amigo(a) y alquilas un video que te gusta mucho.
Estoy contento(a).

1. Tienes una entrevista con el director de la universidad para un trabajo que necesitas.
2. Carlos tiene una infección y piensa que tiene que ir al hospital.
3. Marta y Mario no tienen nada (*nothing*) que hacer—no hay nada interesante en la tele y su computadora no funciona.
4. Compras una nueva computadora. Llegas a casa y cuando tratas de usarla, no funciona. La tienda de computadoras no abre hasta el lunes.
5. Tú y tu familia tienen mucho que hacer. Entre los estudios, el trabajo, los deportes, la familia y los amigos, no hay suficiente tiempo en el día para hacerlo todo.
6. Elena practica deportes por la mañana, trabaja en la biblioteca por la tarde y estudia por la noche. Cuando llega a casa, descansa.
7. La tarea de matemáticas es muy difícil —Martín no comprende las instrucciones. Es muy tarde para llamar a un amigo. Tiene que entregar la tarea muy temprano por la mañana.
8. El abuelo (*grandfather*) de Pedro y Delia está muy enfermo. Pedro y Delia lo visitan en el hospital.

ACTIVIDAD 7 **¿Ser o estar?** Trabaja con un(a) compañero(a) de clase para completar las oraciones. Lean las oraciones y juntos decidan si se debe usar **ser** o **estar.** Escriban la forma correcta del verbo. Luego, escriban por qué se usa **ser** o **estar.**

MODELO: _____*Soy*_____ María Hernández Catina.
razón (*reason*): *identidad*

Razones: nacionalidad, posesión, estado físico, característica física, característica de personalidad, profesión, fecha, hora, estado temporáneo, identidad, posición (*location*), lugar de un evento

1. ¿Cómo _____ usted, profesor Taboada?
razón:

2. _____ un poco cansado hoy.
razón:

3. _____ de España.
razón:

4. ¿Dónde _____ la biblioteca?
razón:

5. Mi padre _____ profesor de lenguas.
razón:

6. Hoy _____ miércoles, el 22 de octubre.
   razón:

7. Nati _____ alta, delgada y tiene el pelo castaño.
   razón:

8. Esta semana Leonardo _____ muy ocupado.
   razón:

9. Este libro, ¿_____ de la profesora?
   razón:

10. ¿Dónde _____ la clase de filosofía?
    razón:

 ACTIVIDAD 8 **¡Pobre Mónica!** Trabaja con un(a) compañero(a) de clase. Miren el dibujo y juntos escriban una descripción de Mónica y de la situación en general. Traten de usar **ser** o **estar** en cada oración y de escribir por lo menos cinco oraciones.

In Spanish-speaking countries, Tuesday the 13th, rather than Friday the 13th, is considered an unlucky day.

Answers Act. 8: *Possible answers:* Mónica es alta y muy delgada. Es estudiante. Está ocupada. Está preocupada. Hoy es martes. La fiesta es hoy en casa de Mónica.

Sonrisas

Standards: In the **Sonrisas** and **Comprensión** sections, students work in the interpretive mode (C 1.2).

COMPRENSIÓN. En tu opinión, ¿cuál de los siguientes adjetivos describen al hombre rubio? ¿Y al hombre moreno?

- ¿Quién está...?

  aburrido / cansado / contento / enfermo / furioso / nervioso / ocupado / preocupado / seguro / triste

- ¿Quién es...?

  activo / antipático / cómico / cuidadoso / divertido / egoísta / extrovertido / impaciente / introvertido / perezoso / serio / simpático / tonto

Answers: El hombre rubio está aburrido, cansado, enfermo, nervioso, preocupado, seguro y triste. El hombre moreno está contento y furioso. El hombre rubio es antipático, egoísta, serio y tonto. El hombre moreno es activo, divertido, extrovertido y simpático.

Gramática útil 3
Talking about everyday events: Stem-changing verbs in the present indicative

CÓMO USARLO

In **Capítulos 1** and **2** you learned the present indicative forms of regular **-ar**, **-er**, and **-ir** verbs in Spanish. There are other Spanish verbs that use the same endings as regular **-ar**, **-er**, and **-ir** verbs in this tense, but they also have a small change in their stem. (Remember that the stem is the part of the infinitive that is left after you remove the **-ar / -er / -ir** ending.)

—¿Qué **piensas** de este asistente electrónico?
—Me gusta, pero **prefiero** éste.
—¿Verdad? Bueno, ¿por qué no le **pides** el precio al dependiente?

What do you think of this electronic assistant?
I like it, but I prefer this one.
Really? Well, why don't you ask the sales clerk the price?

¡Pobre Beto! **Siento** tu frustración.

CÓMO FORMARLO

1. There are three categories of stem-changing verbs in the present indicative.

	o → ue: **encontrar** *(to find)*	e → ie: **preferir** *(to prefer)*	e → i: **pedir** *(to ask for)*
yo	encuentro	prefiero	pido
tú	encuentras	prefieres	pides
Ud. / él / ella	encuentra	prefiere	pide
nosotros / nosotras	encontramos	preferimos	pedimos
vosotros / vosotras	encontráis	preferís	pedís
Uds. / ellos / ellas	encuentran	prefieren	piden

Suggestion: Show students that these are "boot" verbs to help them remember which forms have the stem change. Write out the conjugation of a stem-changing verb (**un verbo que tiene un cambio en el radical**) in two columns (singular and plural). Then draw a line only around the forms that have a stem change. You should be left with a line drawing of a boot.

2. Note that the stem changes in all forms except the **nosotros / nosotras** and **vosotros / vosotras** forms.

3. Remember, all the endings for the present indicative are the same for these verbs as for the other regular verbs you've learned: **-o, -as, -a, -amos, -áis, -an** for **-ar** verbs; **-o, -es, -e, -emos / -imos, -éis / -ís, -en** for **-er** and **-ir** verbs. The only thing that is different here is the change in the stem.

4. Here are some commonly used Spanish verbs that experience a stem change in the present indicative tense.

e → ie

comenzar (a) / empezar (a)	*to begin (to)*
entender	*to understand*
pensar de	*to think (of), have an opinion about*
pensar en	*to think about, to consider*
perder	*to lose*
preferir	*to prefer*
querer	*to want, to love*
sentir	*to feel*

Suggestion: Clarify and contrast **pensar de** and **pensar en**: ¿Qué piensas del presidente? vs. ¿Piensas mucho en el futuro?

o → ue

contar	*to tell, to relate; to count*
dormir	*to sleep*
encontrar	*to find*
jugar*	*to play*
poder	*to be able to*
sonar	*to ring, to go off* (*phone, alarm clock, etc.*)
soñar (con)	*to dream* (*about*)
volver	*to return*

e → i

pedir	*to ask for something*
repetir	*to repeat*
servir	*to serve*

*__Jugar__ is the only **u → ue** stem-changing verb in Spanish. It's grouped with the **o → ue** verbs, since its change is most similar to those.

Actividades

ACTIVIDAD 9 **¿Entiendes?** Tú eres el (la) profesor(a) de la clase de computación. Les preguntas a varias personas si entienden cómo hacer ciertas cosas en la computadora. Tu compañero(a) hace el papel de los varios estudiantes y te contesta.

MODELO: tú: cómo instalar el programa antivirus
Tú: *¿Entiendes cómo instalar el programa antivirus?*
Compañero(a): *Sí, entiendo cómo instalar el programa antivirus.* O: *No, no entiendo cómo instalar el programa antivirus.*

1. ustedes: cómo abrir la aplicación
2. usted: cómo archivar los documentos al disco duro
3. tú: cómo funciona el buscador
4. ellos: cómo cortar la conexión a Internet
5. ustedes: cómo entrar a los grupos de conversación
6. tú: cómo visitar el sitio web de El Corte Inglés

ACTIVIDAD 10 **¿A qué hora vuelves?** Un amigo te pregunta cuándo vuelven a casa tú, tus amigos y varios miembros de tu familia. Escucha la pregunta y escribe la respuesta correcta en una oración completa. Estudia el modelo.

MODELO: Ves: 10:30 A.M.
Escuchas: *¿A qué hora vuelves de la clase de computación?*
Escribes: *Vuelvo de la clase de computación a las diez y media de la mañana.*

1. 4:00 P.M.   3. 3:15 P.M.   5. 7:00 P.M.
2. 1:00 A.M.   4. 8:00 P.M.   6. 11:30 A.M.

ACTIVIDAD 11 **En la clase de español.** Todos los estudiantes en la clase de español están en medio de alguna actividad. Di lo que hace cada persona.

MODELO: Olga (no entender las instrucciones)
Olga no entiende las instrucciones.

1. Joaquín (cerrar el libro)
2. Iris (perder su lugar en el capítulo)
3. Paulo (dormir en su escritorio)
4. Lisa (empezar a hacer la tarea)
5. Arturo (pensar en las vacaciones)
6. Andrés y Marta (jugar en la computadora)
7. Roberto y Humberto (querer ir al gimnasio)
8. Ingrid (preferir hacer la tarea en la computadora)
9. Francisco (no poder abrir la aplicación)
10. la profesora (volver a repetir la tarea)
11. yo (pedir el número de la página de la lectura)
12. yo (repetir la pregunta)

ACTIVIDAD 12 **¡Lo siento!** Invita a tu compañero(a) a tres lugares. Él o ella no puede aceptar tu invitación, y te dice por qué. Luego, tu compañero(a) te invita a ti a tres lugares. Tú no puedes aceptar su invitación y le explicas por qué.

MODELOS: Tú: *¿Quieres ir a tomar un refresco?*
Compañero(a): *Lo siento, no puedo ahora porque tengo clase de computación.*

Compañero(a): *¿Quieres ir al centro de computación a navegar por Internet?*
Tú: *Lo siento, no puedo ahora porque tengo que hacer la tarea.*

ACTIVIDAD 13 **La vida universitaria.** ¿Es la vida del estudiante muy difícil hoy en día? Con tres compañeros de clase, contesten las siguientes preguntas sinceramente. Basándose en las respuestas de sus compañeros, juntos decidan si la vida universitaria produce mucho estrés para el estudiante. Presenten su conclusión a la clase.

1. ¿Sientes mucho estrés? ¿Por qué?
2. ¿A qué hora vuelves a la residencia estudiantil de la universidad?
3. ¿A qué hora duermes? ¿Dónde duermes? ¿Cuántas horas duermes por noche? ¿Duermes lo suficiente?
4. ¿Juegas videojuegos? ¿juegos interactivos? ¿juegos en la red? ¿Cuánto tiempo pasas a diario jugando estos juegos?
5. ¿Pierdes tus llaves (*keys*) con frecuencia? ¿tus gafas? ¿tu dinero (*money*)? ¿tu tarea? ¿tus libros? ¿tus cuadernos? ¿tu mochila?
6. ¿Prefieres tener o no tener un celular o un bíper? ¿Por qué?
7. ¿Piensas en tu futuro? ¿Estás preocupado(a) por tu futuro? ¿Puedes imaginar tu futuro?

Volver + *infinitive* means to go back and do something, or to do it over.

ACTIVIDAD 14 **Los hábitos del universitario.** Haz una gráfica como la de abajo. Si quieres, puedes escribir tus propias preguntas. Luego, hazles las preguntas a diez compañeros de clase. Según sus respuestas, apunta el número de estudiantes en la columna apropiada. Luego, escribe una descripción de tus resultados.

Preguntas	Número de estudiantes
dormir más de seis horas por noche:	6
no dormir más de seis horas por noche:	4
preferir hablar por teléfono para comunicarse:	
preferir escribir e-mail para comunicarse:	
jugar un deporte:	
jugar en Internet:	
jugar videojuegos:	
jugar videos interactivos:	
sentir mucho estrés:	
no sentir mucho estrés:	
pensar en su futuro todos los días:	
no pensar en su futuro todos los días:	
encontrar la vida universitaria difícil:	
encontrar la vida universitaria fácil:	
¿...?	

MODELO: *Seis estudiantes duermen más de seis horas por noche.*
Cuatro estudiantes no duermen más de seis horas por noche.

Gramática útil 4
Describing how something is done: Adverbs

EL MEJOR SERVIDOR DE E-MAIL *

ISOCOR
N-PLEX
http://www.isocor.com

Indudablemente, el producto más versátil... *

N-PLEX es un software de servidor potente e integrado para transmitir información electrónica de forma segura sobre Internet o Intranets. Diseñado especialmente para cumplir las demandas más exigentes de las empresas, organismos gubernamentales y proveedores de acceso a Internet, N-PLEX proporciona un sistema completo y ampliable para realizar intercambio de información electrónica en entornos de redes globales con facilidades de gestión centralizada y remota.

*Según la revista iWorld, N-PLEX de ISOCOR es el mejor software servidor de correo electrónico para Windows NT.

LLAME AHORA PARA INFORMARSE: (91) 677.61.85

Begin the CD-ROM activities. Do the cultural activities and reading and writing practice as you complete the corresponding text sections.

Can you find two -**mente** adverbs in this Spanish advertisement? Based on your knowledge of cognates, can you guess their meanings in English?

Hint: Do you know what the word *indubitably* means in English?

Answers: indudablemente, especialmente

CÓMO USARLO

When you want to say how an activity is carried out (slowly, thoroughly, generally, etc.), you use an adverb.

Generalmente, prefiero usar una contraseña secreta.
Generally I prefer to use a secret password.
Escribo más **rápidamente** en computadora que con bolígrafo.
*I write more **rapidly** on the computer than I do with a pen.*
Este programa es **muy** lento.
*This program is **very** slow.*

CÓMO FORMARLO

LO BÁSICO

An adverb is a word that modifies a verb, an adjective, or another adverb. *Generally, rapidly,* and *very* are all adverbs. You can identify an adverb by asking the question, *"How?"*

1. To form an adverb from a Spanish adjective, it is often possible to add the ending **-mente** to the adjective: **fácil → fácilmente.** If the adjective ends in an **-o,** change it to **-a** before adding **-mente: rápido → rápidamente.**

Suggestion: Reinforce this on the board by writing "-**mente** = -ly".

2. Here are some frequently used Spanish adjectives that can be turned into **-mente** adverbs.

fácil (*easy*)	→	**fácilmente**	**lento** (*slow*)	→	**lentamente**
difícil (*difficult*)	→	**difícilmente**	**rápido** (*fast*)	→	**rápidamente**

3. **-mente** adverbs are also useful to talk about your routine and what you normally do.

frecuentemente	*frequently*	**normalmente**	*normally*
generalmente	*generally*		

Lento and **rápido** can also be used with **muy** for the same effect: **Esta computadora se conecta a Internet muy rápido / muy lento / rápidamente / lentamente.**

4. Here are some other common Spanish adverbs.

Remember, adverbs can be used to modify other adverbs, so it's perfectly acceptable to use **muy** with **frecuentemente** or **mal**, for example!

bastante	*somewhat, rather*	Este sistema es **bastante** lento.
bien	*well*	Tu computadora funciona **bien.**
demasiado	*too much*	Navego **demasiado** por Internet.
mal	*badly*	¡Mi fax-módem funciona muy **mal**!
mucho	*a lot*	Me gustan **mucho** los juegos interactivos.
muy	*very*	Archivo **muy** frecuentemente.
poco	*little*	Chateo **poco** por Internet.

Actividades

Answers Act. 15: 1. fácilmente
2. frecuentemente 3. lentamente
4. Normalmente 5. rápidamente
6. cuidadosamente 7. constantemente
8. tranquilamente

ACTIVIDAD 15 **¿Cómo?** Escucha a Miriam mientras describe su vida a una amiga. Completa sus oraciones. Escoge el adjetivo más lógico del grupo y conviértelo en un adverbio añadiendo el sufijo **-mente.**

constante	cuidadoso	directo	fácil
frecuente	general	lento	normal
inmediato	paciente	tranquilo	rápido
total			

1. Puedes instalar el programa antivirus _____.
2. Yo chateo por Internet _____.
3. Hay algunos sitios web que funcionan _____.
4. _____, navego por Internet dos o tres horas por día.
5. Con este módem interno, puedo hacer una conexión _____.
6. Instalo los programas de software en mi computadora _____.
7. Tengo tarea _____.
8. Los domingos prefiero pasar el día _____.

ACTIVIDAD 16 **¿Cómo te sientes?** Averigua (*Find out*) cómo se sienten tus compañeros de clase en ciertas situaciones. Hazles las siguientes preguntas a varios compañeros y apunta sus respuestas. Luego, dale los resultados de tu encuesta a la clase.

¿Cómo te sientes cuando…

1. vas a tener un examen?
2. tu computadora no funciona bien?
3. recibes la cuenta (*bill*) de tu teléfono celular?
4. la batería de tu teléfono no funciona?
5. pierdes los archivos de tu tarea?
6. ¿…?

Posibles respuestas:

bien	bastante nervioso (triste, preocupado, etc.)
mal	demasiado nervioso (cansado, furioso, etc.)
muy bien	no me afecta
muy mal	¿…?

España

Las riquezas culturales de España. Look at the photos, then read the paragraphs and titles on page 128. Can you match the photos and the correct title to each paragraph? Try to read quickly to catch the gist of each paragraph. Once you have identified the correct title and photo for each paragraph, read the paragraphs again to see if you understood the basic content of each one.

Fotos

Foto 1

Foto 2

Foto 3

Foto 4

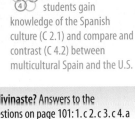

Standards: Here students gain knowledge of the Spanish culture (C 2.1) and compare and contrast (C 4.2) between multicultural Spain and the U.S.

¿Adivinaste? Answers to the questions on page 101: 1. c 2. c 3. c 4. a

Foto 1: the statue of Don Quijote and Sancho Panza in the Plaza de España, Madrid; **Foto 2:** the Alhambra in Granada; **Foto 3:** a **tapas** bar in Madrid; **Foto 4:** *The Triumph of Bacchus* by Diego de Velázquez.

Títulos

La literatura   **La influencia árabe**   **El arte**   **La cocina española**

Answers: **Párrafo 1:** La cocina española, Foto 3; **Párrafo 2:** La literatura, Foto 1; **Párrafo 3:** La influencia árabe, Foto 2; **Párrafo 4:** El arte, Foto 4

Párrafo 1

Las tapas son raciones o porciones pequeñas de comida típicamente española que se sirven en los bares españoles, especialmente en Madrid. Salir a comer tapas con los amigos es mucho más que sólo comer: ¡es una actividad esencial en la vida social española!

Párrafo 2

El ingenioso hidalgo Don Quijote de la Mancha (1605), por el autor español Miguel de Cervantes, se considera la primera novela moderna. Los dos protagonistas, Don Quijote de la Mancha, el idealista sincero, y Sancho Panza, el realista cómico, son unos de los personajes más famosos de la literatura española, y aún de la literatura mundial.

Párrafo 3

En el siglo VIII, colonizadores musulmanes, comúnmente llamados "los moros", conquistan la Península Ibérica. Durante esta época, bajo su influencia, florecen las matemáticas, las ciencias, la arquitectura y las artes decorativas. Las influencias árabes en la arquitectura son muy evidentes por todo el sur de España, en particular en Granada, Córdoba y Sevilla.

Párrafo 4

Los grandes maestros de la pintura española incluyen a El Greco (1541–1614), Diego de Velázquez (1599–1660) y Francisco de Goya (1746–1828). Las obras de El Greco tratan temas religiosos, mientras que las de Velázquez frecuentemente representan mitos y leyendas. Goya es famoso por sus retratos de la familia real y también por sus protestas gráficas contra la violencia y la guerra (*war*).

Internet

Standards: Here students continue acquiring knowledge about Spain (C 2.1) and explore **Sevilla** beyond the classroom setting (C 5.1).

¡CONÉCTATE!

Your class needs to plan a virtual vacation to Sevilla, Spain, in order to get away from all the stress of modern technological living! Divide into four groups. Each group will choose one of the following categories and research it by following links on the *Nexos* website (http://college.hmco.com/languages/spanish/students) to see a list of suggested websites. Each group should come up with a list of three suggestions for their category. Then, based on the group's suggestions, the class will prepare an itinerary for a virtual vacation to Sevilla.

Group 1: Housing / Lodging
Group 2: Entertainment
Group 3: Museums and other cultural sites
Group 4: Where to eat

A LEER

Antes de leer

ESTRATEGIA

Using format clues to aid comprehension

In **Capítulo 3**, you learned to look at the visuals that accompany a magazine or newspaper article to get a general idea of its content. It is also very helpful to look at an article's format. The headline, a section title, and any kind of highlighted text can give you a general idea of the article's content. Also, any sidebars (information presented in a box accompanying the story) can provide helpful hints.

ACTIVIDAD 1 Mira el siguiente artículo de *Netmaní@*, una revista de tecnología e Internet publicada en España. ¿Cuántas de las siguientes claves (*clues*) de formato puedes identificar en el artículo?

- título de sección
- título de artículo
- texto de interés
- texto del lado (*sidebar*)
- citas (*quotations*)
- fotos
- ilustraciones y dibujos
- otros tipos de gráficos

ACTIVIDAD 2 Ahora, estudia las claves de formato para ver si puedes entender el tema principal del artículo. ¿De qué trata el artículo?

- programas para la computadora
- los emoticons (*smiley faces used in cyberspace*)
- técnicas de diseño gráfico para crear los emoticons

Lectura

ACTIVIDAD 3 Ahora lee el artículo completo. Trata de comprender las ideas más importantes. Busca los cognados para comprenderlo mejor.

Preparation: Remind students that they don't need to understand every word. Suggest summarizing each paragraph. Match each statement with a paragraph: **Los smileys son símbolos que expresan las emociones; se usan en los e-mails. Hay muchísimos smileys y hay diccionarios para explicar qué significan.**

Heritage Learners: Research suggests that reading aloud increases fluency and comprehensibility in students learning literacy skills in their native language. Reading aloud works best when the teacher first models reading a passage and then has students take turns reading the same passage until they can pronounce all words correctly and inflect the reading appropriately.

Answers Act. 1: título de sección, título de artículo, texto de interés, texto del lado, otros tipos de gráficos

Answers Act. 2: los emoticons

Optional: It may be helpful to have this vocabulary handy, if students ask or create other emoticons on their own: **punto y coma (;) coma (,) punto (.) dos puntos (:) puntos suspensivos (…) raya (—) guión (-) paréntesis ( ) corchetes { } asterisco ***

Trucos de navegación: Smileys al completo

¿Sabes[1] lo que significa C=}>;*())?
Si estás perdido en el mundo[2] de los smileys, he aquí una solución a tus problemas...

¿Quién no sabe todavía qué son los smileys? Esos populares símbolos, resultado de combinar paréntesis, letras y otros símbolos alfanuméricos, creados[3] para manifestar distintos sentimientos como alegría, diversión, complicidad u otros difícilmente expresables a través del lenguaje escrito[4], pueblan[5] en la actualidad gran parte de los mensajes que se envían[6] por e-mail o se escriben en los grupos de noticias de Usenet.

Aparte de los clásicos :-), :-(, ;-) existen muchísimos más smileys, con una gran diversidad de significados... Una solución para no perderse[7] en este mundillo consiste en recurrir[8] a las recopilaciones de smileys que se han ido realizando[9] últimamente por la Red. Son, claro, los diccionarios de smileys.

Uno de ellos es *The Unofficial Smiley Dictionary* (el diccionario no oficial de smileys), que es uno de los más visitados. Se trata de una colección bastante completa de estos símbolos, divididos en varios grupos, tales como smileys sencillos[10], smileys emocionales o mega smileys, por citar algunos. ■

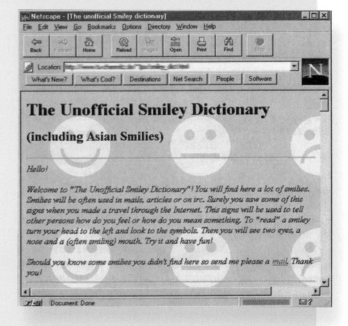

Idioma cibernético

:-)	contento	;-)	sarcástico
:-/	escéptico	*-)	muy contento
>:-[	furioso	:-X	muy discreto
:-D	muy cómico	>>:-[	muy furioso
O:-)	soy un santo	:-(	triste
I-I	dormido	>:->	soy un diablo
:'-(	muy triste	:-I	indiferente
@--->---	romántico (una flor para ti)		

[1]*Do you know* [2]**perdido...** *lost in the world* [3]*created* [4]*written* [5]*populate* [6]**se envían** *people send each other* [7]*to lose oneself* [8]*to fall back on, to resort to* [9]**se han...** *that are being created* [10]*simple*

Después de leer

ACTIVIDAD 4 Ahora di si las siguientes oraciones son **ciertas (C)** o **falsas (F)** según el artículo.

Answers Act. 4: 1. C 2. C 3. F 4. F 5. F

1. _____ Este artículo habla de los smileys, también llamados "emoticons".
2. _____ Hay muchos smileys.
3. _____ Desgraciadamente, no existen diccionarios de los smileys.
4. _____ Los smileys clásicos son :-) y >:-> .
5. _____ >>:-[quiere decir "dormido".

ACTIVIDAD 5 ¿Puedes identificar el equivalente en inglés de los siguientes símbolos?

Answers Act. 5: 1. b 2. d 3. a 4. c

1. _____ |-I
2. _____ O:-)
3. _____ >:->
4. _____ @--->---

a. *I'm a devil.*
b. *asleep*
c. *a flower for you*
d. *I'm a saint.*

ACTIVIDAD 6 En grupos de tres a cuatro estudiantes, creen (*create*) nuevos emoticons para las emociones indicadas. ¡Sean creativos! Cuando terminen, escriban sus emoticons en la pizarra y voten para decidir cuáles van a ser los emoticons "oficiales" para cada emoción indicada.

1. aburrido
2. enfermo
3. nervioso
4. ocupado
5. preocupado
6. seguro

ACTIVIDAD 7 Escribe un e-mail breve a un(a) amigo(a), usando todos los emoticons que puedas. Puedes usar los emoticons del artículo y también los nuevos de la **Actividad 6.**

VOCABULARIO

LA TECNOLOGÍA   *Technology*

El hardware   *Hardware*

La computadora   *Computer*

el altoparlante	*speaker*
el cable	*cable*
el disco duro	*hard drive*
el fax / módem externo	*external fax / modem*
el micrófono	*microphone*
el monitor	*monitor*
el ratón	*mouse*

La computadora portátil   *Laptop computer*

los audífonos	*earphones*
el fax / módem interno	*internal fax / modem*
la impresora	*printer*
el lector de CD-ROM o DVD	*CD-ROM / DVD drive*
la pantalla	*screen*
la tecla	*key*
el teclado	*keyboard*

El software   *Software*

la aplicación	*application*
los archivos	*files*
el ícono del programa	*program icon*
el juego interactivo	*interactive game*
el programa antivirus	*anti-virus program*
el programa de procesamiento de textos	*word-processing program*

Funciones de la computadora   *Computer functions*

archivar	*to file*
conectar	*to connect*
enviar	*to send*
funcionar	*to function*
grabar	*to record*
hacer clic / doble clic	*to click / double click*
instalar	*to install*
tener 512 MB de memoria	*to have 512 MB of memory*

LOS COLORES   *Colors*

amarillo(a)	*yellow*
anaranjado(a)	*orange*
azul	*blue*
blanco(a)	*white*
café / marrón	*brown*
gris	*gray*
morado(a)	*purple*
negro(a)	*black*
rojo(a)	*red*
rosa / rosado(a)	*pink*
verde	*green*

LAS EMOCIONES   *Emotions*

aburrido(a)	*bored*
cansado(a)	*tired*
contento(a)	*happy*
enfermo(a)	*sick*
enojado(a)	*angry*
furioso(a)	*furious*
nervioso(a)	*nervous*
ocupado(a)	*busy*
preocupado(a)	*worried*
seguro(a)	*sure*
triste	*sad*

PRODUCTOS ELECTRÓNICOS
Electronic products

el asistente electrónico	*electronic notebook*
el buscapersonas / bíper	*beeper*
la cámara digital	*digital camera*
la cámara web	*webcam*
el CD portátil / MP3	*portable CD / MP3 player*
el organizador electrónico	*electronic organizer*
el reproductor / grabador de discos compactos	*CD player / burner*
el reproductor / grabador de DVD	*DVD player / burner*
la videocámara	*videocamera*
la videocasetera	*VCR*

FUNCIONES DE INTERNET
Internet functions

el buzón electrónico	electronic mailbox
el buscador	search engine
chatear	to chat
el ciberespacio	cyberspace
la conexión	the connection
cortar la conexión	to go offline
hacer una conexión	to go online
la contraseña	password
el correo electrónico /	e-mail
e-mail	
en línea	online
el enlace	link
el grupo de conversación	chat room
el grupo de debate	news group
la página web	web page
el proveedor de acceso	Internet provider
la red mundial	World Wide Web
el sitio web	web site
el (la) usuario(a)	user

EXPRESIONES DE CORTESÍA
Courtesy expressions

Con permiso.	Pardon me.
Disculpe.	Excuse me.
Lo siento.	I'm sorry.
Perdón.	Excuse me.

VERBOS COMO GUSTAR

encantar	to like a lot
fascinar	to fascinate
importar	to be important to someone; to mind
interesar	to interest, to be interesting
molestar	to bother

OTROS VERBOS*

comenzar (ie)	to begin
contar (ue)	to tell, to relate; to count
dormir (ue)	to sleep
empezar (ie)	to begin
entender (ie)	to understand
jugar (ue)	to play
pedir (i)	to ask for something
pensar (ie) de	to think, have an opinion about
pensar (ie) en	to think about, to consider
perder (ie)	to lose
poder (ue)	to be able to
preferir (ie)	to prefer
querer (ie)	to want; to love
repetir (i)	to repeat

sentir (ie)	to feel
servir (i)	to serve
sonar (ue)	to ring, to go off (phone, alarm clock, etc.)
soñar (ue) con	to dream (about)
volver (ue)	to return

ADJETIVOS

difícil	difficult
fácil	easy
lento	slow
rápido	fast

ADVERBIOS

difícilmente	with difficulty
fácilmente	easily
frecuentemente	frequently
generalmente	generally
lentamente	slowly
normalmente	normally
rápidamente	rapidly
bien	well
demasiado	too much
mal	badly
mucho	a lot
muy	very
poco	little

*Starting now stem-changing verbs will be indicated in vocabulary lists with the stem change in parentheses.

¿Qué tal la familia?

Communication

By the end of this chapter you will be able to:
- talk about and describe your family
- talk about professions
- describe daily routines
- indicate current actions

Cultures

By the end of this chapter you will have learned about:
- Honduras and El Salvador
- nicknames and diminutive expressions
- careers where knowledge of Spanish is helpful
- the Afro-Hispanic **garífuna** culture of Honduras

Standards: The **Garífuna** culture reflects Afro-Caribbean and Central American roots. The practices and the perspectives of the **Garífuna** culture are explored in this chapter (C 2.1). For expansion on this, see *Nexos* website for related links.

Una familia salvadoreña se presenta para una foto en frente de su casa.

RELACIONES FAMILIARES

Nos describimos con relación a diferentes aspectos de nuestra vida: los intereses, la personalidad, las características físicas, la profesión y muchos más. En el mundo hispanohablante, las relaciones familiares son un aspecto muy importante de la identidad personal. En este capítulo, vas a explorar el concepto de la familia y de las relaciones interpersonales.

Los datos

Mira los gráficos y luego indica si las siguientes oraciones se refieren a Honduras o a El Salvador.

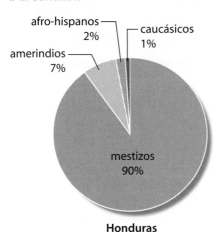

afro-hispanos
2%

caucásicos
1%

amerindios
7%

mestizos
90%

Honduras

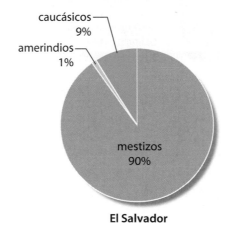

caucásicos
9%

amerindios
1%

mestizos
90%

El Salvador

① Hay más diversidad étnica en este país.
② Hay más amerindios en este país.
③ Hay más caucásicos en este país.

¡Adivina!

¿Qué sabes de Honduras y El Salvador? Di si las oraciones se refieren a Honduras, a El Salvador o a los dos. (Las respuestas están en la página 158.)

① La mayoría de la población es de origen mestizo.
② Hay una pequeña pero significante población afro-hispana.
③ Hay una pequeña pero significante población caucásica.
④ Tiene ruinas de la civilización maya.
⑤ Es el país más pequeño de Centroamérica.

OCÉANO ATLÁNTICO

HONDURAS
Tegucigalpa

San Salvador

OCÉANO
PACÍFICO

EL SALVADOR

¡Adivina! answers: 1. Honduras y El Salvador 2. Honduras 3. El Salvador
4. Honduras 5. El Salvador

135

Vocabulario útil 1

ANILÚ: Son fotos de mi **familia.**

DULCE: ¿De veras? ¿En la computadora?

ANILÚ: Sí, mi **hermanito** Roberto tiene una cámara digital. Saca fotos de la familia y me las manda por Internet.

Suggestion: Draw you own family tree (or make one up) and use it to present vocabulary words in the context of an authentic family, mentioning names and where people live. Point out relationships between relatives and emphasize gender. Take the opportunity to recycle interrogative words with questions like **¿Cómo se llama mi / tu / su madre / padre / etc.?** **¿Cuántos tíos tengo? ¿Dónde vive mi prima?**

Optional: Present family terms in the context of the Spanish Royal Family. There are various websites that offer current information on the Borbón family. Another way to practice family members is by bringing the magazine *People en español* to class and using current pop stars and their families as examples.

Preparation: You may have students who are sensitive about talking about their families. Always give students the option of talking about a family other than their own. Be prepared to field questions on lexical items such as **está muerto(a)**, **está divorciado(a)**, if asked.

Preparation: Write a simple, brief paragraph about the family of the current U.S. president before class, and read it as a model in class.

LA FAMILIA NUCLEAR

la madre (mamá)	*mother*
el padre (papá)	*father*
los padres	*parents*
la esposa	*wife*
el esposo	*husband*
la hija	*daughter*
el hijo	*son*
la hermana (mayor)	*(older) sister*
el hermano (menor)	*(younger) brother*
la tía	*aunt*
el tío	*uncle*
la prima	*female cousin*
el primo	*male cousin*
la sobrina	*niece*
el sobrino	*nephew*
la abuela	*grandmother*
el abuelo	*grandfather*
la nieta	*granddaughter*
el nieto	*grandson*

LA FAMILIA POLÍTICA

la suegra	*mother-in-law*	**el yerno**	*son-in-law*
el suegro	*father-in-law*	**la cuñada**	*sister-in-law*
la nuera	*daughter-in-law*	**el cuñado**	*brother-in-law*

OTROS PARIENTES

la madrastra	*stepmother*	**el hermanastro**	*stepbrother*
el padrastro	*stepfather*	**la media hermana**	*half-sister*
la hermanastra	*stepsister*	**el medio hermano**	*half-brother*

In Spanish, the masculine plural **hermanos** can mean both *brothers* (all males) and *brothers and sisters / siblings* (both males and females).

Notice that **parientes** is a false cognate: it does *not* mean *parents;* it means *family members.* **Los padres** is the correct term for *parents.*

Actividades

ACTIVIDAD 1 **La familia de Anilú.** Con un(a) compañero(a) de clase, háganse preguntas sobre el árbol genealógico (*family tree*) de Anilú. Túrnense nombrando la persona y diciendo cuál es su relación con Anilú.

MODELO: Compañero(a): *¿Quién es Beatriz Vega Chapa?*
Tú: *Es la abuela de Anilú.*

Notice that two surnames are given for the grandparents in Anilú's family tree. In Spanish-speaking countries, a person's first surname comes from his or her father's side, and their second surname comes from his or her mother's side. Anilú's full name will be Anilú Guzmán Villa until she marries. Then she will add her husband's first surname (for example, Rodríguez) after her name: Anilú Guzmán Villa de Rodríguez, and be known simply as Sra. Rodríguez.

ACTIVIDAD 2 **El árbol genealógico.** Dibuja el árbol genealógico de tu familia nuclear. Empieza con tus abuelos y sigue con el resto de tu familia. Luego, en grupos de tres, intercambien sus árboles y háganse preguntas sobre sus familias.

MODELO: Tú: *¿Tom es tu hermano?*
Compañero(a): *Sí, es mi hermano menor. Tiene quince años y es muy divertido.*
Tú: *¿Quién es Elisa?*
Compañero(a): *Es mi sobrina. Es la hija de mi hermana mayor.*

ACTIVIDAD 3 **Mi familia.** Escribe un párrafo corto sobre cada miembro de tu familia nuclear. Para cada individuo, di quién es, cómo se llama y cuántos años tiene. Incluye algunas características físicas y también unas de personalidad. Luego, en grupos de tres lean sus descripciones al grupo. El grupo te hace preguntas sobre cada miembro de tu familia y tú contestas.

¡COMPÁRATE!

En español frecuentemente se usan **palabras diminutivas,** como hace Anilú cuando habla de su **hermanito.** Se forma el diminutivo añadiendo (*adding*) **-ito** o **-ita** a un sustantivo (*noun*): **hermano → hermanito.** (Otras palabras forman el diminutivo añadiendo **-cito / -cita: coche → cochecito.**)

Una palabra diminutiva puede tener dos significados. Uno es para decir que algo o alguien es pequeño o menor: una **casita** es una casa pequeña; una **hermanita** es una hermana menor. El segundo uso del diminutivo es para expresar afecto o cariño (*love, fondness*). Por ejemplo, si Anilú habla de su abuela, la puede llamar **abuelita** para indicar que la quiere mucho.

Para expresar cariño los hispanohablantes también usan mucho los apodos (*nicknames*). Por ejemplo, los personajes del video tienen una variedad de apodos: **Anilú** es apodo de Ana Luisa, **Beto** es apodo de Roberto y **Chela** es apodo de Graciela.

 PRÁCTICA. Con un(a) compañero(a) de clase, contesten las siguientes preguntas sobre los apodos.

1. ¿Tienes apodo? Si tienes uno, ¿te gusta? ¿Por qué?
2. ¿Puedes nombrar apodos que no son formas cortas (*short*) del nombre? Por ejemplo, ¿qué apodos se relacionan con características físicas o de personalidad?
3. En tu opinión, ¿es un apodo una indicación de cariño? ¿Por qué?
4. ¿Te gusta la idea de palabras diminutivas? ¿Por qué? ¿Existe una forma equivalente en inglés?

Vocabulario útil 2

DULCE:	¿Quién es este señor?
ANILÚ:	Es mi papá. Se enoja cuando Roberto le saca fotos. No le gusta salir en fotos. Dice que se ve muy gordo.
DULCE:	¿Qué hace tu papá?
ANILÚ:	Es **arquitecto.** Diseña edificios para negocios.

Notice that when you describe someone's profession, you don't use an article as we would in English: **Es abogada** translates as *She is a lawyer.*

LAS PROFESIONES Y LAS CARRERAS

la abogada

el periodista

la médica

la artista

El policía means a single policeman. **La policía** can mean a single policewoman or the entire police force. You have to extract the correct meaning from context. Other professions whose meaning depends on the context and the article are: **el químico / la química, el físico / la física, el músico / la música, el matemático / la matemática, el guardia / la guardia.**

Notice: Students never know enough vocabulary to cover all of the possibilities. Teach them the phrase "X **trabaja en...**" to give more options while talking about what their relatives and friends do. Help students with new terms and list them on the board.

Suggestion: Practice family terms and professions at the same time with questions like ¿**En qué trabaja tu padre / tu madre / tu tío, etc.?**

el bombero

la carpintera

la policía

el plomero

el arquitecto

MÁS PROFESIONES

el actor / la actriz	*actor / actress*	el hombre / la mujer de negocios	*businessman / businesswoman*
el (la) camarero(a)	*waiter, waitress*	el (la) ingeniero(a)	*engineer*
el (la) cocinero(a)	*cook, chef*	el (la) maestro(a)	*teacher*
el (la) contador(a)	*accountant*	el (la) mecánico(a)	*mechanic*
el (la) dentista	*dentist*	el (la) peluquero(a)	*barber / hairdresser*
el (la) dependiente	*salesclerk*	el (la) programador(a)	*programmer*
el (la) diseñador(a) gráfico(a)	*graphic designer*	el (la) secretario(a)	*secretary*
el (la) dueño(a) de…	*owner of . . .*	el (la) trabajador(a)	*worker*
el (la) enfermero(a)	*nurse*	el (la) veterinario(a)	*veterinarian*
el (la) gerente de	*manager of . . .*		

Actividades

Answers Act. 4: All begin with **Quiere ser…** 1. contador(a) 2. hombre / mujer de negocios 3. ingeniero(a) 4. programador(a) 5. diseñador(a) gráfico(a) 6. artista 7. maestro(a) / profesor(a) 8. periodista

Suggestion: Expand and quiz students with statements like: 1. **Estudia medicina pero quiere trabajar con animales.** 2. **Le gusta servir. Trabaja en un restaurante.** 3. **Es creativo. Trabaja mucho con la computadora.**

Answers Act. 5: 1. primo, enfermero / médico 2. prima, maestra 3. cuñada, periodista 4. sobrino, camarero 5. tío, arquitecto 6. suegro, programador

ACTIVIDAD 4 **Quiere ser…** Tú y tu compañero(a) hablan de varios amigos. Tú le dices a tu compañero(a) qué es lo que estudia esa persona y tu compañero(a) te dice qué quiere ser esa persona.

MODELO: medicina
Tú: *Marcos estudia medicina*
Compañero(a): *Quiere ser médico.*

1. contabilidad
2. administración de empresas
3. ingeniería
4. informática
5. diseño gráfico
6. arte
7. pedagogía
8. periodismo

ACTIVIDAD 5 **Presentaciones.** Estás en la fiesta de un amigo. Él te presenta a varios miembros de su familia. Lee sus presentaciones. Luego, para cada persona, indica cuál es su relación con el narrador y su profesión.

1. Quiero presentarte a Antonio. Él es el hijo de mi tía Rosa. Antonio trabaja en el Hospital Garibaldi. Ayuda a las personas enfermas.

   Nombre: Antonio   *Relación:* _____   *Profesión:* _____

2. Te presento a Miranda. Miranda es la hija de mi tío Ricardo. Miranda enseña francés en el Colegio Del Valle.

   Nombre: Miranda   *Relación:* _____   *Profesión:* _____

3. Mira, te presento a Olga. Olga trabaja para el periódico *El Universal.* Olga es la esposa de mi hermano.

   Nombre: Olga   *Relación:* _____   *Profesión:* _____

4. Quiero presentarte a César. César es el hijo de mi hermano. César trabaja en una pizzería después del colegio.

   Nombre: César   *Relación:* _____   *Profesión:* _____

5. Éste es Raúl. Raúl es el hermano de mi padre. Él diseña casas y edificios.

   Nombre: Raúl   *Relación:* _____   *Profesión:* _____

6. Te presento al señor Domínguez, el padre de mi esposa. Él escribe software para una compañía dot.com.

   Nombre: señor Domínguez *Relación:* _____   *Profesión:* _____

ACTIVIDAD 6 **¿Qué quieres ser?** En grupos de tres, hablen sobre sus planes para el futuro.

MODELO: Tú: *¿Qué profesión te interesa?*
Compañero(a): *¿A mí? Yo quiero ser abogada.*
Tú: *¿Dónde quieres trabajar?*
Compañero(a): *Quiero trabajar aquí, en Los Ángeles.*

ACTIVIDAD 7 **El español y las profesiones.** En Estados Unidos, hay muchas oportunidades profesionales para personas que hablan español. Aquí hay algunas carreras que utilizan el español.

- abogado(a)
- académico(a)
- banquero(a) o financiero(a) que se especializa en Latinoamérica
- enfermero(a)
- hombre / mujer de negocios para una compañía multinacional
- intérprete
- médico(a)
- policía
- profesor(a) o maestro(a) de español
- secretario(a) bilingüe

Con un(a) compañero(a) de clase, contesten las siguientes preguntas.

1. ¿Te interesa alguna de estas carreras? ¿Por qué? ¿Crees que poder hablar español es importante para tu futuro?
2. En Europa, los estudiantes de colegio aprenden inglés y muchas veces otro idioma además de su lengua nativa. ¿Crees que es buena idea? ¿Por qué? ¿Crees que los estadounidenses deben aprender otro idioma además del inglés? ¿Por qué?

¡FÍJATE!

Las profesiones y el género

¿Se dice **la piloto, la pilota, la señora piloto, la mujer piloto?** ¡Qué confusión! Con algunas profesiones existe mucha ambigüedad sobre cómo especificar el género. Frecuentemente, esto ocurre con profesiones tradicionalmente masculinas que ahora incluyen a mujeres. Algunas de estas profesiones son: bombero, ingeniero, general, mecánico, plomero.

La ambigüedad con respecto al género de las profesiones también existe a causa del gran número de opciones gramaticales que el español presenta para especificar el género. Algunas profesiones cambian su terminación y artículo: **el** actor / **la** act**riz**, **el** maestro / **la** maestra, **el** alcalde (*mayor*) / **la** alcald**esa**. Otras profesiones sólo cambian el artículo: **el** gerente / **la** gerente, **el** dentista / **la** dentista. A veces, la palabra **mujer** o **señora** sirve para especificar el género: la **señora** juez (*judge*), la **mujer** policía.

PRÁCTICA. ¿Qué opción (opciones) tiene el inglés para especificar el género en las profesiones? ¿Qué lengua presenta más opciones, el inglés o el español?

Suggestion: Many students don't know what they want to do. Model the following sentence to give students possibilities: **No sé, pero posiblemente arquitecto(a) o...**

Suggestion: To expand on **Actividad 7**, engage students in questions and answers about people that they know. Start with: **Tengo un amigo que es bilingüe. Habla español e inglés. Es banquero. Se llama... Tiene... años.** Then continue: **¿Tienes un amigo (o un conocido) bilingüe? ¿Qué lenguas habla? ¿Dónde trabaja? ¿Qué profesión tiene? ¿Cómo se llama?** etc.

Optional: Have students search the Internet with these prompts. **Busca en Internet para ver qué oportunidades de trabajo existen para personas que hablan español. ¿Cuántas profesiones diferentes puedes encontrar?** (See chapter links on the *Nexos* website.)

Standards / Optional: By comparing the expression of gender in Spanish and English, students develop insight into the nature of language and culture. As a follow up to the **¡Fíjate!** reading, ask students to jot down on a piece of paper some examples of gender expressions in English that they hear in spoken language to make it easier to compare with Spanish examples in the text (e.g., *the lady fireman*).

Optional: For expansion, try this activity with your students: **¿A qué se dedican los siguientes profesionales? ¿Puedes usar tus conocimientos** (*knowledge*) **del inglés y el español para adivinar** (*guess*) **el significado de estas palabras? 1. el otorrinolaringólogo 2. la filatelista 3. el entomólogo 4. la psiquiatra 5. el bibliotecario 6. la ortodontista**

Vocabulario útil 3

ANILÚ: Mamá, ¿está Roberto por allí? Necesito hablar con él.

MAMÁ: No puede venir al teléfono. Se está bañando.

ANILÚ: ¿Está bañándose? ¿A esta hora?

MAMÁ: Acaba de regresar de su partido de fútbol. ¡Ay! ¡No hay ni **toallas** ni **jabón** en el baño! Me tengo que ir. Tengo que llevarle a tu hermano una toalla, el jabón y el **champú**…

EN EL BAÑO   *In the bathroom*

la toalla (de mano)

el cepillo de dientes

el champú

el desodorante

la máquina de afeitar

la pasta de dientes

el jabón

la rasuradora

el maquillaje

el peine

el cepillo

Actividades

ACTIVIDAD 8 **¿Qué necesitan comprar?** Según la situación, ¿qué necesita comprar cada persona?

MODELO: *Él necesita comprar champú.*

 1.

 2.

 3.

 4.

 5.

 6.

ACTIVIDAD 9 **La Farmacia Rivera.** Tú y tu hermano(a) ven un anuncio para la Farmacia Rivera en el periódico. Tú le dices qué quieres comprar y él o ella te dice cuánto dinero necesitas para comprar ese artículo.

(**¡Ojo!** *Dollars* = **dólares** y *cents* = **centavos.**)

MODELO: Tú: *Quiero comprar un cepillo y un peine.*
Hermano(a): *Necesitas tres dólares y setenta y nueve centavos para comprar el cepillo y el peine.*

Farmacia Rivera
¡Todo para la familia!
¡Los mejores precios de la ciudad!

Cepillo y peine "La Bella": $~~4,39~~ $3,79

Champú "Largo y limpio": $~~3,39~~ $2,79

Cepillo de dientes y pasta de dientes "Brillante": $~~4,75~~ $3,75

Desodorante "Frescura": $~~2,69~~ $1,99

Jabón antibacterial "Sanitario": $~~1,49~~ $1,19

Máquina de afeitar "El Varonil": $~~24,99~~ $19,99

Paquete de seis rasuradoras "Para ella": $~~3,97~~ $3,47

Paquete de dos toallas de mano "Elegantes": $~~4,99~~ $3,99

A VER

Antes de ver el video

For additional practice, do the *Nexos* website and / or CD-ROM video exercises.

Answers Act. 1: 1. C 2. F 3. F 4. F 5. C 6. C

ACTIVIDAD 1 Mira las fotos y el guión (*script*) en las páginas 136, 139 y 142 para ver si puedes encontrar la información necesaria para evaluar los siguientes comentarios.

¿Cierto o falso?

1. _____ Este segmento es sobre Anilú y su familia.

2. _____ Conocemos a (*We meet*) Roberto, el hermano de Anilú, a su papá y a su hermana Dulce.

3. _____ El papá de Anilú es abogado.

4. _____ El papá de Anilú tiene una cámara digital.

5. _____ La mamá de Anilú dice (*says*) que Roberto necesita toalla y jabón en el baño.

6. _____ Anilú quiere hablar con su hermano.

a.

ACTIVIDAD 2 Antes de ver el video, mira las fotos a la izquierda (*on the left*) como preparación para el contenido del segmento. A ver si puedes relacionar las fotos y los diálogos que siguen. Escribe la letra de la foto al lado de la parte del diálogo que le corresponde.

b.

_____ 1. Dulce: ¿Qué hace tu papá?
        Anilú: Es arquitecto. Diseña edificios para negocios.

_____ 2. Mamá: Bueno, pero siempre hay que hacer tiempo para llamar a tu mamá.
        Anilú: Sí, mamá, está bien. Perdóname.

_____ 3. Anilú: Mira, ven a ver.
        Dulce: ¿Qué es?
        Anilú: Son fotos de mi familia.   Answers Act. 2: 1. c 2. b 3. a

c.

ESTRATEGIA

Listening for the main idea

When you are listening to Spanish, it's sometimes hard to know what to listen to first. There are often words you don't understand; also, the difference between seeing words on a page and hearing them spoken can be a big one. A good way to organize your viewing task is to focus on getting the main idea of the segment, or of each part of the segment. Don't try to understand every single word, but instead try to get the gist of each scene. Later, with the help of textbook activities and another viewing, some of the other details of the segment will emerge.

El video

Ahora mira el video para el **Capítulo 5.** Trata de entender la idea principal de cada escena.

Después de ver el video

 ACTIVIDAD 3 Conecta cada idea de la derecha (*on the right*) con su escena correspondiente a la izquierda (*on the left*).

1. _____ **Escena 1:** Anilú está mirando (*is looking at*) la computadora.

2. _____ **Escena 2:** Anilú habla con su mamá por teléfono.

3. _____ **Escena 3:** Anilú y Dulce miran una foto en la impresora.

4. _____ **Escena 4:** Roberto llama a Anilú.

5. _____ **Escena 5:** Anilú mira la foto de la fiesta de cumpleaños del abuelo.

a. La mamá de Anilú dice que ella nunca la llama.

b. A Anilú no le gusta la foto pero Roberto cree que es muy cómica.

c. Roberto quiere saber (*to know*) si a Anilú le gustan las fotos.

d. Anilú dice (*says*) que tiene unas fotos digitales.

e. Ven una foto de su papá.

ACTIVIDAD 4 Ahora mira el segmento una o más veces para captar los detalles. Trabaja con un(a) compañero(a) para contestar las siguientes preguntas.

1. ¿Cómo manda Roberto las fotos a Anilú?
2. ¿Qué tipo de edificios (*buildings*) diseña el papá de Anilú y Roberto?
3. ¿Por qué no le gusta al papá cuando Roberto le saca fotos?
4. ¿Qué tiene que llevarle la mamá a Roberto?

Answers Act. 3: 1. d 2. a 3. e 4. c 5. b

Answers, Act. 4: 1. por Internet / en la computadora 2. para negocios 3. Dice que se ve muy gordo. 4. una toalla, jabón y champú

⑤③ Standards: Graciela Kenig's work connects Spanish with other disciplines (C 3.1) and with Spanish-speaking communities at home and around the world (C 5.1). Expand on how Spanish is used in the work place and the market place in your region through class discussion.

¿Te interesa tener una de las profesiones de las cuales habla la Sra. Kenig? To learn more about Graciela Kenig and her advice on careers with Spanish, visit the *Nexos* website (http://college.hmco.com/languages/spanish/students) and follow the links.

VOCES DE LA COMUNIDAD

Graciela Kenig

❝ **Sin duda, ser bilingüe aumenta las posibilidades de trabajo. Mi propia experiencia lo demuestra (*shows it*). De los diez trabajos o posiciones como consultora que he tenido (*I have had*) en los últimos veinte años, nueve se deben directamente al hecho (*fact*) de que hablo inglés y español.** ❞

Graciela Kenig es columnista de *¡Éxito!*, una publicación semanal en lengua española del *Chicago Tribune*. Su columna "Oportunidades" presenta consejos (*advice*) e información general sobre oportunidades profesionales para los bilingües. Kenig también es autora de *Best Careers for Bilingual Latinos: Market Your Fluency in Spanish to Get Ahead on the Job*. Este libro ofrece información importante sobre siete profesiones que presentan oportunidades especiales para los bilingües; entre ellos, la medicina, la tecnología, la publicidad y la educación. Esta exitosa nativa de Argentina es conferencista (*speaker*) profesional y fundadora y presidente de su propia agencia de consultores de servicios profesionales.

¡PREPÁRATE!

Gramática útil 1
Describing daily activities: Irregular *yo* verbs in the present indicative

For more practice of chapter topics, do the Nexos website exercises.

CÓMO USARLO

1. You have already learned the present indicative tense of many verbs. These include regular **-ar**, **-er**, and **-ir** verbs (**hablar, comer, vivir**, etc.), some irregular verbs (**ser, tener, ir**), and some stem-changing verbs (**pensar, poder, dormir**, etc.).

2. Now you will learn some verbs that are regular in all forms of the present indicative except the first-person singular, the **yo** form. Like the other verbs you learned to use in the present indicative tense, these verbs can be used to say what you routinely do, what you are doing at the moment, or what you plan to do in the immediate future.

Todos los días **salgo** para la universidad a las ocho.	*Every day **I leave** for the university at 8:00.*
Ahora mismo, **pongo** mis libros en la mochila y **digo** "hasta luego" a mi compañera de cuarto.	*Right now, **I put / I'm putting** my books in my backpack and **I say / I'm saying,** "See you later" to my roommate.*
Esta noche, **traigo** mis libros a casa otra vez y **hago** la tarea.	*Tonight, **I bring / I'll bring** my books home again and **I do / I'll do** my homework.*

CÓMO FORMARLO

Many irregular **yo** verbs in the present indicative fall into several recognizable categories. Others have to be learned individually.

1. **-go** endings:

hacer	*to make; to do*	**hago,** haces, hace, hacemos, hacéis, hacen
poner	*to put*	**pongo,** pones, pone, ponemos, ponéis, ponen
salir	*to leave, to go out (with)*	**salgo,** sales, sale, salimos, salís, salen
traer	*to bring*	**traigo,** traes, trae, traemos, traéis, traen

Suggestion: You may want to do some old-fashioned drilling to see that students can produce irregular forms. Call out a random subject (**yo, tú, él, ella, ustedes...**) and infinitives from this section. Have students conjugate orally in chorus.

Suggestion: After checking forms, try more meaningful practice. Have a conversation about their life at the university: **¿A qué hora sales de tu casa para la universidad? ¿Qué traes a la universidad? ¿Conduces a la universidad? ¿Conoces a mucha gente en la universidad? ¿A quién(es)?,** etc.

2. **-zco** endings:

conducir	to drive; to conduct	**conduzco,** conduces, conduce, conducimos, conducís, conducen
conocer	to know a person, to be familiar with	**conozco,** conoces, conoce, conocemos, conocéis, conocen
traducir	to translate	**traduzco,** traduces, traduce, traducimos, traducís, traducen

Conducir is used more frequently in Spain. In most of Latin America, the verb **manejar** (a regular **-ar** verb) is used to talk about driving.

3. Other irregular **yo** verbs:

dar	to give	**doy,** das, da, damos, dais, dan
oír	to hear	**oigo,** oyes, oye, oímos, oís, oyen
saber	to know a fact, to know how to	**sé,** sabes, sabe, sabemos, sabéis, saben
ver	to see	**veo,** ves, ve, vemos, veis, ven

Note that **oír** requires a **y** in the **tú, él / ella / Ud.,** and **ellos / ellas / Uds.** forms.

4. Irregular **yo** verbs with a stem change:

decir	to say, to tell	**digo,** dices, dice, decimos, decís, dicen
venir	to come, to attend	**vengo,** vienes, viene, venimos, venís, vienen

5. Remember that these verbs are irregular only in the **yo** form. Otherwise, they follow the rules for regular **-ar, -er,** and **-ir** verbs that you have already learned. **Oír** uses the regular endings but includes a spelling change: the addition of **y** to all forms except the **yo** form.

6. **Saber** vs. **conocer**

Note that **saber** and **conocer** both mean *to know*. It's important to know when to use each one.

◆ Use **saber** to say that you know a fact or information, or that you know how to do something.

Eduardo **sabe** hablar alemán, jugar tenis y bailar flamenco. Además **sabe** dónde están todos los restaurantes buenos de la ciudad.

*Eduardo **knows how** to speak German, play tennis, and dance flamenco. He also **knows** where all the good restaurants in the city are.*

◆ Use **conocer** to say that you know a person or are familiar with a thing.

—¿**Conocen** a Sandra?
—No, pero **conocemos** a su hermana.

*Do you **know** Sandra?*
*No, but we **know** her sister.*

—¿**Conoces** bien Tegucigalpa?
—Sí, pero no **conozco** las otras ciudades de Honduras.

*Do you **know** Tegucigalpa well?*
*Yes, but I don't **know** the other cities in Honduras.*

7. The personal **a**

When you use **conocer** to say that you know a person, you must use the preposition **a** before the noun referring to the person. This preposition is known as

Algún día vas a tener hijos y entonces vas a **saber** cómo es.

One way to remember the difference between **saber** and **conocer** is that **saber** is usually followed by either a verb or a phrase, while **conocer** is often followed by a noun.

Suggestion: To clarify the **saber / conocer** contrast, ask students questions about their classmates: ¿Conoces a Jim de nuestra clase? ¿Qué sabes de él / ella? (su especialidad, su dirección electrónica, etc.)

the personal **a** in Spanish and it must be used whenever a person receives the action of the verb. It has no equivalent in English.

Conocemos **a** Nina y **a** Roberto.   *We know Nina and Roberto.*
¿Ves **a** tus amigos frecuentemente?   *Do you see your friends frequently?*

Actividades

ACTIVIDAD 1 **La mamá de Anilú.** La mamá de Anilú le describe un día normal a una amiga. Da su descripción desde su punto de vista (*viewpoint*).

1. salir del trabajo a las cinco
2. generalmente, traer trabajo a casa
3. cuando llego a casa, venir muy cansada
4. hacer la cena (*dinner*) a las siete
5. poner la mesa (*set the table*) antes de hacer la cena
6. cuando la cena está preparada, decir «todo está listo»
7. conocer a mis hijos muy bien
8. saber que tengo que llamarlos varias veces
9. por fin, oír a los niños apagar la tele
10. dar las gracias por otro día más o menos normal

Ahora escribe un párrafo sobre un día normal en tu vida. Trata de usar los mismos verbos que usa la mamá de Anilú.

 ACTIVIDAD 2 **Cuestionario.** En grupos de tres, háganse las preguntas del siguiente cuestionario. Si quieren, pueden añadir algunas preguntas al cuestionario. Cada uno en el grupo debe contestar cada pregunta.

1. **Tu horario**
   ¿Cuándo haces ejercicio?
   ¿Cuándo haces la tarea?
   ¿Cuándo haces la cena?
2. **Tu vida social**
   ¿Cuántas veces sales cada semana?
   ¿Sales por la noche? ¿Adónde vas?
   ¿Con quién sales los fines de semana?
3. **Tu medio de transporte preferido**
   ¿Tienes coche? ¿Conduces a la universidad?
   ¿Conduces al trabajo?
   ¿Conduces todos los días o usas otro medio de transporte?
4. **Tu tiempo libre**
   ¿Sabes hablar varios idiomas? ¿Cuáles?
   ¿Sabes jugar algún deporte?
   ¿Sabes tocar un instrumento? ¿Cuál?
5. **¿Conoces el mundo?**
   ¿Conoces los países de Europa? ¿Cuáles?
   ¿Conoces Canadá?
   ¿Cuántos estados de EEUU conoces?

ACTIVIDAD 3 **¿Sabes…?** Con un(a) compañero(a), formen preguntas con las siguientes frases. Túrnense para hacerse las preguntas. Luego, inventen nuevas preguntas usando el verbo en cada frase y háganse esas preguntas.

MODELO: conducir para llegar a la universidad
   Tú: *¿Conduces para llegar a la universidad?*
   Compañero(a): *No, no conduzco para llegar a la universidad.*

   Tú: *¿Conduces todos los días?*
   Compañero(a): *No, conduzco tres días por semana.*

1. conocer al presidente de la universidad
2. dar tu contraseña a tus amigos
3. decir siempre la verdad
4. hacer la tarea puntualmente
5. saber navegar por Internet
6. salir frecuentemente con amigos
7. traducir poemas del inglés al español
8. traer la computadora portátil a la clase
9. venir cansado(a) o aburrido(a) de las clases
10. ver televisión por la mañana, la tarde o la noche

 ACTIVIDAD 4 **¿Saber o conocer?** Con un(a) compañero(a), túrnense para hacer las siguientes preguntas. La persona que hace las preguntas tiene que decidir entre los verbos **saber** o **conocer**. Y ¡recuerden la **a** personal!

MODELO: hablar español
   Tú: *¿Sabes hablar español?*
   Compañero(a): *Sí, sé hablar español.*

1. el (la) compañero(a) de cuarto de…
2. Nueva York, París o Londres
3. tocar el violín
4. el (la) profesor(a) de estadística
5. Honduras
6. cómo llegar a la residencia estudiantil de…
7. el (la) nuevo(a) estudiante salvadoreño(a)
8. preparar comida hondureña o salvadoreña
9. dónde está la biblioteca municipal
10. el número del celular de…
11. la dirección electrónica de…

ACTIVIDAD 5 **Sé y conozco.** Escribe cinco cosas que sabes hacer. Luego escribe el nombre de cinco personas o lugares que conoces. Intercambia tu lista con un(a) compañero(a). Tu compañero(a) tiene que informarle a la clase lo que tú sabes y conoces y tú tienes que hacer lo mismo con la lista de tu compañero(a).

MODELO: Tu lista: *Sé jugar tenis.*
   Conozco a muchas personas que juegan tenis.

   Tu compañero(a): *Javier sabe jugar tenis.*
   Conoce a muchas personas que juegan tenis.

Gramática útil 2
Describing daily activities: Reflexive verbs

¡*graduarse*

está de

moda!

Elige la <u>Gafa de sol</u> que más te guste
y llévatela con los cristales <u>Graduados*</u>
...sin <u>ningún coste</u> adicional

This advertisement for graduated-lens sunglasses contains a verb used reflexively. What is it? What play on words does the advertisement make?

Notice that the reflexive pronoun and verb must always match the subject of the sentence: **Nosotros nos bañamos, Ellos se duermen, Mateo se lava,** etc.

Heritage Learners: Although heritage language speakers may use reflexive verbs correctly when speaking, they may not be familiar with the orthographic conventions that apply to these and other pronouns in Spanish. Point out to students that pronouns that follow gerunds or infinitives are attached to the verb. On the other hand, those that precede the verb are written as a separate word. Use the following dictation to practice this rule:

1. Los médicos que no se lavan las manos cuidadosamente después de cada consulta pueden enfermarse. 2. Usualmente, Juan se despierta a las 6:00 para llegar a tiempo a su clase a las 8:00. Hoy va a despertarse más tarde porque no hay clase. 3. Nos conocimos hace un año pero no comenzamos a vernos hasta el mes pasado.

CÓMO USARLO

Answer to questions on the ad: **graduarse**: to graduate from school, graduated lenses

1. So far, you have learned to use Spanish verbs to say what actions people are doing or to describe people and things.

Elena **habla** por teléfono con Eduardo.	*Elena **talks** on the phone with Eduardo.*
La mujer **toca** la guitarra.	*The woman **plays** the guitar.*
Tu hermano **está** cansado y aburrido.	*Your brother **is** tired and bored.*

2. Spanish has another category of verbs, called *reflexive* verbs, where the action of the verb *reflects back* on the person who is doing the action. When you use reflexive verbs in Spanish, they are often translated as *with* or *to myself, yourself, himself, herself, ourselves, yourselves, themselves* in English.

Lidia **se maquilla** todos los días.	*Lidia **puts makeup on** (**herself**) every day.*
Antes de ir a clase, yo **me ducho, me visto** y **me peino**.	*Before going to class, **I shower, get dressed** and **comb my hair**.*

3. Notice how a reflexive verb is always used with a reflexive pronoun. These pronouns always match the subject of the sentence. The action of the verb *reflects back* on the person when the pronoun is used.

Yo me acuesto a las once todos los días.	*I go to bed (**put myself to bed**) at eleven every day.*
Tú te despiertas a las diez los fines de semana.	*You get up (**wake yourself up**) at ten on the weekends.*
Nosotros nos bañamos antes de salir de casa.	*We bathe (**ourselves**) before we leave the house.*
Ellos se afeitan todos los días.	*They shave (**themselves**) every day.*

4. Almost all reflexive verbs can also be used without the reflexive pronoun to express non-reflexive actions, that is, actions that are performed on someone other than oneself.

Mateo **se lava** el pelo todos los días.	*Mateo **washes** his hair every day.*
Mateo **lava** los platos todos los días.	*Mateo **washes** the dishes every day.*

5. Reflexive pronouns can also be used to indicate *reciprocal actions*.

Roque y Rocío **se cortan** el pelo.	*Roque and Rocío **cut each other's** hair.*

CÓMO FORMARLO

LO BÁSICO

- A *reflexive verb* is one in which the action described reflects back on the subject.
- A *reflexive pronoun* is a pronoun that refers back to the subject of the sentence. Reflexive pronouns in English are *myself, yourself, herself, ourselves,* etc.

1. You conjugate reflexive verbs the same way you would any other verb. The only difference is that you must always include the reflexive pronoun.

2. Here is the reflexive verb **lavarse** conjugated in the present indicative tense.

lavarse (*to wash oneself*)	
yo	**me** lav**o**
tú	**te** lav**as**
él / ella / Ud.	**se** lav**a**
nosotros(as)	**nos** lav**amos**
vosotros(as)	**os** lav**áis**
ellos / ellas / Uds.	**se** lav**an**

3. The only difference in the way that reflexive and non-reflexive verbs are conjugated is the addition of the reflexive pronoun to the verb form. Verbs that are irregular or stem-changing when used non-reflexively have the same irregularities or stem changes when used with a reflexive pronoun.

Me despierto a las seis y media.   *I wake (**myself**) up at 6:30.*
Despierto a mi esposo a las siete.   *I wake my husband up at 7:00.*

4. When you use a reflexive verb in its infinitive form, the reflexive pronoun may attach at the end of the infinitive (most common) or go at the beginning of the entire verb phrase.

Voy a acostarme a las once.   OR: **Me voy a acostar** a las once.
Necesito acostarme a las once.   **Me necesito acostar** a las once.
Tengo que acostarme a las once.   **Me tengo que acostar** a las once.

Notice that with **gustar** (and similar verbs), the reflexive pronoun *must* be attached at the end of the infinitive.

Me gusta acostarme a las once.

5. Here are some common reflexive verbs, many of which refer to daily routine. Many reflexive verbs have a stem change, which is indicated in parenthesis.

acostarse (ue) *to go to bed*	**levantarse** *to get up*
afeitarse *to shave oneself*	**maquillarse** *to put on makeup*
bañarse *to take a bath*	**peinarse** *to brush / comb one's hair*
cepillarse el pelo *to brush one's hair*	**ponerse (la ropa)** *to put on (clothing)*
despertarse (ie) *to wake up*	**prepararse** *to get ready*
ducharse *to take a shower*	**quitarse (la ropa)** *to take off (clothing)*
lavarse *to wash oneself*	**secarse el pelo** *to dry one's hair*
lavarse el pelo *to wash one's hair*	**sentarse (ie)** *to sit down*
lavarse los dientes *to brush one's teeth*	**vestirse (i)** *to get dressed*

Standards: Take this opportunity to contrast more examples of reflexive verbs in Spanish with equivalents in English (C 4.1) in written form to demonstrate that the reflexive pronouns do not necessarily translate tangibly to English:

me lavo	I wash (myself)
te cepillas	you brush (your teeth)
nos vestimos	we dress / we get dressed
se duchan	they shower

Remember that when you use a reflexive verb as an infinitive, you still need to change the pronoun to match the subject of the sentence: **Voy a acostarme a las once, pero tú vas a acostarte a medianoche.**

Suggestion: To present these verbs, act out and "ham up" your daily routine using these verbs. A few props like a brush, comb, razor, or makeup will make the presentation memorable and create a context for learning the verbs. Then mime different verbs and have students tell what you're doing; for example, **te acuestas, te afeitas.** Have students mime actions for classmates to identify. Organize TPR-type activities to associate movements with actions.

6. Some Spanish verbs are used with reflexive pronouns to emphasize a change in state or emotion. Spanish has many more verbs that are used this way than English does. Note that some of these verbs (**casarse, comprometerse,** etc.) are usually used to express reciprocal actions, due to the nature of their meaning.

casarse *to get married*	**irse** *to leave, to go away*
comprometerse *to get engaged*	**pelearse** *to have a fight*
despedirse (i) *to say goodbye*	**preocuparse** *to worry*
divertirse (ie) *to have fun*	**quejarse** *to complain*
divorciarse *to get divorced*	**reírse (i)** *to laugh*
dormirse (ue) *to fall asleep*	**reunirse** *to meet, to get together*
enamorarse *to fall in love*	**separarse** *to separate*
enfermarse *to get sick*	

7. Here are some useful words and phrases to use with these verbs.

a veces	*sometimes*
antes	*before*
después	*after*
luego	*later*
nunca	*never*
siempre	*always*
todas las semanas	*every week*
todos los días	*every day*
… veces al día / por semana	*. . . times a day / per week*

Actividades

ACTIVIDAD 6 **Necesito…** Para vernos y sentirnos bien, todos tenemos que hacer ciertas cosas antes o después de participar en ciertas actividades. Escucha las descripciones y escoge el dibujo que le corresponde a cada descripción.

MODELO:

1. _____ 2. _____ 3. _____ 4. _____ 5. _____ 6. _____

Reflexive actions always carry the meaning *to oneself.* Reciprocal actions always carry the meaning *to each other.*

Optional: Bring visuals of a man and woman. Begin by saying: **La mujer y el hombre se casan. ¿Cómo se preparan durante su día especial? ¿Qué hace él? ¿Qué hace ella?**

Reunirse carries an accent on the **u** when conjugated: **se reúnen.**

ACTIVIDAD 7 **De visita.** Estás de visita en la casa de tu compañero(a) y quieres saber más de la rutina diaria de él (ella) y de su familia. Hazle las preguntas de la lista y si quieres, también inventa otras.

MODELOS: padres: acostarse (¿a qué hora?)
   Tú: *¿A qué hora se acuestan tus padres?*
   Compañero(a): *Generalmente se acuestan a las diez o las once de la noche.*

1. tú: lavarse el pelo (¿todos los días?)
2. abuelo: afeitarse (¿cuántas veces por semana?)
3. madre: despertarse (¿tarde o temprano?)
4. hermano: ducharse (¿por la mañana o por la noche?)
5. hermana: maquillarse (¿antes de salir para la universidad?)
6. abuela: dormirse (¿a qué hora?)
7. padre: levantarse (¿a qué hora?)
8. primo: peinarse (¿antes de salir para el colegio?)
9. tú y tus hermanos: lavarse los dientes (¿cuántas veces por día?)

ACTIVIDAD 8 **Preguntas personales.** Tú y tu compañero(a) quieren saber más sobre sus rutinas diarias. Háganse las siguientes preguntas o inventen otras que usen los verbos de la rutina diaria.

1. ¿A qué hora te acuestas durante la semana? ¿Los fines de semana?
2. ¿A qué hora te levantas durante la semana? ¿Los fines de semana?
3. ¿Qué haces después de levantarte?
4. ¿Te afeitas / maquillas todos los días?
5. ¿Prefieres bañarte o ducharte? ¿Prefieres bañarte o ducharte por la mañana o por la noche?
6. ¿Cuántas veces por semana te lavas el pelo?
7. ¿Cuántas veces al día te lavas los dientes?
8. Después de ir al gimnasio, ¿te duchas allí en el gimnasio o esperas a ducharte en casa?
9. ¿…?

ACTIVIDAD 9 **La telenovela.** Miguel y Marta son los protagonistas de una telenovela famosa. Tú eres el (la) guionista (*script writer*) y tienes que escribir una descripción del desarrollo de su relación. Sigue el modelo.

MODELO: divertirse en la fiesta de unos amigos
   Miguel y Marta se divierten en la fiesta de unos amigos.

1. enamorarse después de un mes
2. comprometerse después de un año
3. casarse en la casa de los padres de Marta
4. pelearse frecuentemente
5. quejarse mucho a sus amigos
6. separarse por seis meses
7. divorciarse después de dos años de matrimonio
8. despedirse en el aeropuerto
9. irse a diferentes regiones del país
10. por fin reunirse

Gramática útil 3
Describing actions in progress: The present progressive tense

Begin the CD-ROM activities. Do the cultural activities and reading and writing practice as you complete the corresponding text sections.

Las fotos. ¿Estás viendo las fotos?

Heritage Learners: Keep in mind that heritage language students may use the gerund in ways that are consistent with English, rather than Spanish grammar. Be particularly attentive of incorrect usage of the gerund in three cases:

a. In subject position: ***Nadando** (nadar) es un buen ejercicio.

b. After a preposition: *Lo pusieron en cárcel **por robando** (robar) un carro.

c. In reference to future action: ***Estamos teniendo** (vamos a tener) una fiesta la semana que viene.

CÓMO USARLO

1. The present progressive tense is used in Spanish to describe actions that are in progress at the moment of speaking. It is equivalent to the *is / are + -ing* structure in English.

En este momento estamos llamando a los abuelos.

Right now, we are calling the (our) grandparents.

Están comiendo ahora.

They are eating right now.

2. Note that the present progressive tense is used *much* more frequently in English than it is in Spanish. Whereas in English it is used to describe future plans, in Spanish the present indicative or the **ir + a** + infinitive structure is used instead.

Salimos con la familia este viernes.

We are going out with the family this Friday.

Vamos a salir con la familia este viernes.

We are going to go out with the family this Friday.

3. Use the present progressive in Spanish only to describe actions in which people are engaged at the moment. Do *not* use it to describe routine ongoing activities (use the present indicative), to describe generalized action (use the infinitive), or to describe future actions.

Right now:	No puedo hablar. **Estamos estudiando.**	*I can't talk. **We're studying** (right now).*
BUT:		
Routine:	**Estudio** español, biología, historia e informática.	*I am studying / I study Spanish, biology, history, and computer science.*
Generalized action:	**Estudiar** es importante.	*Studying is important.*
Future:	**Estudio** con Mario el lunes.	*I will study with Mario on Monday.*

4. The Spanish present progressive is hardly ever used in the negative. A form of the present indicative is used instead.

No estudio ahora.

I am not studying now.

CÓMO FORMARLO

LO BÁSICO

A *present participle* is the verb form that expresses a continuing or ongoing action. It is equivalent to the *-ing* form in English.

1. Form the present progressive tense by using the present indicative forms of the verb **estar** (which you learned in **Capítulo 4**) and the present participle.

> **estoy / estás / está / estamos / estáis / están** + present participle

2. Here's how to form the present participle of regular **-ar, -er,** and **-ir** verbs.

-ar verbs	-er / -ir verbs
Remove the **-ar** from the infinitive and add **-ando.**	Remove the **-er / -ir** from the infinitive and add **-iendo.**
caminar → **caminando**	ver → **viendo** escribir → **escribiendo**

Estamos caminando al centro.   *We're walking downtown.*
Estoy viendo la televisión.   *I'm watching television.*
Chali **está escribiendo** su trabajo.   *Chali is writing her paper.*

3. A few present participles are irregular.

leer: **leyendo**   oír: **oyendo**

4. All **-ir** stem-changing verbs show a stem change in their present participle as well.

e → i			
despedirse	**despidiéndose**	reírse	**riéndose**
divertirse	**divirtiéndose**	repetir	**repitiendo**
pedir	**pidiendo**	servir	**sirviendo**
o → u			
dormir	**durmiendo**	morir	**muriendo**

5. As you may have noticed in the list above, to form the present participle of reflexive verbs, you may attach the reflexive pronoun to the end of the present participle, or place it before the entire verb phrase, the same as when you use reflexive verbs in the infinitive. Note that when the pronoun is attached, the new present participle form requires an accent to maintain the correct pronunciation.

Lina **está levantándose** ahora mismo.   *Lina is getting up right now.*
Lina **se está levantando** ahora mismo.

Estoy divirtiéndome mucho.   *I'm having a lot of fun.*
Me estoy divirtiendo mucho.

Suggestion: Give out a series of reflexive verbs with the pronoun unattached and ask students to attach them either orally or on paper; for example:
me estoy riendo → estoy riéndome,
te estás bañando → estás bañándote,
se están peleando → están peleándose,
te estás afeitando → estás afeitándote,
nos estamos enamorando → estamos enamorándonos,
me estoy despidiendo → estoy despidiéndome, etc.

Actividades

Answers Act. 10: *Answers may vary. Sample answers:* 1. —¿Qué está haciendo la profesora? —Está escribiendo en la pizarra. 2. —¿Qué está haciendo la médica? —Está hablando por teléfono. 3. —¿Qué está haciendo la programadora? —Está instalando el programa / escribiendo un programa / navegando por Internet. 4. —¿Qué

ACTIVIDAD 10 **¿Qué están haciendo?** Básandote en los dibujos, pregúntale a un(a) compañero(a) qué está haciendo la persona del dibujo. Menciona la profesión de la persona también.

MODELO: camarero
Tú: *¿Qué está haciendo el camarero?*
Compañero(a): *Está sirviendo la comida.*

1. la profesora 2. la médica 3. la programadora 4. el cocinero 5. la secretaria 6. el bombero

está haciendo el cocinero? —Está preparando la cena. 5. —¿Qué está haciendo la secretaria? —Está mandando / enviando un fax.
6. —¿Qué está haciendo el bombero? —Está descansando / durmiendo.

Ahora, digan qué están haciendo el (la) profesor(a) y sus compañeros de clase en este momento.

MODELOS: *Alberto está comiendo algo.*
La profesora está hablando con un estudiante.

You might want to write down the infinitive verb forms for each person as you listen to the telephone conversation the first time. Then you can write out the sentences after.

ACTIVIDAD 11 **Preparaciones.** La familia González va a una boda (*wedding*) y todos están preparándose. Escucha la conversación telefónica de un miembro de la familia y escribe qué está haciendo cada persona mencionada. Usa la forma del modelo.

MODELO: la prima
La prima está peinándose.

Answers Act. 11: 1. El padre está afeitándose. 2. La madre está bañándose. 3. El hermano está lavándose los dientes. 4. La hermana está secándose el pelo. 5. Los abuelos están vistiéndose. 6. Las tías están maquillándose.

1. el padre
2. la madre
3. el hermano
4. la hermana
5. los abuelos
6. las tías

ACTIVIDAD 12 **¡Imagínense!** Trabaja con un(a) compañero(a) de clase. Juntos hagan una lista de diez personas famosas. Luego, digan qué (en su opinión) están haciendo en este momento. Escriban por lo menos dos frases para cada persona. ¡Sean creativos!

Sonrisas preparation: Before doing the **Expresión** activity on page 157, brainstorm with students a list of verbs and / or other words that might be helpful in writing a description of the executive's day, i.e., **organizar, almorzar, tomar una decisión,** etc.

ACTIVIDAD 13 **¡Chismosos!** Ahora, intercambien sus frases de la **Actividad 12** con las de otra pareja. Juntos escriban una columna de chismes (*gossip*) para una revista semanal. Traten de escribir de una manera interesante y descriptiva. Pueden incluir dibujos de las personas, si quieren.

Sonrisas

EXPRESIÓN. Trabaja con un(a) compañero(a) de clase para imaginar cómo es el día de un presidente de una compañía dot.com (o de otra profesión). ¿Cuál es su rutina diaria? Hagan un horario de un día típico.

MODELO: *Son las ocho de la mañana. Está preparándose para una reunión.*

EXPLORACIONES CULTURALES

Honduras y El Salvador

Países diversos. Mira los grupos de textos y fotos que describen varios aspectos de Honduras y El Salvador. Luego, di si las siguientes oraciones se refieren a la información del **Grupo 1, 2, 3 o 4.**

Grupo	Oración
1.	Esta cultura es un ejemplo de una población afro-hispana.
2.	Muchos edificios de origen español todavía existen en Honduras y El Salvador.
3.	Hay mucha diversidad étnica en El Salvador y Honduras.
4.	Las catedrales de Centroamérica son un símbolo de la fe católica.
5.	Esta ciudad maya es un descubrimiento importante.
6.	Esta cultura también existe en Nicaragua y Belice.
7.	Este sitio tiene más de 1.400 años de edad.
8.	Los amerindios son descendientes de los nativos originales de Centroamérica.

Una mujer garífuna

Grupo 1

¿Quiénes son los garífunas?

Los garífunas son de ascendencia africana, arauaca e indio-caribe. Sus antepasados, exiliados de la isla de San Vicente en 1797, viajaron a la costa Atlántica de Belice, Honduras y Nicaragua. Como no son descendientes de esclavos (*slaves*), la mayor parte de su cultura está intacta, incluso su música y arte tradicionales. Ahora cambios políticos, reformas territoriales, desastres naturales y la economía comienzan a influenciar la comunidad garífuna.

Grupo 2

Un monumento maya

Joya de Cerén, Monumento de la Humanidad de la UNESCO, es un descubrimiento de gran importancia. Es un pueblo (*town*) entero sepultado en el siglo VII por una erupción volcánica.

Como una Pompeya americana, Joya de Cerén es de inestimable valor arqueológico e histórico. Como no sabemos mucho de la vida cotidiana de los mayas, este sitio presenta una oportunidad inigualable para aprender algunos de los secretos de la cultura maya.

Grupo 3

Diversidad étnica

En Centroamérica hay cuatro grupos étnicos principales.
1. **Amerindios,** descendientes directos de las culturas indígenas de la región.
2. **Caucásicos,** descendientes de colonizadores europeos o emigrantes más recientes.
3. **Afro-hispanos,** descendientes de africanos negros.
4. La mezcla de varios grupos: **mestizos** (descendientes de europeos blancos y amerindios), **mulatos** (descendientes de europeos y africanos) y **zambos** (descendientes de africanos y amerindios).

Joya de Cerén

Un mercado al aire libre en Honduras

Grupo 4

La herencia colonial

Es posible ver muchas influencias de la época colonial española por toda Centroamérica. En Honduras y El Salvador, este período empieza en el siglo XVI y termina con la independencia en el siglo XIX. Las iglesias y catedrales son ejemplos muy típicos de la arquitectura colonial. Estos edificios abundan porque la idea de convertir las poblaciones indígenas al catolicismo fue (*was*) muy importante para los colonizadores españoles.

La arquitectura colonial

Internet

¡CONÉCTATE!

El Salvador y Honduras son dos países bastante similares, pero también existen muchas diferencias. Con un grupo de tres a cinco estudiantes, hagan un informe que compare los dos países con relación a uno de los siguientes temas. Usen los enlaces sugeridos en el sitio web de *Nexos* (http://college.hmco.com/languages/spanish/students) para ir a otros sitios web posibles.

Temas posibles:

- origen étnico
- atracciones naturales y geográficas
- museos y atracciones culturales
- deportes
- industrias principales

MODELO: *En Honduras hay...*
En El Salvador también hay... O: *Pero en El Salvador hay...*

A LEER

Antes de leer

ESTRATEGIA

Skimming for the main idea

As you already know, it's important to focus on getting the main idea from an authentic reading in Spanish, rather than trying to understand every single word. Skimming is a reading strategy that helps you get the main idea of each paragraph. When you skim, you read quickly through a paragraph looking for key words and phrases. Together, these help you grasp the main idea of each paragraph.

In the reading that follows, focus on skimming for the main idea of each paragraph. You will have an opportunity to check yourself as you progress through the reading.

ACTIVIDAD 1 Mira otra vez la información del **Grupo 1** de **Exploraciones culturales** (pág. 158). Luego, completa las siguientes oraciones sobre la cultura garífuna.

1. La cultura garífuna es bastante antigua. Tiene aproximadamente... años.
   a. 350   b. 250   c. 200   d. 150

2. Los garífunas son de origen...
   a. español   b. europeo   c. africano   d. latinoamericano

3. Los garífunas todavía tienen su propia...
   a. economía   b. grupo legislativo   c. país   d. cultura

ACTIVIDAD 2 Hay varias palabras que no conoces en el artículo. Trabaja con un(a) compañero(a) de clase para familiarizarse con algunas de las palabras y frases más importantes. Usen los cognados en negrilla **(boldface)** para relacionar las frases en inglés a la derecha (*right*) con las palabras y frases españolas a la izquierda (*left*).

1. _____ a las **culturas** que los rodeaban
2. _____ querían que los dejaran en **paz**
3. _____ están **separados** por fronteras **nacionales**
4. _____ se mantienen... **unidos**
5. _____ los **antecesores** han legado
6. _____ han permanecido fieles a su **pasado**

a. *the **ancestors** have left to them*
b. *they maintain themselves **united***
c. *they are **separated** by **national** borders*
d. *have remained faithful to their **past***
e. *to the **cultures** that surround them*
f. *they wanted to be left in **peace***

Lectura

ACTIVIDAD 3 Ahora lee el siguiente artículo sobre la cultura garífuna de Centroamérica. Presta atención en particular a las frases en negrilla. Éstas son importantes para entender la sección. Después de cada sección, vas a tener la oportunidad de ver si entiendes bien las ideas principales.

LA CULTURA GARÍFUNA

Durante siglos[1] los garífunas, que constituyen un grupo étnico disperso a lo largo de las costas de cinco países, **se han mantenido apartados**[2] de los demás pueblos[3]. Desde el principio, sus antepasados **no buscaron**[4] conquistar ni asimilarse a las culturas que los rodeaban. Sólo querían que los dejaran en paz.

En la actualidad[5], alrededor de 200.000 garífunas viven en Honduras, unos 15.000 en Belice, 6.000 en Guatemala y otros pocos miles en las islas de Barlovento de Nicaragua. **Aunque están separados por fronteras nacionales, los garífunas se mantienen no obstante unidos** en su determinación por preservar su cultura, rica en influencias africanas y americanas.

¿CIERTO O FALSO?

1. Los garífunas querían (*wanted to*) asimilarse a otras culturas.
2. Hay pueblos garífunas en Honduras, Belice, Guatemala y Nicaragua.
3. La cultura garífuna es rica en influencias europeas.

Las comunidades garífunas **conservan celosamente**[6] **su arte, su música, sus artesanías y sus creencias religiosas,** que en conjunto[7] constituyen una forma de vida muy particular. Los antecesores han legado a los garífunas su **música característica, que incorpora canciones y ritmos africanos y americanos,** y un **expresivo lenguaje** que contiene elementos arauacos y caribes —los idiomas originales de los indios caribes— y yoruba, una lengua proveniente de África Occidental. Los garífunas **han permanecido fieles a su pasado.**

¿CIERTO O FALSO?

4. Mantener las tradiciones del arte, de la música y de las creencias religiosas es muy importante para los garífunas.
5. La música garífuna tiene elementos africanos y europeos.
6. La lengua garífuna tiene elementos de lenguas caribes y de una lengua africana.

A través de[8] los siglos, los garífunas sin duda han mantenido el fuego[9] de su vida cultural. En la actualidad, **la libre práctica de sus antiguas tradiciones asegura el conocimiento de su singular historia** y contribuye a acrecentar[10] la riqueza cultural de los países que los albergan[11], compartiendo las sagradas creencias y las ricas expresiones artísticas de sus orgullosos[12] antepasados.

¿CIERTO O FALSO?

7. En realidad, los garífunas no pueden conservar sus tradiciones antiguas.
8. Los garífunas hacen contribuciones culturales a los países donde viven.

Check yourself: 1. F 2. C 3. F 4. C 5. F 6. C 7. F 8. C

---

[1]100 años [2]**se han...** *they kept themselves separate* [3]grupos étnicos [4]**no buscaron** *did not seek to* [5]**En...** Hoy, Ahora mismo [6]*jealously* [7]**en conjunto** como un grupo [8]**A...** *Across, Throughout* [9]*fire* [10]*to strengthen, increase* [11]**los albergan** *shelter them* [12]*proud*

Después de leer

Answers Act. 4: 1. Honduras 2. Tiene elementos de lenguas caribes y de yoruba. 3. Incorpora ritmos africanos y americanos.

ACTIVIDAD 4 Ahora que entiendes las ideas principales de las secciones del artículo, trabaja con un(a) compañero(a) de clase. Lean los párrafos otra vez y luego contesten las siguientes preguntas.

1. ¿Qué país centroamericano tiene la población más grande de garífunas?
2. ¿Cómo es la lengua garífuna?
3. ¿Cómo es la música garífuna?

Preparation: Note that the reading does not offer explicit answers for **Actividad 5.** Brainstorming a few advantages and disadvantages as a class will help groups into the activity.

ACTIVIDAD 5 En grupos de tres a cuatro estudiantes, identifiquen a uno o dos grupos culturales de Estados Unidos o de otros países que mantienen sus tradiciones y costumbres diferentes de las de sus países de residencia. En su opinión, ¿hay beneficios de mantenerse aislados? ¿Hay desventajas (*disadvantages*)?

A ESCRIBIR

Antes de escribir

Notice: The purpose of the activities in the **A escribir** section is to familiarize students with the writing process and the useful strategy of breaking down writing into manageable tasks.

ESTRATEGIA

Writing—Creating a topic sentence

When you write, it's important to know what point you are trying to make or the information you want to convey. Once you have chosen a topic for your written piece, you should be able to write a topic sentence that describes succinctly but completely the key ideas you are trying to get across in each paragraph of your written piece.

In the reading section, you learned to look for the main idea while reading a text. Usually this main idea is expressed by a paragraph's topic sentence. A good paragraph will always contain a topic sentence that communicates the main idea, as well as other sentences that provide supporting detail to back up the main idea.

ACTIVIDAD 1 Con un(a) compañero(a) de clase, miren el artículo sobre la cultura garífuna en la página 161. Analicen cada párrafo para identificar la oración que mejor presente la idea principal del párrafo. Ésta es la **oración temática.** Identifiquen la oración temática para cada uno de los cuatro párrafos. El modelo les da la oración temática del primer párrafo del artículo.

Answers Act. 1: (*Only the first few words in each sentence are provided.*) Paragraph 2: Aunque están separados... Paragraph 3: Las comunidades garífunas conservan... Paragraph 4: En la actualidad...

MODELO: *Durante siglos los garífunas, que constituyen un grupo étnico disperso a lo largo de las costas de cinco países, se han mantenido apartados de los demás pueblos.*

ACTIVIDAD 2 Vas a escribir unas oraciones temáticas para una composición sobre tu profesión futura o sobre la profesión de un(a) pariente que admiras, si prefieres. Primero, limita el tema a un aspecto específico que puedes desarrollar (*develop*) en tres párrafos. Puedes referirte a las técnicas que se presentan en la sección **A escribir** del **Capítulo 4** del **Cuaderno de práctica (*Workbook*).** Después, piensa en tres párrafos que puedes escribir sobre tu tema y escribe una oración temática para cada uno. Sigue el modelo, que trata el tema de las profesiones como ejemplo.

> **Tema:** *Las profesiones*
> **Aspecto específico del tema que vas a tratar:** *La profesión que quiero tener en el futuro*
> **Párrafo 1:** Description of what the profession is
>   **Oración temática:** *Me interesa el diseño gráfico.*
> **Párrafo 2:** Reason you want to have this profession
>   **Oración temática:** *Me gusta esta profesión porque me interesa el arte y también me gusta trabajar en la computadora.*
> **Párrafo 3:** What you need to do to prepare yourself for this profession
>   **Oración temática:** *Para prepararme, necesito tomar una combinación de cursos de diseño gráfico, de arte, de periodismo, de negocios y de computación.*

Escritura

ACTIVIDAD 3 Usando las oraciones temáticas de la **Actividad 1** como modelo, escribe tres oraciones temáticas para tu composición. Usa la organización que se presenta en la **Actividad 2** para ayudarte a organizar tus ideas. Trata de escribir libremente, sin pensar demasiado en los errores o en la ortografía. (Luego vas a tener la oportunidad de revisar tu trabajo.)

Después de escribir

ACTIVIDAD 4 Después de escribir tu borrador, míralo otra vez y revísalo. Usa la siguiente lista para ayudarte con las revisiones.

* ¿Tienen tus oraciones temáticas toda la información necesaria?
* ¿Imitan los modelos de las **Actividades 1** y **2**?
* ¿Hay errores de ortografía?
* ¿Corresponden los sujetos de las oraciones con los verbos correctos?
* ¿Corresponden las formas de los artículos, los sustantivos y los adjetivos?
* ¿Usas correctamente los verbos reflexivos y los verbos irregulares?

Suggestion: To review vocabulary, as a synthesis activity have students review their family trees orally and identify their family members and each one's profession.

LA FAMILIA NUCLEAR   *The nuclear family*

la madre (mamá)	*mother*
el padre (papá)	*father*
los padres	*parents*
la esposa	*wife*
el esposo	*husband*
la hija	*daughter*
el hijo	*son*
la hermana (mayor)	*(older) sister*
el hermano (menor)	*(younger) brother*
la tía	*aunt*
el tío	*uncle*
la prima	*female cousin*
el primo	*male cousin*
la sobrina	*niece*
el sobrino	*nephew*
la abuela	*grandmother*
el abuelo	*grandfather*
la nieta	*granddaughter*
el nieto	*grandson*

LA FAMILIA POLÍTICA   *In-laws*

la suegra	*mother-in-law*
el suegro	*father-in-law*
la nuera	*daughter-in-law*
el yerno	*son-in-law*
la cuñada	*sister-in-law*
el cuñado	*brother-in-law*

OTROS PARIENTES   *Other relatives*

la madrastra	*stepmother*
el padrastro	*stepfather*
la hermanastra	*stepsister*
el hermanastro	*stepbrother*
la media hermana	*half-sister*
el medio hermano	*half-brother*

LAS PROFESIONES Y CARRERAS
Professions and careers

el (la) abogado(a)	*lawyer*
el actor / la actriz	*actor / actress*
el (la) arquitecto(a)	*architect*
el (la) artista	*artist*
el (la) bombero(a)	*firefighter*
el (la) camarero(a)	*waiter, waitress*
el (la) carpintero(a)	*carpenter*
el (la) cocinero(a)	*cook, chef*
el (la) contador(a)	*accountant*
el (la) dentista	*dentist*
el (la) dependiente	*salesclerk*
el (la) diseñador(a) gráfico(a)	*graphic designer*
el (la) dueño(a) de...	*owner of . . .*
el (la) enfermero(a)	*nurse*
el (la) gerente de...	*manager of . . .*
el hombre / la mujer de negocios	*businessman / businesswoman*
el (la) ingeniero(a)	*engineer*
el (la) maestro(a)	*teacher*
el (la) mecánico(a)	*mechanic*
el (la) médico(a)	*doctor*
el (la) peluquero(a)	*barber / hairdresser*
el (la) periodista	*journalist*
el (la) plomero(a)	*plumber*
el (la) policía	*policeman / woman*
el (la) programador(a)	*programmer*
el (la) secretario(a)	*secretary*
el (la) trabajador(a)	*worker*
el (la) veterinario(a)	*veterinarian*

EN EL BAÑO   *In the bathroom*

el cepillo	*hairbrush*
el cepillo de dientes	*toothbrush*
el champú	*shampoo*
el desodorante	*deodorant*
el jabón	*soap*
el maquillaje	*makeup, cosmetics*
la máquina de afeitar	*electric razor*
la pasta de dientes	*toothpaste*
el peine	*comb*
la rasuradora	*razor*
la toalla	*towel*
la toalla de mano	*hand towel*

VERBOS CON LA FORMA *YO* IRREGULAR

conducir (-zc)	to drive; to conduct
conocer (-zc)	to know a person, to be familiar with
dar (doy)	to give
decir (-g) (i)	to say, to tell
hacer (-g)	to make; to do
oír (oigo)	to hear
poner (-g)	to put
saber (sé)	to know a fact, to know how to
salir (-g)	to leave; to go out (*with*)
traducir (-zc)	to translate
traer (-go)	to bring
venir (-g) (ie)	to come
ver (veo)	to see

VERBOS REFLEXIVOS

Acciones físicas   *Physical actions*

acostarse (ue)	to go to bed
afeitarse	to shave oneself
bañarse	to take a bath
cepillarse el pelo	to brush one's hair
despertarse (ie)	to wake up
dormirse (ue)	to fall asleep
ducharse	to take a shower
lavarse	to wash oneself
lavarse el pelo	to wash one's hair
lavarse los dientes	to brush one's teeth
levantarse	to get up
maquillarse	to put on makeup
peinarse	to brush / comb one's hair
ponerse (la ropa)	to put on (*clothing*)
prepararse	to get ready
quitarse (la ropa)	to take off (*clothing*)
secarse el pelo	to dry one's hair
sentarse (ie)	to sit down
vestirse (i)	to get dressed

Estados / emociones   *States / emotions*

casarse	to get married
comprometerse	to get engaged
despedirse (i)	to say goodbye
divertirse (ie)	to have fun
divorciarse	to get divorced
enamorarse	to fall in love
enfermarse	to get sick
irse	to leave, to go away
pelearse	to have a fight
preocuparse	to worry
quejarse	to complain
reírse (i)	to laugh
reunirse	to meet, to get together
separarse	to get separated

OTROS VERBOS

bañar	to swim; to give someone a bath
despertar (ie)	to wake someone up
lavar	to wash
levantar	to raise, to lift
manejar	to drive
quitar	to take off
secar	to dry something
vestir (i)	to dress someone

OTRAS PALABRAS Y EXPRESIONES

a veces	sometimes
antes	before
después	after
luego	later
nunca	never
siempre	always
todas las semanas	every week
...veces al día / por semana	. . . times a day / per week

¿Adónde vas?

Communication

By the end of this chapter you will be able to:
- talk about means of transportation
- say where things are located
- talk about where you are and where you are going
- give directions
- agree and disagree
- indicate and talk about what you plan to buy
- make polite requests and commands
- refer to objects located close to you, farther away, and at a distance

Cultures

By the end of this chapter you will have learned about:
- Mexico
- the indigenous populations of Mexico
- ways to make polite requests in Spanish
- specialty stores and supermarkets
- where Mexico City teens go to have fun

Un policía mexicano les da direcciones a dos turistas en la Ciudad de México.

LA COMUNIDAD LOCAL

El mundo se hace cada día más pequeño. Los avances en la tecnología, las telecomunicaciones y el transporte internacional hacen posible el contacto casi inmediato con el resto del mundo. Pero esto no quiere decir que los vecinos, barrios y centros comerciales de nuestras comunidades locales ya no tienen importancia. En este capítulo vas a explorar la importancia de la comunidad local y tu lugar en ella.

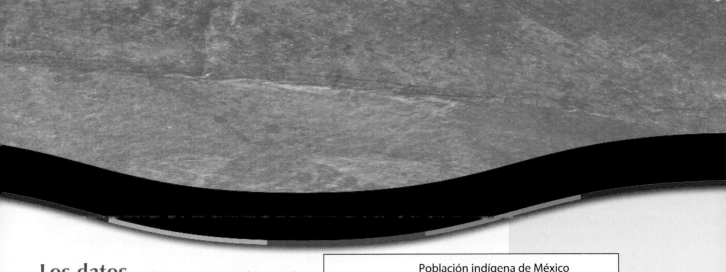

Los datos

Mira la información de los gráficos sobre México y sus varios idiomas. Luego contesta las preguntas.

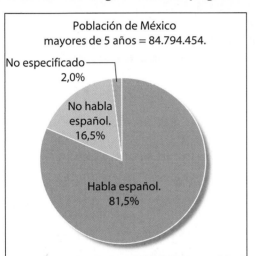

Población de México
mayores de 5 años = 84.794.454.

No especificado
2,0%

No habla
español.
16,5%

Habla español.
81,5%

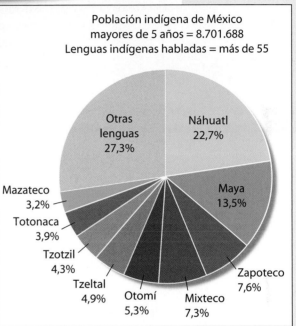

Población indígena de México
mayores de 5 años = 8.701.688
Lenguas indígenas habladas = más de 55

Otras lenguas 27,3%

Náhuatl 22,7%

Mazateco 3,2%

Totonaca 3,9%

Tzotzil 4,3%

Tzeltal 4,9%

Otomí 5,3%

Mixteco 7,3%

Zapoteco 7,6%

Maya 13,5%

❶ ¿Qué idioma habla la mayoría de la población mexicana?
❷ ¿Cuál es la segunda (*second*) lengua indígena en número de hablantes?
❸ ¿Cuál de las siguientes oraciones mejor describe las lenguas indígenas de México?
   a. La mayoría de la población mexicana habla maya.
   b. Hay muchos grupos indígenas, cada uno con su propio (*own*) idioma.
   c. No hay muchos idiomas indígenas en México.

¡Adivina!

¿Qué sabes de México? (Las respuestas están en la página 190.) Di si las siguientes oraciones son ciertas o falsas.

❶ D.F. se refiere al Distrito Federal, otro nombre para la Ciudad de México.
❷ México se divide en estados, como Estados Unidos.
❸ La geografía de México es más o menos igual por todas partes del país.
❹ México tiene dos penínsulas grandes.
❺ México es la fuente (*source*) de dos civilizaciones indígenas prehispánicas muy importantes: la maya y la inca.

Standards: At the beginning of this chapter, interview your class to find out what students know about Mexico. At the end of the chapter, repeat the same questions and compare. Sample questions: ¿Conoces México? ¿Qué partes? ¿Qué sabes de la gente mexicana / la historia / la economía / el arte / la música?

¡IMAGÍNATE!

Vocabulario útil 1

SERGIO: Oye, ¿adónde vas con tanta prisa?

JAVIER: Primero tengo que ir al gimnasio, y después al **centro estudiantil.**

SERGIO: Pero, ¿por qué la prisa, hombre?

JAVIER: Después del centro estudiantil, tengo que ir al **banco** a sacar dinero y después al **súper** para comprar la comida para la cena.

SERGIO: ¿Vas **en bicicleta**?

JAVIER: No, voy **a pie…**

Preparation: Make a transparency or get copies of your campus map. Have students label the places on the map in Spanish and / or move a stick figure around on the map and ask: **¿Dónde está Pedro? ¿Adónde va?**

EN LA UNIVERSIDAD

las canchas de tenis

la piscina

la pista de atletismo

la cancha/el campo de fútbol

el centro estudiantil

el auditorio

el estadio

el dormitorio/ la residencia estudiantil

el edificio

EN LA CIUDAD O EN EL PUEBLO

el aeropuerto	*airport*	la iglesia	*church*
el almacén	*department store*	la joyería	*jewelry store*
el apartamento	*apartment*	el mercado	*market*
el banco	*bank*	el museo	*museum*
el barrio	*neighborhood*	la oficina	*office*
el cajero	*automated teller*	la oficina de	*post office*
automático	*machine*	correos	
	(ATM)	la papelería	*stationery store*
la casa	*house*	el parque	*park*
el centro	*mall*	la pizzería	*pizzeria*
comercial		la plaza	*plaza*
el cine	*cinema*	el restaurante	*restaurant*
el cuarto	*the room*	el supermercado	*supermarket*
la estación de	*train /*	el teatro	*theater*
trenes /	*bus station*	la tienda…	*store*
autobuses		…de música	*music store*
el estacionamiento	*parking lot*	…de ropa	*clothing store*
la farmacia	*pharmacy*	…de videos	*video store*
el hospital	*hospital*	el (la) vecino(a)	*neighbor*

MEDIOS DE TRANSPORTE

a pie	*on foot, walking*
en autobús	*by bus*
en bicicleta	*on bicycle*
en carro / coche / automóvil	*by car*
en metro	*on the subway*
en tren	*by train*
en / por avión	*by plane*

Since many of the places in the city are cognates, cover the right-hand columns and try to identify as many as you can without looking at the English translation.

Other places of worship beside **iglesia** are: **la sinagoga, el templo, la mezquita** (*mosque*).

Suggestion: Introduce vocabulary while discussing your own city or town. Sample questions: ¿**Tenemos un aeropuerto?** ¿**Cómo es el aeropuerto (pequeño o grande)?** ¿**Cómo se llama el centro comercial?** ¿**Cómo se llama el barrio más elegante?** ¿**Cuántos cines hay en…?**

Suggestion: Another helpful context is tourists in Mexico. Start by saying: **Siempre hay muchos turistas en México. ¿Adónde van?** Draw a **plaza** on the board; locate a church at one end. Continue with ¿**Qué hay en la plaza?** You can work in most of the vocabulary words on the **plaza**.

In Mexico, **carro** is more commonly used than **coche**, and **camión** is more common for *bus* than **autobús**.

Actividades

ACTIVIDAD 1 **En la ciudad.** Indica adónde debe ir cada persona, según lo que quiere hacer o comprar. ¡No te preocupes si no entiendes todas las palabras!

1. —Es hora de comer. Tengo muchas ganas de comerme una pizza enorme.

2. —¿Escuchaste el último disco compacto de Albita? ¡Es fenomenal! Tengo que comprar ese CD.

3. —No puedo hacer las compras todavía. Primero necesito ir a sacar dinero.

4. —El doctor dice que necesito esta medicina para controlar mi alergia.

5. —No quiero cocinar en casa. Quiero salir a comer.

6. —Necesito comprar unos cuadernos y bolígrafos para mi clase de literatura.

7. —¿Qué te parece si alquilamos unos videos para ver después de la cena?

Suggestion: Ask students where they buy specific items: ¿**Dónde compras pizzas?** ¿**hamburguesas?** ¿**fruta?** ¿**papel?** ¿**ropa?**

Answers Act. 1: 1. pizzería 2. tienda de música 3. banco / cajero automático 4. farmacia 5. restaurante 6. papelería 7. tienda de videos

In some varieties of Spanish, to indicate playing a sport, **jugar** is used with the preposition **a: jugar al tenis, jugar al fútbol.** Usage of **a** with **jugar** varies from region to region.

ACTIVIDAD 2 **¿Adónde van?** Habla con varios compañeros. ¿Adónde van? ¿Qué van a hacer en ese sitio? También diles adónde vas tú y por qué vas allí.

MODELO: Tú: *¿Adónde vas?*
Compañero(a): *Voy al dormitorio.*
Tú: *¿Qué vas a hacer allí?*
Compañero(a): *Estoy cansado(a). Voy a descansar.*

Ideas posibles:

jugar (al) tenis / fútbol	hacer la tarea
levantar pesas	mirar televisión
correr	estudiar
nadar	cenar
cocinar	trabajar
dormir	¿…?

ACTIVIDAD 3 **¿Vas a pie?** Tu compañero(a) tiene que ir a varios sitios. Pregúntale cómo piensa llegar a esos sitios. Inventa destinos lógicos para cada forma de transporte.

MODELO: Tú: *¿Cómo piensas ir a la fiesta de Carmen?*
Compañero(a): *Voy a ir en autobús.*

 1.

 2.

 3.

 4.

 5.

 6.

La diversidad lingüística en el mundo de habla hispana

Todas las lenguas exhiben variaciones geográficas. El español de México no es exactamente igual al español de Puerto Rico o al español de España. Estas variantes regionales de una lengua se llaman *dialectos*.

En general, el léxico o vocabulario es lo que más varía de una zona dialectal a otra en el mundo hispano. Por ejemplo, algunas de las palabras referentes a los medios de transporte exhiben variación dialectal: **carro, máquina, auto, automóvil** y **coche** se usan en diferentes zonas del mundo hispano. De la misma manera, **autobús, bus, guagua, colectivo, camión, ómnibus** y **micro** son diferentes maneras de referirse a *bus*.

La fonología o pronunciación del español también varía de una zona dialectal a otra. Por ejemplo, en algunos lugares del mundo hispano, la letra **s** se puede pronunciar con aspiración, como el sonido inicial de la palabra *hand*. En los dialectos que aspiran, la palabra **español** se pronuncia frecuentemente como [ehpañol].

Es importante recordar que las diferencias entre los dialectos del español son relativamente pocas. Por esta razón, dos hablantes del español de zonas dialectales muy distantes generalmente pueden comunicarse con facilidad.

PRÁCTICA. ¿Puedes dar unos ejemplos de variación léxica dentro de EEUU o entre los países de habla inglesa del mundo?

Standards: Point out that pronunciation can vary from one region to another in Spanish and English (C 4.1). Help suggest English words by asking **¿Cómo se dice refresco en EEUU?** (e.g., *pop, soda,* etc.) **¿Cómo se dice** *elevator / policeman* **en Inglaterra?** (e.g., *lift, bobby*)

Vocabulario útil 2

DULCE: Pero, mujer, ¿adónde vas con tanta prisa?

CHELA: Quiero ir al gimnasio antes de **hacer las compras** en el supermercado.

DULCE: Pero si no es tarde, son sólo las tres.

CHELA: Ya sé, pero si me da tiempo, quiero ir a la **carnicería** para comprar unos **bistecs**.

Notice: **Carnicería** and **carnecería** are linguistic variants.

In Spanish-speaking countries, the ending **-ía** indicates a store that specializes in a certain product. It is clear what the store specializes in because the name of the store contains the product. Notice the names of stores that end in **-ía** in *Vocabulario útil 1*. Notice that the **í** always carries an accent. Can you name any other specialty stores that end this way?

Suggestion: Converse with students about what they buy where and what products they prefer. Sample questions: ¿Qué compras en la carnicería? ¿Te gusta el bistec / el jamón / el pollo? ¿Comes carne? ¿Qué compras en el supermercado? ¿Prefieres los refrescos o la leche? ¿Cómo vas al supermercado?

HACER LAS COMPRAS...

En la carnicería

En el supermercado

La comida

Actividades

ACTIVIDAD 4 **En el barrio.** Hoy en día, las tiendas especializadas como la carnicería y la panadería no son tan comunes como en el pasado. En las ciudades grandes es más típico ir a un supermercado grande para comprar todos los comestibles en un solo sitio. Los mercados y las tiendas especializadas no pueden competir con los precios de los supermercados más grandes, pero sí ofrecen la oportunidad de hablar con los vecinos y los vendedores en un ambiente agradable e íntimo. Formen grupos de cuatro. Contesten las siguientes preguntas y presenten sus respuestas a la clase.

1. ¿Dónde prefieres hacer las compras, en un supermercado o en pequeñas tiendas especializadas? ¿Por qué?
2. ¿Cuál es el mejor lugar cerca de la universidad para comprar pan? ¿carne? ¿fruta? ¿vegetales?
3. ¿Comes carne? ¿Cuántas veces a la semana comes carne? ¿Dónde?
4. Si eres vegetariano(a), ¿comes mucha fruta y vegetales? ¿Dónde compras la fruta y los vegetales?
5. ¿Qué te importa más cuando haces las compras, el precio de los productos, su calidad (*quality*) o las personas que trabajan en la tienda?
6. ¿Crees que la idea de ir de compras a varias tiendas especializadas es más común en Estados Unidos o en Europa y otros países?

ACTIVIDAD 5 **Las compras.** Formen grupos de cuatro. Cada persona en el grupo debe preparar una lista de las compras que tiene que hacer. Intercambien (*Exchange*) las listas entre el grupo. Túrnense para describir lo que cada persona quiere comprar. Después preparen recomendaciones para cada persona sobre dónde ir de compras.

MODELO: *Mark necesita comprar unas salchichas, pan, queso y unos refrescos. Mark debe ir a la carnicería para las salchichas y al supermercado para el pan, el queso y los refrescos.*

ACTIVIDAD 6 **El día de hoy.** Formen grupos de tres. Cada persona debe preparar una descripción de sus hábitos de consumidor. Intercambien las descripciones y túrnense para leerlas en voz alta. El grupo tiene que adivinar a quién describe cada descripción.

MODELO: Descripción: *Nunca voy al supermercado porque prefiero comer en restaurantes como McDonalds y Burger King. Cuando invito a amigos a comer en casa, voy a una pizzería y compro todo lo que necesito.*
Grupo: *¡Es Mark!*

Optional: Expand these activities with a class chat about transportation. Sample questions: ¿Vas de compras a pie, en coche, en metro? ¿Cuáles son unas ciudades norteamericanas con metro? ¿Conoces unas ciudades en Europa o en otros lugares con metro? ¿Cuánto cuesta ir en metro en… ? En nuestro(a) pueblo / ciudad / campus universitario, ¿cuál es un sitio agradable para ir en bicicleta? ¿Hay autobuses en nuestro(a) pueblo / ciudad / campus universitario? ¿Dónde te gusta ir a pie? ¿Te gusta viajar en avión?

A VER

Antes de ver el video

 **For additional practice, do the** *Nexos* **website and / or CD-ROM video exercises.**

Answers Act. 1: 1. gimnasio 2. centro estudiantil, banco 3. a pie 4. gimnasio, supermercado, carnicería

Answers Act. 2: 1. b 2. c 3. a 4. e 5. d

ACTIVIDAD 1 Mira las fotos y las conversaciones en las páginas 168 y 171. Luego completa las siguientes oraciones sobre las personas de las fotos.

1. Javier habla con Sergio. Javier va al _____.
2. Javier también tiene que ir al _____ y al _____.
3. Javier va a ir _____.
4. Chela habla con Dulce. Chela va al _____, al _____ y si tiene tiempo, a la _____.

ACTIVIDAD 2 Aquí hay una lista de frases que se usan en el video que contienen palabras que no conoces. Trabaja con un(a) compañero(a) de clase para ver si pueden encontrar el equivalente correcto en inglés para cada una.

1. _____ Oye, ¿adónde vas con tanta **prisa**?
2. _____ Tal vez hoy es mi día de **suerte**.
3. _____ Nunca sabes cuándo vas a conocer a la persona de tus **sueños**.
4. _____ **Siga derecho** hasta aquella **esquina**.
5. _____ **En la esquina, doble a la derecha** y camine dos **cuadras**.

a. *You never know when you're going to meet the person of your* ***dreams***.
b. *So, where are you going in such a* ***hurry***?
c. *Perhaps today is my* ***lucky*** *day*.
d. ***At the corner turn (to the) right*** *and walk two* ***blocks***.
e. ***Continue straight*** *until that* ***corner***.

ESTRATEGIA

Watching facial expressions

As you learned in **Capítulo 3,** watching body language can often help you understand what the characters in the video are saying and feeling. The same is true of watching facial expressions: a smile, a frown, a raised eyebrow, or a laugh. These gestures, combined with the actual words you hear, give you a more complete understanding of what the character is trying to express.

El video

Now watch the video segment for **Capítulo 6** without sound. As you watch, focus on the characters' facial expressions and see if they give you a better understanding of what they are saying. Watch it a second time with sound.

Después de ver el video

ACTIVIDAD 3 Completa la tabla siguiente para indicar si las expresiones faciales de las varias personas contribuyen signficativamente al sentido de lo que dicen. Cuando contestas que sí, indica qué emoción expresa cada expresión. (En algunos casos puede haber más de una emoción.)

Answers Act. 3. 1. no 2. sí (humor) 3. sí (curiosidad) 4. no 5. no 6. no 7. sí (humor) 8. sí (melancolía)

Emociones posibles: aburrimiento (*boredom*), celos (*jealousy*), cólera (*anger*), humor, irritación, melancolía, curiosidad

	Sí	No	¿Qué emoción?
1. Javier: Primero tengo que ir al gimnasio y después al centro estudiantil.			
2. Sergio: Dicen que el supermercado es el lugar ideal para conocer a la mujer ideal.			
3. Dulce: ¿A la carnicería? ¿Viene alguna persona especial a cenar?			
4. Chela: Gracias. Nos vemos luego.			
5. Señora: Muchas gracias, joven.			
6. Javier: Siga derecho hasta aquella esquina.			
7. Sergio: Algún día, mi amigo, algún día.			
8. Chela: Sí, todavía sola.			

Conexión cultural. Mira el segmento cultural que está al final del episodio. Luego, en grupos de tres a cuatro, comparen la vida de ciudad en su país con la del mundo hispano.

ACTIVIDAD 4 Ahora mira el video una vez más y pon las actividades de Javier y Chela en el orden correcto. Luego, contesta las siguientes preguntas. Mira el video una vez más para obtener toda la información si te es necesario.

Javier

_____ ir al banco

_____ ir al gimnasio

_____ ir al centro estudiantil

_____ ir al supermercado

Chela

_____ ir al gimnasio

_____ ir a la carnicería

_____ ir al supermercado

1. Según Sergio, ¿el supermercado es el lugar ideal para conocer a quién?
2. ¿Qué va a comprar Javier en el súper?
3. ¿Cómo va a ir Javier?
4. ¿Va alguien especial a la cena de Chela?
5. ¿Adónde quiere ir la mujer que le pide direcciones a Javier?
6. ¿Cuántas oportunidades de conocerse tienen Javier y Chela?

¿Te interesan los programas de Casa Central? ¿Qué servicio te interesa más? To learn more about Ann R. Álvarez and her philanthropic work, see the chapter links on the *Nexos* website (http://college.hmco.com/languages/spanish/students).

VOCES DE LA COMUNIDAD

Ann R. Álvarez

❝ Las jóvenes profesionales deben encontrar su pasión en la vida, perseverar para lograr (*achieve*) sus objetivos profesionales y personales y comprometerse a seguir estudiando y aprendiendo durante toda su carrera. ❞

La puertorriqueña Ann R. Álvarez es presidente de Casa Central Social Services, la mayor organización de servicios sociales hispanos en Chicago. Casa Central tiene como misión crear y ofrecer programas comunitarios que promueven el bienestar de individuos y familias. Los servicios que ofrece Casa Central para familias sin hogares (*homeless*), jóvenes y ancianos se consideran programas modelo al nivel (*level*) nacional. Desde 1989, Ann trabaja incansablemente para aumentar la participación de corporaciones, iglesias y el gobierno en causas y proyectos que beneficien a las diferentes comunidades de Chicago. La revista electrónica *Today's Chicago Woman* seleccionó a Álvarez entre las cien mujeres que están efectuando cambios positivos y significativos en la zona de Chicago, y la revista *Hispanic Business* seleccionó a Casa Central como una de las veinticinco organizaciones filantrópicas hispanas más importantes de Estados Unidos.

Gramática útil 1
Indicating location: Prepositions of location

CÓMO USARLO Suggestion: Write **de** + **el** = **del**; **a** + **el** = **al** on the board for emphasis.

Use prepositions of location to say where something is positioned in relation to other objects, or where it is located in general.

La carnicería está **al lado del** supermercado.

La farmacia está **lejos de** aquí.

El restaurante está **frente a** la iglesia.

El café está **dentro del** almacén.

*The butcher shop is **next to the** supermarket.*

*The pharmacy is **far from** here.*

*The restaurant is **facing** the church.*

*The café is **inside** the department store.*

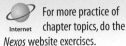

For more practice of chapter topics, do the *Nexos* website exercises.

CÓMO FORMARLO Optional: Return to the concept of the campus map and describe spatial relationships between buildings such as **frente a, lejos de, cerca de,** etc.

1. Commonly used prepositions of location include the following.

al lado de	*next to, on the side of*	La farmacia está **al lado del** hospital.
entre	*between*	La farmacia está **entre** el hospital y la oficina de correos.
delante de	*in front of*	La joyería está **delante del** hotel.
enfrente de	*in front of, opposite*	El joyería está **enfrente del** hotel.
frente a	*in front of, facing, opposite*	La joyería está **frente al** hotel.
detrás de	*behind*	El hotel está **detrás de** la joyería.
debajo de	*below, underneath*	Los libros están **debajo de** la mesa.
encima de	*on top of, on*	El cuaderno está **encima de** los libros.
sobre	*on, above*	La comida está **sobre** la mesa.
dentro de	*inside of*	Las frutas están **dentro del** refrigerador.
fuera de	*outside of*	El pan está **fuera del** refrigerador.
lejos de	*far from*	El súper está **lejos de** la universidad.
cerca de	*close to*	La panadería está **cerca de** la universidad.

En la última cuadra, **frente al** banco, va a ver el centro comercial.

Usage of **enfrente de, delante de,** and **frente a** varies from country to country. However, they are more or less equivalent to each other.

Some of these prepositions can be used without the **de** as adverbs. For example, **El museo está cerca.**

Remember that when **de** or **a** follows a preposition of location, they combine with **el** to form **del** and **al**: **frente al hotel, dentro del refrigerador.**

2. Since these prepositions provide information about *location*, they are frequently used with the verb **estar**, which, as you learned in **Capítulo 4,** is used to say where something is located.

Suggestion: Use yourself, objects, and students to illustrate the prepositions of location. For example, have two or three students stand in front of the class, place yourself between them to illustrate: **Estoy entre A y B.** Walk to the classroom door and show yourself inside and outside of the classroom. Place an object on top of and another object below your desk. Hint: Students will always remember **debajo de,** if you can crawl under your desk! Move from presentation to practice. Gradually elicit prepositions of location from students by placing a pen, book, or student in different locations or using a simple board drawing.

Actividades

Answers Act. 1: Answers will vary. Sample responses: 1. Los apuntes están al lado de la computadora. 2. Los cuadernos están entre la mesa y el fax. 3. El diccionario de español está debajo del escritorio. 4. El CD portátil está enfrente del monitor. 5. Mi asistente electrónico está sobre la mesa. 6. Mi mochila está encima del / sobre el escritorio.

 ACTIVIDAD 1 **¿Dónde está…?** Llegas a clase y te das cuenta (*you realize*) que no tienes varias cosas que necesitas. Llama a tu compañero(a) de cuarto para pedirle que te traiga (*he or she bring*) las cosas que necesitas. Explícale a tu compañero(a) dónde están los siguientes objetos en tu cuarto.

1. los apuntes
2. los cuadernos
3. el diccionario de español
4. el CD portátil
5. mi asistente electrónico
6. mi mochila

 ACTIVIDAD 2 **Nuestro salón de clase.** Ahora, en grupos de tres, describan dónde están varios objetos en su salón de clase.

 ACTIVIDAD 3 **Treviño.** En grupos de tres, estudien el mapa del pueblo de Treviño. Luego, túrnense para describir dónde están situados por lo menos diez edificios o sitios.

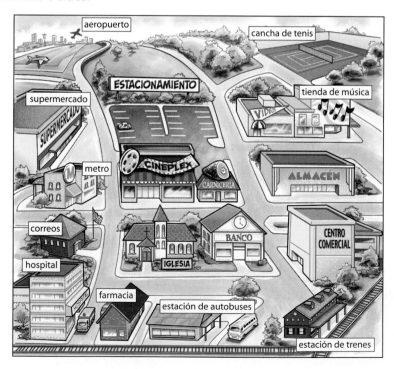

ACTIVIDAD 4 **Nuestra universidad.** Ahora, trabajen en grupos de tres a cinco para dibujar un mapa de su universidad. Incluyan por lo menos seis edificios principales. Luego, alguien en el grupo describe la posición de uno de los edificios y el grupo tiene que adivinar qué edificio se describe. Túrnense para dar las descripciones.

Gramática útil 2
Telling others what to do: Commands with *usted* and *ustedes*

CÓMO USARLO

1. You have already been seeing command forms in direction lines. In Spanish, there are two sets of singular command forms, since there are two ways to address people directly (**tú** and **usted**). The informal commands, which you will learn in **Capítulo 7,** are used with people you would address as **tú.** In this chapter you will learn formal commands, as well as plural commands with **ustedes.**

2. Command forms are not used as frequently in Spanish as they are in English. For example, in **Capítulo 4** you learned that courteous, softening expressions are often used instead of commands: **¿Le importa si uso la computadora?** instead of **Déjeme** (*Let me*) **usar la computadora.**

3. However, one situation in which command forms are almost always used is in giving instructions to someone, such as directions to a specific location.

Siga derecho hasta la esquina. Allí **doble** a la izquierda.	*Continue straight ahead until the corner. Turn left there.*
Camine tres cuadras hasta llegar a la farmacia. Allí **doble** a la derecha y **cruce** la calle. La carnicería está al lado del banco.	*Walk three blocks until you arrive at the pharmacy. There, turn right and cross the street. The butcher shop is next to the bank.*

Mira este anuncio mexicano para un servicio de televisión. ¿Puedes encontrar los dos mandatos formales?

Answers: déjese, prepárese

CÓMO FORMARLO

LO BÁSICO

A *command* form, also known as an *imperative* form, is used to issue a direct order to someone you are addressing: *Vaya* **a la esquina y** *doble* **a la derecha.** (*Go to the corner and turn right.*)

1. Study the following chart that shows the singular formal (**usted**) and plural (**ustedes**) command forms of the verb **seguir** (*to go, to follow*).

	singular	plural
affirmative	**siga**	**sigan**
negative	**no siga**	**no sigan**

2. Here are the rules for forming the **usted** and **ustedes** command forms of most verbs.

◆ Take the **yo** form of the verb in the present indicative. Remove the **-o** and add **-a** for **-er / -ir** verbs or **-e** for **-ar** verbs, to create the **usted** command.

poner: → pongo → pong- + -a → **ponga**

◆ Add an **-n** to the **usted** command form to create the **ustedes** command.

ponga → **pongan**

By using the **yo** form of the present indicative you have already incorporated any irregularities in the verb. Now they automatically carry over into the command form.

Heritage Learners: Some U.S. Spanish speakers may tend to use the diphthongs **ie** and **ue** in infinitives such as **pensar, tener, sentir,** and **empezar.** Emphasize the correct infinitive forms of stem-changing verbs.

infinitive	**yo** form minus the **-o** ending	plus **-e / -en** for **-ar** verbs OR **-a / -an** for **-er / -ir** verbs	**usted / ustedes** command forms
hablar	habl-	+ -e / -en	**hable / hablen**
pensar	piens-	+ -e / -en	**piense / piensen**
tener	teng-	+ -a / -an	**tenga / tengan**
decir	dig-	+ -a / -an	**diga / digan**
escribir	escrib-	+ -a / -an	**escriba / escriban**
servir	sirv-	+ -a / -an	**sirva / sirvan**

3. A few command forms require spelling changes to maintain the original pronunciation of the verb.

◆ verbs ending in **-car**: change the **c → qu**:

buscar: → **busco** → **busque / busquen**

◆ verbs ending in **-zar**: change the **z → c**:

empezar: → **empiezo** → **empiece / empiecen**

◆ verbs ending in **-gar**: change the **g → gu**:

pagar: → **pago** → **pague / paguen**

4. A few verbs have irregular **usted** and **ustedes** command forms.

dar	**dé / den**
estar	**esté / estén**
ir	**vaya / vayan**
saber	**sepa / sepan**
ser	**sea / sean**

5. When you use command forms of reflexive verbs, you attach the reflexive pronoun to the *end* of *affirmative* **usted / ustedes** commands, and place it *before* *negative* **usted / ustedes** commands. A written accent is added to the stressed syllable of the affirmative command form in order to retain the original pronunciation.

Prepárese para una sorpresa.   *Prepare yourself for a surprise.*
No se ponga nervioso.   ***Don't get*** *nervous.*

6. Here are some useful words and phrases, some of which you already know, to use when giving directions. Remember, you will be using **usted** and **ustedes** command forms in this situation since you are talking to people you don't know.

¿Me puede decir cómo llegar a...?   *Can you tell me how to get to . . . ?*
¿Me puede decir dónde queda...?   *Can you tell me where . . . is located?*
Cómo no. Vaya...   *Of course. Go . . .*
   a la avenida   *to the avenue . . .*
   a la calle...   *to the street . . .*
   a la derecha   *to the right*
   a la esquina   *to the corner*
   a la izquierda   *to the left*
   dos cuadras   *two blocks*
   (todo) derecho   *(straight) ahead*

bajar (baje)	*to get down from, to get off of (a bus, etc.)*	**cruzar (cruce)**	*to turn*
		doblar (doble)	*to turn*
caminar (camine)	*to walk*	**seguir (i) (siga)**	*to continue*
		subir (suba)	*to go up, to get on*

One commonly used command in Spanish is **¡Vamos!** (*Let's go!*), which the speaker uses to refer to several people, including himself or herself. Because it includes the speaker in the action, it is used instead of an **ustedes** command form.

Suggestion: Play "Simon Says" (**Simón dice**). Sample prompts: **Digan "adiós", Toquen la cabeza / mesa, Toquen su libro de español, Escriban su nombre en el aire, Den su libro a un compañero, Saquen sus apuntes**, etc.

Actividades

ACTIVIDAD 5 **Los anuncios.** El campo de la publicidad hace uso frecuente de los mandatos formales para tratar de convencer al público que compre o use su producto. Completa los anuncios con mandatos, usando la forma de **usted** de los verbos entre paréntesis.

Answers Act. 5: 1. Abra, Ponga, Tenga 2. Venga, Cocine, Compre 3. espere, Llame, Sirva 4. trabaje, Venga, Descubra 5. Levante, Haga, Reciba 6. Navegue, Visite, Tome, Escriba

1. (abrir, poner, tener)

BANCO MUNDIAL **$**
___ una cuenta en Banco Mundial.
___ su dinero en nuestras manos.
___ confianza en nuestros profesionales.

2. (venir, cocinar, comprar)

SUPERMERCADO CENTRAL
___ al Supermercado Central para hacer las compras.
___ con la comida más fresca y más natural de la ciudad.
___ las comidas favoritas de sus hijos.

3. (esperar, llamar, servir)

PIZZERÍA ITALIA
No ___ .
___ al 555-6677 para ordenar su pizza.
___ la pizza más fresca y deliciosa en su propia casa en menos de treinta minutos.

4. (trabajar, venir, descubrir)

Restaurante París
Esta noche, no ___ en la cocina.
___ *al Restaurante París para disfrutar de nuestro ambiente relajante y nuestro excelente servicio.*
___ *nuestra riquísima cocina francesa.*

5. (levantar, hacer, recibir)

GIMNASIO LA SALUD
___ pesas en un ambiente agradable.
___ ejercicio todos los días para mantenerse en forma.
___ un relajante masaje después de su sesión de ejercicios.

6. (navegar, visitar, tomar, escribir)

CAFÉ CIBERESPACIO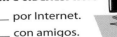
___ por Internet.
___ con amigos.
___ un refresco.
¡ ___ e-mails a todos sus amigos!

Standards: This activity practices presentational communication (C 1.3).

ACTIVIDAD 6 **¡Compre, compre, compre!** Ahora, con un(a) compañero(a), escriban un anuncio comercial para la televisión. Usen el mandato formal con **usted** para convencer a su público. Presenten el anuncio a la clase.

ACTIVIDAD 7 **¡Niños!** Los padres también usan los mandatos con frecuencia al hablar con sus hijos. La señora Díaz tiene que salir esta noche. ¿Qué les dice a sus hijos? Indica sus mandatos en la forma de **ustedes.**

1. empezar la tarea al llegar a casa
2. apagar la computadora después de terminar la tarea
3. ser pacientes con la niñera (*babysitter*)
4. no abrir la puerta
5. no jugar fútbol dentro de la casa
6. no salir de la casa
7. no ir a visitar a sus amigos
8. no comer papitas fritas después de cenar
9. acostarse a las diez
10. cepillarse los dientes antes de acostarse
11. dormir bien
12. estar tranquilos

Answers Act. 7: 1. Empiecen la tarea al llegar a casa. 2. Apaguen la computadora después de terminar la tarea. 3. Sean pacientes con la niñera. 4. No abran la puerta. 5. No jueguen fútbol dentro de la casa. 6. No salgan de la casa. 7. No vayan a visitar a sus amigos. 8. No coman papitas fritas después de cenar. 9. Acuéstense a las diez. 10. Cepíllense los dientes antes de acostarse. 11. Duerman bien. 12. Estén tranquilos.

Optional: To expand on directions, tell students to form groups of three and to pretend that they are throwing a dinner party with three courses for the entire Spanish class. Each course will be at a different residence. Each student gives directions to his / her home.

ACTIVIDAD 8 **¿Cómo llego?** Tu compañero(a) es turista y te pregunta cómo llegar a varios sitios. Dile cómo llegar y dile qué medio de transporte debe usar. Luego, haz tú el papel (*role*) del (de la) turista; tu compañero(a) te va a dar instrucciones. Pueden usar el mapa de la **Actividad 3,** o pueden decirse cómo llegar a sitios en su comunidad.

1. el supermercado
2. el centro comercial
3. el metro
4. la estación de trenes
5. la estación de autobuses
6. las canchas de tenis
7. la oficina de correos
8. el banco

Answers Act. 9: 1. Camine dos cuadras. 2. Doble a la derecha. 3. Siga derecho por una cuadra. 4. Cruce la calle Central. 5. Doble a la izquierda. 6. Camine otra cuadra.

ACTIVIDAD 9 **La oficina de correos.** Escucha la conversación entre un señor y una señorita. La primera vez que escuches la conversación, apunta la información que vas a necesitar. Luego, escribe las instrucciones que le da la señorita al señor para llegar a la oficina de correos. Usa los siguientes verbos en tus oraciones.

1. caminar
2. doblar
3. seguir
4. cruzar
5. doblar
6. caminar

¡COMPÁRATE!

Usamos mandatos con bastante frecuencia en inglés, pero no son tan frecuentes en español. Los mandatos formales pueden parecer (*seem*) un poco descorteses en español, fuera de algunos contextos muy específicos: por ejemplo, para decirle a alguien cómo llegar a un sitio específico, o para dirigirse al público en anuncios y letreros (*signs*).

Cuando los hispanohablantes hablan con alguien que no conocen bien (o que tratan de usted), frecuentemente usan expresiones de cortesía en vez de mandatos formales. Ya sabes usar algunas de estas expresiones: ¿**Le molesta...**?, ¿**Le importa...**? Aquí hay otras que puedes usar para hablar más cortésmente en español.

Me gustaría (+ infinitive)...	*I'd like* (+ *infinitive*) . . .
Por favor, ¿me puede decir...?	*Please, can you tell me . . . ?*
¿Pudiera usted (+ infinitive)**...?**	*Could you* (+ *infinitive*) . . . ?
Quisiera (+ infinitive)**...**	*I'd like* (+ *infinitive*) . . .

—Por favor, **me gustaría** ir a Oaxaca. ¿**Me puede** decir cuándo sale el autobús?

—Cómo no. Sale a las tres y veinte. ¿**Quisiera** reservar un asiento?

—Sí, gracias. ¿**Pudiera** darme un asiento en la ventana, por favor?

PRÁCTICA 1. Con un(a) compañero(a) de clase, escriban una lista de cinco mandatos que les gustaría usar en el salón de clase. Luego, túrnense para decir los mandatos de una forma más cortés, usando las expresiones de cortesía mencionadas.

MODELO: (escrito) *No usen su celular en el salón de clase.*
(hablado) *Por favor, ¿le molesta no usar su celular en el salón de clase?* O:
Por favor, ¿pudiera usted dejar de usar su celular en el salón de clase?

PRÁCTICA 2. Hablen de sus respuestas a las siguientes preguntas sobre la cortesía.

1. ¿Cuándo usas palabras y expresiones en inglés como las que se mencionan arriba? ¿Qué otras palabras y expresiones usas en inglés cuando quieres ser cortés?

2. ¿Crees que la cortesía es muy importante, bastante importante, un poco importante o no muy importante? ¿Por qué? ¿En qué situaciones es importante la cortesía?

Sonrisas

Optional: For expansion, have students generate a detailed list of typical classroom commands and another list of commands used with family members at home. Compare lists.

EXPRESIÓN. En grupos de tres a cuatro personas, piensen en las órdenes que les gustaría dar a los profesores de la universidad. Luego, escriban una lista de sus ideas.

MODELO: *No den tarea para los fines de semana.*

Optional: Expand this activity to have students write at least five commands for their classmates that require moving around or doing something in the classroom. Have some students "command" the class while the class acts these out.

Gramática útil 3
Affirming and negating: Affirmative and negative expressions

CÓMO USARLO

1. There are a number of words and expressions that are used to express affirmatives and negatives in Spanish. Notice that a double negative form is often used in Spanish, where it is hardly ever used in English.

No conozco a **nadie** aquí.   *I don't know anyone here.*
¿Conoces a **alguien** aquí?   *Do you know anyone here?*
No quiero **ni** este libro **ni** ése.   *I don't want this book or that one.*

2. Remember to use the personal **a** that you learned in **Capítulo 5** when you refer to people.

No veo **a** nadie aquí.

CÓMO FORMARLO

1. Here are some frequently used affirmative and negative words in Spanish. You have already learned some of these, such as **también, siempre,** and **nunca.**

alguien	*someone*	nadie	*no one, nobody*
algo	*something*	nada	*nothing*
algún / alguno (a, os, as)	*some, any*	ningún / ninguno (a, os, as)	*none, no, not any*
siempre	*always*	nunca / jamás	*never*
también	*also*	tampoco	*neither, not either*
o... o...	*either / or*	ni... ni...	*neither / nor*

2. Most of these words do not change, regardless of the number or gender of the words they modify. However, the words **alguno** and **ninguno** can also be used as *adjectives*. In this case, they must change to agree with the nouns they modify. Additionally, when they are used before a masculine noun they shorten to **algún** and **ningún.**

—¿Tienes **algún** libro sobre la informática?
—No, no tengo **ningún** libro sobre ese tema. Pero tenemos **algunos** libros muy interesantes sobre la red mundial.
—No, gracias, ya tengo **algunas** revistas. ¿No tienes **ninguna** sugerencia para otros libros?

Do you have a (any) book about computer science?
No, I don't have a (any) book on that subject. But we do have some very interesting books about the World Wide Web.
No, thanks, I already have some magazines. You don't have any suggestions for other books?

An exception to the "no double negative" rule in English is *neither / nor:* Neither Susana *nor* Margarita is coming to the party.

Standards: Emphasize the comparison of the languages by stressing use or giving more examples of double negative in Spanish and pointing out that double negatives in English are considered incorrect and are only present in colloquial speech.

Heritage Learners: If needed, point out that **nadie** is the standard form, though **nadien** may be heard in U.S. Spanish.

¿Viene **alguna** persona especial a cenar?

3. **Alguno** and **ninguno** can also be used as *pronouns* that replace a noun already referred to. In this case, they match the number and gender of the nouns they replace.

—¿Quieres estos **libros**?   *Do you want these **books**?*
—No, gracias, ya tengo **algunos.**   *No, thanks, I already have **some**.*
—¿No quieres una de estas **revistas**?   *Don't you want one of these **magazines**?*
—No, no necesito **ninguna.**   *No, I don't need **any** (**one**).*

4. Notice how in Spanish, unlike English, several negative words can be used in one sentence.

Nunca hay **nadie** aquí.   *There's **never anyone** here.*
Ni viene Laura **ni** Lorenzo   ***Neither** Laura **nor** Lorenzo is coming*
   tampoco.   *either.*

Actividades

Note that the plural forms of ninguno and ninguna, ningunos and ningunas, are hardly ever used.

Notice: Reiterate that **ninguno** and **ninguna** are not used in the plural because "if you don't have any, you don't have even one." This prohibits the use of the plural form.

Notice that when a *negative word precedes the verb*, the word no is not used: Nadie viene. However, when the *negative word comes after the verb*, you must use **no** directly before the verb: **No viene nadie.**

Answers Act. 10: 1. Mis primos también. 2. Mi abuelo tampoco. 3. Mi abuela también. 4. A mis padres también. 5. Mi hermana también. 6. A mis hermanos tampoco. 7. Yo también.

Answers Act. 11: 1. No, no hay ningún supermercado en el barrio. 2. No, nadie puede decirle cómo llegar al centro comercial. 3. No, nunca compro la carne en la Carnicería La Villita. 4. No, no tengo ninguna tienda de ropa preferida. 5. No, no hay ninguna cancha de tenis en el barrio. 6. No, no hay nada bueno en el cine.

Answers Act. 12: 1. Sí, algunos de los estudiantes van a la biblioteca después de clases. / No, nadie va a la biblioteca después de clases. 2. Sí, me gusta comer algo antes de las clases. / No, no me gusta comer nada antes de las clases. 3. Sí, hay algunos cajeros automáticos en la universidad. / No, no hay ningún cajero automático en la universidad. 4. Sí, siempre voy en metro a la universidad. / No, nunca voy en metro a la universidad. 5. Sí, hay algunas tiendas de video cerca de la universidad. / No, no hay ninguna tienda de video cerca de la universidad. 6. O estudio antes de clases o estudio después de clases. / No estudio ni antes de clases ni después de clases.

ACTIVIDAD 10 **¡Yo también!** Un(a) amigo(a) está en tu casa y tú le explicas algunas cosas sobre los hábitos de tu familia. Él (Ella) dice que su familia es igual. Con un(a) compañero(a), improvisen esta situación.

MODELO: Tú: *Mis tíos nunca cenan antes de las ocho de la noche.*
           Amigo(a): *Mis tíos tampoco.*

1. Mis primos siempre se levantan temprano.
2. Mi abuelo nunca se viste informalmente.
3. Mi abuela siempre se viste elegantemente.
4. A mis padres les encanta salir a comer.
5. Mi hermana es fanática de la música rap.
6. A mis hermanos no les gusta levantarse temprano.
7. Yo siempre me baño y me visto elegantemente si voy a una fiesta.

Ahora describe los hábitos verdaderos de tu familia. Tu compañero(a) te dice si su familia es igual o no.

ACTIVIDAD 11 **El visitante.** Un visitante pasa el fin de semana en tu casa. Te hace preguntas sobre tu barrio. Contesta sus preguntas en el negativo. Sigue el modelo.

MODELO: Escuchas: ¿Hay alguna estación de trenes en el barrio?
           Escribes: *No, no hay ninguna estación de trenes en el barrio.*

ACTIVIDAD 12 **Encuesta.** Un encuestador te hace las siguientes preguntas. Primero, contesta la pregunta en el afirmativo. Luego, contesta la pregunta en el negativo. Usa las palabras entre paréntesis en tus respuestas.

MODELO: ¿Comes en la cafetería de la universidad? (siempre / nunca)
           Sí, siempre como en la cafetería de la universidad.
           No, nunca como en la cafetería de la universidad.

1. ¿Algunos de los estudiantes van a la biblioteca después de clases? (algunos / nadie)

2. ¿Te gusta comer algo antes de las clases? (algo / nada)
3. ¿Hay algún cajero automático en la universidad? (algunos / ningún)
4. ¿Vas en metro a la universidad? (siempre / nunca)
5. ¿Hay alguna tienda de video cerca de la universidad? (algunas / ninguna)
6. ¿Estudias antes de clases o después de clases? (o… o… / ni… ni…)

 ACTIVIDAD 13 **El fin de semana.** Vas a pasar el fin de semana en casa de tu compañero(a). Le haces varias preguntas para determinar cómo vas a pasar el fin de semana. Escoge (*Choose*) ideas de la lista o inventa otras. Luego, cambia de papel (*role*) con tu compañero(a). Usa las palabras afirmativas y negativas que acabas de aprender en tus preguntas y tus respuestas.

Posibles ideas:

divertido en la tele
comer en el refrigerador
libro de cocina mexicana
escritora mexicana preferida

revista de música popular
juego interactivo
disco compacto de Paulina Rubio
¿…?

MODELO: Compañero(a): *¿Hay algo divertido en la tele?*
          Tú: *No, no hay nada divertido en la tele.*

Gramática útil 4
Indicating relative position of objects: Demonstrative adjectives and pronouns

CÓMO USARLO

Demonstrative adjectives and pronouns are used to indicate *relative distance* from the speaker. **Este** refers to something that is very close to the speaker. **Ese** refers to something that is a little farther away. **Aquel** refers to something that is at a distance or *over there*. In everyday speech, **ese** and **aquel** are often used interchangeably.

1. Demonstrative adjectives:

Esta casa es muy bonita. También me gusta **esa** casa. Pero **aquella** casa no me gusta nada.

This house is very pretty. I also like that house. But I don't like that house (over there) at all.

2. Demonstrative pronouns:

¡Mira los edificios grandes! ¡**Éste** es grande, pero **ése** es aun más grande, y **aquél** es el más grande de los tres!

Look at the big buildings! This one is big, but that one is even bigger, and that one (over there) is the biggest of the three!

Derecho hasta **aquella** esquina…

CÓMO FORMARLO

LO BÁSICO

A *demonstrative adjective* is used *with* a noun to point out a person or thing and to indicate distance. A *demonstrative pronoun* is used *instead of* a noun to point it out and indicate its distance from the speaker.

Begin the CD-ROM activities. Do the cultural activities and reading and writing practice as you complete the corresponding text sections.

Preparation: Bring three objects to class. Place one close to you, another at medium distance from you, and the third far away from you. Illustrate demonstratives, using Spanish only. Choose objects that will illustrate gender differences.

1. These are the forms for demonstrative adjectives and pronouns.

	Demonstrative adjectives	Demonstrative pronouns
this (*close to speaker*) that (*farther from speaker*)	este, esta, estos, estas ese, esa, esos, esas	éste, ésta, éstos, éstas ése, ésa, ésos, ésas
that (*at a distance from the speaker*)	aquel, aquella, aquellos, aquellas	aquél, aquélla, aquéllos, aquéllas

2. Notice that both demonstrative adjectives and pronouns change to reflect gender and number. Demonstrative adjectives change to reflect the gender and number of the nouns they *modify*. Demonstrative pronouns change to reflect the gender and number of the nouns they *replace*.

3. The only difference between the forms of the demonstrative adjectives and the demonstrative pronouns is that the pronouns are often written with an accent.

4. These words are often used with demonstrative adjectives and pronouns to help indicate relative location.

aquí   *here* (often used with **este**)
allí   *there* (often used with **ese**)
allá   *over there* (often used with **aquel**)

5. Esto and **eso** are often used as neutral pronouns, when referring to a concept, or something that has already been said.

Eso es lo que dijo Séneca sobre la filosofía.
Todo **esto** es muy interesante.

That is what Seneca said about philosophy.
All this is very interesting.

Actividades

ACTIVIDAD 14 **¡Ayuda, por favor!** Completa las siguientes conversaciones con el pronombre o adjetivo demostrativo apropiado.

1.   TÚ: Hola, ¿pudiera usted decirme cómo llegar a las canchas de tenis?
   HOMBRE: Cómo no. Siga usted _____ calle aquí hasta _____ esquina allí, la esquina con la avenida Quintana. Luego vaya todo derecho hasta llegar a un parque muy grande. Las canchas de tenis están en _____ parque.

2.   TÚ: Buenos días. Por favor, ¿pudiera usted decirme cómo ir al aeropuerto?
   MUJER: Claro. Usted debe tomar _____ autobús allí en la calle Francisco. A ver, tengo la ruta aquí en _____ guía de autobuses.
   TÚ: Muy bien. Entonces, ¿_____ autobús es el que necesito tomar?
   MUJER: Sí. _____ autobús lo lleva directamente al aeropuerto.

3.   TÚ: Perdón. ¿Puede usted recomendar un restaurante bueno?
   HOMBRE: Seguro. _____ que está aquí cerca es bastante bueno.
            Pero hay otro allí, mire, al otro lado de la calle, La Criolla.
            _____ sirve comida muy rica. Creo que _____,
            La Criolla, es mi favorito.

4.   TÚ: Hola, busco la sección de música latina.
   MUJER: Muy bien. _____ cintas aquí son de música cubana.
          Allí, en la próxima sección, _____ discos compactos
          son de música mexicana. Y al otro lado de la tienda, allá,
          _____ cintas son de música andina.
     TÚ: ¿Y _____ discos compactos aquí?
   MUJER: ¿_____ allí? _____ discos compactos son de
          música flamenca.

 ACTIVIDAD 15 **En el mercado.** Con un(a) compañero(a) de clase, miren el dibujo de un mercado en México. ¿Qué quieren comprar? Hablen de las cosas que necesitan, usando los adjetivos y pronombres demostrativos correctos.

MODELO: Tú: *¿Qué quieres comprar? ¿Compramos ese queso?*
             Amigo(a): *Sí, y también estas salchichas. ¿Qué más? ...*

 ACTIVIDAD 16 **¿Adónde vamos?** Con un(a) compañero(a) de clase, hagan una lista de dos de los siguientes lugares. Incluyan sitios que están muy cerca de la universidad, un poco lejos y muy lejos.

restaurantes   museos   tiendas de música
cafés   tiendas de ropa   pizzerías

Ahora, hablen de los varios sitios de su lista, usando adjetivos y pronombres demostrativos.

MODELO: Tú: *¿Quieres ir al restaurante Chimichangas? Sirven comida mexicana.*
             Amigo(a): *No, no me gusta ese restaurante. ¿Por qué no vamos a éste, McMurray's? Sirven comida estadounidense.*

México

¿Adivinaste? Answers to the
questions on page 167: 1. C 2. C 3. F
4. C 5. F

Un país de contrastes. Mira el mapa de las nueve zonas culturales de México, según la *Guía Michelin.* Luego, lee los textos en la página 191 y mira las fotos en la página 192. Finalmente, escribe el número del texto (T1, T2, T3, T4, T5) o de la foto (F1, F2, F3, F4) que corresponde a cada zona.

_____ Zona 1: Ciudad de México   _____ Zona 6: Noreste
_____ Zona 2: México Central   _____ Zona 7: Golfo de México
_____ Zona 3: Oeste Central   _____ Zona 8: Costa Pacífico
_____ Zona 4: Noroeste   _____ Zona 9: Yucatán
_____ Zona 5: Baja California

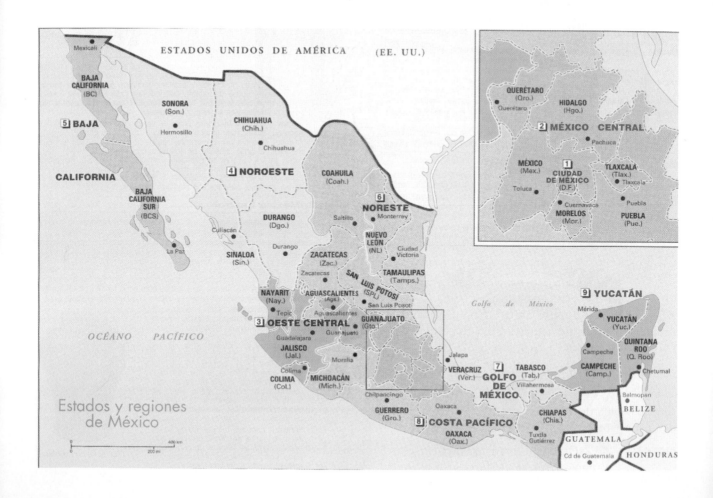

Estados y regiones de México

Texto 1: La comida y la música

En la Sierra Madre Occidental hay cuatro estados que comparten elementos culturales similares. Esta región se conoce por la música norteña, que se caracteriza por sus baladas y rancheras (tipos de canciones mexicanas) con acordeón y guitarra. También es famosa por su comida — la carne asada (*grilled*) y la tortilla de harina (*flour*). Es una zona influenciada por Estados Unidos, especialmente en las áreas cerca de la frontera.

Texto 2: La historia precolombina

En esta parte central del Golfo de México, hay dos estados donde ocurren algunos de los eventos más importantes de la historia mexicana. Los olmecas, la primera civilización de Mesoamérica, se encuentran aquí desde aproximadamente 1800 a. C. (antes de Cristo). Se conocen los olmecas por su sistema de números y por sus estatuas inmensas de cabezas (*heads*) y jaguares. Es en esta región, además, que entran los conquistadores españoles a México.

Texto 3: Cultura y arte

El Distrito Federal, que es la capital del país, es también su estado más pequeño. Aquí abundan el arte y la cultura. Se puede ver el arte de Diego Rivera, Frida Kahlo, Rufino Tamayo y David Siqueiros, entre muchos otros, y se pueden visitar museos de antropología, historia y arquitectura. Sus parques impresionantes, como el Bosque de Chapultepec y la Alameda Central, se combinan con sus avenidas amplias para hacer de esta ciudad una de las grandes ciudades del mundo.

Texto 4: Influencias indígenas

A lo largo de esta región larga y diversa vive la mayoría de los grupos indígenas del país. Todavía mantienen sus tradiciones, lenguas y costumbres. En algunas áreas su influencia es muy marcada, como en los pueblos indígenas cerca de Guatemala. Hay tanta variedad de lenguas, costumbres y comida que casi es posible considerar a estos cuatro estados como cuatro países diferentes.

Texto 5: Los aztecas

Esta región central tiene una historia muy larga. Existe aquí una gran ciudad alrededor de 400 d. C. (después de Cristo). Cuando llegan los aztecas siglos (*centuries*) después, ven la grandeza de las ruinas y nombran el sitio Teotihuacán, que significa "el lugar donde nacieron los dioses (*the gods were born*)". Es el centro del imperio azteca y aquí están las ruinas de las Pirámides del Sol y de la Luna, el templo de Quetzalcóatl y los Palacios de Quetzalpapalotl.

Suggestion: Have students scan Texto 3 and identify names of artists. For expansion, students can research these artists and bring their findings to the classroom. Connecting with the art discipline (C 3.1) through language study is developed, as well as gaining knowledge about the Mexican culture (C 2.2).

Foto 1: Playas del Pacífico   Estos estados son famosos por sus bonitas playas a lo largo del Pacífico. Se distinguen también por la influencia de las culturas indígenas del oeste.

Foto 2: Herencia colonial   Esta región de contrastes incluye tierras áridas, un área industrial y unos ejemplos magníficos de arquitectura colonial. También comparte una frontera con Estados Unidos. Este detalle (*detail*) de una catedral famosa es una buena muestra de la arquitectura colonial.

Foto 3: La naturaleza abundante   Localizada en el océano Pacífico y el Mar de Cortés, ésta es la península más grande del mundo. Es famosa por su diversidad de flora y fauna.

Foto 4: Los mayas   Aproximadamente 900.000 indígenas, que aún hablan maya, viven en esta península, que se conoce por sus antiguas ciudades mayas como Chichén Itzá y Uxmal, sus playas y sus reservas ecológicas.

Internet

¡CONÉCTATE!

Como ves, México es un país muy diverso. Con un grupo de tres a cinco estudiantes, busquen información sobre una de las zonas de arriba. Pueden incluir la siguiente información, u otros datos que les interesen.

- ciudades principales
- industrias principales
- atracciones turísticas
- poblaciones indígenas

Luego, preparen un breve informe y preséntenlo en clase. Usen los enlaces sugeridos en el sitio web de *Nexos* (http://college.hmco.com/languages/spanish/students) para ir a otros sitios web posibles.

A LEER

Antes de leer

Working with unknown grammatical structures

When you read texts that were written for native speakers of Spanish, you will frequently come across grammatical structures you haven't learned yet. This is only natural, since native speakers don't have to worry about using carefully sequenced language the way Spanish textbooks do!

At first, seeing grammatical endings you don't recognize may be intimidating. But if you focus just on getting the meaning of the infinitive of the verb, you can almost always get the general idea of the word. Often you can figure out the tense (present, past, future, etc.) by looking at the context of the rest of the sentence. By not allowing unknown grammatical structures to hold you back, you'll make a great leap forward in your comprehension of authentic texts in Spanish.

Heritage Learners: Have heritage learners list cognates from the reading and compare their Spanish and English spellings. Elicit or point out endings: **-ción (revolución)** = *-tion;* **-dad (formalidad)** = *-ty.*

ACTIVIDAD 1 Aquí tienes algunas frases de la lectura que contienen estructuras gramaticales que no sabes. Mira el significado general del verbo para ver si puedes hacer una correspondencia entre las palabras en español y aquéllas en inglés.

1. _____ es necesario que conozca
2. _____ podrá descifrar
3. _____ esté todo el día conectado al monitor
4. _____ que se encuentre ahí
5. _____ acuda la gente más "nice"
6. _____ estar vestido perfectamente
7. _____ el restaurante que ofrezca

a. *you will be able to decipher*
b. *that may be found there*
c. *it's necessary that you know*
d. *the restaurant that offers*
e. *to be dressed perfectly*
f. *that he is connected to the screen all day*
g. *the nicest people gather*

Answers Act. 1: 1. c 2. a 3. f 4. b 5. g 6. e 7. d

Notice: Present subjunctive forms are formally introduced in Chapter 10. This activity can serve as a preview to the present subjunctive forms by pointing out the endings.

ACTIVIDAD 2 Ahora, mira las frases de la **Actividad 1.** En cada caso, ¿cuál es la forma gramatical que no sabes? Con un(a) compañero(a), hagan una lista de las siete formas gramaticales. ¿Son del tiempo presente o futuro? Usen la siguiente tabla para escribir sus respuestas.

Answers Act. 2: 1. **conozca**, present; 2. **podrá**, future; 3. **esté**, present / **conectado**, present; 4. **se encuentre**, present; 5. **acuda**, present; 6. **estar vestido**, present; 7. **ofrezca**, present

forma gramatical	¿presente o futuro?

Lectura

ACTIVIDAD 3 Vas a leer un artículo sobre adónde van los jóvenes de la Ciudad de México para divertirse. Mientras lees, trata de entender los verbos sin pensar demasiado en las terminaciones o en estructuras gramaticales que no reconoces. Trata de comprender las ideas principales del artículo. No es necesario entender todas las palabras para hacer las actividades.

Los jóvenes se divierten

Alejandro Esquivel

¿Usted sabe cómo se divierten los "teens"? Las maneras de entretenerse en estos tiempos de revolución electrónica, video juegos, DVDs, equipos mp3 y antros son tan heterogéneas como la población que ocupa[1] solamente el Distrito Federal... Es necesario que conozca ciertos perfiles de los jóvenes contemporáneos para entender más su manera de ir por la vida. Es así como podrá descifrar algunos de los códigos[2] de la juventud para saber adónde van y qué hacen... ■

El telemaníaco

Una de las formas de entretener más "ancestrales" es el observar televisión por más de cuatro horas seguidas[3]. A esta joven especie[4] no le interesa ni en lo más mínimo la vida social, pues prefiere observar un maratón entero de Los Simpson a tomar un buen café con sus cuates[5]... Algunos padres prefieren que su "hijito" esté todo el día conectado al monitor, argumentando que es preferible que se encuentre ahí a estar vagabundeando en las calles.

El peace & love

En cuanto a este tipo de jóvenes, les preocupa más lo natural, el amor y la fraternidad entre razas. A diferencia del telemaníaco, éste trata de[6] pasar el menor tiempo posible frente a un televisor. Dentro de sus principales maneras de divertirse está el acudir[7] todos los domingos a la Plaza de Coyoacán, para buscar algún libro y observar los espectáculos culturales que semana a semana ahí se presentan.

El fresa[8]

Este "teen modelo" gusta de asistir a lugares a los cuales acuda la gente más "nice" de la ciudad. Otra forma de diversión son las cenas y los cafés que regularmente se realizan[9] en restaurantes y cafeterías ubicadas[10] en la zona de Bosques de las Lomas y Santa Fe. Al fresa le late[11] bastante asistir a "antros[12]" donde la música comercial sea el hit.

El raver

Los ravers son los encargados de llenar[13] los festivales de música electrónica o raves, ya que éstos sólo son posibles gracias a la asistencia de más de 3 mil personas... La música que se toca es la electrónica y durante los raves se baila sin parar[14] por más de nueve horas continuas y sólo bebiendo agua embotellada. El raver también acude a antros donde solamente se toque electrónica.

El fashion

Otro espécimen fácil de identificar, ya que su preocupación más grande es estar vestido perfectamente. Entre sus grandes pasatiempos es leer revistas de moda[15], pero a la hora de salir trata siempre de asistir al lugar que acaban de inaugurar o al lugar más fashion. También prefiere las cenas en compañía de sus amigos en el restaurante que ofrezca lo último[16] en cocina.

[1]vive [2]codes [3]continuas [4]species [5]amigos [6]**trata de** tries to [7]ir [8]affluent youth [9]**se realizan** take place [10]located [11]**le late** le gusta [12]bar or club, the "in" place [13]**encargados...** in charge of filling [14]to stop [15]**revistas...** fashion magazines [16]**lo último** the latest

Después de leer

 ACTIVIDAD 4 Con un(a) compañero(a), escriban el nombre del grupo de jóvenes que va a cada lugar indicado. En algunos casos, más de un grupo va al lugar.

Answers Act. 4: 1. fresas, ravers
2. ravers 3. peace & love 4. ravers
5. fresas 6. telemaníacos 7. fashion
8. fashion 9. fresas

Lugar	Grupo
1. antros	
2. raves	
3. la Plaza de Coyoacán	
4. festivales de música electrónica	
5. la zona de Bosques de las Lomas	
6. casa	
7. los lugares más "fashion"	
8. restaurantes	
9. cafés	

 ACTIVIDAD 5 En el **Capítulo 4** hay una nota sobre los préstamos del inglés al español. Este artículo tiene muchos ejemplos de este tipo de palabra. Trabaja con un(a) compañero(a) de clase. ¿Pueden encontrar seis préstamos del inglés al español?

Answers Act. 5: *Any 6 of the following:*
teens, DVDs, MP3, monitor, peace & love,
teen, nice, hit, raver, rave, fashion

 ACTIVIDAD 6 Trabaja en un grupo de tres a cuatro estudiantes. ¿Pueden identificar cinco grupos de "tipos" entre los jóvenes estadounidenses? Escriban una lista de los grupos, unas de sus características y adónde van para divertirse. Luego, compartan su lista con la clase entera.

VOCABULARIO

EN LA UNIVERSIDAD   *At the university*

el apartamento	*apartment*
el auditorio	*auditorium*
la cancha / el campo de fútbol	*soccer field*
las canchas de tenis	*tennis courts*
el centro estudiantil	*student center*
el cuarto	*room*
el dormitorio / la residencia estudiantil	*dormitory*
el edificio	*building*
el estadio	*stadium*
la oficina	*office*
la piscina	*swimming pool*
la pista de atletismo	*athletics track*

EN LA CIUDAD O EN EL PUEBLO
In the city or in the town

el aeropuerto	*airport*
el almacén	*store*
el banco	*bank*
el barrio	*neighborhood*
el cajero automático	*automated teller machine (ATM)*
la casa	*house*
el centro comercial	*mall*
el cine	*cinema*
la estación de trenes / autobús	*train / bus station*
el estacionamiento	*parking lot*
la farmacia	*pharmacy*
el hospital	*hospital*
la iglesia	*church*
la joyería	*jewelry store*
el mercado	*market*
el museo	*museum*
la oficina de correos	*post office*
la papelería	*stationery store*
el parque	*park*
la pizzería	*pizzeria*
la plaza	*plaza*
el restaurante	*restaurant*
el supermercado	*supermarket*
el teatro	*theater*

la tienda...	*store*
...de música	*music store*
...de ropa	*clothing store*
...de videos	*video store*
el (la) vecino(a)	*neighbor*

HACER LAS COMPRAS...   *Shopping . . .*

En la carnicería   *At the butcher shop*

el bistec	*steak*
la chuleta de puerco	*pork chop*
el jamón	*ham*
las papitas fritas	*potato chips*
el pavo	*turkey*
el pollo	*chicken*
la salchicha	*sausage*

En el supermercado   *At the supermarket*

la comida	*food*
las frutas	*fruits*
los huevos	*eggs*
la leche	*milk*
el pan	*bread*
el queso	*cheese*
los refrescos	*soft drinks*
los vegetales	*vegetables*
el yogur	*yogurt*

MEDIOS DE TRANSPORTE
Means of transportation

a pie	*on foot, walking*
en autobús	*by bus*
en bicicleta	*on bicycle*
en carro / coche / automóvil	*by car*
en metro	*on the subway*
en tren	*by train*
por avión	*by plane*

Optional: To synthesize vocabulary encourage students to make up group narrations about Pepe or Fabiola, who have to go to the university, then run errands (**hacer mandados**) and then go to the **mercado**. Sample group story: **Fabiola es una chica muy activa. Primero va a la universidad para su clase de educación física. Tiene clase de tenis en las canchas de tenis. Después va al centro estudiantil para comprar un libro. Con una compañera de clase tiene que ir al centro para visitar el museo de arte. Tiene que estudiar el arte para su clase de arte. Después va al supermercado y...** Remind students to use as many vocabulary words as possible.

PARA DECIR CÓMO LLEGAR
Giving directions

¿Me puede decir cómo llegar a...?	*Can you tell me how to get to . . . ?*
¿Me puede decir dónde queda...?	*Can you tell me where . . . is located?*
Cómo no. Vaya...	*Of course. Go . . .*
a la avenida...	*to the avenue . . .*
a la calle...	*to the street . . .*
a la derecha	*to the right*
a la esquina	*to the corner*
a la izquierda	*to the left*
dos cuadras	*two blocks*
(todo) derecho	*(straight) ahead*
bajar	*to get down from, to get off of (a bus, etc.)*
cruzar	*to cross*
doblar	*to turn*
seguir (i)	*to continue*
subir	*to go up, to get on*

EXPRESIONES DE CORTESÍA

Me gustaría (+ infinitive)...	*I'd like (+ infinitive) . . .*
¿Por favor, me puede decir...?	*Please, can you tell me . . . ?*
¿Pudiera Ud. (+ infinitive)...?	*Could you (+ infinitive) . . . ?*
Quisiera (+ infinitive)...	*I'd like (+ infinitive) . . .*

EXPRESIONES AFIRMATIVAS Y NEGATIVAS

algo	*something*
alguien	*someone*
algún, alguno (a, os, as)	*some, any*
jamás	*never*
nada	*nothing*
nadie	*no one, nobody*
ni... ni...	*neither / nor*
ningún, ninguno (a, os, as)	*none, no, not any*
nunca	*never*
o... o...	*either / or*
siempre	*always*
también	*also*
tampoco	*neither, not either*

PREPOSICIONES

al lado de	*next to, on the side of*
cerca de	*close to*
debajo de	*below, underneath*
delante de	*in front of*
dentro de	*inside of*
detrás de	*behind*
encima de	*on top of, on*
enfrente de	*in front of, opposite*
entre	*between*
frente a	*in front of, facing, opposite*
fuera de	*outside of*
lejos de	*far from*
sobre	*on, above*

ADJETIVOS DEMOSTRATIVOS

aquel, aquella, aquellos, aquellas	*those (over there)*
ese, esa, esos, esas	*those*
este, esta, estos, estas	*these*

PRONOMBRES DEMOSTRATIVOS

aquél, aquélla, aquéllos, aquéllas	*those (over there)*
ése, ésa, ésos, ésas	*those*
eso	*that*
éste, ésta, éstos, éstas	*these*
esto	*this*

OTRAS PALABRAS Y EXPRESIONES

allá	*over there*
allí	*there*
aquí	*here*

¿Cuáles son tus pasatiempos preferidos?

CAPÍTULO 7

Communication

By the end of this chapter you will be able to:
- talk about sports and leisure-time activities
- talk about seasons and the weather
- say how you feel using **tener** expressions
- describe your recent leisure-time activities
- suggest activities and plans to friends

Cultures

By the end of this chapter you will have learned about:
- Costa Rica and Panamá
- seasons and the equator
- Fahrenheit and Celsius temperatures
- white-water rafting in Costa Rica

Standards: Refer students to the map of Central America throughout the chapter. A standards-based approach emphasizes *content* and *context,* which links Central America with sports, climate, and natural resources (C 3.1).

Esta mola, una obra de arte tradicional de los kunas de Panamá, conmemora un combate de boxeo.

LOS RATOS LIBRES

¿Trabajas para vivir o vives para trabajar? ¿Cuál es más importante para ti —los ratos libres o el trabajo? ¿Te defines según tu profesión, tus intereses o una combinación de los dos? En este capítulo vamos a explorar cómo pasamos el tiempo libre.

Standards: C 3.1 is met in **Capítulo 7** through mathematics with conversions between Celsius and Fahrenheit and the metric system. Warm up with a few **cierto / falso** items about the metric system and get a sense of general knowledge level: **1. Un kilómetro es más de una milla. (F) 2. Un litro es del sistema métrico. (C) 3. Un milímetro es grande. (F)...** The ¡Conéctate! activities get students virtually out of the classroom and into the Spanish-speaking communities of Panamá and Costa Rica (C 5.1). Start by surveying your students about their prior knowledge: **¿Qué sabes de Costa Rica y Panamá?**

Suggestion: Ask questions like **¿Qué ves en la mola? ¿De qué color es? Describe a las personas en la mola.**

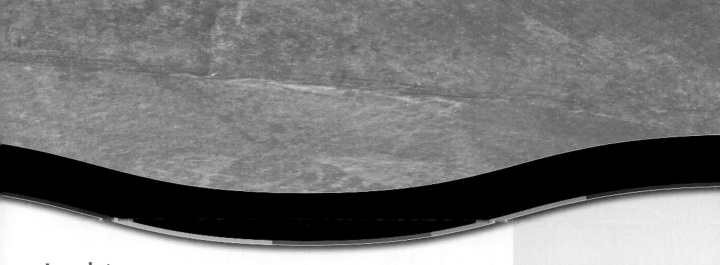

Los datos

Mira la información de las tablas y luego contesta las siguientes preguntas.

Conversiones	Fórmula	Ejemplo
grados C → grados F	(C° × 1.8) + 32 = F°	(30°C × 1.8) + 32 = 86°F
grados F → grados C	(F° − 32) ÷ 1.8 = C°	(86°F − 32) ÷ 1.8 = 30°C
pulgadas a milímetros	pulgadas × 25,4 = mm	70,5" × 25,4 = 1.790,7 mm
milímetros a pulgadas	milímetros ÷ 25,4 = pul.	1.790 mm ÷ 25,4 = 70,5"

❶ ¿Qué significa la palabra **pulgada**?
❷ ¿Cuándo se usa una coma (*comma*) con los números en español? ¿Cuándo se usa un punto (*period*)? ¿Es lo mismo (*the same*) en inglés o es diferente?
❸ ¿Cuántos grados Celsio son 50 grados Fahrenheit?
❹ ¿Cuántas pulgadas son 500 milímetros?

		Costa Rica	Panamá
Temperatura	enero	19,1 C / 66,4 F	26,5 C / 79,7 F
media en...	julio	20,4 C / 68,7 F	26,6 C / 79,9 F
Precipitación anual media		1.793 mm / 70,6 pulgadas	2.512 mm / 98,9 pulgadas

❺ Por lo general, ¿en que país hace más calor (*is it hotter*), en Costa Rica o Panamá?
❻ ¿En que país hay menos precipitación anual?
❼ ¿Cuál de los dos países tiene el clima más tropical?

¡Adivina!

¿Qué sabes de Costa Rica y Panamá? (Las respuestas están en la página 223.)

❶ Este país tiene costa en el Océano Pacífico y en el Mar Caribe.
❷ Estados Unidos construyó un canal en este país y en 1999 se lo cedió al gobierno de ese país.
❸ Este país no tiene fuerzas armadas.
❹ Este país es famoso por sus playas (*beaches*) hermosas.

Preparation: Review the inversion of the comma (,) and period (.). To review this concept ask students to rewrite the following numbers, as they would appear in the Spanish-speaking world: 1,234.5 / .075 / 1,786,905 / 1.33

Preparation: Students may need clarification on the term **media.** Start by writing "20°, 30°, 40°" on the board. Then ask: **¿Cuál es la temperatura media?** Point out Spanish terms: **centígrado, Celsio, Fahrenheit.**

Los datos answers: 1. *inch* 2. with decimals; with numbers one thousand and higher; es diferente 3. 10°C 4. 19,69 pulgadas 5. Panamá 6. Costa Rica 7. Panamá

¡Adivina! answers: 1. Panamá, Costa Rica 2. Panamá 3. Costa Rica 4. Costa Rica

¡IMAGÍNATE!

Vocabulario útil 1

SERGIO:	¿Viste el **partido de fútbol** entre Argentina y México ayer?
JAVIER:	No, llegué tarde a casa.
SERGIO:	Pues, te perdiste un partido buenísimo. Yo lo vi en casa de Arturo.
JAVIER:	¿Ah, sí? ¿Quién ganó?
SERGIO:	Argentina, 2 a 1.
JAVIER:	Me encanta ver los partidos de fútbol internacional por tele.
SERGIO:	Y además del fútbol, ¿qué otros deportes te gustan?
JAVIER:	Las **competencias de natación**, el **ciclismo** y el **boxeo**.
SERGIO:	¿El boxeo? ¡Guau! Yo prefiero el fútbol nacional, el italiano, el español…
JAVIER:	¿Qué piensas de los deportes de **invierno**?
SERGIO:	No sé, hay algunos que me parecen interesantes, como el **hockey sobre hielo** y el **esquí alpino**.

Suggestion: Ask ¿Qué deportes son interesantes / aburridos? ¿Por qué? ¿Te gusta observar o participar en…?

LOS DEPORTES

el boxeo	*boxing*	**el golf**	*golf*
el esquí acuático	*water skiing*	**el hockey sobre hielo**	*ice hockey*
el esquí alpino	*downhill skiing*	**la natación**	*swimming*

ACTIVIDADES DEPORTIVAS

entrenarse	*to train*	**navegar en rápidos**	*to go white-water rafting*
esquiar	*to ski*		
jugar (al) tenis / (al) béisbol / etc.	*to play tennis / baseball / etc.*	**patinar sobre hielo**	*to ice skate*
		practicar / hacer alpinismo	*to hike*
levantar pesas	*to lift weights*		
nadar	*to swim*	**practicar / hacer surfing**	*to surf*

Remember, as you learned in **Capítulo 6, jugar** is used with the preposition **a** in a number of Spanish-speaking countries: **jugar al tenis, jugar al fútbol.** Usage of **a** varies from region to region.

MÁS PALABRAS SOBRE LOS DEPORTES

la competencia	*competition*	**peligroso(a)**	*dangerous*
el equipo	*team*	**la pelota**	*ball*
el lago	*lake*	**la piscina**	*pool*
el partido	*game, match*	**el río**	*river*
el peligro	*danger*	**seguro(a)**	*safe*

OTROS DEPORTES

remar

pescar

montar a caballo

montar en bicicleta

hacer ejercicio

patinar en línea

el fútbol

el tenis

el béisbol

el hockey
sobre hierba

el volibol

el fútbol americano

el básquetbol

el ciclismo

LAS ESTACIONES

el verano

julio

el invierno

la primavera

abril

el otoño

Actividades

Sample Answers Act. 1.: **el parque:** levantar pesas, entrenarse, jugar béisbol / básquetbol / fútbol…; **el océano:** hacer surfing, nadar, remar, pescar, hacer esquí acuático; **el lago:** remar, pescar, nadar, hacer esquí acuático; **la cancha:** tenis, jugar básquetbol / volibol / béisbol; **las montañas:** esquiar, hacer esquí alpino, hacer alpinismo; **el gimnasio:** entrenarse, jugar básquetbol / volibol, levantar pesas, el boxeo; **la piscina:** nadar, jugar volibol, entrenarse; **el río:** navegar en rápidos, remar, pescar, hacer esquí acuático

ACTIVIDAD 1 **En las montañas.** Mira la siguiente tabla. Luego, indica qué deportes se pueden practicar en cada lugar. En algunos casos, puede haber varias posibilidades. Limita tus respuestas a un máximo de tres actividades o deportes por cada lugar.

el parque	el océano	el lago	la cancha
las montañas	el gimnasio	la piscina	el río

ACTIVIDAD 2 **Atletas famosos.** Con un(a) compañero(a) de clase, hagan una lista de atletas famosos. Luego, digan con qué deporte se asocia cada atleta.

MODELO: *Gabrielle Reese*
Gabrielle Reese juega volibol.
Kelly Slater
Kelly Slater hace surfing.

ACTIVIDAD 3 **¡Peligro!** Con un(a) compañero(a) de clase, digan qué deportes creen que son peligrosos y cuáles no lo son. Hagan una lista. Luego, intercambien su lista con la de otra pareja. ¿Tienen las mismas opiniones?

ACTIVIDAD 4 **El deporte preferido.** En grupos de tres o cuatro estudiantes, hagan una lista de sus cinco actividades o deportes preferidos. Luego hagan una lista de los cinco deportes o actividades que no les gustan mucho. Después, intercambien su lista con la lista de otro grupo y hagan comparaciones entre los deportes que más y menos les gustan.

MODELO: *En el Grupo #1, el fútbol es el deporte preferido del grupo.*
En el Grupo #2, el hockey sobre hielo es el deporte preferido del grupo.

Optional: After groups determine the most popular sports from their lists, survey the class as a whole to see which activities are the most popular.

ACTIVIDAD 5 **Las estaciones.** ¿Sabes que los hemisferios norte y sur están en estaciones opuestas durante todo el año? Cuando es el verano en el hemisferio norte, es el invierno en el hemisferio sur. Con un(a) compañero(a) de clase, mira la tabla e indica la estación que corresponde con cada país y mes.

Answers Act. 5: 1. invierno 2. invierno 3. otoño 4. primavera 5. verano 6. otoño 7. verano 8. primavera

Optional. **¿Qué país sudamericano de habla española está en los hemisferios norte y sur a la vez?** (Respuesta: **Ecuador**)

País/mes	Estación
1. Argentina, julio	
2. España, febrero	
3. México, octubre	
4. Uruguay, septiembre	
5. Paraguay, diciembre	
6. Cuba, octubre	
7. Panamá, agosto	
8. Bolivia, octubre	

ACTIVIDAD 6 **En el otoño…** Trabaja con un(a) compañero(a) de clase. Digan qué deportes y actividades les gusta hacer en cada estación.

1. en la primavera
2. en el verano
3. en el otoño
4. en el invierno

Preparation for Act. 6: If your students need extra help / practice with **gustar**, model several examples using your own sports preferences and emphasizing **gusta** + singular, **gustan** + plural, **gusta** + infinitive.

¡FÍJATE!

Los préstamos deportivos

El vocabulario deportivo del español tiene muchas palabras que vienen del inglés; por ejemplo, **jonrón, gol, béisbol, bate, derbi** y **fútbol**. Estas palabras tienen sus raíces en la lengua inglesa, pero es importante recordar que su ortografía, pronunciación y uso gramatical siguen las reglas (*rules*) del español. Todas las consonantes y vocales de *homerun* se adaptan al español para crear **jonrón**. Igualmente, se pronuncia con la erre ("r") múltiple del español que aparece en palabras como **perro** o **rojo**. Además, el plural de **jonrón** es **jonrones**, según las reglas del español. Este proceso de adaptación que afecta a los préstamos se llama "nativización".

PRÁCTICA. ¿Cómo se adaptan las palabras inglesas *baseball, basketball* y *volleyball* para crear las palabras españolas **béisbol, básquetbol** y **volibol**?

Optional: Have your students scan on-line Spanish newspapers in the sport section for evidence of these terms. See if students can identify other **préstamos** that follow the same type of transformation. Another option: Have students listen to a news broadcast with a segment on sports or a sporting event on a Spanish-language television channel. Students listen for and list these or other **préstamos deportivos** that they may hear during the broadcast.

Vocabulario útil 2

JAVIER: Hola, Beto. Qué milagro verte por aquí.

BETO: Ya sé. ¡Odio el gimnasio! No **tengo ganas** de hacer ejercicio en estas malditas máquinas.

SERGIO: ¡Pobre Beto!… ¿Les **tienes miedo** a las "maquinitas"?

BETO: No, ¡no seas ridículo! Yo prefiero jugar tenis, pero hoy no puedo porque **está lloviendo.**

JAVIER: **Tienes razón.** Y además, **hace mucho viento.** Ayer salí a correr pero hoy no tuve otra opción que venir aquí.

BETO: Sí. ¡**Hace mal tiempo** desde el lunes!

EXPRESIONES CON *TENER*

Optional: Dramatize the **tener** expressions by having students act them out for their group or for the whole class to guess.

Heritage Learners: Native speakers need explicit instructions on the use of the **diéresis**. Point out that without the use of the **diéresis, tener vergüenza** would be pronounced with the same sound that appears in **guerra**. Similarly, without the **diéresis, pingüino** would be pronounced with the same sound as that which appears in **guitarra**. Give a dictation of the following to reinforce these concepts:
1. **lingüística** 2. **cigüeña** 3. **manguera**
4. **Guillermo** 5. **guante** 6. **averigüe**
7. **guerrilla** 8. **vergüenza**

tener frío • tener sed • tener sueño • tener calor • tener hambre • tener prisa

tener cuidado	*to be careful*
tener ganas de	*to have the urge to, to feel like*
tener miedo (de, a)	*to be afraid (of)*
tener razón	*to be right, correct*
tener vergüenza	*to be embarrassed*

EL TIEMPO

¿Qué tiempo hace?   *What's the weather like?*

Hace buen tiempo.   *It's nice weather.*
Hace mal tiempo.   *It's bad weather.*
Hace fresco.   *It's cool.*
Hace sol.   *It's sunny.*

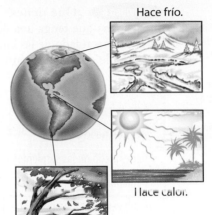

Hace frío.

Hace calor.

Hace viento.

LA TEMPERATURA

grados centígrados   *degrees Celsius*
grados Fahrenheit   *degrees Fahrenheit*
La temperatura está a   *It's 20 degrees*
  20 grados centígrados.   *Celsius.*
La temperatura está a   *It's 70 degrees*
  70 grados Fahrenheit.   *Fahrenheit.*

Está nevando. Nieva.

Está nublado.

Está lloviendo. Llueve.

> You can also say **La temperatura está a 20 grados Celsio(s).**

Actividades

ACTIVIDAD 7   **¡Tengo sueño!** Indica cómo te sientes en las siguientes situaciones. En algunos casos hay más de una respuesta posible.

1. Tienes un examen muy difícil.
2. Es el verano y no tienes aire acondicionado.
3. Tienes una nueva raqueta de tenis.
4. Ya son las ocho de la noche y todavía no has cenado (*haven't eaten dinner*).
5. Acabas de jugar básquetbol por tres horas.
6. Ves una película de terror.
7. Son las tres de la mañana y acabas de estudiar.
8. Es el invierno y no llevas chaqueta.
9. Ya son las diez y tu clase de cálculo empieza a las 9:40.
10. Sabes las respuestas correctas a todas las preguntas.

Answers Act. 7: 1. Tengo miedo. 2. Tengo calor. 3. Tengo ganas de jugar tenis. 4. Tengo hambre. 5. Tengo sed. / Tengo calor. / Tengo sueño. 6. Tengo miedo. 7. Tengo sueño. 8. Tengo frío. 9. Tengo prisa. 10. Tengo razón.

ACTIVIDAD 8 **¿Qué tienes?** Usa la siguiente lista. Pasea por la clase y busca una persona que tenga una de las emociones que se describen en la lista. Escribe los nombres al lado de las emociones. Luego escribe un resumen de tu encuesta. (¡Es posible que no encuentres nombres para todas las categorías!)

Esta persona...	Nombre
siempre tiene calor:	
tiene miedo de las serpientes:	
tiene ganas de viajar a Nepal:	
tiene vergüenza cuando tiene que hablar enfrente de mucha gente:	
nunca tiene sueño:	
siempre tiene razón:	
nunca tiene prisa:	
tiene ganas de hacer surfing:	

MODELO: *Kelly y Sandra siempre tienen calor. Y Jessie...*

ACTIVIDAD 9 **El tiempo.** Di qué tiempo hace por lo general durante las estaciones o meses indicados.

1. el mes de marzo en tu ciudad
2. el mes de agosto en tu ciudad
3. el mes de enero en tu ciudad
4. el mes de octubre en tu ciudad
5. en invierno en Buenos Aires
6. en invierno en Seattle
7. en verano en Miami
8. en invierno en Chicago

 ACTIVIDAD 10 **Prefiero...** Trabaja con un(a) compañero(a) de clase. Identifiquen por lo menos dos actividades que les gusta hacer y dos que no les gusta hacer cuando hace el tiempo indicado. Luego, escriban oraciones completas para hacer un resumen de sus preferencias.

1. cuando hace calor
2. cuando hace frío
3. cuando hace mucho viento
4. cuando nieva
5. cuando llueve

¡COMPÁRATE!

Cuando hablas del tiempo y de la temperatura en español, hay varias cosas importantes que debes saber. Primero, como viste en la **Actividad 5**, los países al norte y al sur del ecuador están en estaciones opuestas. Es decir, cuando en el norte estamos en invierno, los países al sur están en verano. Cuando es otoño en EEUU, allá es primavera.

Segundo, Estados Unidos y los países de habla española usan dos sistemas diferentes de medir (*to measure*) la temperatura. Aquí usamos el sistema Fahrenheit, mientras que en Latinoamérica y España usan el sistema Celsio. El sistema Celsio se usa en la mayoría de los países del mundo y también en las investigaciones científicas. Para ver las fórmulas para convertir temperaturas entre los dos sistemas, mira la página 199.

Finalmente, México, los países del Caribe y varios países de Centroamérica y Sudamérica tienen temporadas de lluvias y temporadas secas (*dry*). Aunque esto es más común en los países más cerca del ecuador, también puede ocurrir cuando corrientes del océano crean condiciones especiales, como en el Noroeste Pacífico de EEUU y en Perú.

PRÁCTICA. Miren las siguientes tablas y contesten las preguntas sobre el tiempo en las dos ciudades. (**tormenta** – *thunderstorm*, **chaparrón** = *cloudburst, downpour*)

Preparation / Optional: For the presentation of ¿**Qué tiempo hace?**, bring in a large colorful weather page from a newspaper, review colors, and ask where the weather is nice, hot, cool, etc.

Answers: 1. 28°, 20° 2. Celsio 3. Llueve. Van a tener tormentas el miércoles y chaparrones el sábado. 4. 33°, 26° 5. Hace más calor en la Ciudad de Panamá. 6. Van a tener chaparrones. 7. El verano es la temporada de lluvias.

1. ¿Cuál es la temperatura máxima en San José? ¿Y la temperatura mínima?
2. ¿Crees que se dan estas temperaturas en grados Celsio o Fahrenheit? (Si necesitas más ayuda, mira la página 199.)
3. ¿Qué tiempo hace en San José el martes 28 de agosto? ¿Qué tiempo va a hacer el miércoles? ¿y el sábado?
4. ¿Cuál es la temperatura máxima en la Ciudad de Panamá? ¿Y la temperatura mínima?
5. ¿Hace más calor en la Ciudad de Panamá o en San José?
6. ¿Cuál es el pronóstico para los días entre el jueves y el sábado en la Ciudad de Panamá?
7. ¿Cuándo es la temporada de lluvias en cada país?

TIEMPO, 28 DE AGOSTO

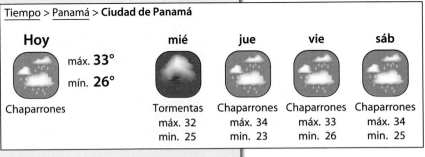

A VER

Antes de ver el video

Preparation: Start students thinking about what they will see in the video by chatting about working out: ¿Haces ejercicio? ¿Dónde? ¿Con quién(es)? ¿Vas al gimnasio frecuentemente o con poca frecuencia? ¿Cuándo haces ejercicio (por la mañana, por la tarde, por la noche)? ¿Te gusta usar las máquinas? ¿Levantas pesas? ¿Corres?

Answers Act. 1: 1. b 2. a 3. c 4. b 5. a 6. c

Answers Act. 2: **A Javier:** le gusta el fútbol / la natación / el ciclismo / el boxeo; no le gusta X (no se indica); **A Sergio:** le gusta el fútbol / el hockey sobre hielo / el esquí alpino; no le gusta X (no se indica); **A Beto:** le gusta el tenis; no le gusta hacer ejercicio en las máquinas (en el gimnasio); **A Dulce:** le gusta jugar tenis; no le gusta el gimnasio

ACTIVIDAD 1 Mira las fotos en las páginas 200 y 204 del **Vocabulario útil.** Luego, completa las siguientes oraciones sobre las personas de las fotos.

1. Javier y Sergio hablan de _____.
   a. los cursos
   b. los deportes
   c. el gimnasio

2. Sergio prefiere _____ sobre el boxeo.
   a. el fútbol nacional
   b. el hockey sobre hielo
   c. el esquí alpino

3. Según Beto, él no les tiene _____ a las máquinas del gimnasio.
   a. frío
   b. hambre
   c. miedo

4. Además, Beto no tiene _____ de hacer ejercicio en el gimnasio.
   a. razón
   b. ganas
   c. vergüenza

5. Beto no puede jugar tenis porque está _____.
   a. lloviendo
   b. nevando
   c. nublado

6. Hoy también hace _____.
   a. calor
   b. sol
   c. viento

ACTIVIDAD 2 Mira la siguiente tabla y fíjate en la información que necesites del video para completarla.

	A Javier...	A Sergio...	A Beto...	A Dulce...
le gusta...				
no le gusta...				

ESTRATEGIA

Listening for details

Previously you have learned to listen for the main idea of a video segment. By doing **Actividad 2,** you will focus on finding specific information. Knowing in advance what to listen for helps you focus on finding key pieces of information. For example, when you ask for directions, you might focus on listening to what turns to take or street names and important landmarks.

El video

Ahora mira el segmento del video para el **Capítulo 7** y completa la tabla de la **Actividad 2.** Si el video no tiene la información necesaria, pon una X en la parte correspondiente de la tabla.

Después de ver el video

ACTIVIDAD 3 Escribe frases completas sobre cada persona que sale en el segmento del video, según la información que usaste (*you used*) para completar la tabla de la **Actividad 2.**

MODELO: *A Javier le gustan la natación,...*

 ACTIVIDAD 4 Con un(a) compañero(a) de clase contesta las siguientes preguntas sobre el video.

1. ¿De qué hablan Javier y Sergio al principio de la escena?
2. ¿Va Beto al gimnasio con frecuencia?
3. ¿Qué dice Sergio sobre la condición física de Beto?
4. ¿Por qué empieza Beto a hacer ejercicio con mucho entusiasmo?
5. ¿Qué le dice Beto a Dulce sobre su rutina diaria? ¿Es cierto o falso?
6. ¿Qué hace Dulce cuando hace ejercicio?

ACTIVIDAD 5 Imagínate una conversación entre Dulce y Beto después de verse en el gimnasio. ¿Qué va a hacer Beto? ¿Va a invitar a Dulce a jugar tenis o va a confesarle que en realidad no se entrena en el gimnasio todos los días? Escribe una conversación breve entre los dos. ¡Usa la imaginación!

Answers Act. 4: 1. Hablan del partido de fútbol entre Argentina y México. 2. no 3. Dice que Beto tiene los músculos de un niño. 4. porque ve que Dulce está en el gimnasio 5. Le dice que va al gimnasio todos los días para levantar pesas. Es falso. 6. Dulce juega tenis.

Standards: Here students can present their version to an audience of listeners to meet C 1.3.

Standards: This spot on Orlando Antigua invites students out of the classroom to use their language and cultural skills to explore Spanish-speaking communities (C 5.1).

Además de Antigua, ¿qué otros deportistas hispanos conoces? ¿Te parece importante que los Harlem Globetrotters tengan un jugador latino? ¿Por qué sí o por qué no? To learn more about Orlando Antigua and his life and sports career, visit the *Nexos* website (http://college. hmco.com/languages/spanish/students) and follow the links.

VOCES DE LA COMUNIDAD

Orlando Antigua

❝ **Las miradas de los niños y sus padres nos recuerdan que todos nuestros esfuerzos bien valen la pena (*are worth it*). Nosotros somos embajadores (*ambassadors*) para el bien. Yo tengo la oportunidad de viajar por todo el mundo y entretener a la gente, hacerlos reír. Pocas personas tienen esa oportunidad.** ❞

Orlando "el Huracán" Antigua es uno de los jugadores más populares de los Harlem Globetrotters. Este nativo de la República Dominicana es también el primer latino en formar parte de este equipo. Además de ser un deportista excepcional, Antigua es una persona de gran valor y determinación. En su segundo año en la escuela secundaria, el joven Antigua fue víctima inocente de un tiroteo (*shooting*). Dos años más tarde, la familia Antigua se vio (*was*) obligada a vivir en las calles del Bronx, al perder su casa. A pesar de (*In spite of*) estos impedimentos, Orlando se convirtió en uno de los mejores jugadores de su escuela secundaria y más tarde de la Universidad de Pittsburgh. En 2001, la revista *Hispanic Business* seleccionó a Antigua como uno de los cien hispanos más influyentes de EEUU.

Gramática útil 1
Talking about what you did: The preterite tense of regular verbs

For more practice of chapter topics, do the *Nexos* website exercises.

¿Quién **ganó**?

Spanish uses another past tense called the *imperfect* to talk about past actions that were routine or ongoing. You will learn more about this tense in **Capítulo 9.**

Heritage Learners: Many heritage language speakers add an -s to the preterite form of the second-person singular: *comistes, *hablastes, *vivistes. When correcting this, point out that many people throughout the Spanish-speaking world also exhibit this tendency. The reason this practice is so widespread is because every other instance of a second-person singular conjugation in Spanish carries an -s. Emphasize that the practice does not correspond to the rules of standard Spanish and should be avoided.

CÓMO USARLO

LO BÁSICO

A *verb tense* is a form of a verb that indicates whether an action occurred in the past, present, or future. You have already been using the present indicative (**Estudio en la biblioteca**) and the present progressive (**Estoy hablando por teléfono**) tenses.

When you want to talk in Spanish about actions that occurred and were completed in the past, you use the *preterite tense*. The preterite is used to describe

◆ actions that began and ended in the past;
◆ conditions or states that existed completely within the past.

Me desperté, leí el periódico y **salí** para el gimnasio.
I woke up, I read the newspaper, and I left for the gym.

Fui secretario bilingüe por dos años.
I was a bilingual secretary for two years.

Estuve muy cansada la semana pasada.
I was very tired last week.

CÓMO FORMARLO

1. To form the preterite tense of regular **-ar, -er,** and **-ir** verbs (including reflexive verbs), you simply remove that ending from the infinitive and add the following endings to the verb stem.

	-ar verb: **bailar**		**-er** and **-ir** verbs: **comer / escribir**	
yo	**-é**	bail**é**	**-í**	com**í**	escrib**í**
tú	**-aste**	bail**aste**	**-iste**	com**iste**	escrib**iste**
Ud. / él / ella	**-ó**	bail**ó**	**-ió**	com**ió**	escrib**ió**
nosotros / nosotras	**-amos**	bail**amos**	**-imos**	com**imos**	escrib**imos**
vosotros / vosotras	**-asteis**	bail**asteis**	**-isteis**	com**isteis**	escrib**isteis**
Uds. / ellos / ellas	**-aron**	bail**aron**	**-ieron**	com**ieron**	escrib**ieron**

2. Notice that the preterite forms of **-er** and **-ir** verbs are the same.

3. Notice that only the **yo** and **Ud. / él / ella** forms are accented.

4. The **nosotros** forms of the preterite and the present indicative of **-ar** and **-ir** verbs are the same. You can tell which is being used by context.

Bailamos todos los fines de semana.   (present)
Bailamos la salsa con Mario ayer.   (past)

Stem-changing verbs that end in -ir also have stem changes in the preterite. You will learn these forms in **Capítulo 8.**

5. All stem-changing verbs that end in **-ar** or **-er** are regular in the preterite.

Me desperté a las ocho cuando **sonó** el teléfono.

Volví temprano de mis vacaciones porque **perdí** mi pasaporte.

I woke up at 8:00 when the telephone *rang.*

I returned early from my vacation because *I lost* my passport.

6. Many of the verbs you have already learned are regular in the preterite tense. A few have some minor changes.

◆ Verbs that end in **-car, -gar,** and **-zar** have a spelling change in the **yo** form to maintain the correct pronunciation.

-car:	**c → qu**	sacar: **saqué,** sacaste, sacó, sacamos, sacasteis, sacaron
-gar:	**g → gu**	llegar: **llegué,** llegaste, llegó, llegamos, llegasteis, llegaron
-zar:	**z → c**	cruzar: **crucé,** cruzaste, cruzó, cruzamos, cruzasteis, cruzaron

◆ Verbs that end in **-eer,** as well as the verb **oír,** change **i** to **y** in the two third-person forms. Note the accent on the **-íste, -ímos,** and **-ísteis** endings.

leer: leí, leíste, leyó, leímos, leísteis, leyeron
creer: creí, creíste, creyó, creímos, creísteis, creyeron
oír: oí, oíste, oyó, oímos, oísteis, oyeron

7. You have already learned the word **ayer.** Here are some other useful time expressions to use with the preterite tense: **anoche** (*last night*), **anteayer** (*the day before yesterday*), **la semana pasada** (*last week*), **el mes pasado** (*last month*), **el año pasado** (*last year*).

Optional: For a simple game that will practice the production of preterite verb endings, divide the class into 2–3 groups. Put students in 2–3 lines ready to approach the blackboard. Call out a subject (**tú, mi padre y yo,** etc.) and an infinitive (**bailar, comer, cruzar,** etc.). Remember to avoid stem-changing -ir verbs at this point. The first students in each line approach the board and write the correct conjugation. Rotate students and track points.

Try a dictation with respect to the use of [c] and [g] in the verbal paradigm, as well as the presence or absence of the accent: 1. navegar / navegué / navegue 2. indicar / indiqué / indique 3. brincar / brinqué / brinque 4. rezar / recé / rece 5. abrazar / abracé / abrace

Notice: Emphasize practice with **jugar** (g → gu) which will be used throughout the chapter. Stress yo form by asking questions like ¿**Jugaste algún deporte ayer / la semana pasada?**

Actividades

ACTIVIDAD 1 **¿Presente o pasado?** Escucha las oraciones e indica si las actividades que se describen ocurren en el presente o el pasado.

	Presente	Pasado
1. esquiar	_____	_____
2. entrenarse	_____	_____
3. navegar en rápidos	_____	_____
4. pescar	_____	_____
5. remar	_____	_____
6. jugar golf	_____	_____
7. patinar sobre hielo	_____	_____
8. nadar	_____	_____

Answers Act. 1: 1. presente 2. presente 3. pasado 4. pasado 5. presente 6. pasado 7. presente 8. pasado

Optional: Have students find out if a partner did any of these activities last week or last month. Then have them report; stress correct third-person forms: **Bob jugó golf y nadó; Sara no practicó estos deportes / ningún deporte** (or give **no hizo nada** for more natural response).

Suggestion: To practice the verb endings, say what you did before class: **Antes de clase, escribí un ensayo, comí un sandwich, llegué a clase.** Start a class conversation asking students questions like: **Antes de la clase de español, ¿leíste el libro de español / el periódico / tu correo electrónico? ¿Comiste? ¿Qué comiste?** etc. Continue by backshifting using other temporal markers like **anoche, ayer, anteayer, la semana pasada,** etc. to expand the question line.

ACTIVIDAD 2 **El calendario de Rosario.** Usa el siguiente calendario para decir qué hizo (*did*) Rosario la semana pasada.

lunes 17	martes 18	miércoles 19	jueves 20	viernes 21	sábado 22	domingo 23
AM: estudiar con Lalo	**AM:** trabajar en la biblioteca	**AM:** almorzar con Neti	**AM:** leer en la biblioteca	**AM:** correr dos millas	**AM:** desayunar con Sergio	**AM:** ¡descansar!
PM: jugar tenis con Fernando	**PM:** salir con Lalo	**PM:** sacar la basura	**PM:** escribir el ensayo para la clase de literatura	**PM:** ¡bailar en la discoteca!	**PM:** entrenarse en el gimnasio	**PM:** comer con Lalo

MODELOS: *El lunes por la mañana Rosario estudió con Lalo.*
O: *El lunes por la mañana Rosario y Lalo estudiaron.*

ACTIVIDAD 3 **Ayer.** Di qué hicieron (*did*) las siguientes personas ayer.

Answers Act. 3: Yo saqué fotos. Usted leyó el periódico. Ellos jugaron fútbol. Ustedes remaron. Elena bebió / tomó un refresco. Julio patinó en línea. Nosotros jugamos tenis. Tú escribiste (una carta). Natalia y Luisa comieron una hamburguesa. Ellas jugaron béisbol.

ACTIVIDAD 4 **La semana pasada.** Ahora, usa el horario de la **Actividad 2** como modelo y complétalo con tu propia información sobre la semana pasada. Luego, trabaja con un(a) compañero(a) de clase para hablar de sus actividades de la semana pasada.

MODELO: Tú: *¿Qué hiciste* (What did you do) *el lunes por la mañana?*
Compañero(a): *Jugué golf. ¿Y tú? ¿Qué hiciste el miércoles por la tarde?*

Gramática útil 2
Talking about what you did: The preterite tense of some common irregular verbs

CÓMO USARLO

As you learned in *Gramática útil 1*, the preterite is a Spanish past tense form that is used to talk about actions that occurred and were completed in the past. It describes actions that began and ended in the past as well as conditions that existed completely within the past.

Fuimos al restaurante.	*We went to the restaurant.*
Hicimos deporte todo el día.	*We played sports all day.*
¡Estuvimos bien cansados!	*We were really tired!*

CÓMO FORMARLO

1. Here are the irregular preterite forms of some frequently used verbs.

	estar	hacer	ir	ser
yo	estuve	hice	fui	fui
tú	estuviste	hiciste	fuiste	fuiste
Ud. / él / ella	estuvo	hizo	fue	fue
nosotros / nosotras	estuvimos	hicimos	fuimos	fuimos
vosotros / vosotras	estuvisteis	hicisteis	fuisteis	fuisteis
Uds. / ellos / ellas	estuvieron	hicieron	fueron	fueron

	dar	ver	decir	traer
yo	di	vi	dije	traje
tú	diste	viste	dijiste	trajiste
Ud. / él / ella	dio	vio	dijo	trajo
nosotros / nosotras	dimos	vimos	dijimos	trajimos
vosotros / vosotras	disteis	visteis	dijisteis	trajisteis
Uds. / ellos / ellas	dieron	vieron	dijeron	trajeron

¿Viste el partido de fútbol entre Argentina y México ayer?

Notice: True beginners will need help pronouncing these irregular forms. Hearing the rhythm of the irregular preterites will help students mnemonically as well.

Suggestion: Model a mini-narrative about what you did with whom yesterday. Chat with students about what they did yesterday: **¿Qué hiciste ayer? ¿Dónde estuviste? ¿Adónde fuiste? ¿Con quién estuviste? ¿A quién viste?** Optional: Have students create a description of all of the things that they did in Spanish class last week using the preterite forms. Cue this with the **nosotros** form.

Ver is irregular only because it does not carry accents on the **yo** and **Ud. / él / ella** forms. **Dar** is irregular because it uses the regular **-er / -ir** endings, rather than the **-ar** endings.

2. Verbs that end in **-cir** follow the same pattern as **traer** and **decir**.

conducir: conduje, condujiste, condujo, condujimos, condujisteis, condujeron
producir: produje, produjiste, produjo, produjimos, produjisteis, produjeron
traducir: traduje, tradujiste, tradujo, tradujimos, tradujisteis, tradujeron

3. Notice that although these irregular verbs do for the most part use the regular endings, they have internal changes to the stem that must be memorized.

4. Notice that none of these verbs requires accents in the preterite.

5. Notice that **ser** and **ir** have the same forms in the preterite. But because the verbs have such different meanings, it is usually fairly easy to tell which one is being used.

Fuimos estudiantes durante esos años.   *We were students during those years.*
Todos **fuimos** a una fiesta muy alegre.   *We all went to a really fun party.*

Actividades

ACTIVIDAD 5   **¿Qué hicieron?** Haz oraciones completas para decir qué pasó la semana pasada.

MODELO: **ir**
     ellos / al parque a jugar tenis
     Ellos fueron al parque a jugar tenis.

estar
1. tú y yo / en las montañas para hacer alpinismo
2. Mónica y Sara / en el gimnasio todos los días
3. usted / en la costa para hacer surfing

ir
4. ustedes / al gimnasio a entrenarse
5. yo / a la biblioteca a estudiar
6. Jorge / al parque a jugar básquetbol

ver
7. yo / una película muy buena
8. nosotros / a Mónica y a Sara en el gimnasio
9. tú / una serpiente en el parque

traer
10. Luis / su pelota de béisbol a mi casa para jugar
11. ellos / su equipo (*equipment*) para jugar hockey sobre hierba
12. tú / tus pesas para entrenarte

 ACTIVIDAD 6   **¿Quién fue?** Con un(a) compañero(a) de clase, digan quiénes fueron las personas indicadas. (En algunos casos, hay más de una respuesta posible.)

MODELO: Abraham Lincoln
     ¿Quién fue Abraham Lincoln?
     Fue presidente de Estados Unidos.

Respuestas posibles: presidente, futbolista, actor / actriz, científico(a), político(a), revolucionario(a)

1. Monsieur y Madame Curie
2. Albert Einstein
3. Sarah Bernhardt y Gloria Swanson
4. George Washington y John F. Kennedy
5. Mahatma Gandhi
6. Che Guevara
7. Jack Lemmon y James Stewart
8. Pelé

 ACTIVIDAD 7 **Las vacaciones.** Averigua qué hizo tu compañero(a) de clase durante sus vacaciones del año pasado. Luego explícale a tu compañero(a) lo que tú hiciste en tus vacaciones del año pasado. Juntos, determinen la siguiente información.

1. ¿Quién viajó más?
2. ¿Quién gastó más dinero?
3. ¿Quién trabajó más?
4. ¿Quién ganó más dinero?
5. ¿Quién hizo más ejercicio?

 ACTIVIDAD 8 **La reunión.** Escucha mientras Cecilia describe qué pasó la semana pasada en la reunión de ex alumnos de su colegio. Primero, completa la tabla con la información necesaria. Luego, escribe oraciones completas según el modelo.

Persona	¿Qué dijo?
yo (Cecilia)	
tú (Rosa Carmen)	
José María	
Marcos	*Es periodista.*
Laura y Sebastián	
Leticia	
Pilar y Antonio	

MODELO: Marcos
Marcos dijo que es periodista.

1. yo
2. tú
3. José María

4. Laura y Sebastián
5. Leticia
6. Pilar y Antonio

Answers Act. 8: 1. Yo dije que estoy casada y que tengo tres hijos. 2. Tú dijiste que trabajas como enfermera (y que te gusta mucho). 3. José María dijo que es profesor de matemáticas. 4. Laura y Sebastián dijeron que son profesores de lenguas (en la misma universidad). 5. Leticia dijo que ahora vive en Seattle (y que le gusta). 6. Pilar y Antonio dijeron que se casaron en 1998 y que son médicos (en el mismo hospital).

Optional: For expansion, explain the word **chisme** or *gossip* to students and state: **Dijeron en la tele que Tom Cruise se casa.** Ask students to think about any gossip items that they have heard recently and jot them down in Spanish. Call on a few students to read **sus chismes** to the class. If they haven't heard of any good gossip, encourage students to make something up!

Gramática útil 3
Referring to something already mentioned: Direct object pronouns

CÓMO USARLO

LO BÁSICO

A *direct object* is a noun or noun phrase that receives the action of a verb: I buy *a book*. We invite *our friends*. *Direct object pronouns* are pronouns that replace direct object nouns or phrases: I buy *it*, We invite *them*. Often you can identify the direct object of the sentence by asking *what?* or *whom?*: We buy *what?* (a book / it) / We invite *whom?* (our friends / them).

You use direct object pronouns in both Spanish and English to avoid repetition and to refer to things or people that have already been mentioned. Look at the following passage in Spanish and notice how much repetition there is.

Quiero hablar con María. Llamo a María por teléfono e invito a María a visitar a mis padres. Visito a mis padres casi todos los fines de semana.

Now read the passage after it's been rewritten using direct object pronouns to replace some of the occasions when the nouns **María** and **padres** were used previously. (The direct object pronouns appear underlined.)

Quiero hablar con María. <u>La</u> llamo por teléfono y <u>la</u> invito a visitar a mis padres. <u>Los</u> visito casi todos los fines de semana.

CÓMO FORMARLO

1. Here are the direct object pronouns in Spanish.

Pues, te perdiste un partido buenísimo. Yo **lo** vi en casa de Arturo.

Optional: Act out the use of direct objects by passing around objects (some masculine, feminine, singular, plural) in the class. Have students tell what they are doing using **pasar** and the direct object pronouns; for example: **Toma la pelota y pásala.** or **¿Qué haces con la pelota? La paso a Jim o Kelly,** etc.

singular		plural	
me	*me*	**nos**	*us*
te	*you (fam.)*	**os**	*you (fam.)*
lo	*you (form. masc.), him, it*	**los**	*you (form. masc.), them, it*
la	*you (form., fem.), she, it*	**las**	*you (form. fem.), them, it*

2. The third-person direct object pronouns in Spanish must agree in gender and number with the noun they replace.

Compramos **el libro.**	→	**Lo** compramos.
Compramos **la raqueta.**	→	**La** compramos.
Compramos **los libros.**	→	**Los** compramos.
Compramos **las raquetas.**	→	**Las** compramos.

3. Pay particular attention to these **lo / la** and **los / las** forms, since they can have a variety of meanings.

Los llamo. → I call them (*group of all men, or men and women*).
I call you (*polite form, more than one person, at least one man in group*).

Las llamo. → I call them (*group of all women*).
I call you (*polite form, all women*).

4. Direct object pronouns always come *before* a *conjugated verb* used by itself.

Me llamas el viernes, ¿no?   *You'll call **me** on Friday, right?*
Te invito a la fiesta.   *I'm inviting **you** to the party.*
No voy a leer este libro. ¿**Lo** quieres?   *I'm not going to read this book. Do you want **it?***

5. When a direct object pronoun is used with an *infinitive* or with the *present progressive*, it may come *before* the conjugated verbs or it may be *attached* to the infinitive or to the present participle.

Te voy a llamar.   OR: Voy a llamar**te**.
Te estoy llamando.   OR: Estoy llamándo**te**.

Notice that when the direct object pronoun attaches to the present participle you must add an accent to the next-to-last syllable of the present participle to maintain the correct pronunciation: **llamándote.**

6. When a direct object pronoun is used with a *command form*, it *attaches to the end of the affirmative command* but *comes before the negative command* form.

Hágalo ahora, por favor.   BUT: **No lo haga** ahora, por favor.

Again notice that when the direct object pronoun attaches to the command form you must add an accent to the next-to-last syllable of command forms of two or more syllables in order to maintain the correct pronunciation: **hágalo.**

7. When you use direct object pronouns with *reflexive pronouns*, the *reflexive pronouns come before the direct object pronouns.*

Me estoy lavando **la cara.**   *I am washing **my face.***
Me **la** estoy lavando.   *I am washing **it.***

Estoy lavándome **la cara.**   *I am washing **my face.***
Estoy lavándome**la.**   *I am washing **it.***

Actividades

ACTIVIDAD 9 **El día horrible de Manuel.** Lee sobre el día horrible de Manuel. Sustituye las palabras **en negrilla (*boldface*)** con complementos directos, según el modelo.

MODELO: Compré **los libros.**
Los compré.

Answers Act. 9 : Los compré, La busqué, no la encontré, lo compré, no los pude comprar (no pude comprarlos), no la encontré, Lo saludé, La escribió, La examiné, no pude repararla (no la pude reparar), Tenemos que llevarla (La tenemos que llevar)

Un día horrible

¡Ayer estuve muy ocupado! Empezaron las clases y tuve que comprar los libros. Compré **los libros** en la librería de la universidad. Pero no encontré el libro para mi clase de cálculo. Tuve que ir a otra librería que me recomendaron. Busqué **la librería,** pero, como no me dieron buenas indicaciones para llegar, ¡no encontré **la librería** hasta después de dos horas! Por fin, vi el libro de clase y compré **el libro.**

Después fui al supermercado para comprar algunos comestibles pero no pude comprar **los comestibles** porque no encontré mi tarjeta de crédito (*credit card*). Volví a la librería para buscar mi tarjeta, pero no encontré **la tarjeta** allí.

Decidí ir a la residencia estudiantil para descansar un poco y hacer un poco de trabajo. Vi a mi compañero de cuarto en la entrada. Saludé a **mi compañero de cuarto.** Él me dijo que me escribió una nota. Escribió **la nota** para decirme que la computadora no funciona bien. Examiné **la computadora,** pero no pude (*I couldn't*) reparar **la computadora.** Tenemos que llevar **la computadora** al centro de computación para hacerle reparaciones. ¡Otra cosa que tengo que hacer!

ACTIVIDAD 10 **Pobre Manuel.** Contesta las preguntas sobre el día horrible de Manuel. Usa un complemento directo en tu respuesta.

MODELO: ¿Encontró Manuel el libro en la librería de la universidad?
No, no lo encontró.

1. ¿Encontró Manuel la librería que le recomendaron sus amigos?
2. ¿Compró los comestibles?
3. ¿Encontró su tarjeta de crédito?
4. ¿Vio a su compañero de cuarto en la residencia estudiantil?
5. Cuando llegó a la residencia estudiantil, ¿pudo hacer su trabajo?
6. ¿Usó la computadora en su cuarto?
7. ¿Tuvo que llevar la computadora al centro de computaciones?
8. ¿Tuvo un día tranquilo?

ACTIVIDAD 11 **Natalia.** El padre de Natalia y Nico es muy exigente (*demanding*). Les hace muchas preguntas. Haz el papel de Natalia y contesta las preguntas de su padre.

MODELOS: Padre: ¿Limpiaron el baño? (sí)
Natalia: *Sí, lo limpiamos.*

Padre: ¿Limpiaste tu cuarto? (no)
Natalia: *No, pero estoy limpiándolo ahora mismo.*

1. ¿Hiciste la tarea? (sí)
2. ¿Prepararon el almuerzo? (no)
3. ¿Hicieron los planes para la fiesta? (no)
4. ¿Leíste la nota de tu mamá? (sí)
5. ¿Viste la lista de comida que debes comprar en el supermercado? (sí)
6. ¿Llamaste a tu abuela? (sí)
7. ¿Tomaron sus vitaminas? (no)
8. ¿Te lavaste los dientes? (no)

ACTIVIDAD 12 **¿Lo leíste?** Trabaja con un(a) compañero(a) de clase. Háganse preguntas y contéstenlas, usando complementos directos. Sigan el modelo.

MODELO: leer / el nuevo libro de Stephen King
Compañero(a): *¿Leíste el nuevo libro de Stephen King?*
Tú: *Sí, lo leí.* O: *No, no lo leí.*

1. ver / la nueva película de Pedro Almodóvar
2. leer / el nuevo libro de Tom Clancy
3. ver / los partidos de básquetbol del WNBA
4. traer / computadora portátil a clase
5. entender / la tarea de la clase de español
6. comprar / las pelotas de tenis
7. comprar / el nuevo CD de Phish
8. ver / los últimos episodios de *Survivor*
9. ver / tus hermanas el mes pasado
10. ¿…?

Sonrisas

Optional: Discuss with the class their own technological preferences and abilities: **¿Prefieres resolver tus propios problemas en tu computadora o prefieres la ayuda de un amigo? ¿Es fácil para ti instalar programas en tu computadora? ¿A quién(es) das tu dirección electrónica? ¿Tienes amigos que pasan demasiado tiempo en Internet?**

EXPRESIÓN. **La cortesía...** En grupos de tres o cuatro estudiantes, hagan una lista de las reglas (*rules*) de cortesía para el teléfono y el correo electrónico. ¿Qué se debe y no se debe hacer?

MODELO: Cuando llamas por teléfono...
No debes llamar muy temprano por la mañana.
Cuando escribes correo electrónico...
Debes escribir mensajes cortos.

Gramática útil 4
Telling friends what to do: *Tú* command forms

Can you find two tú command forms in this ad? Are they regular or irregular?

Answers: ven (irregular), pon (irregular)

CÓMO USARLO

1. You have already learned how to use polite (**usted** and **ustedes**) command forms in **Capítulo 6.** Now you will learn the informal command forms that correspond to people you would normally address as **tú.** (You've been seeing these forms in activity direction lines in the last few chapters.)

Habla con Claudia.	*Talk to Claudia.*
Pero **no hables** con Leo.	*But **don't talk** to Leo.*

2. Since you are using informal command forms to address people who are friends (or small children and animals), you don't need to worry as much about making your requests sound as polite as you do with **usted** forms. However, it never hurts to use one of the softening expressions you learned in **Capítulo 6**! Here they are again, revised to fit an informal context.

¿Me puedes decir... / Me dices...?	*Can you tell me . . .?*
¿Puedes + *infinitive. . .* ?	*Can you + infinitive . . .?*
¿Quieres / Quisieras + *infinitive. . .* ?	*Would you like to . . . + infinitive . . .?*
¿Te importa...?	*Would / Does it matter to you . . .?*
¿Te molesta...?	*Would / Does it bother you . . .?*

CÓMO FORMARLO

Optional: For oral practice, have students imagine that they are preparing for a big Spanish test. Have students come up with advice for each other creating affirmative and negative commands.

1. Unlike the **usted** forms that you learned in **Capítulo 6, tú** commands have one form for affirmative commands and one form for negative commands.

2. To form the affirmative **tú** command form, simply use the **usted / él / ella** present-tense form of the verb.

Affirmative **tú** command forms		
-ar verb	**-er** verb	**-ir** verb
tomar → **toma**	beber → **bebe**	escribir → **escribe**

3. To form the negative **tú** command form, take the affirmative **tú** command, and replace the final vowel with **-es** for **-ar** verbs and with **-as** for **-er / -ir** verbs.

Negative **tú** command forms			
	-ar verb **hablar**	**-er** verb **beber**	**-ir** verb **escribir**
affirmative **tú** command	habla	bebe	escribe
negative **tú** command	no **hables**	no **bebas**	no **escribas**

Notice that the negative **tú** commands are the same as the **usted** command forms, but with an -s added. **Usted** command: **hable**; negative **tú** command: **no hables**.

4. These **tú** command forms are irregular and must be memorized.

	Affirmative **tú** command	Negative **tú** command
decir	di	no digas
hacer	haz	no hagas
ir	ve	no vayas
poner	pon	no pongas
salir	sal	no salgas
ser	sé	no seas
tener	ten	no tengas
venir	ven	no vengas

Notice that the **tú** command for **ser** (**sé**) is the same as the first person of **saber** (**sé**). Context will clarify which is meant: **¡Sé bueno!** vs. **Sé que Manuel es bueno.** The same is true for the command forms of **ir (ve)** and **ver (ve)**: **Ve a clase.** vs. **Ve ese programa.**

5. As with **usted** command forms, *reflexive pronouns* and *direct object pronouns* attach to affirmative **tú** commands and come before negative **tú** commands. Note that you need to add an accent to the next-to-last syllable of the command form when attaching pronouns.

¡Despiértate, ya es tarde!	*Wake up, it's late!*
¡No te acuestes ahora!	*Don't go to bed now!*
Llámame.	*Call me.*
No me llames después de las once.	*Don't call me after 11:00.*

Actividades

Answers Act. 13: 1. No montes... 2. No camines... 3. No hagas... 4. Juega... 5. No patines... 6. No nades... 7. Dúchate... 8. Ten cuidado...

ACTIVIDAD 13 **El campamento.** La semana que viene, tu hermanito va a ir a un campamento de verano. Tú le das algunos consejos antes de salir.

MODELOS: acostarte / temprano   nadar / en el océano
Acuéstate temprano.   *No nades en el océano.*

1. montar en bicicleta / en la carretera (*highway*)
2. caminar / en el parque por la noche
3. hacer / deportes peligrosos
4. jugar / con los otros niños
5. patinar en línea / sin casco (*helmet*)
6. nadar / después de comer
7. ducharse / después de nadar en el lago
8. tener cuidado / al nadar en el lago

Answers Act. 14: **Afirmativo:** 1. Sí, ciérrala, por favor. 2. Sí, ábrelas, por favor. 3. Sí, ponlos en el refrigerador, por favor. 4. Sí, contéstalo, por favor. 5. Sí, apágala, por favor. 6. Sí, sácala, por favor.

Negativo: 1. No, no la cierres. 2. No, no las abras. 3. No, no los pongas en el refrigerador. 4. No, no lo contestes. 5. No, no la apagues. 6. No, no la saques.

ACTIVIDAD 14 **¡Primo!** Vas a quedarte en la casa de tu primo para el verano. Le haces preguntas sobre la casa y tus quehaceres. Escribe sus respuestas, según el modelo.

MODELO: ¿Apago las luces antes de acostarme?
Sí, apágalas, por favor.

1. ¿Cierro la puerta del garaje por la noche?
2. ¿Abro las ventanas si hace calor?
3. ¿Pongo los comestibles en el refrigerador?
4. ¿Contesto el teléfono cuando no estás en casa?
5. ¿Apago la computadora antes de acostarme?
6. ¿Saco la basura los lunes por la noche?

Ahora, contesta la preguntas de arriba con un mandato informal negativo.

MODELO: ¿Apago las luces antes de acostarme?
No, no las apagues.

ACTIVIDAD 15 **Los consejos.** Da un consejo para cada situación.

MODELO: Juan quiere desarrollar sus músculos.
Levanta pesas dos veces por semana.

Magda quiere perder peso pero no quiere hacer ejercicio.
No comas papitas fritas.

1. María desea perder cinco kilos.
2. Pedro quiere entrenarse para un maratón.
3. Pablo quiere mejorar su capacidad aeróbica.
4. Margarita quiere correr más rápido.
5. Francisco quiere ponerse en forma pero no tiene mucho tiempo para hacer ejercicio.

 ACTIVIDAD 16 Trabajen en grupos de tres o cuatro personas. Imagínense que un(a) estudiante nuevo(a) acaba de llegar a su residencia estudiantil. Él (Ella) nunca ha vivido (*has lived*) fuera de su casa paterna. Denle consejos importantes para no tener problemas con sus compañeros de residencia. Sigan el modelo.

MODELO: *No pongas la radio después de las nueve de la noche.*

Panamá y Costa Rica

Similares pero diferentes. Lee los textos sobre Panamá y Costa Rica en las páginas 224–225. Luego completa un diagrama Venn como el de abajo. Pon los números de los comentarios sobre Panamá a la izquierda y los números de los comentarios sobre Costa Rica a la derecha. Los números de los comentarios que se refieren a los dos países van en el centro del diagrama.

1. Los indígenas son una parte importante de la cultura.

2. Los grupos indígenas son los Chorotega, Huetar y Brunca.

3. Tiene un teatro famoso en la ciudad capital.

4. Las famosas molas de los kunas se venden a personas de todo el mundo.

5. Cristóbal Colón exploró este país en 1501 y 1502.

6. Es un país democrático que no tiene fuerzas armadas.

7. La población de ascendencia africana vive en la costa del Mar Caribe.

8. Consiguió su independencia de España en 1821.

9. Fue víctima de muchos ataques de piratas.

10. Tiene muchísimas islas.

11. Es muy popular entre los ecoturistas.

12. La población criolla o mestiza es el grupo étnico más grande del país.

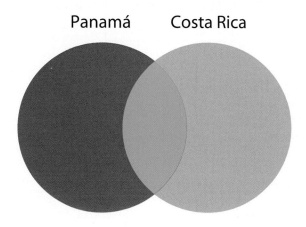

Panamá   Costa Rica

PANAMÁ

PANAMÁ

Grupos étnicos:
- Los criollos o mestizos, que es el grupo étnico más grande.
- Los indígenas, que tienen muchas variantes determinadas por las varias tribus. De estas tribus, tal vez la más famosa son los kunas, conocidos por la fabricación de sus molas tradicionales de colores vivos que se venden internacionalmente.
- La población negra, que son los descendientes africanos que forman las poblaciones de Colón, en el Caribe, y Darién, en la costa pacífica.

Historia:
- Vasco Núñez de Balboa y Cristóbal Colón exploraron el país en 1501 y 1502. Buscando el oro y las riquezas de una civilización indígena legendaria, Balboa "descubrió" el Océano Pacífico en 1513.
- Las colonias españolas sufrieron ataques de piratas ingleses y holandeses durante el siglo XVII. En 1671 el pirata inglés Henry Morgan destruyó la ciudad de Panamá y confiscó sus tesoros (*treasures*).
- Después de ganar la independencia de España en 1821, Panamá pasó por mucha turbulencia política. En 1904, Estados Unidos empezó la construcción del canal de Panamá. En 1999, EEUU cedió el canal al gobierno panameño.

Sitios de interés:
- El archipiélago de San Blas, donde viven los kunas, son unas de las 1.600 islas que pertenecen a Panamá.
- El Parque Nacional de Darién es una de las selvas tropicales más densas y bellas de Centroamérica.
- La ciudad de Panamá es famosa por su celebración de Carnaval y también por los espectáculos de danza y música que se presentan en el Teatro Nacional.

Una mujer kuna vende molas en un mercado panameño.

Heritage Learners: Since many heritage learners have had limited practice reading large numbers in Spanish, it is a good idea to practice numbers whenever the opportunity arises. These readings are good to practice because there are many dates.

Suggestion: Have students calculate and guess the date of the opening of the Panama Canal in Spanish. The Panama Canal opened in 1914.

Costa Rica

COSTA RICA

Grupos étnicos:

- La gran mayoría de la población es criolla—mestizos de ascendencia española e indígena.
- La población negra, que constituye menos del 2 por ciento de la población, vive en su mayoría en la costa caribeña.
- Los grupos indígenas componen menos del 1 por ciento de la población y se distinguen tres etnias indígenas—Chorotega, Huetar y Brunca.

Historia:

- Cristóbal Colón fue el primer europeo en llegar a esta área en 1502. Esperando encontrar riquezas naturales y otros metales preciosos, observó los adornos de oro de los indígenas y nombró el país Costa Rica.
- Costa Rica ganó la independencia de España en 1821 y después de unos conflictos políticos, llegó a ser una democracia en 1889.
- En 1949, el Partido Liberación Nacional creó una constitución nacional, dio el derecho (*right*) de votar a las mujeres y a los afro-costarricenses y abolió las fuerzas armadas.

Sitios de interés:

- Costa Rica es uno de los países de mayor diversidad geográfica del mundo. Su extenso sistema de parques nacionales es famoso por todo el mundo e incluye más de 6.132 km^2 de parques con volcanes, selvas tropicales y playas. Es un lugar muy popular para los ecoturistas.
- El Teatro Nacional, en la capital de San José, es una atracción arquitectónica famosa y también sirve como un centro nacional para el arte, la música y otros eventos culturales.
- Sarchí, un pueblo cerca de San José, es el centro de artesanías costarricenses. Es famoso por sus carretas (*wooden carts*) pintadas en colores brillantes.

El Teatro Nacional en San José es un sitio turístico muy popular.

Internet

¡CONÉCTATE!

En parejas, busquen información en Internet sobre uno de los siguientes temas. Luego, preparen un breve informe para dar a la clase. Usen los enlaces sugeridos en el sitio web de *Nexos* (http://college.hmco.com/languages/spanish/students).

1. la construcción o la historia del canal de Panamá
2. cómo los indios kunas fabrican sus molas (como las de las páginas 198 y 224)
3. por qué Costa Rica decidió abolir las fuerzas armadas
4. las carretas pintadas de Sarchí
5. uno de los parques nacionales de Costa Rica
6. la historia de Balboa en Panamá

A LEER

Antes de leer

Answers Act. 1: 1. 5 (Reventazón, Pacuare, Sarapiquí, Naranjo, Corobicí), 2. Categories I–VI (0 = pool and VII = Niagara Falls)

ACTIVIDAD 1 Mira el siguiente artículo y las fotos sobre la navegación en rápidos en Costa Rica y ojea (*scan*) el artículo rápidamente para encontrar la siguiente información.

1. cuántos ríos (*rivers*) costarricenses se mencionan
2. los niveles (*levels*) de dificultad que se usan para describir los rápidos de los ríos

Answers Act. 2: b.

ACTIVIDAD 2 Después de anotar la información de la **Actividad 1,** di cuál es, en tu opinión, el propósito (*purpose*) de la lectura.

a. describir el paisaje (*scenery*) a lo largo de los ríos de Costa Rica
b. informar a los aficionados de la navegación en rápidos sobre los ríos de Costa Rica
c. darles a los viajeros a Costa Rica una lista de posibles deportes acuáticos

Answers Act. 3: 1. c 2. d 3. a 4. f 5. g 6. e 7. b

ACTIVIDAD 3 Las siguientes palabras aparecen (*appear*) en el artículo. Aunque estas palabras no son cognados, tienen una relación semántica con sus equivalentes en inglés. A ver si puedes identificar el equivalente en inglés de cada palabra a la izquierda.

1. _____ media docena   a. *co-owner*
2. _____ principiantes   b. *peaceful*
3. _____ codueño   c. *half dozen*
4. _____ haber pasado   d. *beginners*
5. _____ poblado   e. *stretches*
6. _____ trechos   f. *to have passed (navigated)*
7. _____ apacible   g. *town, village*

Lectura

ACTIVIDAD 4 Ahora, lee el artículo rápidamente para buscar la idea principal. Luego mira la **Actividad 5** para ver qué información necesitas para completarla. Vuelve al artículo y busca esa información. No olvides usar los cognados, el formato del artículo y las fotos para ayudarte a entender el texto.

Suggestion: Warm up for reading with questions like **¿Te gusta navegar en rápidos? Describe tus experiencias.**

COSTA RICA

Aventuras en los rápidos

Pocos países pueden contar con tan excelentes condiciones para la navegación en rápidos como Costa Rica, donde los retos de este conocido deporte se complementan con la belleza y diversidad de los bosques tropicales.

Quizás[1] las aguas más bravas del país sean aptas sólo para expertos remeros—media docena de equipos olímpicos de kayaks utilizan a Costa Rica como base de entrenamiento—, pero la mayoría de sus ríos rápidos ofrecen condiciones perfectas también para principiantes.

Los navegantes de balsas y kayaks poseen un sistema para evaluar el grado de dificultad de los rápidos y ríos individuales, en una escala que va de la Clase I a la Clase VI— donde el 0 es similar a una piscina y el VII, a las Cataratas del Niágara. Los rápidos de Clase II y III son, por lo general, suficientes para acelerar el ritmo cardíaco. Los de Clase IV pueden ser un poco más peligrosos, mientras que los de Clase V están ya cerca de lo imposible. Los ríos de Clase II y III son magníficos para principiantes. No obstante, resulta recomendable haber pasado, al menos, por un río antes de intentar lanzarse[2] en los de Clase II–IV. Los de Clase IV–V requieren una buena condición física y más experiencia con las balsas.

Las rutas de navegación

El río **Reventazón** posee numerosos tramos[3] navegables. El más popular es la sección Tucurrique (Clase III), que ofrece una excursión segura y emocionante, lo suficientemente fácil para un viaje de primera vez. La sección Peralta (Clase V) es la ruta más difícil de Costa Rica para este tipo de navegación, con rápidos indetenibles y bastante peligro, razón por la cual sólo está abierto para expertos.

El río **Pacuare** (Clase III–IV) es una de las maravillas naturales más impresionantes de Costa Rica. Es un río emocionante de navegar, con numerosos y provocadores rápidos de Clase IV. El Pacuare se navega mejor en un viaje de dos o tres días, lo cual permite un contacto más cercano con el bosque[4] tropical—un área excelente para la observación de pájaros[5].

El **Sarapiquí** (Clase III) es un río hermoso que fluye por el norte de la Cordillera Montañosa Central. La sección de rápidos entre La Virgen y Chilamae proporciona una aventura de navegación en balsa de Clase III, que pasa a través de muchos bosques tropicales y cataratas. La parte más baja del Sarapiquí es un flotador suave que resulta perfecto para niños pequeños.

El **Naranjo** (Clase III–IV) es un río emocionante y provocador que exige[6] cierta experiencia de navegación en balsa. Puede navegarse sólo en meses lluviosos. Queda[7] a un día desde Manuel Antonio y Quepos.

El **Corobicí** (Clase I–II) es un río completamente apacible. Es excelente para los amantes[8] de la naturaleza y puede ser navegado por personas de cualquier edad. En el bosque que viste sus orillas[9] se pueden ver iguanas, monos[10] y una rica variedad de pájaros.

[1]Perhaps [2]**intentar...** to try to throw oneself [3]sections [4]forest [5]birds [6]demands [7]It is located [8]lovers [9]shores [10]monkeys

Después de leer

Answers Act. 5: Reventazón, Clase III–V, una sección tiene la ruta más difícil de Costa Rica que sólo está abierta a expertos; Corobicí, Clase I–II, tiene iguanas, monos y una variedad de pájaros; Sarapiquí; Clase III, una parte es perfecta para los niños pequeños; Naranjo, Clase III–IV, puede navegarse sólo en meses lluviosos; Pacuare, Clase III–IV

ACTIVIDAD 5 Completa la siguiente tabla con información del artículo. Si te es necesario, vuelve al artículo para buscarla.

Río	Clase	Una cosa interesante
Reventazón	III-V	
	I-II	
		Una parte es perfecta para los niños pequeños.
Naranjo		
		Tiene uno de los paisajes más bellos del país.

 ACTIVIDAD 6 Trabajen en grupos de tres a cuatro estudiantes para hablar de los cinco ríos que se describen en el artículo. ¿Cuál les interesa más? Escojan (*Choose*) un lugar para ir de vacaciones con el grupo. Para ayudarles con la decisión, contesten las siguientes preguntas.

1. ¿Cuánta experiencia con la navegación en rápidos tienen las varias personas del grupo?
2. ¿Van a viajar durante la temporada de lluvia (verano) o durante el invierno?
3. ¿A qué distancia de San José están dispuestos (*willing*) a viajar?
4. ¿Cuánto tiempo quieren pasar en el río?
5. ¿Qué les interesa más, la belleza natural o la aventura de los rápidos?

MODELOS: *A mí me gusta...*
Yo prefiero... porque...
Vamos a viajar en...

A ESCRIBIR

Antes de escribir

Preparation: You may want to introduce the phrase **Escribir sin detenerse** to your students to refer to freewriting in class.

 ACTIVIDAD 1 Trabaja con un(a) compañero(a) de clase. Entre los dos van a escribir un artículo de tres párrafos breves para el periódico universitario. Van a describir un pasatiempo interesante que se puede hacer en su pueblo o ciudad. Para empezar, hagan una lista de actividades posibles. (Usen el artículo de la página 227 como modelo para su artículo.)

 ACTIVIDAD 2 Cuando tengan la lista de ideas, escojan (*choose*) la que les gusta más. Juntos, escojan tres aspectos específicos para desarrollar (*to develop*) en los tres párrafos del artículo. Escriban una oración temática para cada uno.

Párrafo 1:
Párrafo 2:
Párrafo 3:

Escritura

ACTIVIDAD 3 Individualmente, usa la información que preparaste con tu compañero(a). Usando las oraciones temáticas que escribiste para la **Actividad 2,** escribe los tres párrafos que forman el primer borrador (*draft*) del artículo. Trata de escribir libremente, sin preocuparte por los errores, la organización, la ortografía o la gramática.

Después de escribir

ACTIVIDAD 4 Ahora trabaja con tu compañero(a) otra vez. Intercambien sus borradores. Usen las dos versiones para crear un solo artículo que contenga lo mejor de los dos borradores.

ACTIVIDAD 5 Ahora, miren juntos la nueva versión del artículo. Usen la siguiente lista para ayudarles a redactarla (*to edit it*).

- ¿Tiene el artículo toda la información necesaria?
- ¿Es interesante e informativo también?
- ¿Usaron pronombres de complemento directo (*direct object pronouns*) para eliminar la repetición?
- ¿Usaron bien las formas del pretérito?
- ¿Usaron las formas correctas de todos los verbos?
- ¿Hay errores de ortografía?

VOCABULARIO

LOS DEPORTES *Sports*

el básquetbol	*basketball*
el béisbol	*baseball*
el boxeo	*boxing*
el ciclismo	*cycling*
el esquí acuático	*water skiing*
el esquí alpino	*downhill skiing*
el fútbol	*soccer*
el fútbol americano	*football*
el golf	*golf*
el hockey sobre hielo	*ice hockey*
el hockey sobre hierba	*field hockey*
la navegación en rápidos	*white-water rafting*
la natación	*swimming*
el tenis	*tennis*
el volibol	*volleyball*

ACTIVIDADES DEPORTIVAS *Sport activities*

entrenarse	*to train*
esquiar	*to ski*
hacer ejercicio	*to exercise*
jugar (ue) (tenis, béisbol, etc.)	*to play (tenis, baseball, etc.)*
montar a caballo	*to ride horseback*
montar en bicicleta	*to ride a bike*
nadar	*to swim*
navegar en rápidos	*to go white-water rafting*
patinar en línea	*to inline skate (rollerblade)*
patinar sobre hielo	*to ice skate*
pescar	*to fish*
practicar / hacer alpinismo	*to hike*
practicar / hacer surfing	*to surf*
remar	*to row*

MÁS PALABRAS SOBRE LOS DEPORTES
More sports words

la competencia	*competition*
el equipo	*team*
el lago	*lake*
el partido	*game, match*
el peligro	*danger*
peligroso(a)	*dangerous*
la pelota	*ball*
la piscina	*pool*
el río	*river*
seguro(a)	*safe*

LAS ESTACIONES *Seasons*

el invierno	*winter*
la primavera	*spring*
el verano	*summer*
el otoño	*fall, autumn*

EXPRESIONES CON *TENER*

tener calor	*to be hot*
tener cuidado	*to be careful*
tener frío	*to be cold*
tener ganas de	*to have the urge to, to feel like*
tener hambre	*to be hungry*
tener miedo (a, de)	*to be afraid (of)*
tener prisa	*to be in a hurry*
tener razón	*to be right*
tener sed	*to be thirsty*
tener sueño	*to be sleepy*
tener vergüenza	*to be embarrassed, ashamed*

EL TIEMPO *Weather*

¿Qué tiempo hace?	*What's the weather like?*
Hace buen / mal tiempo.	*It's nice / bad weather.*
Hace calor.	*It's hot.*
Hace fresco.	*It's cool.*
Hace frío.	*It's cold.*
Hace sol.	*It's sunny.*
Hace viento.	*It's windy.*
Está lloviendo. (Llueve.)	*It's raining.*
Está nevando. (Nieva.)	*It's snowing.*
Está nublado.	*It's cloudy.*

LA TEMPERATURA *Temperature*

grados centígrados	*degrees Celsius*
grados Fahrenheit	*degrees Fahrenheit*
La temperatura está a 20 grados centígrados.	*It's 20 degrees Celsius.*
La temperatura está a 68 grados Fahrenheit.	*It's 68 degrees Fahrenheit.*

PALABRAS RELATIVAS AL TIEMPO

anoche	*last night*
anteayer	*the day before yesterday*
el año pasado	*last year*
el mes pasado	*last month*
la semana pasada	*last week*

¿En qué puedo servirle?

Communication

By the end of this chapter
you will be able to:
- talk about clothing and
  fashion
- shop for various articles
  of clothing and discuss
  prices
- describe recent purchases
  and shopping trips
- talk about buying items
  and doing favors for
  friends
- make comparisons

Cultures

By the end of this chapter
you will have learned about:
- Perú and Ecuador
- traditional clothing vs.
  popular clothing
- Chinese immigration to
  Perú and the U.S.
- attitudes towards jeans
  around the world

Preparation: Ask questions based on the
photo: **¿Es ropa tradicional o de última
moda? ¿De qué colores es la ropa?
Describe los detalles de la ropa.**

Se venden suéteres de alpaca en este mercado ecuatoriano.

ESTILO PERSONAL

¿Tienen mucha importancia para ti la ropa y el estilo personal? ¿Crees que la ropa
es una forma de expresión o es solamente para cubrirse? Para mucha gente, la
ropa es una forma importante de presentarse al mundo e identificarse con los
demás. En este capítulo vamos a explorar los varios aspectos de la moda.

5-2 Standards: In this chapter, students will be able to develop insights into other cultures that are likely to impact them as life-long learners
making decisions in the market place. Have a brief discussion about **la exportación y la importación** of products to the U.S. Start by
asking students where their clothes and other items are from. The culture standard is also met in this chapter through the focus on Perú and
Ecuador. Have students generate what they know about these countries and state what they would like to find out.

Los datos

Mira la información del diagrama. Luego completa cada oración que sigue con la mejor respuesta.

❶ El guanaco es una especie más _____ que las llamas.
   a. moderna
   b. antigua
   c. fuerte

❷ Hay un número casi igual de _____ en el mundo.
   a. guanacos y vicuñas
   b. vicuñas y alpacas
   c. alpacas y llamas

❸ _____ fue domesticado/a por los incas.
   a. El guanaco
   b. La vicuña
   c. La llama

El guanaco
Animal silvestre, progenitor de las llamas, las alpacas y las vicuñas. Unos 500.000 viven en las altas montañas de Argentina y Chile. Es una especie en peligro de extinción.

pelo más suave (*soft*)   pelo menos suave

La vicuña	La alpaca	La llama
Animal domesticado. Más de 120.000 en el centro y sur de Perú. Su pelo se considera una de las fibras más valiosas del mundo.	Animal domesticado. Más de 3,5 millones en Perú. Su pelo es de varios colores y se usa para ropa ligera (*light*) pero caliente.	Animal domesticado. Más de 3,5 millones en Sudamérica, con la mayoría en Perú. Se usa su pelo en la industria textil.

Nota: Las llamas y las alpacas fueron domesticadas por los incas hace 6.000 años.

¡Adivina!

¿Qué sabes de Perú y Ecuador? Indica a qué país o países se refiere cada oración. (Las respuestas están en la página 258.)

❶ En este país están las ruinas del famoso sitio inca de Machu Picchu.
❷ Este país recibió su nombre de un delineador geográfico.
❸ El lago Titicaca, el lago navegable más alto del mundo, está situado entre este país y Bolivia.
❹ Este país ha tenido (*has experienced*) problemas políticos durante las últimas décadas.
❺ Este país tiene como capital la ciudad de Quito, un lugar famoso por su hermosa arquitectura colonial.

Vocabulario útil 1

DEPENDIENTE:	¿En qué puedo servirle, señor?
JAVIER:	Pues, estoy buscando un regalo para mi madre pero no sé, no veo nada.
DEPENDIENTE:	Pues, si le gusta la **ropa** fina, esta **blusa de seda** es muy bonita y además está rebajada.
JAVIER:	No, no le gusta ese color.
DEPENDIENTE:	¿Quizás este **suéter**?
JAVIER:	No. Tampoco necesita suéter.
DEPENDIENTE:	Y las **joyas**, ¿a quién no le gustan las joyas?... ¿Quizás estos **aretes**? Son de **oro** y le dan ese toque de elegancia a cualquier **vestido.**

LAS PRENDAS DE ROPA

Suggestion: Expand discussion of the drawings with ¿Quiénes son las personas en los dibujos? ¿Dónde están? ¿Qué hacen? ¿Qué llevan? ¿Cuántos años tienen (más o menos)? ¿Qué tipo de ropa llevan? ¿Es ropa formal o informal? ¿Llevas este tipo de ropa? ¿Cuándo llevas sudadera / botas / impermeable / etc.?

Optional: Bring in some clothing catalogs and call attention to the broad selection that we have as U.S. consumers. Have students explore the origin of their own clothing by looking at the tags. Get students thinking about where these goods come from and how consumers impact the country of origin.

el suéter · la blusa · la camisa · el saco · la corbata · el vestido · el abrigo · los pantalones cortos · los pantalones · los calcetines · los zapatos de tacón alto · las botas · los zapatos

LAS TELAS

| Está hecho(a) de... | | It's made out of . . . | |
| Están hechos(as) de... | | They're made out of . . . | |

el algodón	cotton	a cuadros	plaid
la lana	wool	a rayas / rayado(a)	striped
el lino	linen	bordado(a)	embroidered
la mezclilla	denim	de lunares	polka-dotted
la piel / el cuero	leather	de un solo color	solid, one single color
la seda	silk		
		estampado(a)	print

LOS ACCESORIOS

LAS JOYAS

la cadena	chain
... (de) oro	(made of) gold
... (de) plata	(made of) silver

The names for articles of clothing can vary greatly from region to region. For example, *jeans* can also be called **vaqueros, tejanos, bluyines,** or **pantalones de mezclilla.**

To say that an item is made of a certain fabric, you need to use **de: botas de cuero, abrigo de piel, camiseta de algodón.**

There is a great deal of variation in the vocabulary for articles of clothing from country to country. For example, in Spain a handbag is **el bolso** and in Mexico it is **la bolsa**; in some places, **la cartera** can also be a handbag, not just a wallet. Other variations are: **los aretes / los pendientes, el anilllo / la sortija, la gorra / el gorro,** and **las gafas / los lentes / los anteojos.**

Suggestion: For some vocabulary words, you can ask about origin: **¿De dónde viene la seda?** (Hint: **Marco Polo.** Answer: **China.**) **¿En qué región se cultiva el algodón en EEUU?** (Answer: **El sureste.**) **¿De dónde viene el cuero o la piel?** (Answer: **Los animales.**), etc. For other vocabulary words, have students sketch **a rayas, de lunares, a cuadros** with their books closed.

Heritage Learners: Words for accessories and articles of clothing show a fair amount of variation throughout the Spanish-speaking world. First, ask students **¿Cómo llamas tú a los siguientes objetos en español?** Have students share with the class the term that they use for items such as earrings, purse, glasses, gym shoes, skirt, swimsuit, and jacket. Involve students in a discussion aimed at showing that, from a linguistic point of view, no word is better than another. Point out that, because of social conventions and historical circumstances, some words are more widely used and accepted than others.

Actividades

Preparation: Personalize this type of activity and describe your clothes in detail. Bring an extra funky scarf or tie and/or have some mismatched or outlandish items to illustrate vocabulary visually and to add humor.

Standards: In **Actividades** 1–7, answers are going to vary according to the students, because in most cases students must provide information and express opinions (C 1.1). A good follow-up to these activities is to ask which groups or pairs did not agree about fashion or other clothes-related matters. See if students can explain any **desacuerdos**.

Heritage Learners: Young Latinos are often torn between the American and Hispanic dress codes. The activities in this section lend themselves to engaging students in a discussion of what might be considered appropriate attire among Hispanics vs. Americans for each of the situations presented.

ACTIVIDAD 1 **Llevo...** Describe qué ropa llevas hoy. ¡No te olvides de incluir los colores!

MODELO: *Llevo unos pantalones negros, una camiseta azul y unos zapatos negros.*

ACTIVIDAD 2 **Me gustan...** Para cada prenda de ropa, indica el tipo de tela y diseño que prefieres. Sigue el modelo.

MODELO: el vestido
Me gustan los vestidos de seda.
O: *Me gustan los vestidos estampados.*

1. el suéter
2. los zapatos de tenis
3. la blusa
4. los pantalones
5. el traje
6. la falda
7. la camiseta
8. la chaqueta

ACTIVIDAD 3 **¿Ropa formal o informal?** Trabaja con un(a) compañero(a) de clase. Digan qué les gusta llevar en las siguientes situaciones. Sean tan específicos como puedan.

1. para estudiar
2. para salir a bailar
3. para trabajar en el jardín
4. para visitar a la familia
5. para ir a clases
6. para ir al gimnasio

ACTIVIDAD 4 **Las estrellas.** Trabajen en grupos de tres a cuatro estudiantes. Primero, hagan una lista de tres personas que son famosas por su manera de vestirse. Luego, usen la imaginación para describir qué llevan en este momento. Incluyan tantos detalles como puedan.

Personas posibles: Madonna, Elton John, Jennifer López, Gwen Stefani, Gwyneth Paltrow, etc.

ACTIVIDAD 5 **Los accesorios.** ¿Quién lleva las siguientes cosas? Para cada accesorio indicado, identifica quién(es) en la clase lo lleva(n). Si nadie lleva el accesorio indicado, di a quién le gusta llevarlo generalmente, o da el nombre de una persona famosa que lo lleva frecuentemente.

MODELOS: una cadena de oro
Stacy lleva una cadena de oro hoy.
O: *Generalmente Stacy lleva una cadena de oro, pero hoy no la lleva.*
los guantes
Nadie lleva guantes ahora mismo. A Michael Jackson le gusta llevar un solo guante.

1. una cadena de oro
2. gafas de sol
3. un sombrero
4. un reloj
5. un pañuelo de seda
6. un brazalete
7. un cinturón de cuero
8. aretes de plata

ACTIVIDAD 6 **¿Qué me pongo?** Descríbele a tu compañero(a) qué ropa y accesorios llevas en las siguientes situaciones. Luego, él o ella hace lo mismo.

1. Es tu primera cita (*date*) con alguien que te gusta mucho.
2. Vas a una recepción para recibir un premio (*prize*).
3. Vas al gimnasio con tu mejor amigo(a).
4. Vas a un concierto de música hip-hop con un grupo de amigos.
5. Vas a una entrevista para un trabajo de verano.
6. Vas a ir a esquiar en las montañas por el fin de semana.

ACTIVIDAD 7 **¡Qué anticuado!** Trabaja con un(a) compañero(a) de clase. Juntos hagan una lista de ropa y accesorios que están de moda en este momento y otra de los que están pasados de moda. Luego, comparen su lista con la de otra pareja. ¿Incluyeron las mismas prendas?

De moda	Pasado de moda

Vocabulario útil 2

DEPENDIENTE: Buenas, señorita. **¿En qué puedo servirle?**

CHELA: La verdad es que estoy buscando un regalo para el cumpleaños de mi mamá pero no tengo ni la menor idea qué comprarle.

DEPENDIENTE: Su mamá seguro es una mujer de muy buen gusto. Tal vez esta blusa de seda…

CHELA: Uy, no, ¡a mamá no le gusta ese color! …

DEPENDIENTE: ¡Ya sé exactamente lo que busca!… Estos aretes de oro son preciosos y **están a muy buen precio** hoy.

CHELA: ¡Qué bonitos! Sí, creo que sí le van a gustar a mamá. **Voy a llevármelos.**

IR DE COMPRAS

El (La) dependiente

¿En qué puedo servirle?	*How can I help you?*
¿Cuál es su talla?	*What is your size?*
Está rebajado(a).	*It's reduced (on sale.)*
Está en venta.	*It's on sale.*
Es muy barato(a).	*It's very inexpensive.*
Está a muy buen precio.	*It's a very good price.*
de buena (alta) calidad	*of good (high) quality*
el descuento	*discount*
la oferta especial	*special offer*

El (La) cliente

¿Cuánto cuesta(n)?	*How much does it (do they) cost?*
¿Lo (La / Los / Las) tiene en una talla...?	*Do you have this in a size . . . ?*
Voy a probármelo(la / las / los).	*I'm going to try it / them on.*
Me queda bien / mal.	*It fits nicely / badly.*
Me queda grande / apretado.	*It's too big / too tight.*
Voy a llevármelo(la / las / los).	*I'm going to take it / them.*
Es (demasiado) caro.	*It's (too) expensive.*

LA MODA

(no) estar de moda	*(not) to be fashionable*
pasado(a) de moda	*out of style*

Actividades

ACTIVIDAD 8 **Por favor...** ¿Qué dices en las siguientes situaciones? Escribe una pregunta o una respuesta para cada situación. En muchos casos, hay más de una respuesta posible.

MODELO: Ves una blusa bonita pero no tiene precio.
¿Cuánto cuesta, por favor?

1. Te pruebas una chaqueta, pero es grande.
2. Decides comprar dos blusas.
3. Ves unos zapatos que te gustan, pero no estás seguro(a) si están en venta.
4. Te pruebas unos zapatos y decides comprarlos.
5. Quieres probarte un vestido en otra talla y se lo pides a la dependiente.
6. Ves unos pantalones que te gustan, pero quieres otro color.
7. El suéter de vicuña es muy fino, pero no sabes si tienes suficiente dinero para comprarlo.
8. Necesitas una talla más grande.

ACTIVIDAD 9 **Situaciones.** Trabaja con un(a) compañero(a) de clase. Representen las siguientes situaciones. Túrnense para hacer los papeles del (de la) dependiente y del (de la) cliente.

Situación 1:

Buscas un regalo para tu novio(a). Quieres algo de muy alta calidad pero a muy buen precio.

Situación 2:

Tienes que ir a una fiesta formal y no sabes qué llevar. Pídele ayuda al (a la) dependiente y compra lo que necesitas.

Situación 3:

Eres un(a) estudiante nuevo(a) en la universidad. Vas a un almacén popular para comprar ropa. ¿Qué debes comprar? Pídele consejos al (a la) dependiente y compra por lo menos dos prendas de ropa.

Situación 4:

Tu prima acaba de tener un bebé. Quieres comprarle un regalo, pero no sabes qué comprar. Escucha las sugerencias del (de la) dependiente y luego compra el regalo.

Standards: Here students work on presentational and interpersonal communication. Have students present their favorite situation to the class as a follow up.

Notice: The word **bebé** is always masculine.

Optional: Mention (or elicit) other ways of shopping: **por Internet, por catálogos. ¿Qué método de compras prefieres?**

¡FÍJATE!

¿Tú o usted?

¿Tú o usted? ¿En qué puedo servirte / servirle? No es siempre fácil para los hablantes nativos del español saber si deben usar el trato formal o informal. Esto es porque las normas de uso varían mucho de una zona dialectal a otra en el mundo de habla hispana. Por ejemplo, en algunos países de Latinoamérica el pronombre formal y sus formas verbales correspondientes se usan hasta en el hogar (*home*), entre padres e hijos y entre esposo y mujer. En otros países, el trato formal está reservado sólo para personas de edad muy avanzada o de rango (*rank*) social muy elevado. Los hispanos reconocen que el usar el trato equivocado (especialmente el **tú**) puede tener consecuencias negativas. Por esta razón, en los comercios y otros establecimientos públicos es preferible usar el tratamiento formal. Esta situación sólo cambia cuando la persona de más edad o rango social invita a la otra persona a "tutearla".

PRÁCTICA. ¿Por qué crees que cuando hay dudas es preferible usar el trato formal al informal? ¿Puedes pensar en una situación donde el uso del trato informal en vez del formal también puede ser ofensivo? ¿Y viceversa?

Suggestion: Ask students whether they would most likely use informal or formal address with the following people in the contexts indicated: **en una fiesta de amigos, con el presidente de México, con un taxista, con un profesor muy viejo y honrado, con alguien que ganó el Premio Nóbel de la Paz, con tu mejor amigo(a) por correo electrónico, con un policía en la calle, con tu perro en casa, con un señor mayor, con unos niños de cinco años en una guardería...**

Vocabulario útil 3

DEPENDIENTE:	Tiene muy buen gusto, señorita. **¿Cómo desea pagar? En efectivo,** ¿verdad?
CHELA:	Sí, gracias.

Preparation: **¿Cuánto cuesta… aproximadamente?** Warm up by asking the class the prices of typical items that cost below 100 dollars (e.g., **tu bolígrafo, un periódico, un refresco,** etc.) and then present numbers over 100.

Optional: Have students research numbers of Latinos or Hispanics in the U.S. (your state, region, or county) from the most recent U.S. Census 2000 and capture these numbers for class discussion. Students can be assigned collecting data on the general population as well, so that they work with a variety of large numbers.

MÉTODOS DE PAGO

¿Cómo desea pagar?	*How do you wish to pay?*
Al contado. / En efectivo.	*In cash.*
Con cheque.	*By check.*
Con cheque de viajero.	*With a traveller's check.*
Con un préstamo.	*With a loan.*
Con tarjeta de crédito.	*With a credit card.*
Con tarjeta de débito.	*With a debit card.*

Cien is used to express the quantity of exactly *one hundred,* as well as before **mil** and **millones. Ciento** is used in combination with other numbers to express quantities from 101–199. Note that with numbers using **-cientos**, the number agrees with the noun it modifies: **doscientas tiendas** but **doscientos mercados.**

LOS NÚMEROS MAYORES DE 100

100 cien	**800 ochocientos(as)**
101 ciento uno	**900 novecientos(as)**
102 ciento dos, etc.	**1.000 mil**
200 doscientos(as)	**2.000 dos mil, etc.**
300 trescientos(as)	**5.000 cinco mil**
400 cuatrocientos(as)	**10.000 diez mil**
500 quinientos(as)	**100.000 cien mil**
600 seiscientos(as)	**1.000.000 un millón**
700 setecientos(as)	**2.000.000 dos millones, etc.**

Actividades

ACTIVIDAD 10 **Para pagar.** Por lo general, ¿cómo vas a pagar en las siguientes situaciones? Di cuánto crees que te va a costar cada compra.

MODELO: Compras un café grande en Starbucks.
Dos dólares y treinta centavos.

1. Compras un vestido / un traje nuevo.
2. Compras los libros para las clases.
3. Compras un pasaje (*ticket*) en avión.

4. Compras frutas en el mercado.
5. Compras una cadena de oro.
6. Compras unos recuerdos (*souvenirs*) durante tus vacaciones.
7. Cenas en un restaurante muy elegante.
8. Vas al cine para ver una película.
9. Pagas el alquiler (*rent*) de tu apartamento.
10. Compras una casa nueva.
11. Compras un automóvil nuevo.

 ACTIVIDAD 11 Trabaja con un(a) compañero(a) de clase. Juntos escojan seis objetos del dibujo y representen una escena como la del modelo. Túrnense para hacer el papel del (de la) dependiente y el (la) cliente. Sigan el modelo.

MODELO: el café
         Tú: *Un café grande, por favor.*
         Compañero(a): *Muy bien. Son dos dólares y veinticinco centavos. ¿Cómo desea pagar?*
         Tú: *En efectivo. Aquí lo tiene.*

A VER

Antes de ver el video

Answers Act. 1: 1. a. C b. C c. F d. F e. C
2. a. C b. F c. F d. C e. F 3. no

ACTIVIDAD 1 Mira las páginas 234, 237 y 240 para familiarizarte con los tres personajes del video de este capítulo. Luego, contesta las siguientes preguntas. Algunas de las oraciones se relacionan con los segmentos de video de capítulos anteriores.

1. ¿Qué sabes de Javier? Di si las siguientes oraciones son ciertas (**C**) o falsas (**F**).

   a. _____ A Javier le gustan los deportes y también le gusta cocinar.

   b. _____ Javier conoce a Dulce.

   c. _____ Javier no conoce a Sergio.

   d. _____ Javier tiene novia (*girlfriend*).

   e. _____ A Javier le interesa la natación, el ciclismo y el boxeo.

2. ¿Qué sabes de Chela? Di si las siguientes oraciones son ciertas o falsas.

   a. _____ Chela es reportera para la estación de la universidad.

   b. _____ A Chela no le gusta ir al gimnasio.

   c. _____ Chela es una persona muy frívola.

   d. _____ Chela conoce a Anilú.

   e. _____ Chela tiene novio (*boyfriend*).

3. ¿Se conocen Chela y Javier?

Answers Act 2: 1. para su mamá
2. una tienda de ropa para mujeres
3–4. *Answers will vary.*

 ACTIVIDAD 2 En el episodio para este capítulo, Chela y Javier independientemente buscan un regalo para sus madres. Mira otra vez las fotos y las conversaciones en las secciones del **Vocabulario útil.**

1. ¿Para quién buscan un regalo Chela y Javier?
2. ¿En qué tipo de tienda están?
3. ¿Cuáles de los accesorios y prendas de ropa del vocabulario pueden ser un regalo bueno para la mamá de Chela y la de Javier?
4. ¿Cuáles de los accesorios y prendas de ropa del vocabulario no son un regalo bueno para la mamá de Chela y la de Javier, según ellos?

Using background knowledge to anticipate content

Often if you have a rough idea of what a video segment is about before you watch it, you can predict what some of its content will be. Think about the topic and think about what kinds of situations will be likely to arise. Ask yourself what kind of language you associate with these situations. By organizing your thoughts in advance, you prepare yourself to understand the content more easily.

Your background knowledge about this video segment includes the knowledge that Javier and Chela are both shopping for a gift for their mothers in a clothing store. How does that help you prepare for viewing the video?

 ACTIVIDAD 3 Basándose en la información de las **Actividades 1** y **2,** hagan una predicción sobre qué va a ocurrir en el video para este capítulo. (**Ideas:** ¿Qué tipo de preguntas van a hacer Chela y Javier? ¿Qué palabras y frases van a usar? ¿Qué tipos de regalos van a considerar? ¿Van a conocerse por fin?)

| Predicción sobre Javier y Chela: |
| Predicción sobre los regalos: |

El video

 Ahora mira el episodio para el **Capítulo 8.** No te olvides de enfocarte en las predicciones que hiciste sobre Javier, Chela y los regalos posibles.

Después de ver el video

ACTIVIDAD 4 Ahora contesta las siguientes preguntas sobre el video.

1. ¿Acertaste con tus predicciones sobre Javier y Chela?
2. ¿Cómo te ayudó la información anterior (*background knowledge*) a entender el contenido del video?

ACTIVIDAD 5 Contesta las siguientes preguntas para ver si entendiste bien el segmento de video.

1. ¿Compró Javier una blusa para su mamá? ¿y Chela?
2. ¿Compró Javier un suéter para su mamá? ¿y Chela?
3. ¿Qué compraron Javier y Chela para sus mamás?
4. ¿Por qué no les gustó la blusa a Javier y a Chela? ¿y el suéter?
5. ¿Sabemos cuánto costaron los aretes?
6. ¿Cómo pagaron Javier y Chela?
7. ¿Qué pensó el dependiente sobre la relación entre Javier y Chela?

Answers Act. 5: 1. no, no 2. no, no 3. unos aretes 4. No les gusta el color de la blusa. La mamá de Javier no necesita suéter. La mamá de Chela no usa ese estilo. 5. no 6. en efectivo 7. Piensa que son hermanos.

ACTIVIDAD 6 Escribe un resumen corto de la acción del video para este capítulo. Escribe por lo menos seis oraciones que describan la conversación entre el dependiente y Javier y luego entre el dependiente y Chela. Usa las formas del pretérito que aprendiste en el **Capítulo 7.**

 Conexión cultural. Mira el segmento que está al final del episodio. Luego, en grupos de tres o cuatro, hablen de lo que hace la gente en su tiempo libre. ¿Cuáles son las actividades más populares entre sus amigos? ¿Son algunos los mismos que son populares en el mundo hispano?

VOCES DE LA COMUNIDAD

Carolina Herrera

“ Todos hemos visto (*have seen*) diseñadores que hacen ropa muy bonita que no queda bien. Ellos venden una colección, pero no la próxima. **”**

Elegantes, clásicos, puros… éstos son algunos de los adjetivos que frecuentemente se escuchan en relación con los diseños de Carolina Herrera, una de las figuras más importantes de la moda contemporánea. Desde su primera colección en 1980, las creaciones de Herrera han contado con (*have been certain of*) la admiración de un público internacional. Actualmente, sus colecciones de moda y de perfumes para hombres y mujeres se venden en las tiendas más elegantes de EEUU, Latinoamérica y Europa. Originalmente de Venezuela, hoy en día Herrera reside en Nueva York desde donde maneja su gran imperio internacional con Adriana, su hija menor, quien, según la diseñadora, es su más importante colaboradora.

¿Te gusta la idea de vestirte con ropa de diseñadores famosos? ¿Por qué sí o por qué no? ¿Tienes algunas prendas de ropa de diseñadores famosos? To learn more about Carolina Herrera and her fashion empire, visit the *Nexos* website (http://college.hmco.com/languages/spanish/students) and follow the links.

Suggestion: For a group discussion: ¿Quiénes llevan ropa de diseño? ¿Quiénes son otros diseñadores? ¿Qué tipo de diseños prefieres (elegante / barroco / simple / clásico / juvenil / lujoso / bohemio / orgánico / práctico / serio / profesional / convencional)? ¿Qué estilo de ropa llevas para ir a una fiesta formal / para una entrevista / para un puesto de gerente en una compañía / para ir de camping?

¡PREPÁRATE!

Gramática útil 1
Talking about what you did: The preterite tense of more irregular verbs

CÓMO USARLO

1. In Spanish, as in most languages, many of the verbs you use most often are irregular. In this chapter you will learn the preterite forms of **andar, haber, poder, poner, querer, saber, tener,** and **venir.** Notice that many of these verbs are also irregular in the present indicative.

2. The verbs **conocer, saber, poder,** and **querer** have slight changes in meaning when they are used in the preterite (as opposed to their meaning in the present indicative).

	present indicative meaning	preterite meaning
conocer	*to know someone, to be acquainted with*	*to meet*
saber	*to know a fact*	*to find out some information*
poder	*to be able to do something*	*to accomplish something*
no poder	*not to be able to*	*to try to do something and fail*
querer	*to want; to love*	*to try to do something*
no querer	*to not want, love*	*to refuse to do something*

Elena **quiso** llamarme pero **no pudo** encontrar su celular.

Conocí al padre de Beto y **supe** que Beto está en Colombia.

Pude completar el trabajo pero **no quise** ir a la oficina.

*Elena **tried** to call me but **was unable (failed)** to find her cell phone.*

*I **met** Beto's father and **found out** that Beto is in Colombia.*

*I **succeeded in** finishing the work, but I **refused** to go to the office.*

3. Notice that while the rest of these verbs are irregular in the preterite, **conocer** is regular in this tense. Its only irregularity is its **yo** form in the present tense: **conozco.**

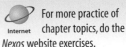

For more practice of chapter topics, do the *Nexos* website exercises.

Standards: Students compare regular with irregular forms of the Spanish language and present tense of verbs that have a change in meaning in the preterite.

Preparation: Review regular forms and emphasize their *pronunciation* to make it easier to memorize. Emphasize the stressed syllables in the first and third person singular in **hablé, leí, visité, habló, leyó, visitó.** Stressing the last syllable helps students internalize the difference between **habló** and **hablo.**

Heritage Learners: When reviewing the preterite of irregular verbs, notice that some heritage language speakers tend to conjugate **venir** in the preterite with an **-e** instead of an **-i** in the verbal root: *veniste, *venimos, *venieron. Another verb that is particularly problematic for heritage learners is **caber** in the preterite. Practice the forms of **caber** with groups of high beginners only.

CÓMO FORMARLO

Here are the preterite forms of these irregular verbs. Some verbs are somewhat similar in their irregular stems, so they are grouped together to help you memorize them more easily.

andar: **anduve, anduviste, anduvo, anduvimos, anduvisteis, anduvieron**
tener: **tuve, tuviste, tuvo, tuvimos, tuvisteis, tuvieron**

poder: **pude, pudiste, pudo, pudimos, pudisteis, pudieron**
poner: **puse, pusiste, puso, pusimos, pusisteis, pusieron**
saber: **supe, supiste, supo, supimos, supisteis, supieron**
haber: **hay → hubo**

querer: **quise, quisiste, quiso, quisimos, quisisteis, quisieron**
venir: **vine, viniste, vino, vinimos, vinisteis, vinieron**

Actividades

ACTIVIDAD 1 **En el centro comercial.** Di qué pasó en el centro comercial hoy. Sigue el modelo.

MODELO: Mario
Mario bebió un refresco grande.

Optional: Have students expand their statements: **Mario tuvo sed y compró / bebió un refresco enorme.**

Verbos posibles: beber, querer tomar una siesta pero no poder, comer pizza, andar mucho, poder encontrar muchas cosas, conocer, saber las últimas noticias, venir, poner en la mesa, querer jugar golf

1. Adela
2. Ernesto
3. Arcely
4. Miguel
5. Leo
6. Néstor
7. Beti

ACTIVIDAD 2 **La vida universitaria.** Con un(a) compañero(a) de clase, háganse y contesten las siguientes preguntas.

1. ¿Cómo supiste que te habían aceptado (*had accepted*) en la universidad? ¿Cuándo lo supiste?
2. ¿Viniste a la universidad como estudiante nuevo(a), estudiante de intercambio o te transferiste de otra universidad? ¿Te gustó la universidad cuando llegaste por primera vez?
3. ¿Pudiste traer todas tus cosas a la universidad? ¿Qué cosas no pudiste traer?
4. ¿Conociste a muchas personas la primera semana de clases? ¿Cuántas, más o menos?
5. ¿Tuviste que estudiar mucho el semestre / trimestre pasado? ¿Recibiste buenas notas?
6. ¿Aprendiste algo interesante el semestre / trimestre pasado? ¿Qué fue?
7. ¿Tuviste tiempo para hacer mucho ejercicio? ¿Anduviste mucho el semestre / trimestre pasado?
8. ¿Pudiste tomar todas tus clases preferidas?

ACTIVIDAD 3 **El semestre o trimestre pasado.** Mira el siguiente formulario. Luego, pregúntales a tus compañeros de clase si hicieron las actividades indicadas el semestre o trimestre pasado. Cuando encuentres a alguien que responde que sí, escribe su nombre en el espacio correspondiente. Sigue el modelo.

MODELO: venir a la universidad con mucha ropa nueva
—*¿Viniste a la universidad con mucha ropa nueva?*
—*No, no vine con mucha ropa nueva.* O:
—*Sí, vine con mucha ropa nueva.* (Escribe su nombre en el formulario.)

¿Quién...?	Nombre
tener que estudiar todos los fines de semana	
no conocer a su compañero(a) de cuarto antes de llegar a la universidad	
poner un refrigerador y un televisor en su cuarto	
venir a las clases sin hacer la tarea	
no poder dormir antes de los exámenes importantes	
venir a la universidad con mucha ropa nueva	
tener sueño en las clases	
no querer comer la comida de la cafetería	

Gramática útil 2
Talking about what you did: The preterite tense of -ir stem-changing verbs

Starting with this chapter, all -ir stem-changing verbs will be shown with both of their stem changes in parentheses. The first letter or letters show the present-tense stem change and the second letter shows the preterite stem change.

Heritage Learners: Stem changing verbs are particularly problematic for heritage language speakers. Emphasize that diphthongs [ie] and [ue] seldom appear in infinitives. On the other hand, the i / e alternation in forms like **sentí** and **sintió** creates uncertainty as to which forms of the verb carry one vowel versus the other. Pay special attention to review and practice these verbs. Practice by moving from infinitive to present to preterite: **pedir** → él pide, él pidió; **dormir** → ella duerme, ella durmió; **vestir** → yo visto, yo vestí; **poder** → nosotros podemos, nosotros pudimos; **preferir** → ustedes prefieren, ustedes prefirieron, etc.

CÓMO FORMARLO

1. As you learned in **Capítulo 7**, the only stem-changing verbs that also change in the preterite are verbs that end in **-ir**. Present-tense stem-changing verbs that end in **-ar** and **-er** do not change their stem in the preterite.

2. In the preterite, **-ir** stem-changing verbs only experience the stem change in the third-person singular (**usted / él / ella**) and third-person plural (**ustedes / ellos / ellas**) forms.

◆ Verbs that change **e → ie** in the present change **e → i** in the preterite.

> **preferir:** preferí, preferiste, **prefirió,** preferimos, preferisteis, **prefirieron**
>
> Similar verbs you already know: **divertirse, sentirse**
> New verb of this kind: **sugerir (ie, i)** *to suggest*

◆ Verbs that change **e → i** in the present also change **e → i** in the preterite.

> **pedir:** pedí, pediste, **pidió,** pedimos, pedisteis, **pidieron**
>
> Similar verbs you already know: **despedirse, reírse, repetir, seguir, servir, vestir, vestirse**
> New verbs of this kind: **conseguir (i, i)** *to get, to have;* **sonreír (i, i)** *to smile*

◆ Verbs that change **o → ue** in the present change **o → u** in the preterite.

> **dormir:** dormí, dormiste, **durmió,** dormimos, dormisteis, **durmieron**
>
> New verb of this kind: **morirse (ue, u)** *to die*

Actividades

Answers Act. 4: Te divertiste, me divertí, fui, insistió, sugirió, consiguieron, vimos, pudimos, preferimos, se vistió, me reí, seguimos, nos despedimos, vine, hiciste

ACTIVIDAD 4 **Olivia y Belkys.** Completa la conversación con la forma correcta del pretérito de los verbos indicados. Después, di si, en tu opinión, Belkys tiene razón en sentirse tan avergonzada (*embarrassed*).

OLIVIA: ¿Qué tal tu día de compras? ¿(divertirse) _____?

BELKYS: No, no (divertirse) _____ ni un poquito y además no compré nada.

OLIVIA: ¡No te lo creo! ¿Tú, sin comprar nada? ¡Imposible!

BELKYS: Pero es la verdad. Yo (ir) _____ con Gerardo porque él
(insistir) _____ en acompañarme. Él (sugerir) _____
ir al centro porque le gustan los trajes en una tienda allí.

OLIVIA: ¿Pero ustedes no (conseguir) _____ comprar nada?

BELKYS: No. Los dos (ver) _____ unas cosas bonitas, pero no
(poder) _____ encontrar nada a buen precio. Por eso,
(preferir) _____ no comprar nada.

OLIVIA: ¡Qué pena!

BELKYS: Y lo peor es que Gerardo (vestirse) _____ de traje viejo,
muy pasado de moda, verde, con rayas amarillas. Yo casi me muero
de vergüenza.

OLIVIA: ¡Pobrecita! ¡Imagínate el horror!

BELKYS: Bueno, tú te ríes, ¡pero te digo que yo no (reírse) _____ en
toda la tarde! Nosotros (seguir) _____ buscando en todas
las tiendas del centro. Por fin (despedirse) _____ y yo
(venir) _____ directamente aquí para contarte toda la
historia.

OLIVIA: Ay, chica, tranquila. Por lo menos ¡tú me (hacer) _____ reír
un poco!

ACTIVIDAD 5 **Me sentí…** Di cómo se sintieron las siguientes personas en las
situaciones indicadas.

MODELO: tu tía / después de perder el trabajo
Se sintió desilusionada.

Emociones posibles: contento, triste, cansado, nervioso, preocupado, ocupado,
furioso, aburrido, desilusionado, animado, feliz

1. tú / antes de tus exámenes finales
2. tú y tu mejor amigo(a) / al final del semestre o trimestre
3. tu mejor amigo(a) / cuando estuvo enfermo(a)
4. tus padres / cuando saliste para la universidad
5. tu primo(a) / después de perder el partido de fútbol
6. tus amigos / en una película de tres horas y media
7. tu compañero(a) de cuarto / antes de la visita de sus padres
8. tú / después de conocer a una persona simpática

ACTIVIDAD 6 **En la U.** Con un(a) compañero(a) de clase, háganse las siguientes
preguntas sobre su llegada a la universidad y luego contéstenlas.

1. ¿Cómo te sentiste cuando llegaste a la universidad la primera vez?
2. ¿Qué te sugirió tu familia cuando viniste a la universidad?
3. ¿Le pediste ayuda a tu familia para traer todas tus cosas a la universidad?
4. ¿Te divertiste el primer semestre / trimestre? ¿Qué hiciste?
5. ¿Preferiste vivir en una residencia estudiantil o en un apartamento?
6. ¿Conseguiste un trabajo el primer semestre / trimestre?
7. ¿Siguieron tú y tus amigos la misma carrera de estudios?

Answers Act. 5: *Answers may vary.*
1. Me sentí nervioso(a). 2. Nos sentimos
contentos(as). 3. Él / Ella se sintió
cansado(a). 4. Se sintieron tristes.
5. Se sintió furioso(a). 6. Se sintieron
aburridos. 7. Se sintió nervioso(a).
8. Me sentí animado(a).

Optional: Expand **Actividad 6** with
additional questions: ¿Usaste el
Internet para comprar lo básico para
la universidad? ¿los libros? ¿la ropa?
¿Hablaste por celular para contactar
a amigos o parientes? ¿Usaste tu
asistente electrónico para organizar
tu horario de clases? ¿Qué hiciste tu
primer día en la universidad / de
clases?, etc.

Gramática útil 3
Saying who is affected or involved: Indirect object pronouns

Standards: Notice that students are asked to compare (C 4.1) English and Spanish structures of indirect and direct objects.

Preparation: For visual and kinetic learners, bring objects to class to pass around. Illustrate the indirect object pronouns and have students describe actions that they see and do using object pronouns; for example: **Le dio el libro nuevo. Me pasaste las llaves. La profesora nos devolvió la tarea.**

CÓMO USARLO

LO BÁSICO

- An *indirect object* is a noun or noun phrase that indicates for whom or to whom an action is done: *I bought a gift for **Beatriz**. We asked **the teachers** a question.*
- *Indirect object pronouns* are used to replace indirect object nouns: *I bought a gift for **her**. We asked **them** a question.* Often you can identify the indirect object of the sentence by asking *to or for whom?* about the verb: *We bought a gift **for whom?*** (Beatriz / her) / *We asked a question **to whom?*** (the teachers / them).

1. In **Capítulo 7** you learned how to use direct object pronouns to avoid repetition. In this chapter you will learn how you can also use indirect object pronouns to avoid repetition and to clarify what person is being referred to.

2. Look at the following passage and see if you can figure out to whom the boldface indirect object pronouns refer.

Fui al almacén el miércoles. Tenía una lista larga de compras. **Le** compré unos jeans y una camisa a Miguel. También **le** compré una corbata. A Susana y a Carmen **les** compré unas camisetas. También tuve que comprar**les** calcetines. Además **me** compré una falda bonita y un reloj.

CÓMO FORMARLO

1. Although English uses the same set of pronouns for direct object pronouns and indirect object pronouns, in Spanish there are two slightly different sets.

2. Notice that the only difference between the direct object pronouns and the indirect object pronouns is in the two third-person pronouns. Instead of **lo / la,** the indirect object pronoun is **le.** And instead of **los / las,** the indirect object pronoun is **les.** The indirect object pronouns **le** and **les** do not have to agree in gender with the nouns they replace, as do the direct object pronouns **lo, la, los,** and **las.**

¿En qué puedo **servirle,** señor?

Notice that these are the same pronouns you learned to use with **gustar** and similar verbs in **Capítulos 2** and **4.**

Indirect object pronouns			
me	*to / for me*	**nos**	*to / for us*
te	*to / for you*	**os**	*to / for you (fam. pl.)*
le	*to / for you (form. sing.) / him / her*	**les**	*to / for you (form., pl.) / them*

3. As with direct object pronouns, indirect object pronouns always come before a conjugated verb used alone.

Te traje el periódico.   *I brought **you** the newspaper.*
Nos dieron un regalo bonito.   *They gave **us** a nice gift.*

4. When an indirect object pronoun is used with an infinitive or with the present progressive, it may come before the conjugated verb, or it may be attached to the infinitive or to the present participle.

Te voy a dar el libro.	OR:	Voy a dar**te** el libro.
Te estoy comprando el CD.	OR:	Estoy comprándo**te** el CD.

Notice that when the indirect object pronoun attaches to the present participle, you must add an accent to the next-to-last syllable of the present participle to maintain the correct pronunciation.

5. When an indirect object pronoun is used with a command form, it attaches to the end of the affirmative command but comes before the negative command form.

Cómprame / Cómpreme el libro ahora, por favor.	BUT:	**No me compres / No me compre** el libro ahora, por favor.

Again notice that when the indirect object pronoun attaches to the command form you must add an accent to the next-to-last syllable of command forms of two or more syllables in order to maintain the correct pronunciation.

6. As you learned in **Capítulo 4,** if you want to emphasize or clarify to or for whom something is being done, you can use **a** + the person's name, or **a** + prepositional pronoun (**mí, ti, usted, nosotros, vosotros, ustedes, ellos, ellas**). Note that when **a** + pronoun is used, there is often no direct translation in English.

Les escribo una carta **a ustedes.**	*I'm writing **you** a letter.*
Le doy el regalo **a Lucas.**	*I'm giving the gift **to Lucas.***
Les traigo el periódico **a mis padres.**	*I bring the newspaper **to my parents.***

Prepositional pronouns can follow *any* preposition, not just **a.** Other prepositions you know include **con:** *with* (with con, **mí** and **ti** change to **conmigo** and **contigo**); **de:** *from, of;* **sin:** *without.*

Actividades

ACTIVIDAD 7 **¡Ay, Hernando!** Completa la siguiente conversación con el complemento indirecto correcto. Después de completarla, léela otra vez para ver si entiendes por qué se usa cada complemento indirecto.

Answers Act. 7: 1. le 2. me 3. te 4. me 5. me 6. les 7. me 8. Le 9. me 10. me

HERNANDO: Oye, tengo que ir al centro. ¿Quieres acompañarme?

SEBASTIÁN: Cómo no. Tengo que (1) comprar _____ un regalo a mi hermanito para el día de su santo.

HERNANDO: Y yo (2) _____ voy a comprar unos jeans y una camiseta nueva.

SEBASTIÁN: ¿Tú con interés en la moda? Hombre, ¿qué (3) _____ pasa?

HERNANDO: Es Lidia. Ahora que salimos juntos los fines de semana (4) _____ dice que toda mi ropa está pasada de moda.

SEBASTIÁN: ¡No (5) _____ digas! A las mujeres... ¡(6) _____ importa demasiado la ropa!

HERNANDO: Y lo peor es que no tengo mucho dinero. ¿Crees que (7) _____ den un descuento en la tienda donde trabaja Julio?

SEBASTIÁN: Oye, vale la pena (*it's worthwhile*) ir a ver. ¿(8) _____ dijiste a Julio que necesitas comprar ropa?

HERNANDO: Sí. Pero (9) _____ dijo que debemos ir al almacén en el centro. Además dijo que los precios en su tienda son demasiado caros y la calidad no es muy buena.

SEBASTIÁN: Bueno, parece que él no nos puede ayudar. Entonces, ¿vamos directamente al almacén?

HERNANDO: De acuerdo. Oye, ¿no (10) _____ puedes prestar un poco de dinero?

SEBASTIÁN: ¡Hombre! Nunca cambias...

Answers Act. 8: 1. Le compró una cartera a su padre. 2. Les compró camisetas a sus abuelos. 3. Le compró una pulsera de oro a su madre. 4. Me compró unos guantes de piel. 5. Les compró unos pantalones cortos a los niños. 6. Nos compró unos zapatos de tenis.

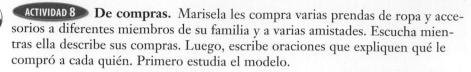

ACTIVIDAD 8 **De compras.** Marisela les compra varias prendas de ropa y accesorios a diferentes miembros de su familia y a varias amistades. Escucha mientras ella describe sus compras. Luego, escribe oraciones que expliquen qué le compró a cada quién. Primero estudia el modelo.

MODELO: Escuchas: A mi tía le encantan las blusas bordadas. Cuando estaba de vacaciones en Ecuador, le compré una blusa bordada muy bonita.
Escribes: *Le compró una blusa bordada a su tía.*

Personas:	Prendas o accesorios:
1. padre	pulsera de oro
2. madre	cartera
3. abuelos	guantes de piel
4. tía	zapatos de tenis
5. niños	camisetas
6. yo	blusa bordada
7. nosotros	pantalones cortos

 ACTIVIDAD 9 **De vez en cuando.** Trabaja con un(a) compañero(a) de clase. Juntos digan para quiénes hacen las actividades indicadas. Sigan el modelo. Usen cada verbo por lo menos una vez.

MODELO: comprar un café
De vez en cuando le compro un café a mi compañero(a) de cuarto.
O: Nunca le compro un café a nadie.

Acción	Objeto directo	Objeto indirecto
escribir	cartas	mi madre / padre
dar	flores	mis padres
comprar	regalos	mi amigo(a)
contar	chismes	mis amigos
mandar	notas de agradecimiento	mi profesor(a)
pedir	favores	mis profesores
contar	chistes	mi novio(a)
hacer	ayuda	mi compañero(a) de cuarto
traer	ropa	mis compañeros(as) de cuarto
¿...?	¿...?	

Frases útiles: de vez en cuando (*sometimes*), frecuentemente, muchas veces, todas las semanas, todos los días, rara vez (*hardly ever*), nunca, casi

 ACTIVIDAD 10 **¿Quién?** Con un(a) compañero(a), háganse preguntas sobre las acciones de sus compañeros de clase. Pueden usar las ideas de la lista o pueden inventar otras. Asegúrense de usar verbos que requieren el uso del objeto indirecto.

MODELO: Tú: *¿Quién le regaló ropa a su novio(a)?*
Compañero(a): *Dahlia le regaló un traje a su novio Jesús para su cumpleaños.*

1. regalar ropa
2. decir siempre la verdad
3. pagar los estudios
4. escribir mensajes electrónicos
5. ayudar con la tarea
6. ¿...?

Gramática útil 4
Making comparisons: Comparatives and superlatives

AR MODA

¡Canasta!

LOS BOLSOS DE MIMBRE, RAFIA Y
CUERDA SON EL ACCESORIO BÁSICO
DEL VERANO, TANTO PARA IR A LA
PISCINA COMO SI SALES DE NOCHE

FOTOS: **GEMA LÓPEZ** ESTILISMO: **JUAN ANTONIO FRÍAS**

**Can you find the
comparative words in this
text? Are they making an
equal or unequal
comparison?**

Answers: tanto ... como; equal
comparison

CÓMO USARLO

LO BÁSICO

Comparatives compare two or more objects. *Superlatives* indicate that one object
exceeds or stands above all others. In English we use *more* and *less* with adjectives,
adverbs, nouns, and verbs to make comparisons, and we also add *-er* to the end of
most one- or two-syllable adjectives: *more expensive, cheaper.* To form superlatives
we use *most / least* with adjectives or add *-est* to the end of most one- or two-
syllable adjectives: *the most expensive, the cheapest.*

1. Comparatives in Spanish use **más** (*more*) and **menos** (*less*) to make comparisons between people, actions, and things. **Más** and **menos** can be used with
nouns, adjectives, verbs, and adverbs.

Nouns: Hay **más libros** en esta tienda que en aquélla.
          *There are **more books** in this store than in that one.*

Adjectives: Este libro es **menos interesante** que ése.
          *This book is **less interesting** than that one.*

Verbs: Yo **leo menos** que él.
          *I **read less** than he (does).*

Adverbs: Él lee **más lentamente** que yo.
          *He reads **more slowly** than I (do).*

Begin the CD-ROM
activities. Do the cultural
activities and reading and writing
practice as you complete the
corresponding text sections.

2. Superlative forms indicate that something exceeds all others: *the most, the least.*

Este libro es **interesantísimo.**
  Es **el más interesante** de todos.

*This book is **really interesting**. It's the **most interesting** of all of them.*

CÓMO FORMARLO

1. Regular comparatives. Comparisons can be *equal* (as many as) or *unequal* (more than, less than). Comparatives can be used with nouns, adjectives, adverbs, and verbs.

Notice that of all the words used in these comparative forms (**tanto, tan, más, menos, como,** and **que**) only **tanto** changes to reflect number and gender.

Notice: Point out to students that **más bueno** and **más malo** are the comparative forms of **bueno** and **malo** when these adjectives refer to the moral quality of people. Therefore, **Pepe es más bueno que su hermano** means that Pepe is a better person, (from a moral standpoint), than his brother. On the other hand, **mejor** and **peor** are the comparative forms of **bueno** and **malo** when they refer to the quality of an object (**Esta pluma es mejor que la otra**) or the capacity of an individual within a field of expertise (**Juan es mejor médico que Luis**).

	equal comparisons	unequal comparisons
noun	**tanto** + noun + **como** (**Tanto** agrees with the noun.) Tengo **tanto dinero como** tú. Tengo **tantas tarjetas de crédito como** tú.	**más / menos** + noun + **que** (**Más / menos** do not agree with the noun.) Tengo **más dinero que** tú. Tengo **menos tarjetas de crédito que** tú.
adjective	**tan** + adjective + **como** Este reloj es **tan caro como** ése.	**más / menos** + adjective + **que** Este reloj es **más caro que** ése, pero es **menos caro que** aquél.
verb	verb + **tanto como** **Compro tanto como** tú.	verb + **más / menos** + **que** Ella **compra menos que** yo, pero él **compra más que** yo.
adverb	**tan** + adverb + **como** Pago mis cuentas **tan rápidamente como** tú.	**más / menos** + adverb + **que** Ella paga sus cuentas **más rápidamente que** yo, pero él paga **menos rápidamente que** yo.

2. Irregular comparatives. Some adjectives and adverbs have irregular comparative forms.

◆ Adjectives

bueno → **mejor:**	Este libro es **bueno,** pero ese libro es **mejor.**
malo → **peor:**	Esta tienda es **mala,** pero esa tienda es **peor.**
joven → **menor:**	Los dos somos **jóvenes,** pero Remedios es **menor** que yo.
viejo → **mayor:**	Martín no es **viejo,** pero es **mayor** que Remedios.

Menor and **mayor** are usually used to refer to people, although they can be used in place of **más grande** (**mayor**) and **más pequeño** (**menor**) when referring to objects. If you wish to say that one object is *older* or *newer* than another, use **más viejo** or **más nuevo.**

◆ Adverbs

bien → **mejor:**	Lorena canta muy **bien,** pero Alfonso canta **mejor.**
mal → **peor:**	Nosotros bailamos **mal,** pero ellos bailan **peor.**

3. Superlatives

◆ In order to say that a person or thing is extreme in some way, add **-ísimo** to the end of an adjective. (If the adjective ends in a vowel, remove the vowel first.)

> fácil → **facilísimo** (*very easy*)   contento → **contentísimo** (*extremely happy*)

◆ To say that a person or thing is *the most* or *the least*... use the following formula. (Do not use this formula with the **-ísimo** ending—choose one or the other!)

> noun + **más / menos** + adjective + **de**

Roberto es **el estudiante más popular de** la universidad.
Ellas son **las dependientes más trabajadoras del** almacén.

> These superlative forms must change to reflect the gender and number of the nouns they modify: **unos aretes carísimos, unas camisetas baratísimas,** etc.

> Notice that the accent is always on the first **í** of **-ísimo**. If the adjective has an accent, it is dropped when you add **-ísimo: difícil → dificilísimo.**

> Notice that the article and the adjective must agree with the noun: **el estudiante popular, las dependientes trabajadoras.**

Actividades

ACTIVIDAD 11 **El almacén Toneti.** Escucha el anuncio sobre Toneti, un almacén grande. Pon una X al lado de cada objeto que se menciona. **¡Ojo!** Asegúrate de que la descripción de cada objeto es la correcta.

1. _____ las mochilas más baratas
2. _____ las mochilas más grandes
3. _____ la selección más grande de zapatos
4. _____ los zapatos de tenis más populares
5. _____ los pantalones menos caros del centro
6. _____ los pantalones más caros del centro
7. _____ las camisetas de la más alta calidad
8. _____ las camisetas más bonitas del centro

Answers Act.. 11: *Items mentioned are:* 1, 2, 4, 5, and 7

ACTIVIDAD 12 **La rebaja.** Haz comparaciones entre los precios de varias prendas de ropa y accesorios. Sigue el modelo.

MODELO: caro: las botas ($50) / los zapatos de tenis ($40)
Las botas son más caras que los zapatos de tenis.
Los zapatos de tenis son menos caros que las botas.

1. caro: los suéteres ($25) / las camisetas ($15)
2. caro: las camisetas ($15) / los vestidos ($50)
3. caro: las blusas ($30) / las camisetas ($15)
4. caro: las botas ($50) / los vestidos ($50)
5. barato: los vestidos ($50) / los suéteres ($25)
6. barato: las blusas ($30) / las botas ($50)
7. barato: los vestidos ($50) / los zapatos de tenis ($40)
8. barato: las camisetas ($15) / las blusas ($30)

Answers Act. 12: 1. Los suéteres son más caros que… / Las camisetas son menos caras que… 2. Las camisetas son menos caras que… / Los vestidos son más caros que… 3. Las blusas son más caras que… / Las camisetas son menos caras que… 4. Las botas son tan caras como… / Los vestidos son tan caros como… 5. Los vestidos son menos baratos que… / Los suéteres son más baratos que… 6. Las blusas son más baratas que… / Las botas son menos baratas que… 7. Los vestidos son menos baratos que… / Los zapatos de tenis son más baratos que… 8. Las camisetas son más baratas que… / Las blusas son menos baratas que…

ACTIVIDAD 13 **Las personas famosas.** Haz comparaciones según el modelo.

MODELO: cantar: Britney Spears o Madonna
Britney Spears canta peor que Madonna.
O: *Britney Spears canta mejor que Madonna.*
O: *Britney Spears canta tan bien como Madonna.*

1. cantar: Jennifer López o Gwen Stefani
2. bailar: Ricky Martin o Gloria Estefan
3. cocinar: tu mejor amigo(a) o tu madre
4. jugar tenis: Venus Williams o Serena Williams
5. jugar golf: Tiger Woods o tu padre
6. patinar sobre hielo: tú o tu mejor amigo(a)
7. nadar: tú o tu hermano(a)
8. jugar béisbol: Nomar Garciaparra o Sammy Sosa
9. hacer esquí acuático: tú o tus amigos
10. tocar la guitarra: Eric Clapton o Carlos Santana

 ACTIVIDAD 14 **En el centro comercial.** Trabaja con un(a) compañero(a) de clase. Juntos miren el dibujo y hagan todas las comparaciones que puedan. Usen las palabras y expresiones útiles por lo menos una vez cada una.

Palabras y expresiones útiles: tanto como, más, menos, tan como, mejor, peor, el (la) más... de todos, el (la) menos... de todos

ACTIVIDAD 15 **Nuestros amigos.** Trabaja con un(a) compañero(a) de clase. Primero piensen en seis personas que conozcan los dos. Luego hagan comparaciones según el modelo.

MODELOS: cómico
Sean es más cómico que Jason.
hablar rápido
Sean habla más rápido que Jason.

Palabras y frases útiles: cómico, joven, viejo, alto, extrovertido, introvertido, hablar rápido, comer despacio (*slowly*), viajar frecuentemente, jugar tenis (u otro deporte) bien, correr rápido, entrenarse frecuentemente

Optional: Comparatives and superlatives can be fun to apply to the demographics of your class. Try questions like: **¿Quién es el (la) más alto(a) / bajo(a) / divertido(a) / atlético(a) de la clase?, ¿mayor?, ¿menor?, etc.** Have students interview each other about ages, possessions, number of classes, etc., so that they will be able to make comparisons: **¿Cuántas horas estudias cada semana? … estudia tantas horas como… ¿Cuántos libros (CDs, jeans, hermanos, etc.) tienes?, etc.**

Sonrisas

Standards: Explore language comparisons in English. Have students generate similar expressions in English to express **estar más loco que un zapato.** Example: To be crazier than a loon (nut), etc.

EXPRESIÓN. En grupos de tres a cuatro estudiantes, trabajen para completar la comparación **"Es más loco(a) que un…"** de una manera diferente. Después de crear una lista de posibilidades, escojan una y hagan una tira cómica semejante a la de arriba.

Perú y Ecuador

Influencias andinas. Mira la siguiente tabla y la lista de palabras que aparece arriba de la tabla. Los siguientes textos contienen información sobre cada uno de estos lugares o cosas. Mientras lees, ¿puedes poner diez de las palabras de la lista en la columna correcta de la tabla? (**¡Ojo!** En algunos casos, una cosa o un lugar puede referirse a los dos países.)

el cuy (*guinea pig*)   los aimaraes   los bananos   los nazca
las flores   la vicuña   los Andes   el cultivo genético
las papas   el quechua   el algodón   la alpaca
el volcán Cotopaxi   los incas   la irrigación   el cóndor
el café   el cacao   el tomate   Charles Darwin

	Ecuador	Perú
idiomas		
flora y fauna		
geografía y ciencia		
grupos indígenas		

¡CONÉCTATE!

Después de leer la lectura sobre Ecuador y Perú, trabaja con un(a) compañero(a) de clase. Hagan una investigación por Internet para buscar información sobre uno de los siguientes temas. Incluyan por lo menos tres datos interesantes sobre el tema. Usen los enlaces sugeridos en el sitio web de *Nexos* (http://college.hmco.com/languages/spanish/ students) para ir a otros sitios web posibles.

1. la mítica ciudad incaica de Machu Picchu
2. la exótica flora y fauna de las Islas Galápagos
3. productos de la vicuña o la alpaca
4. expediciones para escalar las montañas de Ecuador
5. recetas (*recipes*) para preparar cuy

Ecuador, un país mágico

Ecuador es un pequeño país de gran diversidad. En medio de sus montañas altas hay ciudades que reflejan la influencia española, pero que también celebran su pasado indígena. La población indígena desciende de las grandes civilizaciones inca y aimara. Cada valle tiene sus costumbres, tradiciones, música, comida e incluso dialectos individuales. Los idiomas predominantes son el quechua, la lengua de los incas, y el español, la lengua que enseñan en las escuelas. La mayoría de los ecuatorianos son perfectamente bilingües.

Unas iguanas de las Islas Galápagos

Es el territorio de la llama, de la vicuña, de la alpaca y del cóndor. La gran altitud del país resulta en una abundancia de luz solar, que permite cultivar una gran variedad de flores que se exportan a todo el mundo. En la costa hay cultivos típicos de los trópicos—bananos, arroz, cacao, café y piñas.

Siendo un país montañoso, Ecuador ofrece vistas y paisajes espectaculares. Cotopaxi, el volcán activo más alto del planeta, se encuentra aquí. A 1.000 kilómetros de la costa están las Islas Galápagos, que son únicas por su belleza pero aun más por su flora y fauna. Las condiciones naturales de las islas no han cambiado (*have not changed*) hace siglos, resultando en ecosistemas permanentes que permitieron a Charles Darwin demostrar su teoría de la evolución, usando la flora y la fauna de estas islas.

Perú lo tiene todo.

Perú es un país de contrastes. Desde los impresionantes picos de los Andes hasta los valles secretos de la selva amazónica, la mayor parte del país se mantiene en estado virgen. Aunque sus ciudades grandes son muy modernas, los habitantes del resto del país mantienen sus costumbres ancestrales.

Se considera a la civilización incaica de Perú como una de las civilizaciones más antiguas del mundo. Los incas fueron uno de los primeros grupos en desarrollar la agricultura y el cultivo de animales domesticados. Hace unos 10.000 años los incas inventaron sistemas de irrigación e hicieron modificaciones genéticas en las plantas que cultivaron. Entre sus más grandes contribuciones están el cultivo de 128 plantas nativas, como la papa, el algodón, el tomate y la papaya, y animales como la llama, la vicuña, la alpaca y el cuy.

El territorio que hoy día llamamos Perú también fue la cuna (*cradle*) de otras civilizaciones aun más antiguas como las de Chavín, Tiahuanaco, Vicús, Nazca, Paracas y Mochica-Chimú, convirtiéndose en el más grande y poderoso (*powerful*) imperio de Sudamérica en la época prehispánica. La mayoría de la población peruana habla español, la lengua oficial, pero también existe una variedad de lenguas nativas, de las cuales el quechua es el idioma más hablado. Los indígenas de la selva amazónica tienen sus propias lenguas con sus propios dialectos también.

Las alturas de la ciudad incaica de Machu Picchu

Optional: Test your students' knowledge about the two focus countries in this chapter using comparatives and superlatives with these statements (**cierto o falso**). 1. Ecuador es más grande que Perú. (F) 2. Ecuador tiene menos habitantes que Perú. (C) 3. Perú tiene más selva (jungla) que Ecuador. (C) 4. Las islas Galápagos de Ecuador son famosísimas. (C) Add that the Galapagos Islands, about 600 miles off the coast of Ecuador, are well known for their unusual plant and animal species. The British biologist Charles Darwin studied on the islands before writing *The Origin of the Species* in 1859.

Optional: During the sixteenth and seventeenth centuries, Peru was the *only* Spanish Viceroyalty in South America and a powerful center of government in Colonial Latin America.

Línea férrea en Perú

Es común considerar a EEUU como un país de gran diversidad étnica, a causa de su larga historia de inmigración desde otros países. Sin embargo (*Nevertheless*), mucha gente no sabe que los países de Latinoamérica también son sitios de gran inmigración. En el siglo XIX, por ejemplo, Perú tuvo una ola (*wave*) de inmigración desde China, similar a la que ocurrió en EEUU durante los años 1840 hasta 1880. Hoy día hay muchas comunidades chinas y asiáticas en las ciudades principales de Perú, y, aunque en menor grado, en otras partes de Sudamérica y América Central también.

La época de la inmigración china a Perú empezó en el año 1849 cuando el gobierno (*government*) autorizó la inmigración relacionada con la agricultura. Entre los años 1849 y 1974 llegaron más de 100.000 chinos a Perú, la mayoría para trabajar en las haciendas de agricultura en la costa. La ola más grande de inmigrantes chinos ocurrió entre 1861 y 1875, cuando miles de trabajadores vinieron para construir los ferrocarriles (*railroads*) y participar en el cultivo de algodón.

Hoy la presencia china es muy fuerte en Perú. La fusión de costumbres y tradiciones chinas y peruanas se nota en la forma en que hablan español los peruanos y también en costumbres como la preferencia por el arroz en la comida. Existe una variedad de organizaciones chino-peruanas que promueven la armonía y la fusión entre las dos culturas.

 PRÁCTICA. En grupos de tres a cuatro personas, hablen de los siguientes temas.

1. ¿Pueden pensar en otros países, además de EEUU, que tienen una historia de mucha inmigración de otros países? ¿Qué eventos históricos causaron esos períodos de inmigración?
2. En su opinión, ¿hay beneficios de tener muchos inmigrantes en un país? ¿Hay desventajas (*disadvantages*)? ¿Existen diferencias entre los distintos grupos de inmigrantes y las razones por las cuales decidieron inmigrar?
3. Hablen sobre los orígenes étnicos de sus familias. ¿De dónde inmigraron originalmente sus antepasados (*ancestors*)?

A LEER

Antes de leer

ACTIVIDAD 1 Las siguientes palabras están en el artículo de la página 262, que trata de la popularidad de los jeans por todo el mundo. ¿A qué palabras inglesas son similares?

1. overoles   2. cachemira   3. apliques

Answers Act. 1: overalls, cashmere, appliqués

ACTIVIDAD 2 El artículo que vas a leer en este capítulo trata de la influencia de los jeans en la moda internacional. Antes de leer el artículo, escribe cinco a siete palabras que tú asocias con los jeans y con la mezclilla.

ACTIVIDAD 3 Las siguientes frases del artículo contienen palabras que no conoces. A ver si puedes emparejar (*match*) las frases de las dos columnas para adivinar el sentido de las palabras **en negrilla**.

Answers Act. 3: 1. c 2. d 3. a 4. b

1. _____ algo moderno, permanente y **novedoso...**

2. _____ El jean es muy dúctil... lo puedes **doblar...**

3. _____ puedes **guardar**lo sin que ocupe mucho espacio

4. _____ Hace ver **varonil** a cualquier hombre.

a. *you can **store** it without it taking up much space*

b. *It makes any man look **manly**.*

c. *something modern, permanent, and* ***novel*** *. . .*

d. *A pair of jeans is very flexible . . . you can **fold** it . . .*

Lectura

ACTIVIDAD 4 Lee el artículo de un periódico ecuatoriano en la siguiente página. ¿Hay unas de las palabras que escribiste para la Actividad 2 en el artículo?

Standards: Here students read and reflect about cultural products and practices. In this case, the product is jeans. Ask students to tell everything that they know about the history of jeans, denim fabric, jeans styles over the years, etc., to warm up for the reading. Whether assigned or read in class, remind students to look for cognates and stress that they needn't understand every word. Encourage multiple readings. Reading out loud offers pronunciation practice.

El jean impone su encanto

Hace un siglo, el jean se creó para usar en sectores laborales estadounidenses donde el trabajo arduo hizo la ropa fuerte una necesidad. Ahora, al pasar los siglos, este material sigue siendo algo moderno, permanente y novedoso...

Los atractivos del jean han sobrepasado[1] los límites del tiempo y de las fronteras. Los clásicos pantalones jeans y los overoles todavía son populares y, además, les dan la posibilidad a sus usuarios de combinarlos de mil maneras. Se pueden usar hasta en ocasiones más elegantes si se usan con una chaqueta o con una blusa de seda o un saco de cachemira. Los beneficios de esta tela son innumerables. Por ejemplo, es común ver carteras de jean, zapatos con tacones de mezclilla y gorras, chalecos, chompas[2], sombreros, mochilas, monederos y otros accesorios de la moda que rompen con los diseños tradicionales y se modernizan al usar esta tela tan tradicional y moderna a la vez.

Pero, ¿qué es lo que puede ofrecer el jean a los hombres y a las mujeres de esta época? Escuchemos sus testimonios. ★

- "Usar jean es sentirse más joven, a pesar de la edad real que tengas."
- "El jean es muy dúctil, por lo que lo puedes doblar y guardarlo sin que ocupe mucho espacio."
- "Es resistente a cualquier trato."
- "Se lava y sigue como si nada..."
- "Puedes llevar libros o bloques de cemento, sabe cuál es su función."
- "El cuero es para gente mayor. El jean siempre será[3] joven."
- "Hace ver varonil a cualquier hombre."
- "Es de los materiales más durables y que además no pasa de moda. Un jean puedes llevarlo años y mientras más rasgado, más en onda[4]."
- "Los brazaletes de jean son súper chéveres[5]."
- "El jean es discreto cuando debe serlo, pero también sensual cuando le has dado ese papel[6]."
- "Sobre el jean puedes poner cualquier tipo de apliques..."
- "Es de lo más práctico para vestir. Sólo necesitas un pantalón y falda y la mitad de tus problemas están resueltos[7]."

[1]**han...** *have surpassed* [2]**suéteres** [3]**va a ser** [4]**más rasgado...** *the more ripped, the more in style* [5]*cool* [6]**le...** *you have given it that role* [7]*resolved*

Después de leer

ACTIVIDAD 5 Vuelve a la lista de palabras y asociaciones que hiciste para la **Actividad 2.** ¿Te ayudó pensar en este tema antes de leer el artículo? ¿Pudiste predecir algunas de las ideas del texto? ¿Por qué sí o por qué no?

ACTIVIDAD 6 Trabaja con un grupo de tres a cuatro estudiantes. Juntos contesten las siguientes preguntas sobre la lectura.

1. ¿Con qué país asocia el autor del artículo los jeans?
2. ¿Con qué prendas de ropa sugiere el autor combinar los jeans?
3. ¿Qué otras prendas o accesorios son de mezclilla?
4. Hagan una lista de por lo menos cinco aspectos positivos de los jeans que se mencionan en los "testimonios".

ACTIVIDAD 7 En la opinión de la gente de otros países, los jeans son un símbolo de los Estados Unidos (¡junto con la hamburguesa y los autos grandes!). Hablen en grupo sobre las siguientes preguntas. Luego, cada persona debe escribir un resumen corto de la conversación.

1. ¿Hay una diferencia entre una prenda de ropa muy popular y una prenda de ropa "tradicional"? Por ejemplo, en Perú y Ecuador, la ropa tradicional generalmente se refiere a la ropa que usa la gente indígena de la región andina. Los peruanos que viven en las ciudades se visten en estilos más modernos e internacionales.
2. En la opinión de ustedes, ¿existe una "ropa tradicional americana"? (Piensen en las regiones geográficas y en los grupos étnicos del país.) Si existe, ¿cómo es?
3. Cuando la gente de otros países piensa en "la ropa americana", ¿a qué tipo de ropa se refieren? En la opinión de ustedes, ¿es correcta o falsa esta imagen del estilo estadounidense?

Answers Act. 6: 1. Estados Unidos 2. una chaqueta, una blusa de seda, un saco de cachemira 3. carteras, zapatos con tacones, gorras, chalecos, chompas, sombreros, mochilas, monederos 4. *Answers will vary. Sample responses:* sentirse más joven, son muy flexibles, son resistentes a cualquier trato, son buenos para todas las situaciones, son varoniles, son durables, no pasan de moda, los puedes llevar años, son discretos pero sensuales, puedes poner apliques sobre los jeans, son muy prácticos

VOCABULARIO

LAS PRENDAS DE ROPA *Articles of clothing*

el abrigo	*coat*
la blusa	*blouse*
las botas	*boots*
los calcetines	*socks*
la camisa	*shirt*
la camiseta	*t-shirt*
el chaleco	*vest*
la chaqueta	*jacket (outdoor, non-suit coat)*
la falda	*skirt*
el impermeable	*raincoat*
los jeans	*jeans*
los pantalones	*pants*
los pantalones cortos	*shorts*
el saco	*jacket, sports coat*
la sudadera	*sweatpants*
el suéter	*sweater*
el traje	*suit*
el traje de baño	*bathing suit*
el vestido	*dress*

LOS ZAPATOS *Shoes*

las botas	*boots*
las sandalias	*sandals*
los zapatos	*shoes*
los zapatos de tacón alto	*high-heeled shoes*
los zapatos de tenis	*tennis shoes*

LAS TELAS *Fabrics*

Está hecho(a) de... / Están hechos(as) de...	*It's made out of . . . / They're made out of . . .*
el algodón	*cotton*
el cuero	*leather*
la lana	*wool*
el lino	*linen*
la mezclilla	*denim*
la piel	*leather*
la seda	*silk*
a cuadros	*plaid*
a rayas / rayado(a)	*striped*
bordado(a)	*embroidered*
de lunares	*polka-dotted*
de un solo color	*solid (color)*
estampado(a)	*print*

LOS ACCESORIOS *Accessories*

la bolsa	*purse*
la bufanda	*scarf*
la cartera	*wallet*
el cinturón	*belt*
las gafas de sol	*sunglasses*
la gorra	*cap*
los guantes	*gloves*
el sombrero	*hat*

LAS JOYAS *Jewelry*

el anillo	*ring*
los aretes	*earrings*
el brazalete	*bracelet*
la cadena	*chain*
el collar	*necklace*
los pendientes	*earrings*
la pulsera	*bracelet*
el reloj	*watch*
el oro	*gold*
la plata	*silver*

LA MODA *Fashion*

(no) estar de moda	*(not) to be fashionable*
pasado(a) de moda	*out of style*

IR DE COMPRAS *Going shopping*

El (La) dependiente *The clerk*

¿Cuál es su talla?	*What is your size?*
¿En qué puedo servirle?	*How can I help you?*
Es muy barato.	*It's very inexpensive.*
Está a muy buen precio.	*It's a very good price.*
Está en venta.	*It's on sale.*
Está rebajado(a).	*It's reduced / on sale.*
de buena (alta) calidad	*of good (high) quality*
el descuento	*discount*
la oferta especial	*special offer*

El (La) cliente   *The customer*

¿Cuánto cuesta(n)?	*How much does it (do they) cost?*
Es (demasiado) caro.	*It's (too) expensive.*
¿Lo (La / Los / Las) tiene en una talla...?	*Do you have it / them in a size . . .?*
Me queda bien / mal.	*It fits nicely / badly.*
Me queda grande / apretado(a).	*It's too big / too tight.*
Voy a llevármelo(la / los / las).	*I'm going to take it / them.*
Voy a probármelo(la / los / las).	*I'm going to try it / them on.*

MÉTODOS DE PAGO   *Forms of payment*

¿Cómo desea pagar?	*How do you wish to pay?*
Al contado.	*In cash.*
Con cheque.	*By check.*
Con cheque de viajero.	*With a traveller's check.*
Con un préstamo.	*With a loan.*
Con tarjeta de crédito.	*With a credit card.*
Con tarjeta de débito.	*With a debit card.*
En efectivo.	*In cash.*

LOS NÚMEROS MAYORES DE 100
Numbers above 100

cien	*one hundred*
ciento uno	*one hundred and one*
ciento dos, etc.	*one hundred and two, etc.*
doscientos(as)	*two hundred*
trescientos(as)	*three hundred*
cuatrocientos(as)	*four hundred*
quinientos(as)	*five hundred*
seiscientos(as)	*six hundred*
setecientos(as)	*seven hundred*
ochocientos(as)	*eight hundred*
novecientos(as)	*nine hundred*
mil	*one thousand*
dos mil, etc.	*two thousand, etc.*
cinco mil	*five thousand*
diez mil	*ten thousand*
cien mil	*one hundred thousand*
un millón	*one million*
dos millones, etc.	*two million, etc.*

COMPARACIONES

más [noun / adjective / adverb] que	*more [noun / adjective / adverb] than*
menos [noun / adjective / adverb] que	*less [noun / adjective / adverb] than*
[verb] más / menos que	*[verb] more / less than*
tan [adjective / adverb] como	*as [adjective / adverb] as*
tanto(a) [noun] como	*as much [noun] as*
tantos(as) [noun] como	*as many [noun] as*
[verb] tanto como	*[verb] as much as*
mayor	*older; more*
mejor	*better*
menor	*younger; less*
peor	*worse*

PRONOMBRES DE COMPLEMENTO INDIRECTO

me	*to / for me*
te	*to / for you (fam. sing.)*
le	*to / for you (form. sing.), him, her, it*
nos	*to / for us*
os	*to / for you (fam. pl.)*
les	*to / for you (form., pl.), them*

PRONOMBES PREPOSICIONALES

mí	*me*
ti	*you (fam. sing.)*
usted	*you (form. sing.)*
él	*him*
ella	*her*
nosotros(as)	*us*
vosotros(as)	*you (fam. pl.)*
ustedes	*you (form. pl.)*
ellos	*them (male or mixed group)*
ellas	*them (female)*
conmigo	*with me*
contigo	*with you*

VERBOS

andar	*to walk*
conseguir (i, i)	*to get, to obtain*
morirse (ue, u)	*to die*
sonreír (i, i)	*to smile*
sugerir (ie, i)	*to suggest*

¿Qué te apetece?

CAPÍTULO 9

Communication

By the end of this chapter you will be able to:
- talk about food and cooking
- shop for food
- order in a restaurant
- talk about what you used to eat and cook
- say what you do for others

Cultures

By the end of this chapter you will have learned about:
- Bolivia and Paraguay
- traditional foods
- ordering in a restaurant
- bilingual countries in North and South America

Una mujer boliviana vende legumbres en un mercado al aire libre.

Unas salteñas

SABORES

¿Comes para vivir o vives para comer? La comida da sabor a las reuniones entre familia y amigos y juega un papel integral en todas las culturas del mundo. En este capítulo, vamos a examinar la comida y la importancia que tiene en nuestra vida.

Los datos

Mira la información del diagrama. Luego contesta las siguientes preguntas.

Paraguay   Bolivia

el bori de gallina:
una sopa de pollo

la so'o: una sopa
de verduras y
albóndigas
(*meatballs*)

el mbeju:
un panqueque
con queso

el bife (*beef*)

el maíz (*corn*)

la batata
(*sweet potato*)

los chuños:
un tipo de
papa/patata

el satja: una sopa
de pollo

la salteña:
una empanada
de carne

Comidas típicas paraguayas y bolivianas

① ¿Qué comidas típicas tienen en común los dos países?
② ¿En qué país es popular un tipo de sopa de pollo?
③ ¿Qué es la so'o? ¿y la salteña?
④ ¿Cuáles de estas comidas tienen nombres indígenas?
⑤ Piensa en cinco comidas "típicas" de EEUU. ¿Cuál es el origen de cada una?

¡Adivina!

¿Qué sabes de Bolivia y Paraguay? Indica a qué país o países se refiere cada oración. (Las respuestas están en la página 288.)

① Este país es uno de los pocos países con una biosfera no contaminada.
② Este país recibió su nombre del libertador Simón Bolívar.
③ El mayor complejo hidroeléctrico del mundo se encuentra en este país.
④ Este país no tiene costas.
⑤ Este país es el único en el mundo que tiene dos ciudades capitales.
⑥ Este país tiene dos idiomas oficiales, el español y el guaraní.

Vocabulario útil 1

CHELA: Quedamos en vernos a las ocho en punto en el **restaurante.** No llegó hasta las ocho y media. Cuando llegó, no ofreció explicaciones y no se disculpó. El **camarero** nos trajo los **menús** pero en ese momento sonó el celular de Sergio. Habló por teléfono —no sé con quién— por diez minutos enteros mientras yo esperaba. Por fin colgó y **ordenamos.** Yo pedí el **pollo asado** y él pidió el **lomo de res.**

Heritage Learners: The term *waiter* or **el camarero** has many variants. Ask students what other words they know for **camarero/a.** Examples: **mozo/a, garzón, mesero/a, mesonero/a,** etc. Often the variations are tied to dialects and the type of restaurant.

Usage and meaning of **bocadillo** and **sandwich** vary throughout the Spanish-speaking world. In general, a **bocadillo** is made with crusty bread similar to the French baguette. A **sandwich** is typically made of pre-sliced loaf-style bread.

Green beans are referred to as **habichuelas** only in the Caribbean. In Spain, they are referred to as **judías verdes,** and in other countries you might see them referred to as **vainas verdes.**

With a partner, go through all the items on the menu and decide whether they are masculine or feminine. Check your answers in the **Vocabulario** section on pages 296–297.

Food terms vary tremendously from country to country and region to region. For example, *cake* can be **pastel** or **torta;** *pork* can be **puerco** or **cerdo;** *banana* can be **plátano, banana,** or **guineo.** When you travel, be prepared to come across a variety of foods that you don't recognize and different names for foods that you do.

EN EL RESTAURANTE MIRAMAR

Cómo ordenar y pagar

Camarero(a), ¿me puede traer el menú?	*Waiter (Waitress), could you please bring me the menu?*
¿Me puede recomendar algo ligero / fuerte?	*Can you recommend something light / filling?*
Para plato principal, voy a pedir…	*For the main course, I would like to order . . .*
Para tomar, quiero…	*To drink, I want . . .*
De postre, voy a pedir…	*For dessert, I would like to order . . .*
¿Me puede traer la cuenta, por favor?	*Can you bring me the check, please?*
¿Cuánto debo dejar de propina?	*How much should I leave as a tip?*

Suggestion: As you introduce these words to students, ask them about their preferences in each category: **¿Prefieres caldo de pollo o sopa de fideos?** Ask students which local restaurants specialize in particular items: **¿Qué restaurante se especializa en mariscos / hamburguesas / pasta / pizza?** Have students identify what they would eat on certain occasions: **¿Qué tomas para una comida romántica / una comida rápida / una comida vegetariana? ¿Cuándo pagan tus padres o abuelos o cuándo paga otra persona?**

Notice: In many Spanish-speaking countries the restaurant bill is paid by one person and rarely divided up, as is often the custom in the U.S. You might want to share with your students that friends and relatives use the expression **te (le / os / les) invito** to offer to pay. The rationale is that everyone will pay the bill at some point and the cost will eventually even out.

EL MENÚ

Desayuno

cereal	*cereal*
huevos revueltos	*scrambled eggs*
huevos estrellados	*eggs, sunny-side up*
pan tostado	*toast*

Almuerzo

Ensaladas

ensalada mixta	*mixed salad*
ensalada de lechuga y tomate	*lettuce and tomato salad*
ensalada de papas	*potato salad*

Sopas

caldo de pollo	*chicken soup*
sopa de fideos	*noodle soup*
gazpacho	*cold, tomato-based soup (Spain)*

Sándwiches (o bocadillos)

sándwich de jamón y queso con aguacate	*ham and cheese sandwich with avocado*
hamburguesa	*hamburger*
hamburguesa con queso	*cheeseburger*
perro caliente	*hot dog*
...con papas fritas	*. . . with French fries*

Bebidas y refrescos

café	*coffee*
té o té helado	*hot or iced tea*
agua mineral	*mineral water*
jugo de fruta	*fruit juice*
leche	*milk*
limonada	*lemonade*
vino blanco/tinto	*white/red wine*
cerveza	*beer*

A la carta

Vegetales

frijoles refritos	*refried beans*
zanahorias	*carrots*
bróculi	*broccoli*
espárragos	*asparagus*
guisantes	*peas*
habichuelas	*green beans*

Postres

flan	*custard*
galletas	*cookies*
pastel	*cake*
helado de vainilla/chocolate	*vanilla/chocolate ice cream*

Frutas

naranja	*orange*
manzana	*apple*
plátano	*banana*
fresas	*strawberries*
uvas	*grapes*
melón	*cantaloupe*

Platos principales

Carnes

lomo de res	*prime rib*
bistec	*steak*
chuleta de puerco	*pork chop*
guisado	*beef stew*
pollo asado	*roasted chicken*
pollo frito	*fried chicken*
arroz con pollo	*chicken with rice*

Mariscos

almejas	*clams*
camarones	*shrimp*
langosta	*lobster*

Pescados

atún	*tuna*
salmón	*salmon*
bacalao	*cod*
trucha	*trout*

Actividades

ACTIVIDAD 1 **¡Tengo hambre!** Tienes mucha hambre. ¿Qué vas a pedir para comer y tomar en las siguientes situaciones?

1. Te despertaste tarde y no tienes mucho tiempo para desayunar antes de ir a la oficina.

2. Acabas de correr cinco millas en una carrera para una organización benéfica (*charity*).

3. Estás en una cita con una persona que es vegetariana y quieres hacer una buena impresión.

4. Es tu cumpleaños y estás en un restaurante elegante con varios amigos para celebrarlo.

5. Tu jefe quiere salir a comer contigo para hablar sobre algunos problemas de la oficina.

6. Sales a cenar con tus padres para su aniversario.

 Standards: In **Actividades 2** and **3** students are asked to use presentational skills. By presenting through role-play, students will be able to express longer thoughts and ideas with more extended discourse than the frequent question / answer format in the language class.

ACTIVIDAD 2 **El menú.** Con un(a) compañero(a), preparen un menú para las siguientes personas. Incluyan tres comidas y también algunas meriendas (*snacks*) si creen que le hacen falta a esa persona. Incluyan todos los detalles necesarios, incluso lo que debe tomar esa persona con cada comida o merienda.

1. una persona que está a dieta

2. una persona muy activa que necesita muchas calorías

3. una pareja que sale a cenar para celebrar su aniversario

4. un estudiante universitario que no tiene mucho dinero

5. una persona que acaba de despertarse y va a correr un maratón hoy

Optional: Suggest service learning beyond the classroom. Have students explore local opportunities for Spanish practice in community and religious centers in your area.

ACTIVIDAD 3 **En el restaurante.** En grupos de tres, representen una de las siguientes situaciones. Pueden preparar un guión antes de representar la situación a la clase.

Situación 1: Es el cumpleaños de tu novio(a) y están en un restaurante elegante para la celebración. El (La) camarero(a) es un actor (actriz) a quien no le gusta su trabajo y en realidad no debe servirle comida a la gente.

Situación 2: Tu jefe te invita a cenar. Estás un poco nervioso(a) porque no sabes de lo que quiere hablar. El (La) camarero(a) es un(a) viejo(a) amigo(a) tuyo(a) y te hace muchas recomendaciones, pero tú no tienes hambre y no quieres lo que te sugiere.

Vocabulario útil 2

CHELA: Empezamos a comer. Inmediatamente, Sergio llamó al camarero. ¡Pobre camarero! Sergio fue muy descortés con él. Le dijo que la **sopa** estaba **congelada**, que el **bróculi** no estaba **fresco** y ¡que la **carne** estaba **cruda**! Mandó toda la comida a la cocina. ¡Qué vergüenza! No sabía qué hacer. Mientras esperábamos sus platos, **se enfriaron** los míos.

Suggestion: Practice these verbs by asking students to fill in the blanks orally. Examples: Tengo que [pelar] las zanahorias para una ensalada (o las papas antes de cocerlas). Tengo que [freír] para preparar huevos fritos. Tengo que [mezclar] los ingredientes para preparar un pastel. Tengo que [unir] varios ingredientes para preparar una salsa mexicana. Tengo que [hervir] los huevos para hacer huevos duros.

LAS RECETAS

Los ingredientes

el aceite de oliva	olive oil	la mantequilla	butter
el ajo	garlic	la sal y la pimienta	salt and pepper
el azúcar	sugar	la mayonesa	mayonnaise
la cebolla	onion	la mostaza	mustard
la harina	flour	el vinagre	vinegar

La preparación

a fuego suave / lento	at low heat	molido(a)	crushed, ground
al gusto	to taste	picante	spicy
al hilo	stringed	agregar, añadir	to add
al horno	roasted (in the oven)	calentar (ie) (en el microondas)	to heat (in the microwave)
a la parrilla	grilled		
al vapor	steamed	cocer (ue)	to cook (on the stove)
		enfriarse	to get cold
congelado(a)	frozen	freír (i, i)	to fry
crudo(a)	raw	hervir (ie, i)	to boil
dorado(a)	golden; browned	hornear	to bake in the oven
fresco(a)	fresh	mezclar	to mix
frito(a)	fried	pelar	to peel
hervido(a)	boiled	picar	to chop, mince
		unir	to mix together, incorporate

Las medidas — Measurements

un kilo	kilo (approximately 2.2 lbs.)	la cucharada	tablespoonful
un medio kilo	half a kilo	la cucharadita	teaspoonful
la libra	pound	la docena	dozen
		el paquete	package
el litro	liter	el pedazo	piece, slice
el galón	gallon	el trozo	chunk, piece

Suggestion: Have an oral chat with students about what they like to eat and what they know how to prepare. Lead with questions like: ¿Te gusta preparar la comida? ¿Qué sabes preparar / cocer / freír / hornear? ¿Sabes preparar la comida al horno / a la parrilla / en el microondas? ¿Te gusta la comida frita? ¿Cuál es un ejemplo de comida frita? ¿Te gusta la comida picante / congelada / fresca / con mucha sal?

Suggestion: ¿Dónde se usan los kilos y dónde se usan las libras? ¿Qué cosas compras por kilo / por litro / . . . ?

Actividades

Picadillo is a spicy mincemeat typical of Latin America.

ACTIVIDAD 4 **Picadillo boliviano.** Lee la siguiente receta para un picadillo boliviano. Con un(a) compañero(a), contesten las siguientes preguntas para ver si entendieron las instrucciones.

PICADILLO

Ingredientes

15 papas peladas y cortadas al hilo
1/2 kg. de cadera de res
5 vainas de ají colorado molido y frito
2 cebollas
1 tomate
1 cucharilla de pimienta
1/4 cucharilla de comino
aceite
sal

Suggestion: Point out the command forms (3rd person singular) in the recipe. Take the opportunity to briefly review them.

Preparación

Pique la carne muy menuda, el tomate en cuadritos y la cebolla finamente picada. En una sartén con poco aceite, fría la cebolla hasta que esté transparente. Añada la pimienta, el comino, la sal al gusto y la carne. Cuando la carne esté dorada, agregue el tomate, deje cocer 5 minutos e incorpore el ají colorado y 1/2 taza de agua. Deje secar a fuego suave el guiso. Aparte fría las papas en abundante aceite caliente. En el momento de servir, una las papas y el guisado de carne. Mezcle bien.

1. ¿Qué debes hacer con las quince papas?
2. ¿Qué debes hacer con la carne antes de freírla?
3. ¿Cómo debes cortar el tomate?
4. ¿Qué debes hacer con la cebolla?
5. ¿Qué le vas a añadir a la cebolla después de freírla?
6. ¿Cuándo puedes agregar el tomate?
7. Después de agregar el tomate, ¿que más le tienes que añadir al guiso?
8. Mientras el guiso se seca a fuego suave, ¿qué debes hacer con las papas?
9. ¿Qué debes hacer al final?

Answers Act 4: 1. Pelarlas y cortarlas al hilo. 2. Picarla muy menuda. 3. En cuadritos. 4. Picarla finamente y freírla en una sartén con poco aceite hasta que esté transparente. 5. La pimienta, el comino, sal al gusto y la carne. 6. Cuando la carne esté dorada. 7. El ají colorado y media taza de agua. 8. Freírlas aparte en abundante aceite caliente. 9. Unir las papas y el guisado de carne y mezclar bien.

ACTIVIDAD 5 **Telecocina.** Escoge una receta sencilla, como la del picadillo boliviano, y escríbela en una tarjeta. ¡Vas a explicarle a la clase cómo preparar tu plato favorito! Pero lo vas a tener que hacer sin estufa y horno. La clase puede hacerte preguntas durante tu demostración. Imagínate que tu presentación se está transmitiendo por televisión.

Vocabulario útil 3

CHELA: Después de la cena, otro desastre. El camarero nos servía el café cuando sonó el celular de Sergio otra vez. Decidió tomar la llamada en privado. Al levantarse, se pegó en la **mesa** y tiró el café por todo el **mantel**.

DULCE: ¡Uy, qué horror! ¡Parece de película!

CHELA: Sí, ¡de película de horror! Y ¡no me lo vas a creer!, pero después de todo eso, ¡no le dejó propina al pobre camarero! ¡Yo tuve que regresar a dejársela!

Preparation: Bringing paper plates, plastic utensils, cups, napkins, tablecloth, etc., is a good way to present and practice these words. Have students use prepositions as they tell you where to place items to set a place setting.

LA MESA

Cómo poner la mesa   *Setting the table*

el mantel · el vaso · la taza · la copa · el cuchillo · el tenedor · el plato hondo · la servilleta · la cuchara · el plato

Optional, Act. 5: Vary by supplying several other simple recipes for the students to act out. Also, having students role-play a famous chef can add some humor to the presentation. Additionally, students can bring in ingredients and / or finished product and present.

Actividades

ACTIVIDAD 6   **¡Necesito un tenedor!** Un(a) amigo(a) da una cena para varios invitados y te pide que lo (la) ayudes. Al oír los comentarios de los invitados, te das cuenta que necesitan ciertos utensilios. ¿Qué le hace falta a cada persona?

1. «No puedo tomar el caldo de pollo.»
2. «Me gustaría tomarme un té caliente.»
3. «Quisiera un poco de agua mineral, por favor.»
4. «Voy a abrir una botella de vino tinto.»
5. «No puedo cortar este bistec.»
6. «Este arroz se ve delicioso.»
7. «¿En qué debo servir el gazpacho?»
8. «Necesito algo para limpiarme las manos.»

Tomar, not **comer,** is used to refer to eating soup.

Answers Act. 6: 1. una cuchara 2. una taza 3. un vaso 4. unas copas 5. un cuchillo 6. un tenedor 7. unos platos hondos 8. una servilleta

ACTIVIDAD 7   **La cena.** En grupos de cuatro, representen la siguiente situación frente a la clase. Pueden preparar un guión si quieren.

Tú y tres amigos van a dar una fiesta para celebrar algo importante. Los cuatro se juntan para planear el menú. No están de acuerdo sobre varias decisiones.

- dónde va a ser la fiesta
- qué platos van a cocinar
- quién va a preparar qué platos
- cómo los van a preparar
- qué refrescos van a servir
- a quiénes van a invitar
- ¿...?

Standards: This activity is in the presentational mode. Also encourage high beginners to research a variety of **menús** that are easily located on the Internet for additional ideas.

Antes de ver el video

 ACTIVIDAD 1 El video para este capítulo tiene lugar en un restaurante. Chela le describe a Dulce la cena que tuvo la noche anterior con Sergio. Trabaja con un(a) compañero(a) de clase y contesten las siguientes preguntas sobre lo que ya saben de Chela y Sergio.

For additional practice, do the *Nexos* website and / or CD-ROM video exercises.

1. ¿Qué sabes de la personalidad de Chela? Piensa en tres adjetivos que la describan.
2. ¿Qué sabes de la personalidad de Sergio? Piensa en tres adjetivos diferentes que lo describan.
3. En su opinión, ¿son Chela y Sergio compatibles? ¿Por qué sí o por qué no?

ESTRATEGIA

Using visuals to aid comprehension

In the video segment you are going to see, you can gain a lot of information from just looking at the visuals on the screen. In some cases, the scenes and images you see also help you to understand the language that you hear. When watching video, it is important to pay attention to the visuals as well as to the spoken conversation.

Answers Act. 2: 1. d 2. b 3. a 4. c

ACTIVIDAD 2 Antes de ver el video, mira las siguientes fotos del video. Luego escoge la oración que mejor describe la idea principal de cada foto.

1. _____   2. _____   3. _____   4. _____

Ideas principales
a. Parece que Sergio llegó muy tarde a la cita.
b. A Chela no le gustó nada la conversación telefónica que tuvo Sergio.
c. Sergio fue muy descortés con el camarero.
d. A Sergio no le importó mucho el accidente que tuvo con el café.

El video

Mira el episodio para el **Capítulo 9.** No te olvides de enfocarte en las imágenes del video para ayudarte a entender la acción y los comentarios de Chela.

Suggestion: Tell students that Chela's body language will be easy to follow in this video segment. Have students make a list of her gestures and facial expressions. There are also examples of expressive intonation that can be pointed out. Students can hear and practice this simple example: **por favor** (polite, pleading, asking for patience) and **por favor** (impolite, don't bother me with this).

Answers Act. 3: *Order:* 2, 4, 5, 1, 3, 6

Optional: Ask a student or two to volunteer a personal experience to the class: **¿Quién tuvo una mala experiencia en un restaurante alguna vez? ¿Qué pasó?**

Después de ver el video

ACTIVIDAD 3 Pon en orden correcto los ejemplos de la descortesía de Sergio, según los comentarios de Chela.

_____ "Habló por teléfono —no sé con quién— por diez minutos enteros mientras yo esperaba."

_____ "...Sergio llamó al camarero. ¡Pobre camarero! Sergio fue muy descortés con él."

_____ "Decidió tomar la llamada en privado. Al levantarse, se pegó en la mesa y tiró el café por todo el mantel."

_____ "Quedamos en vernos a las ocho en punto en el restaurante. No llegó hasta las ocho y media."

_____ "Habló de sí mismo por una eternidad y mientras hablaba no dejaba de arreglarse el pelo."

_____ "...después de todo eso, ¡no le dejó propina al pobre camarero!"

ACTIVIDAD 4 En tu opinión, ¿crees que a Sergio le pareció una cena agradable? Escribe una conversación breve entre Sergio y Beto en la que Sergio describe la cena desde su punto de vista.

Optional: For expansion, ask students: **¿Cuáles son los restaurantes latinos que tú conoces? Y, ¿qué sabes de ellos?**

¿Te gusta experimentar con platillos nuevos o prefieres la comida tradicional? ¿Te interesa comer en el restaurante "¡Pasión!" y probar la Nueva Cocina Latina? To learn more about Guillermo Pernot and his cuisine, visit the *Nexos* website (http://college.hmco.com/languages/spanish/students) and follow the links.

VOCES DE LA COMUNIDAD

Guillermo Pernot

Guillermo Pernot explica por qué su restaurante se llama "¡Pasión!", diciendo: "La comida se parece a mis sentimientos — poderosa (*powerful*), compleja y con mucho sabor (*flavor*)".

Guillermo Pernot es dueño (*owner*) y chef del restaurante "¡Pasión!" de Filadelfia. Este nativo de la Argentina es uno de los pioneros de la Nueva Cocina Latina, un nuevo estilo culinario que combina los sabores de la cocina tradicional y contemporánea de Centro y Sur América. La cocina de Pernot se caracteriza por su uso del pescado crudo y cocido y una abundante variedad de frutas y vegetales. *¡Ceviche!*, el nuevo libro de cocina de Pernot y su co-autora Aliza Green, es una innovadora colección de platillos tales como ensalada de papaya, ceviche de langosta y picadillo de atún.

Puedes ver a Pernot en el programa de televisión *Ready, Set, Cook.*

Guillermo Pernot ha recibido (*has received*) algunos de los honores más altos de la industria culinaria de EEUU y en 1999, la revista *Philadelphia Magazine* escogió a "¡Pasión!" como el mejor restaurante nuevo de Filadelfia.

Gramática útil 1
Talking about what you used to do: The imperfect tense

For more practice of chapter topics, do the *Nexos* website exercises.

Habló por teléfono, no sé con quién, por diez minutos enteros mientras yo **esperaba**.

CÓMO USARLO

1. You have already learned to talk about completed actions and past events using the *preterite tense* in Spanish.

2. Spanish has another past-tense form known as the *imperfect tense*. The imperfect is used to talk about *ongoing actions* or *conditions* in the past.

3. Use the *imperfect tense* to talk about the following events or situations in the past.

◆ to talk about what you *habitually did* or *used to do*

Todos los días, **desayunaba** a las ocho y luego **caminaba** a la escuela.	*Every day* **I used to eat breakfast** *at eight and then* **I walked** *to school.*

◆ to describe an *action in progress* in the past

Vivíamos en Asunción con mi prima Enedina y sus padres.	*We were living* *in Asunción with my cousin Enedina and her parents.*

◆ to *tell the time* in the past

Por lo general, **eran** las diez de la noche cuando **comíamos**.	*It was usually* *ten at night when* *we would eat dinner.*

◆ to describe *emotional or physical conditions* in the past

Todos **estábamos** muy contentos y nadie se enfermó ese año. **Nos sentíamos** muy afortunados.	*We were* *all very happy and no one got sick that year.* *We felt* *very fortunate.*

◆ to describe *ongoing weather conditions* in the past

Llovía mucho en Paraguay en esa época.	*It rained* *a lot in Paraguay during that time.*

◆ to tell someone's *age* in the past

Enedina **tenía** quince años ese año.	*Enedina* **was** *fifteen that year.*

4. The imperfect tense is generally translated into English in different ways. For example, **comía** can be translated as *I ate* (routinely), *I was eating, I would eat,* or *I used to eat.*

CÓMO FORMARLO

1. Here are the imperfect forms of regular verbs, which includes almost all Spanish verbs. Notice that **-er** and **-ir** verbs share the same endings, and that the **yo** and **usted / él / ella** forms are identical for all verbs.

	cenar	comer	pedir
yo	cen**aba**	com**ía**	ped**ía**
tú	cen**abas**	com**ías**	ped**ías**
usted / él / ella	cen**aba**	com**ía**	ped**ía**
nosotros / nosotras	cen**ábamos**	com**íamos**	ped**íamos**
vosotros / vosotras	cen**abais**	com**íais**	ped**íais**
ustedes / ellos / ellas	cen**aban**	com**ían**	ped**ían**

2. There are no stem changes in the imperfect tense.

3. There are only three irregular verbs in the imperfect.

	ir	ser	ver
yo	**iba**	**era**	**veía**
tú	**ibas**	**eras**	**veías**
usted / él / ella	**iba**	**era**	**veía**
nosotros / nosotras	**íbamos**	**éramos**	**veíamos**
vosotros / vosotras	**ibais**	**erais**	**veíais**
ustedes / ellos / ellas	**iban**	**eran**	**veían**

> Heritage Learners: It is very common for heritage language speakers to spell the imperfect endings **-aba, -abas, -ábamos,** and **-aban** with **v,** rather than **b.** Call special attention to the correct spelling of these forms. Also, remind students that the imperfect endings **-ía, -ías, -íamos,** and **-ían** always take an accent over the **i.**

> Notice the use of accents on the **nosotros / nosotras** form of **-ar** verbs, and on *all* forms of the **-er** and **-ir** verbs.

> **Ver** is irregular only in that the **e** is maintained before adding the regular **-er** imperfect endings.

Actividades

ACTIVIDAD 1 **Sergio.** Sergio describe su vida cuando tenía catorce años y estaba en el colegio. Cambia sus oraciones del presente al imperfecto para saber cómo era su vida.

1. Me levanto a las seis de la mañana todos los días.
2. Tomo el desayuno en casa.
3. Salgo a correr dos millas antes de ir al colegio.
4. Voy al colegio en autobús.
5. Almuerzo en la cafetería del colegio.
6. Tengo clases hasta las cuatro de la tarde.
7. Estudio en la casa de mi novia hasta las ocho y media de la noche.
8. Me acuesto a las diez de la noche.

> Answers Act. 1: 1. Me levantaba a las seis de la mañana todos los días. 2. Tomaba el desayuno en casa. 3. Salía a correr dos millas antes de ir al colegio. 4. Iba al colegio en autobús. 5. Almorzaba en la cafetería del colegio. 6. Tenía clases hasta las cuatro de la tarde. 7. Estudiaba en la casa de mi novia hasta las ocho y media de la noche. 8. Me acostaba a las diez de la noche.

ACTIVIDAD 2 **En la secundaria.** Entrevista a un(a) compañero(a). Quieres saber más de su vida cuando estaba en la secundaria. Puedes usar las siguientes preguntas para tu entrevista, o puedes hacerle las preguntas que quieras. Túrnense para hacer la entrevista.

1. ¿A qué hora empezaban las clases?
2. ¿A qué hora te levantabas / desayunabas?
3. ¿Comías en la cafetería de la escuela o llevabas tu propia comida?
4. Si llevabas tu propio almuerzo, ¿quién lo preparaba?
5. ¿Qué comías de almuerzo?
6. ¿Trabajabas después de la escuela?
7. ¿Cuántas horas de tarea hacías?
8. ¿Participabas en algún deporte?
9. ¿Ibas a fiestas los fines de semana? ¿Solo(a) o con tus amigos?
10. ¿Eras miembro de algún club u organización en tu escuela?
11. ¿Tenías novio(a)?
12. ¿Qué hacías con tus amigos?

 ACTIVIDAD 3 **Los veranos de mi niñez.** ¿Cómo pasabas los veranos cuando eras niño(a)? Escribe una descripción de lo que te acuerdas de los veranos de tu niñez, o de un verano en particular que fue importante u horrible. Léele tu descripción a un(a) compañero(a) y escucha la descripción de él (ella). Usa las siguientes preguntas como guía si quieres.

- ¿Dónde pasabas los veranos? ¿Con quién(es)?
- ¿Qué hacías?
- ¿Qué te gustaba hacer? ¿Por qué?
- ¿Qué no te gustaba hacer? ¿Por qué?
- ¿Cuáles eran tus actividades preferidas del verano?
- ¿…?

Gramática útil 2
Talking about the past: Choosing between the preterite and the imperfect tenses

No **sabía** qué hacer. Mientras **esperábamos** sus platos, **se enfriaron** los míos.

CÓMO USARLO

1. As you have learned, the preterite tense is generally used in Spanish to express past actions and describe past events that are viewed as completed and over. The imperfect is used to describe past actions or conditions that are viewed as habitual or ongoing.

2. Sometimes the choice between the preterite and the imperfect is not clear-cut. It may depend on the speaker's judgment of the event. However, here are some general guidelines for using the two tenses.

Preterite	Imperfect
1. Relates a *completed past action* or a *series of completed past actions*. **Comimos** en ese restaurante la semana pasada. Ayer, **fuimos** al restaurante, **pedimos** el menú, **comimos** y luego **salimos** para ir al teatro.	1. Describes *habitual or routine past actions*. **Comíamos** en ese restaurante todas las semanas. Siempre **íbamos** al restaurante, **pedíamos** el menú, **comíamos** y luego **salíamos** para ir al teatro.
2. Focuses on the *beginning* or *end* of a past event. La cena **comenzó** a las nueve, pero no **terminó** hasta medianoche.	2. Focuses on the *duration* of the event in the past, rather than its beginning or end. **Cenábamos** desde las nueve hasta medianoche.
3. Relates a *completed past condition* that is viewed as completely over and done with at this point in time (usually gives a time period associated with the condition). Manuel **estuvo** enfermo por dos semanas después de comer en ese restaurante, pero ahora está bien.	3. Describes *past conditions*, such as time, weather, emotional states, age, and location, that were ongoing at the time of description (no focus on beginning or end of condition). El restaurante **era** famoso por su comida latinoamericana y **estábamos** muy contentos con los platos que pedimos.
4. Relates an *action that interrupted* an ongoing action. Ya comíamos el postre cuando por fin Miguel **llegó** al restaurante.	4. Describes *ongoing background events* in the past that were interrupted by another action. Ya **comíamos** el postre cuando por fin Miguel llegó al restaurante.

3. Notice that certain words and phrases related to time may suggest when to use the imperfect and when to use the preterite. These are not hard-and-fast rules, but general indicators.

Preterite	Imperfect
de repente (*suddenly*) **por fin** (*finally*) **ayer** **la semana pasada** **el mes / el año pasado** **una vez / dos veces**, etc.	**generalmente / por lo general** **normalmente** **todos los días / meses / años** **todas las semanas** **frecuentemente** **típicamente**

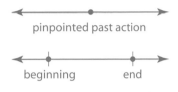

4. In **Capítulo 8** you learned that some verbs (**querer, poder, conocer,** and **saber**) have a different meaning in the preterite tense. This change in meaning does not occur in the imperfect tense.

Quise traer un plato boliviano a la fiesta, pero **no pude** encontrar los ingredientes.	*I **tried** to bring a Bolivian dish to the party, but **I failed** to find the ingredients.*
Quería ir a la fiesta, pero no **podía** salir de la oficina.	*I **wanted** to go to the party, but I couldn't **leave** the office.*
Durante la cena en el restaurante, **conocí** a un hombre que es cocinero profesional y **supe** cómo hacer salteñas perfectas.	*During the dinner at the restaurant, I **met** a man who is a professional chef and I **found out** how to make the perfect salteñas.*
En Bolivia, **conocía** a un hombre que era cocinero profesional y él **sabía** cómo hacer salteñas perfectas.	*In Bolivia I **knew** a man who was a professional chef and he **knew** how to make perfect salteñas.*

CÓMO FORMARLO

Review the preterite forms presented in **Capítulos 7** and **8,** as well as the imperfect forms presented in **Gramática útil 1** (on pages 276–277 of this chapter).

Actividades

ACTIVIDAD 4 **Picadillo boliviano.** ¡Pobre Amelia! Ella describe lo que le pasó cuando estaba preparando un picadillo boliviano para su familia. Escribe las oraciones según el modelo. Ponle mucha atención al uso del pretérito y el imperfecto.

MODELO: picar la carne / sonar el teléfono
Picaba la carne cuando sonó el teléfono.

1. pelar las papas / empezar a llover
2. freír la cebolla / entrar mi hermano a la cocina empapado (*drenched*)
3. cortar el tomate en cuadritos / llegar papá del trabajo muerto de hambre
4. añadir la sal, la pimienta y el comino / mi hermanito poner la tele
5. agregar el tomate / mi hermanita decidir ayudarme
6. dorar la carne / (ellos) anunciar en la tele que venir un huracán
7. secar el guiso a fuego suave / llegar mamá de la oficina
8. freír las papas en aceite caliente / empezar la tormenta
9. mezclar las papas y el guisado / sentarse todos a la mesa
10. servir el picadillo / cortarse la electricidad

ACTIVIDAD 5 **¡Qué decepción!** Anoche, Ricardo y Elena fueron a un restaurante a cenar. Elena le describe la cita a su amiga Fernanda. Completa su descripción con las formas correctas del pretérito y del imperfecto de los verbos entre paréntesis.

Anoche Ricardo y yo (1. ir) a un restaurante elegante. No (2. tener) reservación y por eso no (3. sentarse) hasta las diez de la noche. Los dos (4. estar) muertos de hambre. Yo (5. ordenar) una ensalada mixta, pollo asado con habichuelas, flan y un café. Ricardo (6. pedir) una ensalada de papa, lomo de res y un helado de vainilla. Nosotros (7. hablar) de la película que (8. acabar) de ver cuando (9. regresar) el camarero a la mesa. Él nos (10. explicar) que no (11. haber) ni lomo ni pollo y nos (12. preguntar) si (13. querer) una hamburguesa. Ricardo (14. enojarse) mucho y le preguntó si por favor no nos (15. poder) recomendar algo más apetitoso. El camarero (16. sonreír) y (17. decir) que todo lo que (18. quedar) en la cocina (19. ser) ¡hamburguesas y papas fritas! Con el hambre que (20. tener) los dos, (21. decidir) ordenar las hamburguesas. Yo no (22. querer) dejarle buena propina porque había sido (*had been*) un poco descortés, pero Ricardo (23. insistir) en que no (24. ser) su culpa y le (25. dejar) una propina exagerada.

ACTIVIDAD 6 **Los veranos de Chela.** Escucha mientras Chela describe cómo pasaba los veranos cuando era niña. En un papel aparte, haz dos columnas como las siguientes. Mientras escuchas, escribe los verbos en el pretérito en la primera columna y los verbos en el imperfecto en la segunda columna.

Acciones: visitar a los abuelos, vivir en un pueblito, llevar su computadora, sorprenderse, levantarse muy temprano, ir a dar una vuelta por el centro, estar triste, la computadora no funcionar, salir al pueblo, no usar más la computadora

Completed action in the past	Action in progress or habitual action in the past
	visitaba

ACTIVIDAD 7 **¡Qué horror!** A veces salimos con alguien que no conocemos muy bien y la cita es un desastre. Esto le pasó a Chela cuando salió con Sergio en el video. ¿Has tenido alguna vez una cita desastrosa? Escribe una narración que describa esa cita o una cita imaginaria. Incluye muchos detalles y pon atención al uso del pretérito y del imperfecto.

- ¿Adónde fueron?
- ¿Qué hicieron?
- ¿Qué pasó durante la cita?
- ¿Qué hizo él / ella que te avergonzó (*embarrassed you*) o molestó?
- ¿Cómo te sentías?
- ¿Cómo respondiste?
- ¿...?

¡FÍJATE!

El pretérito y el imperfecto

En español, al hablar del pasado podemos enfocarnos en tres aspectos diferentes de una acción: su comienzo, un punto intermedio o su terminación. El punto de vista (*point of view*) que el hablante adopta sobre una acción determina si va a usar el pretérito o el imperfecto. Por ejemplo, en la oración **A las ocho preparé la cena,** el pretérito sirve para enfocarse en el comienzo de la acción. Por contraste, en la oración **A las ocho preparaba la cena,** el uso del imperfecto indica un momento intermedio durante el cual ocurrió la acción. El pretérito también sirve para indicar el final de una acción, como, por ejemplo, en la oración **A las ocho me caí.**

El pretérito y el imperfecto permiten hacer referencia a una acción pasada con gran precisión. Sin embargo (*Nevertheless*), a veces el hablante sólo tiene interés en comunicar que una acción pasada ocurrió, sin querer destacar ningún aspecto específico de aquella acción. En tal caso, el hablante usa el pretérito, como en la oración **En 1998 viví en La Paz.**

PRÁCTICA. Identifica cuáles de los verbos indicados se pueden expresar con el imperfecto en español. ¿Cómo se puede expresar más claramente el momento intermedio de una acción en inglés?

1. While I *washed* the dishes, my son *cleared* the table.
2. I *burned* myself when I *took* the cake out of the oven.

Elicit or point out that, in English, the *was* + *-ing* form of the verb can more clearly express the middle of an action.

Gramática útil 3
Avoiding repetition: Double object pronouns

How many object pronouns can you find in this ad? Are they direct or indirect object pronouns? How can you tell?

Te is an indirect object pronoun. You can tell it is indirect because it comes before the direct pronoun la. La refers to música; te refers to the person who is reading the ad.

CÓMO USARLO

1. You have already learned to use direct object pronouns **(me, te, lo, la, nos, os, los, las)** in **Capítulo 7**. In **Capítulo 8** you learned to use indirect object pronouns **(me, te, le, nos, os, les).**

2. Remember that you use direct object pronouns to replace the direct object of a sentence. The direct object receives the action of the verb.

Preparé **la comida.** → **La** preparé.

3. Remember that you use indirect object pronouns to replace the indirect object of a sentence. The indirect object says who the object or action is for.

Preparé la comida (para **ti**) → **Te** preparé la comida.

4. Sometimes you will want to use direct and indirect object pronouns together. In this situation, they are called *double object pronouns*.

Preparé la comida (para **ti**). → **Te la** preparé.
Organicé un almuerzo especial (para **ellos**). → **Se lo** organicé.

Heritage Learners: Point out that object pronouns are attached to infinitives, affirmative commands, and present participles. Use dictation exercises to practice this rule, as well as to practice placing the accent when double objects are used.

CÓMO FORMARLO

1. Here are the indirect and direct object pronouns in Spanish. They stay the same when used together, except for the third-person singular and third-person plural. In those two cases, **se** replaces **le** and **les** as the indirect object pronoun.

Indirect object	Direct object
me	me
te	te
le → se	lo / la
nos	nos
os	os
les → se	los / las

2. When you use double object pronouns, follow these rules.

◆ The *indirect object pronoun* comes *before* the *direct object pronoun*. This is true whether the pronouns are used before the verb or attached to the end of the verb (infinitives, affirmative command forms, present participles).

Pedí una sopa. **Me la** sirvieron inmediatamente.
Luego pedí una ensalada. Le dije al camarero: "Por favor, **tráigamela** con un poco de pan".

◆ Remember that with *negative command forms*, the double object pronouns must come *before the verb*.

Quiero un postre, pero **no me lo traiga** inmediatamente.

◆ When double object pronouns are used with conjugated verbs and infinitives, they may go *before the conjugated verb* or *attach to the infinitive*.

Me lo van a servir en unos minutos.   O: Van a **servírmelo** en unos minutos.

Remember, when pronouns are attached to the end of infinitives, command forms, and present participles, an accent is placed on the verb to maintain the original pronunciation: **tráigamela.**

♦ When using the direct object pronouns **lo, la, los,** and **las** with the indirect object pronouns **le** or **les,** change **le / les** to **se.** (Notice that you use **se** to replace both **le** and **les.**)

Ileana **le** preparó **una ensalada** a Susana.

Ileana **se la** preparó (a Susana).

Susana **le** llevó **los ingredientes** a Ileana.

Susana **se los** llevó (a Ileana).

Ileana y Susana **les** prepararon **la cena** a sus padres.

Ileana y Susana **se la** prepararon (a sus padres).

Actividades

Answers Act. 8: 1. **Papá:** Hija, no te lo voy a comprar / No voy a comprártelo. **Tú:** Adelita quería un helado. Su papá no se lo compró. 2. **Papá:** Hijos, no se las voy a comprar / No voy a comprárselas. **Tú:** Adán y Adelita querían unas hamburguesas. Su papá no se las compró. 3. **Papá:** Hijo, sí te los voy a comprar / Voy a comprártelos. **Tú:** Adán quería unos plátanos. Su papá se los compró. 4. **Papá:** Hija, sí te la voy a comprar. / Voy a comprártela. **Tú:** Adelita quería una ensalada mixta. Su papá se la compró. 5. **Papá:** Hijos, no se las voy a comprar. / No voy a comprárselas. **Tú:** Adán y Adelita querían unas papas fritas. Su papá no se las compró. 6. **Papá:** Hija, sí te las voy a comprar / Voy a comprártelas. **Tú:** Adelita quería unas fresas. Su papá se las compró. 7. **Papá:** Hijo, no te la voy a comprar / No voy a comprártela. **Tú:** Adán quería una galleta. Su papá no se la compró.

ACTIVIDAD 8 **Adán y Adelita.** El padre de Adán y Adelita cree que sus hijos sólo deben comer comida nutritiva. Nunca les compra comida rápida y no les permite comer postres llenos de azúcar. Primero, haz el papel del padre y contesta las preguntas de sus hijos. Luego, di si les compró o no les compró las comidas que querían.

MODELO: **Adán:** Papá, quiero un perro caliente.
Papá: *Hijo, no te lo voy a comprar.* O: *Hijo, no voy a comprártelo.*
Tú: *Adán quería un perro caliente. Su papá no se lo compró.*

1. **Adelita:** Papá, quiero un helado.
2. **Adán y Adelita:** Papá, queremos unas hamburguesas.
3. **Adán:** Quiero unos plátanos.
4. **Adelita:** Papá, quiero una ensalada mixta.
5. **Adán y Adelita:** Papá, queremos unas papas fritas.
6. **Adelita:** Papá, quiero unas fresas.
7. **Adán:** Papá, quiero una galleta.

ACTIVIDAD 9 **Miguel.** La mamá de Miguel le pregunta si ha hecho varias cosas para los diferentes miembros de su familia. ¿Cómo contesta Miguel? Sigue el modelo.

Answers Act. 9: 1. Sí, se lo preparé. 2. Sí, se las compré. 3. Sí, se la serví. 4. Sí, se las traje. 5. Sí, me los compré. 6. Sí, te la di. 7. Sí, se las calenté. 8. Sí, nos las dieron.

MODELO: ¿Le serviste la leche a tu prima?
Sí, se la serví.

1. ¿Le preparaste el café a tu abuelo?
2. ¿Les compraste las galletas a tus tíos?
3. ¿Le serviste la sopa de fideos a tu hermano?
4. ¿Nos trajiste las servilletas?
5. ¿Te compraste los plátanos?
6. ¿Me diste la receta para el picadillo?
7. ¿Les calentaste las tortillas a tu primos?
8. ¿Les dieron las gracias tus primos a tu hermana y a ti?

ACTIVIDAD 10 **A la hora de comer.** Es la hora de comer en casa de Emilia Gutiérrez. La señora Gutiérrez le da instrucciones a Emilia. Escucha lo que le dice y escoge la frase que mejor complete sus instrucciones.

Answers Act. 10: 1. c 2. h 3. f 4. g 5. d 6. b 7. e 8. a

1. _____ a. Ábremelo, por favor.
2. _____ b. Prepáraselo, por favor.
3. _____ c. Sírvesela, por favor.
4. _____ d. Sírveselo, por favor.
5. _____ e. ¿Nos las calientas, por favor?
6. _____ f. Llévaselas, por favor.
7. _____ g. Dáselo, por favor.
8. _____ h. Tráemelo, por favor.

ACTIVIDAD 11 **¿Qué quieres para tu cumpleaños?** Con un(a) compañero(a), túrnense para representar la siguiente situación. Usen los pronombres dobles por lo menos dos veces en su conversación. Pueden practicar antes de representarle la situación a la clase. (Nota que los verbos **dar, traer, servir, preparar** y **comprar** frecuentemente requieren dos pronombres porque indican una acción hacia otra persona.)

Es tu cumpleaños y tus amigos quieren saber qué regalos quieres. Te van a dar una fiesta y también quieren saber qué comidas quieres que preparen. Eres muy exigente (*demanding*): quieres muchas cosas y te gusta una variedad de comidas. Pide todo lo que te apetezca (*you desire*).

MODELO: **Amigo(a):** ¿Qué quieres para tu cumpleaños?
Tú: Me gustaría tener el último CD de Shakira.
Amigo(a): Vamos a comprártelo. ¿Y qué más quieres?
Tú: …

Standards: This activity hones presentational skills (C 1.3). Taping (video or audio) offers students the opportunity to hear / view their own presentations and auto-critique them.

Gramática útil 4
Indicating for whom actions are done and what is done routinely: The uses of *se*

Begin the CD-ROM activities. Do the cultural activities and reading and writing practice as you complete the corresponding text sections.

Al levantarse, **se** pegó en la mesa y tiró el café por todo el mantel.

Ask students if they can identify which use of **se** is demonstrated in the video caption. (reflexive)

CÓMO USARLO

You have used the pronoun **se** in several different ways. Here's a quick review of its uses, plus one new use.

Use **se**...	
to replace **le** or **les** when they are used with a direct object pronoun.	Marta **le** dio un regalo a Selena. Marta **se** lo dio.
with reflexive verbs, when using **usted / ustedes** and **él / ella / ellos / ellas** forms.	Ustedes **se** vistieron y salieron para la oficina. Ella **se** vistió después de ducha**rse**.
to give general and impersonal information about "what is done."	**Se sirve** comida paraguaya en ese restaurante. **Se venden** libros bolivianos en esa librería.

1. When using the **se** + verb construction shown at the bottom of the chart, notice that the verb is in the third-person singular **(sirve)** if the noun that follows is singular, or in the third-person plural **(venden)** if the noun is plural.

Se venden empanadas aquí.	*They sell empanadas here.*
Se busca camarero.	*They are looking for a waiter*.

2. Se can also be used with a *singular verb and no noun* to say what an unspecified person does. (This use is similar to the "one does" use in English.)

Se come muy bien en ese restaurante.	*One eats well in that restaurant.*
Se viaja con gran confort en ese tren.	*One travels in great comfort on that train.*

Actividades

ACTIVIDAD 12 **Los anuncios clasificados.** Vas a escribir unos anuncios clasificados para el periódico universitario. Algunas personas te describen lo que necesitan o buscan. Escribe la primera línea de cada anuncio según lo que te dicen.

MODELO: —Me voy a graduar este año y tengo muchos libros usados que quiero vender.
      Se venden libros usados.

1. —Soy director y quiero montar (*put together*) una obra de teatro. Busco tres actores y una actriz.
2. —Vamos a hacer un Festival Boliviano y necesitamos voluntarios para ayudar con todos los detalles.
3. —Voy a estudiar al extranjero este semestre y quiero alquilar mi apartamento.
4. —Para las Navidades queremos darles ropa y juguetes a los niños pobres. Aceptamos donaciones de ropa y juguetes usados.

Sonrisas

⑤ Standards: The communities standard (C 5.2) is met as learners experience the wit, wisdom, and common sense of a vignette that exemplifies a learning moment for life and humor that promotes personal enjoyment in the target language.

 EXPRESIÓN. En grupos de tres a cuatro estudiantes, contesten las siguientes preguntas sobre la tira cómica.

1. ¿Por qué se usa un verbo singular con los dos primeros letreros?
2. ¿Por qué se usa un verbo plural con los dos últimos letreros?
3. ¿Crees que el niño va a recibir dinero de la gente que ve su letrero? ¿Por qué?
4. Piensen en unos letreros cómicos para los siguientes lugares. Luego, compartan sus ideas con otro grupo. ¿Qué grupo tiene los letreros más creativos?

   a. restaurante
   b. tienda
   c. hospital

   d. consultorio (*office*) de un dentista
   e. taller de un mecánico
   f. la pizarra en la clase de español

Optional: Have students explain the **Sonrisas** cartoon in their own words in Spanish to check their comprehension.

Bolivia y Paraguay

¿Adivinaste? Answers to the questions on page 267: 1. Paraguay 2. Bolivia 3. Paraguay 4. Bolivia y Paraguay 5. Bolivia 6. Paraguay

Answers: oración 1 = párrafo 5; oración 2 = párrafo 2; oración 3 = párrafo 6; oración 4 = párrafo 4; oración 5 = párrafo 1; oración 6 = párrafo 3

La tradición y la innovación. Lee los siguientes párrafos sobre Bolivia y Paraguay. Luego, empareja la oración en el cuadro con el párrafo que describe.

Párrafo	Oración
	1. Una gigante presa (*dam*) es una de las atracciones turísticas más populares de toda Sudamérica.
	2. Este país es un poco diferente de los otros países sudamericanos por dos razones.
	3. Las misiones son una parte importante de la historia de este país.
	4. Las riquezas naturales de este país atraen a muchos turistas.
	5. La gran influencia indígena en este país es obvia por todas partes.
	6. Los instrumentos indígenas forman la base de la música andina.

Bolivia: rica en variadas tradiciones

Párrafo 1

En Bolivia hay más de treinta grupos indígenas; los grupos más grandes son los quechuas, los aimaraes y los tupí-guaraníes. Esta diversidad de culturas resulta en una variedad de tipos de ropa tradicional, artesanías, bailes y música, que atraen a turistas de todo el mundo.

Párrafo 2

Bolivia recibió su nombre de Simón Bolívar, el héroe de la independencia de cinco países sudamericanos. A diferencia de los otros países de Sudamérica, Bolivia no tiene ni costas ni playas. Además, es el único país en Latinoamérica con dos capitales. La Paz es la capital administrativa del gobierno y Sucre es la capital constitucional.

Carnaval en Oruro, Bolivia

Párrafo 3

La música andina se encuentra por toda Bolivia y es popular por todo el mundo. Unos de los instrumentos indígenas típicos y tradicionales son las quenas, los sicus y las flautas que imitan el sonido (*sound*) del viento en los Andes. El charango es una pequeña guitarra y es muy popular en la música de la región.

The **charango** is made from the shell of the armadillo.

Paraguay: pasado y futuro

Párrafo 4

Paraguay es uno de los países menos contaminados del planeta. Por eso, hay muchas áreas naturales que no han cambiado (*haven't changed*) desde hace siglos, paraísos ecológicos que atraen a visitantes de todo el mundo. La flora y fauna de este país son bien conocidas por los ecoturistas, que llegan para visitar sitios como las ciénagas (*swamps*) del altiplano del Paraná y los secos llanos (*plains*) del Chaco.

Párrafo 5

Itaipú es el mayor complejo hidroeléctrico del mundo. Se encuentra en el río Paraná y es una empresa binacional, construida y operada por Brasil y Paraguay. El complejo provee el 24% de las necesidades de energía eléctrica de Brasil y el 95% de los requisitos del Paraguay. Es una atracción turística inmensa con casi 11 millones de visitantes desde 1977.

El complejo hidroeléctrico Itaipú

Párrafo 6

Las misiones jesuitas de Latinoamérica fueron construidas (*were constructed*) por la orden religiosa Compañía de Jesús entre 1609 y 1768. Estos misioneros jesuitas españoles y portugueses viajaron a las áreas más remotas de Sudamérica donde establecieron misiones, convirtieron a los indígenas al catolicismo y les enseñaron su idioma. La Misión de Trinidad del Paraná en Paraguay es quizás la más interesante de las misiones jesuitas que quedan, y ha sido declarada Patrimonio Universal de la Humanidad.

Internet

¡CONÉCTATE!

Trabaja con un(a) compañero(a) de clase. Hagan una investigación por Internet para buscar información sobre dos de las siguientes cosas o lugares. Usen los enlaces sugeridos en el sitio web de *Nexos* (http://college.hmco.com/languages/spanish/students).

1. los instrumentos nativos que se usan en la música andina
2. la presa gigante de Itaipú en el río Paraná
3. la vida de los guaraníes hoy día en Paraguay
4. la vida de los aimaraes a orillas del lago Titicaca
5. ¿...?

¡COMPÁRATE!

¿Sabes cuántos países oficialmente bilingües hay en las Américas? Tal vez la respuesta te va a sorprender. Hay dos: —Paraguay y Canadá. Paraguay es el único país hispanohablante en las Américas que reconoce dos idiomas oficiales: el español y el guaraní. Esta situación existe porque Paraguay siempre ha sido (*has been*) un país bicultural. La herencia indígena de los guaraníes se ha integrado (*has integrated itself*) casi completamente con la cultura hispanohablante paraguaya.

Las escuelas, las oficinas del gobierno y los medios de comunicación paraguayos se comunican con el pueblo paraguayo en los dos idiomas. Aunque el guaraní siempre ha sido una lengua de tradición oral, ha tenido (*has had*) una tradición escrita desde el siglo XVIII, cuando los misionarios católicos vieron la necesidad de crear un alfabeto guaraní para comunicarse con la gente indígena.

Existen varios diccionarios guaraní-español. Además, a causa de la historia de inmigración de Alemania a Paraguay, también existen diccionarios trilingües —guaraní-español-alemán.

 PRÁCTICA. En grupos de tres a cuatro personas, hablen de los siguientes temas.

1. ¿Les gusta la idea de tener más de un idioma oficial? ¿Por qué?
2. Si EEUU tuviera (*had*) más de una lengua oficial, ¿cuál sería (*would be*) la otra lengua?
3. ¿Cuánto saben de Canadá y sus idiomas oficiales? ¿Saben cuál es el otro idioma, además del inglés? ¿Han viajado (*Have you traveled*) a las partes de Canadá que lo hablan?

A LEER

Antes de leer

ESTRATEGIA

Setting a time limit

One of the best ways to learn Spanish is by reading it. Developing your reading skills will help you avoid spending too much time trying to understand every single word in a reading. In previous chapters, you have learned strategies to help you focus on getting the main idea without becoming too bogged down in the details. Another good way to do this is to set yourself a time limit. Reading under deadline pressure forces you to focus on what's important, rather than on trying to understand every single word.

ACTIVIDAD 1 Vas a leer un ensayo (*essay*) humorístico de un periodista boliviano, Hernán Maldonado. Describe un incidente que le dejó sin muchas ganas de comer en la oficina. Hay varias palabras desconocidas en el ensayo. Mira el dibujo para familiarizarte con estos términos.

La jornada laboral

ACTIVIDAD 2 En este ensayo, el autor describe la tentación de comer **salteñas** en la oficina, aunque está prohibido por la presidenta de la organización. Con un(a) compañero(a) de clase, contesten las siguientes preguntas para prepararse para algunas de las ideas del ensayo.

1. ¿Les gusta comer mientras estudian o trabajan?
2. ¿Creen que en EEUU es aceptable comer y beber en la oficina o en cualquier otro sitio de trabajo? ¿Hay sitios donde no es aceptable comer y beber? ¿Cuáles son?
3. ¿Creen que en EEUU somos más o menos informales con respecto a la comida que en otros países del mundo? ¿Pueden dar unos ejemplos?

Optional: See the *Nexos* website for links to **salteña** recipes. Assign students to visit links and report back to class what a **salteña** is in their own words. The sites also have pictures of **salteñas**, as does the chapter-opening spread, to clarify that the word is not a cognate and the reading is not about saltine crackers.

Lectura

Preparation: Have students scan true-false statements in **Actividad 4** to focus their reading.

Suggestion: Depending on the level of your class, break the reading down into parts and check comprehension by using true-false or either-or questions after each part.

Notice: The reading has a variety of verbs that contrast preterite and imperfect. Try having students underline or circle each type to call attention to the contrast.

ACTIVIDAD 3 Ahora, lee el artículo por primera vez. Trata de entender sólo las ideas principales. Pregúntate "¿Qué pasó?" mientras lees. Toma quince minutos y lee el ensayo por completo.

Los bocadillos en las oficinas
por Hernán Maldonado

FINALMENTE PARECE HABERSE superado una etapa[1] en la que no sé todavía por qué razones se prohibía terminantemente en las oficinas comer un bocadillo en medio de una jornada laboral.

Aunque en la mayor parte de las oficinas siempre existe un cuartito que sirve de comedor[2], el 90 por ciento de los empleados, a la hora de su "lunch", comen sobre sus escritorios. Nunca he podido[3] hacer algo similar y yo creo que se trata de un trauma que arrastro desde el primer y único año en que me desempeñé[4] como funcionario público.

Era el año 1969 y fungía[5] como Jefe de Relaciones Públicas del Consejo Nacional del Menor (Coname). Nuestras oficinas funcionaban en el Ministerio del Trabajo. Por razones de espacio, lo que antes era una sola oficina había sido dividida[6] en 10 oficinas con paredes de cartón.

Todos los días, a golpe de 10 de la mañana, acudía al edificio una mujer potosina[7] que vendía salteñas. Al comienzo traía sólo una pequeña canasta, pero como sus bocadillos tuvieron amplia aceptación, al poco tiempo apareció con un balay[8].

Todo andaba sobre ruedas[9] hasta que una mañana la presidenta de Coname, la señora Elsa Omiste de Ovando, prohibió que los empleados comieran salteñas en horas de oficina.

Como doña Elsa prefería despachar[10] desde su casa, la prohibición contra las salteñas fue relajándose y poco a poco, todo volvió a ser como antes, de manera que una mañana mi secretaria me dijo: "Señor Maldonado, la potosina está en la puerta, ¿pedimos?" "¡Por supuesto!" le respondí.

Justamente en ese momento se escucharon gritos en la puerta del edificio: "¿Quién me está comiendo salteñas? ¿Me van a hacer caso[11] o no? ¡Boten[12] a esa mujer de aquí!"

Me quedé congelado mientras escuchaba a nuestra presidenta entrar cubículo por cubículo, abriendo personalmente cajones, profiriendo gritos, dando órdenes. Me sentí despedido.

Y entonces se volvió al escritorio de mi secretaria. Hizo la misma revisión, incluyendo el basurero, y yo esperaba que en cualquier segundo gritaría en triunfo al encontrar las cuatro salteñas. Pero no encontró nada y salió furiosa. Yo no podía creerlo.

Mi secretaria estaba con la vista fija en la pared, como hipnotizada. "¿Qué hizo con las salteñas?" le pregunté.

"Estoy sentada sobre ellas, señor Maldonado", me dijo. Estaba petrificada.

[1]**parece...** *an era seems to have passed* [2]*dining room* [3]**Nunca...** *I have never been able* [4]**me desempeñé** yo trabajé [5]trabajaba [6]**había...** *had been divided* [7]**acudía...** llegaba al edificio una mujer de Potosí (ciudad en Bolivia) [8]**balay** *large basket* [9]**Todo...** Todo iba muy bien, sin problemas [10]trabajar [11]**hacer caso** *pay attention, obey* [12]**Boten** *Throw out*

Después de leer

ACTIVIDAD 4 Di si las siguientes oraciones sobre la lectura son ciertas o falsas.

1. _____ El autor no come en su oficina a causa de una experiencia traumática que tuvo cuando era joven.

2. _____ La secretaria del autor vendía salteñas en la oficina.

3. _____ A la presidenta de la agencia no le gustaba que los empleados comieran (*would eat*) en la oficina.

4. _____ La presidenta siempre estaba en la oficina, espiando a los empleados.

5. _____ Un día la presidenta vino a la oficina y vio que los empleados comían salteñas.

6. _____ La presidenta buscó las salteñas en todas las oficinas.

7. _____ El autor no tenía miedo de la presidenta.

8. _____ La secretaria del autor no pudo esconder (*to hide*) sus salteñas.

ACTIVIDAD 5 Completa las siguientes oraciones sobre la lectura para ver cuánto entendiste.

Preparation: Have students read
Actividad 5 before reading a second
time. Have pairs of students work on the
answers together.

Answers Act. 5: 1. a 2. b 3. a 4. a 5. a
6. b 7. a

1. El autor trabajaba en una oficina donde la _____ prohibió el consumo de comida en la oficina.
   a. presidenta
   b. secretaria

2. Una mujer potosina vendía _____ todos los días.
   a. bocadillos
   b. salteñas

3. La presidenta trabajaba fuera _____ la mayoría de los días.
   a. de la oficina
   b. del comedor

4. Como la presidenta no estaba en la oficina, los empleados _____.
   a. comían las salteñas en la oficina
   b. salían temprano de la oficina

5. Un día el autor y su secretaria acababan de _____ cuando entró la presidenta.
   a. comprar salteñas
   b. hablar con la potosina

6. Tuvieron que poner las salteñas _____.
   a. en el basurero
   b. donde la presidenta no podía verlas

7. Cuando salió la presidenta, la secretaria dijo que _____.
   a. se sentó sobre las salteñas
   b. comió todas las salteñas muy rápidamente

ACTIVIDAD 6 En grupos de tres o cuatro, contesten las siguientes preguntas sobre las ideas de la lectura.

1. En su opinión, ¿es exagerada la reacción de la presidenta? ¿por qué sí o por qué no?
2. ¿Creen que esta situación puede ocurrir en una oficina estadounidense ahora? ¿Y hace veinte años (*20 years ago*)?
3. Hay gente que cree que es descortés comer los comestibles que tienen un olor fuerte (*strong smell*) —como la pizza y las palomitas (*popcorn*)— en la oficina. ¿Están de acuerdo? ¿por qué sí o por qué no?
4. ¿Hay situaciones cuando es descortés comer en público? Por ejemplo: ¿en la iglesia? ¿en una clase? ¿en una ceremonia de graduación? ¿Cómo se decide cuándo es apropiado y cuándo no lo es?

A ESCRIBIR

Antes de escribir

 ACTIVIDAD 1 Trabaja con un(a) compañero(a) de clase. Van a escribir tres párrafos cortos que describan una experiencia con la comida. Escojan uno de los siguientes temas y piensen en una historia que quieren contar.

1. la primera vez que cociné
2. la primera vez que fui a un restaurante elegante
3. mis experiencias culinarias en un país extranjero

ACTIVIDAD 2 Después de establecer su tema, miren la tabla y complétenla, usando las oraciones modelo como guía.

	Oración temática (que comunica la idea principal del párrafo)	Detalles y ejemplos que ilustran la oración temática
Párrafo 1: Comienzo / fondo (*background*) de la historia (Recuerden que se usa **el imperfecto** para describir.)	*Yo tenía trece años y tenía una familia muy grande.*	*Era el menor de seis hijos y a veces me sentía un poco tímido en la presencia de mis hermanos mayores...*
Párrafo 2: La acción de la historia (Por lo general se usa **el pretérito** para relatar la acción de una historia. Se usa el **imperfecto** para describir las emociones de los participantes y los estados del pasado.)	*Un día tuve que preparar la cena para mi familia entera.*	*Tenía miedo porque no sabía cocinar muy bien y creía que no podía hacerlo. Miraba los libros de recetas...*
Párrafo 3: El fin de la historia y el resultado	*Aunque la cena estaba muy rica, el postre salió crudo.*	*Mis hermanos se rieron, pero no se burlaron de mí (they didn't make fun of me).*

Escritura

ACTIVIDAD 3 Ahora, escriban su historia. Miren la lista de expresiones de la página 279 **(Gramática útil 2)** para unas frases útiles.

Después de escribir

 ACTIVIDAD 4 Intercambien su borrador con el de otra pareja de estudiantes. Usen la siguiente lista para ayudarlos a corregirlo (*to edit it*).

- ¿Tiene su historia toda la información necesaria?
- ¿Es interesante?
- ¿Usaron bien las formas del pretérito? ¿y las del imperfecto?
- ¿Usaron complementos directos e indirectos para eliminar la repetición?
- ¿Hay errores de ortografía?

VOCABULARIO

EN EL RESTAURANTE   *At the restaurant*

el menú   *menu*

El desayuno   *Breakfast*

el cereal   *cereal*
los huevos estrellados   *eggs sunny-side up*
los huevos revueltos   *scrambled eggs*
el pan tostado   *toast*

El almuerzo   *Lunch*

Las ensaladas   *Salads*
la ensalada de fruta   *fruit salad*
la ensalada de lechuga   *lettuce and tomato salad*
  y tomate
la ensalada de papa   *potato salad*
la ensalada mixta   *tossed salad*

Las sopas   *Soups*
el caldo de pollo   *chicken soup*
el gazpacho   *cold tomato soup (Spain)*
la sopa de fideos   *noodle soup*

Los sandwiches (los bocadillos)   *Sandwiches*
con papas fritas   *with French fries*
la hamburguesa   *hamburger*
la hamburguesa con   *cheeseburger*
  queso
el perro caliente   *hot dog*
el sandwich de jamón   *ham and cheese sandwich with*
  y queso con   *avocado*
  aguacate

Los platos principales   *Main dishes*

Las carnes   *Meats*
el arroz con pollo   *chicken with rice*
el bistec   *steak*
la chuleta de puerco   *pork chop*
el guisado   *beef stew*
el lomo de res   *prime rib*
el pollo asado   *roasted chicken*
el pollo frito   *fried chicken*

Los mariscos   *Shellfish*
las almejas   *clams*
los camarones   *shrimp*
la langosta   *lobster*

Los pescados   *Fish*
el atún   *tuna*
el bacalao   *cod*
el salmón   *salmon*
la trucha   *trout*

A la carta   *À la carte*

Los vegetales   *Vegetables*
el bróculi   *broccoli*
los espárragos   *asparagus*
los frijoles (refritos)   *(refried) beans*
los guisantes   *peas*
las habichuelas   *green beans*
las zanahorias   *carrots*

Los postres   *Desserts*

el flan   *custard*
la galleta   *cookie*
el helado de vainilla /   *vanilla / chocolate ice cream*
  chocolate
el pastel   *cake*

Las frutas   *Fruit*

las fresas   *strawberries*
la manzana   *apple*
el melón   *cantaloupe*
la naranja   *orange*
el plátano   *banana*
las uvas   *grapes*

Las bebidas y los refrescos   *Beverages*

el agua mineral   *sparkling water*
el café   *coffee*
la cerveza   *beer*
el jugo de fruta   *fruit juice*
la leche   *milk*
la limonada   *lemonade*
el té / té helado   *hot / iced tea*
el vino blanco / tinto   *white / red wine*

Cómo ordenar y pagar   *How to order and pay*

Camarero(a), ¿me puede traer el menú?	*Waiter (Waitress), could you please bring me the menu?*
¿Me puede recomendar algo ligero / fuerte?	*Can you recommend something light / filling?*
Para plato principal, voy a pedir…	*For the main course, I would like to order . . .*
Para tomar, quiero…	*To drink, I want . . .*
De postre, voy a pedir…	*For dessert, I would like to order . . .*
¿Me puede traer la cuenta, por favor?	*Can you bring me the check, please?*
¿Cuánto debo dejar de propina?	*How much should I leave as a tip?*

LAS RECETAS   *Recipes*

Los ingredientes   *Ingredients*

el aceite de oliva	*olive oil*
el ajo	*garlic*
el azúcar	*sugar*
la cebolla	*onion*
el comino	*cumin*
la harina	*flour*
la mantequilla	*butter*
la mayonesa	*mayonnaise*
la mostaza	*mustard*
la sal y la pimienta	*salt and pepper*
el vinagre	*vinegar*

La preparación   *Cooking preparation*

a fuego suave / lento	*at low heat*
al gusto	*to taste*
al hilo	*stringed*
al horno	*roasted (in the oven)*
a la parrilla	*grilled*
al vapor	*steamed*
congelado(a)	*frozen*
crudo(a)	*raw*
dorado(a)	*golden; browned*
fresco(a)	*fresh*
frito(a)	*fried*
hervido(a)	*boiled*
molido(a)	*crushed, ground*
picante	*spicy*
agregar	*to add*
añadir	*to add*
calentar (ie)	*to heat*
cocer (ue)	*to cook*
enfriarse	*to get cold*
freír (i, i)	*to fry*

hervir (ie, i)	*to boil*
mezclar	*to mix*
pelar	*to peel*
picar	*to chop, mince*
unir	*to mix together, incorporate*

Las medidas   *Measurements*

la cucharada	*tablespoonful*
la cucharadita	*teaspoonful*
la docena	*dozen*
el galón	*gallon*
el kilo	*kilo*
la libra	*pound*
el litro	*liter*
el medio kilo	*half a kilo*
el paquete	*package*
el pedazo	*piece, slice*
el trozo	*chunk*

LA MESA   *The table*

Cómo poner la mesa   *Setting the table*

la copa	*wine glass, goblet*
la cuchara	*spoon*
el cuchillo	*knife*
el mantel	*tablecloth*
el plato	*plate*
el plato hondo	*bowl*
la servilleta	*napkin*
la taza	*cup*
el tenedor	*fork*
el vaso	*glass*

OTRAS PALABRAS Y EXPRESIONES

Expresiones para usar con el imperfecto

frecuentemente	*frequently*
generalmente / por lo general	*generally*
normalmente	*normally*
típicamente	*typically*
todas las semanas	*every week*
todos los días / meses / años	*every day / month / year*

Expresiones para usar con el pretérito

ayer	*yesterday*
de repente	*suddenly*
el mes / el año pasado	*last month / year*
por fin	*finally*
la semana pasada	*last week*
una vez / dos veces, etc.	*once, twice, etc.*

¿Cómo es tu casa?

Communication

By the end of this chapter you will be able to:
- talk about your childhood
- describe houses and apartments and their furnishings
- talk about household tasks
- indicate numerical order
- talk about the duration of past and present events
- say what people want others to do
- emphasize ownership

Cultures

By the end of this chapter you will have learned about:
- Guatemala and Nicaragua
- Habitat for Humanity projects in Nicaragua and Guatemala
- Nicaragua and its poetic tradition
- historical houses in Guatemala and Nicaragua

Standards: In this chapter, students relate their study of culture to philanthropy, international outreach, and volunteerism as they learn about the cultures of Nicaragua and Guatemala.

Esta humilde casa en León, Nicaragua, data del siglo XIX y es el lugar de nacimiento (*birthplace*) del famoso poeta nicaragüense, Rubén Darío. El poeta la describió así: "La casa era una vieja construcción a la manera colonial, cuartos seguidos, un largo corredor, un patio con su pozo (*well*), árboles".

Esta elegante casa fue construida en 1636 por Don Luis de las Infantas Mendoza y Venegas. Gracias al cuidadoso trabajo de conservación iniciado por la familia Popenoe durante los años treinta, la casa ahora sirve como un auténtico ejemplo de cómo vivía una familia en Antigua, Guatemala, durante la época colonial.

AMBIENTES

Los ambientes juegan un papel muy importante en nuestras vidas y en nuestros recuerdos. En este capítulo, vamos a hablar de los lugares y de la importancia que tienen en nuestras vidas, en el presente igual que en el pasado.

Los datos

Mira las fotos de las dos casas históricas en la página 298: el Museo Rubén Darío y la Casa Popenoe. Primero lee la información al lado de las fotos y luego indica si las siguientes oraciones se refieren al Museo Rubén Darío o a la Casa Popenoe.

❶ ¿Cuál de estas casas es más o menos una casa típica?
❷ ¿Cuál de estas casas es una mansión?
❸ ¿Cuál de las casas es más antigua?
❹ Si quieres saber más sobre la niñez de un poeta, ¿qué casa vas a visitar?
❺ Si quieres saber más sobre la época colonial de Centroamérica, ¿qué casa vas a visitar?

Los datos answers: 1. Museo Rubén Darío 2. Casa Popenoe 3. Casa Popenoe 4. Museo Rubén Darío 5. Casa Popenoe

¡Adivina! answers: 1. F 2. C 3. F 4. C 5. F 6. C 7. C 8. C

¡Adivina!

¿Qué sabes de Guatemala y Nicaragua? Di si las siguientes oraciones son ciertas o falsas. (Las respuestas están en la página 324.)

❶ Cristóbal Colón nunca llegó a Nicaragua.
❷ La ganadora del Premio Nóbel de la Paz, Rigoberta Menchú Tum, es de Guatemala.
❸ El *Popol Vuh* es el libro sagrado de los indígenas nicaragüenses.
❹ Hoy día todavía se hablan más de veinte dialectos maya-quiché en Guatemala.
❺ Guatemala es el país más grande de Centroamérica.
❻ Hay volcanes activos en Nicaragua.
❼ Hay muchas montañas y selvas tropicales en Guatemala, que es también uno de los países con el mayor número de volcanes del mundo.
❽ El poeta nicaragüense más importante, Rubén Darío, se considera como el padre del modernismo, un movimiento literario a finales del siglo XIX.

¡IMAGÍNATE!

Vocabulario útil 1

BETO: Cuando era niño, me gustaba preparar la comida para mi familia.

DULCE: ¿En serio? Yo creía que a los chicos no les gustaba hacer nada en la casa. Mis hermanos siempre decían que el trabajo de casa era para las mujeres.

BETO: ¡Qué anticuado! Yo no pienso así. Me crié en **el centro de la ciudad.** Somos muy modernos los hombres de la ciudad.

DULCE: ¿De veras? Qué bueno. En mi casa, mis hermanas y yo teníamos que hacer los quehaceres domésticos, pero mis hermanos sólo hacían lo que tenía que ver con **el garaje** o **el jardín.**

Ordinal numbers must agree in gender with the nouns they modify: **el segundo piso, la tercera oficina.** They are usually used in front of the noun. **Primero** and **tercero** shorten to **primer** and **tercer** when used before a masculine singular noun: **primer piso, tercer dormitorio** (but **primera casa, tercera ciudad.**)

Ordinal numbers can be used without nouns when it is clear what they are referring to: **Mi casa es *la cuarta* de la calle. Primero** and **tercero** are not shortened when used without a noun: **Este piso es *el tercero*, pero vamos *al primero*.**

In most Spanish-speaking countries, people refer to the ground floor (what we consider the first floor) as **la planta baja.** What we call the second floor is then referred to as **el primer piso,** the third as **el segundo piso,** etc. In Spain, speakers may use the word **planta** instead of **piso** to refer to the floor of a building, because, there, **piso** also means *apartment.*

ÁREAS DE LA CIUDAD

las afueras	*the outskirts*
el apartamento	*apartment*
el barrio	*neighborhood*
...comercial	*business district*
...residencial	*residential neighborhood*
el centro de la ciudad	*downtown*
los suburbios	*suburbs*
los vecinos	*neighbors*

LA CASA

el garaje	*garage*	el pasillo	*hallway*
el jardín	*garden, yard*	el patio	*patio*
la lavandería	*laundry room*	el sótano	*basement, cellar*
la oficina	*office*		

NÚMEROS ORDINALES

primer(o)	*first*	sexto	*sixth*
segundo	*second*	séptimo	*seventh*
tercer(o)	*third*	octavo	*eighth*
cuarto	*fourth*	noveno	*ninth*
quinto	*fifth*	décimo	*tenth*

Suggestion: This vocabulary lends itself to a discussion of **¿Dónde vives? ¿Vives en el centro o en las afueras (o en el campo)?** Have students interview a classmate about where they live now.

Notice: **Los suburbios** can have a negative connotation in the Spanish-speaking world, where it can mean ghettos or shantytowns on the outskirts of a town or city.

Heritage Learners: As is the case with English, the vocabulary for parts of the house varies from one Spanish-speaking country to the other. Have heritage learners work as a group to pool the words they use and also interview native speakers they know to gather as many variants as possible. As a follow-up, students can place these variants on a map of the Spanish-speaking world.

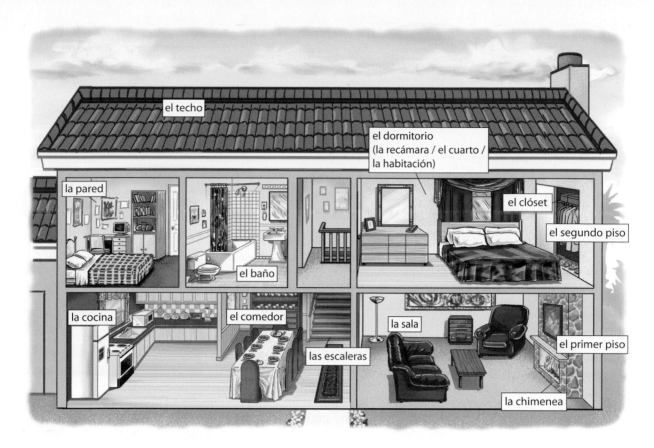

el techo

el dormitorio
(la recámara / el cuarto /
la habitación)

la pared

el clóset

el segundo piso

el baño

la cocina

el comedor

la sala

el primer piso

las escaleras

la chimenea

Actividades

 ACTIVIDAD 1 **¿En qué cuarto estás?** Di en qué cuarto o lugar de la casa está tu compañero(a) de clase basándote en lo que él (ella) te dice que está haciendo.

MODELO: Compañero(a): Estoy preparando la comida.
Tú: *Estás en la cocina.*

1. Estoy lavando la ropa.
2. Estoy mirando un programa en la tele.
3. Estoy cenando con mi familia.
4. Me estoy lavando los dientes.
5. Estoy subiendo al segundo piso.
6. Estoy cambiándole el aceite al carro.
7. Estoy regando (*watering*) las plantas.
8. Estoy trabajando en la computadora.

 ACTIVIDAD 2 **¿Dónde vives?** En grupos de cuatro, describan el barrio donde viven, qué tipo de casa tienen y cómo llegan a la universidad de su casa. Añadan todos los detalles personales que quieran. Tus compañeros pueden hacerte preguntas si no les das suficiente información.

MODELO: *Yo vivo en un barrio residencial en las afueras de la ciudad. Hay aparta-mentos y también casas individuales. Vivo en un apartamento en el segundo piso. Es una casa de veinte apartamentos. No hay tiendas muy cerca. Manejo para llegar a la universidad.*

Al final, informen a otro grupo o a la clase quién vive más lejos de la universidad y cuál es el modo de transporte más común.

Suggestion: Instructors can draw a building with many floors, introduce the words **edificio** (*building*) and **rascacielos** (*skyscraper*) and label floors to illustrate the ordinal numbers. Add names and ask questions like **¿En qué piso vive Marta?**

Answers Act. 1: 1. Estás en la lavandería. 2. Estás en la sala / en el dormitorio / en la cocina, etc. 3. Estás en el comedor. 4. Estás en el baño. 5. Estás en las escaleras. 6. Estás en el garaje. 7. Estás en el jardín. 8. Estás en la oficina.

If you or any members of your group live on campus, describe the neighborhood where you grew up.

ACTIVIDAD 3 **Mi casa.** En grupos de tres, háganse preguntas y describan su casa. Averigüen cómo es, cuántos cuartos tiene, si hay jardín y garaje, etc. Pueden describir la casa de su niñez o donde vive su familia ahora.

MODELOS: Compañero(a): *¿Cuántos pisos tiene tu casa?*
Tú: *Dos pisos.*
Compañero(a): *¿Cuántos dormitorios hay en tu casa?*
Tú: *Hay tres dormitorios, dos en el segundo piso y uno en el primero.*

¡COMPÁRATE!

La provisión de vivienda (*housing*) en Centroamérica siempre es difícil, a causa de los desastres naturales que ocurren con frecuencia en esta región—los terremotos (*earthquakes*), los huracanes, las erupciones volcánicas y las inundaciones (*floods*). La organización estadounidense Hábitat para la Humanidad trabaja con los países de Centroamérica (y de otras partes del mundo) para ayudar con la construcción de casas.

Las familias beneficiarias participan activamente en la planificación y la construcción de sus casas, que cuestan aproximadamente $1,000 dólares estadounidenses por casa. El modelo básico de una casa de Hábitat mide (*measures*) de 36 a 42 m² y es diseñada para resistir los terremotos. Tiene pisos de baldosas (*floor tiles*), paredes de bloc o ladrillo (*brick*) y techos de cinc. Consiste en un cuarto principal y dos dormitorios.

Hábitat empezó a trabajar en Guatemala en 1979, y éste fue el primer país en América Latina y el segundo país fuera de EEUU donde trabajó. Se estableció en Nicaragua en 1984. Hábitat jugó un papel (*played a role*) muy importante en la región después del Huracán Mitch, que devastó partes de Guatemala y gran parte de Nicaragua y Honduras en 1998. La organización inició un proyecto para ayudar a las víctimas, construyendo casas en las áreas más afectadas.

Hábitat para la Humanidad también opera en Estados Unidos, donde empezó sus primeros proyectos de construcción. Muchos estadounidenses, jóvenes y mayores, han participado (*have participated*) como voluntarios en sus programas de construcción de casas en áreas pobres o para ayudar a las víctimas de desastres naturales.

 PRÁCTICA. En grupos de tres a cuatro personas, hablen de los siguientes temas.

1. ¿Les gusta la idea de Hábitat para la Humanidad? ¿Creen que sus proyectos benefician a la gente de Guatemala y Nicaragua?
2. Comparen una casa de Hábitat para la Humanidad con la casa donde viven o donde viven sus familias. ¿Cuántas diferencias pueden identificar?
3. ¿Conocen algunas áreas de EEUU donde hay casas de Hábitat para la Humanidad?
4. ¿Les gusta la idea de trabajar en un proyecto de Hábitat para la Humanidad en Nicaragua o Guatemala? ¿Por qué sí o por qué no?

Vocabulario útil 2

BETO: No me parece justo. Yo **tendía las camas, pasaba la aspiradora, lavaba los platos** igual que mis hermanas.

DULCE: Pues eres único.

BETO: Sí, mi mamá decía que yo era su ayudante preferido. **Barría el piso, sacaba la basura, ponía la mesa, limpiaba los baños, planchaba, sacudía las alfombras…**

DULCE: Oye, me estás tomando el pelo, ¿verdad? Yo no conozco a ningún niño tan trabajador.

LOS QUEHACERES DOMÉSTICOS

Dentro de la casa

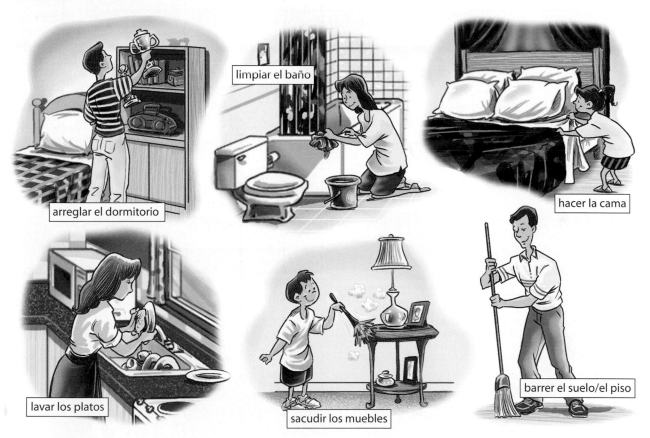

limpiar el baño

hacer la cama

arreglar el dormitorio

lavar los platos

sacudir los muebles

barrer el suelo/el piso

Optional: Throughout this chapter there are vocabulary words that lend themselves to graphics. Bring visuals of homes and floor plans with or without furniture and / or have students sketch and label their living spaces to present, reinforce, and make the vocabulary words three dimensional.

Dentro de la casa

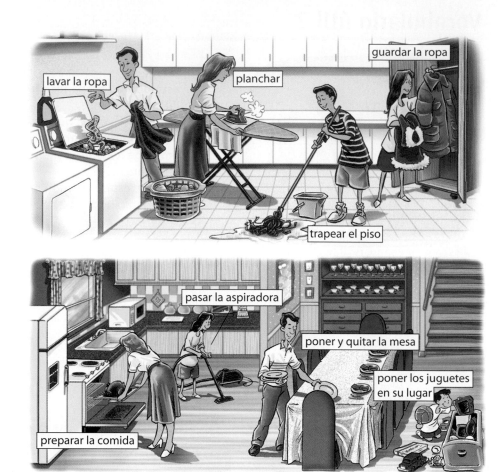

lavar la ropa

planchar

guardar la ropa

trapear el piso

pasar la aspiradora

poner y quitar la mesa

poner los juguetes en su lugar

preparar la comida

Fuera de la casa

darle de comer al perro y al gato

regar las plantas

sacar la basura

sacar a pasear al perro

cortar el césped

hacer el reciclaje

LOS MUEBLES Y DECORACIONES

- el cuadro
- el sillón
- la alfombra
- la persiana
- la cama
- el tocador/la cómoda
- la mesita de noche
- la silla
- la lámpara
- la mesa
- el espejo
- las cortinas
- el sofá

Notice: Although the word **persiana** can be translated as *Venetian blind,* **persiana** conjures different visual images depending on the country. Writer Julia Álvarez from the Dominican Republic calls attention to the nuance of the term **persiana** in the first poem in "Bilingual Sestina" (*The Other Side / El Otro Lado*). "Bilingual Sestina" is written principally in English.

Optional: **¿Participas en juegos virtuales como** "Sim City" **donde puedes planear una ciudad virtual? ¿Qué tipo de casa / ciudad te gustaría crear?** Suggest that interested students do a **búsqueda** of "Sim City Spanish" and download old versions for free.

Actividades

ACTIVIDAD 4 **¿Dónde pongo esto?** Un(a) amigo(a) acaba de mudarse (*has just moved*) a un nuevo apartamento. Tú le vas a ayudar a poner todos sus muebles y decoraciones en su lugar. Pregúntale dónde van ciertas cosas. Él (Ella) va a decirte dónde quiere cada cosa.

MODELO: Tú: *¿Dónde pongo el sillón?*
Compañero(a): *Pon el sillón en la sala, por favor.*

Answers Act. 4: *Answers may vary.*
1. ¿Dónde pongo el sofá? Pon el sofá en la sala, por favor. 2. ¿Dónde pongo la mesita de noche? Pon la mesita de noche en el dormitorio, por favor. 3.¿Dónde pongo el tocador / la cómoda? Pon el tocador / la cómoda en el dormitorio, por favor. 4. ¿Dónde pongo la lámpara? Pon la lámpara en la mesita de noche, por favor. 5. ¿Dónde pongo el espejo? Pon el espejo en el baño, por favor. 6. ¿Dónde pongo la alfombra? Pon la alfombra en el pasillo, por favor.

1.

2.

3.

4.

5.

6.

ACTIVIDAD 5 **¿A quién le toca?** En grupos de tres, representen la siguiente situación. Ustedes tres son compañeros(as) de cuarto y ¡su apartamento es un desastre! Decidan entre sí (*among yourselves*) quién va a hacer cada quehacer. Pueden negociar si quieren.

MODELO: No hay platos limpios para la cena.

Compañero(a) #1: *¿Quién va a lavar los platos?*

Compañero(a) #2: *Yo los puedo lavar si [Compañero(a) 3] hace las compras.*

Compañero(a) #3: *Estás loco(a). Prefiero sacar la basura.*

Compañero(a) #1: *Bueno, los lavo yo.*

Problema	Nombre / Tarea
No hay platos limpios para la cena.	[Nombre] va a lavar los platos.
El perro tiene mucha hambre.	
Las plantas están secas.	
El suelo de la cocina está sucio (*dirty*).	
Hay mucho polvo (*dust*) en los muebles.	
Mañana es día de reciclaje.	
Hay varias bolsas de basura.	
El perro tiene que salir.	
La alfombra está sucia.	
El baño es un desastre.	

Vocabulario útil 3

BETO: Pues, exagero un poco, pero sí me gustaban algunos de los quehaceres.

DULCE: ¿Como cuáles?

BETO: Pues, a ver, me gustaba limpiar **el refrigerador...**

Suggestion: When introducing appliances, ask questions like: ¿En qué cuarto / habitación de la casa se encuentra...? ¿Para qué se usa...?

LOS ELECTRODOMÉSTICOS

el abrelatas eléctrico	*electric can opener*
la aspiradora	*vacuum cleaner*
la estufa	*stove*
la lavadora	*washer*
el lavaplatos	*dishwasher*
la licuadora	*blender*
el microondas	*microwave*
la plancha	*iron*
el refrigerador	*refrigerator*
la secadora	*dryer*
el televisor	*television set*
la tostadora	*toaster*

Actividades

ACTIVIDAD 6 **¿Qué necesitas?** Identifica el electrodoméstico que necesitas en cada situación.

1. Tienes que lavar ropa esta noche porque no tienes nada que ponerte mañana.
2. Tienes que abrir una lata (*can*) de atún.
3. Tu ropa está muy arrugada (*wrinkled*) porque la acabas de sacar de la maleta.
4. Quieres pan tostado con los huevos revueltos.
5. Tienes ganas de tomar un batido de frutas (*smoothie*).
6. No tienes mucho tiempo para preparar la cena así que decides comer un paquete de comida preparada.
7. Quieres enfriar la botella de vino.
8. Quieres limpiar la alfombra.

Sample answers Act. 6: 1. Necesito la lavadora. 2. Necesito el abrelatas eléctrico. 3. Aquí está la plancha. 4. La tostadora está en la cocina. 5. La licuadora está en la cocina. 6. ¿Sabes usar el microondas? 7. Ponla en el refrigerador. 8. Usa la aspiradora.

ACTIVIDAD 7 **La casa nueva.** En grupos de tres, representen la siguiente situación a la clase. Pueden preparar un guión si quieren.

Tres amigos(as) van a ser compañeros(as) de casa. Tienen que comparar qué tienen y qué necesitan para la casa nueva. La casa tiene tres dormitorios, una sala grande, una cocina y dos baños.

- ¿Qué muebles y electrodomésticos tienen entre los tres?
- ¿Qué necesitan comprar?
- ¿En qué cuartos quieren poner los distintos muebles y electrodomésticos?

Optional: This activity can be done as **La casa soñada** using an example from **Las casas de los ricos y famosos**.

Antes de ver el video

ACTIVIDAD 1 En el episodio del video de este capítulo Beto y Dulce van de picnic. Piensa en los picnics que tú conoces. ¿Qué cosas probablemente vas a ver en el video?

ACTIVIDAD 2 Contesta las siguientes preguntas sobre Beto y Dulce.

1. ¿Qué recuerdas de la personalidad de Beto? ¿Es una persona muy sincera o exagera la realidad de vez en cuando?
2. ¿Qué recuerdas de la personalidad de Dulce? ¿Es una persona introvertida o extrovertida? ¿Es seria? ¿Le gusta reírse un poco de las personas muy serias?

Notice: You may want to point out that non-native speakers rely heavily on this type of *extra-linguistic* information to figure out situations in which they do not understand every word. Besides **el tono de la voz,** what other nonverbal clues do you see in the clip that communicate attitude or information?

ESTRATEGIA

Listening to tone of voice

In this chapter's video segment, pay particular attention to the tone of voice that Dulce and Beto use as they speak.

In many cases, what they say does not completely reflect what they are actually thinking and feeling.

How can you tell when Beto is exaggerating, when he becomes nervous or embarrassed, and when he relaxes? How can you tell when Dulce is surprised, when she is skeptical, and when she is teasing Beto?

Listen carefully to the characters' tone of voice (**el tono de la voz**) to help you understand what additional information lies beneath their surface commentary.

Lee los siguientes comentarios del video. Luego, mientras miras el video, presta atención particular al tono de voz que usan Beto y Dulce. Si crees que el tono contradice el comentario, escribe **C**; si crees que añade más información, marca **A**. Si crees que el tono no afecta el comentario, no escribas nada.

1. _____ Dulce: Hace mucho tiempo que no voy de picnic.

2. _____ Beto: Cuando era niño, me gustaba preparar la comida para mi familia.

3. _____ Dulce: ¿De veras? Qué bueno.

4. _____ Beto: Sí, mi mamá decía que yo era su ayudante preferido.

5. _____ Dulce: ¡Vas a ser un padre excelente!

6. _____ Beto: Mira, prueba éstos, los compré en el supermercado.

7. _____ Dulce: ¿No los preparaste tú?

8. _____ Beto: La verdad es que a mí no me gusta cocinar.

9. _____ Dulce: ¡Planchabas! ¡Limpiabas los baños! ¡Cocinabas! ¡Súper-Chico!

El video

Mira el episodio del video para el **Capítulo 10.** No te olvides de enfocarte en el tono de voz de Dulce y Beto para entender qué quieren decir en realidad.

Después de ver el video

Di si los siguientes comentarios sobre el video son ciertos **(C)** o falsos **(F).**

1. _____ Dulce está muy contenta con el picnic.

2. _____ Beto dice que preparaba la comida para su familia.

3. _____ En la familia de Dulce, los hijos también preparaban la comida.

4. _____ Beto se crió en el centro de la ciudad y se considera un hombre moderno.

5. _____ En realidad, Beto sí hacía las camas, pasaba la aspiradora y lavaba los platos.

6. _____ Dulce cree que Beto está exagerando.

7. _____ Dulce habla en serio cuando dice que Beto es el hombre ideal y va a ser un excelente padre.

8. _____ Beto se pone (*becomes*) nervioso y confiesa que no preparó la comida.

ACTIVIDAD 5 Trabaja con un(a) compañero(a) de clase. Basándose en la información del video, y también en lo que comprendieron del tono de voz de los dos personajes, escriban la historia verdadera de Beto. ¿Cómo era de niño? ¿Qué hacía y no hacía? Escriban por lo menos cinco oraciones que describan la realidad de su niñez.

 Conexión cultural. Mira el segmento cultural que está al final del episodio. Después, en grupos de tres o cuatro, digan cuáles de los platos mencionados en el video ustedes conocen o les gustaría probar. Cuando viajen a otros países, ¿creen que es importante probar la comida allí? ¿Por qué sí o no? Identifiquen algunos platos típicos que deben conocer los visitantes a su país.

VOCES DE LA COMUNIDAD

Francisco X. Alarcón

La tortilla

Cada tortilla
es una sabrosa (*tasty*)
ronda de aplausos
para el sol (*sun*)

Francisco X. Alarcón es uno de los autores más populares y reconocidos de libros bilingües para niños en EEUU. Sus versos celebran su herencia mexicana y su niñez en un barrio latino de Los Ángeles. Con un lenguaje sencillo y juguetón (*simple and playful*), Alarcón recuerda las canciones de su abuela, las fiestas mexicanas, los jardines de su barrio y el mundo fantástico de la imaginación de los niños.

Además de su colección de poesías infantiles, Alarcón es autor de varios libros de poesía para adultos. Su obra poética para niños y adultos ha recibido premios (*has received prizes*) nacionales de gran prestigio. También es autor de varios libros de texto de español y es profesor en la Universidad de California en Davis, donde se especializa en la enseñanza de español para los hablantes nativos de esta lengua.

¿A qué se refiere Alarcón cuando habla de una "ronda de aplausos"? Para contestar esta pregunta, piensa en el movimiento que hacen las manos para formar una tortilla. To learn more about Francisco X. Alarcón and his work visit the *Nexos* website (http://college.hmco.com/languages/spanish/students) and follow the links.

Gramática útil 1
Expressing hopes and wishes: The subjunctive mood

CÓMO USARLO

LO BÁSICO

- As you know, a *verb tense* is a form of a verb that indicates *when* an action took place, is taking place, or will take place. The present indicative, the present progressive, the preterite, and the imperfect are all *verb tenses*.
- *Mood* refers to a verb form that expresses *attitudes* towards actions and events.

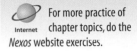

For more practice of chapter topics, do the *Nexos* website exercises.

1. In Spanish, as well as English, verbs can be used to express *time* (with tenses) and to express *attitudes* (moods). You have already learned the *indicative mood*, which is used to make statements, ask questions, and express objective, factual, or real information, and the *imperative mood*, which is used to give commands.

2. You are going to learn another mood, the *subjunctive mood*, which allows the speaker to express a variety of subjective nuances, such as hopes, wishes, desires, doubts, and opinions. The subjunctive is also used to express unknown or hypothetical situations. Although the subjunctive mood exists in English, it is often only used in literature or in formal written communication.

3. The subjunctive mood has tenses, just like the indicative mood does. You are going to learn the *present subjunctive*, which, like the present indicative, is used to express what happens regularly, what is happening now, and what is about to happen. The difference is that the present subjunctive views these present-tense events through a subjective, emotional, or contrary-to-fact filter.

4. In this chapter, you will focus on forming the present subjunctive correctly and using it to express how people wish to influence the actions of others.

Compare the following sentences that contrast the uses of the present indicative and the present subjunctive.

Heritage Learners: Research on U.S. Spanish indicates that, by and large, second- and even third-generation U.S. Hispanics use the Spanish present subjunctive correctly; however, other subjunctive tenses present serious difficulties for these students. The present subjunctive is a good indicator of the degree of native speaker proficiency of heritage language speakers. Students who have difficulties with the present subjunctive are likely to encounter problems with many other basic aspects of the language.

Present indicative	Present subjunctive
Marilena **visita** a su familia.	Su abuela **quiere que** Marilena **visite** a su familia.
Gonzalo **necesita** el libro de su amigo.	Gonzalo **necesita que** su amigo le **dé** su libro.
Marta no **recomienda** el concierto.	Marta no **recomienda que vayamos** al concierto.

Cuando yo tenga hijos, **quiero que aprendan** a ser responsables desde muy pequeños.

5. Notice that in the sentences above, the subjunctive is only used when there is a change of subject; in other words, when someone else wishes another person to take (or not take) some sort of action. This change of subject is signaled by the word **que.** Follow this formula.

Person 1	+ indicative verb	+ **que**	+ Person 2	+ subjunctive verb
Adela	**quiere**	**que**	**Elmer**	***venga* a la fiesta.**
Adela	*wants*	*(that)*	*Elmer*	*to come (come)*
				to the party.

6. Here are some verbs that you can use to express what others wish, need, request, desire, or want others to do (or not to do!).

aconsejar	*to advise*	**permitir**	*to permit, allow*
desear	*to wish*	**prohibir**	*to forbid*
esperar	*to hope*	**querer**	*to wish, to want*
insistir en	*to insist*	**recomendar (ie)**	*to recommend*
mandar	*to order*	**requerir (ie, i)**	*to require*
necesitar	*to need*	**sugerir (ie, i)**	*to suggest*
pedir (i, i)	*to ask, request*		

CÓMO FORMARLO

1. To form the subjunctive, take the present indicative **yo** form of the verb, delete the **-o,** and add the following subjunctive endings. Using the **yo** form of the verb makes sure that any irregularities such as stem changes are automatically carried over into the present subjunctive forms.

	hablar	comer	escribir
yo	hable	coma	escriba
tú	hables	comas	escribas
usted / él / ella	hable	coma	escriba
nosotros / nosotras	hablemos	comamos	escribamos
vosotros / vosotras	habléis	comáis	escribáis
ustedes / ellos / ellas	hablen	coman	escriban

2. **-Ar** and **-er** stem-changing verbs follow the same stem-changing pattern that they use in the present indicative (i.e., all forms reflect a stem change except the **nosotros** and the **vosotros** forms). However, **-ir** stem-changing verbs show a stem change in the **nosotros** and the **vosotros** forms as well.

-ar verb: pensar	piense, pienses, piense, pensemos, penséis, piensen
-er verb: poder	pueda, puedas, pueda, podamos, podáis, puedan
-ir verb: pedir	pida, pidas, pida, pidamos, pidáis, pidan
-ir verb: sugerir	sugiera, sugieras, sugiera, sugiramos, sugiráis, sugieran

Remember that if there is no change of subject in the sentence, the infinitive is used: **Adela quiere invitar a Elmer a la fiesta.**

Note that often the subjunctive translates into English as an infinitive.

Suggestion: Put contrasting sentences on the board to illustrate to students the difference between a one-clause and two-clause sentence.

Marta quiere ir a clase. (una cláusula)

Marta quiere que *José* vaya a clase. (dos cláusulas)

Notice the similarity between the subjunctive forms and the **usted / ustedes** command forms, both of which are based on the idea of using "opposite vowel endings." (To review formation of the **usted / ustedes** command forms, see page 180 in **Capítulo 6.**)

Capítulo 10   ¿Cómo es tu casa?

Note that the stem-changing verbs **dormir** and **morir** show an additional **o → u** change in the **nosotros** and **vosotros** forms.

> dormir: **d**u**erma, d**u**ermas, d**u**erma, d**u**rmamos, d**u**rmáis, d**u**erman**
> morir: **m**u**era, m**u**eras, m**u**era, m**u**ramos, m**u**ráis, m**u**eran**

3. Spelling-change verbs in the preterite (**-car** verbs: **c → qu**, **-gar** verbs: **g → gu,** and **-zar** verbs: **z → c**) have the same spelling change in all forms of the present subjunctive.

	buscar (c → qu)	llegar (g → gu)	comenzar (z → c)
yo	bus**que**	lle**gue**	comien**ce**
tú	bus**ques**	lle**gues**	comien**ces**
usted / él / ella	bus**que**	lle**gue**	comien**ce**
nosotros / nosotras	bus**quemos**	lle**guemos**	comen**cemos**
vosotros / vosotras	bus**quéis**	lle**guéis**	comen**céis**
ustedes / ellos / ellas	bus**quen**	lle**guen**	comien**cen**

4. The following verbs have irregular present subjunctive forms.

	dar	estar	ir	saber	ser
yo	dé	esté	vaya	sepa	sea
tú	des	estés	vayas	sepas	seas
usted / él / ella	dé	esté	vaya	sepa	sea
nosotros / nosotras	demos	estemos	vayamos	sepamos	seamos
vosotros / vosotras	deis	estéis	vayáis	sepáis	seáis
ustedes / ellos / ellas	den	estén	vayan	sepan	sean

Suggestion: Practicing these forms in rote fashion a few times can be helpful to emphasize pronunciation because some learners will drop the verb ending into the *schwa* sound to avoid making the choice between subjunctive and indicative endings.

Suggestion: Practice verb endings by having students substitute the second subject: 1. Quiero que Marta (tú / ellos, Jorge / Felipe y yo) *escriba* con frecuencia. 2. Quiero que tú (Mirella y Fabiola / el señor, la profesora / vosotros) me *des* el libro. 3. Necesito que tú (ellos / Patricio, vosotros / Juan y Fernando) *vayas* a la pizarra. 4. Requerimos que tú (Beto y él / Uds. / los estudiantes / vosotros) *saques* la basura cada día.

Actividades

ACTIVIDAD 1 **Abuelita quiere que…** Miguelín, Andrea y Arturo son hermanos. Están de visita en casa de su abuelita. Ella quiere que ellos la ayuden con algunos de los quehaceres. Escucha los mandatos que les da a los niños. Completa las siguientes oraciones según el modelo.

MODELO: Escuchas: Miguelín, por favor, dale de comer al gato.
Escribes: Abuelita quiere que Miguelín *le dé de comer al gato.*

1. Insiste en que Arturo y Andrea _____.

2. Necesita que alguien _____.

3. Espera que los niños _____.

4. Sugiere que los niños _____.

5. Le pide a Andrea que _____.

6. Quiere que todos _____.

Answers Act. 1: 1. … pongan los juguetes en su lugar 2. … saque la basura 3. … hagan las camas 4. … limpien los baños 5. … prepare el almuerzo 6. … se diviertan

Answers Act. 2: *Verbs of main clause may vary.* 1. Espero que no hagas mucho ruido después de las nueve de la noche. 2. No permito que tengas un perro o gato. 3. Espero que prepares la cena dos o tres veces por semana. 4. Recomiendo que limpies el baño una vez por semana. 5. Prohibo que invites a amigos a quedarse la noche. 6. Sugiero que pagues la renta a tiempo. 7. Necesito que pases la aspiradora una vez por semana. 8. Pido que laves los platos la misma noche que los usas. 9. Quiero que seamos buenos(as) amigos(as).

Optional: This activity can be repeated looking for several roommates to produce all of the verbs in the plural form.

ACTIVIDAD 2 **Compañero de cuarto.** Buscas un(a) compañero(a) de cuarto, pero tienes requisitos muy específicos. Di lo que esperas de un(a) compañero(a) de cuarto.

Verbos útiles:

(no) esperar	necesitar
permitir	pedir
recomendar	querer
prohibir	insistir
sugerir	

MODELO: no fumar / dentro de la casa
Insisto en que no fumes dentro de la casa.

1. no hacer mucho ruido después de las nueve de la noche

2. tener un perro o gato

3. preparar la cena dos o tres veces por semana

4. limpiar el baño una vez por semana

5. invitar a amigos a quedarse la noche

6. pagar la renta a tiempo

7. pasar la aspiradora una vez por semana

8. lavar los platos la misma noche que los usas

9. (nosotros / as) ser buenos(as) amigos(as)

ACTIVIDAD 3 **¡Quiero que limpies tu cuarto!** Tu compañero(a) de cuarto te está volviendo loco(a) porque no hace sus quehaceres y hace otras cosas que te molestan. Dile lo que quieres que haga y lo que quieres que no haga. Luego, tu compañero(a) te va a decir a ti lo que él (ella) quiere que tú hagas y no hagas.

MODELO: Tú: *Quiero que pongas los platos en el lavaplatos después de comer.*
Compañero(a): *Pues, insisto en que no dejes tu ropa en la secadora después de usarla.*

ACTIVIDAD 4 **Sugerencias.** Acabas de conocer a Daniel, un nuevo estudiante de Nicaragua que sabe muy poco de la universidad. Basándote en tu experiencia, hazle seis sugerencias a Daniel sobre los estudios, la vida universitaria, la vida social, dónde vivir, etc. Trata de usar algunos de los siguientes verbos: **aconsejar, desear, esperar, insistir en, mandar, necesitar, pedir, permitir, prohibir, querer, recomendar, requerir, sugerir.**

MODELO: *Sugiero que no vivas en un apartamento porque es más difícil conocer a otros estudiantes. Recomiendo que comas en… y que vayas a…*

Sonrisas

Learners experience the wit, wisdom, and common sense of a vignette of life-long learning. This vignette can launch a discussion of **estereotipos femeninos y masculinos**. Ask students **¿Estás de acuerdo con…?**

EXPRESIÓN. En grupos de tres a cuatro estudiantes, imaginen el escenario al revés: la mujer es la quien necesita que su esposo haga varias cosas. Vuelvan a escribir (*Rewrite*) la tira cómica con esta perspectiva nueva.

¿Conoces a alguien como el esposo, que siempre necesita que otros hagan todo para él o ella? ¿Qué cosas pide?

Gramática útil 2
Emphasizing ownership: Stressed possessives

Heritage Learners: The stressed possessives present two spelling challenges for heritage language speakers. Many heritage language speakers tend to spell **tuyo** and **suyo** with an **i** rather than a **y**. Second, students tend to forget that the forms of **mío** always carry an accent. Be sure to remind students of correct spelling.

CÓMO USARLO

1. You have already learned how to express possession in Spanish using possessive adjectives and phrases with **de**.

Es **tu** habitación.	*It's **your** bedroom.*
Es la habitación **de Nati**.	*It's **Nati's** bedroom.*

2. When you wish to emphasize, contrast, or clarify who owns something, you can also use stressed possessives.

Stressed possessives		Unstressed possessive	
Es la casa **mía**.	*It's **my** house.*	Es **mi** casa.	*It's **my** house.*
¡La casa es **mía**!	*That house is **mine!***		
La casa es **mía**, no **suya**.	*The house is **mine**, not **yours / his / hers**.*		

3. Stressed possessives must agree in number and gender with the noun they modify: **un libro mío, la calculadora mía, los videos míos, las mochilas mías.**

4. Stressed possessives may be used as adjectives with a noun, in which case they follow the noun: **Es el coche *mío*.** If it's clear what is being referred to, the noun may be dropped: **—¿De quién es el coche? —Es *mío*.**

5. Stressed possessives can also be used as pronouns that replace the noun. Notice that the article is maintained: **Le gusta *el coche mío*.** → **Le gusta *el mío*.**

CÓMO FORMARLO

Here are the stressed possessive forms in Spanish.

person	singular	plural	
yo	mío, mía	míos, mías	*my, mine*
tú	tuyo, tuya	tuyos, tuyas	*your, yours*
usted / él / ella	suyo, suya	suyos, suyas	*your, yours, his, her, hers, its*
nosotros / nosotras	nuestro, nuestra	nuestros, nuestras	*our, ours*
vosotros / vosotras	vuestro, vuestra	vuestros, vuestras	*your, yours*
ustedes / ellos / ellas	suyo, suya	suyos, suyas	*your, yours, their, theirs*

¡FÍJATE!

Dar énfasis

Los posesivos que acabas de estudiar, los llamados **posesivos tónicos,** son el único tipo de posesivo que se puede usar para dar énfasis en español. Por eso, para destacar (*to emphasize*) el concepto de posesión, es posible decir **Es el libro MÍO,** pero no **Es MI libro.** Es importante recordar que los artículos tampoco se pueden enfatizar (*to emphasize*) en español, aunque éstos se enfatizan comúnmente en inglés: *This is THE book to read.*

Numerosos estudios lingüísticos han comprobado (*have proven*) que las estrategias más comunes que emplean los hablantes nativos del español para enfatizar algo incluyen la repetición de palabras (**Juan es alto alto**), el cambio de orden de las palabras de una oración (**Juan es alto → Es alto Juan**) y la adición de palabras tales como **muy, sí, especialmente** y **sumamente** (**Juan es sumamente alto**).

En general, el español hace poco uso del tono o la acentuación para dar énfasis. Al contrario, el inglés emplea estas características muy frecuentemente para dar énfasis. Si has mirado (*have watched*) la televisión o escuchado (*listened to*) la radio en español, es posible que tengas la impresión de que el español es una lengua mucho más monótona que el inglés. La razón es que el inglés utiliza los contrastes de entonación y la acentuación mucho más que el español.

PRÁCTICA. Considera las siguientes traducciones de la oración inglesa *"This is THE apartment for me."* Pensando en la información de arriba, ¿cuál es la única traducción técnicamente correcta de esta frase? Justifica tu respuesta.

Answer: #2

1. Éste es EL apartamento para mí.
2. Este apartamento sí es para mí.
3. Éste es MI apartamento.

Actividades

ACTIVIDAD 5 **La fiesta.** La fiesta se ha terminado y el anfitrión (*host*) quiere estar seguro de que los invitados se lleven todas sus cosas. Tú conoces todos los artículos de ropa de tus amigos. Contesta las preguntas del anfitrión. Sigue el modelo.

MODELO: Anfitrión: ¿Es éste el impermeable de Martín? (gris)
Tú: *No, no es suyo. El suyo es gris.*

1. ¿Es éste tu abrigo? (negro)
2. ¿Es ésta la bufanda de María? (azul)
3. ¿Son éstos los guantes de Miguel? (de piel)
4. ¿Son éstas las botas de ustedes? (de otra marca)
5. ¿Es ésta tu gorra? (de lana)
6. ¿Son éstas las bolsas de Ana y Adela? (verdes)
7. ¿Es éste el saco de Pablo? (de un solo color)

Answers Act. 5: 1. No, no es mío. El mío es negro. 2. No, no es suya. La suya es azul. 3. No, no son suyos. Los suyos son de piel. 4. No, no son nuestras. Las nuestras son de otra marca. 5. No, no es mía. La mía es de lana. 6. No, no son suyas. Las suyas son verdes. 7. No, no es suyo. El suyo es de un solo color.

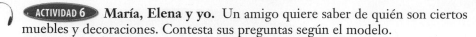

ACTIVIDAD 6 **María, Elena y yo.** Un amigo quiere saber de quién son ciertos muebles y decoraciones. Contesta sus preguntas según el modelo.

MODELO: yo
Escuchas: ¿De quién es esta lámpara?
Escribes: *Es mía.*

1. María
2. Elena
3. tú
4. Elena
5. María
6. yo

Gramática útil 3
Expressing ongoing events and duration of time: **Hace / Hacía** with time expressions

Hace mucho tiempo que no voy de picnic.

CÓMO USARLO

1. **Hace** and **hacía** are used to talk about ongoing actions and their duration. They can also be used to say how long it has been since someone has done something or since something has occurred. Look carefully at the following formulas and model sentences.

◆ To express an action that has been occurring over a period of time and is still going on

hace + period of time + **que** + present indicative

Hace tres años que vivimos en este barrio.

We've been living in this neighborhood *for three years.*

◆ To say *how long it has been since you have done something*

hace + period of time + **que** + **no** + present indicative

Hace seis meses que no salimos de la ciudad.

We haven't left the city *in six months.*

◆ To express how long ago an event took place

preterite + **hace** + period of time

Vine aquí **hace tres años.**

*I came here **three years ago.***

♦ To say *how long an action had been going on in the past* before another more recent past event

> **hacía** + period of time + **que** + imperfect

Cuando nos mudamos a esta nueva casa, **hacía cinco años que vivíamos** en ese apartamento.

*When we moved to this new house, **we had been living** in that apartment **for five years**.*

2. Use the following formulas to ask *questions* with **hace** and **hacía.**

♦ To ask *how long an action or event has been going on* (**hace** + present indicative)

¿Cuánto tiempo hace que vives aquí?

How long have you been living here?

♦ To ask *how long it has been since an action or event has been going on* (**hace** + **no** + present)

¿Cuánto tiempo hace que no hablas con tus abuelos?

How long has it been since you spoke to your grandparents?

♦ To ask *how long ago an action took place* (**hace** + preterite)

¿Cuánto tiempo hace que hablaste con tus abuelos?

How long ago did you speak to your grandparents?

♦ To ask *how long an action or event had been going on* in the past (**hacía** + imperfect)

¿Cuánto tiempo hacía que no podías ir a la escuela?

How long had you not been able to go to school?

Suggestion: Have students answer questions to practice **hace:** ¿Cuánto tiempo hace que vives aquí / vives en el mismo sitio / estudias español / asistes a nuestra universidad / etc.?

Notice that in all these examples only the forms **hace** and **hacía** are used.

Actividades

ACTIVIDAD 7 **¡Odio los quehaceres!** Odias los quehaceres. Di cuánto tiempo hace que no haces ciertos quehaceres en tu casa.

MODELO: no pasar la aspiradora (dos meses)
Hace dos meses que no paso la aspiradora.

1. no limpiar el baño (tres semanas)
2. no preparar la comida en casa (una semana)
3. no cortar el césped (seis semanas)
4. no trabajar en el jardín (un mes)
5. no limpiar el garaje (tres años)
6. no arreglar el sótano (dos años)
7. no trapear el piso (un mes)

Preparation: Emphasize that in **Actividad 7** the actions are still going on.

Answers Act. 7: 1. Hace tres semanas que no limpio el baño. 2. Hace una semana que no preparo la comida en casa. 3. Hace seis semanas que no corto el césped. 4. Hace un mes que no trabajo en el jardín. 5. Hace tres años que no limpio el garaje. 6. Hace dos años que no arreglo el sótano. 7. Hace un mes que no trapeo el piso.

ACTIVIDAD 8 **¿Y tú?** Túrnense para preguntarle a un(a) compañero(a) cuánto tiempo hace que él o ella no hace ciertos quehaceres.

MODELO: Tú: *¿Cuánto tiempo hace que no lavas la ropa?*
Compañero(a): *Hace dos semanas que no lavo la ropa.*

ACTIVIDAD 9 **¿Cuánto tiempo hace?** Túrnense para preguntarle a un(a) compañero(a) cuánto tiempo hace que participó en ciertas actividades. Puedes usar ideas de la lista o puedes inventar tus propias preguntas.

Ideas
estudiar español en…
comprar tu carro
hablar con tus abuelos
mudarte a tu apartamento
conocer a tu novio(a)
¿…?

MODELO: Tú: *¿Cuánto tiempo hace que estudiaste español en Nicaragua?*
Compañero(a): *Estudié español en Nicaragua hace cinco años.*

ACTIVIDAD 10 **Hacía cinco años que…** Manuel y su familia se mudaron de Guatemala a Estados Unidos hace muchos años. Manuel recuerda cuando él se graduó del colegio. ¿Qué dice?

MODELO: nosotros / vivir en Estados Unidos (cinco años)
Cuando me gradué del colegio, hacía cinco años que vivíamos en Estados Unidos.

1. yo / estudiar inglés (diez años)
2. papá / trabajar con la compañía GE (dos años)
3. mamá / tomar clases de computación (tres años)
4. mi novia y yo / conocerse (un año)
5. nosotros / alquilar nuestra casa (dos años)
6. mi hermano / estudiar en la Universidad de Los Ángeles (tres años)

Gramática útil 4
Choosing between *por* and *para*

Can you figure out why por is used in this ad and not para?

Answer: **Por** is used because it is expressing motion through or around a place; also a fixed expression.

por dentro la belleza y elegancia de las maderas nobles naturales de roble o sapelly barnizadas.
por fuera el acabado y la dureza del aluminio lacado al fuego.

CÓMO USARLO

1. You have already learned some expressions that use the prepositions **por** (por favor, por lo general) and **para** (Para plato principal, voy a pedir...).

2. **Por** and **para** are often translated with the same words in English, but they are not used interchangeably in Spanish. Here are some guidelines to help you use them correctly.

Use **por...**	
to describe the *method by which an action is carried out*.	Viajamos **por** avión. Hablamos **por** teléfono. Nos comunicamos **por** Internet.
to give a *cause or reason*.	Miguel está preocupado **por** su salud. Elena está nerviosa **por** el examen.
to give a *time of day*.	Vamos al café **por** la tarde. **Por** las noches, comemos en casa.
to describe *motion through or around* a place.	Pasamos **por** la playa todas las mañanas. Vas **por** el centro de la ciudad y luego doblas a la izquierda.
to express the idea of an *exchange*.	Pagué doce dólares **por** el espejo. ¡Gracias **por** todo!
to say that something was done on *behalf of someone else*.	Lo hice **por** mi hermano porque estaba enfermo. Puedo hablar **por** ellos.
to express *units of measurement*.	Venden las naranjas **por** kilo. Venden la canela **por** gramos.
to express *duration of time*.	Estuvimos en el restaurante **por** dos horas. Fuimos a Bolivia **por** tres semanas.
in certain *fixed expressions*.	**por ejemplo** (*for example*) **por eso** (*so, that's why*) **por favor** (*please*) **por fin** (*finally*) **por lo menos** (*at least*) **por supuesto** (*of course*)

Optional: For high beginners, you may want to add more idioms with **por**: por aquí, por algo, por casualidad, por suerte, por todas partes, por otra parte, por si acaso.

Optional: With heritage learners and
high beginners, you may want to
introduce **estar para** = *to be about to* /
estar por = *to be in favor of.*

Use **para...**	
to indicate *destination*.	Salimos **para** un parque en las afueras y nos perdimos.
to indicate a *recipient* of an object or action.	El cuadro es **para** Angélica. Limpié la casa **para** mis padres.
to indicate a *deadline or specific time in the future*.	Hicimos reservaciones en el restaurante **para** la próxima semana. Tengo que escribir un informe **para** mañana.
to express *intent or purpose*.	Estas lámparas son **para** la sala. Vinieron temprano **para** limpiar la casa.
to indicate an *employer*.	Trabajo **para** la universidad.
to make a *comparison*.	**Para** estudiante, tiene mucho dinero. **Para** mí, la sopa de ajo es la mejor de todas.

3. To aid your understanding of these two prepositions, here are some ways they are translated into English.

Por	Para
(*in exchange*) *for*	*for* (deadline)
during, in	*toward, in the direction of*
through, along	*for* (recipient or purpose)
on behalf of	*in order to* + verb
for (duration of an event)	*for* . . . (in comparison with others)
by (transportation)	*for* (employer)

Actividades

Answers Act. 11: 1. para 2. para 3. por 4. por 5. por 6. para 7. para 8. por 9. por 10. Para

ACTIVIDAD 11 **¡Vamos a Nicaragua!** Ernesto va a viajar a Nicaragua. Completa su descripción con **por** o **para** para saber más de su viaje con su familia.

1. Vamos a ir a Nicaragua _____ las vacaciones.

2. Vamos principalmente _____ visitar a mis tíos.

3. Vamos a viajar _____ avión.

4. Hicimos las reservaciones _____ Internet.

5. Pagamos muy poco _____ los boletos.

6. Mañana voy a llamar a mis tíos _____ decirles nuestra hora de llegada.

7. Mi tío trabaja _____ una compañía de telecomunicaciones en Nicaragua.

8. Nos vamos a quedar en Managua _____ un mes.

9. Queremos viajar _____ todo el país.

10. _____ mí, va a ser una experiencia inolvidable.

 ACTIVIDAD 12 **¿Por o para?** Vas a hacerle cinco preguntas a tu compañero(a). Usa elementos de las cuatro columnas para formar las preguntas. Luego, él o ella te va a hacer cinco preguntas a ti. Sé creativo(a) con tus preguntas y sincero(a) con tus respuestas.

Columna A	Columna B	Columna C	Columna D
¿Te gusta?	hacer compras	por	Internet
¿Prefieres?	hacer reservaciones	para	compañía (internacional, etc.)
¿Quieres?	esperar a un amigo		restaurante (cine, etc.)
¿...?	preferir viajar		avión (autobús, tren)
	pagar demasiado		los libros de texto (los CDs, etc.)
	comprar un regalo		[nombre de persona]
	trabajar		teléfono (correo electrónico, carta, etc.)
	salir temprano		dos (o más) horas
	hacer planes		la próxima semana (mes, año)
	comunicarte		¿...?
	¿...?		

MODELOS: *¿Te gusta hacer compras por Internet?*
Cuando haces reservaciones, ¿prefieres hacerlas por Internet o por teléfono?
Cuando termines la universidad, ¿quieres trabajar para una compañía internacional o doméstica?

Guatemala y Nicaragua

Una gran presencia en Centroamérica. Lee los siguientes textos sobre Guatemala y Nicaragua. Luego completa un diagrama Venn como el siguiente. Pon los números de los comentarios sobre Guatemala a la izquierda y los de los comentarios sobre Nicaragua a la derecha. Los números de los comentarios que se refieren a los dos países van en el centro del diagrama.

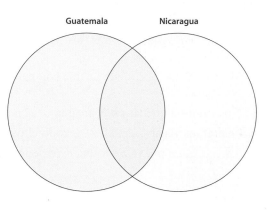

1. Hace frontera con cuatro países.
2. Hace frontera con dos países.
3. Tiene costas en el mar Caribe y en el océano Pacífico.
4. Más del 55% de la población es de ascendencia maya.
5. El 77% de la población es mestiza.
6. Tiene una tradición literaria muy importante.
7. Tiene muchos volcanes.
8. La agricultura es una fuente económica muy importante.
9. Se encuentran ruinas y templos mayas en este país.
10. Es el país más grande de Centroamérica.

¡CONÉCTATE!

Internet

Después de leer sobre Guatemala y Nicaragua, trabaja con un(a) compañero(a) de clase. Busquen información sobre dos de los siguientes temas en Internet. Usen los enlaces sugeridos en el sitio web de *Nexos* (http://college.hmco.com/language/spanish/students) para ir a otros sitios web posibles. Luego preparen un breve informe para la clase.

1. los dialectos maya-quiché
2. Miguel Ángel Asturias
3. el *Popol Vuh*
4. Rubén Darío
5. las huellas de Acahualinca
6. ¿…?

Guatemala

La geografía y el clima

Guatemala tiene fronteras con México, Belice, Honduras y El Salvador; al noreste de Guatemala está el mar Caribe y al sur está el océano Pacífico. En Guatemala abundan las montañas, excepto en la región de El Petén, que es un área de selvas tropicales. Guatemala es también uno de los países del mundo con el mayor número de volcanes. Muchos de los cráteres de sus antiguos volcanes se han convertido en (*have become*) lagos altos y hermosos; el lago Atitlán, que está a una altitud de 1.562 metros, es uno de estos lagos. Guatemala tiene una variedad de climas: no hace ni mucho frío ni mucho calor.

La economía

Guatemala es un país agrícola, con una economía basada en la agricultura y la ganadería. Sus productos principales son el café, el algodón y el banano, y exporta al mercado internacional una variedad de maderas de más de 300 especies.

Los mayas

La cultura indígena de mayor influencia por toda Guatemala es la cultura maya. Hoy día en el país se hablan más de veinte lenguas de la familia maya-quiché, y la mayoría de los guatemaltecos son de ascendencia maya—más del 55% de la población. Estos descendientes mantienen vivas las tradiciones culturales de los mayas; todavía llevan el traje indígena típico y practican las mismas artesanías con los mismos colores y diseños.

Una selva tropical
en El Petén

Tikal y Uacaxtún en El Petén son las dos antiguas ciudades mayas más importantes de Guatemala. Tikal tiene cinco templos mayas en forma de pirámide; uno de estos templos mide 70 metros de altura. Otro de estos templos, el cual está en Uacaxtún y tal vez sea la pirámide maya más antigua de Centroamérica, es un observatorio astronómico.

El *Popol Vuh*

"La biblia" de los maya-quiché es el *Popol Vuh*. Este libro sagrado describe la creación de los hombres, las mujeres y el mundo entero. En la Biblioteca Newberry de Chicago hay un manuscrito del *Popol Vuh* que data del siglo XVIII y que fue copiado (*was copied*) por fray Francisco Ximénez, un sacerdote español; al lado del texto en quiché está la traducción al español hecha por Ximénez.

Mujeres mayas
en Guatemala

Las letras

Dos guatemaltecos son recipientes del Premio Nóbel: Miguel Ángel Asturias y Rigoberta Menchú Tum. El escritor Miguel Ángel Asturias, quien recibió el Premio Nóbel de Literatura en 1967, es un novelista famoso cuya obra maestra se titula *El señor Presidente*. En 1992, la escritora y activista Rigoberta Menchú Tum recibió el Premio Nóbel de la Paz. En su autobiografía, *Me llamo Rigoberta Menchú y así me nació la conciencia* (1983), la autora nos relata las injusticias que han sufrido los maya-quiché desde la colonización española.

Nicaragua

La geografía y el clima

Nicaragua tiene fronteras con Honduras y Costa Rica; al este está el mar Caribe y al oeste el océano Pacífico. Nicaragua, un país muy montañoso, es el más grande de Centroamérica. Tiene unos cincuenta y ocho volcanes, seis de los cuales están todavía activos. Nicaragua también se conoce por sus bonitos lagos. Entre ellos están el Managua (también llamado Xolotlán) y el lago Nicaragua (o Cocibolca), que es uno de los lagos de agua dulce (*freshwater*) más grandes del mundo. Nicaragua tiene buen clima en su interior; las costas son húmedas y calurosas, aunque es menos húmedo en la costa oeste.

El lago de Managua

La economía

Como Guatemala, Nicaragua también es un país agrícola. Sus productos principales son el café y algodón, y también el cacao, la caña de azúcar, el plátano, el maíz, el tabaco, el trigo y el sésamo.

La historia

Antes de la llegada de Cristóbal Colón, varios grupos indígenas vivían en Nicaragua: los nicaraos, los chorotegas, los chontales y los mosquitos (llamados también 'misquitos' en otras partes de Centroamérica). Cuando Colón llegó allí en 1502, durante su cuarto y último viaje, él era la primera persona de Europa que había venido a la región. Hoy día, 77 por ciento de la población de Nicaragua es mestiza, una mezcla de los europeos y los indígenas. Sólo en la Costa de los Mosquitos viven indígenas puros—un 4% de la población total de Nicaragua.

Las huellas de Acahualinca

Las huellas de Acahualinca

En Acahualinca, a orillas del lago de Managua, hay unas famosas huellas (*footprints*) antiguas que, según los expertos, tienen más de seis mil años de edad. Aunque hay varias teorías sobre su origen, no se sabe exactamente cómo fue que aparecieron. Una de las hipótesis más interesantes sugiere que se formaron cuando unas personas que se escapaban de una erupción volcánica pisaron (*they stepped on*) la lava caliente que encontraban a su paso.

Las letras

Nicaragua tiene fama de ser un país de poetas. El más famoso de éstos es Rubén Darío (1867–1916), cuya colección de poesía y prosa *Azul* (1888), según los críticos, inició el modernismo, un movimiento literario de gran importancia a finales del siglo XIX. Otros grandes poetas nicaragüenses del pasado son Azarías Pallais, Salomón de la Selva y Alfonso Cortés. Los nuevos poetas como Rosario Murillo y Ernesto Cardenal se inspiran tanto en la política y la sociedad actuales de Nicaragua como en su pasado histórico.

Antes de leer

Understanding poetry

Up until now, all of the readings you have encountered have been nonfiction—web pages, magazine articles, and the like. You are now going to read several poems, fictional pieces of literature. When you read nonfiction, you usually read to obtain factual information. When you read fiction and literature, you read to be entertained or enlightened.

Rhyme (**La rima**) is one aspect of most poetry. Words rhyme when they share similar sounds, for example, **pino** and **fino.** Blank verse (**El verso libre**) is a kind of poetry that does not follow the usual rules of rhyme. Instead, it relies on the sounds of words and the division of lines to create its own sense of rhythm and motion.

ACTIVIDAD 1 Los poemas que vas a leer incluyen un poema de Rubén Darío (1867–1916), considerado el poeta más importante de Nicaragua, y otro de un poeta nicaragüense vanguardista, José Coronel Urtecho (1906–1994). Estos poemas, entre otros, aparecen en un sitio web que se llama "Dariana". Primero, lee la información sobre Darío que aparece en la sección **Exploraciones culturales** (p. 326). Luego lee el siguiente comentario del sitio web y contesta las preguntas a continuación.

"Se ha dicho que el mejor producto de exportación de Nicaragua es su poesía. Y toda nuestra mejor poesía y, por qué no, nuestra misma nicaraguanidad nacen (are born) *y se fundamentan en Rubén Darío... Darío pronosticó que un día su poesía, indefectiblemente, iría a las muchedumbres* (would reach the masses). *Valga esta humilde página y esta todo-abarcante* (all-encompassing) *tecnología para intentarlo."*

Rubén Darío (1867–1916)

1. Según este comentario, ¿cuál es el mejor producto de exportación de Nicaragua?
2. ¿Creía Darío que muchas o pocas personas leerían (*would read*) su poesía?
3. ¿Cómo ayuda la tecnología a implementar la visión de Darío?

Answers Act. 1: 1. la poesía 2. Sí. 3. Con Internet, su poesía llega fácil y rápidamente a todas partes del mundo.

ACTIVIDAD 2 Lee las siguientes preguntas sobre los poemas a continuación. Después, lee los poemas rápidamente y contesta las preguntas. Luego vas a leer los poemas más detalladamente.

1. ¿Cuál de los poemas se escribe en rima? ¿Se escribe uno en verso libre?
2. Busca un ejemplo de dos palabras que riman.
3. Busca el uso de la repetición de palabras en los dos poemas. Escribe dos ejemplos de la repetición de una palabra o de palabras semejantes.
4. ¿Cuál es el tema principal de los dos poemas?

Lectura

ACTIVIDAD 3 Ahora lee los poemas con más detalle. Recuerda que no es necesario entender todas las palabras para apreciar los poemas. Escucha los sonidos (*sounds*) de las palabras y trata de entender la idea principal de cada poema.

—⚹— RUBÉN DARÍO

Amo, amas

AMAR[1], AMAR, AMAR, AMAR SIEMPRE, CON TODO
el ser y con la tierra y con el cielo[2],
con lo claro del sol y lo oscuro del lodo[3]:
amar por toda ciencia y amar por todo anhelo[4].

Y cuando la montaña de la vida
nos sea dura y larga y alta y llena de abismos,
amar la inmensidad que es de amor encendida[5]
¡y arder[6] en la fusión de nuestros pechos[7] mismos!

[1]*to love* [2]**con la tierra...** *with the earth and with the sky* [3]*mud* [4]*wish, desire* [5]*burning, on fire* [6]*to burn* [7]*hearts* (literally, *chests*)

—ᵐᵛ— JOSÉ CORONEL URTECHO

Dos canciones de amor para el otoño

I

CUANDO YA NADA PIDO
y casi nada espero
y apenas puedo nada[8]
es cuando más te quiero.

II

BASTA[9] QUE ESTÉS, QUE SEAS
Que te pueda llamar, que te llame María
Para saber quién soy y conocer quién eres
Para saberme tuyo y conocerte mía
Mi mujer entre todas las mujeres.

[8]**apenas...** *There's nothing to be done, I can do no more.* [9] **Basta...** Es bastante

Después de leer

ACTIVIDAD 4 A ver si comprendiste bien los dos poemas. Trabaja con un(a) compañero(a) de clase para contestar las siguientes preguntas.

Answers Act. 4: 1. c 2. optimista; *Answers will vary.* 3. *Answers will vary.* 4. a 5. optimista; *Answers will vary.* 6. *Answers will vary.*

"Amo, amas" de Darío

1. ¿Cuál de las siguientes oraciones mejor expresa la idea central del poema?
    a. El amor es duro (*hard*) y difícil.
    b. El amor es como una montaña alta que es difícil escalar.
    c. El amor verdadero es eterno, como la naturaleza.

2. ¿Es optimista o pesimista la actitud del poeta? ¿Por qué?
3. ¿Están de acuerdo con el mensaje del poema?

"Dos canciones de amor para el otoño, I, II" de Coronel Urtecho

4. ¿Cuál de las siguientes oraciones mejor expresa la idea central del primer poema?
    a. Cuando el autor no tiene esperanza es cuando está más enamorado.
    b. El autor no pide ni espera el amor, porque no lo quiere.
    c. El autor no puede querer a nadie porque no tiene esperanza.

5. ¿Es optimista o pesimista la actitud del poeta? ¿Por qué?
6. ¿Cuál de los poemas les gustó más? ¿Por qué?

VOCABULARIO

ÁREAS DE LA CIUDAD   *Parts of the city*

las afueras	*the outskirts*
el apartamento	*apartment*
el barrio	*neighborhood*
... comercial	*business district*
... residencial	*residential neighborhood*
el centro de la ciudad	*downtown*
los suburbios	*suburbs*
los vecinos	*neighbors*

LA CASA   *La casa*

el baño	*bathroom*
la chimenea	*fireplace*
el clóset	*closet*
la cocina	*kitchen*
el comedor	*dining room*
el dormitorio (la recámara, el cuarto, la habitación)	*bedroom*
las escaleras	*stairs*
el garaje	*garage*
el jardín	*garden*
la lavandería	*laundry room*
la oficina	*office*
la pared	*wall*
el pasillo	*hallway*
el patio	*patio*
el primer piso (segundo, etc.)	*first floor (second, etc.)*
la sala	*living room*
el sótano	*basement, cellar*
el techo	*roof*

NÚMEROS ORDINALES   *Ordinal numbers*

primer(o)	*first*
segundo	*second*
tercer(o)	*third*
cuarto	*fourth*
quinto	*fifth*
sexto	*sixth*
séptimo	*seventh*
octavo	*eighth*
noveno	*ninth*
décimo	*tenth*

LOS QUEHACERES DOMÉSTICOS
Household chores

Dentro de la casa   *Inside the house*

arreglar el dormitorio	*to straighten up the bedroom*
barrer el suelo (el piso)	*to sweep the floor*
guardar la ropa	*to put away the clothes*
hacer la cama	*to make the bed*
lavar los platos (la ropa)	*to wash the dishes (the clothes)*
limpiar el baño	*to clean the bathroom*
pasar la aspiradora	*to vacuum clean*
planchar	*to iron*
poner los juguetes en su lugar	*to put the toys where they belong*
poner y quitar la mesa	*to set and to clear the table*
preparar la comida	*to prepare the food*
sacudir los muebles	*to dust the furniture*
trapear el piso	*to mop the floor*

Fuera de la casa   *Outside the house*

cortar el césped	*to mow the lawn*
darle de comer al perro (gato)	*to feed the dog (cat)*
hacer el reciclaje	*to do the recycling*
regar (ie) las plantas	*to water the plants*
sacar a pasear al perro	*to take the dog for a walk*
sacar la basura	*to take out the garbage*

LOS MUEBLES Y DECORACIONES
Furniture and decorations

la alfombra	*rug, carpet*
la cama	*bed*
las cortinas	*curtains*
el cuadro	*painting, print*
el espejo	*mirror*
la lámpara	*lamp*
la mesa	*table*
la mesita de noche	*night table*
la persiana	*Venetian blind*
la silla	*chair*
el sillón	*armchair*
el sofá	*sofa*
el tocador (la cómoda)	*dresser*

LOS ELECTRODOMÉSTICOS *Appliances*

el abrclatas cléctrico	*electric can opener*
la aspiradora	*vacuum cleaner*
la estufa	*stove*
la lavadora	*washer*
el lavaplatos	*dishwasher*
la licuadora	*blender*
el microondas	*microwave*
la plancha	*iron*
el refrigerador	*refrigerator*
la secadora	*dryer*
el televisor	*television set*
la tostadora	*toaster*

VERBOS

aconsejar	*to advise*
desear	*to wish*
esperar	*to hope*
insistir en	*to insist*
mandar	*to order*
necesitar	*to need*
pedir (i, i)	*to ask, request*
permitir	*to permit, allow*
prohibir	*to forbid*
querer	*to wish; to want*
recomendar (ie)	*to recommend*
requerir (ie)	*to require*
sugerir (ie, i)	*to suggest*

ADJETIVOS POSESIVOS

mío, mía, míos, mías	*my, mine*
tuyo, tuya, tuyos, tuyas	*your, yours*
suyo, suya, suyos, suyas	*your, yours, his, her, hers, its, their, theirs*
nuestro, nuestra, nuestros, nuestras	*our, ours*
vuestro, vuestra, vuestros, vuestras	*your, yours*

OTRAS PALABRAS Y EXPRESIONES

para	*for; by* (a deadline); *toward, in the direction of; for* (a specific recipient, employer, or purpose); *in order to* (+ verb); *for . . .* (in comparison with others)
por	(in exchange) *for; during; through, along; on behalf of; for* (duration of an event); *by* (a means of transportation)
por ejemplo	*for example*
por eso	*so, that's why*
por favor	*please*
por fin	*finally*
por lo menos	*at least*
por supuesto	*of course*

¿Qué quieres ver?

CAPÍTULO 11

Miembros del Ballet Nacional de Caracas interpretan un ballet en el Teatro Teresa Carreño.

Communication

By the end of this chapter you will be able to:
- talk about popular and high culture
- express preferences and make suggestions about entertainment
- express emotion and wishes
- express doubt and uncertainty
- express unrealized desires and unknown situations

Cultures

By the end of this chapter you will have learned about:
- Venezuela and Colombia
- a Colombian soap opera
- a Venezuelan television program dedicated to Internet users
- electronics in Venezuela, Colombia, and the U.S.
- learning: acquisition and usage

Preparation: This chapter deals with many personal preferences. Introduce, review, and reinforce verbs of preference and selection throughout the chapter: **elegir, encantar, gustar, preferir, querer,** etc.

Preparation: Review the difference between **la televisión (lo que uno mira)** and **el televisor (el aparato).** The variation with **el / la radio** can be pointed out here also.

Suggestion: Follow up to analyze and personalize the data on page 333: **¿Por qué es importante el número de televisores / radios? ¿Qué indica sobre la economía de un país? ¿Qué indica sobre preferencias culturales? ¿Cuántos televisores / radios tienes? En general, ¿prefieres mirar la televisión o escuchar la radio?,** etc.

Point out that **billón** refers to a different quantity than English *billion.* The latter stands for 1000 millions. In Spanish, on the other hand, **un billón** is a million millions: *Billion:* 1,000,000,000; **Billón:** 1.000.000.000.000

Heritage Learners: Heritage language learners need practice reading and writing large numbers. Dictate numbers for students to write in numeral form. Have students dictate to each other large numbers and correct each other's work.

CULTURAS

¿Qué significa la palabra **cultura** para ti? ¿Quiere decir el arte, el ballet, los museos, el teatro, la ópera? ¿O, en tu opinión, se refiere más bien a la televisión, las películas, la música popular y la radio? ¿Qué tipo de actividad cultural te gusta más? En este capítulo vamos a hablar de diversiones culturales y cómo nos gusta pasar el tiempo libre.

 Standards: In this chapter, students will explore Venezuelan and Colombian cultures (both high and daily life culture) and compare them with their own.

Los datos

Mira la información de los gráficos. Luego di si las siguientes oraciones son ciertas o falsas.

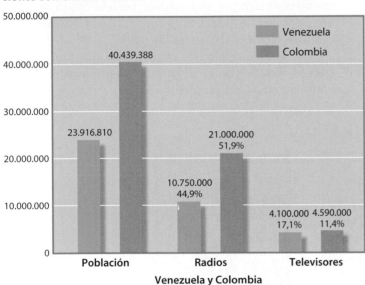

Venezuela y Colombia

- Venezuela
- Colombia

23.916.810
40.439.388
10.750.000 / 44,9%
21.000.000 / 51,9%
4.100.000 / 17,1% 4.590.000 / 11,4%

Población   Radios   Televisores

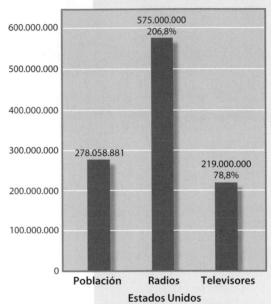

Estados Unidos

278.058.881
575.000.000 / 206,8%
219.000.000 / 78,8%

Población   Radios   Televisores

❶ _____ En Colombia, más del 50% de la población tiene radios.

❷ _____ En Venezuela un porcentaje más alto de la población tiene radios que en Colombia.

❸ _____ En Venezuela un porcentaje más alto de la población tiene televisores que en Colombia.

❹ _____ En Estados Unidos, hay más televisores que personas.

¡Adivina!

¿Qué sabes de Colombia y Venezuela? Indica si las siguientes oraciones se refieren a Colombia, a Venezuela o a los dos países. (Las respuestas están en la página 352.)

❶ Este país tiene una gran historia en las artes cinematográficas.
❷ Este país tiene una producción importante de esmeraldas.
❸ La leyenda de El Dorado proviene de este país.
❹ El principal producto de exportación de este país es el petróleo.
❺ "El Libertador" Simón Bolívar nació y vivió en este país.

OCÉANO ATLÁNTICO

★ Caracas

VENEZUELA

OCÉANO PACÍFICO

★ Bogotá

COLOMBIA

Vocabulario útil 1

JAVIER: ¿Qué clase de **películas** te gustan?

ANILÚ: Me encantan **las comedias románticas**. Quiero ver una película que me haga reír. ¿Y tú?

JAVIER: Bueno, está bien. Podemos ver una comedia.

ANILÚ: No contestaste mi pregunta.

JAVIER: A ver… me gustan **los dramas**… y **los documentales** me parecen siempre informativos. Leí **una crítica** de una película que parece muy buena… **Los críticos** la **calificaron con cuatro estrellas.**

ANILÚ: ¡La crítica! Yo nunca leo las críticas. En primer lugar, **los críticos** no saben de lo que hablan. Y en segundo lugar, prefiero formar mis propias opiniones.

CLASES DE PELÍCULA

la comedia (romántica)

los dibujos animados

el documental

el drama

el misterio

la película de acción

la película de ciencia ficción

la película de horror / terror

SOBRE LA PELÍCULA

el título	*title*
doblado(a)	*dubbed*
una película titulada…	*a movie called . . .*
con subtítulos en inglés	*with subtitles in English*
Se trata de…	*It's about . . .*
la estrella de cine	*movie star*

LA CRÍTICA

calificar / clasificar con cuatro estrellas	*to give a four-star rating*
el (la) crítico(a)	*critic*
la reacción crítica	*critical reaction*
la reseña / la crítica	*review*

EL ÍNDICE DE AUDIENCIA

apto(a) para toda la familia	*G (for general audiences)*
se recomienda discreción	*PG-13 (parental discretion advised)*
prohibido para menores	*R (minors restricted)*

EN EL CINE

los chocolates	*chocolates*
los dulces	*candy*
la entrada / el boleto	*ticket*
las palomitas	*popcorn*

Notice: There are many countries that have no rating system at all. The rating of movies according to content is a concept associated with the norms of American culture that has spread to other countries.

Actividades

Preparation: Before doing the activities, research current movie titles in Spanish (see Internet). List about ten current or classic movie titles on the board. Allow students to guess which English titles they correspond to and use them as a basis for discussion during the following activities.

ACTIVIDAD 1 **Las películas más populares en Colombia.** Con un(a) compañero(a), di qué clase de películas son las siguientes y cuál es su índice de audiencia. Túrnense para describir las películas. ¿Pueden adivinar cuáles son los títulos en inglés? ¿Cuáles tienen más ingresos (*revenue*)?

2001		
Orden de popularidad	**Película**	**Ingresos en pesos colombianos**
1	Harry Potter	1.045.585
2	La momia regresa	703.556
3	El planeta de los simios	696.214
4	Límite vertical	666.454
5	Gatos y perros	539.993

MODELO: Tú: Harry Potter *es una película de acción y un poco de terror. Las estrellas de la película son Daniel Radcliffe, Rupert Grint y Emma Watson. Es apta para toda la familia.*

ACTIVIDAD 2 **¿Qué clase de película es?** En grupos de tres, cada persona escribe en unos pedacitos de papel el título de dos películas conocidas. Pongan los seis papelitos en el medio del grupo. La primera persona escoge un papelito y dice algo sobre la película. La segunda persona trata de adivinar el título de la película, y la tercera persona dice qué clase de película es.

MODELO: Tú: *Los actores principales son Tom Hanks y Meg Ryan. Se trata de dos personas que se comunican por Internet.*
Compañero(a) #1: *Es* You've Got Mail.
Compañero(a) #2: *Es una comedia romántica.*

ACTIVIDAD 3 **¿Quieres ir al cine?** Quieres invitar a tu compañero(a) al cine, pero no sabes qué clase de películas le gustan. Conversen sobre sus preferencias y decidan qué película quieren ver. Pueden comentar sobre la reacción crítica, las reseñas que hayan leído y el índice de audiencia. ¡No tienen que estar de acuerdo sobre la película que quieren ver!

Remember the phrase **me gustaría** (*I would like to*)? You can also use **me encantaría** (*I would love to*).

MODELO: Compañero(a): *¿Quieres ir al cine?*
Tú: *Sí, me gustaría.*
Compañero(a): *¿Qué clase de películas te gustan?*
Tú: *Me encantan los dramas. Hay una película clásica que me gustaría ver:* Casablanca *con Humphrey Bogart.*
Compañero(a): *A mí no me gustan los dramas. Prefiero ver una película de acción...*

Vocabulario útil 2

ANILÚ: Dame ese **control** un momento. Voy a **cambiar de canal.** ¡Odio a esa **entrevistadora!**

JAVIER: ¿Te gusta **la ópera**?

ANILÚ: ¡La ópera! ¡Ni muerta! Prefiero **los musicales, los shows** grandes de Broadway.

JAVIER: ¿Y qué clase de **música** te gusta?

ANILÚ: Tiene que ser **pop.**

JAVIER: A ver, vamos a hacer cuentas. A mí me gustan los documentales y los dramas, las palomitas, la ópera y **la música clásica.** Leo las críticas antes de salir a ver una película y me gusta escoger la película antes de salir de casa.

ANILÚ: Uy, no nos va muy bien, ¿eh?

LA TELEVISIÓN

el cable	*cable television*	**la estación**	*station*
cambiar el / de canal	*to change the channel*	**grabar**	*to videotape; to record*
el control remoto	*remote control*	**por satélite**	*by satellite dish*
en vivo	*live*	**la teleguía**	*TV guide*
el episodio	*episode*		

LOS PROGRAMAS DE TELEVISIÓN

la teleserie   *TV series*

Heritage Learners: Research suggests that heritage language speakers watch a considerable amount of Spanish-language television and listen to Spanish-language radio. Discuss students' favorite shows, channels, and personalities.

las noticias

el programa de concursos

el programa de entrevistas

la telecomedia

el teledrama

la telenovela

Other types of music are: **la música alternativa, el jazz, la música folk, las baladas.**

LA GENTE EN LA TELEVISIÓN

el (la) entrevistador(a)	*interviewer*
el (la) locutor(a)	*announcer*
el (la) participante	*participant*
el (la) presentador(a)	*host of the show*
el público	*audience*
el (la) televidente	*TV viewer*

LA MÚSICA

la música clásica	*classical music*
la música country	*country music*
la música moderna	*modern music*
la música mundial	*world music*
la música pop	*pop music*
el R & B	*rhythm and blues*
el rap	*rap*
el rock	*rock*

ARTE Y CULTURA *The arts*

el baile / la danza	*dance*	el musical	*musical*
la escultura	*sculpture*	la ópera	*opera*
el espectáculo	*show*	la pintura	*painting*
la exposición de arte	*art exhibit*	el show	*show*
la obra teatral	*play*		

Notice: Point out to students that **el show** is synomous with **el espectáculo.** Unlike English, **el show** is not used for theatrical presentations or dramas.

Actividades

Standards: Here students practice C 1.1 by engaging in conversations, expressing preferences, and exchanging opinions to engage in interpersonal communication.

 ACTIVIDAD 4 **¡Dame ese control!** Con una(a) compañero(a), identifica los siguientes programas de televisión, di si te gustan y también di por qué sí o no. Luego, describe un programa del mismo género que te guste más. Explica por qué tu programa es superior al de la lista.

1. Es un programa de entrevistas en vivo. La entrevistadora entrevista a estrellas de cine y cantantes o habla de temas como "Las mujeres a quienes no les gusta la tele".
2. Es una telecomedia. El humor se extrae de los problemas que ocurren entre un periodista deportivo y su esposa. También ocurren problemas con el hermano del periodista, que es policía, y los padres del periodista que son vecinos.
3. Es un programa de concursos. La locutora es una señora de muy mal humor que siempre insulta a los participantes cuando no pueden contestar las preguntas que ella les hace. Cada segundo que demoran (*they delay*) en contestar disminuye el premio total, lo cual crea un clima de bastante tensión.
4. Es un teledrama que se sitúa en la Casa Blanca en la capital de los Estados Unidos. El presidente y su administración tratan de resolver problemas de importancia nacional e internacional.
5. Es un programa de noticias internacionales y nacionales. El locutor y reportero canadiense presenta su punto de vista de una manera muy informativa y razonable.

ACTIVIDAD 5 **¿Qué clase de arte te interesa?** Completa las siguientes oraciones con las palabras correctas de la lista.

1. Me encanta ＿＿ de Rodin.
2. ＿＿ de Picasso son mundialmente reconocidas.
3. En el mundo del ＿＿, Isadora Duncan fue reina (*queen*).
4. ＿＿ *Phantom of the Opera* de Andrew Lloyd Webber tuvo mucho éxito por el mundo.
5. *Cat on a Hot Tin Roof* de Tennessee Williams es una ＿＿ fenomenal.
6. Quiero ir al Museo de Arte Moderno en Nueva York para ver ＿＿ latinoamericano.
7. ¿Cuál es tu ＿＿ favorita? Yo creo que la mía es *Carmen*.

a. baile
b. ópera
c. la escultura
d. la exposición de arte
e. las pinturas
f. el musical
g. obra teatral

ACTIVIDAD 6 **Tus preferencias musicales.** Habla con tu compañero(a) sobre sus preferencias musicales. Primero, identifica dos cantantes o grupos musicales que pertenecen a cada una de las categorías. Luego, comparen sus preferencias musicales. Finalmente, informen a otra pareja sobre sus preferencias y ellos harán lo mismo.

Categorías
la música pop
la música country
la música mundial
el R & B
el rap
el rock

MODELO: Tú: *¿Conoces la música de Shakira?*
Compañero(a): *No, ¿qué clase de música es?*
Tú: *Es música pop, pero ella misma escribe las canciones. ¿Qué clase de música te gusta a ti?*

ACTIVIDAD 7 **Una cita a ciegas** (*blind date*). Vas a salir en una cita a ciegas, pero antes de salir, decides que debes hablar con la persona por teléfono para tratar de decidir adónde van y qué van a hacer en la cita. Como sabes muy poco de los gustos de la persona, vas a tener que hacerle muchas preguntas sobre sus preferencias. Trabaja con un(a) compañero(a) e incluye en la conversación el tema de las películas, la televisión, la música, el arte y la cultura. Al final de la conversación telefónica, tienen que haber decidido (*to have decided*) adónde van a ir en su cita. Explíquenle a otra pareja en la clase qué decidieron hacer en su cita y ellos harán lo mismo.

Optional: As a follow up to **Actividad 7**, have one pair report their blind dates to another in groups of four.

MODELO: Tú: *¿Qué te gustaría hacer el viernes por la noche?*
Compañero(a): *No sé. Creo que hay un concierto en el Auditorio Nacional muy bueno. ¿Qué clase de música te gusta?*

As a variation, you can dramatize your phone conversation in front of the class.

¡COMPÁRATE!

To learn more about *Alta Densidad*, visit the *Nexos* website (http://college.hmco.com/languages/spanish/students) and follow the links.

Investiga el sitio web de *Alta Densidad*. Sigue los enlaces para ir a unos de sus sitios recomendados. Haz un breve resumen de tus reacciones a *Alta Densidad* y su sitio web.

Suggestion: If possible, view the website in class or prior to answering the questions.

Venezuela es el tercer mercado de Internet más grande en Latinoamérica, después de Brasil y México. Uno de los resultados de este aumento en el uso venezolano de Internet es que empiezan a salir programas de televisión venezolanos dedicados al uso de la computadora y de Internet.

Alta Densidad es un programa de la compañía venezolana Globovisión, que se transmite semanalmente en Venezuela y por toda Latinoamérica. El programa se enfoca en el uso de Internet y en cuestiones tecnológicas. Tiene un sitio web que suplementa la información del programa y que contiene información sobre programas previos.

Ofrece noticias, ayuda, práctica, reportajes de video y enlaces a sitios web interesantes. El sitio web de *Alta Densidad* también ofrece la innovadora "Pez (*Fish*) Cam". César Miguel, la mascota del programa, es un pez que se filma veinticuatro horas al día. Millones y millones de internautas pueden mirarlo día y noche gracias a la primera webcam subacuática.

El programa y sitio web también ofrecen encuestas sobre cuestiones tecnológicas. Una encuesta reciente dio los siguientes resultados.

	Sí	No	Me da igual. (*It doesn't matter to me.*)	No sé.
1. ¿Te da miedo usar tu tarjeta de crédito en Internet?	82,1%	13,8%	4,1%	—
2. ¿Te gustan las páginas web con muchos movimientos y animaciones?	79,1%	15,4%	5,2%	0,3%
3. ¿Te interesa escuchar publicidad por tu celular a cambio de (*in exchange for*) mejores tarifas?	61,6%	35,2%	—	3,2%

 PRÁCTICA. En grupos de tres a cuatro personas, hablen de los siguientes temas.

1. ¿Conocen algún programa dedicado al uso de las computadoras o Internet? ¿Crees que es bueno tener este tipo de programa en televisión?
2. ¿Les interesa ver un episodio de *Alta Densidad?* ¿Por qué sí o por qué no?
3. ¿Les gusta la idea de la Pez Cam? ¿Por qué sí o por qué no? ¿Conocen otros sitios web que tengan cámaras web? ¿Cuáles?
4. Háganse las preguntas de las encuestas. ¿Son los resultados de la clase similares a los de las personas entrevistadas? Si son diferentes, ¿en qué áreas se diferencian?

A VER

Antes de ver el video

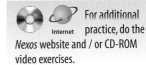

ACTIVIDAD 1 Cuando van al cine, ¿qué hacen? Con un(a) compañero(a) de clase, piensen en las cosas que hacen antes de salir para el cine y las que hacen después de llegar allí. Hagan una lista de unas seis a ocho cosas.

MODELO: *Decidimos qué tipo de película vamos a ver.*

ACTIVIDAD 2 ¿Qué les gusta o no les gusta a Anilú y a Javier? Combina la información que ya sabes sobre estos dos personajes con la información de las páginas 334 y 337. Llena la tabla con todos los datos que puedas. (Después de ver el video, vas a completar la tabla con la información nueva.)

For additional practice, do the *Nexos* website and / or CD-ROM video exercises.

Answers Act. 2 & 3: **Anilú:** las comedias románticas, los chocolates en el cine, la música pop, los musicales, los shows de Broadway; **Javier:** los documentales, las palomitas en el cine, las críticas de películas, hacer planes, la ópera, la música clásica

	Anilú	Javier
las comedias románticas		
los documentales		
las palomitas en el cine		
los chocolates en el cine		
las críticas de películas		
hacer planes		
la ópera		
la música pop		
la música clásica		
los musicales		
los shows de Broadway		

ESTRATEGIA

Listening for sequencing words

As you listen to this chapter's video segment, pay attention to sequencing words that help you understand the order in which things occur. Words such as **primero, segundo, luego, en primer lugar** (*in the first place*), **antes, después,** and **mientras** (*while, during*) can help you order the information in the video and aid your comprehension.

El video

Ahora mira el episodio del video para el **Capítulo 11.** No te olvides de enfocarte en las palabras de la tabla para ayudarte a entender la información del video.

Después de ver el video

ACTIVIDAD 3 Mira el video y vuelve a completar la tabla de la **Actividad 2** con los datos que faltan.

ACTIVIDAD 4 Mira el video otra vez y usa las palabras de la estrategia **(primero, en primer lugar, en segundo lugar, antes, después o mientras)** para completar las siguientes oraciones. Después de completarlas, indica quién dijo cada una.

1. —_____, los críticos no saben de lo que hablan.

2. —¿Quieres ver la tele? Aquí tienes el control remoto _____ me esperas.

3. —Leo las críticas _____ de ir a ver una película y me gusta escoger la película _____ de salir de casa.

4. —Y _____, prefiero formar mis propias opiniones.

 ACTIVIDAD 5 ¿A quién se describe? Trabaja con un(a) compañero(a) de clase para decir si las siguientes oraciones se refieren a Javier **(J)** o a Anilú **(A).**

1. _____ Quiere ver la guía de películas en el periódico.

2. _____ Le gustan las comedias románticas.

3. _____ Le gustan los documentales.

4. _____ Le gusta leer las críticas de las películas.

5. _____ Prefiere comer palomitas durante una película.

6. _____ Le gusta comer chocolates en el cine.

7. _____ Le encantan los musicales y la música pop.

8. _____ Le gusta ir a la ópera.

ACTIVIDAD 6 ¿A quién se parecen más? Trabajen en grupos de tres a cuatro personas. Usen la tabla de la **Actividad 2.** Cada persona debe dar sus preferencias para cada categoría. Indiquen el número de personas que se parecen a Anilú y el número de las que se parecen a Javier.

¿Estás de acuerdo con de León que la música puede enseñar valores importantes a los niños y ofrecerles una alternativa a las pandillas? To learn more about Sonia Marie de León de Vega and her musical projects, visit the *Nexos* website (http://college.hmco.com/languages/spanish/students) and follow the links.

VOCES DE LA COMUNIDAD

Sonia Marie de León de Vega

❝ ¿Por qué andar con una pandilla (*gang*) cuando se puede formar parte de una orquesta? Con la música, los niños aprenden el valor (*value*) del trabajo, ven resultados y aprenden a ser disciplinados. ❞

Sonia Marie de León de Vega es directora de la Orquesta Santa Cecilia. De León de Vega fundó esta orquesta en 1992 para llevar la música clásica a las comunidades latinas en el área de Los Ángeles. Esta misión se cumple a través de (*is accomplished through*) dos programas especiales de la orquesta: uno es una serie de conciertos que se ofrecen en los barrios hispanos del Sur de California, y el otro es un programa especial para niños hispanos en zonas urbanas pobres.

Tanto por sus talentos musicales, como por su servicio a la comunidad latina, de León de Vega es una de las mujeres directoras de mayor renombre (*renown*) internacional. Ella tiene el honor de haber sido (*having been*) la primera mujer en ser invitada a dirigir un concierto ante el Papa en la Ciudad del Vaticano. En el año 2000, la red de televisión Univisión la reconoció como una de las mujeres latinas más sobresalientes (*outstanding*) del estado de California. Un año más tarde, la revista *Hispanic Business* seleccionó a de León de Vega entre los 100 hispanos más importantes de Estados Unidos.

¡PREPÁRATE!

Gramática útil 1
Expressing emotion and wishes: The subjunctive with impersonal expressions and verbs of emotion

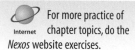 **Internet** For more practice of chapter topics, do the *Nexos* website exercises.

Suggestion: It is helpful to restate that the subjunctive occurs in the second clause of a two-clause sentence.

Optional: Point out that **alegrar** may be used like **gustar: Me alegra que Julio venga** vs. **Me alegro de que Julio venga.**

Ojalá (*I wish, I hope*) is a word of Arabic origin meaning "May Allah grant." This and other Arabic words entered the Spanish language during almost eight centuries of Arab inhabitation of Spain.

The use of **que** is optional with **ojalá**, but is used in the rest of the sentences to signal the beginning of the dependent clause.

CÓMO USARLO

LO BÁSICO

- *An independent clause* is a phrase containing a verb that *can stand alone* as a complete sentence: **Estoy muy contento.**

- *A dependent clause* is a phrase containing a verb that *cannot stand alone* as a complete sentence: **...que ustedes vengan al teatro.**

- *A complex sentence* combines both independent and dependent clauses: **Estoy muy contento de que ustedes vengan al teatro.**

In **Capítulo 10,** you learned to use the present subjunctive with verbs of volition—verbs that express what people want, need, hope, or wish other people will do. In this chapter, you will learn three more uses of the present subjunctive.

You may want to review the present subjunctive forms you learned in **Capítulo 10** to refresh your memory.

1. In addition to verbs of volition, Spanish speakers also use the present subjunctive when they express emotion, use generalized impersonal expressions, or use the Spanish word **ojalá.**

Me alegro de que puedas venir.	*I'm happy that you can come.*
Es importante que lleguemos temprano al cine.	*It's important that we arrive early at the theater.*
Ojalá (que) la película **sea** buena.	*I hope the movie is good.*

2. Notice that the model sentences above all follow the pattern you learned in **Capítulo 10.** These sentences are complex sentences where a verb or expression in the independent clause triggers the use of the subjunctive in the dependent clause.

Notice that there is always a change of subject from the independent clause to the dependent clause.

independent clause (verb of emotion, impersonal expression, or *ojalá*)	*que*	dependent clause (verb in subjunctive)
A mis amigos les **encanta**	que	**haya** muchos cines aquí.
Es importante	que	ustedes **vengan** con nosotros.
Ojalá	(que)	la película **sea** buena.

3. Remember, in situations where there is no use of **que** and no change of subject, there is also no use of the subjunctive.

Me alegro de poder ir al concierto.   vs.   Me alegro de **que tú puedas** ir al concierto.

Es importante llegar a tiempo.   vs.   Es importante **que lleguemos** a tiempo.

4. Here are some verbs and expressions that are frequently used with the subjunctive. Notice that some of these are the same or similar to the verbs of volition you learned in **Capítulo 10.** This is because the subjunctive is usually used to describe situations that involve emotion, which includes volition.

Es mejor que reconsideremos esta cita.

Remember that the verbs **encantar, fascinar, sorprender,** and **molestar** are used like **gustar.** They are used with the indirect object pronouns **me, te, le, nos, os,** and **les,** rather than with the subject pronouns **yo, tú, usted, él, ella, nosotros(as), vosotros(as), ustedes, ellos,** and **ellas.**

verbs of emotion, positive and neutral		
alegrarse de	estar contento(a) de	ojalá
encantar	fascinar	sorprender (*to surprise*)
esperar	gustar	

verbs of emotion, negative		
molestar	temer (*to fear*)	
sentir (*to feel sorry, to regret*)	tener miedo de	

impersonal expressions		
es bueno	es imprescindible (*essential*)	es mejor
es extraño (*strange*)	es interesante	es necesario
es fantástico	es (una) lástima	es obvio
es horrible	es lógico	es ridículo
es importante	es malo	es terrible

Actividades

ACTIVIDAD 1 **Me molesta que…** ¿Qué piensas del mundo del cine y la televisión? Escribe tus reacciones en oraciones completas.

MODELO: (no) me sorprende que / salir tantas películas malas
Me sorprende que salgan tantas películas malas.

1. (no) me molesta que / Hollywood hacer tantas películas de acción
2. (no) me sorprende que / las telenovelas ser tan populares
3. (no) es lógico que / los actores recibir más dinero que los directores
4. (no) es importante que / las películas extranjeras ser dobladas
5. (no) me molesta que / los refrescos costar tanto en el cine
6. (no) me sorprende que / los críticos siempre tener las mismas opiniones

ACTIVIDAD 2 **Felipe.** Felipe lleva dos años en Hollywood buscando trabajo como actor. Escucha la descripción de la vida de Felipe. Usando la frase indicada, expresa tu opinión sobre la situación de Felipe.

MODELO: Lees: Es fantástico que…
Escuchas: Felipe piensa que quiere ser estrella de cine.
Escribes: *Es fantástico que quiera ser estrella de cine.*

1. Es mejor que…
2. Es importante que…
3. Es imprescindible que…
4. Es una lástima que…
5. Es una pena que…
6. Es necesario que no…

ACTIVIDAD 3 **Yo creo que…** Te gusta mucho ir al cine y ver la televisión, pero tienes opiniones muy fuertes sobre ciertos aspectos de la industria. Expresa tus opiniones sobre los siguientes temas a un(a) compañero(a). Usa las frases de emoción o las expresiones impersonales para formar tus oraciones.

1. el salario de los actores principales
2. los presupuestos (*budgets*) de más de ochenta millones de dólares
3. el precio de las entradas
4. el precio de las palomitas y los chocolates en el cine
5. los anuncios en la tele
6. la programación en la tele
7. las telenovelas
8. el nivel de violencia en las películas y los programas de televisión

MODELO: *Es ridículo que les paguen veinte millones de dólares a los actores principales de una película.*

El aprendizaje y la adquisición

Los lingüistas que estudian cómo se aprenden las lenguas extranjeras reconocen que existen dos procesos cognitivos muy diferentes: el **aprendizaje** (*learning*) y la **adquisición**. El aprendizaje se basa en el análisis y la práctica de las reglas (*rules*) de grámatica. La adquisición se basa en el uso espontáneo de la lengua en situaciones comunicativas.

Un conocido estudio sobre el subjuntivo realizado por el difunto lingüista Tracy Terrell muestra la diferencia entre estos dos procesos. Un grupo de estudiantes de español de la Universidad de California en Irvine recibió instrucción y práctica con las reglas del uso del subjuntivo. Después, los estudiantes participaron en dos actividades destinadas a evaluar su dominio del subjuntivo. En la primera actividad, un examen tradicional de gramática, los estudiantes recibieron calificaciones muy altas. En la segunda, los estudiantes participaron en una conversación natural en español. Sorprendentemente (*Surprisingly*), los mismos estudiantes que recibieron calificaciones muy altas en el examen previo, no hicieron uso correcto del subjuntivo en la conversación espontánea. Terrell concluyó que sus estudiantes habían aprendido (*had learned*) el subjuntivo pero no lo habían adquirido (*had not acquired it*). Para llegar a usar el subjuntivo de manera comunicativa, ellos tendrían que (*would have to*) escucharlo en uso y practicarlo más en la conversación.

PRÁCTICA. En tu opinión, ¿qué implicaciones tiene este estudio? ¿Crees que existe una diferencia similar cuando aprendes actividades tales como manejar un automóvil, practicar un deporte o tocar un instrumento musical?

Preparation: You might want to introduce this topic briefly by asking ¿**Saben Uds. explicar la diferencia entre lo que se llama en inglés** *book learning* **y** *performance or practical knowledge?* Explain or have students explain the difference: **El aprendizaje es lo que uno sabe describir sobre cierto tema. La adquisición es lo que uno sabe hacer con esta misma información en la práctica.**

Gramática útil 2
Expressing doubt and uncertainty: The subjunctive with expressions of doubt and disbelief

CÓMO USARLO

1. Another group of verbs and expressions that trigger the use of the subjunctive are expressions of doubt and uncertainty.

No creo que funcione el televisor.	*I don't think the TV is working.*
No estoy segura de que yo pueda repararlo.	*I'm not sure I can fix it.*
Dudo que podamos ver el programa.	*I doubt we'll be able to watch the program.*

2. Because speakers are expressing situations that they doubt are certain, or expect not to occur, they use the subjunctive. Notice that in this usage, you do not need to have a change in subject: **No estoy segura de que yo pueda repararlo.**

3. Here are some verbs and expressions that are used to express doubt and uncertainty with the subjunctive.

dudar	*to doubt*	**no es cierto**	*it's not certain*
es dudoso	*it's doubtful / unlikely*	**no es probable**	*it's not probable / likely*
es improbable	*it's improbable / unlikely*	**no es seguro**	*it's not sure*
		no es verdad	*it's not true*
no creer	*to not believe*	**no estar seguro(a) de**	*to not be sure*

4. When speakers use similar expressions to express belief or certainty (**creer, estar seguro[a], es cierto, es seguro),** the present indicative—and not the present subjunctive—is used.

Creo que **funciona** el televisor.	*I think the TV is working.*
Estoy segura de que puedo repararlo.	*I'm sure I can repair it.*
Es cierto que podemos ver el programa.	*It's certain that we can watch the program.*

Actividades

ACTIVIDAD 4 **Dudo que...** En tu vida como televidente, has formado muchas opiniones negativas de la industria televisiva. ¡Dudas de todo! Di lo que dudas.

MODELO: ese episodio / ser nuevo *Dudo que ese episodio sea nuevo.*

1. las noticias / ser interesantes
2. los programas de realidad / existir en veinte años
3. esa telecomedia / hacerme reír
4. ese participante / ganar el concurso
5. ese programa de entrevistas / gustarle al público
6. el show de los Óscars / terminar a tiempo
7. la presentadora / ser original en sus comentarios
8. ese teledrama / durar más de un año

ACTIVIDAD 5 **La música.** Hay muchos tipos de música hoy día, y las preferencias del público varían mucho. Escribe seis oraciones sobre la industria musical, combinando frases de las tres columnas para expresar tus opiniones.

Columna 1	**Columna 2**	**Columna 3**
no creer	la música pop	existir en… años
no estar seguro(a) de	la música clásica	ser tan popular en el futuro
dudar / es dudoso	la música country	controlar el mercado en… años
no es probable / es improbable	la música mundial	cambiar de ritmo y tema en el futuro
no es cierto / no es seguro	el rap	tener el público en el futuro que tiene hoy
	el rock	encontrarse en conciertos para jóvenes
	¿…?	¿…?

MODELO: *No creo que el rock exista en cincuenta años.*

ACTIVIDAD 6 **Mi futuro.** Conversa sobre tu futuro con un(a) compañero(a). Usando el subjuntivo con algunas expresiones de duda, cuéntale a tu compañero(a) cuatro o cinco predicciones sobre tu futuro. Él (Ella) igualmente te contará (*will tell you*) cuatro a cinco predicciones sobre su futuro.

MODELO: *Es improbable que tenga una casa grande en Hollywood y una carrera como director de cine.*

Sonrisas

⑤ Standards: C 5.2 is addressed as learners experience the wit, wisdom, and common sense of a vignette about life-long learning. This cartoon can launch a discussion on **la felicidad**: ¿Cuáles son los elementos (o ingredientes) necesarios para la felicidad en la vida? ¿Dudas que... sea posible? ¿Dudas que sea posible lograrlo? ¿Crees que es importante ser flexible en la vida?

EXPRESIÓN. En grupos de tres a cuatro estudiantes, den sus reacciones a los siguientes lemas (*slogans*). Usen expresiones como **dudo que, estoy seguro(a) de que, no es cierto que, es probable que** y **no es probable que.**

1. El tiempo es oro.
2. El mundo es un pañuelo (*handkerchief*).
3. La mala suerte (*luck*) y los tontos caminan del brazo (*arm in arm*).
4. La práctica hace al maestro.
5. Donde una puerta se cierra, cien se abren.

¿Tienes la misma duda que los niños? ¿Por qué sí o por qué no?

Gramática útil 3

Expressing unrealized desires and unknown situations:
The subjunctive with nonexistent and indefinite situations

¿Quién dijo que no hay nada que valga la pena en la TV?

¡Sí! Envíeme más información gratis y sin compromiso.

Nombre_____

Dirección_____

Ciudad_____

Estado_____ Zona Postal_____

Teléfono (   )_____

Inglés sin Barreras
640 S. San Vicente, Los Angeles, CA 90048
(800) 411-6666

Look at this ad for a television program that teaches English. Can you figure out why the subjunctive is used? (**Valga** is the subjunctive form of **valer**; the expression **valer la pena** means *to be worthwhile*.)

Answer: The subjunctive is used because it is expressing a supposedly nonexistent situation.

CÓMO USARLO

1. So far, you have practiced using the subjunctive in dependent clauses that begin with **que**. These dependent clauses in the subjunctive follow independent clauses that contain:

- verbs of volition

  Mis amigos **prefieren** que **vayamos** al teatro.

- impersonal expressions

  Es ridículo que las entradas **cuesten** treinta dólares.

- verbs and expressions of emotion

  ¡**Qué lástima** que no **puedas** acompañarnos!

- ojalá

  Ojalá que **vengas** la próxima vez.

- expressions of doubt

  No estoy seguro de que todos **podamos** ir.

2. You also use the subjunctive when you refer to people, places, or things that either don't exist or may not exist (you don't know). These references to nonexistent or unknown things occur in dependent clauses (beginning with **que**) that require the subjunctive.

- Doesn't exist:

No veo a nadie aquí que nos **pueda** ayudar.
I don't see anyone here who can help us.

No hay ningún café que **esté** abierto después de medianoche.
There isn't a single café that is open after midnight.

- Unknown—don't know if it exists:

Busco un teatro que **se especialice** en comedias.
I'm looking for a theater that specializes in comedies.

Necesito hablar con un director que **sepa** colaborar con los actores.
I need to talk to a director who knows how to collaborate with the actors.

Notice that with the verb **buscar**, you do not use the personal **a** when referring to people: **Busco un actor que sepa hacer papeles cómicos.** BUT: **Veo a un actor que hace papeles cómicos.**

Suggestion: Introduce terms in Spanish **existe** vs. **no existe** and **definido** vs. **indefinido**, so that students can actively identify sentences according to these categories.

3. When you *know or believe* that something or someone exists, you use the present indicative in the dependent **que** clause.

Veo a alguien que nos **puede** ayudar.
I see someone who can help us.

En este barrio **hay** un café que **está** abierto después de medianoche.
In this neighborhood there is a café that is open after midnight.

Conozco un teatro que **se especializa** en comedias.
I know of a theater that specializes in comedies.

Voy a hablar con un director <u>que</u> *I'm going to talk* to a director (that I
<u>sabe</u> colaborar con los actores. know of) *who **knows how** to
collaborate with the actors.*

4. Notice that these sentences follow the same pattern as the other complex
sentences you have learned: independent clause + **que** + dependent clause with
subjunctive.

Optional: Read the following sentences and have students identify them as: **existe, no existe, definido, indefinido. 1. Busco una casa que <u>tenga</u> 3 baños. (indefinido) 2. Tengo un coche que <u>es</u> rojo. (existe, definido) 3. No hay nadie aquí que <u>hable</u> francés. (no existe) 4. Conozco a muchos que <u>hablan</u>** (cont. below)

Actividades

ACTIVIDAD 7 **Los deseos de la productora.** La productora tiene una visión
particular para un musical que quiere montar (*present*) en Broadway. ¿Qué dice
ella que busca, quiere o necesita para desarrollar su visión?

MODELO: querer: escoger una obra (tener posibilidades cómicas)
Quiero escoger una obra que tenga posibilidades cómicas.

1. buscar: una actriz (poder hablar francés, inglés y español)
2. necesitar: un banco (prestarnos [*to lend us*] los fondos)
3. querer: un director (saber algo de musicales)
4. buscar: un teatro (no ser ni muy pequeño ni muy grande)
5. necesitar: un asistente (poder manejar muchos detalles)
6. buscar: un actor (no ser muy conocido todavía)
7. querer: un público (apreciar el arte del teatro cómico)

ACTIVIDAD 8 **El productor ejecutivo.** Escucha al productor ejecutivo de
un musical. Él describe lo que va a necesitar para poder montar un musical.
Escucha su descripción y escribe lo que él dice que necesita en cada persona que
busca.

MODELO: Escuchas: Primero, vamos a necesitar un director. El director tiene
que tener mucha experiencia en el teatro.
Ves: director / tener
Escribes: *Necesita un director que tenga experiencia en el teatro.*

1. actores / poder 3. diseñador / ser
2. conductor / saber 4. productor / ser

ACTIVIDAD 9 **¡Somos directores!** Con un(a) compañero(a), ustedes van a
ser escritores(as) o directores(as) de una telecomedia sobre las experiencias de
estudiantes universitarios que estudian español. Escriban seis oraciones que
describan su visión. Usen el subjuntivo para describir esas cosas y personas que
buscan para ejecutar su plan. Piensen en las siguientes preguntas antes de
empezar.

• ¿Qué cualidades quieren que tenga su telecomedia?
• ¿Qué tipo de actor / actriz buscan para representar al (a la) profesor(a)?
• ¿Cómo quieren que sean los estudiantes?
• ¿Qué tipo de situaciones van a representar?

MODELO: *Queremos escribir una telecomedia que sea divertida.*

español. (existe) 5. Quiero hablar con alguien que <u>hable</u> portugués. (indefinido) 6. Tengo un amigo que <u>habla</u> árabe. (existe, definido)

Suggestion: Have students describe their ideal roommate, teacher, or spouse. **Quiero un(a) compañero(a) que…** Note that use of the subjunctive or indicative in adjective clauses is not always hard-and-fast. For example, **Busca una palabra en el cuento que quiere / quiera decir guapo.** Use of the subjunctive is probably more common; however, use of the indicative would suggest you know that the word exists, even if it hasn't yet been identified. You may want to emphasize with students that, if there's any doubt or uncertainty about whether something exists, the subjunctive is used.

Answers Act. 7: 1. Busco una actriz que pueda hablar francés, inglés y español. 2. Necesito un banco que nos preste los fondos. 3. Quiero un director que sepa algo de musicales. 4. Busco un teatro que no sea ni muy pequeño ni muy grande. 5. Necesito un asistente que pueda manejar muchos detalles. 6. Busco un actor que no sea muy conocido todavía. 7. Quiero un público que aprecie el arte del teatro cómico.

Answers Act. 8: 1. Necesita actores que puedan cantar. 2. Necesita un conductor que sepa conducir piezas largas. 3. Necesita un diseñador que sea experto en la historia de la Revolución francesa. 4. Necesita un productor que sea muy organizado y eficiente.

Venezuela y Colombia

¿Adivinaste? Answers to the questions on page 333: 1. Venezuela 2. Colombia 3. Colombia 4. Venezuela 5. Venezuela

Standards: Here students gain knowledge about products and explore perspectives of Colombia and Venezuela through art and media (C 2.2).

Arte y cultura. Mira las fotos y luego lee los textos que siguen. Escoge los títulos y las fotos que corresponden a los textos. Trata de leer rápidamente para entender la idea central del texto. Después de identificar el título y la foto correspondientes, lee los textos de nuevo para ver si entendiste el contenido de cada uno.

Fotos

Foto 1

Foto 2

Foto 3

Foto 4

Títulos

Título 1: Una escena artística y moderna

Título 2: Un arte puramente colombiano

Título 3: Raíces indígenas y venezolanas

Título 4: Una nueva estrella colombiana

Suggestion: Try other pre-reading techniques like dividing your class into four groups. Have each group scan a different reading and list the 10 key words crucial to understanding the theme and gist of the reading. Have each group list their words on the board and use them to preview the readings.

Answers: **Texto 1:** Foto 2, Título 3; **Texto 2:** Foto 3, Título 4; **Texto 3:** Foto 4, Título 1; **Texto 4:** Foto 1, Título 2

Texto 1

Patricia Velásquez hizo su debut como actriz en 1999 en la película francesa *Le jaguar*, pero es mejor conocida por su papel en la popular película norteamericana *La momia regresa*. En esta película Velásquez hace el papel de Anck-Su Namun, la enemiga de la egiptóloga Evelyn (Rachel Wiesz), mujer y colega del aventurero Rick O'Connell (Brendan Fraser). Las escenas de pelea entre Evelyn y Anck-Su Namun, al estilo de las artes marciales, son unas de las más emocionantes de la película.

Velásquez es una venezolana de Maracaibo. Al principio de su carrera, trabajaba como modelo para unos de los diseñadores más famosos del mundo y apareció en revistas internacionales como *Sports Illustrated, Elle* y *Vogue*. También fue una de las primeras modelos de Latinoamérica que se hizo popular en Europa.

Su físico exótico resulta de la unión de un padre venezolano y una madre indígena de la tribu Guajira Wayú. La actriz está orgullosa (*proud*) de su herencia mixta y lo menciona en muchas de sus entrevistas con la prensa internacional. Es también activista que se dedica a una variedad de causas: el fomento (*promotion*) de la comunidad hispana, la igualdad para los grupos indígenas y la lucha contra el SIDA infantil.

Texto 2

Este cantante colombiano ya ha ganado (*has won*) tres premios Grammy latinos a la joven edad de 28 años. Se llama Juanes, que viene de una combinación de Juan y Esteban, parte de su nombre original Juan Esteban Aristizábal. Es cantante, compositor, productor y guitarrista, y en este momento, parece que no hay nada que este talentoso joven no pueda hacer.

Aunque empezó su carrera musical a la edad de 15 años, en el año 2001 Juanes sorprendió a la industria internacional de entretenimiento al recibir siete nominaciones al Grammy, el mayor número hasta ahora en la historia de los Grammy para un artista latino. Las tres nominaciones que ganó son Mejor Album Rock ("Fíjate bien"), Mejor Canción Rock y Mejor Nuevo Artista.

Juanes admite influencias musicales tan diversas como Led Zeppelin, los tangos de Carlos Gardel, Metallica, Silvio Rodríguez, Jimmy Hendrix y Eminem. "Yo vengo de una escuela musical basada en el folclor colombiano y latinoamericano, pero por cosas de la vida, desde los 14 años comencé a escuchar mucho rock y otras cosas. [Mi música]... pasa por todos estos lados pero no se queda en ninguno establecido."

Texto 3

Muchos críticos de arte y arquitectura creen que el Complejo Cultural Teresa Carreño es la obra arquitectónica y cultural más importante construida en Venezuela en los últimos cien años. Tiene su origen en la reestructuración urbanística de la ciudad de Caracas que empezó en los años 50 del siglo XX, cuando surgió la idea de construir un teatro moderno para la capital venezolana.

El centro incorpora varias salas y espacios para la presentación del arte, en todas sus formas. Las salas José Félix Ribas y Ríos Reyna se dedican al teatro, la danza, la ópera, el ballet y conciertos y otras expresiones populares. Otros espacios, llamados "espacios alternativos", sirven para las más diversas manifestaciones escénicas, desde lo clásico hasta lo popular, pasando por el folclor y las expresiones infantiles.

El centro también es sede (*home*) de varias orquestas, un coro de ópera profesional y una de las compañías venezolanas de ballet con mayor prestigio. La estructura arquitectónica del teatro incluye obras escultóricas de una variedad de artistas. "El Teresa" tiene la meta (*goal*) de apoyar (*to support*) el desarrollo de las artes, ofrecer oportunidades para entretenimiento a todos y elevar el nivel cultural de Venezuela.

Texto 4

Ana Mercedes Hoyos es tal vez la pintora colombiana con mayor éxito (*success*) fuera de su país natal. Los expertos comparan su fama con la de un Fernando Botero o de un Alejandro Obregón. Sus obras se venden en las Casas Sotheby's y Christie's de Nueva York, y se exponen en diferentes galerías de Japón, Brasil, España, Cuba, Francia y Argentina.

Hoyos nació en Bogotá en 1942 y empezó a exponer sus pinturas en 1966. Sus obras ocupan un lugar entre lo abstracto y lo realista, entre lo figurativo y lo geométrico. Unas se acercan al "pop art" de los años 60, mientras otras reflejan más la influencia del ancestro africano en los países del Caribe.

Durante su carrera, la artista se interesó en hacer recreaciones de famosos bodegones (o naturalezas muertas) de la historia del arte internacional, incluyendo obras de Caravaggio, Zurbarán, Cezanne y Lichtenstein. Luego hizo una serie de obras figurativas con motivos nacionales, "Bodegones de Palenque".

Internet

Suggestion: Organize the follow-up presentation like this: **Al volver, pónganse en grupos según su tema de investigación, compartan la información que han encontrado trabajando solo o con compañeros. Después hagan una síntesis para la clase.**

¡CONÉCTATE!

En grupos de tres o cuatro, hagan una investigación en Internet sobre uno de los siguientes temas. Usen los enlaces sugeridos en el sitio web de *Nexos* (http://college.hmco.com/languages/spanish/students) para ir a otros sitios web posibles. Presenten su informe a la clase.

Grupo 1: La industria televisiva o cinematográfica de Venezuela
Grupo 2: La industria petrolera de Venezuela
Grupo 3: La arquitectura histórica en el barrio de La Candelaria en Bogotá
Grupo 4: La pintura y escultura de Fernando Botero

A LEER

Antes de leer

Using prefixes and suffixes to aid in comprehension

Whenever you read authentic Spanish texts that were written for native speakers, there will always be words that you don't understand. You have learned to identify cognates and to use a bilingual dictionary to help you guess the meaning of unknown words. Analyzing prefixes and suffixes is another good way to try to understand words you don't know. Prefixes (such as the English *un-* and *non-*) attach to the beginnings of words, so that all words with that prefix share that part of their meaning. Suffixes (such as, in English, *-ly* and *-tion*) attach to the ends of words. Paying attention to prefixes and suffixes can help you extend your Spanish vocabulary.

Standards: Here students explore C 4.1 with language comparisons between Spanish and English prefixes and suffixes.

 ACTIVIDAD 1 Trabaja con un(a) compañero(a) de clase. Miren la siguiente tabla de prefijos y sufijos. Escriban un ejemplo en español para cada uno. Usen palabras que ya conocen o palabras de la lectura.

Prefijos	Sufijos	
re-	-cia	-dad
tele-	-ivo	-ista
in-	-ción	-ado
pro-	-mente	-al

Suggestion: Point out that English *-tion* usually corresponds to Spanish *-ción*, while English *-sion* and *-ssion* correspond to *-sión* in Spanish. Here are some examples to use: nation – **nación;** passion – **pasión;** *experimentation* – **experimentación;** *version* – **versión;** *diction* – **dicción.**

Answers Act. 1: *Answers may vary.* re-: re-transmisión; tele-: telenovela, televidentes; in-: inigualado; pro-: protagonista, profesional, -cia: inocencia; -ivo: exclusivo; -ción: confección, relación, adquisición; -mente: simplemente, recientemente; -dad: ingenuidad, integridad; -ista: economista; -ado: inigualado, privado; -al: profesional

 ACTIVIDAD 2 Miren sus palabras en la tabla de la **Actividad 1.** Estudien los prefijos y los sufijos. Luego, traten de asociar los siguientes prefijos y sufijos ingleses con los españoles. ¿Son similares o diferentes en los dos idiomas?

1. tele-
2. -ly
3. -ive
4. -sion / -tion
5. re-
6. -ity
7. -ence
8. -ist
9. -al
10. -ed
11. pro-

Answers Act. 2: 1. tele- 2. -mente 3. -ivo 4. -ción 5. re- 6. -dad 7. -cia 8. -ista 9. -al 10. -ado 11. pro-

ACTIVIDAD 3 Van a leer un artículo sobre una telenovela colombiana muy popular. Antes de leer, hablen de las siguientes preguntas sobre las telenovelas.

1. En su opinión, ¿hay una diferencia entre las telenovelas que se transmiten durante el día y las teleseries dramáticas que se ponen por la noche? (Piensen en, por ejemplo, las diferencias entre *All My Children* o *General Hospital* y *Buffy the Vampire Slayer, The West Wing* y *ER.*)
2. ¿Cuál es la telenovela más popular que conocen? ¿Y la teleserie?
3. ¿Miran telenovelas? ¿Miran teleseries dramáticas? ¿Qué prefieren, las telenovelas o las teleseries?

Lectura

To see Univision's schedule for *Eco Moda* and *Betty la Fea*, go to the *Nexos* website (http://college.hmco.com/languages/spanish/students) and follow the links.

ACTIVIDAD 4 Lee el artículo sobre la telenovela más popular de Latinoamérica en el año 2000. No te olvides de usar los prefijos y los sufijos para ayudarte a entender las palabras que no conozcas.

Yo soy Betty, la Fea

Esta telenovela, mejor conocida simplemente como "Betty" o "Betty la Fea", ha sido[1] un fenómeno inigualado en la historia de los canales de televisión privados de Colombia. Desde su inicio el 25 de octubre de 2000, se ha convertido[2] en la telenovela más vista[3] en todos los países donde se transmite, que incluyen Ecuador, Panamá, Venezuela, Guatemala, Costa Rica, la República Dominicana, Honduras, Bolivia y Argentina.

Sinopsis

Se trata de una serie que cuenta la vida de Beatriz Pinzón, una brillante y excelente economista, buena hija y amiga, pero que tiene un gran defecto: ser muy fea. El único novio que tuvo en su vida la abandonó pocos días después de empezar su relación; por ello Betty piensa que se va a quedar soltera[4] para siempre.

Por esta razón, mientras las chicas de su edad se dedicaban a salir por las noches a bares y discotecas de moda, Betty estudiaba para triunfar como una auténtica profesional. Betty, que ya tiene 26 años, sigue viviendo con sus padres, ya que no hay ningún hombre que quiera formar parte de su vida. Después de buscar trabajo durante un largo período de tiempo, la contratan como secretaria del presidente de Eco Moda, una de las empresas más grandes de confección[5] de Colombia.

Betty

En la serie, la protagonista Betty representa la ingenuidad y la inocencia. Los televidentes se identifican con ella cuando se encuentra metida[6] en un mundo nuevo y extraño—el de la alta moda. Rodeada por[7] las intrigas entre las modelos bellas, los diseñadores y los hombres y mujeres de negocios, Betty lucha para mantener su integridad y adelantar su carrera profesional.

En realidad, la actriz que interpreta el papel de Betty, Ana María Orozco, no es nada fea. Pero el papel de Betty ha sido el triunfo más importante de su vida profesional.

¡Tal ha sido la popularidad de Betty que ya hay "muñecas[8] Betty" de varios tamaños y estilos, incluso un modelo para el mercado estadounidense!

Betty viene a Estados Unidos

A causa del éxito[9] tremendo de Betty por toda Latinoamérica, el canal estadounidense Univisión recientemente confirmó su adquisición de los derechos exclusivos en Estados Unidos y Puerto Rico del catálogo de telenovelas de RCN de Colombia. Esta adquisición incluye no sólo los

Ana María Orozco como Betty la Fea y con su apariencia normal

Notice: In Spanish-speaking cultures, identifying individuals by their physical characteristics is an accepted practice. People commonly identify each other by hair color, height, and other physical characteristics and do not consider it offensive. Nicknames such as **gordito** may even be used affectionately.

derechos para la re-transmisión de "Betty la Fea", sino también los derechos para una nueva serie basada en "Betty", con Ana María Orozco como protagonista, cuyo título es "Eco Moda".

"Eco Moda" ya se transmite por Univisión, que describe la nueva serie así:

"Betty fue, por largo tiempo, un Patito Feo[10], pero ahora está viviendo el cuento de hadas[11] que siempre soñó. De secretaria ha pasado a ser la presidente de la prestigiosa casa de modas, Eco Moda. Está casada con Armando, su antiguo jefe, y tiene una hija de un año de edad. Sus fantasías se han vuelto[12] realidad y Eco Moda es su segundo hogar. Sin embargo, debido a los cambios económicos que afectan a América Latina, Eco Moda busca expandir sus operaciones más allá de las fronteras colombianas... Con todos estos cambios, Betty espera que ocurra lo peor, no sólo en el área profesional, sino también la emocional…"

[1]**ha sido** *has been* [2]**se... has become** [3]*viewed* [4]*single* [5]*fashion, couture* [6]*placed* [7]**Rodeada...** *Surrounded by* [8]*dolls* [9]*success* [10]**Patito...** *Ugly Duckling* [11]**cuento...** *fairytale* [12]**se...** *have become*

Después de leer

ACTIVIDAD 5 Trabaja con un(a) compañero(a) de clase para contestar las siguientes preguntas sobre la lectura.

1. ¿Qué país produjo la telenovela "Betty la Fea"?
2. ¿En qué países se puede ver esta telenovela?
3. ¿Cómo es Betty? (Den por lo menos tres adjetivos.)
4. ¿Quién es Ana María Orozco?
5. ¿Qué es "Eco Moda"?
6. ¿Qué canal estadounidense adquirió los derechos para transmitir "Betty" en EEUU?
7. ¿Les gustaría ver unos episodios de "Betty"? ¿Por qué sí o no?
8. ¿Les gusta la idea de una protagonista fea? ¿Por qué sí o no?

ACTIVIDAD 6 En grupos de tres a cuatro personas, den unas ideas posibles para un nuevo episodio de "Eco Moda". ¿Qué pasa hoy con Betty? Mira la lista de protagonistas de "Eco Moda" como inspiración. (¡No tienen que usar todos los personajes!) Luego, escribe un breve resumen de la trama (*plot*) de un episodio.

Protagonistas

Betty: presidente de Eco Moda

Kenneth: un especialista de modas de EEUU cuyos (*whose*) cambios dramáticos provocan una rebelión entre los empleados

Natasha: la nueva secretaria ejecutiva, que recibe demasiada atención de los hombres de la compañía

Freddy: el mensajero vanidoso de Eco Moda, su gran amor es Aura María

Gabriela: una bella mexicana que sabe mucho de la moda y posiblemente enemiga secreta de Betty

Nicolás: un adolescente en cuerpo (*body*) de hombre, el mejor amigo de Betty, ya un poco aislado de ella después de su boda

Armando: esposo de Betty, muy aficionado a las mujeres y celoso del éxito fenomenal de Betty

Hugo: el diseñador talentoso pero extremadamente superficial

Aura María: novia de Freddy, una mujer impulsiva y muy, muy coqueta

Heritage Learners: A good number of heritage language students may be familiar with "Yo soy Betty, la Fea" or other popular soap operas in Spanish. Have students compare and contrast Spanish-language soaps and English-language soaps with regard to the role of women, the representation of social class, the themes, the importance of the family, etc.

Notice: Point out to students or have them find the sentence that is an example of nonexistence with the subjunctive. **Betty, que ya tiene 26 años, sigue viviendo con sus padres, ya que no hay ningún hombre que quiera formar parte de su vida.**

Answers Act. 5: 1. Colombia 2. Colombia, Ecuador, Panamá, Venezuela, Guatemala, Costa Rica, la República Dominicana, Honduras, Bolivia y Argentina y pronto en EEUU 3. fea, brillante, ingenua, inocente, excelente economista, buena hija y amiga 4. la actriz que hace el papel de Betty 5. la nueva serie basada en "Betty" (o, el nombre de la compañía donde trabaja Betty) 6. Univisión 7. *Answers will vary.* 8. *Answers will vary.*

Heritage Learners: Point out that **trama** is feminine, not to be confused with other words that are irregular in gender and problematic for heritage language students: **el problema, el poema, el poeta, el tema.** These words all descend from Greek.

To read more about these characters, go to the *Nexos* website (http://college.hmco.com/languages/spanish/students) and follow the links.

Optional: Try this writing exercise in "nutshelling" or summarizing. First have students write the brief summary outlined in **Actividad 6.** Next have students rewrite their summaries with the stipulation that it be reduced to only three sentences. The last step is to compress the summary to only one sentence in length.

A ESCRIBIR

 Preparation: If possible, have students view a Spanish movie together or an episode of "Betty" to make this a class activity.

ESTRATEGIA

Prewriting—Creating an outline

In **Capítulo 9** you learned how to write a paragraph using a topic sentence and supporting details. In this chapter, you will create an outline that shows the organization of a piece of writing that is composed of more than one paragraph. When you are writing compositions longer than a single paragraph, an outline is a useful way to organize your thoughts and ideas before you begin writing.

Antes de escribir

ACTIVIDAD 1 Trabaja con un(a) compañero(a) de clase.

1. Juntos, piensen en un programa de televisión, una película, una pieza de música o una exposición de arte que los dos conocen bien. Van a escribir una reseña de cuatro párrafos breves.

2. Después de seleccionar una obra, hagan una lista de opiniones, datos (*facts*) y ejemplos que puedan usar en su reseña. Escriban todo lo que puedan; van a tener la oportunidad de organizar sus ideas en la **Actividad 3.**

MODELO: película: *Vanilla Sky*
actores: *Tom Cruise, Penélope Cruz, Cameron Díaz*
temas y ideas: *película de misterio, de acción; Se trata de un hombre que tuvo un accidente de coche...; es una versión americana de una película española,* etc.

ACTIVIDAD 2 Miren su lista de ideas y traten de hacer un bosquejo (*outline*) como el siguiente. Recuerden que cada párrafo debe tener una oración temática y detalles que se relacionen con esa oración.

I. **Párrafo 1: Introducción**
  A. Reacción general a la obra: *Me gustó mucho la exposición de arte colombiano...*
  B. Ejemplo 1: *Tenía obras de una gran variedad de artistas. Es bueno que...*
  C. Ejemplo 2: *Se trataba de varias épocas históricas y estilos de arte y me sorpende que...* (etc.)

II. **Párrafo 2: Primer aspecto que se relaciona con la reacción general**
  A. Detalle o ejemplo 1: *Primero, todas las obras trataron el tema de..., aunque no es cierto que...*
  B. Detalle o ejemplo 2: *Segundo, incluyó obras de Fernando Botero, Ana Mercedes Hoyos... y creo que...*

III. Párrafo 3: Segundo aspecto que se relaciona con la reacción general
    A. Detalle o ejemplo 1: *Al principio, la exposición empezó con obras indígenas del siglo XV... La única cosa que me molesta es que...*
    B. Detalle o ejemplo 2: *Luego incluyó pinturas, esculturas, fotografías... Ojalá que...*

IV. Párrafo 4: Conclusión
    A. Reacción general otra vez: *En fin, es una exposición muy completa...*
    B. Una o dos oraciones que apoyan (*support*) esta reacción: *Incluye obras de todos los artistas colombianos más famosos...*

Escritura

ACTIVIDAD 3 Usa el bosquejo para escribir tu reseña. Aquí hay unas frases que te puedan ser útiles (*useful*) mientras escribes.

En primer /
    segundo lugar...
Después...
Luego...
En fin...
Dudo que...
No es cierto...
Creo que...
Es bueno / malo /
    extraño / obvio / una
    lástima / lógico…
Me molesta que...
Temo que...
Me alegro de que...
Ojalá que...
Me sorprende que...

Después de escribir

ACTIVIDAD 4 Intercambia tu borrador con el de otro(a) estudiante. Usen la siguiente lista como guía para revisar el borrador de su compañero(a).

1. ¿Incluye la reseña toda la información del bosquejo?
2. ¿Hay oraciones que son difíciles de entender?
3. ¿Usaron expresiones de emoción y transiciones como **primero, segundo, luego, antes,** etc.?
4. ¿Hay errores de ortografía?
5. ¿Usaron las formas correctas de todos los verbos?
6. ¿Hay concordancia (*agreement*) entre los artículos, los sustantivos (*nouns*) y los adjetivos?
7. ¿Usaron bien el subjuntivo con los verbos y expresiones de negación, de duda y de emoción?

VOCABULARIO

CLASES DE PELÍCULA *Movie genres*

la comedia (romántica)	*(romantic) comedy*
los dibujos animados	*cartoons; animated film*
el documental	*documentary*
el drama	*drama*
el misterio	*mystery*
la película...	*movie, film*
... de acción	*action*
... de ciencia ficción	*science fiction*
... de horror / terror	*horror*

SOBRE LA PELÍCULA *About the movie*

con subtítulos en inglés	*with subtitles in English*
doblado(a)	*dubbed*
la estrella de cine	*movie star*
una película titulada...	*a movie called . . .*
Se trata de...	*It's about . . .*
el título	*title*

LA CRÍTICA *Critique, review*

calificar / clasificar con cuatro estrellas	*to give a four-star rating*
el (la) crítico(a)	*critic*
la reacción crítica	*critical reaction*
la reseña / la crítica	*review*

EL ÍNDICE DE AUDIENCIA *Ratings*

apto(a) para toda la familia	*G (for general audiences)*
se recomienda discreción	*PG-13 (parental discretion advised)*
prohibido para menores	*R (minors restricted)*

EN EL CINE *At the movies*

los chocolates	*chocolates*
los dulces	*candy*
la entrada / el boleto	*ticket*
las palomitas	*popcorn*

LA TELEVISIÓN *Television broadcasting*

el cable	*cable television*
cambiar el / de canal	*to change the channel*
el control remoto	*remote control*
en vivo	*live*
el episodio	*episode*
la estación	*station*
grabar	*to videotape; to record*
por satélite	*by satellite dish*
la teleguía	*TV guide*

LOS PROGRAMAS DE TELEVISIÓN
Television programs

las noticias	*news*
el programa de concursos	*game show*
el programa de entrevistas	*talk show*
la telecomedia	*sitcom*
el teledrama	*drama series*
la telenovela	*soap opera*
la teleserie	*TV series*

LA GENTE EN LA TELEVISIÓN *People on TV*

el (la) entrevistador(a)	*interviewer*
el (la) locutor(a)	*announcer*
el (la) participante	*participant*
el (la) presentador(a)	*presenter; host (of the show)*
el público	*audience*
el (la) televidente	*TV viewer*

LA MÚSICA *Music*

la música clásica	*classical music*
la música country	*country music*
la música moderna	*modern music*
la música mundial	*world music*
la música pop	*pop music*
el R & B	*rhythm and blues*
el rap	*rap*
el rock	*rock*

ARTE Y CULTURA   *The arts*

el baile / la danza	*dance*
la escultura	*sculpture*
el espectáculo	*show*
la exposición de arte	*art exhibit*
la obra teatral	*play*
el musical	*musical*
la ópera	*opera*
la pintura	*painting*
el show	*show*

VERBOS Y EXPRESIONES DE DUDA

dudar	*to doubt*
es dudoso	*it's doubtful / unlikely*
es improbable	*it's improbable / unlikely*
no creer	*to not believe*
no es cierto	*it's not certain*
no es probable	*it's not probable / likely*
no es seguro	*it's not sure*
no es verdad	*it's not true*
no estar seguro(a) de	*to not be sure of*

EXPRESIONES IMPERSONALES

es bueno	*it's good*
es extraño	*it's strange*
es fantástico	*it's fantastic*
es horrible	*it's horrible*
es importante	*it's important*
es imprescindible	*it's extremely important*
es (una) lástima	*it's a shame*
es lógico	*it's logical*
es malo	*it's bad*
es mejor	*it's better*
es necesario	*it's necessary*
es obvio	*it's obvious*
es ridículo	*it's ridiculous*
es terrible	*it's terrible*

VERBOS Y EXPRESIONES DE EMOCIÓN POSITIVAS Y NEGATIVAS

alegrarse de	*to be happy about*
encantar	*to enchant; to please*
esperar	*to wait; to hope*
estar contento(a) de	*to be pleased about*
fascinar	*to fascinate*
gustar	*to like, to please*
molestar	*to bother*
ojalá (que)	*I wish, I hope*
sentir (ie, i)	*to feel sorry, to regret*
sorprender	*to surprise*
temer	*to fear*
tener miedo de	*to be afraid (of)*

¿Qué síntomas tienes?

Communication

By the end of this chapter you will be able to:

- talk about health and illness
- describe aches and parts of the body
- express probable outcomes
- express yourself precisely with the subjunctive and the indicative
- talk about future activities

Cultures

By the end of this chapter you will have learned about:

- Equatorial Guinea, Morocco, and the Canary Islands (Spain)
- healing properties of typical foods in Equatorial Guinea, Morocco, and the Canary Islands
- immigration issues between Europe and Africa
- Eric Moussambani, an Equatorial Guinean Olympic swimmer
- specialized medical language

Standards: Spanish-speaking Africa is frequently not included in the first year curriculum. Here students acquire knowledge about the estimated 700,000 Spanish-speakers in Africa.

Optional: You may want to point out that the Kingdom of Morocco was one of the first countries abroad to recognize American independence formally in 1777. Morocco's Sultan enjoyed correspondence with Benjamin Franklin that led to a peace treaty with the African nation in 1780.

Un médico habla con su paciente sobre sus síntomas y cómo se siente hoy.

EL BIENESTAR

El bienestar se refiere no solamente a la salud física sino a la salud mental también. Cada persona tiene su propia manera de poner en equilibrio su vida—sea el ejercicio, los deportes, la reflexión y la meditación o la dieta y la nutrición. En este capítulo vamos a explorar las prácticas y los problemas que se relacionan con el bienestar.

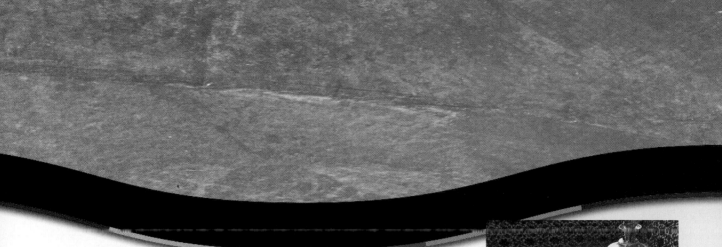

Los datos

Standards: Here students connect their Spanish studies to medicine and health (C 3.1).

Mira los datos sobre los ingredientes de unos platos típicos de Marruecos, Guinea Ecuatorial y las Islas Canarias y sus beneficios para la salud. Luego, di si las siguientes oraciones son ciertas o falsas.

Los datos answers: 1. F 2. C 3. F 4. C 5. C 6. C

Islas Canarias	Marruecos	Guinea Ecuatorial
berros (*watercress*): alergias, artritis; plato: potaje de berros	**menta:** resfriados, gripe; plato: té de menta	**ajo:** corazón, sangre, antibiótico natural; plato: salsa de pili-pili
perejil (*parsley*): asma, contusiones; plato: mojo verde (con cilantro)	**canela** (*cinnamon*): náuseas, estómago; plato: keftas (*meatballs*)	**cardamomo:** estómago, intestinos; plato: sopa de pollo con cardamomo

El té de menta

① _____ El ajo es beneficioso para las personas con alergias.
② _____ Si tienes asma, debes comer mojo verde.
③ _____ La menta y la canela son buenas para los resfriados.
④ _____ El cardamomo y la canela benefician el estómago.
⑤ _____ El potaje de berros puede mejorar la artritis.
⑥ _____ El ajo puede combatir las bacterias.

¡Adivina!

¿Qué sabes de las Islas Canarias, Marruecos y Guinea Ecuatorial? Indica si las siguientes oraciones se refieren a las Islas Canarias, Marruecos, Guinea Ecuatorial o a una combinación de los tres. (Las respuestas están en la página 382.)

① Estas islas forman una de las diecisiete comunidades autónomas de España.
② Este país comprende cinco islas en la costa oeste de África.
③ Dos ciudades ubicadas (*located*) en este país—Ceuta y Melilla—son plazas de soberanía (*sovereignty*) española.
④ El español es la lengua oficial.
⑤ Aunque es una parte de España, hay mucha influencia africana aquí.
⑥ Es el país africano más cercano a Europa.

¡Adivina! answers: 1. Islas Canarias 2. Guinea Ecuatorial 3. Marruecos 4. Guinea Ecuatorial, Islas Canarias 5. Islas Canarias 6. Marruecos

363

¡IMAGÍNATE!

Vocabulario útil 1

JAVIER:	Dime, ¿qué **síntomas** tienes?
BETO:	Uy, tengo **una tos** terrible y **estornudo** muchísimo.
JAVIER:	¿Te tomaste la temperatura?
BETO:	Sí. Parece que tengo **fiebre**. También **me duele la garganta**. ¡Y no se me quita este **dolor de cabeza**!

Notice: Be sure to emphasize cognates (**estómago**), associations with Latin-based medical terms (**ojos** and ophthalmology), and exceptions like **la mano.**

Suggestion: While presenting body parts, get students out of their seats and present vocabulary through movement, pointing at the body parts during presentation and later through TPR-type activities like the game "Simon says"/"**Simón dice.**" For example, **Simón dice: toca la nariz / mueve la cabeza,** etc.

EL CUERPO

el corazón	*heart*
la garganta	*throat*
el pulmón (los pulmones)	*lung(s)*
la sangre	*blood*
el tobillo...	*ankle . . .*
quebrado / roto	*broken*
torcido	*twisted*

Optional: Drawing activities where students sketch and label body parts are a good follow-up to reinforce the vocabulary.

Heritage Learners: Remind students, especially heritage learners, that possessive adjectives are not used when talking about body parts: **Me duele *la* cabeza,** not **Me duele *mi* cabeza.**

LOS SÍNTOMAS

el catarro/el resfriado

el dolor de cabeza

la tos

el dolor de garganta

la fractura

la fiebre

la herida

el dolor de estómago
las náuseas

Use **tener** to say you have an allergy: **Tengo alergia a la penicilina.** Use **tener** or **sentir** to say you are nauseous: **Tengo náuseas después de comer. Siento náuseas cuando viajo por avión.**

la alergia	*allergy*	**la gripe**	*flu*
la enfermedad	*sickness, illness*	**la infección**	*infection*

Suggestion: While presenting these, dramatize the maladies. Students can be assigned specific words to act out; their classmates guess which concepts they are trying communicate.

cortarse	*to cut oneself*
desmayarse	*to faint*
dolerle (ue) (a uno)	*to hurt*
estar congestionado(a)	*to be congested*
estar mareado(a)	*to feel dizzy*
estornudar	*to sneeze*
lastimarse	*to hurt, injure oneself*
palpitar	*to palpitate*
resfriarse	*to get chilled; to catch cold*
toser	*to cough*
vomitar	*to throw up*

Doler follows the same pattern as the verb **gustar: Me duele el estómago. / Le duelen las rodillas.**

Actividades

ACTIVIDAD 1 **Beto.** Beto no se siente nada bien. Completa sus comentarios con las conclusiones más lógicas de la segunda columna.

Answers Act. 1: 1. j 2. f 3. d 4. h / i 5. h / i 6. a 7. e 8. b

1. _____ Me corté el dedo.
2. _____ Estaba mareado.
3. _____ Tuve náuseas.
4. _____ Estoy estornudando mucho.
5. _____ Estoy congestionado.
6. _____ No quiero comer.
7. _____ Tengo mucho calor.
8. _____ Me caí y me lastimé el tobillo.

a. Tengo dolor de estómago.
b. Tengo el tobillo torcido.
c. Me lastimé el hombro.
d. Vomité.
e. Tengo fiebre.
f. Me desmayé.
g. Tengo una fractura en la mano.
h. Tengo alergia en la primavera.
i. Tengo catarro.
j. Me salió sangre.

Answers Act. 2: 1. las piernas, los pies 2. la oreja, el oído 3. los dedos, la mano 4. los pulmones, la nariz, la boca 5. la nariz 6. los ojos 7. el estómago 8. la mano, los dedos 9. el codo 10. los ojos

 ACTIVIDAD 2 **El cuerpo.** ¿Qué parte o partes del cuerpo usas para hacer las siguientes cosas?

1. para caminar
2. para oír
3. para tocar la guitarra
4. para respirar
5. para oler
6. para leer
7. para la digestión
8. para escribir
9. para doblar el brazo
10. para llorar

ACTIVIDAD 3 **Una vez...** Con un(a) compañero(a), háganse las siguientes preguntas sobre la salud.

- ¿Qué tuviste la última vez que estabas enfermo(a)?
- ¿Te has roto (*Have you broken*) el brazo o la pierna alguna vez? ¿Cómo ocurrió?
- ¿Tienes alergia a alguna comida o medicina? Explica.
- ¿Qué haces cuando tienes gripe?
- ¿Te has desmayado (*Have you fainted*) alguna vez? Explica.
- ¿Tienes náuseas en ciertas situaciones? ¿Cuáles?
- ¿Has tenido (*Have you had*) una fractura o una herida alguna vez? ¿Cómo ocurrió?

(5) **Standards / Optional:** You may want to alert students that there are volunteer or service learning opportunities in many communities where Spanish students can help local Spanish-speaking populations fill out general medical history and personal data forms in clinics without being completely fluent in both languages. (C 5.1)

Vocabulario útil 2

JAVIER: Pobre hombre. ¿Quieres que te lleve al **médico?**

BETO: No, hombre, no es para tanto. Creo que es una gripe, es todo. Me tomé unas aspirinas y voy a **guardar cama** unos cuantos días a ver si se me pasa.

You can use **el (la) doctor(a)** or **el (la) médico(a)** to refer to a medical doctor in Spanish. Even **la médico** has been popularized recently.

Heritage Learners: Medical vocabulary presents a good opportunity to review / practice Spanish and English spelling rules. Point out that English *ph-* corresponds to Spanish **f-** (*pharmacy*, **farmacia**). English *psy-* in words like *psychiatry* and *psychology* are usually spelled with **si-** or **psi-** in Spanish: **(p)siquiatría** and **(p)sicología,** respectively. Note also that the suffix *-ology* corresponds to **-ología** in Spanish, with an accent. In addition, remind heritage language students that the initial **h** in words like **hepatitis, hospital,** and **homeopático** is silent. For more spelling rules, see ¡**Fíjate!** p. 368.

EN EL CONSULTORIO DEL MÉDICO

el chequeo médico	*physical, checkup*	**la sala de emergencias**	*emergency room*
la cita	*appointment*	**la sala de espera**	*waiting room*
la clínica	*clinic*	**la salud**	*health*

INSTRUCCIONES Y PREGUNTAS

Lo (La) voy a examinar.	*I'm going to examine you.*	**Abra la boca.**	*Open your mouth.*
¿Qué le duele?	*What hurts?*	**Respire hondo.**	*Breathe deeply.*
¿Qué síntomas tiene?	*What are your symptoms?*	**Saque la lengua.**	*Stick out your tongue.*
		Trague.	*Swallow.*

Le voy a...
... hacer un análisis de sangre / orina.
... poner una inyección.

I'm going to . . .
. . . *give you a blood / urine test.*
. . . *give you an injection.*

... poner una vacuna.	... *vaccinate you.*
... recetar una medicina.	... *prescribe a medicine.*
... tomar la presión.	... *take your blood pressure.*
... tomar la temperatura.	... *take your temperature.*
... tomar una radiografía.	... *take an X-ray.*

CONSEJOS

Le aconsejo que...	*I advise you to . . .*
... coma alimentos nutritivos.	*. . . eat healthy foods.*
... duerma más.	*. . . sleep more.*
... guarde cama.	*. . . stay in bed.*
... haga ejercicio regularmente.	*. . . exercise regularly.*
... lleve una vida sana.	*. . . lead a healthy life.*
¡Ojalá se mejore pronto!	*Hopefully you'll get better soon!*

Actividades

ACTIVIDAD 4 Los síntomas. Los pacientes le describen sus síntomas a la doctora Ruiz. ¿Cómo responde la doctora? En parejas, túrnense para hacer los papeles de la doctora y del (de la) paciente. Pueden usar las respuestas sugeridas en la segunda columna o pueden inventar sus propias respuestas.

MODELO: El (La) paciente: Tengo fiebre y dolor de cabeza.
La Dra. Ruiz: *Le voy a tomar la temperatura.*

1. _____ Me está palpitando mucho el corazón.

2. _____ Necesito perder peso.

3. _____ Voy a viajar a Guinea Ecuatorial.

4. _____ Me rompí la pierna esquiando.

5. _____ Estoy muy cansado y congestionado.

6. _____ Hay mucha diabetes en mi familia.

7. _____ No tengo tiempo para cocinar. Siempre como comida rápida.

8. _____ Me duele mucho la garganta.

a. Le aconsejo que guarde cama.

b. Le voy a tomar la presión.

c. Le voy a poner una vacuna contra la hepatitis.

d. Le voy a hacer un análisis de sangre.

e. Le aconsejo que haga ejercicio regularmente.

f. Le voy a recetar una medicina.

g. Le voy a tomar una radiografía.

h. Le aconsejo que coma alimentos nutritivos.

ACTIVIDAD 5 ¡Estoy enfermo(a)! Con un(a) compañero(a), representa la siguiente situación: uno de ustedes está muy enfermo(a) y le describe su situación al (a la) doctor(a). El (La) doctor(a) te examina y te da consejos. Túrnense para hacer los papeles de paciente y médico.

MODELOS: Compañero(a): *¿Cómo está de salud?*
Tú: *No muy bien. El otro día me desmayé y estoy muy congestionado(a).*
Compañero(a): *¿Qué otros síntomas tiene?*
Tú: *Pues, no duermo muy bien por la noche...*

¡FÍJATE!

El lenguaje médico

Adenopatias laterocervicales, inguinales y axilares, exantema máculo-papuloso muy pruriginoso, hepatoesplenomegalia, nefromegalia con insuficiencia hepática aguda durante su estancia en el hospital, meningitis aséptica.

Como lo demuestra (*demonstrates*) el texto de arriba, la medicina tiene su propio lenguaje altamente especializado que puede resultar incomprensible para las personas que no tienen entrenamiento técnico. Sin embargo, muchos términos médicos son similares en inglés y español, debido a que el vocabulario médico y científico tiene sus raíces (*roots*) en el latín y el griego. Esto permite que un médico que no habla español comprenda el informe médico anterior. Para facilitar la comprensión de los términos científicos y médicos sólo basta con tener en consideración algunas correspondencias básicas entre las dos lenguas.

español		inglés	
f-	farmacia, física	ph-	pharmacy, physics
(p)si-	(p)sicología, (p)siquiatría	psy-	psychology, psychiatry
inm-	inmunología	imm-	immunology
c-	cólera, tecnología	ch-	cholera, technology
-ología	oncología, dermatología	-ology	oncology, dermatology
t-	terapia, patología	th-	therapy, pathology
-ólogo	patólogo, ginecólogo	-ologist	pathologist, gynecologist

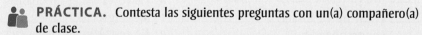 **PRÁCTICA.** Contesta las siguientes preguntas con un(a) compañero(a) de clase.

1. Consideren el informe médico. ¿Comprenden de qué se trata? ¿Reconocen algunas palabras?
2. ¿Qué vocabulario especializado emplea el campo profesional en el cual está interesado cada uno de ustedes? Hagan una lista de cinco palabras para cada campo profesional.
3. ¿Por qué existen los lenguajes técnicos? ¿Qué función cumplen estas lenguas para los que las usan?

Optional: You may want to point out any special classes that your university offers in Spanish for the health professionals or medical Spanish.

Vocabulario útil 3

DULCE: ¿No **te recetó** nada el médico? Puedo pasar por **la farmacia** para recogértelo.

BETO: No necesito **medicinas** sino compañía agradable. ¿Por qué no vienes a visitarme?

Pharmacies in most Spanish-speaking countries focus more on selling medications and remedies and less on toiletries, cosmetics, and other products, as in the U.S. The **farmacia** often substitutes for a visit to a doctor for routine injuries or illnesses, because the pharmacists in Spanish-speaking countries are trained to diagnose and treat minor problems.

EN LA FARMACIA

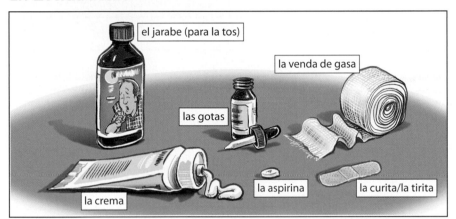

el jarabe (para la tos)
la venda de gasa
las gotas
la crema
la aspirina
la curita/la tirita
las muletas
el yeso

el antibiótico	*antibiotic*	**la píldora**	*pill*
las hierbas	*herbs*	**la receta**	*prescription*
la pastilla	*tablet*	**la vitamina**	*vitamin*

Optional: Have students design survey questions about health habits, for example: ¿**Tomas vitaminas todos los días?**

Actividades

ACTIVIDAD 6 **¿Qué te recetó el médico?** Tu compañero(a) no se siente bien. Tú eres su médico(a). ¿Qué le recetas o aconsejas?

MODELO: Compañero(a): Tengo una tos horrible.
Tú: *Le voy a recetar un jarabe para la tos.*

1. Tengo un dolor de cabeza fuerte.
2. Me rompí el brazo.
3. No puedo dormir.
4. Me siento muy cansado(a).
5. Tengo una gripe muy fuerte.
6. Me pusieron un yeso porque me rompí la pierna.
7. Me corté el dedo.
8. Tengo los ojos muy rojos.
9. Me duelen los oídos.
10. Tengo dolor de espalda.
11. Me duele la garganta.
12. Tengo la piel muy seca.

Answers Act. 6: *Answers may vary.* 1. Tómese estas aspirinas. 2. Le voy a poner un yeso. 3. Le voy a recetar unas píldoras para dormir. 4. Tómese estas vitaminas. 5. Le voy a recetar unos antibióticos. 6. Va a necesitar unas muletas. 7. Póngase esta curita. 8. Le voy a recetar unas gotas. 9. Le voy a recetar unas gotas. 10. Le voy a recetar unas pastillas. 11. Le voy a recetar unos antibióticos. 12. Va a tener que comprar una crema para la piel.

Optional: Ask students about their personal experiences with **yesos** and **muletas**. Get students to tell their stories; this provides a good review of the past tenses and **hace** + expressions of time.

¡Imagínate!   369

Antes de ver el video

 For additional
practice, do the
Nexos website and / or CD-ROM
video exercises.

ACTIVIDAD 1 El episodio de este capítulo se enfoca en Beto, que está enfermo. Javier habla con él en su apartamento y Dulce lo llama por teléfono. Mira las fotos y las conversaciones de las páginas 364 y 366, y luego llena la tabla con los síntomas que identifiques.

Síntomas
está estornudando, tiene una tos...

 ACTIVIDAD 2 ¿Qué cosas hacen los amigos para ayudar a alguien que está enfermo? En parejas hagan una lista de por lo menos cuatro cosas que pueden hacer para ayudar a una persona que esté enferma.

¿Qué puedes hacer para ayudar a un(a) amigo(a) enfermo(a)?
1.
2.
3.
4.

Optional: Try a dictation to illustrate the pronunciation differences: **1.** la fiebre **2.** el síntoma **3.** la píldora **4.** la náusea **5.** el vómito **6.** la diarrea **7.** la fatiga **8.** la infección **9.** el antibiótico

ESTRATEGIA

Listening for cognates and key words

As you have learned throughout your study of Spanish, when listening to authentic speech, it is important to listen for key words to help you get the general meaning of what is being said. In this chapter's video segment, many of the key words are related to illness and remedies, and many of these words are cognates with English. However, while you might recognize these words immediately in their written form, you must listen carefully for them, since they are pronounced quite differently in Spanish and in English.

ACTIVIDAD 3 Trabaja con un(a) compañero(a) de clase y túrnense para pronunciar estos cognados. Fíjense en las diferencias del inglés que se oyen al pronunciarlos. Luego, mientras ves el video, pon un círculo alrededor de los cognados que oigas.

Answers Act. 3: paciente, síntomas, médico, medicinas, aspirinas, farmacia, temperatura

Cognados relacionados con la salud

paciente	hospital	síntomas	emergencia
apendicitis	médico	medicinas	drogas
aspirinas	inyección	farmacia	temperatura

El video

Mira el episodio del video para el **Capítulo 12.** No te olvides de identificar las palabras que oigas de la **Actividad 3.**

Después de ver el video

ACTIVIDAD 4 Pon un círculo alrededor de la palabra o las palabras clave en cada oración. El número entre paréntesis te indica el número de palabras clave que debes marcar.

1. **Javier:** Dime, ¿qué síntomas tienes? (1)
2. **Beto:** Uy, tengo una tos horrible y estornudo muchísimo. (2)
3. **Javier:** ¿Te tomaste la temperatura? (1)
4. **Beto:** Sí. Parece que tengo fiebre. También me duele la garganta. (2)
5. **Beto:** ¡Y no se me quita este dolor de cabeza! (2)
6. **Javier:** ¿Quieres que te lleve al médico? (2)
7. **Beto:** Creo que es una gripe, es todo... voy a guardar cama unos cuantos días a ver si se me pasa. (3)

Preparation: Depending on the level of your class, you may want to generate a definition of **palabra(s) clave** before you begin the activity. Or, have students work in pairs.

Answers Act. 4: *Answers may vary.*
1. síntomas 2. tos, estornudo
3. temperatura 4. fiebre, garganta
5. dolor, cabeza 6. lleve, médico 7. gripe, guardar, cama

 ACTIVIDAD 5 Ahora, trabaja con un(a) compañero(a) de clase. Comparen sus respuestas en la **Actividad 4.** ¿Escogieron las mismas palabras clave? Si no, hablen de por qué escogieron ciertas palabras.

 ACTIVIDAD 6 Contesten las siguientes preguntas sobre el video. Usen las palabras clave para encontrar las respuestas.

1. ¿Qué síntomas tiene Beto?
2. ¿Qué ofrece hacer Javier?
3. ¿Qué prefiere hacer Beto por unos días?
4. ¿Qué cosas le da Javier a Beto?
5. ¿Qué le va a traer Javier a Beto después de las clases?
6. ¿Qué enfermedad tiene Beto, según su conversación con Dulce?
7. ¿Qué ofrece hacer Dulce?
8. ¿Qué prefiere Beto que haga Dulce?

Answers Act. 6: 1. estornuda, tiene tos, fiebre, dolor de garganta, dolor de cabeza 2. llevarlo al médico
3. guardar cama 4. aspirinas y agua
5. algo caliente (como una sopa de pollo) y unos videos 6. la gripe 7. pasar por la farmacia para recogerle la medicina
8. que venga a visitarlo

ACTIVIDAD 7 ¿Qué pasa cuando se enferman ustedes? En grupos de tres a cuatro estudiantes, cada persona debe completar la siguiente tabla. Luego, juntos escriban un resumen de sus respuestas.

(5) Standards / Optional: Have students look for local Spanish-speaking communities by asking them to look for advertisements of doctors, dentists, or other health care workers who advertise in Spanish in the Yellow Pages. Ask them to bring an example of an advertisement to class. (C 5.1)

¿Crees que es una buena idea que los pacientes vean médicos de la misma nacionalidad cuando sea posible? Por ejemplo, los latinos componen aproximadamente el 35% de la población de California, pero se estima que sólo el 4% de los médicos de ese estado son latinos. ¿Cuál es tu opinión? To learn more about Dr. Emilio Carrillo and his intercultural views on medicine, visit the *Nexos* website (http://college.hmco.com/languages/spanish/students) and follow the links.

Cuando tienes resfriado o una gripe ligera (*light*)…	Sí	No
¿guardas cama?		
¿vas al médico?		
¿tomas medicinas como aspirinas o jarabes para la tos?		
¿vas a clases?		
¿duermes mucho?		
¿sales con los amigos?		
¿vas a la biblioteca?		
¿comes alimentos especiales?		
¿bebes mucha agua?		
¿haces ejercicio?		
¿les pides consejos a tus amigos?		

 Conexión cultural. Mira el segmento cultural que está al final del episodio. Después, en grupos de tres o cuatro, comparen lo que hace la gente en su país cuando sale para divertirse con lo que acabas de ver en el video.

VOCES DE LA COMUNIDAD

El Dr. Emilio Carrillo

"En la sociedad multicultural de hoy, para ofrecer cuidado médico de calidad, los doctores tienen que comprender cómo las experiencias socio-culturales de los pacientes afectan sus creencias y comportamiento hacia asuntos (*behavior toward things*) relacionados con la salud."

Los médicos más eficientes se enfocan no sólo en el cuidado fisiológico de sus pacientes sino también en sus necesidades emocionales, sociales y culturales. Por esta razón, el doctor Emilio Carrillo, director médico del New York Hospital Community Health Plan y profesor de la Facultad de Medicina de la Universidad de Cornell, ha creado un currículum para los residentes médicos con énfasis en la competencia intercultural. Carrillo también es co-fundador de la Organización Nacional Boricua / Latina de Salud, una organización estudiantil con la misión de aumentar el número de latinos en las profesiones médicas y de educar al público sobre temas relacionados con la salud de la población latina. En 1997, Carrillo recibió el prestigioso premio de la Asociación Médica Nacional de Hispanos por su labor en pro de los latinos y su investigación en los campos del cuidado médico primario y la prevención de enfermedades.

¡PREPÁRATE!

Gramática útil 1
Expressing possible outcomes: The subjunctive and indicative with conjunctions

Alivio más rápido.
Tan pronto abras el frasco de Vicks® VapoRub®, sentirás la sensación de respirar con mayor facilidad. Ni las pastillas ni el jarabe pueden hacer esto.
Alivio rápido.

Siga las indicaciones.   www.vicks.com

For more practice of chapter topics, do the *Nexos* website exercises.

Look at the ad for a salve that helps with respiratory problems and identify the verb used in the subjunctive. Can you explain why the subjunctive is used here?

Answer: **abras;** subjunctive is necessary because it is used with **tan pronto** (**como** is implied).

CÓMO USARLO

LO BÁSICO

A *conjunction* is a word or phrase that links two clauses in a sentence. In the sentence **Voy a llamar a la farmacia para que tenga lista tu receta, para que** is the conjunction.

1. As you have learned so far in your study of the subjunctive mood, your decision to use the subjunctive often depends on what you are expressing. The subjunctive is used after verbs or expressions of *uncertainty, doubt, disbelief, volition, negation,* and *emotion.*

2. Certain conjunctions also require the use of the subjunctive. With some conjunctions, the subjunctive is always used. With other conjunctions, either the subjunctive or the indicative may be used, depending upon the context.

Remember that the situations referred to in number 1 are places where the subjunctive is used in a dependent clause that begins with **que.**

¡Prepárate!   **373**

3. The following groups of conjunctions are either used with the subjunctive only, or may be used with both the subjunctive and the indicative.

♦ Conjunctions that require the subjunctive:

a menos que	*unless*	**en caso de que**	*in case*
antes (de) que	*before*	**para que**	*so that*
con tal (de) que	*so that, provided that*	**sin que**	*without*

♦ Conjunctions that may be used with the subjunctive or indicative, depending on context:

aunque	*although*	**en cuanto**	*as soon as*
cuando	*when*	**hasta que**	*until*
después (de) que	*after*	**tan pronto como**	*as soon as*

4. Examine the following sentences to see how and when the subjunctive is used.

No te vas a mejorar **a menos que *tomes*** tu medicina todos los días.	*You won't get better **unless you take** your medicine every day.*
El médico dice que puedo hacer ejercicio **con tal de que no *me sienta*** peor.	*The doctor says I can exercise **as long as I don't feel** worse.*
Voy a ir al hospital **en cuanto *llegue*** Nati de la oficina.	*I'm going to the hospital **as soon as** Nati **arrives** from the office (whenever that may be).*
Fui al hospital **en cuanto *llegó*** Nati de la oficina.	*I went to the hospital **as soon as** Nati **arrived** from the office (she has already arrived).*
Debes quedarte en cama **hasta que** nos ***llame*** el médico.	*You should stay in bed **until** the doctor **calls** us (whenever that may be).*
Cuando estás enfermo, te quedas en cama **hasta que** te ***llama*** el médico.	*When you are sick, you stay in bed **until** the doctor **calls** you (habitual action).*

5. In the case of the conjunctions that require the subjunctive, the subjunctive is used because the action expressed in the dependent clause has not yet taken place and is an unrealized event, with respect to the action described in the main clause.

Voy al hospital **antes de que venga** la niñera.	*I'm going to the hospital **before** the babysitter **arrives.** (I'm leaving now, she's not here, I don't know when she will come.)*

6. With conjunctions that may be used with the subjunctive or the indicative, the use of subjunctive or indicative depends upon whether or not the action described is habitual (indicative), whether it has already occurred (indicative), or whether it has yet to occur (subjunctive).

Siempre voy al hospital **tan pronto como viene** la niñera.	*I always go to the hospital **as soon as** the babysitter **arrives.** (habitual action)*

Suggestion: Students need basic practice with these expressions to reinforce their meaning. Try some examples and open-ended statements like: **Voy a hablar español fuera de clase en cuanto... Voy a estudiar más español para que... Voy a repasar la gramática española hasta que...**

Heritage Learners: Do not assume that heritage language speakers are familiar with conjunctions such as **con tal de que, a menos que,** and **tan pronto como.** Conjunctions such as these are primarily found in the written language, which students may be less familiar with.

Fui al hospital **tan pronto como vino** la niñera.

Voy al hospital **tan pronto como venga** la niñera.

*I went to the hospital **as soon as** the babysitter **arrived.** (past action)*

*I'm going to the hospital **as soon as** the babysitter **arrives.** (future action— I have no idea when it will occur)*

7. Aunque is a slightly different case. When used with the subjunctive, it may mean that the speaker does not know what the current situation is, or is dismissing its importance, whatever it may be. When used with the indicative, it indicates that the situation is, in fact, true.

Aunque esté enfermo, Arturo siempre asiste a sus clases.

Even though he may be sick (we don't know right now if he is sick / it doesn't matter if he is sick or not), Arturo always attends his classes.

Aunque está enfermo, Arturo asiste a sus clases.

Even though he is sick (right now), Arturo attends his classes.

Actividades

ACTIVIDAD 1 **La mamá de Beto.** Completa las recomendaciones de la mamá de Beto con una de las siguientes conjunciones adverbiales: **con tal de que, a menos que, aunque, en caso de que, para que** y **sin que.**

MODELO: Puedes ir a esquiar *con tal de que* no te resfríes.

1. Tienes que ir a la clínica _____ te receten unos antibióticos.

2. No vas a perder peso _____ hagas ejercicio regularmente.

3. Tienes que hablar con el médico _____ necesites una vacuna para tu viaje a Marruecos.

4. No pueden saber si te rompiste el brazo _____ te tomen una radiografía.

5. Si no guardas cama, no te vas a mejorar _____ te tomes todas las medicinas.

6. Puedes jugar tenis todos los días _____ no te lastimes.

ACTIVIDAD 2 **El doctor Serna.** Vas a hacerte tu chequeo médico con el doctor Serna. ¿Qué te dice? Usando elementos de las tres columnas, escribe lo que te dice en oraciones completas. Sigue el modelo.

MODELO: *Te van a llamar cuando esté lista la receta.*

Te van a llamar	en cuanto	guardar cama unos cuantos días
Ve a casa a descansar	hasta que	no empezar a llevar una vida sana
Come algo	después de que	estar lista la receta
Pregunta por mí		dormir bien
Te vas a sentir mejor	tan pronto como	tomarse el antibiótico
Vas a tener más energía	cuando	ir a la farmacia
No vas a estar feliz	antes de que	llamar por los resultados de tu análisis

ACTIVIDAD 3 **A menos que…** Completa las siguientes oraciones. Trabaja con un(a) compañero(a) para completar las oraciones de una manera lógica.

1. Voy a sacar buenas notas este semestre / trimestre a menos que…
2. Necesito hacer ejercicio para que…
3. Pienso viajar después de graduarme de la universidad con tal de que…
4. Voy a tratar de ahorrar mucho dinero en caso de que…
5. No voy a tomar ese curso hasta que…
6. Tengo que hacer una investigación en Internet antes de que…
7. Voy a buscar trabajo tan pronto como…
8. ¿…?

Sonrisas

⑤ Standards: This **Sonrisas** can launch a discussion on ¿Qué es lo que hay que hacer para ayudar a los niños a crecer bien?

 EXPRESIÓN. En grupos de tres a cuatro estudiantes, escriban lemas (*slogans*) para los siguientes productos. Sigan el modelo y ¡sean creativos!

MODELO: una almohada (*pillow*) para viajeros
Para que siempre duermas bien, no importa dónde estés.

1. el agua mineral
2. el asiento de seguridad para los bebés
3. una bebida fortificada para deportistas
4. unos zapatos atléticos
5. un casco (*helmet*) para los ciclistas
6. un abrigo de invierno

Gramática útil 2
Expressing yourself precisely: Choosing between the subjunctive and indicative moods

In this and the last few chapters, you have learned the basic situations and contexts in which the subjunctive mood is used. Here is a summary that contrasts their uses in general.

Use the subjunctive.

- after expressions of emotion

  Me alegro de **que te sientas** mejor.
  Es una lástima **que estés** enfermo.

- after expressions of doubt and uncertainty

  Dudo **que** el médico **sepa** la respuesta.
  No es verdad **que** los antibióticos siempre **sean** un remedio eficaz.

- after impersonal expressions, **ojalá,** and verbs expressing opinions, wishes, desires, and influence

  Es importante **que sigas** las instrucciones de la enfermera.
  Ojalá **tengamos** tiempo para comer una cena nutritiva hoy.
  Mis amigos quieren **que** yo **vaya** con ellos al gimnasio.

- in a **que** clause to refer to unknown or nonexistent situations

  Busco un médico **que tenga** experiencia con medicina geriátrica.

- after certain conjunctions to refer to events that have not yet taken place or that may not take place

  Voy a llamar al médico para que te **dé** una receta.
  Antes de que **vayas** al médico, debes hacer una lista de preguntas.
  Voy a la farmacia en cuanto **salga** del trabajo.

- after **aunque** to express situations that may or may not be true, or are considered irrelevant

  Aunque el médico no **esté,** voy a su oficina.

Use the indicative:
- after expressions of certainty

  Estoy seguro de que el médico **sabe** la respuesta.

- in a **que** clause with known or definite situations

  Sé que tu médico **tiene** experiencia con medicina geriátrica.

- after certain conjunctions to express past or habitual actions

  Elena salió para el hospital después de que yo **llegué.**
  Siempre duermo cuando **llego** del trabajo.

- after **aunque** when a situation is a reality

  Aunque ya **es** tarde, voy a llamar al médico.

Remember that all these uses of the subjunctive are either in a dependent clause that begins with **que** or a conjunction (such as **cuando** or **para que**), or after **ojalá.**

Suggestion: Point out the Appendix at the back of the book that lists verbs conjugated by tense and mode for reference.

Dudo que estés de ánimo para tener compañía.

Use an infinitive:

◆ after expressions of emotion when there is no change of subject

Estoy contenta de **sentirme** mejor.

◆ after verbs of volition or influence when there is no change of subject

Mis amigos quieren **ir** al gimnasio.

◆ after impersonal expressions to make generalized statements

Es importante **seguir** las instrucciones de la enfermera.

Actividades

Answers Act. 4: 1. No lo conoce.
2. No la conoce. 3. Lo conoce. 4. No lo
conoce. 5. La conoce. 6. Lo conoce.

ACTIVIDAD 4 **En el consultorio.** Estás en la sala de espera del consultorio y escuchas a varias personas comentar sobre diferentes personas. Según lo que dicen, ¿conocen o no conocen a las personas que mencionan? Escucha los comentarios y luego marca la respuesta apropiada.

MODELO: Escuchas: ¿Me puedes recomendar un médico que me ayude con mis alergias?
Marcas: ✓ No lo / la conoce.

1. _____ Lo / La conoce.
   _____ No lo / la conoce.

2. _____ Lo / La conoce.
   _____ No lo / la conoce.

3. _____ Lo / La conoce.
   _____ No lo / la conoce.

4. _____ Lo / La conoce.
   _____ No lo / la conoce.

5. _____ Lo / La conoce.
   _____ No lo / la conoce.

6. _____ Lo / La conoce.
   _____ No lo / la conoce.

Answers Act. 5: 1. me llamaste
2. eches de menos 3. tomes, se acaben
4. puedas 5. quieres 6. te vas 7. te aburras
8. te sientas 9. quieras

ACTIVIDAD 5 **El buen amigo.** Un buen amigo va a visitar a su colega que acaba de salir del hospital. Completa sus comentarios con los verbos entre paréntesis. Piensa bien si se requiere el subjuntivo o el indicativo en cada caso.

MODELO: Me alegro de que (tú / estar) en casa.
Me alegro de que estés en casa.

1. Vine directo a tu casa después de que (tú / llamarme).
2. Dudo que (tú / echar de menos) la comida del hospital.
3. Es importante que (tú / tomar) todos los antibióticos hasta que (acabarse).
4. Es una lástima que no (tú / poder) salir por dos semanas.
5. Sé que no (tú / querer) guardar cama por tanto tiempo.
6. Estoy seguro de que (tú / irte) a recuperar pronto.
7. Te traje unas revistas para que no (tú / aburrirse).
8. Vamos a la playa en cuanto (tú / sentirte) mejor.
9. Llámame cuando (tú / querer).

ACTIVIDAD 6 **Mi salud.** En tu clase de salud, tu profesor te pide que describas tu salud y tus actitudes hacia la salud. Con un(a) compañero(a), escribe siete oraciones que usen las siguientes frases.

MODELO: es importante
Es importante que te hagas un chequeo médico una vez al año.

antes de
Siempre leo todas las instrucciones antes de tomarme las píldoras.

1. cuando
2. dudo que
3. antes de que
4. es importante que
5. estoy seguro(a) de que
6. para que
7. querer

Gramática útil 3
Talking about future activities: The future tense

CÓMO USARLO

Begin the CD-ROM activities. Do the cultural activities and reading and writing practice as you complete the corresponding text sections.

1. You have already learned to use the present tense of **pensar** and **ir** + **a** + infinitive to talk about the future.

Pienso ser enfermera.　　　　*I plan to become a nurse.*
Voy a ir al médico el viernes.　*I'm going to go to the doctor on Friday.*

2. Additionally, Spanish has a separate tense, the future tense, which you can use to talk about events that have not yet occurred. This tense is equivalent to the *will* + infinitive future tense used in English.

Hablaré con el médico cuando pueda.　*I will talk to the doctor when I can.*

3. Most Spanish speakers use **ir** + **a** + infinitive or the present indicative to talk about future events that are about to happen, and the future tense for events that are further away in time or in more formal contexts.

Voy al gimnasio esta tarde.　　*I'm going to the gym this afternoon.*
Voy a correr en el parque mañana.　*I'm going to run in the park tomorrow.*
El próximo mes **iré** a la playa con mi familia.　*Next month I will go to the beach with my family.*

4. Spanish speakers also use the future tense to speculate about current situations.

—¿**Dónde estará** el médico? Hace una hora que lo esperamos.　*Where could the doctor be? We've been waiting for him for an hour.*
—**Tendrá** una emergencia en el hospital.　*He must have an emergency at the hospital.*

Heritage Learners: Sociolinguistic studies have shown that U.S. Spanish favors the **ir** + **a** + infinitive construction over the morphological future. For this reason, heritage learners may need extensive practice with the formation and use of this tense. Also, remind students that, although the progressive (or *-ing* form) can be used in English to refer to future actions (*I'm taking an exam tomorrow*), it can never serve this function in Spanish.

Notice that all foms except the first-person plural (**nosotros**) have a written accent on the final syllable.

Tendrás que tomar mis exámenes también.

Notice: Emphasize pronunciation with the future tense to get the accent on the last syllable.

CÓMO FORMARLO

1. Future-tense endings are the same for **-ar, -er,** and **-ir** verbs. The future endings attach to the end of the *infinitive*, rather than to a verb stem.

yo	-é	hablaré	nosotros / as	-emos	hablaremos
tú	-ás	hablarás	vosotros / as	-éis	hablaréis
Ud. / él / ella	-á	hablará	Uds. / ellos / ellas	-án	hablarán

2. The following verbs are irregular in the future tense. They attach the regular future endings to the irregular stems shown, rather than to the infinitive.

irregular, no pattern		
decir	**dir-**	diré, dirás, dirá, diremos, diréis, dirán
hacer	**har-**	haré, harás, hará, haremos, haréis, harán
e is dropped from infinitive		
poder	**podr-**	podré, podrás, podrá, podremos, podréis, podrán
querer	**querr-**	querré, querrás, querrá, querremos, querréis, querrán
saber	**sabr-**	sabré, sabrás, sabrá, sabremos, sabréis, sabrán
d replaces the final vowel		
poner	**pondr-**	pondré, pondrás, pondrá, pondremos, pondréis, pondrán
salir	**saldr-**	saldré, saldrás, saldrá, saldremos, saldréis, saldrán
tener	**tendr-**	tendré, tendrás, tendrá, tendremos, tendréis, tendrán
venir	**vendr-**	vendré, vendrás, vendrá, vendremos, vendréis, vendrán

3. The future tense of **hay** is **habrá.**

Habrá una reunión en el hospital el viernes.

There will be a meeting in the hospital on Friday.

Actividades

Answers Act. 7: 1. Sí, (No, no) perderé peso este año. 2. Sí, (No, no) haré ejercicio cinco veces por semana. 3. Sí, (No, no) pondré más atención en lo que como. 4. Sí, (No, no) tendré más tiempo para descansar. 5. Sí, (No, no) saldré menos en días de entresemana. 6. Sí, (No, no) seguiré las recomendaciones del médico. 7. Sí, (No, no) dormiré ocho horas al día. 8. Sí, (No, no) llevaré una vida sana desde hoy en adelante.

ACTIVIDAD 7 **El Año Nuevo.** Todos resolvemos cambiar de hábitos para el Año Nuevo. Vas a escuchar dos veces unas preguntas sobre tus resoluciones. Di si harás o no harás lo que se pregunta. Escribe las respuestas en oraciones completas. Primero estudia el modelo.

MODELO: Escuchas: ¿Vas a hacer una cita para un chequeo médico?

Escribes: *Sí, haré una cita para un chequeo médico.*

O: *No, no haré una cita para un chequeo médico.*

ACTIVIDAD 8 **¿Qué les pasará?** Ahora que conoces a los personajes del video, vas a tratar de predecir qué les va a pasar en el futuro. Escribe por lo menos dos oraciones para cada personaje (o personajes) en la lista.

MODELO: Sergio y Javier
Sergio y Javier serán atletas profesionales. Viajarán por todo el mundo para competir en torneos internacionales.

1. Beto
2. Anilú
3. Chela
4. Sergio y Javier
5. Dulce y Beto
6. Dulce

Posibles futuros:

ser [¿qué profesión?]
trabajar [¿dónde?]
casarse [¿con quién?]
salir [¿con quién?]
tener [¿cuántos?] hijos
vivir en [¿qué ciudad?]
viajar [¿adónde?]
hacer [¿...?]
saber [¿...?]
¿...?

ACTIVIDAD 9 **¿Qué hará el doctor?** Estás en el consultorio y especulas sobre qué hará o no hará el doctor para resolver tu problema. ¿Qué te preguntas? Sigue el modelo.

MODELO: tomar una radiografía
¿Me tomará una radiografía?

1. tomar la presión
2. poner una inyección
3. hacer un análisis de sangre
4. recetar unos antibióticos
5. decir que todo está bien
6. haber una solución para mi problema

ACTIVIDAD 10 **El futuro.** Todos tenemos ideas de lo que vamos a hacer en el futuro: dónde vamos a vivir, qué profesión vamos a practicar, qué clase de casa vamos a tener, cómo va a ser nuestra familia y así. Hazle seis preguntas a tu compañero(a) sobre su futuro. Escribe un párrafo que describa el futuro de tu compañero(a) según sus respuestas. Luego, si hay algunas predicciones que tienen en común, explícalas.

MODELO: Las predicciones de mi compañero: *Será programador y trabajará en una compañía que produce juegos para la computadora. Estará casado con tres hijos y tendrá una casa grande en las afueras de Nueva York. Sus hijos asistirán a una escuela privada. Tendrá un Porsche, un Ferrari y un Lamborghini.*
Las predicciones que tenemos en común: *Los dos estaremos casados y tendremos hijos.*

Answers Act. 9: 1. ¿Me tomará la presión? 2. ¿Me pondrá una inyección? 3. ¿Me hará un análisis de sangre? 4. ¿Me recetará unos antibióticos? 5. ¿Me dirá que todo está bien? 6. ¿Habrá una solución para mi problema?

Islas Canarias, Marruecos y Guinea Ecuatorial

Raíces e influencias africanas. En parejas, miren el mapa y las tarjetas de información sobre las tres regiones en las páginas 383–384. Luego, miren los siguientes comentarios y fotos y traten de escribir el número del comentario o de la foto en la categoría correspondiente de la tarjeta del país apropiado. El primer comentario ya está en la categoría correcta y puede servir como ejemplo. Hay tres comentarios y una foto para cada país.

¿Adivinaste? Answers to the questions on page 363: 1. Islas Canarias 2. Guinea Ecuatorial 3. Marruecos 4. Guinea Ecuatorial, Islas Canarias 5. Islas Canarias 6. Marruecos

Standards / Optional: This section offers an opportunity to explore some topics about which American students generally know very little. Use the ¡Conéctate! section to have students search for additional cultural information (C 2.1, 2.2) and explore Spanish-speaking communities (C 5.1) around the world. You may want to assign different topics to different groups (possible topics: How did the Canary Islands become part of Spain? What is the current government or state of economy in Guinea Ecuatorial?) or have students generate their own topics.

Answers: **Canarias:** Geografía 1; Sociedad e historia 5, 7, 11 / **Marruecos:** Geografía 3, 10; Sociedad e historia 6, 9 / **Guinea Ecuatorial:** Gobierno y economía 2; Geografía: 4; Sociedad e historia 8, 12.

Comentarios

1. El Teide es la montaña más alta de toda España.
2. Recientemente se descubrieron reservas petroleras cerca de la costa de este pequeño país, que ahora es una de las regiones más importantes para la exploración petrolera de toda la región africana al sur del desierto del Sahara.
3. Es común hacer una excursión en camello al desierto grande de este país.
4. Hay muchos bosques pluviales (*rain forests*) para explorar en Bioko y Río Muni.
5. Antes de la llegada de los conquistadores españoles, los guanches, una tribu indígena, vivían en estas islas. Después de la conquista estuvieron bajo el control de España.
6. La cocina de este país es notable por sus couscouses, kebabs y su té de menta.
7. Cristóbal Colón hizo una parada (*stop*) en estas islas españolas antes de viajar al Nuevo Mundo.
8. Además de hablar español y francés, los habitantes de este país hablan fang y bubi.
9. Los mercados de artesanía de las ciudades principales de este país son famosos por todo el mundo.

Fotos

10. Las montañas Atlas Mayor son unas de las montañas más altas de toda África.

11. Se celebra el Carnaval con mucho entusiasmo en Santa Cruz de Tenerife.

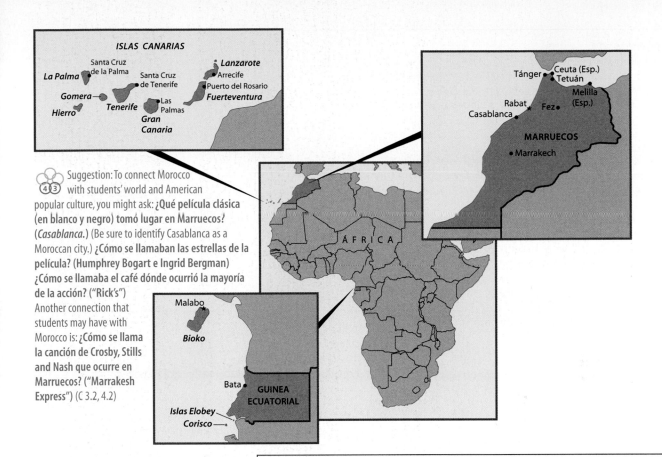

ISLAS CANARIAS

La Palma • Santa Cruz de la Palma
Gomera • Santa Cruz de Tenerife
Hierro • Tenerife
Gran Canaria • Las Palmas

Lanzarote • Arrecife
Puerto del Rosario
Fuerteventura

Tánger • Ceuta (Esp.)
Tetuán
Rabat • Fez • Melilla (Esp.)
Casablanca
MARRUECOS
• Marrakech

ÁFRICA

Malabo
Bioko
Bata • GUINEA ECUATORIAL
Islas Elobey
Corisco

Suggestion: To connect Morocco with students' world and American popular culture, you might ask: **¿Qué película clásica (en blanco y negro) tomó lugar en Marruecos?** (*Casablanca.*) (Be sure to identify Casablanca as a Moroccan city.) **¿Cómo se llamaban las estrellas de la película?** (Humphrey Bogart e Ingrid Bergman) **¿Cómo se llamaba el café dónde ocurrió la mayoría de la acción?** ("Rick's") Another connection that students may have with Morocco is: **¿Cómo se llama la canción de Crosby, Stills and Nash que ocurre en Marruecos?** ("Marrakesh Express") (C 3.2, 4.2)

Las Islas Canarias

Gobierno y economía
- Parte de la Unión Europea, comunidad autónoma de España
- La exportación de flores es una industria importante.

Geografía
- Estas islas cerca de la costa de África son un archipiélago volcánico.
- Hay gran diversidad ecológica, desde un clima tropical hasta desiertos con dunas.

Sociedad e historia
- Turistas vienen aquí de toda Europa para visitar sus playas y disfrutar de su clima templado.
- Hay muchas atracciones en Tenerife, como discotecas, jardines botánicos y un lago artificial.
- La Laguna, la primera capital de Tenerife, tiene muchos edificios coloniales, incluso una casa de 400 años de edad que se ha convertido (*has been converted*) en El Museo de Historia de Tenerife.

12. Se ve la influencia española en las plazas y en la arquitectura de Malabo.

Marruecos

Gobierno y economía

- Se retiró la administración española de Marruecos en 1976, pero las ciudades de Melilla y Ceuta siguen bajo control español.
- Se divide el país en cuatro provincias, cada una con un gobernador designado por el rey (*king*).

Geografía

- El desierto del Sahara Occidental está en este país.
- Tiene costas en el mar Mediterráneo y en el océano Atlántico.
- Las escenas de sus cordilleras de montañas son impresionantes y dramáticas.

Sociedad e historia

- Las paredes blancas y las secciones laberínticas e históricas de ciudades como Rabat y Fez son famosas por todo el mundo.
- La gente habla árabe oficialmente, pero también se oyen el español, el francés y el inglés.
- El golf y el windsurfing son deportes muy populares aquí.

Guinea Ecuatorial

Gobierno y economía

- El jefe del estado es Obiang Nguema.
- Hay un movimiento nacional de liberación contra el gobierno actual.

Geografía

- Comprende varias islas además del territorio continental de África.
- Bioko, la isla más importante, se formó en una erupción volcánica.

Sociedad e historia

- Los grupos indígenas ancestrales de este país son los pigmeos y los bantú.
- Ganó la independencia de España en 1968.
- Entre los meses de octubre y junio en Malabo hay una fiesta de calle permanente que atrae tanto a visitantes como a gente local.

Internet

¡CONÉCTATE!

En grupos de tres o cuatro, hagan una investigación en Internet sobre uno de los siguientes temas. Usen los enlaces sugeridos en el sitio web de *Nexos* (http://college.hmco.com/languages/spanish/students) para ir a otros sitios web posibles. Presenten su informe a la clase.

Tema 1: un itinerario para un viaje por Marruecos que incluya por lo menos cinco sitios de interés

Tema 2: una descripción de Las Hijas del Sol, unas cantantes guineanas que son famosas en España y toda Europa

Tema 3: una descripción breve de las Islas Canarias, con énfasis en las diferencias geográficas entre las islas

Tema 4: ¿...?

¡COMPÁRATE!

To find comparable statistics for the United States, go to the *Nexos* website (http://college.hmco.com/languages/spanish/students) and follow the links.

La inmigración es un dilema mundial. En años recientes han aumentado (*have increased*) los problemas relacionados con la inmigración en Europa. Los inmigrantes dejan sus países de origen por cuestiones de salud, trabajo, política y hambre en busca de una vida mejor. Una vez que entran a un país europeo, pasan fácilmente a otros países de la Unión Europea porque ahora no se requiere un pasaporte para cruzar las fronteras individuales.

Durante 2001, la llegada de inmigrantes a Canarias desde África creció dramáticamente, como las siguientes estadísticas lo muestran (*show*). Además de los inmigrantes legales, también llegan muchos inmigrantes indocumentados, viajando en botes pequeños llamados "pateras", aunque el pasaje a Canarias es peligroso y muchos mueren durante el viaje.

Unos inmigrantes indocumentados en una patera

Heritage Learners: The reading on immigration: Note that **inmigración** is written with **nm**. The double **m** does not exist in Spanish, hence: **inmediatamente, inmenso, comentario**, etc.

	2000	2001
Número de inmigrantes legales a Canarias	895.000	1.300.000 (+45,3%)
Número de inmigrantes indocumentados a Canarias	2.104	2.830 (+34,5%)
Número de inmigrantes indocumentados a Canarias interceptados en pateras en ruta a Canarias y deportados	15.190	17.692 (+16,5%)

Cuando los inmigrantes indocumentados llegan a Canarias, muchas veces viven en condiciones poco saludables mientras buscan trabajo y evitan (*avoid*) a los oficiales de inmigración. Los campamentos para los inmigrantes que esperan la deportación también pueden estar infestados de varias enfermedades y muchas veces les faltan agua potable y suficiente comida.

Actualmente, los gobiernos de los países africanos, de España y de la U.E. consideran soluciones para el problema. Pero mientras las condiciones de vida en África no mejoren, es probable que la inmigración a Canarias sea un problema creciente durante los próximos años del nuevo milenio.

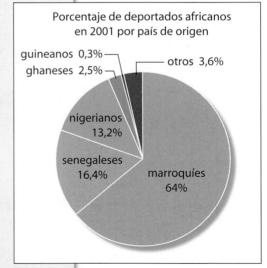

Porcentaje de deportados africanos en 2001 por país de origen

guineanos 0,3%
ghaneses 2,5%
otros 3,6%
nigerianos 13,2%
senegaleses 16,4%
marroquíes 64%

 PRÁCTICA. En grupos de tres a cuatro personas, hablen de los siguientes temas.

1. En su opinión, ¿es la inmigración un problema en EEUU? ¿Por qué sí o no? Comparen la situación en Canarias con la de EEUU.
2. ¿Deben los gobiernos proveer asistencia básica a los inmigrantes indocumentados? ¿Por qué sí o no?
3. Si los otros países no dejan entrar más de un cierto número de inmigrantes legales de cada país, ¿qué puede hacer la gente que vive en países con problemas graves de hambre, guerra, etc.? ¿Debemos ayudar a países con problemas o mantenernos fuera del debate?

A LEER

Antes de leer

Verb tenses can also help you figure out the chronology of events. For example, this article uses the verb **había** (*had*) with past participles (**ido** = *gone*, **hecho** = *done*, **visto** = *seen*, **nadado** = *swum*). This tense, the past perfect, indicates that the actions described occurred prior to other past tense actions. You will learn more about the past perfect in **Capítulo 13.**

Suggestion: As a warm-up, ask your class to name Olympic figures whom they admire and tell why.

Answers Act. 1: 3, 2, 5, 4, 1

ESTRATEGIA

Understanding a chronology

Many newspaper and magazine articles are written to show when certain events occurred over a period of time. You can find these shifts in the timeline by looking for words that signal a transition. When you read the article on pages 387–388, look for words such as **antes de, después de, hace** + time, **luego, durante, ahora,** and **recientemente** to help you order events in time.

ACTIVIDAD 1 Trabaja con un(a) compañero(a) de clase. Juntos hagan una cronología de los eventos de la lista, basándose en las palabras cronológicas y los tiempos de los verbos. Los eventos describen las experiencias de Eric Moussambani, un nadador de Guinea Ecuatorial en las Olimpiadas de Sydney en 2000.

_____ Hace unos meses, Eric compitió en un evento en Canarias y terminó penúltimo (*next to last*).

_____ Durante los Juegos Olímpicos de 2000, Eric se hizo (*became*) famoso por completar su evento con el peor tiempo en más de cien años.

_____ Eric dice que competirá en las Olimpiadas de 2004.

_____ Eric se entrena para los Juegos Olímpicos de 2004.

_____ Antes de los Juegos Olímpicos de 2000, Eric no pudo entrenarse mucho.

 ACTIVIDAD 2 Miren las oraciones de la **Actividad 1.** Para cada oración, indiquen las palabras que les ayudaron a decidir en qué orden debe ir la oración.

Lectura

Answers Act. 3: Durante: Párrafos 1, 2, 4; Inmediatamente después: Párrafo 5, Recientemente: Párrafo 6; En el futuro: Párrafo 7; *Words chosen for right-hand side of table will vary.*

ACTIVIDAD 3 Lee el artículo sobre Eric Moussambani, un nadador guineano que se hizo famoso por su falta de habilidad y entrenamiento. Presta atención particular a la secuencia de los párrafos. Cuando termines la lectura, escribe los números de los párrafos que se refieren a la cronología indicada en la primera columna de la tabla. Luego, vuelve a la lectura para buscar las palabras que te ayudaron a decidir la cronología y escríbelas en la segunda columna.

Orden cronológico	Palabras que indican la cronología (pasado, presente, futuro)
Antes de las Olimpiadas: *Párrafo 3*	*tuvo, antes de, podía, estaba, querían, tenía, había, sabía, temía, pudiera, necesitaba*
Durante las Olimpiadas:	
Inmediatamente después de las Olimpiadas:	
Recientemente:	
En el futuro:	

Eric Moussambani:
Un héroe improbable

Párrafo 1

En el año 2000, Eric Moussambani fue tal vez el atleta más famoso de los Juegos Olímpicos de Sydney. El guineano ecuatorial, que mide[1] sólo cinco pies y medio, tenía 22 años. Cuando entró a la piscina olímpica para completar los 100 metros libres, era la primera vez que había visto una piscina tan grande y llevaba sólo cuatro meses nadando. Nunca había nadado más de 50 metros completos en toda su vida. Entró al agua como atleta desconocido. Salió famoso, recipiente de una ovación tremenda de los espectadores.

Párrafo 2

Eric Moussambani completó su evento con el peor tiempo en más de cien años: 1:52.72, más del triple del récord mundial. Pero sí completó su evento, que no era nada cierto cuando empezó a nadar.

Párrafo 3

En realidad, Eric nunca tuvo la oportunidad de entrenarse mucho antes de ir a los Juegos. Sólo podía entrenarse en los ríos salvajes de su país, llenos de tiburones y caimanes[2], o en piscinas muy pequeñas. No hay una piscina olímpica en toda Guinea Ecuatorial; la más grande es una de 20 metros en un hotel en Malabo. Pero Eric no podía usarla sino cuando estaba vacía[3] y los huéspedes[4] del hotel no querían nadar. Tenía que arreglar sus prácticas para las horas menos populares y había días enteros cuando no podía practicar. No tenía ni entrenador ni tenía un bañador de cuerpo completo[5], como los otros atletas, sino uno más tradicional de pantalones cortos. No sabía hacer los virajes[6] y temía que no pudiera respirar[7] durante el tiempo que necesitaba para nadar 100 metros.

Párrafo 4

Pero cuando llegó su "momento Olímpico" y unos atletas de otros países se descalificaron en vez de competir, Eric tuvo el coraje de entrar a la piscina y completar su evento. Ian Thorpe, la estrella australiana de natación, dijo de Eric: "Vi nadar a Eric en la televisión y fue sorprendente la tremenda ovación que tuvo por parte del público presente. Fue algo increíble. Esto es lo que son las Olimpiadas—es darles la oportunidad a atletas de todo el mundo de nadar en el mayor evento que existe."

Párrafo 5

Después de los Juegos Olímpicos, Eric se hizo famoso y tuvo la oportunidad de viajar por todo el mundo. Sigue hablando con varias compañías de ropa atlética, como Nike y Speedo, sobre la posibilidad de actuar como patrocinador[8] de sus líneas acuáticas. Y, claro, sigue entrenándose y compitiendo.

Párrafo 6

Recientemente finalizó en penúltimo lugar en la Primera Travesía Bahía Gran Tarajal de 800 metros, que tuvo lugar en Fuerteventura, Canarias. Pero Eric se acusa de falta de[9] entrenamiento. "Nadar con olas[10] es muy incómodo y yo no estoy acostumbrado, pero tampoco me preocupa haber quedado[11] en la penúltima posición. Aún me falta mucho para alcanzar[12] mi nivel."

Párrafo 7

Sus esperanzas para el futuro no terminan aquí. Del 2004 dice: "Si yo tuviera[13] un buen entrenador, seguro que podría[14] aspirar a una medalla en los Juegos de Atenas". Ya es cierto que Eric no es la única persona que espera que él tenga la oportunidad de competir otra vez en el escenario mundial.

[1]*measures* [2]**tiburones...** *sharks and crocodiles* [3]*empty* [4]*guests* [5]**bañador...** *full-body bathing suit* [6]*turns* [7]**no...** *he wouldn't be able to breathe* [8]*sponsor* [9]**falta...** *lack of* [10]*waves* [11]**haber...** *to have come in* [12]*achieve* [13]**Si...** *If I had* [14]*I could*

Después de leer

ACTIVIDAD 4 Trabaja con un(a) compañero(a) de clase y contesten las siguientes preguntas sobre la lectura.

1. ¿Qué récord Olímpico batió (*broke*) Eric?

2. ¿Podía entrenarse en una piscina olímpica antes de ir a los Juegos? ¿Por qué?

3. ¿Por qué era peligroso para Eric practicar en los ríos de Guinea Ecuatorial?

4. ¿Cómo reaccionaron los espectadores al ver a Eric nadar?

5. ¿Qué hizo Eric después de las Olimpiadas?

6. ¿Para qué se entrena ahora?

Answers Act. 4: 1. Batió el récord para el peor tiempo en los 100 metros libres en más de cien años. 2. No, porque no hay una piscina olímpica en Guinea Ecuatorial y sólo podía nadar en la piscina del hotel cuando no había huéspedes. 3. Había caimanes y tiburones. 4. Le dieron una ovación tremenda. 5. Viajó por todo el mundo. 6. Se entrena para las Olimpiadas de 2004.

ACTIVIDAD 5 En grupos de tres a cuatro personas, hablen de los siguientes temas.

1. Eric pudo participar en los Juegos Olímpicos de 2000 porque tuvo la suerte de recibir un "wild card" que lo dejó entrar sin tener que calificarse. En su opinión, ¿es eso una idea buena o mala? ¿Por qué?

2. Aunque mucha gente cree que Eric es un héroe por completar su evento, otras personas (entre ellas, muchos guineanos) creen que Eric se convirtió en una broma (*joke*) mundial y que debe tener vergüenza de su récord en las Olimpiadas. ¿Qué opinan? ¿Es héroe o es atleta desacreditado?

3. Ian Thorpe, el nadador australiano, mide seis pies y cuatro pulgadas. Eric es mucho más bajo. En los eventos atléticos, ¿qué importancia tienen los atributos físicos de los atletas y qué importancia tiene el entrenamiento? En su opinión, ¿cuál es más importante? ¿Por qué?

ACTIVIDAD 6 En grupos de tres a cuatro personas, imagínense que son periodistas que acaban de ver nadar a Eric en unas Olimpiadas del futuro. ¿Qué pasó? Escriban un artículo breve de dos párrafos en que incluyen los datos del evento y una cita (*quote*) imaginaria de Eric. ¡Sean creativos!

VOCABULARIO

EL CUERPO   *The body*

la boca	*mouth*
el brazo	*arm*
la cabeza	*head*
el codo	*elbow*
el corazón	*heart*
el cuello	*neck*
el dedo	*finger, toe*
la espalda	*back*
el estómago	*stomach*
la garganta	*throat*
el hombro	*shoulder*
la lengua	*tongue*
la mano	*hand*
la nariz	*nose*
el oído	*inner ear*
los ojos	*eyes*
la oreja	*outer ear*
el pecho	*chest*
el pie	*foot*
la pierna…	*leg*
el pulmón (los pulmones)	*lung(s)*
la sangre	*blood*
el tobillo…	*ankle*
… quebrado / roto	*broken*
… torcido	*twisted*

LOS SÍNTOMAS   *Symptoms*

la alergia	*allergy*
el catarro / el resfriado	*cold*
el dolor…	*pain, ache*
… de cabeza	*headache*
… de estómago	*stomachache*
… de garganta	*sore throat*
la enfermedad	*sickness, illness*
la fiebre	*fever*
la fractura	*fracture*
la gripe	*flu*
la herida	*injury, wound*
la infección	*infection*
las náuseas	*nausea*
la tos	*cough*
cortarse	*to cut oneself*
desmayarse	*to faint*

dolerle (ue) (a uno)	*to hurt*
estar congestionado(a)	*to be congested*
estar mareado(a)	*to feel dizzy*
estornudar	*to sneeze*
lastimarse	*to hurt, injure oneself*
palpitar	*to palpitate*
resfriarse	*to get chilled; to catch cold*
toser	*to cough*
vomitar	*to throw up*

EN EL CONSULTORIO DEL MÉDICO
In the doctor's office

el chequeo médico	*physical, checkup*
la cita	*appointment*
la clínica	*clinic*
la sala de emergencias	*emergency room*
la sala de espera	*waiting room*
la salud	*health*

INSTRUCCIONES Y PREGUNTAS

Lo (La) voy a examinar.	*I'm going to examine you.*
¿Qué le duele?	*What hurts?*
¿Qué síntomas tiene?	*What are your symptoms?*
Abra la boca.	*Open your mouth.*
Respire hondo.	*Breathe deeply.*
Saque la lengua.	*Stick out your tongue.*
Trague.	*Swallow.*
Le voy a…	*I'm going to . . .*
… hacer un análisis de sangre / orina.	*. . . give you a blood/urine test.*
… poner una inyección.	*. . . give you an injection.*
… poner una vacuna.	*. . . vaccinate you.*
… recetar una medicina.	*. . . prescribe a medicine.*
… tomar la presión.	*. . . take your blood pressure.*
… tomar la temperatura.	*. . . take your temperature.*
… tomar una radiografía.	*. . . take an X-ray.*

CONSEJOS   *Advice*

Le aconsejo que...	*I advise you to . . .*
... coma alimentos nutritivos.	*. . . eat healthy foods.*
... duerma más.	*. . . sleep more.*
... guarde cama.	*. . . stay in bed.*
... haga ejercicio regularmente.	*. . . exercise regularly.*
... lleve una vida sana.	*. . . lead a healthy life.*
¡Ojalá se mejore pronto!	*Hopefully you'll get better soon!*

EN LA FARMACIA   *At the pharmacy*

el antibiótico	*antibiotic*
la aspirina	*aspirin*
la crema	*cream*
la curita / la tirita	*(small) bandaid*
las gotas	*drops*
las hierbas	*herbs*
el jarabe (para la tos)	*(cough) syrup*
las muletas	*crutches*
la pastilla	*tablet*
la píldora	*pill*
la receta	*prescription*
la venda de gasa	*gauze bandage*
la vitamina	*vitamin*
el yeso	*cast*

CONJUNCIONES ADVERBIALES

Con el subjuntivo

a menos que	*unless*
antes (de) que	*before*
con tal (de) que	*so that, provided that*
en caso de que	*in case*
para que	*so that*
sin que	*without*

Con el subjuntivo o el indicativo

aunque	*although, even though*
cuando	*when*
después (de) que	*after*
en cuanto	*as soon as*
hasta que	*until*
tan pronto como	*as soon as*

¿Te gusta trabajar con la gente?

CAPÍTULO 13

Un maestro chileno le enseña cómo dibujar a una estudiante joven.

METAS PROFESIONALES

¿Vives para trabajar o trabajas para vivir? No importa cuál sea tu respuesta—todos participamos en la fuerza laboral de una u otra manera. Somos ciudadanos mundiales, no sólo residentes de una nación. Todos contribuimos a la economía global, y por eso es importante entender qué pasa en el mundo. En este capítulo vamos a hablar del trabajo y de las noticias del día, y cómo los dos nos afectan.

Los datos

Mira la información del gráfico y contesta las siguientes preguntas.

Los datos answers: 1. Chile, EEUU 2. Chile, EEUU 3. Uruguay, EEUU

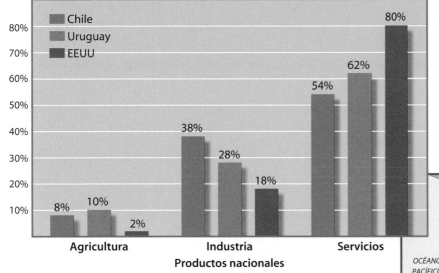

Chile
Uruguay
EEUU

	Agricultura	Industria	Servicios

80%
70%
60%
50%
40%
30%
20%
10%

8% 10% 2% 38% 28% 18% 54% 62% 80%

Productos nacionales

① ¿Cuál de los países depende menos de productos del sector de servicios? ¿Qué país depende más de ese sector?
② ¿Qué país produce el porcentaje de productos industriales más alto? ¿Y el porcentaje más bajo?
③ ¿Qué país tiene la producción de productos agrícolas más alta? ¿Y la más baja?

¡Adivina!

¿Qué sabes de Uruguay y Chile? Indica si las siguientes oraciones se refieren a Uruguay o a Chile. (Las respuestas están en la página 412.)

① Tiene un enorme desierto.
② De todos los países latinoamericanos, este país tiene el porcentaje más grande de personas de ascendencia europea.
③ La Isla de Pascua (*Easter Island*), o Rapa Nui, es parte de este país.
④ Aquí se pueden observar los pingüinos en Tierra del Fuego.

¡Adivina! answers: 1. Chile 2. Uruguay 3. Chile 4. Chile

CHILE
OCÉANO PACÍFICO
Santiago★
URUGUAY
★ Montevideo
OCÉANO ATLÁNTICO

393

¡IMAGÍNATE!

Vocabulario útil 1

SERGIO:	Podríamos hablar de las **noticias del día**, si quieres.
ANILÚ:	No, gracias. ¿De qué vamos a hablar? ¿Del **crimen,** de la **política** o de la **economía**? Me pongo hasta más nerviosa.
SERGIO:	Tienes razón. No había pensado en eso.

Use **discriminar a** to say *discriminate against* and **discriminar por** to say *discriminated against:* **Eduardo no discrimina a nadie, pero se siente discriminado por sus colegas.**

Optional: Have students give actual examples for these current event words; i.e., **Hay una guerra en..., Se encuentra mucha discriminación en...**, etc.

LAS NOTICIAS DEL DÍA

la campaña	*campaign*
el (la) ciudadano(a)	*citizen*
el crimen	*crime*
el desastre natural	*natural disaster*
la (des)igualdad	*(in)equality*
la discriminación	*discrimination*
la economía	*economy*
las fuerzas armadas	*armed forces*
la globalización	*globalization*
el gobierno	*government*
la guerra	*war*
el huracán	*hurricane*
el (la) líder	*leader*
la paz mundial	*world peace*
la política	*politics*
el proceso electoral	*election process*
el terremoto	*earthquake*
el terrorismo	*terrorism*
la violencia	*violence*
iniciar	*to initiate*
luchar contra	*to fight against*
participar en	*to participate in*
sobrevivir	*to survive, overcome*
sufrir (las consecuencias)	*to suffer (the consequences)*
tomar medidas	*to take steps or measures*
votar	*to vote*

la contaminación (del aire)

la inundación

el ejército

las elecciones

la huelga

la manifestación

Actividades

ACTIVIDAD 1 **¿En qué te hace pensar?** Escribe una o dos oraciones sobre cada tema. Trata de incluir un ejemplo reciente de ese fenómeno.

MODELOS: la contaminación del aire
Dicen que la contaminación del aire de la Ciudad de México es la peor del mundo.
un desastre natural
Un desastre natural que no olvidaremos pronto es el huracán Mitch que devastó a Honduras en 1998.

1. la contaminación (del aire, del agua, de la radiación)
2. las elecciones (locales, nacionales)
3. un desastre (natural, causado por el hombre)
4. la economía (local, nacional, global)
5. una huelga (de hambre, de estudiantes, de activistas verdes)
6. el crimen (violento, empresarial, electrónico)
7. una manifestación (pacífica, violenta)
8. la guerra (fría, mundial, civil)

ACTIVIDAD 2 **Las noticias de hoy.** En parejas, pongan en orden del 1 al 6 los siguientes temas, desde el problema más serio (#1) hasta al problema menos serio (#6), según su opinión. Luego, den ejemplos de las noticias del día sobre cada tema que justifique su clasificación.

_____ el terrorismo
_____ el crimen
_____ la discriminación (contra...)
_____ la economía
_____ la violencia (doméstica / en la televisión)
_____ la guerra (contra las drogas, en...)

Optional: Have students work in pairs to complete the activity. Or, have them report recent events.

Other natural disasters are: **el tornado, la erupción volcánica**, and **el incendio forestal** (*forest fire*).

Preparation: If your classroom is not wired, print out a few copies of digital Spanish press from a variety of Spanish-speaking countries and populations in the U.S. Use for **Actividad 2**; have students examine in groups and discuss different style conventions (dates, abbreviations, etc.) in these online newspapers.

Vocabulario útil 2

SERGIO: Pues, desde mi punto de vista, no tienes nada de qué preocuparte. Tienes muy **buena presencia, te llevas bien con la gente,** y me imagino que eres muy **responsable.**

ANILÚ: Oye, ¿quién eres? ¿Te pagó alguien para animarme?

SERGIO: No, no, no seas tan desconfiada. Sólo quería ayudarte.

ANILÚ: No, de veras. ¿No me digas que estás **solicitando el mismo puesto**?

SERGIO: No, no, y aunque fueras mi **competencia,** te ayudaría. ¿Trajiste tu **currículum vitae**?

ANILÚ: Sí, lo tengo en **el maletín.**

SERGIO: Perfecto. Ahora, en una **entrevista,** la cosa más importante es cómo **tus habilidades** satisfacen plenamente **los requisitos del puesto.**

Suggestion: Chat about this theme, introducing new vocabulary words: **¿Piensas solicitar un puesto para el verano? ¿Vas a tener muchas entrevistas? ¿Dónde? ¿Con quiénes? ¿Cómo piensas prepararte para las entrevistas?** Continue with general questions: **¿Es importante ser puntual? ¿Qué habilidades tienes? ¿Cuáles son unos ejemplos de beneficios que te interesan? ¿Trabajas? ¿Dónde? ¿A tiempo parcial / completo?**

For **el currículum vitae,** you might also encounter **el curriculum** (without the accent mark), **el currículo, el historial personal,** and **la hoja de vida.**

PARA SOLICITAR EMPLEO

La entrevista

El (La) candidato(a)

detallista	*detail-oriented*
disponible	*available*
emprendedor(a)	*enterprising*
puntual	*punctual*
responsable	*responsible*
llevarse bien con la gente	*to get along with people*
tener...	*to have . . .*
...algunos conocimientos de...	*. . . some knowledge of . . .*
...buena presencia	*. . . a good presence*
...(mucha) experiencia en...	*. . . (a lot of) experience in . . .*
...las habilidades necesarias	*. . . the necessary skills*

El puesto

el ascenso	*promotion*
el aumento de sueldo	*salary increase, raise*
los beneficios	*benefits*
el contrato	*contract*
la (des)ventaja	*(dis)advantage*
el (la) empleado(a)	*employee*
el requisito	*requisite, requirement*
el seguro médico	*medical insurance*
averiguar	*to look into, investigate*
contratar	*to hire*
despedir (i, i)	*to fire*
dirigir	*to direct*
emplear	*to employ*
hacer informes	*to write reports*
jubilarse	*to retire*
requerir (ie, i)	*to require*
satisfacer	*to satisfy*
supervisar	*to supervise*
trabajar a tiempo completo	*to work full time*
trabajar a tiempo parcial	*to work part time*

Optional: You may want to point out that **retirarse** is a variant of **jubilarse.**

LOS NEGOCIOS

Optional: You may want to point out that **empresa** is a variant of **compañía.**

la bolsa (de valores)	*stock market*
la compañía multinacional	*multinational corporation*
los costos	*costs*
el desarrollo	*development*
el (la) empresario(a)	*businessman / woman*
la fábrica	*factory*
las ganancias y las pérdidas	*profits and losses*
la industria	*industry*
el presupuesto	*budget*
las telecomunicaciones	*telecommunications*

Actividades

ACTIVIDAD 3 **El candidato ideal.** Escribe una o dos oraciones que describan al (a la) candidato(a) ideal para los siguientes puestos. Debes incluir vocabulario del **Vocabulario útil 2,** pero también puedes usar vocabulario que aprendiste antes para describir a la gente.

MODELO: secretario(a)
El secretario ideal es puntual, responsable y se lleva bien con la gente. También es inteligente y sabe resolver problemas fácilmente.

1. dependiente de una tienda de videos
2. gerente de una oficina
3. detective
4. periodista
5. actor (actriz)
6. espía
7. médico forense
8. ¿...?

Suggestion: Warm up for these activities with questions like: **¿Cómo se buscan los empleos buenos? (en el periódico, en la red, hablando con contactos profesionales) ¿Es buena idea poner tu currículum en la red?**

Optional: List additional occupations and allow students to consider any they choose. Possibilities: **taxista, policía, guía turística, gaucho, piloto, peluquero(a).**

ACTIVIDAD 4 **Los negocios.** Contesta las siguientes preguntas en oraciones completas.

MODELO: ¿Te gustaría trabajar para una compañía multinacional?
Me gustaría trabajar para una compañía multinacional. Me imagino que los sueldos y los beneficios son buenos y es posible que tenga la oportunidad de viajar.

1. ¿Te gustaría trabajar para una compañía multinacional? ¿Por qué sí o por que no?
2. ¿Es más importante para ti tener un buen sueldo, un buen seguro médico o muchas vacaciones? Explica.
3. ¿Cuáles son los factores que se deben considerar en el ascenso de un(a) empleado(a)?
4. ¿Cómo debe ser una persona que supervisa a otras? ¿Por qué crees eso?
5. Describe detalladamente tu puesto ideal.

ACTIVIDAD 5 **La entrevista.** Con un(a) compañero(a), representen una entrevista de un(a) candidato(a) para uno de los puestos en los anuncios clasificados que siguen. El (La) entrevistador(a) debe tener una lista de preguntas que quiere hacerle al (a la) candidato(a). El (La) candidato(a) debe tener una lista de sus habilidades y razones por las cuales sería (*would be*) el (la) perfecto(a) empleado(a) para ese puesto.

MODELO: Candidato(a): *Hola. Yo soy... y estoy aquí para solicitar el puesto de...*
Entrevistador(a): *Mucho gusto, señor / señora / señorita... Siéntese, por favor...*

Auto Venta

SE BUSCA VENDEDOR(A) DE CARROS

Solicitamos persona responsable, con buena presencia, que se lleva muy bien con la gente. Experiencia en ventas y algunos conocimientos de contabilidad. Trabajo a tiempo completo. Beneficios incluyen sueldo generoso más comisión, seguro médico y vacaciones pagadas. Llame al 4-23-89-67 para solicitar una entrevista.

Teletrabajos

SE SOLICITA TELEMARKETER

Se solicita persona detallista, puntual, responsable, de buena presencia y amable por teléfono. Disponible los fines de semana. Trabajo a tiempo parcial. Experiencia no necesaria. Sueldo según experiencia. Ascenso garantizado para la persona emprendedora. Enviar fax de su currículum al 3-21-89-64.

¡COMPÁRATE!

Si piensas solicitar empleo en un país hispanohablante y necesitas escribir una carta o e-mail de presentación (*cover letter or e-mail*), ten cuidado con los servicios de traducción en Internet. Estos servicios de traducción que abundan en la red son una tentación para muchas personas que no saben el español muy bien o no quieren aprenderlo. A pesar de que estos servicios son útiles (*useful*) hasta cierto punto, la calidad de las traducciones que producen varía mucho y todavía no alcanza el nivel (*doesn't achieve the level*) de una persona que estudia y aprende el idioma. Muchas veces los servicios gratis ofrecen traducciones muy malas y los más caros ni siquiera toman en cuenta (*take into account*) los factores culturales y lingüísticos que afectan la calidad de una traducción buena.

Mira los e-mails a la derecha. El primero es el original, escrito en inglés. El segundo es una versión española escrita por un servicio de traducción. El tercer e-mail es el mismo mensaje escrito por una persona que habla el español muy bien.

 PRÁCTICA. En grupos de tres a cuatro personas, contesten las siguientes preguntas.

1. ¿Qué diferencias se notan entre las dos versiones en español?

2. ¿Cuál de los dos mensajes en español les parece más formal o cortés? ¿Por qué? Comparen las dos versiones otra vez. ¿Pueden encontrar algunos errores en la traducción del servicio?

3. ¿Creen que es una buena idea usar servicios de traducción cibernéticos en las siguientes situaciones? ¿Por qué?

   • para solicitar empleo en un país de habla española
   • para escribir una carta a un amigo chileno que sabe un poco de inglés, pero que prefiere comunicarse en español
   • para traducir un documento que imprimiste de la red

4. Escriban un mensaje en inglés de dos a tres oraciones. Luego, busquen unos servicios gratis de traducción en Internet. Usen los enlaces sugeridos en el sitio web de *Nexos* para ir a unos sitios web posibles. Cada persona del grupo debe ir a un servicio diferente para buscar una traducción. Luego, comparen sus traducciones. ¿Son muy similares o muy diferentes? ¿Pueden decidir cuál es la mejor?

Fecha: 15 de mayo, 2004
Para: Tráfico Gráfico, S.A. <recursos@tgsa.com>
De: Michael McDonald <mmcdonald@att.net>
Re: Web designer job

Dear Sir or Madam:

I am writing in order to apply for the position of web designer that you advertised in the local paper this Sunday. I am attaching my résumé. I look forward to hearing from you soon.

All the best,

Michael McDonald

Fecha: 15 de mayo, 2004
Para: Tráfico Gráfico, S.A. <recursos@tgsa.com>
De: Michael McDonald <mmcdonald@att.net>
Re: Diseñador de telaraña

Estimado Señor o la Señora:

Escribo para aplicar para la posición de diseñador de telaraña que usted anunció en el papel local este domingo. Conecto mi résumé. Espero con ansia oír de usted pronto.

Todo mejor,

Michael McDonald

Fecha: 15 de mayo, 2004
Para: Tráfico Gráfico, S.A. <recursos@tgsa.com>
De: Michael McDonald <mmcdonald@att.net>
Re: Diseñador de sitios web

Muy estimados señores:

Me dirijo a ustedes con el propósito de solicitar empleo como diseñador de sitios web, puesto que anunciaron en el periódico local del domingo previo. Adjunto encontrarán mi currículum vitae.

Sin más por el momento y a la espera de su respuesta, los saluda atentamente,

Michael McDonald

A VER

Antes de ver el video

 ACTIVIDAD 1 En el episodio de este capítulo, Sergio y Anilú se conocen por primera vez. Los dos hablan en una oficina, donde Anilú va a tener una entrevista de trabajo con el jefe de la compañía. ¿Qué recuerdan de Sergio y de Anilú? Con un(a) compañero(a) de clase, completen la siguiente tabla, indicando con una X si las características indicadas describen a Sergio, a Anilú o a los dos.

 For additional Internet practice, do the *Nexos* website and / or CD-ROM video exercises.

Answers Act. 1: *Answers may vary slightly. Suggested response:* **Sergio:** egoísta, extrovertido, un poco dramático; **Anilú:** extrovertida, poco convencional, un poco dramática

Características	Sergio	Anilú
tímido(a)		
egoísta		
extrovertido(a)		
poco convencional		
un poco dramático(a)		
aburrido(a)		

ACTIVIDAD 2 Las entrevistas de trabajo, sean en EEUU o sean en el mundo hispanohablante, son similares. Con un(a) compañero(a) de clase, hagan una lista de las cosas que uno debe hacer para prepararse para una entrevista de trabajo.

Ideas: estar bien vestido(a) / llegar a tiempo para la entrevista / practicar las respuestas a preguntas posibles / traer un currículum / averiguar información sobre la empresa / ¿...?

ESTRATEGIA

Watching for transitions and listening for words that signal a change in the conversation

In this chapter's video segment, you'll notice that several times Sergio wants to change the topic of the conversation or stall for time while he thinks of something to say. When people converse, this can be done by actions and by words. As you watch the video segment, watch for the actions and words Sergio uses to either change the topic or stall for a little more time.

ACTIVIDAD 3 Mientras miras el video, haz una lista de por lo menos una acción y dos palabras, expresiones o preguntas que usa Sergio para cambiar de tema y / o para darse más tiempo antes de contestar. Para (*Stop*) el video y vuelve a mirar el episodio si es necesario.

Acciones	Palabras, expresiones, preguntas

El video

Mira el episodio del **Capítulo 13.** No te olvides de enfocarte en las acciones y palabras que necesitas para completar la tabla de la **Actividad 3.**

Después de ver el video

ACTIVIDAD 4 Trabaja con un(a) compañero(a) de clase para contestar las siguientes preguntas sobre el video.

1. ¿En qué ocasiones cambia Sergio de tema cuando habla con Anilú?
2. Al final, sabemos por qué cambia de tema. ¿Cuál es la razón?
3. ¿Por qué está tan nerviosa Anilú?
4. ¿Cómo trata Sergio a Anilú, con mucha o poca simpatía? ¿Cómo saben cuál es su actitud?
5. ¿Por qué no quiere Anilú hablar de las noticias del día?
6. ¿Cómo es Anilú, según Sergio?
7. En la **Actividad 2,** miren la lista de cosas que un candidato para un puesto debe hacer. ¿Cuántas de las cosas aquí—y en su lista—hizo Anilú?
8. En su opinión, ¿cómo va a ser la entrevista entre Anilú y el jefe, buena o mala?

ACTIVIDAD 5 Trabaja con un(a) compañero(a) de clase y representen una de las siguientes escenas.

1. la conversación entre Sergio y su padre
2. la entrevista entre Anilú y el padre de Sergio

ACTIVIDAD 6 Con tu compañero(a) de la **Actividad 5,** busquen a otra pareja de estudiantes que representaron la misma conversación que ustedes. Luego, combinen sus ideas y escriban una conversación que contenga ideas y oraciones de las dos conversaciones.

Suggestion: You may want to pause the video in appropriate spots to show students how to look for information in segments.

Optional / Standards: Compare with similar expressions in English. Many students are not aware that they use these conventions in their native tongue as well. Point out filler words like "um..." and expressions used to change the subject like "on the other hand." See if students can come up with other examples. (C 4.1)

Answers Act. 3: *Examples:* **Acciones:** looks down at a newspaper but we don't see it, puts hand out for curriculum vitae; **Palabras, expresiones, preguntas: De todas maneras, pues, se puede decir, mira**

Answers Act 4: 1. Cuando ella le pregunta para qué está en la oficina. 2. Porque el jefe es su papá. 3. Porque no le dieron otro puesto que había solicitado. 4. La trata con mucha simpatía. Sugiere hablar de otros temas y ensayar / practicar para la entrevista. 5. Porque la ponen aún más nerviosa. 6. Tiene buena presencia, se lleva bien con la gente y probablemente es muy responsable. 7. *Answers will vary.* 8. *Answers will vary.*

Standards: **Actividades 5** and **6** offer opportunities for students to communicate in the presentational mode. (C 1.1, 1.3)

Gaddi Vásquez

" A través de sus esfuerzos dignos, los Voluntarios de Peace Corps se han convertido en algunos de los mejores embajadores de este país, sembrando comprensión y buena voluntad alrededor del mundo. En el siglo 21, los Estados Unidos tiene el más alto nivel de diversidad étnica y cultural en toda su historia y estamos comprometidos a lograr que los rangos (*ranks*) de nuestra agencia reflejen esa misma diversidad. "

Gaddi Vásquez es el director del Cuerpo de Paz de Estados Unidos. Hijo de trabajadores migrantes mexicanos, Vásquez es la personificación del sueño americano. Fue el primer miembro de su familia en recibir un título universitario. Entre 1987 y 1995 fue supervisor del Condado de Orange en California y antes de ocupar su posición actual, fue el vicepresidente de la compañía eléctrica Southern California Edison Company. Además, Vásquez tiene una larga historia de servicio comunitario y es miembro ejecutivo de varias organizaciones benéficas.

Como director del Cuerpo de Paz, Vásquez se ha propuesto doblar el número de voluntarios, promover el desarrollo de iniciativas comunitarias e incrementar el número de voluntarios de grupos minoritarios.

¿Te interesa la idea de participar en los proyectos del Cuerpo de Paz? To learn more about Gaddi Vásquez and the Peace Corps, visit the *Nexos* website at http://college.hmco.com/languages/spanish/students and follow the links.

Gramática útil 1
Talking about what has occurred: The present perfect tense

Can you find the present perfect form in the headline of this advertisement for a bank?

Answer: ha estado

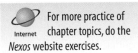

For more practice of chapter topics, do the *Nexos* website exercises.

Heritage Learners: Heritage language students may need extensive practice forming the present perfect. They might not know how to conjugate the verb **haber** or how to spell the forms. Common spelling errors include omitting the **h**, or placing it following the vowel, as in **eh, ahs, ah, ehmos...** Point out that all forms of the verb **haber** start with **h**. Give a dictation and ask students to pick out the forms of the verb **haber.** Ask them to discuss the strategies that they used to accomplish this task. Did they translate from English? Did they look for a past participle? Sample dictation: **1. Va a estudiar más este semestre. 2. Ha estado muy enfermo. 3. Él asiste a clases de química. 4. ¿Ya han entrevistado al alcalde? 5. Todavía no hemos estudiado para el examen. 6. Va a haber elecciones este mes.**

CÓMO USARLO

LO BÁSICO

- A *past participle* is a verb form that expresses an action that has been completed. In the sentence *I have **walked** to the office every day this week, walked* is the past participle, used with the auxiliary verb *to have.*
- An *auxiliary verb* is a verb that is used with another verb. **Estar** is one example of a Spanish auxiliary verb you have already learned. You used it to form the present progressive with the present participle: **Estoy trabajando ahora.**

1. The present perfect tense is used to talk about actions that have already been completed at the time of speaking. It is used similarly to the preterite, but the present perfect usually gives a greater sense of immediacy to the completion of the action and usually focuses on its relation to the present. Compare the following two sentences.

He hablado con el gerente de la compañía.

I have spoken with the director of the company.

Hablé con el gerente de la compañía.

I spoke with the director of the company.

The first sentence implies a more recent conversation and, because it relates to the present, hints that there may be more information still to come. In the second sentence, the action is viewed as completed and done with.

2. Spanish-speakers' use of the present perfect tense, as compared to the preterite, varies from country to country. For example, in Spain the present perfect is used more frequently to talk about past actions than it is in many Latin American countries.

CÓMO FORMARLO

1. The present perfect tense is formed using a present-tense form of the auxiliary verb **haber** and the past participle of a second verb.

◆ The past participle is formed by removing the **-ar, -er,** or **-ir** ending from the verb and adding the following endings. Notice that the same endings are used for both **-er** and **-ir** verbs.

-ar verb: **trabajar**   **-er** verb: **conocer**   **-ir** verb: **imprimir**

-ado: trabajado   **-ido: conocido**   **-ido: imprimido**

◆ Conjugated forms of **haber** are used with the past participle.

Present perfect tense		
yo	he	
tú	has	
Ud. / él / ella	ha	+ **trabajado / conocido / imprimido**, etc.
nosotros(as)	hemos	
vosotros(as)	habéis	
Uds. / ellos / ellas	han	

2. A number of verbs have irregular past participles.

abrir: **abierto**	morir: **muerto**	satisfacer: **satisfecho**
decir: **dicho**	poner: **puesto**	ver: **visto**
escribir: **escrito**	romper: **roto**	volver: **vuelto**
hacer: **hecho**		

3. When an **-a, -e,** or **-o** precedes the **i** in **-ido,** place an accent on the **i** to maintain the correct pronunciation: **leído, traído, oído.** No accent is used, however, when the **i** of **-ido** is preceded by **-u: construido, destruido.**

Haber means *to have,* as does the verb **tener,** but the difference is that **haber** is almost always used with another verb, as an auxiliary verb, while **tener** is used alone. The invariable forms **hay** (*there is, there are*) and **había** (*there was, there were*) also come from **haber.**

Verbs that end in **-rir** follow the same pattern as **abrir: descubrir → descubierto.** Verbs that end in **-ver** (except **ver**), use the **-uelto** ending: **resolver → resuelto.**

Heritage Learners: Ask students why these forms need an accent: **creer, leer, atraer, caer, traer,** and **oír.** What would they sound like without an accent? This kind of discussion provides a good review of the rules of accentuation that apply to vowel sequences.

4. When using a form of **haber** and the past participle to form the present perfect tense, the form of **haber** changes to agree with the subject. The present participle does not change.

Elena ha tenido una entrevista con esa compañía tres veces.	*Elena **has** had an interview with that company three times.*
Yo sólo **he** tenido una entrevista con ellos.	*I **have** only had one interview with them.*

5. The past participle may also be used as an adjective with the verb **estar.** When it is used this way, it changes its form to reflect number and gender, as do all adjectives.

Han escrito los informes ayer.	(past participle used in present perfect)
Los informes ya **están escritos.**	(past participle used as an adjective)
He arreglado la computadora.	(past participle used in present perfect)
La computadora **está arreglada.**	(past participle used as an adjective)

6. When the past participle of reflexive verbs is formed, the reflexive pronoun goes *before* the auxiliary verb. The same is true with direct and indirect object pronouns.

Ya **me he preparado** para la reunión.	*I **have** already **prepared myself** for the meeting.*
¿El informe? Sí, **lo he escrito.**	*The report? Yes, **I have written it.***

Note that, unlike in English, an adverb cannot separate the auxiliary verb from the past participle; the two components making up the Spanish present perfect tense are never split by another word: *I **have** already **applied** for the job,* but **ya he solicitado** el puesto.

Actividades

ACTIVIDAD 1 **Antes de la entrevista.** Es el día antes de la entrevista de Anilú y su mamá quiere saber si Anilú se ha preparado bien. Escucha la conversación entre Anilú y su madre. Marca con una X las cosas que Anilú sí ha hecho para prepararse para la entrevista. Luego, escribe una oración para cada cosa que sí ha hecho y una oración para cada cosa que no ha hecho.

MODELO: *Anilú ha preparado su currículum vitae.*

___X___ preparar su currículum vitae

_____ revisar su currículum vitae varias veces

_____ completar la solicitud que le mandaron

_____ hacer una lista de sus habilidades

_____ averiguar cuáles son los requisitos del puesto

_____ practicar su presentación frente al espejo

_____ escoger lo que se va a poner

_____ confirmar la hora de la entrevista

ACTIVIDAD 2 **¿Qué hemos hecho?** Todos queremos cambiar el mundo. ¿Qué han hecho tus compañeros, tu familia, tu gobierno y tú para combatir los problemas de hoy? Haz seis oraciones usando elementos de las tres columnas. Asegúrate que el verbo esté en el presente perfecto.

MODELO: *El gobierno ha tomado medidas para combatir el terrorismo. Mi amigo Geraldo ha participado en una manifestación contra la desigualdad.*

él (mi amigo...)	participar	la discriminación
ella (mi amiga...)	votar	la paz mundial
nosotros	iniciar	la economía global
ustedes	escribir	la desigualdad
usted	tomar medidas	combatir el terrorismo
el gobierno	para / contra	reducir la contaminación
el (la) profesor(a) de...	luchar contra	del aire
mi (*miembro de familia*)	estudiar	en las elecciones
los estudiantes	¿...?	presidenciales
¿...?		una manifestación contra...
		una huelga en...
		artículos sobre...
		¿...?

Suggestion: You may want to mention that the **presente perfecto** is also called the **pretérito perfecto**.

Answers Act. 3: *Questions may vary slightly.* 1. ¿Alguna vez has esquiado en los Andes? 2. ¿Alguna vez has probado un vino chileno? 3. ¿Alguna vez has viajado a Punta del Este? 4. ¿Alguna vez has visto los glaciares de Tierra del Fuego? 5. ¿Alguna vez has conocido a un gaucho uruguayo?

ACTIVIDAD 3 **Alguna vez.** Trata de informarte más sobre tu compañero(a) y las cosas que ha hecho y no ha hecho en su vida. Hazle preguntas sobre su pasado usando el presente perfecto, luego que él o ella te haga preguntas sobre el tuyo. Puedes usar las ideas en los dibujos o puedes inventar tus propias preguntas.

MODELO: Tú: *¿Alguna vez has visitado la Isla de Pascua?*
Compañero(a): *No, nunca he visitado la Isla de Pascua, pero algún día me gustaría hacerlo.*

visitar la Isla de Pascua

1. esquiar en los Andes

2. probar un vino chileno

3. viajar a Punta del Este

4. ver los glaciares de Tierra del Fuego

5. conocer a un gaucho uruguayo

ACTIVIDAD 4 **Las metas (*goals*) que he logrado (*have achieved*) y no he logrado.** Escribe cinco actividades o metas que son importantes para ti. Di si hasta este momento las has logrado o no. Luego, en grupos de cuatro o cinco, comparen sus metas y escriban conclusiones sobre las metas que tienen en común.

MODELO: Meta: *completar el curso de español*
Yo: *No he completado el curso de español.*
Grupo: *En el grupo, nadie ha completado el curso de español.*

Gramática útil 2
Talking about events that took place prior to other events: The past perfect tense

CÓMO USARLO

1. The past perfect tense, like the present perfect tense, is a compound tense (auxiliary verb + verb). It is used to describe past actions that occurred *prior to* other past actions.

Ya **había escrito** el informe cuando la jefa me lo pidió.

*I **had** already **written** the report when the boss asked me for it.*

2. The past perfect tense is frequently used in combination with another verb in the *preterite*, since it describes a past action that occurred *before* another past action.

Ya me **habían llamado** cuando **llegué** a la oficina.

*They **had** already **called** me when **I arrived** at the office.*

CÓMO FORMARLO

1. The past perfect tense uses the same past participles that you learned to use when forming the present perfect tense.

2. You use the *imperfect tense forms* (instead of the present tense forms) of the verb **haber** with the past participle to form the past perfect.

Es que **había solicitado** otro puesto y acabo de recibir la mala noticia que no me lo dieron.

Suggestion: Place **había hablado** on a time line with **he hablado** so that students can see that it is a temporal backshift from *have spoken* to *had spoken*. Contrast with **Ayer hablé con el jefe** to show preterite.

Suggestion: Introduce the term **pluscuamperfecto** so that students are familiar with grammatical terms in Spanish.

Past perfect tense		
yo	había	
tú	habías	
Ud. / él / ella	había	
nosotros(as)	habíamos	+ **trabajado / conocido / imprimido**, etc.
vosotros(as)	habíais	
Uds. / ellos / ellas	habían	

3. All of the other rules you learned about the present perfect also apply to the past perfect.

♦ **Haber** changes to agree with the subject.

Naty había escrito la carta la semana pasada.
Los gerentes habían escrito dos cartas adicionales.

◆ When the past participle is used as an adjective with **estar,** it changes to reflect number and gender.

Las preparaciones para la reunión ya **estaban hechas.**
La presentación para los directores no **estaba lista.**

◆ All reflexive and object pronouns precede the form of **haber** and the past participle.

Gonzalo **se había preparado** mucho antes de la entrevista.
La jefa me pidió el informe, pero **se lo había dado** a su secretario para copiar.

Actividades

ACTIVIDAD 5 **¡Pobrecito!** ¡Pobre señor Malapata! Necesita encontrar trabajo pero cada vez que hace algo para lograrlo, nada le sale bien. Estudia el modelo y combina las dos oraciones para describir su situación en una oración nueva. Pon atención al uso del pluscuamperfecto en la oración.

MODELO: Buscó el periódico para leer los anuncios clasificados. Su hijo lo puso en la basura.
Cuando buscó el periódico para leer los anuncios clasificados, su hijo ya lo había puesto en la basura.

1. Solicitó el puesto de gerente. Le ofrecieron el puesto a otro candidato.

2. Decidió solicitar el puesto de supervisor. Tres otros candidatos lo solicitaron.

3. El día de la entrevista, fue a buscar el carro. Su esposa se llevó el carro.

4. Bajó a la plataforma del metro. El tren salió.

5. Llegó a la entrevista. El jefe se fue.

6. Lo llamaron para ofrecerle el puesto. Aceptó otro puesto menos lucrativo.

ACTIVIDAD 6 **La clase de ciencias políticas.** Soledad describe su primer año en la universidad. Antes de llegar a la U, no había entendido la importancia de participar en la política del país y del mundo. La clase de ciencias políticas le despertó la conciencia y por eso ella y varios amigos hicieron muchas cosas que nunca habían hecho antes. Escucha a Soledad mientras ella describe su primer año en la U. Escribe una oración que describa lo que ella y sus amigos nunca habían hecho antes. Primero, estudia el modelo.

MODELO: (ella) votar en elecciones nacionales
Nunca había votado en elecciones nacionales.

1. (ellas) contribuir con dinero y tiempo a la campaña de un candidato político

2. (ella) interesarse en la política y la economía global

3. (ella) participar en una manifestación

4. (ellos) ser voluntarios

5. (ella) escribir ensayos para el periódico universitario

6. (ellos) abrir los ojos sobre los problemas globales

ACTIVIDAD 7 **Antes de llegar a la universidad.** Quieres informarte más sobre las cosas que tu compañero(a) había hecho o no había hecho antes de llegar a la universidad. Hazle seis preguntas sobre su pasado; luego él o ella te hará seis preguntas. Puedes usar las ideas de la lista o puedes inventar otras.

MODELO: Tú: *¿Tomaste (Has tomado) clases de español antes?*
Compañero(a): *No, antes de llegar a la universidad, nunca había tomado una clase de español.*
O: *Sí, lo había estudiado un año en la escuela secundaria.*

Ideas
trabajar fuera de casa
viajar al extranjero
vivir fuera de casa
entrevistarse para un puesto
tener tu propio carro
compartir tu habitación
cocinar
¿...?

Standards: Encourage students to expand their histories by giving additional detail. (C 1.1, 1.3)

Optional: Ask students to make a list of 3–5 things they had never done before being at the university: **Antes de llegar a la universidad, yo nunca...** Have them compare answers with a partner or use the ideas in **Actividad 7**.

Gramática útil 3
Expressing doubt, emotion, and will: The present perfect subjunctive

CÓMO USARLO

1. In **Capítulos 10–12,** you learned to use the subjunctive mood to express a variety of reactions and emotions.

2. The present perfect subjunctive is used in the same contexts where you use the present subjunctive. The difference is that you are using the present perfect subjunctive in a *past-tense context*, rather than a present-tense context. The present perfect subjunctive, like the present perfect indicative, describes actions that recently occurred or have a bearing on the present.

Begin the CD-ROM activities. Do the cultural activities and reading and writing practice as you complete the corresponding text sections.

You may want to review the uses of the subjunctive mood on page 377 of **Capítulo 12**.

¡Me alegro de que hayas conseguido el puesto!
I'm happy that you have gotten the position!

Dudo que hayan terminado el proyecto.
I doubt that they have finished the project.

Es bueno que él haya estudiado los informes antes de la reunión.
It's good that he has studied the reports before the meeting.

Ojalá que hayamos hecho todo antes de las siete.
I hope that we have done everything before 7:00.

No hay nadie en la oficina **que haya cumplido** el curso de xtml.
There is no one in the office who has completed the xtml course.

Cuando hayas leído los reportajes, debes hablar con la directora.
When you have read the reports, you should talk to the director.

Tráeme el contrato **tan pronto como lo haya firmado el jefe,** por favor.
Bring me the contract as soon as the boss has signed it, please.

Es posible que **haya buscado** trabajo en alguna u otra ocasión.

Suggestion: Put the following in 3 columns on the board and have students create sentences first in the present subjunctive, then in the present perfect subjunctive: (Col 1) **es bueno, dudo, ojalá, es seguro, lamento, quiero, prohibo** (Col 2) **que Roberto** (Col 3) **venir, salir, conseguir el puesto,...**

Suggestion: To review adjective clauses, have students complete the following, first in the present, then in the present perfect: **No hay nadie en esta clase que...** Start off the activity by giving or eliciting a model: **... sepa tocar cinco instrumentos / sea millonario / haya ido a Uruguay / haya escalado los Andes.** Do similar practice with adverbial clauses.

Heritage Learners: Research indicates that the perfect forms of the subjunctive are not widely used by second- and third-generation U.S. Hispanics. Some students, for example, may be able to understand the forms but have little or no productive abilities with them. Others may neither understand them nor use them. Start out by testing students' ability to understand these forms. If they show little or very limited receptive skills, do not expect productive command. Situations such as the following sample can be used to check students' familiarity: **Elena tuvo una entrevista de trabajo hoy por la mañana. (a) Espero que le ofrezcan el trabajo. (b) Espero que le hayan ofrecido el trabajo. (c) Las dos respuestas son posibles.**

CÓMO FORMARLO

The present perfect subjunctive uses the same past participles you have already learned, and follows the same rules as the present perfect tense. The only difference is that it uses the present subjunctive forms of the verb **haber,** rather than its present indicative forms.

Present perfect subjunctive		
yo	**haya**	
tú	**hayas**	
Ud. / él / ella	**haya**	**+ trabajado / conocido / imprimido,** etc.
nosotros(as)	**hayamos**	
vosotros(as)	**hayáis**	
Uds. / ellos / ellas	**hayan**	

Actividades

ACTIVIDAD 8 **El siglo veintiuno.** Expresa tu opinión sobre los siguientes temas de este siglo. Puedes usar los elementos de las columnas o puedes inventar tus propias ideas. Usa el presente perfecto del subjuntivo en tu comentario.

MODELOS: *Es una pena que haya aumentado la contaminación del aire en las ciudades grandes del mundo como Nueva York y la Ciudad de México en los últimos años.*

Temo que el terrorismo haya escalado drásticamente a través del mundo en las últimas décadas.

siento que	aumentar la contaminación del aire	últimamente
me alegro de que		en los últimos años
es bueno que	ocurrir tantos desastres naturales	recientemente
temo que		hasta ahora
es una pena que	los gobiernos: (no) hacer lo suficiente contra las drogas	hasta el momento
dudo que		en las últimas décadas
¿...?	el terrorismo: escalar drásticamente a través del mundo	
	conseguir la paz mundial	
	lograr (*to achieve*) la igualdad	
	acabarse la discriminación	

ACTIVIDAD 9 **Mi opinión.** Imagínate que los siguientes sucesos han ocurrido. Da tu opinión sobre cada noticia. Sigue el modelo.

MODELO: Tuvieron un huracán devastador en Centroamérica.
Es una pena que hayan tenido un huracán devastador en Centroamérica.

1. Tuvieron una serie de tornados en el sur de Estados Unidos. Varias personas murieron. Pero muchas familias fueron salvadas por los bomberos y la policía.
2. Ya terminaron las elecciones presidenciales en Uruguay. Se condujeron de una manera pacífica y democrática. La mayoría de la población votó en paz.

3. La tasa de desempleo bajó en Chile. La tasa de inflación también bajó. La economía está muy fuerte.
4. La guerra fría terminó. Los líderes internacionales declararon la paz mundial. Los gobiernos están de acuerdo sobre el futuro de sus relaciones.

 ACTIVIDAD 10 **Esta clase.** Con un(a) compañero(a), hagan una lista de seis cosas que crean que nadie en su clase haya hecho hasta ahora.

MODELO: *No hay nadie en esta clase que haya escalado los Andes. No hay nadie en esta clase que haya visto las estatuas de Rapa Nui.*

EXPRESIÓN. En grupos de tres a cuatro estudiantes, imagínense la siguiente situación: Horacio ha conseguido un nuevo puesto. Hay mucho trabajo que hacer y el jefe quiere saber qué ha hecho Horacio mientras él (el jefe) estaba de vacaciones. Escriban una conversación entre Horacio y el nuevo jefe, y entre las otras personas de la oficina (si quieren incluir a otras personas). Luego, representen la escena enfrente de la clase.

Chile y Uruguay

Dos economías fuertes. En parejas, miren los dos textos y las fotos. Después de leer los textos, indiquen cuál de las doce oraciones o grupos de oraciones de los textos puede servir como un resumen apropiado para cada foto.

Texto 1: Chile

(1) Chile tiene una increíble variedad geográfica, gracias a su extensión alargada del norte al sur. Desde un impresionante desierto hasta los glaciares de Tierra del Fuego en Patagonia, este país es una maravilla de contrastes. (2) Su diversidad geográfica significa que el país tiene una gran diversidad industrial también. Chile está entre los países sudamericanos con las economías más fuertes, aun con los recientes problemas económicos mundiales, y tiene una reputación muy sólida entre las empresas de inversiones (*investments*) internacionales.

(3) Una de las industrias mejor conocidas de Chile es la vinicultura, o la producción de vinos, los cuales Chile exporta a todo el mundo. Sus socios (*partners*) de exportación son: primero EEUU, segundo Japón, y luego vienen el Reino Unido y Brasil. (4) Chile también exporta minerales como el cobre, maderas (*woods*), pescado y metales industriales como el acero y el hierro (*steel and iron*).

(5) El turismo también es una industria muy importante para el país. Destinaciones como Tierra del Fuego, con sus glaciares y pingüinos, Viña del Mar, con sus bonitas playas, y Santiago, con sus atracciones urbanas y culturales, son populares entre turistas de todo el mundo. (6) La Isla de Pascua, o Rapa Nui en su lengua nativa, también atrae a visitantes internacionales. En su mayor parte, esta isla misteriosa, con sus estatuas con cabezas enormes, vive del turismo, pero también es importante aquí la industria pesquera, con énfasis en la exportación de langostas.

Texto 2: Uruguay

(7) Este país es el que muestra más influencia europea de toda Latinoamérica, ya que tiene el porcentaje más grande de personas de ascendencia europea. La mayoría de los inmigrantes vinieron a Uruguay desde España, Portugal e Italia durante el siglo XIX. (8) Aunque es un país pequeño, tiene la economía más fuerte del continente después de Chile; y como Chile, también tiene una posición de confianza muy alta entre los analistas económicos mundiales.

(9) La economía uruguaya siempre ha sido influida por la de Argentina, su vecino al oeste, y los recientes problemas económicos de Argentina han impactado fuertemente a Uruguay, en particular con relación a la industria turística. (10) Punta del Este, un balneario (*seaside resort, spa*) muy popular entre turistas argentinos, ha sufrido una marcada disminución de turistas durante los últimos años, pero todavía sirve como un destino turístico ideal para la gente adinerada (*wealthy*) que quiera practicar el windsurfing o ver carreras internacionales de automóviles de fórmulas especiales.

(11) Uruguay, junto con Argentina, es la tierra original del gaucho, el famoso y mítico vaquero (*cowboy*) de las canciones y la historia. Como el país es en su mayor parte llano (*flat*) con tierras fértiles, la industria ganadera (*cattle*) siempre ha sido muy importante, y la carne y los artículos de cuero son unas de las exportaciones uruguayas más importantes. (12) Otros productos que Uruguay exporta son el arroz, la lana y los productos de leche. Aunque Uruguay exporta a Europa y a EEUU, el mercado principal para sus productos son los países de Mercosur, la organización que une (*unites*) a las economías de Uruguay, Paraguay, Brasil y Argentina.

Foto B: _____

Foto A: _____

Foto C: _____

Foto D: _____

Internet

¡CONÉCTATE!

En grupos de tres o cuatro, hagan una investigación en Internet sobre uno de los siguientes temas. Usen los enlaces sugeridos en el sitio web de *Nexos* (http://college.hmco.com/languages/spanish/students) para ir a otros sitios web posibles. Después de hacer la investigación, presenten su informe a la clase.

Tema 1: las momias recientemente descubiertas en el desierto de Atacama de Chile
Tema 2: la historia de Rapa Nui, o la Isla de Pascua
Tema 3: los gauchos de Uruguay y la industria ganadera
Tema 4: los balnearios y baños termales de Uruguay
Tema 5: la economía de Chile o Uruguay
Tema 6: el Mercosur

Las lenguas de América

Muchos lingüistas opinan que la economía global representa una amenaza (*threat*) mundial a la diversidad lingüística. La preservación lingüística es algo sumamente importante para Latinoamérica, donde se encuentran un gran número de lenguas indígenas.

En Chile se estima que hay casi un millón de hablantes de mapu-dugun, la lengua de una de las poblaciones indígenas de esta zona, los mapuches. Además del mapu-dugun, en el territorio chileno se escuchan otras doce lenguas indígenas. Entre éstas figuran el aimara (también hablado en Bolivia), el rapa nui y el quechua chileno.

De todas las naciones de Latinoamérica, México es la más plurilingüe, con más de 280 lenguas indígenas. Otras naciones con un gran número de lenguas nativas son:

- Perú (90)
- Colombia (76)
- Guatemala (52)
- Venezuela (39)

Al otro extremo están Uruguay y Cuba, en las cuales (*in which*) ya no se registra el uso de lenguas indígenas. Sin embargo (*Nevertheless*), en Uruguay se hablan varias lenguas europeas. Se estima, por ejemplo, que hay más de 79.000 hablantes de italiano en este país, 28.000 hablantes de alemán y 28.000 hablantes de portugués.

 PRÁCTICA. Contesta las siguientes preguntas con un(a) compañero(a) de clase.

1. En su opinión, ¿es importante preservar las lenguas indígenas de Latino-américa? ¿Por qué sí o no?
2. ¿Pueden nombrar algunas de las lenguas indígenas que se hablan en EEUU?

Notice: Here are a few examples of indigenous languages in North America: Algonkian, Arapaho, Cree Mohegan, Ojibwa, Cheyenne, Blackfoot, Navajo, Yup'ik, Passamaquoddy.

Antes de leer

Clustering words and phrases

When you read texts in Spanish, it is sometimes helpful to go through each sentence and group together the words and phrases that convey similar ideas. This is especially useful when the reading contains many long or complex sentences. Additionally, punctuation such as commas, semicolons, dashes, and parentheses are often good places to look for the beginning or end of clusters.

For example, look at the following sentence from this chapter's reading on etiquette in the Internet. The circles indicate how you might cluster the sentence's words and phrases in order to help you break it down into more manageable chunks.

(Además del sentido común) (los buenos modales, la cortesía, el respeto, la consideración y la tolerancia) (éstas son algunas reglas) (que debemos todos observar) (al comunicarnos a través de la red.)

There is no right or wrong way to cluster words; the goal is just to break up long sentences into smaller chunks that are meaningful to you as a reader.

 ACTIVIDAD 1 Con un(a) compañero(a) de clase, analicen las siguientes oraciones de la lectura. Juntos hagan círculos que indiquen los grupos de palabras que ven en la oración.

Remind students that there is no single correct way to break down the sentences.

1. Cuando nos comunicamos con otra persona frente a frente o por teléfono, utilizamos gestos, expresiones y / o modulaciones de la voz que ayudan a nuestro interlocutor a interpretar nuestro mensaje.

2. Al contestar algún mensaje, deje alguna cita para que se sepa a qué se está refiriendo usted, pero, por favor, recorte todo lo demás.

3. Las letras MAYÚSCULAS se pueden usar para sustituir acentos o para enfatizar, pero NO escriba todo en mayúsculas, pues esto se interpreta en la red como que ¡USTED ESTÁ GRITANDO!

4. Si decide informarle a alguien de algún tipo de error, hágalo cortésmente, y si es posible, en un e-mail privado en lugar de un e-mail público que recibirá la lista o grupo de discusión.

ACTIVIDAD 2 Con el (la) mismo(a) compañero(a) de clase, miren los grupos de palabras que identificaron en la **Actividad 1.** ¿Por qué juntaron (*did you group*) estas palabras? Miren las siguientes explicaciones y decidan cuál afectó más sus decisiones.

1. similar meaning
2. the punctuation around them
3. same parts of speech
4. complete phrase

ACTIVIDAD 3 Vas a leer un artículo que apareció en el sitio web del periódico uruguayo *Diario La República*. El artículo trata de la etiqueta en Internet y cómo debemos portarnos (*behave*) cuando nos comunicamos en el ciberespacio. Como el uso de la red y del correo electrónico se hace cada vez más importante en el trabajo y en la vida privada, es esencial que nos comuniquemos con cortesía y claridad. Antes de leer el artículo, haz una lista de por lo menos cinco cosas que debemos o no debemos hacer cuando usamos Internet.

Lectura

ACTIVIDAD 4 Lee el artículo sobre la Netiquette en la página 417. No te olvides de agrupar las palabras relacionadas para ayudarte a entender algunas de las oraciones más largas.

Después de leer

Suggestion: Chat with students about their e-mail habits and opinions: **¿Sigues tú las normas de la etiqueta en la red? ¿Cuáles son los tres consejos más importantes? Una pregunta indiscreta: ¿Cuál es el error más grave que has hecho por correo electrónico?**

Answers Act. 5: 1. C 2. F, No debes usar el correo electrónico... 3. C 4. F, Cuando contestes un e-mail, no debes...; 5. F, No debes usar una lista de distribución para...; 6. C 7. F, No debes enviar avisos sobre viruses...; 8. C

ACTIVIDAD 5 Trabaja con un(a) compañero(a) de clase para indicar si los siguientes consejos sobre la Netiquette son ciertos o falsos, según el artículo. Si un comentario es falso, corríjanlo.

1. _____ La tolerancia es una parte importante de la Netiquette.

2. _____ El correo electrónico es bueno para comunicar las cosas que tienes miedo de decir frente a frente.

3. _____ No debes enviar anexos grandes a una lista de distribución.

4. _____ Cuando contestes un e-mail, debes incluir todos los comentarios anteriores, aunque sean muy largos.

5. _____ Una lista de distribución es una buena manera de comunicar tus opiniones sobre la política y la religión.

6. _____ Debes mantener privada la información de una lista como las direcciones y los números de teléfono.

7. _____ Debes enviar avisos sobre viruses posibles a todos los participantes de una lista de distribución.

8. _____ Si decides corregir los errores de un novato, debes hacerlo en privado, no enviando un mensaje a la lista entera.

EN LA OFICINA

La Netiquette (etiqueta en la red)

Cuando nos comunicamos con otra persona frente a frente o por teléfono, utilizamos gestos, expresiones y / o modulaciones de la voz que ayudan a nuestro interlocutor a interpretar nuestro mensaje. Esas importantes ayudas audiovisuales de la comunicación no están presentes en la comunicación escrita, por lo que es más difícil transmitir ciertas ideas, conceptos o sentimientos.

La Netiquette es una serie de reglas[1] de etiqueta que todos debemos conocer y seguir al comunicarnos a través de la red.

Además del sentido común, los buenos modales[2], la cortesía, el respeto, la consideración y la tolerancia, éstas son algunas reglas que todos debemos observar al comunicarnos a través de la red:

• Tenga siempre en mente que al otro lado de su pantalla hay un ser humano real, con sus propias ideas y sentimientos. Nunca escriba nada que no le diría[3] frente a frente a otra persona.
• Mantenga sus comunicados breves y al grano[4].
• No envíe a una lista de distribución anexos[5] largos, como archivos gráficos. El procedimiento correcto es ponerlos en algún lugar en la red y enviar el URL a la lista para que los interesados puedan tener acceso a ellos.
• Al contestar algún mensaje, deje alguna cita[6] para que se sepa a qué se está refiriendo usted, pero, por favor, recorte[7] todo lo demás.
• Nunca conteste un e-mail cuando esté enojado o molesto.

• Sea cuidadoso con información personal o privada. No envíe a una lista de distribución datos de otras personas, como dirección o número de teléfono.
• Asegúrese de que está enviando su correo electrónico al destinatario correcto **antes** de oprimir[8] el botón de "Enviar".
• Las letras MAYÚSCULAS se pueden usar para sustituir acentos o para enfatizar, pero **no** escriba todo en mayúsculas, pues esto se interpreta en la red como que ¡USTED ESTÁ GRITANDO[9]!
• No utilice una lista de distribución para promocionar ni adelantar causas religiosas, filosóficas, políticas, comerciales o para promover su propio sitio web.
• Si usted recibe un mensaje de aviso[10] sobre un virus que se contagia por correo electrónico o algo similar, **no** escriba a su lista de distribución para alertar a todos los miembros. Lo más seguro es que se trata de uno de tantos *hoaxes* que abundan en la red. Notifique sólo a los administradores de la lista y ellos investigarán.

Todo el mundo fue un novato[11] alguna vez y muchos de ellos no tuvieron la oportunidad de leer el *Netiquette*. Por lo tanto, cuando alguien cometa algún error, sea bondadoso[12] con él. Quizás no sea necesario mencionar nada si el error fue mínimo. Tener buenos modales no nos da derecho a corregir a los demás. Si decide informarle a alguien de algún tipo de error, hágalo cortésmente, y si es posible, en un e-mail privado en lugar de un e-mail público que recibirá la lista o grupo de discusión. Dé a la gente el beneficio de la duda. Puede ser que la otra persona haya cometido el error sin darse cuenta. Sobre todo, ¡no sea Ud. arrogante!

[1] *rules*
[2] *manners*
[3] **no...** *you would not say*
[4] **al...** al punto
[5] *attachments*
[6] *quotation*
[7] quite
[8] *to push*
[9] *shouting*
[10] *warning*
[11] *newbie, novice*
[12] simpático

 ACTIVIDAD 6 En grupos de tres a cuatro estudiantes, hablen de las reglas del Netiquette del artículo. ¿Están de acuerdo con todas? Miren las listas de reglas posibles que anotaron en la **Actividad 3.** ¿Hay algunas que quieran añadir a la lista? Después de hablar, hagan una lista de las "Diez Reglas de Oro" para comunicarse en Internet. Luego, comparen su lista con la de otro grupo.

Optional: Ask students to prioritize the list: **Pon las reglas del artículo en orden de importancia.**

A ESCRIBIR

Antes de escribir

Writing—Writing from charts and diagrams

When you are writing something that includes a lot of information, it is often helpful to group the information into categories before you begin writing. These categories then serve as the different paragraphs of your written piece, while the facts within the categories serve as supporting details.

Option or preparation: You may want to distribute ads from Spanish-language newspapers or provide ads for common student jobs.

ACTIVIDAD 1 Vas a escribir una carta o e-mail de presentación para el trabajo que se describe en el siguiente anuncio de trabajo. Completa la siguiente tabla con tus datos personales en preparación para escribir tu carta o e-mail de presentación.

Datos personales
Estudios y títulos
Experiencia profesional
Otros conocimientos o habilidades

Se buscan jóvenes
Buena imagen, dinámicos y con afán de superación[1], incorporación inmediata
Categoría: Área comercial, verano
Subcategoría: Comercial / Vendedor, verano
Lugar de trabajo: Montevideo, Uruguay
Número de vacantes: 20

Se requiere:
• Estudios de colegio, título universitario no es necesario
• Formación continuada a cargo de la empresa[2]
• Experiencia laboral no es necesaria

Se recomienda:
• Conocimiento de español
• Conocimiento de programas de software

Otros datos
Licencia de manejar: No
Vehículo propio: No
Disponibilidad para viajar: Sí
Disponibilidad de cambio de residencia: Sí

Se ofrece:
Remuneración de $6,00/hora, con comisión, trabajo completo, costos de traslado remunerados por la empresa

Otros datos
Interesados enviar C.V. por fax: 2/907622

Suggestion: After the chart is filled out, have students cross out irrelevant experience(s) or skill(s) for the **empleo** named.

[1] **afán...** *desire to succeed*
[2] **formación...** *ongoing training by the company*

ACTIVIDAD 2 Trabaja con un(a) compañero(a) de clase. Van a escribir una carta o e-mail de presentación para un trabajo. Necesitan incluir toda la información necesaria, pero deben tratar de que su carta no sea demasiado larga. Van a escribir una carta o e-mail de cuatro párrafos. Miren los datos que anotaron en la tabla de la **Actividad 1** y decidan cuáles son los más importantes. Luego, pongan esta información en el siguiente orden.

Párrafo 1: Preséntate y menciona el empleo que solicitas.
Párrafo 2: Describe brevemente tu preparación profesional y personal.
Párrafo 3: Habla de otros conocimientos o habilidades que tienes que pueden ser útiles para el puesto.
Párrafo 4: Despídete e incluye los datos personales necesarios para que se pongan en contacto contigo.

Escritura

ACTIVIDAD 3 Ahora escribe el borrador de tu carta o e-mail. Usa el modelo como ejemplo. También puedes usar expresiones y palabras de la siguiente lista.

Introducción

Me dirijo a ustedes para / en relación con...

Estudios / Experiencia / Otros conocimientos

Permítanme destacar (*to point out*)...
Quisiera señalar (*to point out*)...
Me gustaría añadir...
Además de...
Estoy dispuesto(a) a concretar una entrevista con ustedes si consideran adecuado mi currículum.

<fecha>

<dirección de la compañía>

Estimados señores:

<párrafo 1: introducción>

<párrafo 2: estudios y experiencia>

<párrafo 3: otros conocimientos>

En espera de su respuesta, los saluda atentamente,

<firma, si es una carta>
<tu nombre, dirección, teléfono, e-mail>

Optional: You may want to introduce other options for a business letter. **Más saludos: Muy distinguida señorita, Muy señor mío. Más despedidas: Un saludo cordial, Sinceramente suyo, De usted muy cordialmente.**

Notice: Formal business correspondence in Spanish generally has a more formal and sometimes flowery tone than in English business correspondence whose hallmarks are brevity and clarity. (C 2.1, C 4.1)

Después de escribir

 ACTIVIDAD 4 Intercambia tu borrador con otro(a) estudiante. Usen la siguiente lista como guía al corregir el borrador de la otra persona.

- ¿Incluye la carta toda la información necesaria sin ser demasiado larga?
- ¿Describe la carta claramente los estudios, la experiencia y los conocimientos de tu compañero(a)?
- ¿Se usó bien el subjuntivo con los verbos y expresiones negativas, de duda y de emoción?
- ¿Se usaron las formas correctas de todos los verbos?
- ¿Hay concordancia (*agreement*) entre los artículos, los sustantivos (*nouns*) y los adjetivos?
- ¿Hay errores de ortografía?

Después de hacer todas las correcciones necesarias, escribe la versión final de tu carta.

VOCABULARIO

LAS NOTICIAS DEL DÍA   *Current events*

la campaña	*campaign*
el (la) ciudadano(a)	*citizen*
la contaminación (del aire)	*(air) pollution*
el crimen	*crime*
el desastre natural	*natural disaster*
la (des)igualdad	*(in)equality*
la discriminación	*discrimination*
la economía	*economy*
el ejército	*the army*
las elecciones	*elections*
las fuerzas armadas	*armed forces*
la globalización	*globalization*
el gobierno	*government*
la guerra	*war*
la huelga	*strike*
el huracán	*hurricane*
la inundación	*flood*
el (la) líder	*leader*
la manifestación	*demonstration*
la paz mundial	*world peace*
la política	*politics*
el proceso electoral	*election process*
el terremoto	*earthquake*
el terrorismo	*terrorism*
la violencia	*violence*
iniciar	*to initiate*
luchar contra	*to fight against*
participar en	*to participate in*
sobrevivir	*to survive, overcome*
sufrir (las consecuencias)	*to suffer (the consequences)*
tomar medidas	*to take steps or measures*
votar	*to vote*

PARA SOLICITAR EMPLEO   *Applying for a job*

La entrevista   *The Interview*

la competencia	*the competition*
el currículum vitae	*curriculum vitae, résumé*
darse la mano	*to shake hands*
el formulario	*form*
el maletín	*briefcase*
la solicitud	*application*
la tarjeta	*business card*

El (La) candidato(a)   *The Candidate*

detallista	*detail-oriented*
disponible	*available*
emprendedor(a)	*enterprising*
llevarse bien con la gente	*to get along with people*
puntual	*punctual*
responsable	*responsible*
tener...	*to have . . .*
...algunos conocimientos de...	*. . . some knowledge of . . .*
...buena presencia	*. . . a good presence*
...(mucha) experiencia en...	*. . . (a lot of) experience in . . .*
...las habilidades necesarias	*. . . the necessary skills*

El puesto   *The job, position*

el ascenso	*promotion*
el aumento de sueldo	*salary increase, raise*
los beneficios	*benefits*
el contrato	*contract*
la (des)ventaja	*(dis)advantage*
el (la) empleado(a)	*employee*
el requisito	*requisite, requirement*
el seguro médico	*medical insurance*

El puesto (cont.)

averiguar	*to look into, investigate*
contratar	*to hire*
despedir (i, i)	*to fire*
dirigir	*to direct*
emplear	*to employ*
hacer informes	*to write reports*
jubilarse	*to retire*
requerir (ie, i)	*to require*
satisfacer (like **hacer**)	*to satisfy*
supervisar	*to supervise*
trabajar a tiempo completo	*to work full time*
trabajar a tiempo parcial	*to work part time*

LOS NEGOCIOS   *Business*

la bolsa (de valores)	*stock market*
la compañía multinacional	*multinational corporation*
los costos	*costs*
el desarrollo	*development*
el (la) empresario(a)	*businessman / woman*
la fábrica	*factory*
las ganancias y las pérdidas	*profits and losses*
la industria	*industry*
el presupuesto	*budget*
las telecomunicaciones	*telecommunications*

PARTICIPIOS PASADOS IRREGULARES

abierto	*open*
dicho	*said*
escrito	*written*
hecho	*done*
muerto	*dead*
puesto	*placed*
roto	*broken*
satisfecho	*satisfied*
visto	*seen*
vuelto	*returned*

¿Te gustaría ir conmigo?

CAPÍTULO 14

Communication

By the end of this chapter you will be able to:
- talk about travel and make travel plans
- describe animals and geography
- hypothesize and speculate
- express doubt, emotion, and reactions about past events

Cultures

By the end of this chapter you will have learned about:
- Argentina
- transportation and travel in Argentina and the U.S.
- **el agroturismo**
- noted Argentine author Jorge Luis Borges, a literary hoax concerning him, and the Internet
- the use of **vos** forms in Latin America

Un guía habla con un grupo de turistas en la Plaza de Mayo en Buenos Aires.

COMUNIDAD GLOBAL

Un refrán español dice que "El mundo es un pañuelo (*handkerchief*)", y es verdad. Hoy es posible viajar en poco tiempo a los lugares más remotos del mundo. También es posible hablar instantáneamente por teléfono o Internet con personas que están al otro lado del planeta. La posibilidad de visitar todos los países del mundo ya no es un sueño—¡es una realidad! En este capítulo, vamos a hablar de los viajes a otros países y de las bellezas naturales que nos esperan allí.

Los pingüinos magallanes de la península Valdés en Patagonia atraen a turistas de todo el mundo.

Las Cataratas del Iguazú están en el río Iguazú entre Argentina y Brasil en medio de una densa y remota selva tropical.

Bariloche es un centro turístico a las orillas del lago Nahuel Huapí en la región andina de Argentina.

Los datos

Mira las fotos y la información y luego di si las siguientes oraciones son ciertas o falsas.   *Los datos* answers: 1. C 2. C 3. F 4. C

❶ _____ Bariloche es un centro turístico en los Andes de Argentina.

❷ _____ Hay pingüinos en Argentina.

❸ _____ Las Cataratas del Iguazú están cerca de varias ciudades grandes.

❹ _____ El lago Nahuel Huapí está cerca de Bariloche.

¡Adivina!   ¡Adivina! answers: 1. F 2. C 3. C 4. F 5. C

¿Qué sabes de Argentina? Indica si las siguientes oraciones son ciertas o falsas. (Las respuestas están en la página 443.)

❶ _____ Argentina es el país más grande de Sudamérica.

❷ _____ Es posible esquiar en las montañas de Argentina durante los meses de julio y agosto.

❸ _____ Muchos argentinos son de ascendencia italiana, inglesa, alemana, judía y eslava.

❹ _____ Durante su larga historia, Argentina siempre ha tenido una de las economías más estables de Latinoamérica.

❺ _____ Hay gauchos en Argentina, como en Chile.

¡IMAGÍNATE!

Vocabulario útil 1

JAVIER: ¡Qué suerte!, ¿verdad? Bueno, si resulta que es una oferta legítima. Ojalá que sí. Sí, un fin de semana en las playas de Flamingo, ¡gratis! Necesito unas vacaciones, ¿sabes? Un viaje a la costa me vendría bien... Sí, sí, dice que incluye **el boleto de ida y vuelta,** ¡por **avión!**

Optional: You might want to point out that Flamingo Beach is in the west coast province of Guanacaste on the Pacific Rim. Costa Rica is home to 5% of the entire world's biodiversity. It is the second smallest Central American nation and has many beaches on the Caribbean and Pacific coasts, along with rain forests, cloud forests, and seven active volcanoes.

Suggestion: Introduce vocabulary through a chat about travel: **¿Te gusta viajar? ¿Adónde? ¿Usas una agencia de viajes? ¿Has viajado al extranjero? ¿Te gustaría hacer un tour en grupo con un itinerario preestablecido o prefieres viajar independientemente?**

La guía turística is a *tourist guidebook*; however, **el / la guía** can also be used to mean a male or female *tour guide*.

Suggestion: **Describe una ruta probable para viajar a Argentina desde donde estamos ahora.**

PARA VIAJAR

la agencia de viajes	*travel agency*
la guía turística	*tourist guide book*
el itinerario	*itinerary*
cambiar dinero	*to exchange money*
hacer una reservación	*to make a reservation*
hacer un tour	*to take a tour*
viajar al extranjero	*to travel abroad*

EN EL AEROPUERTO Y DENTRO DEL AVIÓN

la puerta (de embarque)

el asiento de ventanilla

el pasajero de clase turista

la pasajera de primera clase

la tarjeta de embarque

el asiento de pasillo

el (la) asistente de vuelo	*flight attendant*
el boleto / el billete	*ticket*
... de ida	*one-way*
... de ida y vuelta	*round-trip*
con destino a...	*with destination to . . .*
hacer escala en...	*to make a stopover in . . .*
la lista de espera	*waiting list*
la llegada	*arrival*
el pasaje	*ticket*
el retraso / la demora	*delay*
la salida	*departure*
el vuelo	*flight*
abordar	*to board*
desembarcar	*to disembark, get off (the plane)*

Actividades

ACTIVIDAD 1 **En el aeropuerto.** ¿Qué tienes que hacer en el aeropuerto en las siguientes situaciones? Escoge la mejor opción de la segunda columna. ¡OJO! Una de las opciones se puede usar en dos de las situaciones.

1. _____ Quieres facturar el equipaje.

2. _____ Es hora de abordar el vuelo a Buenos Aires.

3. _____ Acabas de llegar al destino y quieres recoger la maleta.

4. _____ Quieres cambiar tu asiento de ventanilla por un asiento de pasillo.

5. _____ El vuelo está lleno pero quieres esperar para ver si al final queda un asiento vacío.

6. _____ Tomas un vuelo internacional y tienes que enseñar el pasaporte.

7. _____ Tienes el boleto y estás en la puerta, pero no te dejan abordar.

a. Tienes que ir al mostrador de la línea aérea.

b. Tienes que mostrar el boleto para conseguir una tarjeta de embarque.

c. Tienes que poner tu nombre en la lista de espera.

d. Tienes que ir a la puerta de embarque.

e. Tienes que pasar por la aduana.

f. Tienes que ir a la sala de equipajes.

Answers Act. 1: 1. a 2. d 3. f 4. a 5. c 6. e 7. b

ACTIVIDAD 2 **Vamos de viaje.** Vas a viajar a Buenos Aires con un(a) amigo(a). Llamas a la agencia Buen Viaje para hacer las reservaciones de avión. Tu compañero(a) hace el papel del (de la) agente y te hace preguntas sobre tus planes. Contesta sus preguntas.

Agente: Tienes que averiguar adónde quiere viajar, cuándo quiere viajar, cuántos pasajes necesita, si quiere boletos de ida y vuelta, qué clase de boletos quiere... Al final, pide el número de teléfono del (de la) pasajero(a) para llamarlo(la) después con toda la información necesaria.

Pasajero(a): Vas a viajar a Buenos Aires con un(a) amigo(a). Anota las fechas de tu viaje antes de llamar y prepárate para contestar las preguntas del (de la) agente.

Vocabulario útil 2

JAVIER: Sí, **el hotel** también, **habitación doble, aire acondicionado, desayuno incluido, piscina...** ¡un verdadero paraíso! Bueno, me tengo que ir. Tengo que estar en la Agencia de Viajes Futura a las dos para recoger el paquete.

EL HOTEL

el ascensor	*elevator*
la conexión a Internet	*Internet connection*
el conserje	*concierge*
el desayuno incluido	*breakfast included*
la estampilla	*postage stamp*
la habitación doble	*double room*
... con / sin baño / ducha	*with / without bath / shower*
... de fumar / de no fumar	*smoking / non-smoking*
el (la) huésped(a)	*hotel guest*
el lavado en seco	*dry cleaning*
la recepción	*reception desk*
registrarse	*to register*
el servicio despertador	*wake-up call*
la tarjeta postal	*postcard*

It is much more common to hear **la huésped** rather than **la huéspeda** in everyday speech.

LA HABITACIÓN SENCILLA

el aire acondicionado

con baño y ducha

el botones

el secador de pelo

NO FUMAR

la televisión por cable

la llave

Actividades

ACTIVIDAD 3 **El huésped.** El señor García viaja a Buenos Aires para completar unos negocios de su compañía. Él expresa varias opiniones y necesidades. Según su comentario, indica qué cosa, servicio o persona va a necesitar. Escoge de la segunda columna.

Answers Act. 3: 1. c 2. f 3. i 4. a 5. k 6. g 7. b 8. l 9. j

1. _____ Hace mucho calor afuera. No puedo soportar (*to stand, tolerate*) el calor.

2. _____ Tengo que poder comunicarme con la oficina vía correo electrónico todos los días.

3. _____ No soporto un cuarto que huele a humo (*smells like smoke*) de cigarrillo.

4. _____ Tengo que secarme el pelo antes de ir a la reunión.

5 _____ Tengo que despertarme temprano y no traje mi despertador.

6. _____ Como voy a tener varias reuniones con clientes de mi compañía, voy a tener que usar el mismo traje varias veces.

a. el secador de pelo
b. el botones
c. el aire acondicionado
d. la televisión por cable
e. la llave
f. la conexión a Internet
g. el lavado en seco
h. la recepción
i. una habitación de no fumar
j. unas estampillas
k. el servicio despertador
l. el conserje

(cont. next page)

(cont.)

7. ____ Tengo muchas maletas y no puedo con ellas solo.

8. ____ Tengo que llevar a mis clientes a cenar y quiero llevarlos a los mejores restaurantes. No conozco los restaurantes de Buenos Aires.

9. ____ Escribí varias tarjetas postales para mi familia y quisiera enviárselas.

 ACTIVIDAD 4 **¡No hay aire acondicionado!** Con un(a) compañero(a), representen la siguiente situación: uno de ustedes es recepcionista en el Hotel Colonial y el otro es huésped(a). El (La) huésped(a) tiene muchas preguntas y quiere muchos servicios. El hotel es un poco antiguo y no tiene todas las comodidades modernas. Túrnense para hacer el papel de recepcionista y huésped(a). Si eres el (la) huésped(a), decide si te quieres quedar en este hotel o si prefieres buscar otro.

Servicios que <u>no</u> ofrece el Hotel Colonial
aire acondicionado
secador de pelo
servicio despertador
televisión por cable
conexión a Internet
ascensor
desayuno incluido
baño en la habitación
habitación de no fumar
estacionamiento gratis

MODELO: Compañero(a): *Quiero una habitación, por favor.*
Tú: *Muy bien, señor(a). ¿Sencilla o doble?*
Compañero(a): *Sencilla, por favor, pero tiene que tener aire acondicionado...*

Vocabulario útil 3

JAVIER: Ya sabía que no podía ser. Yo nunca me gano nada.
CHELA: Yo tampoco. Y ¡tenía unas ganas de ir a **la playa**!
JAVIER: ¡Yo ya casi podía oler **el mar**!
CHELA: Ay, sí, ¿verdad? El sol contra tu cara, **la arena** debajo de los pies... He tenido tanto trabajo... me parecía un sueño poder tomar un descanso.
JAVIER: Y salir de la ciudad. Estoy tan cansado de tanto estudiar. Si tuviera el dinero, me iría inmediatamente.

LA GEOGRAFÍA

LA ISLA

Heritage Learners: Additional practice with heritage speakers are: **suroeste, sureste, noroeste,** and **noreste.**

el cielo

las ruinas

la selva tropical

el mar/
el océano

el cañón

el volcán

el río

el desierto

el bosque

el lago

la arena

la playa

norte

oeste · este

sur

Actividades

ACTIVIDAD 5 **Me encanta la naturaleza.** Con un(a) compañero(a), túrnense para hablar de su viaje ideal. ¿Adónde les gustaría viajar? ¿Por qué? ¿Qué pueden hacer allí?

MODELO: Tú: *Me encantaría viajar a Mar del Plata en la costa atlántica. Para mí, el viaje ideal siempre incluye una playa.*

Compañero(a): *¿Sabes lo que me interesa? La selva tropical. Hay muchas especies de plantas y pájaros que me encantaría ver.*

ACTIVIDAD 6 **¡Odio la naturaleza!** Con un(a) compañero(a), túrnense para hablar del viaje que nunca les gustaría hacer. ¿Por qué?

MODELO: Tú: *No tengo ningún interés en ir al desierto. Odio el calor y la arena.*

Compañero(a): *Dicen que los volcanes son impresionantes, pero no quiero acercarme mucho.*

¡COMPÁRATE!

Actualmente existe mucho interés en temas relacionados con el medio ambiente (*environment*) y la naturaleza. Por esta razón el ecoturismo se ha convertido en una industria global. Pero en Argentina, un país donde la agricultura siempre ha sido sumamente importante, existe otro tipo de turismo también: el **agroturismo.**

El agroturismo es muy popular en Buenos Aires, donde los "agroturistas" pueden viajar a corta distancia de la ciudad y tener una experiencia rural auténtica en una de las muchas estancias (*ranches*) de la provincia de Buenos Aires que están abiertas al turismo. Como la vida en la ciudad es muy agitada, muchas personas quieren volver, aunque sea por unos días, a la tranquilidad de la vida rural y tradicional que vivían los argentinos hace unos cien años.

Típicamente los visitantes a estas estancias participan en tareas campestres (*rural*), como la fabricación de alimentos caseros (*homemade*), como el pan y el queso artesanal, o hacen excursiones a caballo para explorar la naturaleza cerca de la estancia. Es común que grupos estudiantiles pasen períodos breves de vacaciones en estas estancias, cuidando de los animales domésticos y cultivando productos agrícolas como el trigo (*wheat*) y las frutas.

 PRÁCTICA. En grupos de tres a cuatro personas, contesten las siguientes preguntas.

1. ¿Les gusta la idea del agroturismo? ¿Por qué sí o por qué no?
2. ¿Creen que es importante para los residentes de ciudades grandes tener experiencias rurales o ponerse en contacto con la naturaleza? ¿Por qué sí o por qué no?
3. ¿Creen que el agroturismo puede llegar a ser popular en EEUU también? ¿Por qué sí o por qué no?
4. ¿Ven algunas semejanzas (*similarities*) entre la vida tradicional de Argentina y la de EEUU hace unos cien años?

A VER

Antes de ver el video

 ACTIVIDAD 1 En el video para este capítulo Javier y Chela por fin se van a conocer. Con un(a) compañero(a) de clase, hagan unas predicciones. ¿Que va a pasar cuando se conozcan? ¿Van a estar en la misma excursión? ¿Van a llevarse bien (*get along well*) o mal? ¿Qué más?

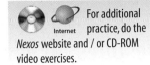

For additional practice, do the *Nexos* website and / or CD-ROM video exercises.

 ACTIVIDAD 2 Trabaja con un(a) compañero(a) de clase para hablar de varios viajes que han hecho. ¿Cuáles han sido sus favoritos? ¿Cuáles han sido los peores? ¿Por qué?

 ACTIVIDAD 3 Trabaja con un(a) compañero(a) de clase. ¿Han tenido una experiencia personal con el fraude? Por ejemplo:

1. una oferta de viajar a un sitio para quedarte "gratis" en un hotel
2. una carta o un e-mail que te ofrece la oportunidad de ganar mucho dinero sin hacer nada (o muy poco)
3. un e-mail de una persona que no revela su verdadera identidad electrónica pero que te promete dinero u otras cosas valiosas (*valuable*)
4. una carta, mensaje de teléfono o e-mail que te dice que has ganado un premio (*prize*) en un concurso (*contest*)
5. ¿...?

¿Cómo reaccionas a esas experiencias?

ESTRATEGIA

Integrating your viewing strategies

Now that you have learned a variety of video-viewing strategies, take a moment to review them, and place a check mark beside the ones you've found most helpful in previous chapters.

_____ viewing a segment several times
_____ using questions as an advance organizer
_____ watching body language to aid in comprehension
_____ watching without sound
_____ listening for the main idea
_____ watching facial expressions
_____ listening for details
_____ using background knowledge to anticipate content

_____ using visuals to aid comprehension
_____ listening to tone of voice
_____ listening for sequencing words
_____ listening for cognates and key words
_____ watching for transitions and listening for words that signal a change in the conversation

Optional: Survey your class to find out the top three most commonly identified viewing strategies. Incorporate this information into your teaching.

ACTIVIDAD 4 Mientras ves el video para este capítulo, trata de identificar una o dos estrategias de la lista anterior que te ayudaron a entender el episodio. Si no estás seguro(a) de las estrategias, ¿qué es lo que más te ayuda a entender el video?

El video

Mira el episodio para el **Capítulo 14.** No te olvides de enfocarte en las estrategias que se usan para entender el contenido del segmento.

Después de ver el video

ACTIVIDAD 5 Con un(a) compañero(a) de clase, contesten las siguientes preguntas sobre el video.

1. ¿Qué tiene Chela?
2. ¿Qué cree que ha ganado?
3. ¿Adónde tiene que ir ella para recoger (*to pick up*) el boleto y el itinerario?
4. ¿Qué cree Javier que ha ganado?
5. ¿Cuándo tiene que ir al sitio indicado para recoger el paquete?
6. Cuando Chela y Javier van al sitio indicado, ¿qué encuentran?
7. Según Javier, si tuviera (*if he had*) dinero, ¿qué haría (*would he do*)?
8. ¿Qué pasa al final del episodio?
9. Expliquen la reacción de Sergio, Beto, Anilú y Dulce.

ACTIVIDAD 6 Trabaja con otros tres compañeros de clase y representen la conversación que tuvieron Dulce, Anilú, Beto y Sergio antes del comienzo del episodio con Chela y Javier. ¿Por qué hicieron lo que hicieron?

ACTIVIDAD 7 Con un(a) compañero(a), escriban la carta que Dulce, Anilú, Beto y Sergio les mandaron a Javier y Chela. Vuelvan a ver el episodio varias veces para sacar todos los detalles sobre el viaje que ofrece la carta misteriosa.

Conexión cultural. Mira el segmento cultural que está al final del episodio. Luego, en grupos de tres o cuatro, decidan cuál de las ciudades o países les gustaría conocer y expliquen por qué. Finalmente, hagan un itinerario de lugares que debe ver un(a) turista en su estado o país.

VOCES DE LA COMUNIDAD

Omar Edmundo Pascucci

"En los últimos treinta años me he navegado el mundo entero. Me encanta explorar diferentes culturas, lenguas, regiones, cocinas y hasta climas. Es por eso que disfruto tanto de (*I enjoy so much*) mi trabajo. Sin embargo, no hay nada más dulce (*nicer*) que el retorno a casa después de una larga temporada. "

Omar Edmundo Pascucci es Jefe de Cubierta (*Chief Officer*) del barco *Grandeur of the Seas* de Royal Caribbean. Con una tripulación (*crew*) de más de 760 personas, y una capacidad para casi 2.500 pasajeros, este lujoso crucero es una pequeña ciudad, completa con tiendas, gimnasios, restaurantes, salones de baile, biblioteca, cines y piscinas. Como Jefe de Cubierta, Pascucci es responsable por la navegación, las rutas, la carga y los oficiales de guardia de su barco. Su trabajo lo lleva a puertos de escala como Barcelona, Málaga, Nápoles, Malta, Grecia, el canal de Panamá, Quebec y México. Típicamente, Pascucci alterna cuatro meses de viajes con tres meses de descanso en su hogar en Los Ángeles, California. Nacido en la Argentina, Pascucci es egresado (*graduate*) de la Escuela Náutica Nacional de Argentina y oficial de la marina mercante.

Preparation: Warm up by asking students the questions from the student anno: **¿Te gustaría ganarte la vida viajando? ¿Qué ventajas y desventajas presenta este tipo de trabajo?**

¿Te gustaría ganarte la vida viajando? ¿Qué ventajas y desventajas presenta este tipo de trabajo? To learn more about Omar Edmundo Pascucci and cruise ships on the Royal Caribbean line, visit the *Nexos* website (http://college.hmco.com/languages/spanish/students) and follow the links.

Gramática útil 1

**Expressing doubt, emotion, volition, and nonexistence in the past:
The imperfect subjunctive**

Internet For more practice of chapter topics, do the *Nexos* website exercises.

CÓMO USARLO

1. When you use verbs that express influence, doubt, and emotion within a past-tense or hypothetical context, the imperfect subjunctive—instead of the present subjunctive—is used in the dependent clause.

Los niños **querían** que sus padres **compraran** un auto nuevo para el viaje.	*The children **wanted** their parents to **buy** a new car for the trip.*
Era necesario que **estudiaras** los mapas antes del viaje.	*It **was** necessary that **you studied** the maps before the trip.*
No **había** nadie que **supiera** tanto de la región como tú.	*There **was** no one who **knew** the region as well as you.*

2. The imperfect subjunctive is used in the following situations.

main clause verb is in the *imperfect, preterite,* or *past perfect* →	dependent clause verb is in the *imperfect subjunctive*
Los turistas nos **pedían** que... *The tourists **asked** (us) that . . .*	... los **lleváramos** a las montañas. *. . . we **take** them to the mountains.*
Los turistas **se alegraron** de que... *The tourists **were happy** that . . .*	... los **pudiéramos** llevar. *. . . we **could** take them.*
Yo **había dudado** que... *I **had doubted** that . . .*	... **tuviéramos** tiempo para el viaje. *. . . we **had** time for the trip.*

Heritage Learners: Research shows that heritage language speakers lack familiarity with the formal registers of language. Have students transform commands into formal and polite requests for practice. Encourage students to generate as many polite forms as they can for each command: Pásame el agua. Cállense que no oigo nada. ¿Cómo? Siéntate. Dime tu nombre. Oye, ¿dónde queda el Museo de Arte Moderno? Ayúdame con la tarea. Dame cambio para un dólar. Tráeme el menú.

3. The imperfect subjunctive forms of **poder** and **querer** are often used in present-tense situations to express requests more courteously.

Quisiera hacerle una pregunta. ¿**Pudiera** ayudarme con el itinerario?	*I **would like** to ask you a question.* ***Could you (please)** help me with the itinerary?*

4. Note that when the main clause uses **decir** in the preterite or the imperfect, the verb used in the dependent clause varies, depending upon what is meant.

Marta **dijo** que el viaje **era**
fenomenal.
Marta **dijo** que **nos quedáramos** en
su casa.

*Marta **said** that the trip **was**
phenomenal.*
*Marta **told** us **to stay** in her house.*

In the first example, you are merely reporting what Marta said. This is known
as indirect discourse and is often used in newspaper accounts to quote someone's speech. In the second example, Marta is expressing a wish or desire, which
means that the subjunctive is required because it says what she wants us to do.
Look carefully at past-tense sentences with **decir** to see which meaning is being
expressed.

COMO FORMARLO

1. To form the imperfect subjunctive, take the **ustedes / ellos / ellas** form of
the preterite tense. Remove the **-on** ending and add the new endings shown
in the following chart. Notice that this formula is the same for **-ar, -er,** and
-ir verbs.

regular **-ar** verb: **viajar**		regular **-er** verb: **ver**		regular **-ir** verb: **salir**	
viajaron → viajar-		**vieron → vier-**		**salieron → salier-**	
viajara	viajáramos	viera	viéramos	saliera	saliéramos
viajaras	viajarais	vieras	vierais	salieras	salierais
viajara	viajaran	viera	vieran	saliera	salieran

irregular verb: **ir**		stem-change verb: **pedir**	
fueron → fuer-		**pidieron → pidier-**	
fuera	fuéramos	pidiera	pidiéramos
fueras	fuerais	pidieras	pidierais
fuera	fueran	pidiera	pidieran

2. Because you are forming the imperfect subjunctive from an already conjugated preterite form, this form already reflects any irregularities of the verb in
the preterite, and any spelling or stem changes.

Actividades

🎧 **ACTIVIDAD 1** **Las recomendaciones.** Quieres viajar a Buenos Aires. Hablas
con una agente de viajes de la Agencia Paraíso. Escucha sus recomendaciones y
escribe una oración que explique qué te recomendó. Sigue el modelo.

MODELO: comprar
Me recomendó que comprara un boleto de ida y vuelta.

1. llegar
2. no llevar
3. facturar
4. quedarse
5. reservar
6. registrarse

Suggestion: Review conjugation of
the following verbs in the third person
plural of the preterite tense: **1.** cantar,
cantaron 2. pagar, **pagaron 3.** dar,
dieron 4. conocer, **conocieron**
5. perder, **perdieron 6.** traer, **trajeron**
7. ver, **vieron 8.** querer, **quisieron**
9. hacer, **hicieron 10.** poner, **pusieron**
11. llevar, **llevaron 12.** deber, **debieron**
13. leer, **leyeron 14.** salir, **salieron**
15. decir, **dijeron**

Notice that you must put an accent
on the **nosotros** form in order to
maintain the correct pronunciation.

You may want to review irregular
preterite and preterite stem-
changing verbs in **Capítulos 7** and **8**
in order to refresh your memory on
these conjugations.

Suggestion: It is important to contrast
pronunciation between the third person
plural of the preterite and the imperfect
subjunctive form. Try a listening activity
where students write **I (indicativo)** and
S (subjuntivo) according to what they
hear: **1.** durmieran, S **2.** sintieron, I
3. cerraron, I **4.** jugaran, S
5. estuvieran, S **6.** facturaran, S
7. supieron, I (*Review special meaning:
they found out*) **8.** pudieran, S
9. hubieron, I **10.** fueran, S

Suggestion: You may want to have
students take notes as they listen and
then formulate the sentences.

Answers Act. 1: **1.** Me recomendó que
llegara al aeropuerto con tres horas
de anticipación. **2.** Me recomendó que
no llevara más de una maleta. **3.** Me
recomendó que facturara el equipaje en
vez de cargarlo. **4.** Me recomendó que me
quedara en el Hotel Rioplatense. **5.** Me
recomendó que reservara una habitación
doble con baño. **6.** Me recomendó
que me registrara en el hotel
inmediatamente al llegar a la ciudad.

ACTIVIDAD 2 **Los primos.** Tus primos vinieron a visitarte. Tenían ciertas expectativas del viaje. ¿Qué esperaban?

MODELO: el vuelo: salir a tiempo
Esperaban que el vuelo saliera a tiempo.

1. sus maletas: llegar con ellos

2. el avión: no hacer escala en ningún sitio

3. el retraso: no ser tan largo

4. la línea aérea: servirles algo de comer durante el vuelo

5. nosotros: recogerlos en el aeropuerto

6. ustedes: llevarlos al hotel

7. el hotel: tener conexión a Internet

8. el botones: ser más cortés

ACTIVIDAD 3 **Óscar.** Viajas con tu amigo Óscar. ¡A Óscar le gusta quejarse de todo! Después del viaje le explicas a otro amigo de qué dudaba Óscar. Sigue el modelo.

MODELO: Óscar: ¡El agente no nos va a poner en la lista de espera!
Tú: *Dudaba que el agente nos pusiera en la lista de espera.*

1. ¡El vuelo no va a salir a tiempo!

2. ¡No nos van a servir el almuerzo en el vuelo!

3. ¡No vamos a desembarcar a tiempo!

4. ¡No vamos a encontrar las maletas en la sala de equipajes!

5. ¡El hotel no va a tener televisión por cable!

6. ¡El secador de pelo en el baño no va a funcionar!

7. ¡La habitación no va a incluir el desayuno!

8. ¡La habitación no va a estar limpia!

ACTIVIDAD 4 **Los consejos.** Los amigos y la familia siempre nos dan consejos sobre nuestra vida. Explícale a tu compañero(a) seis consejos que te dieron amigos o parientes y el resultado de esos consejos. Luego, que tu compañero(a) te explique a ti.

Frases útiles:
Mis padres me pidieron que...
Mi hermano(a) me aconsejó que...
Mi amigo(a)... me sugirió que...
Mis amigos querían que...
Mi tío(a) me recomendó que...
Mi abuelo(a) insistió en que...

MODELO: *Mis amigos querían que fuera a Buenos Aires con ellos. Decidí ir con ellos y nos divertimos mucho.*

Gramática útil 2
Saying what might happen or could occur: The conditional

Can you find the conditional form in the headline of this ad? Why do you think it is used here?

Answer: **deberías**; the conditional is used to convey the idea "should"

CÓMO USARLO

LO BÁSICO

So far you have learned a number of *tenses* (the present, the present progressive, the present perfect, the past perfect, the preterite, the imperfect, and the future) and two *moods* (the indicative and subjunctive moods). As you recall, *tenses* are associated with *time,* while *moods* reflect *how the speaker views the event* he or she is describing.

1. Both English and Spanish speakers use a mood called the *conditional* to talk about events that *might or could happen* in the future. The conditional is used because the speaker is saying *what could or might occur, under certain conditions.*

Ojalá que me toque la lotería. **Usaría** el dinero para viajar por toda Latinoamérica. Primero **iría** a Buenos Aires y luego **vería** las Cataratas del Iguazú.	*I hope I win the lottery.* **I would use** *the money to travel all over Latin America. First* **I would go** *to Buenos Aires and later* **I would see** *Iguazú Falls.*

2. The conditional is used to soften requests or make suggestions in a more courteous way. Verbs frequently used in this way are **poder** and **querer,** similar to the use in the imperfect subjunctive that you learned on pages 434–435.

pages 434–435.

¿Podría decirme cuándo sale el autobús para Buenos Aires?	*Can you* (*please*) *tell me when the bus for Buenos Aires leaves?*
¿Querría usted cambiar de asiento?	*Would you like* *to change seats?*

> The imperfect subjunctive is the most polite way to make non-command requests: **¿Pudiera Ud. ayudarme?** Next is the conditional (**¿Podría Ud. ayudarme?**), followed by the present tense, which is the least formal: **¿Puede Ud. ayudarme?**

3. The conditional may also be used to speculate about events that have already occurred, similar to the way that the future tense is used to speculate about current events. It is often used this way with expressions such as **tal vez** and **quizás** (*perhaps*).

No sé por qué llegó tan tarde el tren. **Tal vez habría** nieve.	*I don't know why the train arrived so late.* ***Perhaps there was*** *snow.*

CÓMO FORMARLO

1. The formation of the conditional is very similar to the formation of the future tense, which you learned in **Capítulo 12.** As with the future, you add a set of endings to the full *infinitive*, not the *stem*, of regular **-ar, -er,** and **-ir** verbs. Here are the conditional endings.

yo	**-ía**	**viajaría**	nosotros(as)	**-íamos**	**viajaríamos**
tú	**-ías**	**viajarías**	vosotros(as)	**-íais**	**viajaríais**
Ud. / él / ella	**-ía**	**viajaría**	Uds. / ellos / ellas	**-ían**	**viajarían**

> Notice that the conditional endings are identical to the imperfect tense endings for **-er** and **-ir** verbs.

2. The following verbs are irregular in the conditional. They attach the regular conditional endings to the irregular stems shown, not the infinitive.

> Notice that these are the same verbs that have irregular stems in the future tense.

irregular, no pattern:		
decir	**dir-**	diría, dirías, diría, diríamos, diríais, dirían
hacer	**har-**	haría, harías, haría, haríamos, haríais, harían
***e* is dropped from infinitive:**		
poder	**podr-**	podría, podrías, podría, podríamos, podríais, podrían
querer	**querr-**	querría, querrías, querría, querríamos, querríais, querrían
saber	**sabr-**	sabría, sabrías, sabría, sabríamos, sabríais, sabrían
***d* replaces the final vowel:**		
poner	**pondr-**	pondría, pondrías, pondría, pondríamos, pondríais, pondrían
salir	**saldr-**	saldría, saldrías, saldría, saldríamos, saldríais, saldrían
tener	**tendr-**	tendría, tendrías, tendría, tendríamos, tendríais, tendrían
venir	**vendr-**	vendría, vendrías, vendría, vendríamos, vendríais, vendrían

3. The conditional form of **hay** is **habría.**

Habría un problema.	*There must have been a problem.*

Actividades

ACTIVIDAD 5 **Buenos Aires.** Imagínate que vives en Buenos Aires. ¿Qué harías?

MODELO: vivir en el barrio de San Telmo
Viviría en el barrio de San Telmo.

1. ir a ver una ópera en el Teatro Colón
2. comprar una chaqueta de piel
3. buscar un bar donde bailan el tango
4. comer bistec a la parrilla en una de las parrillas famosas
5. salir de compras en la Avenida 9 de Julio
6. visitar Mar del Plata con mis amigos
7. pasar las tardes en la Plaza de Mayo

ACTIVIDAD 6 **Las situaciones.** Escucha las siguientes situaciones y decide cuál de las explicaciones de la segunda columna es la más lógica para cada situación.

1. _____
2. _____
3. _____
4. _____
5. _____
6. _____

a. Perdería el número de teléfono de la casa.
b. Su vuelo se demoraría.
c. Tendría una emergencia en el hospital.
d. Estaría enfermo.
e. Cambiarían de hotel.
f. Se les olvidaría.

ACTIVIDAD 7 **En esa situación...** En grupos de tres o cuatro, lean las siguientes situaciones. Luego cada persona en el grupo tiene que hacer por lo menos una sugerencia para la persona en la situación.

1. Acabas de llegar a Salta. En el hotel, al buscar tu tarjeta de crédito, te das cuenta de que te han robado. Sólo tienes un poco de dinero en efectivo. ¿Qué harías?

2. Un amigo tuyo va a graduarse. Le han ofrecido un trabajo muy bueno en Detroit, pero su novia va a estar en Nueva York. Además, quieren casarse pronto. No sabe si aceptar el puesto o pedirle a su novia que renuncie a su trabajo y se vaya con él. ¿Qué debería hacer tu amigo?

3. Tienes unos amigos a quienes les interesa la cinematografía. Quieren hacer un documental sobre el tango. Saben un poco de español, pero no mucho. Tienen que ir a Argentina para hacer las entrevistas para el documental. ¿Qué necesitarían hacer?

4. ¿...? (Inventen otra situación dentro del grupo.)

Gramática útil 3
Expressing the likelihood that an event will occur: Si clauses with the subjunctive and the indicative

Begin the CD-ROM activities. Do the cultural activities and reading and writing practice as you complete the corresponding text sections.

Si tuviera el dinero, **me iría** inmediatamente.

Suggestion: Model and have students generate events that are likely to occur like: **Si vamos a la clase de español, hablaremos en español, escucharemos al (a la) profesor(a)... Si vamos de viaje al extranjero...**

CÓMO USARLO

1. The conditional is often used with **si** (*if*) and the imperfect subjunctive to talk about situations that are contrary to fact or very unlikely to occur (at least in the speaker's opinion). The **si** clause is the dependent clause that expresses the unlikely hypothesis, while the main clause expresses what would occur in the contrary-to-fact situation.

Si me dieran el trabajo, **viajaría** a Argentina, Uruguay y Chile.	*If they give me (were to give me) the job, I would travel to Argentina, Uruguay and Chile.*
Si tuviéramos el dinero y el tiempo, **haríamos** un viaje de seis meses después de graduarnos de la universidad.	*If we had (were to have) the money and the time, we would make a six-month trip after graduating from the university.*

2. In situations where you think an outcome is *likely* to occur, use the present indicative in the **si** clause and the future or **ir** + **a** + infinitive in the main clause.

Si tengo tiempo, **haré / voy a hacer** las reservaciones hoy.	*If I have time (and I think I will), I will make / am going to make the reservations today.*
Si estás mejor mañana, **vendrás / vas a venir** en el tren con nosotros.	*If you are better tomorrow (and you probably will be), you will come / are going to come on the train with us.*

3. To summarize:

Note that you do not use the present subjunctive with **si**. You either use the present indicative (**Si tengo el tiempo...**) if you are fairly certain that the event will occur, or the imperfect subjunctive (**Si tuviera el tiempo...**) if you consider it unlikely.

Suggestion: Model several sentences that will be seen as concretely hypothetical like: **Si ganara un millón de dólares, viajaría al Cono Sur. Si ganaras un millón de dólares, ¿qué harías?**

Si clause to express unlikely outcome	*Si* clause to express likely outcome
Si + *imperfect subjunctive* is used with the *conditional*.	**Si** + *present indicative* is used with the *future* or **ir** + **a** + *infinitive*.
Si tuviera el dinero, **haría** un viaje. (*If [in the unlikely situation that] I were to have the money, I would take a trip.*)	**Si tengo** el dinero, **haré / voy a hacer** un viaje. (*If I have the money—and I think I will—I will take / am going to take a trip.*)

Heritage Learners: The sequence of tenses in conditional clauses varies considerably from country to country. Be aware that heritage language speakers that use these are reflecting the standards of their own community, rather than showing an incorrect mastery of this grammar point. Possible variations include: **Si tuviera más tiempo, fuera al gimnasio. Si tendría más tiempo, iría al gimnasio. Si hubiera tenido más tiempo, hubiera ido al gimnasio. Si habría tenido más tiempo, habría ido al gimnasio.**

Actividades

ACTIVIDAD 8 **Estoy seguro(a).** Escribe seis oraciones usando elementos de las dos columnas. Usa **si** + **el futuro** o **ir** + **a** + **infinitivo** para señalar que estás seguro(a) de que vas a hacer las cosas en la segunda columna. Luego, escribe por lo menos una oración que no use elementos de la lista sino elementos de tu propia imaginación.

Preparation / Optional: Have students write this activity. Collect their responses, read them aloud, and have students guess whose future plans are whose.

MODELO: *Si viajo al extranjero, iré a Argentina.*

viajar al extranjero	ver el Gran Cañón
tener el tiempo	pasar unos días en Mar del Plata
viajar al suroeste de EEUU	hacer una excursión a la selva tropical
estar en México	de Brasil
tener el dinero	subir las pirámides de Teotihuacán
ir a Sudamérica /	ir a Argentina
Centroamérica	ir a ver los volcanes en Costa Rica
¿...?	¿...?

ACTIVIDAD 9 **¿Qué harías?** Túrnense para hacerle preguntas a su compañero(a) sobre lo que haría en diferentes situaciones. Pueden usar las ideas de la lista o pueden inventar otras.

MODELO: Compañero(a): *Si ganaras la lotería, ¿qué harías?*
Tú: *Me compraría una casa de veinte habitaciones.*

Si...
ganar la lotería
poder ir a cualquier lugar
vivir en Buenos Aires
ser millonario(a)
trabajar para una línea aérea
viajar al extranjero
tener el tiempo
conocer al presidente de Argentina
tener cinco hijos
poder conocer a cualquier persona
¿...?

¿Qué harías?
¿...?

ACTIVIDAD 10 **Mis planes para el futuro.** Con un(a) compañero(a), hablen sobre sus planes para el futuro. Algunas cosas saben con certitud que las van a hacer, otras las quisieran hacer y otras son sueños. Cada uno(a) debe mencionar por lo menos cuatro cosas que piensa hacer.

MODELO: Tú: *Si ahorro suficiente dinero, voy a visitar a una amiga en París.*
Compañero(a): *Si pudiera, yo pasaría un año en Argentina mejorando mi español.*

Sonrisas

Standards: This activity fosters interpersonal expression among students where they will express their opinions. (C 1.1)

 EXPRESIÓN. En grupos de tres a cuatro estudiantes, hagan lo siguiente.

1. Pongan las ideas de la segunda estudiante en orden de importancia: 1 es para la idea más importante y 4 es para la idea menos importante.
2. Añadan dos ideas más a la lista.
3. Luego, hagan una lista de cinco cosas egoístas o superficiales que harían, empezando con hacer la televisión por cable un derecho constitucional.
4. Al final, pongan las ideas de la segunda lista en orden de importancia.
5. Comparen sus listas con las de otro grupo. ¿Están de acuerdo? ¿Qué diferencias hay?

Argentina

 Un país de contrastes. Con un(a) compañero(a), miren el mapa, los textos y las fotos en las páginas 443–445. Luego, traten de asociar los textos y las fotos con los números indicados en el mapa. (Cada número en el mapa corresponde con una de las fotos o uno de los textos.)

¿Adivinaste? Answers to the questions on page 423: 1. F 2. C 3. C 4. F 5. C

Answers: 1: Foto E 2: Foto F 3: Texto B 4: Texto C 5: Texto D 6: Texto A 7: Foto G

Texto A:

Cuando se habla de Argentina, muchas personas piensan en los gauchos, esas figuras míticas tan populares en la literatura argentina de los siglos XVIII y XIX. Vivían (y todavía viven) en varias regiones del país, pero se asocian más con las llanuras (*plains*) fértiles en el centro del país, que es muy parecido al oeste estadounidense. Con sus tradiciones pintorescas y su música vibrante de acordeón, los gauchos son una parte importante de la herencia argentina.

Texto B:

Se llaman las Islas Malvinas en español, pero también se conocen como Las Falklands. La posesión de este territorio siempre ha sido un punto de conflicto político entre Inglaterra y Argentina. En 1982, estalló (*broke out*) una guerra entre los dos países sobre la posesión de estas islas. Aunque Inglaterra ganó la guerra, todavía quedan problemas políticos que resultaron del conflicto.

Notice: The **Islas Malvinas** are also known in the English-speaking world as the Falkland Islands. There are two large islands and about 200 smaller ones. British rule was established in the islands in 1833. Argentina, who also claims the islands, invaded in 1982. Air, sea, and land battles broke out between the two countries. Argentina withdrew its forces later in 1982.

Texto C:

Tierra del Fuego es una isla al extremo sur de Argentina. La capital de la región, Ushuaia, es el área poblada más austral (*southern*) del globo, a unos pocos kilómetros de distancia de Antártida. Charles Darwin vino a esta región en los años 1840, en su famoso viaje del *Beagle*, cuando exploró y documentó la rara flora y fauna de la Patagonia.

Texto D:

Las Cataratas del Iguazú se encuentran en la frontera entre Argentina y Brasil, en el centro de una selva tropical, donde el río Iguazú cae unos 76 metros desde las alturas (*heights*) de la selva hasta las rocas de abajo. Las cataratas consisten en más de 275 cascadas separadas, y hasta 350 durante la temporada lluviosa. Dos aeropuertos internacionales, uno de Argentina y otro de Brasil, sirven este remoto sitio, el cual se encuentra a dos días en coche de Buenos Aires.

Foto E:

Aconcagua, a unos 6.200 metros de altura, es el pico más alto del hemisferio sur. Muchos alpinistas intentan la peligrosa subida cada año.

Foto F:

Buenos Aires, que se encuentra en la boca del Río de la Plata, tiene un marcado sabor (*flavor*) europeo. Los porteños, también llamados rioplatenses, disfrutan de una ciudad llena de cafés, que muchos comparan con París.

Internet

5·2 Standards: Besides directly seeking information about the Argentine culture, by gathering research on the web, students will interact with virtual communities of Spanish-speakers such as travel agencies, institutions, international organizations, etc. Encourage your students to do web searches in Spanish to ensure more direct contact with the language and culture.

¡CONÉCTATE!

En grupos de tres o cuatro, escojan una de las regiones de Argentina que ya estudiaron. Luego, cada persona debe buscar información por Internet o en la biblioteca sobre un aspecto de la región. Usen los enlaces sugeridos en el sitio web de *Nexos* (http://college.hmco.com/languages/spanish/students) para ir a otros sitios web posibles. Después de hacer su investigación, juntos preparen un informe para presentar a la clase.

Regiones	Aspectos
Buenos Aires	geografía
Bariloche y los lagos de los Andes	historia breve
la Pampa	diversiones
las Cataratas del Iguazú	medios de transporte
el pico Aconcagua	
Tierra del Fuego	
las Islas Malvinas	

Foto G:

Bariloche es un conocido centro turístico de esquí en los Andes. Situado a orillas del lago Nahuel Huapí, Bariloche ofrece una variedad de deportes invernales para los turistas que vienen de todo el mundo para gozar de (*to enjoy*) esta región de lagos y montañas.

¡FÍJATE!

El voseo

Ninguna presentación sobre la lengua española puede considerarse completa sin hablar del tema del **voseo.** Este término se refiere al uso del pronombre **vos** en la segunda persona del singular, en vez de **tú,** para expresar la familiaridad. El voseo se encuentra por muchas zonas de Centro y Sudamérica, donde adopta diferentes aspectos según la región. En algunas zonas, vos tiene su propia conjugación verbal: **vos amá(i)s, vos queré(i)s, vos bebé(i)s.** En otras, vos se emplea con las formas verbales del pronombre **tú: vos hablas, vos quieres, vos bebes.** Y en otras zonas el pronombre **tú** acompaña a las formas verbales de vos: **tú amás, tú querés, tú vivís.**

El valor social del voseo también varía mucho de una región a otra. En algunos países, por ejemplo en Chile y Perú, el voseo se considera una manera de hablar de las clases bajas (*lower*). En otros países, el voseo se acepta sólo entre familiares y amigos, mientras que **tú** es la forma aceptada en situaciones formales. En Argentina, el voseo es aceptado por todas las clases sociales y es considerado un símbolo de la argentinidad.

 PRÁCTICA. Contesta las siguientes preguntas con un(a) compañero(a) de clase.

1. ¿Existe una forma similar al voseo en inglés?
2. ¿Puedes pensar en unas diferencias regionales en tu país con relación a la manera familiar o coloquial de hablar?
3. ¿Quién usa estas formas? ¿Tienen un significado (*meaning*) social?

A LEER

Antes de leer

Standards: Here students interpret the poems as cultural products, which offer wisdom and lessons of life-long learning. (C 1.2, C 2.2, C 5.2)

ESTRATEGIA

Understanding an author's point of view

When you read any piece of writing, it's important to understand why the author has written it. Is it to inform, to persuade, to entertain, to enlighten, to share emotion? Recognizing the author's point of view is an important tool to use when reading in Spanish. In this chapter, you are going to read two poems. When you read a poem, what do you think the author's purpose is in writing it? Is it to share emotions and experiences? To entertain? To enlighten? Keep these ideas in mind as you read this chapter's poems.

ACTIVIDAD 1 Los dos poemas que vas a leer tratan de los pensamientos de dos autores mientras reflexionan sobre sus vidas. Con un(a) compañero(a) de clase, contesten las siguientes preguntas.

1. ¿Cómo describirían su vida hasta este punto: feliz, triste, emocionante, aburrida? ¿Qué palabras la describen mejor?
2. ¿Qué cosas no volverían a hacer (*not do over again*) si tuvieran la oportunidad de empezar la vida de nuevo? ¿Qué cosas sí harían otra vez?
3. ¿Creen que sería posible escribir su autobiografía ahora o preferirían esperar unos años? ¿Cuántos años querrían esperar?
4. ¿Creen que las actitudes hacia la vida y la muerte evolucionan con la edad? Traten de dar unos ejemplos para apoyar su opinión.

ACTIVIDAD 2 Uno de los poemas que van a leer, "Instantes" (que también ha aparecido con el título "Último poema"), es un misterio literario. Ha sido falsamente atribuido a Jorge Luis Borges, un famoso poeta argentino, pero no se sabe realmente quién lo escribió. Una cosa sí es cierta: este fraude ha continuado diseminándose por Internet, donde todavía es fácil encontrar el poema atribuido a Borges. Con un(a) compañero(a) de clase, contesten las siguientes preguntas sobre los fraudes y los engaños (*hoaxes*) de Internet.

1. ¿Pueden pensar en obras literarias que hayan sido falsamente atribuidas? (Por ejemplo, había un discurso atribuido a Kurt Vonnegut que se diseminaba por Internet que resultó ser escrito por una periodista estadounidense.) ¿Hay historias o anécdotas (como las leyendas urbanas) que ustedes conocen que al final resultaron ser falsas? ¿Cómo creen que empiezan estos engaños y por qué?

2. En su opinión, ¿qué papel juega Internet en la diseminación de información falsa? ¿Han encontrado información incorrecta en Internet? ¿Cómo pueden averiguar si la información que encuentran en Internet es verdadera o no?

3. ¿Creen que las personas que diseminan engaños o información falsa lo hacen a propósito o por accidente? En su opinión, ¿por qué lo hacen?

Lectura

ACTIVIDAD 3 Ahora lee los dos poemas. Mientras los lees, trata de identificar el punto de vista de cada autor. Trata de entender el sentido general de cada poema; no es necesario entender todas las palabras.

MI VIDA ENTERA

Jorge Luis Borges

AQUÍ OTRA VEZ, LOS LABIOS[1] MEMORABLES, ÚNICO Y
    SEMEJANTE A VOSOTROS.
Soy esa torpe[2] intensidad que es un alma.[3]
He persistido en la aproximación de la dicha[4] y
    en la privanza del pesar.[5]
He atravesado[6] el mar.
He conocido muchas tierras; he visto una mujer
    y dos o tres hombres.
He querido a una niña altiva[7] y blanca y de una
    hispánica quietud.
He visto un arrabal[8] infinito donde se cumple una
    insaciada mortalidad de ponientes.[9]
He paladeado[10] numerosas palabras.
Creo profundamente que eso es todo y que ni veré
    ni ejecutaré cosas nuevas.
Creo que mis jornadas[11] y mis noches se igualan en
    pobreza y en riqueza a las de Dios y a las
    de todos los hombres.

[1]*lips* [2]*awkward* [3]*soul* [4]felicidad, alegría [5]**privanza...** el privilegio de la tristeza [6]cruzado [7]arrogante [8]barrio, suburbio [9]**insaciada...** *incalculable number of tireless sunsets* [10]*tasted, savored* [11]días (de trabajo)

Suggestion: Work on the poems in class—paraphrasing and giving students a guided reading—and then have them reread as homework.

Suggestion: Point out or elicit that **Mi vida entera** has many verbs in the present perfect tense and that in **Instantes / Último poema** the conditional tense dominates the poem. Besides reviewing these tenses, be sure to point out the different rhythm and tone that these structures (**haber** + past participle and **-ía**) create in literature.

Instantes (o Último poema)

Autor desconocido

Si pudiera vivir nuevamente mi vida,
En la próxima trataría de cometer más errores.
No intentaría ser tan perfecto,
me relajaría más.

Sería más tonto de lo que he sido,
de hecho tomaría muy pocas cosas
con seriedad.
Sería menos higiénico.

Correría más riesgos,[1] haría más viajes,
contemplaría más atardeceres,[2]
subiría más montañas, nadaría más ríos.

Iría a más lugares adonde nunca he ido,
comería más helados y menos habas,[3]
tendría más problemas reales
y menos imaginarios.

Yo fui una de esas personas que vivió
sensata y prolíficamente cada minuto
de su vida; claro que tuve momentos
de alegría.

Pero si pudiera volver atrás trataría
de tener solamente buenos momentos.

Por si no lo saben, de eso está
hecha la vida, sólo de momentos;
no te pierdas el ahora.

Yo era uno de esos que nunca iban
a ninguna parte sin termómetro,
una bolsa de agua caliente,
un paraguas y un paracaídas.[4]

Si pudiera volver a vivir,
viajaría más liviano.[5]

Si pudiera volver a vivir comenzaría
a andar descalzo[6] a principios de la
primavera y seguiría así
hasta concluir el otoño.

Daría más vueltas en calesita,[7]
contemplaría más amaneceres[8]
y jugaría con más niños, si
tuviera otra vez la vida por delante.

Pero ya tengo 85 años
y sé que me estoy muriendo.

---

[1]*risks* [2]*sunsets* [3]frijoles [4]*parachute* [5]*lightly* [6]sin zapatos [7]**daría...** *I would take more rides on the merry-go-round*
[8]*sunrises, dawns*

Después de leer

ACTIVIDAD 4 Contesta las siguientes preguntas sobre los poemas con un(a) compañero(a) de clase.

Answers Act. 4: 1."Mi vida entera" b; "Instantes" c 2. b 3. a 4–8. *Answers will vary.*

1. En su opinión, ¿cuál es el punto de vista de cada autor? (Puede haber una respuesta diferente para cada poema.)
   a. para dar información
   b. para compartir emociones
   c. para persuadir al lector a cambiar su punto de vista

2. ¿Cuál de las siguientes oraciones es la idea principal del poema "Mi vida entera"?
   a. Hasta ahora no he hecho mucho, pero en el futuro voy a hacer cosas importantes.
   b. Soy una persona típica. He hecho algunas cosas pero nunca voy a hacer algo notable.
   c. Es importante viajar por todo el mundo, así harás cosas importantes en el futuro.

3. ¿Cuál de las siguientes oraciones es la idea principal del poema "Instantes"?
   a. Hay muchas cosas que el autor cambiaría si pudiera vivir la vida otra vez.
   b. Es importante tener cuidado y protegerse de los peligros de la vida.
   c. El autor analiza su vida y está muy contento con todo lo que hizo.

4. Para ustedes, ¿cuál de los dos poemas es el más difícil de entender?

5. ¿Cómo es el tono de "Mi vida entera"?

6. ¿Cómo es el tono de "Instantes"?

7. ¿Qué les parece la idea de que "Instantes" fuera escrito por Borges? ¿Les parece posible? ¿Por qué sí o por qué no?

8. ¿Cuál de los poemas les gusta más? ¿Por qué?

ACTIVIDAD 5 En grupos de tres a cuatro personas, piensen en los temas de los dos poemas: las experiencias y cómo uno debe vivir su vida. Usando la forma de "Instantes", hagan una lista de las cosas que cambiarían si pudieran vivir otra vez.

MODELO: *Si pudiéramos vivir nuevamente la vida…*
…estaríamos más con los amigos y pasaríamos menos tiempo solos…, etc.

PARA VIAJAR   *Travel*

la agencia de viajes	*travel agency*
la guía turística	*tourist guide book*
el itinerario	*itinerary*
cambiar dinero	*to exchange money*
hacer una reservación	*to make a reservation*
hacer un tour	*to take a tour*
viajar al extranjero	*to travel abroad*

EN EL AEROPUERTO Y DENTRO DEL AVIÓN
At the airport and in the plane

abordar	*to board*
la aduana	*customs*
el asiento	*seat*
... de pasillo	*aisle*
... de ventanilla	*window*
el (la) asistente de vuelo	*flight attendant*
el boleto / el billete	*ticket*
... de ida	*one-way*
... de ida y vuelta	*round-trip*
con destino a...	*with destination to . . .*
desembarcar	*to disembark, get off (the plane)*
facturar el equipaje	*to check your baggage*
hacer escala en...	*to make a stopover in . . .*
la línea aérea	*airline*
la lista de espera	*waiting list*
la llegada	*arrival*
la maleta	*suitcase*
el mostrador	*counter; check-in desk*
el pasaje	*ticket*
el (la) pasajero(a)	*passenger*
... de clase turista	*coach*
... de primera clase	*first class*
el pasaporte	*passport*
la puerta (de embarque)	*(departure) gate*
el retraso / la demora	*delay*
la sala de equipajes	*baggage claim*
la salida	*departure*
la tarjeta de embarque	*boarding pass*
el vuelo	*flight*

EL HOTEL   *Hotel*

el aire acondicionado	*air conditioning*
el ascensor	*elevator*
el botones	*bellboy*
la conexión a Internet	*Internet connection*
el conserje	*concierge*
el desayuno incluido	*breakfast included*
la estampilla	*postage stamp*
la habitación sencilla / doble	*single / double room*
... con / sin baño / ducha	*with / without bath / shower*
... de fumar / de no fumar	*smoking / non-smoking*
el (la) huésped(a)	*hotel guest*
el lavado en seco	*dry cleaning*
la llave	*key*
la recepción	*reception desk*
registrarse	*to register*
el secador de pelo	*hairdryer*
el servicio despertador	*wake-up call*
la tarjeta postal	*postcard*
la televisión por cable	*cable TV*

LA GEOGRAFÍA   *Geography*

este	*east*
oeste	*west*
norte	*north*
sur	*south*
la arena	*sand*
el bosque	*forest*
el cañón	*canyon*
el cielo	*sky*
el desierto	*desert*
la isla	*island*
el lago	*lake*
el mar	*sea*
el océano	*ocean*
la playa	*beach*
el río	*river*
las ruinas	*ruins*
la selva tropical	*tropical jungle*
el volcán	*volcano*

Heritage Learners: Since this is the final chapter of the book, it is appropriate to ask heritage language speakers of Spanish to reflect on how they plan to continue to improve their knowledge of Spanish. Suggest the following activities: keeping a journal in Spanish, committing to reading for fifteen minutes a day, reading an online newspaper in Spanish once a week, keeping a personal dictionary of new words encountered, volunteering to work in community organizations that serve Hispanics. Ask for other ideas from students.

REFERENCE MATERIALS

Regular Verbs

SIMPLE TENSES

Infinitive	Past participle / Present participle	Indicative						Subjunctive		
		Present	Imperfect	Preterite	Future	Conditional	Present	Imperfect*	
cantar *to sing*	cantado cantando	canto cantas canta cantamos cantáis cantan	cantaba cantabas cantaba cantábamos cantabais cantaban	canté cantaste cantó cantamos cantasteis cantaron	cantaré cantarás cantará cantaremos cantaréis cantarán	cantaría cantarías cantaría cantaríamos cantaríais cantarían	cante cantes cante cantemos cantéis canten	cantara cantaras cantara cantáramos cantarais cantaran	
correr *to run*	corrido corriendo	corro corres corre corremos corréis corren	corría corrías corría corríamos corríais corrían	corrí corriste corrió corrimos corristeis corrieron	correré correrás correrá correremos correréis correrán	correría correrías correría correríamos correríais correrían	corra corras corra corramos corráis corran	corriera corrieras corriera corriéramos corrierais corrieran	
subir *to go up, to climb up*	subido subiendo	subo subes sube subimos subís suben	subía subías subía subíamos subíais subían	subí subiste subió subimos subisteis subieron	subiré subirás subirá subiremos subiréis subirán	subiría subirías subiría subiríamos subiríais subirían	suba subas suba subamos subáis suban	subiera subieras subiera subiéramos subierais subieran	

*In addition to this form, another one is less frequently used for all regular and irregular verbs: cantase, cantases, cantase, cantásemos, cantaseis, cantasen; corriese, corrieses, corriese, corriésemos, corrieseis, corriesen; subiese, subieses, subiese, subiésemos, subieseis, subiesen.

Commands

Person	Affirmative	Negative	Affirmative	Negative	Affirmative	Negative
tú	canta	no cantes	corre	no corras	sube	no subas
usted	cante	no cante	corra	no corra	suba	no suba
nosotros	cantemos	no cantemos	corramos	no corramos	subamos	no subamos
vosotros	cantad	no cantéis	corred	no corráis	subid	no subáis
ustedes	canten	no canten	corran	no corran	suban	no suban

STEM-CHANGING VERBS: *-AR* AND *-ER* GROUPS

Type of change in the verb stem	Subject	Indicative Present	Subjunctive Present	Commands Affirmative	Commands Negative	Other -ar and -er stem-changing verbs
-ar verbs **e > ie** pensar *to think*	yo tú él/ella, Ud. nosotros/as vosotros/as ellos/as, Uds.	**pienso** **piensas** **piensa** pensamos pensáis **piensan**	**piense** **pienses** **piense** pensemos penséis **piensen**	— **piensa** **piense** pensemos pensad **piensen**	— no **pienses** no **piense** no pensemos no penséis no **piensen**	atravesar *to go through, to cross;* cerrar *to close;* despertarse *to wake up;* empezar *to start;* negar *to deny;* sentarse *to sit down.* Nevar *to snow* is only conjugated in the third-person singular.
-ar verbs **o > ue** contar *to count, to tell*	yo tú él/ella, Ud. nosotros/as vosotros/as ellos/as, Uds.	**cuento** **cuentas** **cuenta** contamos contáis **cuentan**	**cuente** **cuentes** **cuente** contemos contéis **cuenten**	— **cuenta** **cuente** contemos contad **cuenten**	— no **cuentes** no **cuente** no contemos no contéis no **cuenten**	acordarse *to remember;* acostar(se) *to go to bed;* almorzar *to have lunch;* colgar *to hang;* costar *to cost;* demostrar *to demonstrate, to show;* encontrar *to find;* mostrar *to show;* probar *to prove, to taste;* recordar *to remember*
-er verbs **e > ie** entender *to understand*	yo tú él/ella, Ud. nosotros/as vosotros/as ellos/as, Uds.	**entiendo** **entiendes** **entiende** entendemos entendéis **entienden**	**entienda** **entiendas** **entienda** entendamos entendáis **entiendan**	— **entiende** **entienda** entendamos entended **entiendan**	— no **entiendas** no **entienda** no entendamos no entendáis no **entiendan**	encender *to light, to turn on;* extender *to stretch;* perder *to lose*
-er verbs **o > ue** volver *to return*	yo tú él/ella, Ud. nosotros/as vosotros/as ellos/as, Uds.	**vuelvo** **vuelves** **vuelve** volvemos volvéis **vuelven**	**vuelva** **vuelvas** **vuelva** volvamos volváis **vuelvan**	— **vuelve** **vuelva** volvamos volved **vuelvan**	— no **vuelvas** no **vuelva** no volvamos no volváis no **vuelvan**	mover *to move;* torcer *to twist.* Llover *to rain* is only conjugated in the third-person singular.

STEM-CHANGING VERBS: *IR* VERBS

Type of change in the verb stem	Subject	Indicative		Subjunctive		Commands	
		Present	**Preterite**	**Present**	**Imperfect**	**Affirmative**	**Negative**
-ir verbs **e > ie or i** **Infinitive:** sentir *to feel* **Present participle:** sintiendo	yo tú él/ella, Ud. nosotros/as vosotros/as ellos/as, Uds.	**siento** **sientes** **siente** sentimos sentís **sienten**	sentí sentiste **sintió** sentimos sentisteis **sintieron**	**sienta** **sientas** **sienta** **sintamos** **sintáis** **sientan**	**sintiera** **sintieras** **sintiera** **sintiéramos** **sintierais** **sintieran**	— **siente** **sienta** **sintamos** sentid **sientan**	— no **sientas** no **sienta** no **sintamos** no **sintáis** no **sientan**
-ir verbs **o > ue or u** **Infinitive:** dormir *to sleep* **Present participle:** durmiendo	yo tú él/ella, Ud. nosotros/as vosotros/as ellos/as, Uds.	**duermo** **duermes** **duerme** dormimos dormís **duermen**	dormí dormiste **durmió** dormimos dormisteis **durmieron**	**duerma** **duermas** **duerma** **durmamos** **durmáis** **duerman**	**durmiera** **durmieras** **durmiera** **durmiéramos** **durmierais** **durmieran**	— **duerme** **duerma** **durmamos** dormid **duerman**	— no **duermas** no **duerma** no **durmamos** no **durmáis** no **duerman**

Other similar verbs: advertir *to warn;* arrepentirse *to repent;* consentir *to consent,* to *pamper;* convertir(se) *to turn into;* divertir(se) *to amuse (oneself);* herir *to hurt,* to *wound;* mentir *to lie;* morir *to die;* preferir *to prefer;* referir *to refer;* sugerir *to suggest*

Type of change in the verb stem	Subject	Indicative		Subjunctive		Commands	
		Present	**Preterite**	**Present**	**Imperfect**	**Affirmative**	**Negative**
-ir verbs **e > i** **Infinitive:** pedir *to ask for,* to *request* **Present participle:** pidiendo	yo tú él/ella, Ud. nosotros/as vosotros/as ellos/as, Uds.	**pido** **pides** **pide** pedimos pedís **piden**	pedí pediste **pidió** pedimos pedisteis **pidieron**	**pida** **pidas** **pida** **pidamos** **pidáis** **pidan**	**pidiera** **pidieras** **pidiera** **pidiéramos** **pidierais** **pidieran**	— **pide** **pida** **pidamos** pedid **pidan**	— no **pidas** no **pida** no **pidamos** no **pidáis** no **pidan**

Other similar verbs: competir *to compete;* despedir(se) *to say good-bye;* elegir *to choose;* impedir *to prevent;* perseguir *to chase;* repetir *to repeat;* seguir *to follow;* servir *to serve;* vestir(se) *to dress,* to *get dressed*

VERBS WITH SPELLING CHANGES

	Verb type	Ending	Change	Verbs with similar spelling changes
1	**bus**c**ar** *to look for*	**-car**	• Preterite: yo bus**qué** • Present subjunctive: bus**que**, bus**ques**, bus**que**, bus**quemos**, bus**quéis**, bus**quen**	comunicar, explicar *to explain* indicar *to indicate*, sacar, pescar
2	**conocer** *to know*	*vowel* + **-cer** or **-cir**	• Present indicative: cono**zco**, conoces, conoce, and so on • Present subjunctive: cono**zca**, cono**zcas**, cono**zca**, cono**zcamos**, cono**zcáis**, cono**zcan**	nacer *to be born*, obedecer, ofrecer, parecer, pertenecer *to belong*, reconocer, conducir, traducir
3	**vencer** *to win*	*consonant* + **-cer** or **-cir**	• Present indicative: ven**zo**, vences, vence, and so on • Present subjunctive: ven**za**, ven**zas**, ven**za**, ven**zamos**, ven**záis**, ven**zan**	convencer, torcer *to twist*
4	**leer** *to read*	**-eer**	• Preterite: le**yó**, le**yeron** • Imperfect subjunctive: le**yera**, le**yeras**, le**yera**, le**yéramos**, le**yerais**, le**yeran** • Present participle: le**yendo**	creer, poseer *to own*
5	**llegar** *to arrive*	**-gar**	• Preterite: yo lle**gué** • Present subjunctive: lle**gue**, lle**gues**, lle**gue**, lle**guemos**, lle**guéis**, lle**guen**	colgar *to hang*, navegar, negar *to negate, to deny*, pagar, rogar *to beg*, jugar
6	**coger** *to take*	**-ger** or **-gir**	• Present indicative: co**jo**, coges, coge, and so on • Present subjunctive: co**ja**, co**jas**, co**ja**, co**jamos**, co**jáis**, co**jan**	escoger, proteger, recoger *to collect, to gather*, corregir *to correct*, dirigir *to direct*, elegir *to elect, to choose*, exigir *to demand*
7	**seguir** *to follow*	**-guir**	• Present indicative: si**go**, sigues, sigue, and so on • Present subjunctive: si**ga**, si**gas**, si**ga**, si**gamos**, si**gáis**, si**gan**	conseguir, distinguir, perseguir
8	**huir** *to flee*	**-uir**	• Present indicative: hu**yo**, hu**yes**, hu**ye**, huimos, huís, hu**yen** • Preterite: huí, huiste, hu**yó**, huimos, huisteis, hu**yeron** • Present subjunctive: hu**ya**, hu**yas**, hu**ya**, hu**yamos**, hu**yáis**, hu**yan** • Imperfect subjunctive: hu**yera**, hu**yeras**, hu**yera**, hu**yéramos**, hu**yerais**, hu**yeran** • Present participle: hu**yendo** • Commands: hu**ye** tú, hu**ya** usted, hu**yamos** nosotros, huíd vosotros, hu**yan** ustedes, no hu**yas** tú, no hu**ya** usted, no hu**yamos** nosotros, no hu**yáis** vosotros, no hu**yan** ustedes	concluir, contribuir, construir, destruir, disminuir, distribuir, excluir, influir, instruir, restituir, substituir
9	**abrazar** *to embrace*	**-zar**	• Preterite: yo abra**cé** • Present subjunctive: abra**ce**, abra**ces**, abra**ce**, abra**cemos**, abra**céis**, abra**cen**	alcanzar *to achieve*, almorzar, comenzar, empezar, gozar *to enjoy*, rezar *to pray*

COMPOUND TENSES

	Indicative					Subjunctive	
	Present perfect	Past perfect	Preterite perfect	Future perfect	Conditional perfect	Present perfect	Past perfect
	he	había	hube	habré	habría	haya	hubiera
	has	habías	hubiste	habrás	habrías	hayas	hubieras
	ha	había	hubo	habrá	habría	haya	hubiera
	hemos	habíamos	hubimos	habremos	habríamos	hayamos	hubiéramos
	habéis	habíais	hubisteis	habréis	habríais	hayáis	hubierais
	han	habían	hubieron	habrán	habrían	hayan	hubieran
	cantado corrido subido	cantado corrido subido	cantado corrido subido	cantado corrido subido	cantado corrido subido	cantado corrido subido	cantado corrido subido

All verbs, both regular and irregular, follow the same formation pattern with **haber** in all compound tenses. The only thing that changes is the form of the past participle of each verb. (See the chart below for common verbs with irregular past participles.) Remember that in Spanish, no word can come between **haber** and the past participle.

COMMON IRREGULAR PAST PARTICIPLES

Infinitive	Past participle		Infinitive	Past participle	
abrir	**abierto**	*opened*	morir	**muerto**	*died*
caer	caído	*fallen*	oír	oído	*heard*
creer	creído	*believed*	poner	**puesto**	*put, placed*
cubrir	**cubierto**	*covered*	resolver	**resuelto**	*resolved*
decir	**dicho**	*said, told*	romper	**roto**	*broken, torn*
descubrir	**descubierto**	*discovered*	(son)reír	(son)reído	*(smiled) laughed*
escribir	**escrito**	*written*	traer	traído	*brought*
hacer	**hecho**	*made, done*	ver	**visto**	*seen*
leer	leído	*read*	volver	**vuelto**	*returned*

Reflexive Verbs

REGULAR AND IRREGULAR REFLEXIVE VERBS: POSITION OF THE REFLEXIVE PRONOUNS IN THE SIMPLE TENSES

Infinitive	Present participle	Reflexive pronouns	Indicative					Subjunctive	
			Present	Imperfect	Preterite	Future	Conditional	Present	Imperfect
lavarse	lavándome	**me**	lavo	lavaba	lavé	lavaré	lavaría	lave	lavara
to wash	lavándote	**te**	lavas	lavabas	lavaste	lavarás	lavarías	laves	lavaras
oneself	lavándose	**se**	lava	lavaba	lavó	lavará	lavaría	lave	lavara
	lavándonos	**nos**	lavamos	lavábamos	lavamos	lavaremos	lavaríamos	lavemos	laváramos
	lavándoos	**os**	laváis	lavabais	lavasteis	lavaréis	lavaríais	lavéis	lavarais
	lavándose	**se**	lavan	lavaban	lavaron	lavarán	lavarían	laven	lavaran

REGULAR AND IRREGULAR REFLEXIVE VERBS: POSITION OF THE REFLEXIVE PRONOUNS WITH COMMANDS

Person	Affirmative	Negative	Affirmative	Negative	Affirmative	Negative
tú	lávate	no te laves	ponte	no te pongas	vístete	no te vistas
usted	lávese	no se lave	póngase	no se ponga	vístase	no se vista
nosotros	lavémonos	no nos lavemos	pongámonos	no nos pongamos	vistámonos	no nos vistamos
vosotros	lavaos	no os lavéis	poneos	no os pongáis	vestíos	no os vistáis
ustedes	lávense	no se laven	pónganse	no se pongan	vístanse	no se vistan

REGULAR AND IRREGULAR REFLEXIVE VERBS: POSITION OF THE REFLEXIVE PRONOUNS IN COMPOUND TENSES*

	Indicative										Subjunctive		
Reflexive Pronoun	Present Perfect		Past Perfect		Preterite Perfect		Future Perfect		Conditional Perfect		Present Perfect		Past Perfect
me	he		había		hube		habré		habría		haya		hubiera
te	has	lavado	habías	lavado	hubiste	lavado	habrás	lavado	habrías	lavado	hayas	lavado	hubieras	lavado
se	ha	puesto	había	puesto	hubo	puesto	habrá	puesto	habría	puesto	haya	puesto	hubiera	puesto
nos	hemos	vestido	habíamos	vestido	hubimos	vestido	habremos	vestido	habríamos	vestido	hayamos	vestido	hubiéramos	vestido
os	habéis		habíais		hubisteis		habréis		habríais		hayáis		hubiérais	
se	han		habían		hubieron		habrán		habrían		hayan		hubieran	

*The sequence of these three elements—the reflexive pronoun, the auxiliary verb **haber,** and the present perfect form—is invariable and no other words can come in between.

REGULAR AND IRREGULAR REFLEXIVE VERBS: POSITION OF THE REFLEXIVE PRONOUNS WITH CONJUGATED VERB + INFINITIVE**

	Indicative										Subjunctive		
Reflexive Pronoun	Present		Imperfect		Preterite		Future		Conditional		Present		Imperfect
me	voy a		iba a		fui a		iré a		iría a		vaya a		fuera a	
te	vas a	lavar	ibas a	lavar	fuiste a	lavar	irás a	lavar	irías a	lavar	vayas a	lavar	fueras a	lavar
se	va a	poner	iba a	poner	fue a	poner	irá a	poner	iría a	poner	vaya a	poner	fuera a	poner
nos	vamos a	vestir	íbamos a	vestir	fuimos a	vestir	iremos a	vestir	iríamos a	vestir	vayamos a	vestir	fuéramos a	vestir
os	vais a		ibais a		fuisteis a		iréis a		iríais a		vayáis a		fuerais a	
se	van a		iban a		fueron a		irán a		irían a		vayan a		fueran a	

The reflexive pronoun can also be placed after the infinitive: voy a lavarme,** voy a poner**me,** voy a vestir**me,** and so on.
Use the same structure for the present and the past progressive: **me** estoy lavando / estoy lavándo**me; me** estaba lavando / estaba lavándo**me.**

Irregular Verbs
ANDAR, CABER, CAER

Infinitive	Past participle / Present participle	Indicative					Subjunctive	
		Present	Imperfect	Preterite	Future	Conditional	Present	Imperfect
andar *to walk; to go*	andado andando	ando andas anda andamos andáis andan	andaba andabas andaba andábamos andabais andaban	**anduve** **anduviste** **anduvo** **anduvimos** **anduvisteis** **anduvieron**	andaré andarás andará andaremos andaréis andarán	andaría andarías andaría andaríamos andaríais andarían	ande andes ande andemos andéis anden	**anduviera** **anduvieras** **anduviera** **anduviéramos** **anduvierais** **anduvieran**
caber *to fit; to have enough space*	cabido cabiendo	**quepo** cabes cabe cabemos cabéis caben	cabía cabías cabía cabíamos cabíais cabían	**cupe** **cupiste** **cupo** **cupimos** **cupisteis** **cupieron**	**cabré** **cabrás** **cabrá** **cabremos** **cabréis** **cabrán**	**cabría** **cabrías** **cabría** **cabríamos** **cabríais** **cabrían**	**quepa** **quepas** **quepa** **quepamos** **quepáis** **quepan**	cupiera cupieras cupiera cupiéramos cupierais cupieran
caer *to fall*	caído cayendo	**caigo** caes cae caemos caéis caen	caía caías caía caíamos caíais caían	caí caíste **cayó** caímos caísteis **cayeron**	caeré caerás caerá caeremos caeréis caerán	caería caerías caería caeríamos caeríais caerían	**caiga** **caigas** **caiga** **caigamos** **caigáis** **caigan**	cayera cayeras cayera cayéramos cayerais cayeran

Commands

Person	andar		caber		caer	
	Affirmative	Negative	Affirmative	Negative	Affirmative	Negative
tú	anda	no andes	cabe	no **quepas**	cae	no **caigas**
usted	ande	no ande	**quepa**	no **quepa**	**caiga**	no **caiga**
nosotros	andemos	no andemos	**quepamos**	no **quepamos**	**caigamos**	no **caigamos**
vosotros	andad	no andéis	cabed	no **quepáis**	caed	no **caigáis**
ustedes	anden	no anden	**quepan**	no **quepan**	**caigan**	no **caigan**

DAR, DECIR, ESTAR

Infinitive	Past participle Present participle	Indicative					Subjunctive	
		Present	Imperfect	Preterite	Future	Conditional	Present	Imperfect
dar *to give*	dado dando	**doy** das da damos dais dan	daba dabas daba dábamos dabais daban	**di** diste dio dimos disteis dieron	daré darás dará daremos daréis darán	daría darías daría daríamos daríais darían	**dé** des dé demos deis den	diera dieras diera diéramos dierais dieran
decir *to say, to tell*	dicho diciendo	**digo** dices dice decimos decís dicen	decía decías decía decíamos decíais decían	**dije** dijiste dijo dijimos dijisteis dijeron	diré dirás dirá diremos diréis dirán	diría dirías diría diríamos diríais dirían	diga digas diga digamos digáis digan	dijera dijeras dijera dijéramos dijerais dijeran
estar *to be*	estado estando	estoy estás está estamos estáis están	estaba estabas estaba estábamos estabais estaban	estuve estuviste estuvo estuvimos estuvisteis estuvieron	estaré estarás estará estaremos estaréis estarán	estaría estarías estaría estaríamos estaríais estarían	esté estés esté estemos estéis estén	estuviera estuvieras estuviera estuviéramos estuvierais estuvieran

Commands

Person	dar		decir		estar	
	Affirmative	Negative	Affirmative	Negative	Affirmative	Negative
tú	da	no des	**di**	no digas	**está**	no estés
usted	**dé**	no **dé**	diga	no diga	**esté**	no esté
nosotros	**demos**	no **demos**	digamos	no **digamos**	estemos	no estemos
vosotros	dad	no **deis**	decid	no digáis	estad	no estéis
ustedes	**den**	no **den**	**digan**	no **digan**	**estén**	no estén

HABER*, HACER, IR

Infinitive	Past participle / Present participle	Indicative					Subjunctive	
		Present	Imperfect	Preterite	Future	Conditional	Present	Imperfect
haber* *to have*	habido habiendo	**he** **has** **ha** **hemos** habéis **han**	había habías había habíamos habíais habían	**hube** **hubiste** **hubo** **hubimos** **hubisteis** **hubieron**	**habré** **habrás** **habrá** **habremos** **habréis** **habrán**	**habría** **habrías** **habría** **habríamos** **habríais** **habrían**	**haya** **hayas** **haya** **hayamos** **hayáis** **hayan**	hubiera hubieras hubiera hubiéramos hubierais hubieran
hacer *to do*	hecho haciendo	**hago** haces hace hacemos hacéis hacen	hacía hacías hacía hacíamos hacíais hacían	**hice** **hiciste** **hizo** **hicimos** **hicisteis** **hicieron**	**haré** **harás** **hará** **haremos** **haréis** **harán**	**haría** **harías** **haría** **haríamos** **haríais** **harían**	**haga** **hagas** **haga** **hagamos** **hagáis** **hagan**	hiciera hicieras hiciera hiciéramos hicierais hicieran
ir *to go*	ido yendo	**voy** **vas** **va** **vamos** **vais** **van**	**iba** **ibas** **iba** **íbamos** **ibais** **iban**	**fui** **fuiste** **fue** **fuimos** **fuisteis** **fueron**	iré irás irá iremos iréis irán	iría irías iría iríamos iríais irían	**vaya** **vayas** **vaya** **vayamos** **vayáis** **vayan**	fuera fueras fuera fuéramos fuerais fueran

*Haber also has an impersonal form **hay.** This form is used to express "There is, There are." The imperative of **haber** is not used.

Commands

Person	hacer		ir	
	Affirmative	Negative	Affirmative	Negative
tú	**haz**	no hagas	ve	no vayas
usted	**haga**	no haga	vaya	no vaya
nosotros	**hagamos**	no hagamos	vamos	no vayamos
vosotros	haced	no hagáis	id	no vayáis
ustedes	**hagan**	no hagan	vayan	no vayan

JUGAR, OÍR, OLER

Infinitive	Past participle / Present participle	Indicative					Subjunctive	
		Present	Imperfect	Preterite	Future	Conditional	Present	Imperfect
jugar *to play*	jugado jugando	juego juegas juega jugamos jugáis juegan	jugaba jugabas jugaba jugábamos jugabais jugaban	jugué jugaste jugó jugamos jugasteis jugaron	jugaré jugarás jugará jugaremos jugaréis jugarán	jugaría jugarías jugaría jugaríamos jugaríais jugarían	juegue juegues juegue juguemos juguéis jueguen	jugara jugaras jugara jugáramos jugarais jugaran
oír *to hear, to listen*	oído oyendo	oigo oyes oye oímos oís oyen	oía oías oía oíamos oíais oían	oí oíste oyó oímos oísteis oyeron	oiré oirás oirá oiremos oiréis oirán	oiría oirías oiría oiríamos oiríais oirían	oiga oigas oiga oigamos oigáis oigan	oyera oyeras oyera oyéramos oyerais oyeran
oler *to smell*	olido oliendo	huelo hueles huele olemos oléis huelen	olía olías olía olíamos olíais olían	olí oliste olió olimos olisteis olieron	oleré olerás olerá oleremos oleréis olerán	olería olerías olería oleríamos oleríais olerían	huela huelas huela olamos oláis huelan	oliera olieras oliera oliéramos olierais olieran

Commands

Person	jugar		oír		oler	
	Affirmative	Negative	Affirmative	Negative	Affirmative	Negative
tú	juega	no juegues	oye	no oigas	huele	no huelas
usted	juegue	no juegue	oiga	no oiga	huela	no huela
nosotros	juguemos	no juguemos	oigamos	no oigamos	olamos	no olamos
vosotros	jugad	no juguéis	oíd	no oigáis	oled	no oláis
ustedes	jueguen	no jueguen	oigan	no oigan	huelan	no huelan

PODER, PONER, QUERER

Infinitive	Past participle / Present participle	Indicative					Subjunctive	
		Present	Imperfect	Preterite	Future	Conditional	Present	Imperfect
poder *to be able to, can*	podido pudiendo	**puedo** **puedes** **puede** podemos podéis **pueden**	podía podías podía podíamos podíais podían	**pude** **pudiste** **pudo** **pudimos** **pudisteis** **pudieron**	**podré** **podrás** **podrá** **podremos** **podréis** **podrán**	**podría** **podrías** **podría** **podríamos** **podríais** **podrían**	**pueda** **puedas** **pueda** podamos podáis **puedan**	pudiera pudieras pudiera pudiéramos pudierais pudieran
poner* *to put*	puesto poniendo	**pongo** pones pone ponemos ponéis ponen	ponía ponías ponía poníamos poníais ponían	**puse** **pusiste** **puso** **pusimos** **pusisteis** **pusieron**	**pondré** **pondrás** **pondrá** **pondremos** **pondréis** **pondrán**	**pondría** **pondrías** **pondría** **pondríamos** **pondríais** **pondrían**	**ponga** **pongas** **ponga** **pongamos** **pongáis** **pongan**	pusiera pusieras pusiera pusiéramos pusierais pusieran
querer *to want, to wish; to love*	querido queriendo	**quiero** **quieres** **quiere** queremos queréis **quieren**	quería querías quería queríamos queríais querían	**quise** **quisiste** **quiso** **quisimos** **quisisteis** **quisieron**	**querré** **querrás** **querrá** **querremos** **querréis** **querrán**	**querría** **querrías** **querría** **querríamos** **querríais** **querrían**	**quiera** **quieras** **quiera** queramos queráis **quieran**	quisiera quisieras quisiera quisiéramos quisierais quisieran

*Similar verbs to **poner**: **imponer, suponer.**

Commands**

Person	poner		querer	
	Affirmative	Negative	Affirmative	Negative
tú	**pon**	no **pongas**	**quiere**	no **quieras**
usted	**ponga**	no **ponga**	**quiera**	no **quiera**
nosotros	**pongamos**	no **pongamos**	queramos	no queramos
vosotros	poned	no **pongáis**	quered	no queráis
ustedes	**pongan**	no **pongan**	**quieran**	no **quieran**

Note: The imperative of **poder is used very infrequently and is not included here.

SABER, SALIR, SER

Infinitive	Past participle / Present participle	Indicative					Subjunctive	
		Present	Imperfect	Preterite	Future	Conditional	Present	Imperfect
saber *to know*	sabido sabiendo	sé sabes sabe sabemos sabéis saben	sabía sabías sabía sabíamos sabíais sabían	supe supiste supo supimos supisteis supieron	sabré sabrás sabrá sabremos sabréis sabrán	sabría sabrías sabría sabríamos sabríais sabrían	sepa sepas sepa sepamos sepáis sepan	supiera supieras supiera supiéramos supierais supieran
salir *to go out, to leave*	salido saliendo	salgo sales sale salimos salís salen	salía salías salía salíamos salíais salían	salí saliste salió salimos salisteis salieron	saldré saldrás saldrá saldremos saldréis saldrán	saldría saldrías saldría saldríamos saldríais saldrían	salga salgas salga salgamos salgáis salgan	saliera salieras saliera saliéramos salierais salieran
ser *to be*	sido siendo	soy eres es somos sois son	era eras era éramos erais eran	fui fuiste fue fuimos fuisteis fueron	seré serás será seremos seréis serán	sería serías sería seríamos seríais serían	sea seas sea seamos seáis sean	fuera fueras fuera fuéramos fuerais fueran

Commands

Person	saber		salir		ser	
	Affirmative	Negative	Affirmative	Negative	Affirmative	Negative
tú	sabe	no sepas	sal	no salgas	sé	no seas
usted	sepa	no sepa	salga	no salga	sea	no sea
nosotros	sepamos	no sepamos	salgamos	no salgamos	seamos	no seamos
vosotros	sabed	no sepáis	salid	no salgáis	sed	no seáis
ustedes	sepan	no sepan	salgan	no salgan	sean	no sean

SONREÍR, TENER*, TRAER

Infinitive	Past participle / Present participle	Indicative					Subjunctive	
		Present	Imperfect	Preterite	Future	Conditional	Present	Imperfect
sonreír *to smile*	sonreído / sonriendo	**sonrío** / **sonríes** / **sonríe** / sonreímos / sonreís / **sonríen**	sonreía / sonreías / sonreía / sonreíamos / sonreíais / sonreían	sonreí / sonreíste / **sonrió** / sonreímos / sonreísteis / **sonrieron**	sonreiré / sonreirás / sonreirá / sonreiremos / sonreiréis / sonreirán	sonreiría / sonreirías / sonreiría / sonreiríamos / sonreiríais / sonreirían	**sonría** / **sonrías** / **sonría** / **sonriamos** / **sonriáis** / **sonrían**	sonriera / sonrieras / sonriera / sonriéramos / sonrierais / sonrieran
tener* *to have*	tenido / teniendo	**tengo** / **tienes** / **tiene** / tenemos / tenéis / **tienen**	tenía / tenías / tenía / teníamos / teníais / tenían	**tuve** / **tuviste** / **tuvo** / **tuvimos** / **tuvisteis** / **tuvieron**	**tendré** / **tendrás** / **tendrá** / **tendremos** / **tendréis** / **tendrán**	**tendría** / **tendrías** / **tendría** / **tendríamos** / **tendríais** / **tendrían**	**tenga** / **tengas** / **tenga** / **tengamos** / **tengáis** / **tengan**	tuviera / tuvieras / tuviera / tuviéramos / tuvierais / tuvieran
traer *to bring*	traído / trayendo	**traigo** / traes / trae / traemos / traéis / traen	traía / traías / traía / traíamos / traíais / traían	**traje** / **trajiste** / **trajo** / **trajimos** / **trajisteis** / **trajeron**	traeré / traerás / traerá / traeremos / traeréis / traerán	traería / traerías / traería / traeríamos / traeríais / traerían	**traiga** / **traigas** / **traiga** / **traigamos** / **traigáis** / **traigan**	trajera / trajeras / trajera / trajéramos / trajerais / trajeran

Commands

Person	sonreír Affirmative	Negative	tener Affirmative	Negative	traer Affirmative	Negative
tú	**sonríe**	no **sonrías**	**ten**	no **tengas**	trae	no **traigas**
usted	**sonría**	no **sonría**	**tenga**	no **tenga**	**traiga**	no **traiga**
nosotros	**sonriamos**	no **sonriamos**	**tengamos**	no **tengamos**	**traigamos**	no **traigamos**
vosotros	sonreíd	no **sonriáis**	tened	no **tengáis**	traed	no **traigáis**
ustedes	**sonrían**	no **sonrían**	**tengan**	no **tengan**	**traigan**	no **traigan**

*Many verbs ending in -tener are conjugated like **tener: contener, detener, entretener(se), mantener, obtener, retener.**

VALER, VENIR*, VER

Infinitive	Past participle / Present participle	Indicative					Subjunctive	
		Present	Imperfect	Preterite	Future	Conditional	Present	Imperfect
valer *to be worth*	valido valiendo	valgo vales vale valemos valéis valen	valía valías valía valíamos valíais valían	valí valiste valió valimos valisteis valieron	valdré valdrás valdrá valdremos valdréis valdrán	valdría valdrías valdría valdríamos valdríais valdrían	valga valgas valga valgamos valgáis valgan	valiera valieras valiera valiéramos valierais valieran
venir* *to come*	venido viniendo	vengo vienes viene venimos venís vienen	venía venías venía veníamos veníais venían	vine viniste vino vinimos vinisteis vinieron	vendré vendrás vendrá vendremos vendréis vendrán	vendría vendrías vendría vendríamos vendríais vendrían	venga vengas venga vengamos vengáis vengan	viniera vinieras viniera viniéramos vinierais vinieran
ver *to see*	visto viendo	veo ves ve vemos veis ven	veía veías veía veíamos veíais veían	vi viste vio vimos visteis vieron	veré verás verá veremos veréis verán	vería verías vería veríamos veríais verían	vea veas vea veamos veáis vean	viera vieras viera viéramos vierais vieran

*Similar verb to venir: prevenir

Commands

Person	valer Affirmative	valer Negative	venir Affirmative	venir Negative	ver Affirmative	ver Negative
tú	vale	no valgas	ven	no vengas	ve	no veas
usted	valga	no valga	venga	no venga	vea	no vea
nosotros	valgamos	no valgamos	vengamos	no vengamos	veamos	no veamos
vosotros	valed	no valgáis	venid	no vengáis	ved	no veáis
ustedes	valgan	no valgan	vengan	no vengan	vean	no vean

SPANISH-ENGLISH GLOSSARY

The vocabulary includes the active vocabulary presented in the chapters and many receptive words. Exceptions are verb conjugations, regular past participles, adverbs ending in **-mente**, superlatives, diminutives, and proper names of individuals and most countries. Active words are followed by a number that indicates the chapter in which the word appears as an active item. **P** refers to the opening pages that precede Chapter 1.

The gender of nouns is indicated except for masculine nouns ending in **-o** and feminine nouns ending in **-a**. Stem changes and spelling changes are shown for verbs, e.g., **dormir (ue, u); buscar (qu).**

The following abbreviations are used. Note that the *adj.*, *adv.*, and *pron.* designations are used only to distinguish similar or identical words that are different parts of speech.

adj.	adjective	*fam.*	familiar	*irreg.*	irregular verb	*p.p.*	past participle
adv.	adverb	*form.*	formal	*m.*	masculine	*pron.*	pronoun
f.	feminine	*inf.*	infinitive	*pl.*	plural	*s.*	singular

A

a to; **~ cambio de** in exchange for; **~ menos que** unless, 12; **~ pesar de** in spite of; **~ pie** on foot, walking, 6; **~ través de** across, throughout

abierto (*p.p. of* **abrir**) open, 13

abogado(a) lawyer, 5

abordar to board, 14

abrelatas eléctrico (*m. s.*) electric can opener, 10

abrigo coat, 8

abril April, 1

abrir to open, 3; **Abran los libros.** Open your books. P

abuelo(a) grandfather (grandmother), 5

abundancia abundance

aburrido(a) boring, 2; bored, 4

aburrimiento boredom

académico(a) academic

accesorio accessory, 8

acción (*f.*) action, 5

aceite (*m.*) **de oliva** olive oil, 9

acero steel

aconsejar to advise, 10

acostarse (ue) to go to bed, 5

acrecentar (ie) to strengthen; to increase

actividad (*f.*) activity, P; **~ deportiva** sports activity, 7

activo(a) active, 2

actor (*m.*) actor, 5

actriz (*f.*) actress, 5

actualidad (*f.*): **en la~** at the present time

acudir to go; to attend

adelantar to get ahead, to promote

adelante ahead

además besides

adinerado(a) rich, wealthy

adiós good-bye, 1

adivinar to guess; **Adivina.** Guess. P

administración (*f.*) **de empresas** business administration, 3

¿adónde? (to) where?

adquisición (*f.*) acquisition

aduana customs, 14

aeropuerto airport, 6

afán (*m.*) desire

afeitarse to shave oneself, 5

afueras (*f. pl.*) outskirts, 10

agencia de viajes travel agency, 14

agosto August, 1

agregar (gu) to add, 9

agrícola agricultural

agua (*f.*) (*but:* **el agua**) water; **~ dulce** fresh water; **~ mineral** sparkling water, 9

aguacate avocado, 9

aire (*m.*) **acondicionado** air conditioning, 14

ajedrez (*m.*) chess

ajo garlic, 9

al (a + el) to the, 3

albergar (gu) to shelter

albóndiga meatball

alcalde (alcadesa) mayor

alcanzar (c) to achieve

alegrarse de to be happy about, 11

alemán (alemana) German, 2

alemán (*m.*) German language, 3

alergia allergy, 12

alfabeto alphabet

alfombra rug, carpet, 10

algo something, 6

algodón (*m.*) cotton, 8

alguien someone, 6

algún, alguno(a)(s) some, any, 6

alistar to recruit; to enroll

allá over there, 6

allí there, 6

alma (*f.*) (*but:* **el alma**) soul

almacén (*m.*) store, 6

almeja clam, 9

almohada pillow

almuerzo lunch, 9

alpinismo: hacer ~ to hike, 7

alquilar videos to rent videos, 2

alquiler (*m.*) rent

alrededor de around

altitud (*f.*) altitude, height

altivo(a) arrogant

alto(a) tall, 2

altoparlante (*m., f.*) speaker, 4

altura height

amanecer (zc) to dawn

amante (*m., f.*) lover
amarillo(a) yellow, 4
ambiente (*m.*) atmosphere; **medio ~** (*m.*) environment
ambigüedad (*f.*) ambiguity
ambos(as) both
amenaza threat
amigo(a) friend, P
amor (*m.*) love
análisis (*m.*) **de sangre/orina** blood/urine test, 12
anaranjado(a) orange (*in color*), 4
andar (*irreg.*) to walk, 8
anexo attachment
anfitrión (*m.*) host
anillo ring, 8
anoche last night, 7
anónimo(a) anonymous
Antártida Antarctica
anteayer the day before yesterday, 7
antecesor(a) ancestor
anteojos (*m. pl.*) eyeglasses
antepasado(a) ancestor
antes before, 5; **~ (de) que** before, 12
antibiótico antibiotic, 12
anticuado(a) antiquated, old-fashioned
antipático(a) unpleasant, 2
anuncio personal personal ad
añadir to add, 9
año year, 3; **~ pasado** last year, 7; **tener** (*irreg.*) **... ~** to be . . . years old, 1;
apacible mild, gentle
apagar (gu) to turn off, 2
aparecer (zc) to appear
apariencia física physical appearance
apartamento apartment, 6
apenas scarcely
apetecer (zc) to long for
aplicación (*f.*) application, 4
apodo nickname
apoyar to support
apreciar to appreciate
aprender to learn, 3
aprendizaje (*m.*) learning
apropiado(a) appropriate
apto(a) apt, fit; **~ para toda la familia** rated G (for general audiences), 11
apuntes (*m.*) notes, P
aquel/aquella(s) (*adj.*) those (over there), 6

aquél/aquélla(s) (*pron.*) those (over there), 6
aquí here, 6
árbol (*m.*) tree; **~ genealógico** family tree
archivar to file, 4
archivo file, 4
arena sand, 14
arete (*m.*) earring, 8
argentino(a) Argentinian, 2
arquitecto(a) architect, 5
arquitectura architecture, 3
arreglar el dormitorio to straighten up the bedroom, 10
arroz (*m.*) **con pollo** chicken with rice, 9
arrugado(a) wrinkled
arte (*m.*) art, 3; **~ y cultura** the arts, 11
artesanía handicrafts
artículo article, 1
artista (*m., f.*) artist, 5
asado(a) grilled
ascenso (job) promotion, 13
ascensor (*m.*) elevator, 14
asegurarse to make sure
asiento seat, 14; **~ de pasillo** aisle seat, 14; **~ de ventanilla** window seat, 14
asistente: ~ (*m., f.*) **de vuelo** flight attendant, 14; **~** (*m.*) **electrónico** electronic notebook, 4
asistir a to attend, 3
aspiradora vacuum cleaner, 10
aspirina aspirin, 12
ataque (*m.*) attack
atardecer (*m.*) late afternoon
atún (*m.*) tuna, 9
audiencia audience
audífonos (*m. pl.*) earphones, 4
auditorio auditorium, 6
aumentar to increase
aumento de sueldo salary increase, 13
aun even
aún yet (*in negative contexts*); still
aunque although, even though, 12
autobús: en ~ by bus, 6
automóvil: en ~ by car, 6
avenida avenue, 1
avergonzado(a) embarrassed
avergonzar (ue) (c) to embarrass
averiguar (gü) to find out; to look into, to investigate, 13
avión (*m.*) airplane, 14

aviso warning
ayer yesterday, 3
ayuda help
ayudar to help
azúcar (*m., f.*) sugar, 9; **caña de ~** sugar cane
azul blue, 4

B

bacalao codfish, 9
bailar to dance, 2
baile (*m.*) dance, 3
bajar to get down from, to get off of (*a bus, etc.*), 6
bajo(a) short (*in height*), 2
baldosa paving stone
balneario seaside resort, spa
banco (commercial) bank, 6
bañador(a) bather
bañar to swim; to give someone a bath, 5; **bañarse** to take a bath, 5
baño bathroom, 10
barco boat
barrer el suelo/el piso to sweep the floor, 10
barrio neighborhood, 6; **~ residencial** residential neighborhood, suburbs, 10; **~ comercial** business district, 10
básquetbol (*m.*) basketball, 7
Bastante bien. Quite well. 1
basura garbage, 10; **sacar la ~** to take out the garbage, 10
basurero wastebasket
batir to beat; to break
beber to drink, 3
bebida beverage, 9
béisbol (*m.*) baseball, 7
belleza beauty
bello(a) beautiful
beneficio benefit, 13
berro watercress
besar to kiss
bicicleta: en ~ on bicycle, 6; **montar en ~** to ride a bike, 7
bien well, 4; **~, gracias.** Fine, thank you. 1; **(no) muy ~** (not) very well, 1
bienestar (*m.*) well-being
bienvenido(a) welcome
bilingüe bilingual
billete (*m.*) ticket, 14; **~ de ida** one-way ticket, 14; **~ de ida y vuelta** round-trip ticket, 14
biología biology, 3

bíper (*m.*) beeper, 4
bistec (*m.*) steak, 6
blanco(a) white, 4
blusa blouse, 8
boca mouth, 12
bocadillo sandwich, 9
boda wedding
bodegón (*m.*) tavern
boleto ticket, 11; **~ de ida** one-way ticket, 14; **~ de ida y vuelta** round-trip ticket, 14
bolígrafo ballpoint pen, P
boliviano(a) Bolivian, 2
bolsa purse, 8; **~ de valores** stock market, 13
bombero(a) fire fighter, 5
bondadoso(a) kind; good
bonito(a) pretty
bordado(a) embroidered, 8
borrador (*m.*) rough draft
bosque (*m.*) forest, 14; **~ tropical/pluvial** rainforest
bosquejo outline
bota boot, 8
bote (*m.*) boat
botones (*m. s.*) bellboy, 14
boxeo boxing, 7
brazalete (*m.*) bracelet, 8
brazo arm, 12
breve brief
bróculi (*m.*) broccoli, 9
broma joke
bueno(a) good, 2; **Buenas noches.** Good night. Good evening. 1; **Buenas tardes.** Good afternoon. 1; **Buenos días.** Good morning. 1; **es bueno** it's good, 11
bufanda scarf, 8
buscador (*m.*) search engine, 4
buscapersonas (*m. s.*) beeper, 4
buscar (qu) to look for, 2
buzón (*m.*) **electrónico** electronic mailbox, 4

C

caballo: montar a ~ to ride horseback, 7
cabeza head, 12; **dolor** (*m.*) **de ~** headache, 12
cable (*m.*) cable, 4; cable television, 11
cabo end
cacao chocolate
cachemira cashmere
cadena chain, 8
caer (*irreg.*) to fall

café (*m.*) coffee, 9; (*adj.*) brown, 4
cafetería cafeteria, 3
caimán (*m.*) alligator
cajero automático automated bank teller, ATM, 6
cajón (*m.*) large box; drawer
calcetín (*m.*) sock, 8
calculadora calculator, P
cálculo calculus, 3
caldo de pollo chicken soup, 9
calentar (ie) to heat, 9
calidad (*f.*) quality; **de buena (alta) ~** of good (high) quality, 8
calificación (*f.*) evaluation
calle (*f.*) street, 1
calor: Hace ~. It's hot., 7; **tener** (*irreg.*) **~** to be hot, 7
caluroso(a) warm
cama bed, 10; **guardar ~** to stay in bed , 12; **hacer la ~** to make the bed, 10
cámara: ~ digital digital camera, 4; **~ web** webcam, 4
camarero(a) waiter (waitress), 5
camarón (*m.*) shrimp, 9
cambiar: ~ dinero to exchange money, 14; **~ el canal** to change the channel, 11
cambio change; exchange rate; **a ~ de** in exchange for
caminar to walk, 2
camisa shirt, 8
camiseta t-shirt, 8
campaña campaign, 13
campestre rural
campo: ~ de estudio field of study, 3; **~ de fútbol** soccer field, 6
caña de azúcar sugar cane
canadiense (*m., f.*) Canadian, 2
canasta basket
cancha soccer field, 6; **~ de tenis** tennis court, 6
candidato(a) candidate, 13
canela cinnamon
cañón (*m.*) canyon, 14
cansado(a) tired, 4
cantante (*m., f.*) singer
cantar to sing, 2
capítulo chapter, P
característica trait; **~ de la personalidad** personality trait, 2; **~ física** physical trait, 2
Caribe (*m., f.*) Caribbean (sea)
cariño love, fondness
carne (*f.*) meat, 9

carnicería butcher shop, 6
caro: Es (demasiado) caro(a). It's (too) expensive. 8
carpintero(a) carpenter, 5
carrera career, 5
carreta wooden cart
carro: en ~ by car, 6
carta: a la ~ à la carte, 9
cartera wallet, 8
cartón (*m.*) cardboard
casa house, 6
casarse to get married, 5
casco helmet
casero(a) homemade
caso: en ~ de que in case, 12; **hacer ~** to pay attention, to obey
catarata waterfall
catarro cold (*e.g., headcold*), 12
catorce fourteen, P
CD (*m.*) compact disc, P; **~ portátil/MP3** portable CD/MP3 player, 4
cebolla onion, 9
celebración (*f.*) celebration
celos: tener (*irreg.*) **~** to be jealous
celoso(a) jealous
cena dinner
cenar to eat dinner, 2
censo census
centavo cent
centro center; **~ comercial** mall, 6; **~ de computación** computer center, 3; **~ de comunicaciones** media center, 3; **~ de la ciudad** downtown, 10; **~ estudiantil** student center, 6
Centroamérica Central America
cepillarse el pelo to brush one's hair, 5
cepillo brush, 5; **~ de dientes** toothbrush, 5
cerca de close to, 6
cereal (*m.*) cereal, 9
cero zero, P
cerrar (ie) to close; **Cierren los libros.** Close your books. P
cerveza beer, 9
chaleco vest, 8
champú (*m.*) shampoo, 5
chaparrón (*m.*) cloudburst, downpour
chaqueta jacket (*outdoor, non-suit coat*), 8
chatear to chat, 4
Chau. Bye, Good-bye, 1

cheque (*m.*)   check; **pagar con ~ / con ~ de viajero**   to pay by check / with a traveler's check, 8

chequeo médico   physical, checkup, 12

chévere   terrific, great (*Cuba, Puerto Rico*)

chico(a)   boy (girl), P

chileno(a)   Chilean, 2

chimenea   fireplace, 10

chino   Chinese language, 3

chino(a)   Chinese, 2

chisme (*m.*)   gossip

chismoso(a)   gossiping

chocolate (*m.*)   chocolate, 11

chuleta de puerco   pork chop, 6

ciberespacio   cyberspace, 4

ciclismo   cycling, 7

ciego(a)   blind; **cita a ciegas**   blind date

cielo   sky, 14

cien   one hundred, P; **~ mil**   one hundred thousand, 8

ciencias (*f. pl.*)   science, 3; **~ políticas**   political science, 3

científico(a)   scientific

ciento uno   one hundred and one, 8

cierto(a)   certain; **no es cierto**   it's not certain, 11

cinco   five, P; **~ mil**   five thousand, 8

cincuenta   fifty, P

cine (*m.*)   cinema, 6; movies, 11

cinta   audiotape, P

cinturón (*m.*)   belt, 8

cita   appointment, 12; quotation; **~ a ciegas**   blind date

ciudad (*f.*)   city, 6

ciudadano(a)   citizen, 13

claridad (*f.*)   clarity

clase (*f.*)   class, P; **~ baja**   lower class; **~ de película**   movie genre, 11

clasificar (qu) con cuatro estrellas   to give a four-star rating, 11

clic: hacer ~/doble ~   to click/ double click, 4

cliente (*m., f.*)   customer, 8

clínica   clinic, 12

clóset (*m.*)   closet, 10

cobre (*m.*)   copper

cocer (-z) (ue)   to cook, 9

coche: en ~   by car, 6

cocina   kitchen, 10

cocinar   to cook, 2

cocinero(a)   cook, chef, 5

código   code

codo   elbow, 12

colectivo   bus

cólera   anger

collar (*m.*)   necklace, 8

colombiano(a)   Colombian, 2

colonia   neighborhood, 1

color (*m.*)   color, 4; **de un solo ~**   solid (colored), 8

coma   comma

comedia (romántica)   (romantic) comedy, 11

comedor (*m.*)   dining room, 10

comenzar (ie) (c)   to begin, 4

comer   to eat, 3; **~ alimentos nutritivos**   to eat healthy foods, 12; **darle de ~ al perro/gato**   to feed the dog/cat, 10

cómico(a)   funny, 2

comida   food, 6

comino   cumin, 9

¿cómo?   how? 3; **¿~ desea pagar?**   How do you wish to pay? 8; **¿~ es?**   What's he/she/it like? 2; **¿~ está (usted)?** (*s. form.*)   How are you? 1; **¿~ están (ustedes)?** (*pl.*)   How are you? 1; **¿~ estás (tú)?** (*s. fam.*)   How are you? 1; **¿~ te/le/les va?**   How's it going with you? 1; **~ no.**   Of course. 6; **¿~ se dice…?**   How do you say . . . ? P; **¿~ se llama?** (*s. form.*)   What's your name? 1; **¿~ te llamas?** (*s. fam.*)   What's your name? 1

cómoda   dresser, 10

compañero(a) de cuarto   room-mate, P

compañía multinacional   multinational corporation, 13

comparación (*f.*)   comparison, 8

compartir   to share, 3

competencia   competition, 7

competir (i, i)   to compete

complicidad (*f.*)   complicity

comportamiento   behavior

comprar   to buy, 2

compras: hacer las ~   to go shopping, 6

comprender   to understand, 3

comprensión (*f.*)   understanding

comprometerse   to get engaged, 5

computación (*f.*)   computer science, 3

computadora   computer, P; **~ portátil**   laptop computer, 4

común   common

comunicación (*f.*) **pública**   public communications, 3

con   with; **~ destino a**   with destination to, 14; **~ tal (de) que**   so that, provided that, 12

concordancia   agreement

concurso   contest

conducir (zc)   to drive, to conduct, 5

conectar   to connect, 4

conexión (*f.*)   connection, 4; **~ a Internet**   Internet connection, 14; **hacer una ~**   to go online, 4

confección (*f.*)   confection

conferencista (*m., f.*)   speaker

congelado(a)   frozen, 9

congestionado(a): estar ~   to be congested, 12

conmigo   with me, 8

conocer (zc)   to meet; to know a person, to be familiar with, 5

conocimientos: tener (*irreg.*) **algunos ~ de**   to have some knowledge of, 13

conseguir (i, i)   to get, to obtain, 8

consejo   advice, 12

conserje (*m., f.*)   concierge, 14

consultorio del médico   doctor's office, 12

contabilidad (*f.*)   accounting, 3

contado: al ~   in cash, 8

contador(a)   accountant, 5

contaminación (*f.*) **(del aire)**   (air) pollution, 13

contar (ue)   to tell, to relate, 4; to count; **~ con**   to be certain of

contento(a)   happy, 4; **estar ~ de**   to be pleased about, 11

contestar   to answer; **Contesten.** Answer. P

contigo   with you (*fam.*), 8

contracción (*f.*)   contraction, 3

contrario: al ~   on the contrary

contraseña   password, 4

contratar   to hire, 13

contrato   contract, 13; **~ prenupcial**   prenuptial agreement

control (*m.*) **remoto**   remote control, 11

conversación (*f.*)   conversation

convertir (ie, i)   to change

copa   wine glass, goblet, 9

coraje (*m.*)   courage

corazón (*m.*)   heart, 12

cordillera mountain range
corregir (i, i) (j) to correct
correo electrónico e-mail, 4
correr to run, 3
cortar to cut, 12; **~ el césped** to mow the lawn, 10; **~ la conexión** to go offline, 4; **cortarse** to cut oneself, 12
cortesía courtesy, 4
cortina curtain, 10
corto(a) short (*in length*)
costarricense (*m., f.*) Costa Rican, 2
costo cost, 13
cotidiano(a) daily
crear to create
creativo(a) creative
creer (en) to believe (in), 3; **no creer** to not believe, 11
crema cream, 12
crimen (*m.*) crime, 13
crítica criticism; critique, review, 11
crítico(a) critic, 11
cronología chronology
crucero cruise ship
crudo(a) raw, 9
cruzar (c) to cross, 6
cuaderno notebook, P
cuadra (city) block, 6
cuadro painting; print, 10
cuadros: a ~ plaid, 8
¿cuál? what? which one? 3; **¿~ es tu/su dirección (electrónica)?** (*s. fam./form.*) What's your (e-mail) address? 1; **¿~ es tu/su número de teléfono?** (*s. fam./ form.*) What is your phone number? 1
¿cuáles? what? which ones? 3
cuando when, 12
¿cuándo? when? 3; **¿~ es tu cumpleaños?** When is your birthday? 1
cuanto: en ~ as soon as, 12; **en ~ a** in relation to
¿cuánto(a)? how much? 3; **¿Cuánto cuesta(n)?** How much does it (do they) cost? 8
¿cuántos(as)? how many? 3
cuarenta forty, P
cuarto room, P; bedroom, 10
cuarto(a) fourth, 10
cuate(a) friend, buddy
cuatro four, P
cuatrocientos(as) four hundred, 8
cubano(a) Cuban, 2

cuchara spoon, 9
cucharada tablespoonful, 9
cucharadita teaspoonful, 9
cuchillo knife, 9
cuello neck, 12
cuenta check, bill, 9
cuento de hadas fairy tale
cuero leather, 8
cuerpo body, 12
cuestionario questionnaire
cuidado: tener (*irreg.*) **~** to be careful, 7; **¡~!** careful!
cuidadoso(a) cautious, 2
culinario(a) culinary
cultura culture
cuna cradle
cuñado(a) brother- in-law (sister-in-law), 5
curita (small) bandaid, 12
currículum vitae (*m.*) curriculum vitae, résumé, 13
curso básico basic course, 3
cuy (*m.*) guinea pig
cuyo(a) whose

D

danza dance, 11
dar (*irreg.*) to give, 5; **~ información personal** to give personal information, 1; **~ la hora** to give the time, 3; **~le de comer al perro/gato** to feed the dog/cat, 10
darse la mano to shake hands, 13
dato fact; piece of information
De nada. You're welcome. 1
debajo de below, underneath, 6
deber (+ *inf.*) should, ought to (*do something*), 3
décimo(a) tenth, 10
decir (*irreg.*) to say, to tell, 5; **~ cómo llegar** to give directions, 6; **~ la hora** to tell the time, 3; **Se dice...** It's said . . . , P
decoración (*f.*) decoration, 10
dedo finger, toe, 12
definido(a) definite, 1
dejar to leave, to stop, 2; **~ de** (+ *inf.*) to stop (*doing something*), 3
del (**de** + **el**) from the, of the, 3
delante de in front of, 6
delgado(a) thin, 2
demasiado(a) too much, 4
demora delay, 14
demostrar (ue) to demonstrate, to show
demostrativo(a) demonstrative, 6

dentista (*m., f.*) dentist, 5
dentro de inside of, 6; **~ la casa** inside the house, 10
dependiente (*m., f.*) salesclerk, 5
deporte (*m.*) sport, 7
derecha: a la ~ to the right, 6
derecho: (todo) ~ (straight) ahead, 6
desarrollar to develop
desarrollo development, 13
desastre (*m.*) disaster; **~ natural** natural disaster, 13
desayuno breakfast, 9; **~ incluido** breakfast included, 14
descalificar (qu) to disqualify
descalzo(a) barefoot
descansar to rest, 2
descortés rude
describir to describe, 2
descubrir to discover, 3
descuento discount, 8
desear to want; to wish, 10
desembarcar (qu) to disembark, 14
desempeñarse to manage
desengaño disillusionment
desierto desert, 14
desigualdad (*f.*) inequality, 13
desilusión (*f.*) disappointment
desmayarse to faint, 12
desodorante (*m.*) deodorant, 5
despachar to dispatch; to wait on
despacio (*adv.*) slowly; (*adj.*) slow
despedido(a) fired (*from a job*)
despedir (i, i) to fire, 13; **despedirse (i, i)** to say good-bye, 1
despertar (ie) to wake someone up, 5; **despertarse (ie)** to wake up, 5
después after, 5; **~ (de) que** after, 12
destacar (qu) to emphasize
destino: con ~ a with destination to, 14
desventaja disadvantage, 13
detalle (*m.*) detail
detallista detail-oriented, 13
detrás de behind, 6
día (*m.*) day, 3; **~ de la semana** day of the week, 3; **~ de las Madres** Mother's Day, 3; **todos los días** every day, 3
dialecto dialect
dibujo drawing, P; **~ animado** cartoon; (*pl.*) animated film, 11
diccionario dictionary, P
dicha happiness

dicho saying; (*p.p. of* **decir**) said, 13
diciembre December, 1
diccinueve nineteen, P
dieciocho eighteen, P
dieciséis sixteen, P
diecisiete seventeen, P
diez ten, P; **~ mil** ten thousand, 8
diferencia difference
difícil difficult, 4
dinero money
dirección (*f.*) address
dirigir (j) to direct, 13
disco duro hard drive, 4
discreción: se recomienda ~ rated PG-13 (parental discretion advised), 11
discriminación (*f.*) discrimination, 13
Disculpe. Excuse me. 4
diseñador(a) gráfico(a) graphic designer, 5
diseño design; **~ gráfico** graphic design, 3
disfrutar (la vida) to enjoy (life)
disponibilidad (*f.*) availability
disponible available, 13
dispuesto(a) willing
disquete (*m.*) disk, P
diversidad (*f.*) diversity
diversión (*f.*) amusement
divertido(a) fun, entertaining, 2
divertirse (ie, i) to have fun, 5
divorciarse to get divorced, 5
doblado(a) dubbed, 11
doblar to turn, 6; to fold
doce twelve, P
docena dozen, 9
doctor(a) doctor
documental (*m.*) documentary, 11
dólar (*m.*) dollar
doler (ue) to hurt, 12
dolor (*m.*) pain, ache, 12; **~ de cabeza** headache, 12; **~ de estómago** stomachache, 12; **~ de garganta** sore throat, 12
domesticado(a) tame, tamed
domingo Sunday, 2
dominicano(a) Dominican, 2
don (doña) title of respect used with male (female) first name, 1
¿dónde? where? 3; **¿~ tienes la clase de... ?** Where does your . . . class meet? 3; **¿~ vives/vive?** (*s. fam./form.*) Where do you live? 1
dondequiera: por ~ everywhere
dorado(a) golden, browned, 9

dormir (ue, u) to sleep, 4; **dormirse (ue, u)** to fall asleep, 5
dormitorio bedroom, 10; **~ estudiantil** dormitory, 6
dos two, P; **~ mil** two thousand, 8
doscientos(as) two hundred, 8
drama (*m.*) drama, 11
ducharse to take a shower, 5
dudar to doubt, 11
dudoso(a) doubtful, unlikely, 11
dueño(a) owner, 5
dulce (*m.*) candy, 11; (*adj.*) sweet
duro(a) hard

E

economía economy, 3
ecuador (*m.*) equator
ecuatoriano(a) Ecuadoran, 2
edad (*f.*) age
edificio building, 6
educación (*f.*) education, 3
efectivo: en ~ in cash, 8
egoísta selfish, egotistic, 2
ejemplo example, 10; **por ~** for example, 10
ejercicio: hacer ~ to exercise, 7
ejército army, 13
el (*m.*) the, 1
él he, 1; him, 8
elección (*f.*) election, 13
electricidad (*f.*) electricity
electrodoméstico appliance, 10
elefante (*m.*) elephant
ella she, 1; her, 8
ellos(as) they, 1; them, 8
e-mail (*m.*) e-mail, 4
embajador(a) ambassador
emergencia emergency, 12
emoción (*f.*) emotion, 4
empapado(a) drenched
emparejar to match
empezar (ie) (c) to begin, 4
empleado(a) employee, 13
emplear to employ, 13
emprendedor(a) enterprising, 13
empresario(a) businessman/woman, 13
en in, on, at; **~ autobús/tren** by bus/train, 6; **~ bicicleta** on bicycle, 6; **~ carro/coche/automóvil** by car, 6; **~ caso de que** in case, 12; **~ cuanto** as soon as, 12; **~ cuanto a** in relation to; **~ línea** online, 4; **~ metro** on the subway, 6; **~ realidad** actually
enamorarse to fall in love, 5

Encantado(a). Delighted to meet you. 1
encantar to like a lot, 4; to enchant, to please, 11
encima de on top of, on, 6
encuentro encounter; meeting
encuesta survey
enero January, 1
enfatizar (c) to emphasize
enfermarse to get sick, 5
enfermedad (*f.*) sickness, illness, 12
enfermero(a) nurse, 5
enfermo(a) sick, 4
enfrente de in front of, opposite, 6
enfriarse to get cold, 9
engañar to fool
engaño hoax
enlace (*m.*) link, 4
enojado(a) angry, 4
ensalada salad, 9; **~ de fruta** fruit salad, 9; **~ de lechuga y tomate** lettuce and tomato salad, 9; **~ de papa** potato salad, 9; **~ mixta** tossed salad, 9
ensayo essay
enseñar to teach
entender (ie) to understand, 4
entonces then
entrada ticket (*to a movie, concert, etc.*), 11
entre between, 6
entregar (gu) to turn in; **Entreguen la tarea.** Turn in your homework. P
entrenador(a) trainer
entrenarse to train, 7
entresemana during the week, on weekdays, 3
entretener (*like* **tener**) to entertain
entrevista interview, 13
entrevistador(a) interviewer, 11
enviar to send, 4
episodio episode, 11
equilibro: poner en ~ to balance
equipaje (*m.*) baggage, luggage, 14; **facturar el ~** to check one's baggage, 14
equipo team, 7
erupción (*f.*) **volcánica** volcanic eruption
escala: hacer ~ en to make a stopover in, 14
escaleras (*f. pl.*) stairs, 10
esclavo(a) slave
escoger (j) to choose
esconder to hide

escribir to write, 3; **Escriban en sus cuadernos.** Write in your notebooks. P

escrito (*p.p. of* **escribir**) written, 13

escritorio desk, P

escuchar to listen; ~ **música** to listen to music, 2; **Escuchen la cinta/el CD.** Listen to the tape/CD. P

escultura sculpture, 11

ese (esa) (*s. adj.*) that, 6

ése (ésa) (*s. pron.*) that one, 6

eso: por ~ so, that's why, 10

esos (esas) (*pl. adj.*) those, 6

ésos (ésas) (*pl. pron.*) those (ones), 6

espalda back, 12

España Spain

español (española) Spanish, 2

español (*m.*) Spanish language, 3

espárragos (*m.pl.*) asparagus, 9

especie (*f.*) species

espectáculo show, 11

espejo mirror, 10

esperanza wish, hope

esperar to hope, 10; to wait, 11

esposo(a) husband (wife), 5

esquí (*m.*) ski, skiing; ~ **acuático** water skiing, 7; ~ **alpino** downhill skiing, 7

esquiar to ski, 7

esquina corner, 6

estación (*f.*) season, 7; station, 11; ~ **autobús** bus station, 6; ~ **de trenes** train station, 6

estacionamiento parking lot, 6

estadio stadium, 6

estadística statistics, 3

estado state, 5; ~ **civil** marital status

Estados Unidos United States

estadounidense (*m., f.*) U. S. citizen, 2

estampado(a) print, 8

estampilla postage stamp, 14

estancia ranch

estar (*irreg.*) to be, 1; ~ **congestionado(a)** to be congested, 12; ~ **contento(a) de** to be pleased about, 11; ~ **mareado(a)** to feel dizzy, 12

estatura height (*of a person*)

este (*m.*) east, 14

este (esta) (*s. adj.*) this, 6

éste (ésta) (*s. pron.*) this one, 6

estilo style

estos(as) (*pl. adj.*) these, 6

estómago stomach, 12; **dolor** (*m.*) **de ~** stomachache, 12

estornudar to sneeze, 12

éstos(as) (*pl. pron.*) these (ones), 6

estrategia strategy

estrella de cine movie star, 11

estudiante (*m., f.*) student, P

estudiar to study; ~ **en la biblioteca (en casa)** to study at the library (at home), 2; **Estudien las páginas… a…** Study pages . . . to . . . P

estudio studio, 3

estufa stove, 10

Europa Europe

evitar to avoid

exhibir to exhibit

exigir (j) to demand

éxito success

exótico(a) exotic, strange

exposición (*f.*) **de arte** art exhibit, 11

expresar preferencias to express preferences, 2

expresión (*f.*) expression, 1

extraño(a) strange, 11

extrovertido(a) extroverted, 2

F

fábrica factory, 13

fácil easy, 4

facturar el equipaje to check one's baggage, 14

falda skirt, 8

falso(a) false

familia family; ~ **nuclear** nuclear family, 5; ~ **política** in-laws, 5

fantasía fantasy

fantástico(a) fantastic, 11

farmacia pharmacy, 6

fascinar to fascinate, 4

fatal terrible, awful, 1

fax (*m.*) **externo/interno** external/internal fax, 4

favor: por ~ please, 1

febrero February, 1

fecha date, 3; **¿A qué ~ estamos?** What is today's date? 3

felicidad (*f.*) happiness

femenino(a) feminine

feo(a) ugly, 2

ferrocarril (*m.*) railroad

fiebre (*f.*) fever, 12

filantrópico(a) philanthropic

filosofía philosophy, 3

fin (*m.*) end; intention; ~ **de semana** weekend, 2; **por ~** finally, 9

final final

financiero(a) financial

física physics, 3

físico(a) physical, 5

flan (*m.*) custard, 9

flor (*f.*) flower

florecer (zc) to flower, to flourish

flotador(a) floating

fondo background

formulario form, 13

fortaleza fortress

foto (*f.*) photo, P; **sacar fotos** to take photos, 2

fractura fracture, 12

francés (francesa) French, 2

francés (*m.*) French language, 3

frecuentemente frequently, 4

freír (i, i) to fry, 9

frente a in front of, facing, opposite, 6

fresa strawberry, 9

fresco(a) fresh, 9; **Hace fresco.** It's cool. 7

frijoles (*m.*) **(refritos)** (refried) beans, 9

frío(a) cold; **Hace frío.** It's cold. 7; **tener** (*irreg.*) **frío** to be cold, 7

frito(a) fried, 9

frontera border

fruta fruit, 6

fuego fire; **a ~ suave/lento** at low heat, 9

fuente (*f.*) source

fuera de outside of, 6; ~ **de la casa** outside the house, 10

fuerte strong, filling (*e.g., a meal*), 9

fuerzas armadas armed forces, 13

funcionar to function, 4

funciones (*f.*) **de la computadora** computer functions, 4

fundador(a) founder

furioso(a) furious, 4

fútbol (*m.*) soccer, 7; ~ **americano** football, 7

G

gafas (*f. pl.*) **de sol** sunglasses, 8

galleta cookie, 9

galón (*m.*) gallon, 9

ganadería cattle, livestock

ganado cattle

ganancia profit, 13

ganar to win; to earn (*money*)

ganas: tener (*irreg.*) ~ **de** to have the urge to, to feel like, 7

garaje (*m.*) garage, 10

garganta throat, 12; **dolor** (*m.*) **de ~** sore throat, 12

gato(a) cat, 2

gazpacho cold tomato soup (*Spain*), 9

general: por lo ~ generally, 9

género genre

generoso(a) generous, 2

geografía geography, 3

gerente (*m., f.*) manager, 5

gimnasio gymnasium, 3

globalización (*f.*) globalization, 13

gobernador(a) (*m.*) governor

gobierno government, 13

golf (*m.*) golf, 7

gordo(a) fat, 2

gorra cap, 8

gotas (*f. pl.*) drops, 12

gozar (c) to enjoy

grabador (*m.*) **de discos compactos/ DVD** CD/DVD recorder, 4

grabar to record, 4; to videotape, 11

gracias: Muchas ~. Thank you very much. 1

grado degree; **~ centígrado** Cclsius degree, 7; **~ Fahrenheit** Fahrenheit degree, 7

gráfica graph

grande big, great, 2

grano: al ~ to the point

gripe (*f.*) flu, 12

gris gray, 4

gritar to shout, to scream

grito scream

grupo group; **~ de conversación** chat room, 4; **~ de debate** news group, 4

guagua bus (*Cuba, Puerto Rico*)

guante (*m.*) glove, 8

guapo(a) handsome, attractive, 2

guardar to store; **~ cama** to stay in bed , 12; **~ la ropa** put away the clothes, 10

guatemalteco(a) Guatemalan, 2

guerra war, 13

guía turística tourist guide, brochure, 14

guión (*m.*) script

guionista (*m., f.*) script writer

guisado beef stew, 9

guisante (*m.*) pea, 9

guitarra guitar, 2

gustar to like, to please, 11; **A mí/ti me gusta...** I/You like . . . , 2; **A... le gusta...** He/She likes . . . , 2; **A... les gusta...** They/You (*pl.*)

like . . . , 2; **Me gustaría** (+ *inf.*) ... I'd like (+ *inf.*) . . . , 6

gusto taste; **al ~** to individual taste, 9; **El ~ es mío.** The pleasure is mine. 1; **Mucho ~.** My pleasure. 1; **Mucho ~ en conocerte.** A pleasure to meet you. 1

H

haba (*f.*) (*but:* **el haba**) bean

habichuela green bean, 9

habilidades necesarias necessary skills, 13

habitación (*f.*) bedroom, 10; **~ con baño/ducha** room with a bath/shower, 14; **~ de fumar/de no fumar** smoking/non-smoking room, 14; **~ doble** double room, 14; **~ sencilla** single room, 14; **~ sin baño/ducha** room without a bath/shower, 14

habitante (*m., f.*) inhabitant

hablar por teléfono to talk on the telephone, 1

hacer (*irreg.*) to make, to do, 5; **Hace buen/mal tiempo.** It's nice/bad weather. 7; **Hace calor/fresco/frío.** It's hot/cool/ cold. 7; **Hace sol/viento.** It's sunny/windy. 7; **~ alpinismo** to hike, 7; **~ caso** to pay attention, to obey; **~ clic/doble clic** to click/double click, 4; **~ ejercicio** to exercise, 7; **~ el reciclaje** to do the recycling, 10; **~ escala en** to make a stopover in, 14; **~ informes** to write reports, 13; **~ la cama** to make the bed, 10; **~ las compras** to go shopping, 6; **~ preguntas** to ask questions, 3; **~ surfing** to surf, 7; **~ un análisis de sangre/orina** to give a blood/urine test, 12; **~ un tour** to take a tour, 14; **~ una conexión** to go online, 4; **~ una reservación** to make a reservation, 14; **Hagan la tarea para mañana.** Do the homework for tomorrow. P

hambre (*f.*) (*but:* **el hambre**) hunger; **tener** (*irreg.*) **~** to be hungry, 7

hamburguesa hamburger, 9; **~ con queso** cheeseburger, 9

hardware (*m.*) hardware, 4

harina flour, 9

hasta until, 12; **~ luego.** See you later, 1; **~ mañana.** See you to-morrow. 1; **~ pronto.** See you soon. 1; **~ que** until, 12

hay there is, there are, 1

hecho fact

hecho(a) (*p. p.*) done, 13; **Está ~ de...** It's made out of . . . , 8

helado de vainilla/chocolate vanilla/chocolate ice cream, 9

herencia heritage

herida injury, wound, 12

hermanastro(a) stepbrother (stepsister), 5

hermano(a) (menor, mayor) (younger, older) brother (sister), 5

hermoso(a) handsome, beautiful

hervido(a) boiled, 9

hervir (ie, i) to boil, 9

hierba herb, 12

hierro iron

hijo(a) son (daughter), 5

hilo: al ~ stringed, 9

himno hymn

hispano(a) Hispanic

hispanohablante Spanish-speaking

historia history, 3

hockey (*m.*) **sobre hielo/hierba** ice/field hockey, 7

hogar (*m.*) home; **sin ~** homeless

hoja dc papcl sheet of paper, P

hola hello, 1

hombre (*m.*) man, P; **~ de negocios** businessman, 5

hombro shoulder, 12

hondureño(a) Honduran, 2

honesto(a) honest

hora hour; time; **dar** (*irreg.*) **la ~** to give the time, 3; **decir la ~** to tell the time, 3

horario schedule

horno oven; **al ~** roasted (in the oven), 9

horrible horrible, 11

hospital (*m.*) hospital, 6

hotel (*m.*) hotel, 14

hoy today, 3; **~ es martes treinta.** Today is Tuesday the 30th. 3; **¿Qué día es ~?** What day is today? 3

huelga strike, 13

huella footprint

huésped(a) hotel guest, 14

huevo egg, 6; **~ estrellado** egg sunny-side up, 9; **~ revuelto** scrambled egg, 9

humanidades (*f. pl.*) humanities, 3

húmedo(a) humid
humilde humble
huracán (*m.*) hurricane, 13

I

ícono del programa program icon, 4
identidad (*f.*) identity
idioma (*m.*) language, 3
iglesia church, 6
igualdad (*f.*) equality, 13
Igualmente. Likewise. 1
impaciente impatient, 2
impermeable (*m.*) raincoat, 8
importante important, 11
importar to be important, to matter, 4
imprescindible extremely important, 11
impresionante impressive
impresora printer, 4
imprimir to print, 3
improbable improbable, unlikely, 11
impulsivo(a) impulsive, 2
incendio forestal forest fire
increíble incredible
indefinido(a) indefinite, 1
índice (*m.*) index; **~ de audiencia** movie ratings, 11
indígena indigenous
industria industry, 13; **~ ganadera** cattle-raising industry
infección (*f.*) infection, 12
influencia influence
influir (y) to influence
informática computer science, 3
informe (*m.*) report; **hacer informes** to write reports, 13
ingeniería engineering, 3
ingeniero(a) engineer, 5
inglés (inglesa) English, 2
inglés (*m.*) English language, 3
ingrediente (*m.*) ingredient, 9
ingreso revenue
iniciar to initiate, 13
inmigración (*f.*) immigration
insistir to insist, 10
instalar to install, 4
instrucción (*f.*) instruction, 12
instructor(a) instructor, P
inteligente intelligent, 2
intentar to attempt
intercambiar to exchange
interesante interesting, 2
interesar to interest, to be interesting, 4

Internet (*m.* or *f.*) Internet
intérprete (*m., f.*) interpreter
íntimo(a) intimate
introvertido(a) introverted, 2
inundación (*f.*) flood, 13
invierno winter, 7
inyección (*f.*) injection, 12
ir (*irreg.*) to go, 3; **~ a** (+ *inf.*) to be going to (*do something*), 3; **~ de compras** to go shopping, 8; **irse** to leave, to go away, 5
irresponsable irresponsible, 2
isla island, 14
italiano(a) Italian, 2
italiano (*m.*) Italian language
itinerario itinerary, 14
izquierda: a la ~ to the left, 6

J

jabón (*m.*) soap, 5
jamás never, 6
jamón (*m.*) ham, 6
japonés (japonesa) Japanese, 2
japonés (*m.*) Japanese language, 3
jarabe (*m.*) **(para la tos)** (cough) syrup, 12
jardín (*m.*) garden, 10
jeans (*m. pl.*) jeans, 8
jornada laboral workday
joven young, 2
joyas (*f. pl.*) jewelry, 8
joyería jewelry store, 6
jubilarse to retire, 13
juego interactivo interactive game, 4
jueves (*m.*) Thursday, 3
jugar (ue) (gu) to play, 4; **~ tenis (béisbol, etc.)** to play tennis (baseball, etc.), 7
jugo de fruta fruit juice, 9
juguete (*m.*) toy, 10
juguetón (juguetona) playful
julio July, 1
junio June, 1
juntar to group
juventud (*f.*) youth

K

kilo kilo, 9; **medio ~** half a kilo, 9

L

la (*f.*) the, 1
labio lip
lado side; **al ~ de** next to, on the side of, 6
ladrillo brick

lago lake, 7
lámpara lamp, 10
lana wool, 8
langosta lobster, 9
lanzarse (c) to throw oneself
lápiz (*m.*) pencil, P
lástima: es una ~ it's a shame, 11
lastimarse to hurt/injure oneself, 12
lavado en seco dry cleaning, 14
lavadora washer, 10
lavandería laundry room, 10
lavaplatos (*m. s.*) dishwasher, 10
lavar to wash, 5; **~ los platos (la ropa)** to wash the dishes (the clothes), 10
lavarse to wash oneself, 5; **~ el pelo** to wash one's hair, 5; **~ los dientes** to brush one's teeth, 5
le to/for you (*form. s.*), to/for him, to/for her, 8
lección (*f.*) lesson, P
leche (*f.*) milk, 6
lector (*m.*) **de CD-ROM o DVD** DVD/CD-ROM drive, 4
leer (y) to read, 3; **Lean el Capítulo 1.** Read Chapter 1. P
lejos de far from, 6
lema (*m.*) slogan
lengua language, 3; tongue, 12; **sacar la ~** to stick out one's tongue, 12
lentes (*m. pl.*) eyeglasses
lento(a) slow, 4
les to/for you (*form. pl.*), to/for them, 8
letrero sign
levantar to raise, to lift, 5; **~ pesas** to lift weights, 2
levantarse to get up, 5
libra pound, 9
librería bookstore, 3
libro book, P
licencia de manejar driver's license
licuado de fruta fruit shake, smoothie
licuadora blender, 10
líder (*m., f.*) leader, 13
ligero(a) light, lightweight, 9
limonada lemonade, 9
limpiar el baño to clean the bathroom, 10
lindo(a) pretty, 2
línea: ~ aérea airline, 14; **en ~** online, 4
lingüístico(a) linguistic

lino linen, 8
lista de espera waiting list, 14
literatura literature, 3
litro liter, 9
llamar to call, 2; **llamarse** to name, 2; **Me llamo…** My name is . . . , 1
llano(a) flat
llanura plain
llave (*f.*) key (*to a lock*), 14
llegada arrival, 14
llegar (gu) to arrive, 2
llevar to take, to carry; **~ una vida sana** to lead a healthy life, 12; **llevarse bien con la gente** to get along well with people, 13
llover to rain; **Está lloviendo. (Llueve.)** It's raining. 7
lobo wolf
locutor(a) announcer, 11
lógico(a) logical, 11
lograr to achieve
lomo de res prime rib, 9
los (las) (*pl.*) the, 1
luchar (contra) to fight (against), 13
luego later, 5
lugar (*m.*) place; **~ de nacimiento** birthplace
lujoso(a) luxurious
lunares: de ~ polka-dotted, 8
lunes (*m.*) Monday, 3
luz (*f.*) light; **~ solar** sunlight

M

madera wood
madrastra stepmother, 5
madre (*f.*) mother, 5
maestro(a) teacher, 5
maíz (*m.*) corn
mal badly, 4
maleta suitcase, 14
maletín (*m.*) briefcase, 13
malo(a) bad, 2
mamá mother, 5
mañana morning, 3; tomorrow, 3; **de la ~** in the morning (*with precise time*), 3; **por la ~** during the morning, 3
mandar to send; to order, 10
mandato command
manejar to drive, 5
manifestación (*f.*) demonstration, 13
mano (*f.*) hand, 12; **darse la ~** to shake hands, 13
mantel (*m.*) tablecloth, 9
mantequilla butter, 9

manzana apple, 9
maquillaje (*m.*) makeup, 5
maquillarse to put on makeup, 5
máquina de afeitar electric razor, 5
mar (*m., f.*) sea, 14
maravilla wonder
marcar (qu) to mark; to point out
mareado(a): estar ~ to feel dizzy, 12
marisco shellfish, 9
marrón brown, 4
martes (*m.*) Tuesday, 3
marzo March, 1
más more; **~ que** more than, 8
masculino(a) masculine
matemáticas (*f. pl.*) mathematics, 3
mayo May, 1
mayonesa mayonnaise, 9
mayor older, greater, 8
mayoría majority
mayúsculo(a) capital (letter)
me to/for me, 8
mecánico(a) mechanic, 5
medio(a) hermano(a) half-brother (half-sister), 5
medianoche (*f.*) midnight, 3
medicina medicine, 3
médico(a) doctor, 5
medida measurement, 9
medio ambiente (*m.*) environment
mediodía (*m.*) noon, 3
medios de transporte means of transportation, 6
medir (i, i) to measure
meditación (*f.*) meditation
mejilla cheek
mejor better, 8; **es ~** it's better, 11
melón (*m.*) cantaloupe, 9
menor younger; less, 8
menos: ~ que less than, 8; **a ~ que** unless, 12; **por lo ~** at least, 10
mensajero(a) messenger
mentiroso(a) dishonest, lying, 2
menú (*m.*) menu, 9
mercadeo marketing, 3
mercado market, 6
merecer (zc) to deserve
merienda snack
mes (*m.*) month, 3; **~ pasado** last month, 7
mesa table, P; **poner la ~** to set the table, 9; **quitar la ~** to clear the table, 10
mesita de noche night table, 10
meta goal
metro: en ~ on the subway, 6
mexicano(a) Mexican, 2

mezcla mix
mezclar to mix, 9
mezclilla denim, 8
mi (*adj.*) my, 3
mí (*pron.*) me, 8
micro bus (*Chile*)
micrófono microphone, 4
microondas (*m. s.*) microwave, 10
miedo: tener (*irreg.*) **~ (a, de)** to be afraid (of), 7
mientras while, during
miércoles (*m.*) Wednesday, 3
mil (*m.*) one thousand, 8
millón (*m.*): **un ~** one million, 8; **dos millones** two million, 8
mío(a) (*adj.*) my, 10; (*pron.*) mine, 10
mirar televisión to watch television, 2
misionero(a) missionary
mismo(a) same; **lo mismo** the same (thing)
misterio mystery, 11
mitad (*f.*) half
mixto(a) mixed
mochila backpack, P; knapsack
moda fashion, 8; **(no) estar de ~** (not) to be fashionable, 8; **pasado(a) de ~** out of style, 8
modales (*m. pl.*) manners
módem (*m.*) **externo/interno** external/internal modem, 4
molestar to bother, 4
molido(a) crushed, ground, 9
monitor (*m.*) monitor, 4
mono monkey
montañoso(a) mountainous
montar to ride; **~ a caballo** to ride horseback, 7; **~ en bicicleta** to ride a bike, 7
monte (*m.*) mountain
morado(a) purple, 4
morirse (ue, u) to die, 8
mortalidad (*f.*) mortality
mostaza mustard, 9
mostrador (*m.*) counter; check-in desk, 14
mostrar (ue) to show
muchacho(a) boy (girl), P
muchedumbre (*f.*) crowd
mucho a lot, 4; **~ que hacer** a lot to do; **No ~.** Not much. 1
mudarse to move (*change residence*)
muebles (*m. pl.*) furniture, 10
muerto(a) dead, 13
mujer (*f.*) woman, P; **~ de negocios** businesswoman, 5

muleta crutch, 12
mundial: música ~ world music, 11
mundo world
muñeca doll
museo museum, 6
música music, 3; **~ clásica** classical music, 11; **~ country** country music, 11; **~ moderna** modern music, 11; **~ mundial** world music, 11; **~ pop** pop songs, 11
musical musical, 11
muy very, 2

N

nacer (zc) to be born
nacionalidad (*f.*) nationality, 2
nada nothing, 1; **De ~.** You're welcome. 1
nadar to swim, 7
nadie no one, nobody, 6
naranja orange (*fruit*), 9
nariz (*f.*) nose, 12
narrador(a) narrator
natación (*f.*) swimming, 7
naturaleza nature; **~ muerta** still life
náuseas (*f. pl.*) nausea, 12
navegación (*f.*) navegation
navegar (gu): ~ en rápidos to go white-water rafting, 7; **~ por Internet** to surf the Internet, 2
necesario(a) necessary, 11
necesitar to need, 2
negocio business, 3
negro(a) black, 4
nervioso(a) nervous, 4
nevar to snow, 7; **Está nevando. (Nieva.)** It's snowing. 7
ni... ni neither . . . nor, 6
nicaragüense (*m., f.*) Nicaraguan, 2
nieto(a) grandson (granddaughter), 5
niñero(a) baby-sitter
ningún, ninguno(a) none, no, not any, 6
niño(a) boy (girl), P
nivel (*m.*) level
noche (*f.*) night, 3; **de la ~** in the evening (*with precise time*), 3; **por la ~** during the evening, 3
nombre (*m.*) name; **Mi ~ es...** My name is . . . , 1; **~ completo** full name
normal normal, 4
norte (*m.*) north, 14
Norteamérica North America

nos to/for us, 8
nosotros(as) we, 1; us, 8
nota grade, P
noticias (*f. pl.*) news, 11; **~ del día** current events, 13
novato(a) newbie, novice
novecientos(as) nine hundred, 8
novedoso(a) novel, new
novelista (*m., f.*) novelist
noveno(a) ninth, 10
noventa ninety, P
noviembre November, 1
novio(a) boyfriend (girlfriend)
nublado: Está ~. It's cloudy. 7
nuera daughter-in-law, 5
nuestro(a) (*adj.*) our, 3; (*pron.*) ours, 10
nueve nine, P
número number, 8; **~ ordinal** ordinal number, 10
nunca never, 5

O

o... o either . . . or, 6
obra teatral play, 11
obvio(a) obvious, 11
océano ocean, 14
ochenta eighty, P
ocho eight, P
ochocientos(as) eight hundred, 8
octavo(a) eighth, 10
octubre October, 1
ocupado(a) busy, 4
odio hatred
oeste (*m.*) west, 14
oferta especial special offer, 8
oficina office, 6; **~ de correos** post office, 6
oído inner ear, 12
oír (*irreg.*) to hear, 5
ojalá (que) I wish, I hope, 11; **¡~ se mejore pronto!** Hopefully you'll get better soon! 12
ojear to scan
ojo eye, 12
ola wave
ómnibus (*m.*) bus
once eleven, P
onda: en ~ in style
ópera opera, 11
oprimir to push
opuesto(a) opposite
oración (*f.*) sentence
ordenar to order, 9
oreja outer ear, 12

organización (*f.*) **benéfica** charity
organizador (*m.*) **electrónico** electronic organizer, 4
orgulloso(a) proud
originar to originate
orilla shore
oro gold, 8
ortografía spelling
os to/for you (*fam. pl.*), 8
otoño fall, autumn, 7

P

paciente (*m., f.*) patient, 2
padrastro stepfather, 5
padre (*m.*) father, 5; **padres** (*m. pl.*) parents, 5
pagar (gu) to pay, 9
página page, P; **~ web** web page, 4
pago: método de ~ form of payment, 8
país (*m.*) country
paisaje (*m.*) scenery
pájaro bird
palomitas (*f. pl.*) popcorn, 11
palpitar to palpitate, 12
pan (*m.*) bread, 6; **~ tostado** toast, 9
panameño(a) Panamanian, 2
pandilla gang
pantalla screen, 4
pantalones (*m. pl.*) pants, 8; **~ cortos** shorts, 8
pañuelo handkerchief
papá (*m.*) father, 5
papas fritas (*f. pl.*) French fries, 9
papel role; paper; **hoja de ~** sheet of paper, P
papelería stationery store, 6
papitas fritas (*f. pl.*) potato chips, 6
paquete (*m.*) package, 9
para for, toward, in the direction of, in order to (+ *inf.*), 10; **~ que** so that, 12
paracaídas (*m.*) parachute
parada stop
paraguayo(a) Paraguayan, 2
parar to stop
parecer (zc) to seem
pared (*f.*) wall, P
pariente (*m., f.*) family member, relative, 5
parque (*m.*) park, 6
párrafo paragraph
parrilla: a la ~ grilled, 9
participante (*m., f.*) participant, 11

participar en   to participate in, 13
partido   game, match, 7
pasaje (*m.*)   ticket, 14
pasajero(a)   passenger, 14; **~ de clase turista**   coach passenger, 14; **~ de primera clase**   first class passenger, 14
pasaporte (*m.*)   passport, 14
pasar   to pass (by), 2; **~ la aspiradora** to vacuum clean, 10
pasear: sacar a ~ al perro   to take the dog for a walk, 10
pasillo   hallway, 10
pasta de dientes   toothpaste, 5
pastel (*m.*)   cake, 9
pastilla   tablet, 12
patinar   to skate, 2; **~ en línea** to inline skate (rollerblade), 7; **~ sobre hielo**   to ice skate, 7
patio   patio, 10
patrocinador(a)   sponsor
pavo   turkey, 6
paz (*f.*)   peace; **~ mundial**   world peace, 13
pecho   chest, 12
pedazo   piece, slice, 9
pedir (i, i)   to ask for (*something*), 1; to request, 10; **~ la hora**   to ask for the time, 3
peinarse   to brush/comb one's hair, 5
peine (*m.*)   comb, 5
pelar   to peel, 9
pelearse   to have a fight, 5
película   movie, film, 11; **~ de acción**   action movie, 11; **~ de ciencia ficción**   science fiction movie, 11; **~ de horror/terror** horror movie, 11; **~ titulada...** movie called . . . , 11
peligro   danger, 7
peligroso(a)   dangerous, 7
pelirrojo(a)   redheaded , 2
pelo   hair; **~ castaño/rubio** brown/blond hair, 2
pelota   ball, 7
peluquero(a)   barber/hairdresser, 5
pendiente (*m.*)   earring, 8
pensar (ie)   to think, 4; **~ de**   to have an opinion about, 4; **~ en (de)** to think about, to consider, 4
penúltimo(a)   next-to-last
peor   worse, 8
pequeño(a)   small, 2
perder (ie)   to lose, 4; **perderse (ie)** to lose oneself, to get lost

pérdida   loss, 13
Perdón.   Excuse me. 4
perejil (*m.*)   parsley
perezoso(a)   lazy, 2
periódico   newspaper
periodismo   journalism, 3
periodista (*m., f.*)   journalist, 5
permiso: Con ~.   Pardon me. 4
permitir   to permit, to allow, 10
pero   but, 2
perro(a)   dog, 2; **perro caliente** hot dog, 9
persiana   Venetian blind, 10
personalidad (*f.*)   personality
peruano(a)   Peruvian, 2
pesar: a ~ de   in spite of
pesas: levantar ~   to lift weights, 2
pescado   fish (*caught*), 9
pescar (qu)   to fish, 7
pez (*m.*)   fish (*alive*)
piano   piano, 2
picante   spicy, 9
picar (qu)   to chop, to mince, 9
pie (*m.*)   foot, 12; **a ~**   on foot, walking, 6
piel (*f.*)   leather, 8
pierna   leg, 12; **~ quebrada/rota** broken leg, 12
píldora   pill, 12
pimienta   pepper, 9
pingüino   penguin
pintar   to paint, 2
pintoresco(a)   picturesque
pintura   painting, 3
pirata (*m.*)   pirate
pisar   to step on
piscina   swimming pool, 6
piso   floor; **primer (segundo, etc.) ~** first (second, etc.) floor, 10
pista de atletismo   athletics track, 6
pizarra   chalkboard, P
pizzería   pizzeria, 6
placer: Un ~.   My pleasure. 1
plancha   iron, 10
planchar   to iron, 10
plata   silver, 8
plátano   banana, 9
plato   plate, 9; **~ hondo**   bowl, 9; **~ principal**   main dish, 9
playa   beach, 14
plaza   plaza, 6
plomero(a)   plumber, 5
poblar (ue)   to populate
pobre   poor
poco   little, small amount, 4

poder (*m.*)   power; (*irreg.*)   to be able to, 4
poderoso(a)   powerful
poesía   poetry
poeta (poetisa)   poet
policía (*m., f.*)   policeman (policewoman), 5
política   politics, 13
político(a)   political
pollo   chicken, 6; **~ asado**   roasted chicken, 9; **~ frito**   fried chicken, 9
polvo   dust
poner (*irreg.*)   to put, 5; **~ en equilibro**   to balance; **~ la mesa** to set the table, 9; **~ mis juguetes en su lugar**   to put my toys where they belong, 10; **~ una inyección** to give an injection, 12; **~ una vacuna**   to vaccinate, 12; **ponerse (la ropa)**   to put on (clothing), 5
por   for, during, in, through, along, on behalf of, by, 10; **~ avión**   by plane, 6; **~ ejemplo**   for example, 10; **~ eso**   so, that's why, 10; **~ favor**   please, 1; **~ fin**   finally, 9; **~ lo menos**   at least, 10; **~ satélite**   by satellite dish, 11; **~ supuesto**   of course, 10
¿por qué?   why? 3
porcentaje (*m.*)   percentage
porque   because, 3
portarse   to behave
postre (*m.*)   dessert, 9
pozo   well; hole
practicar (qu)   to practice; **~ alpinismo**   to hike, 7; **~ deportes**   to play sports, 2; **~ surfing**   to surf, 7
precio: Está a muy buen ~.   It's a very good price. 8
preferencia   preference
preferir (ie, i)   to prefer, 4
pregunta   question, 12; **hacer preguntas**   to ask questions, 3
premio   prize
prenda de ropa   article of clothing, 8
preocupado(a)   worried, 4
preocuparse   to worry, 5
preparación (*f.*)   preparation, 9
preparar   to prepare, 2; **~ la comida** to prepare the food, 10; **prepararse** to get ready, 5
prepararse   to get ready, 5
preposición (*f.*)   preposition, 6
presa   dam

presentador(a)   host (*of a show*), 11
presentar a alguien   to introduce someone, 1
préstamo   loan, 8
presupuesto   budget, 13
primavera   spring, 7
primer(o)(a)   first, 10; **~ primer piso**   first floor, 10
primo(a)   cousin, 5
principiante(a)   beginner
prisa   haste, hurry; **tener** (*irreg.*) **~** to be in a hurry, 7
probable   probable, likely, 11
probarse (ue): Voy a probármelo/la(los/las).   I'm going to try it (them) on. 8
proceso electoral   election process, 13
producto electrónico   electronic product, 4
profesión (*f.*)   profession, 5
profesor(a)   professor, P
programa (*m.*)   program; **~ antivirus** anti-virus program, 4; **~ de concursos**   game show, 11; **~ de entrevistas**   talk show, 11; **~ de procesamiento de textos** word-processing program, 4; **~ de televisión**   television program, 11
programador(a)   programmer, 5
prohibido para menores   rated R (minors restricted), 11
prohibir   to forbid, 10
promover (ue)   to promote
pronombre (*m.*)   pronoun, 1
propina   tip, 9
propósito   purpose
proveedor (*m.*) **de acceso**   Internet service provider, 4
provocador(a)   provocative
próximo(a)   next
psicología   psychology, 3
publicidad (*f.*)   public relations, 3
publicitario(a) (*adj.*)   pertaining to advertising
público   audience, 11
pueblo   town, 6
puerta   door, P; **~ (de embarque)** (departure) gate, 14
puertorriqueño(a)   Puerto Rican, 2
puesto   job, position, 13
puesto (*p.p. of* **poner**)   placed, 13
pulgada   inch
pulmón (*m.*)   lung, 12
pulsera   bracelet, 8

punto de vista   viewpoint
punto   period
puntual   punctual, 13

Q

¿qué?   what? which? 3; **¿~ hay de nuevo?**   What's new? 1; **¿~ hora es?**   What time is it? 3; **¿~ le duele?**   What hurts (you)? 12; **¿~ significa…?**   What does . . . mean? P; **¿~ síntomas tiene?** What are your symptoms? 12; **¿~ tal?**   How are things going? 1; **¿~ te gusta hacer?**   What do you like to do? 2
quebrado(a)   broken, 12
quedar   to fit; **Me queda bien/mal.** It fits nicely/badly. 8; **Me queda grande/apretado.**   It's too big/too tight. 8; **quedar(se)**   to remain; to be
quehacer (*m.*) **doméstico**   house-chore, 10
quejarse   to complain, 5
querer (*irreg.*)   to want, to love, 4; to wish, 10
queso   cheese, 6
¿quién(es)?   who? 3; **¿De ~ es?** Whose is this? 3; **¿De ~ son?** Whose are these? 3
química   chemistry, 3
quince   fifteen, P
quinientos(as)   five hundred, 8
quinto(a)   fifth, 10
quisiera (+ *inf.*)   I'd like (+ *inf.*), 6
quitar   to take off, to remove 5; **~ la mesa**   to clear the table, 10; **quitarse (la ropa)**   to take off (one's clothing), 5
quizás   perhaps

R

R & B   Rhythm and Blues, 11
radiografía: tomar una ~   to take an X-ray, 12
raíz (*f.*)   root
rango   rank
rap (*m.*)   rap, 11
rápido(a)   fast, 4
rasgar (gu)   to tear up
rasuradora   razor, 5
ratón (*m.*)   mouse, 4
rayado(a)   striped, 8
rayas: a ~   striped, 8
razón (*f.*)   reason; **tener** (*irreg.*) **~** to be right, 7

reacción (*f.*) **crítica**   critical reaction, 11
realidad: en ~   actually
realizarse (c)   to take place
rebajado(a): estar ~.   to be reduced (in price)/on sale. 8
recámara   bedroom, 10
recepción (*f.*)   reception desk, 14
receta   recipe, 9; prescription, 12
recetar una medicina   to prescribe a medicine, 12
recibir   to receive, 3
reciclaje (*m.*)   recycling, 10
recomendar (ie)   to recommend, 10
reconocer (zc)   to recognize
recorte (*m.*)   cutting
recuerdo   souvenir
recurrir   to fall back on, to resort to
red (*f.*)   web, Internet; **~ mundial** World Wide Web, 4
redactar   to edit
reflejar   to reflect
reflexión (*f.*)   reflection
refresco   soft drink, 6; beverage, 9; **tomar un ~**   to have a soft drink, 2
refrigerador (*m.*)   refrigerator, 10
regalo   present, gift
regar (ie) (gu) las plantas   to water the plants, 10
registrarse   to register, 14
regla   rule
regresar   to return, 2
regular   so-so, 1
reina   queen
reírse (*irreg.*)   to laugh, 5
relajarse   to relax
reloj (*m.*)   watch, 8
remar   to row, 7
remero(a)   rower
renombre (*m.*)   renown
renovar (ue)   to renovate
repente: de ~   suddenly, 9
repetir (i, i)   to repeat, 4; **Repitan.** Repeat. P
reproductor (*m.*) **de discos com-pactos/DVD**   CD/DVD recorder, 4
requerir (ie, i)   to require, 10
requisito   requisite, 13
reseña   review, 11
reservación (*f.*)   reservation, 14
resfriado   cold (*e.g., headcold*), 12
resfriarse   to get chilled; to catch cold, 12
residencia estudiantil   dorm, 3

respirar to breathe; **Respire hondo.** Breathe deeply. 12

responder to respond, 1

responsable responsible, 2

restaurante (*m.*) restaurant, 6

resuelto (*p.p. of* **resolver**) determined

resumen: en ~ in short, to sum up

reto challenge

retraso delay, 14

reunión (*f.*) meeting

reunirse to meet, to get together, 5

revista magazine

rey (*m.*) king

ridículo(a) ridiculous, 11

riesgo risk

rima rhyme

río river, 7

riqueza wealth

rock (*m.*) rock (music), 11

rodeado(a) surrounded

rojo(a) red, 4

ropa clothing, 5

rosa rose, 4

rosado(a) pink, 4

roto (*p.p. of* **romper**) broken, 13

rubio(a) blond(e), 2

rueda wheel

ruina ruin, 14

ruta route

S

sábado Saturday, 2

saber (*irreg.*) to know (*a fact, information*), 5; **~** (+ *inf.*) to know how (*to do something*), 5

sabor (*m.*) flavor

sacar (**qu**) to take out; **~ a pasear al perro** to take the dog for a walk, 10; **~ fotos** to take photos, 2; **~ la basura** to take out the garbage, 10; **~ la lengua** to stick out one's tongue, 12

sacerdote (*m.*) priest

saco jacket, sports coat, 8

sacudir los muebles to dust the furniture, 10

sal (*f.*) salt, 9

sala living room, 10; **~ de emergencias** emergency room, 12; **~ de equipajes** baggage claim, 14; **~ de espera** waiting room, 12

salchicha sausage, 6

salida departure, 14

salir (*irreg.*) to leave, to go out, 5

salmón (*m.*) salmon, 9

salón (*m.*) **de clase** classroom, P

salud (*f.*) health, 3

saludable healthy

saludar to greet, 1

saludo greeting

salvadoreño(a) Salvadoran, 2

salvaje wild, untamed

salvavidas (*m. s.*) lifejacket

sandalia sandal, 8

sandwich (*m.*) sandwich, 9; **~ de jamón y queso con aguacate** ham and cheese sandwich with avocado, 9

sangre (*f.*) blood, 12

satisfacer (*like* **hacer**) to satisfy, 13

satisfecho (*p.p. of* **satisfacer**) satisfied, 13

secador (*m.*) **de pelo** hairdryer, 14

secadora dryer, 10

secar (**qu**) to dry (*something*), 5; **secarse** (**qu**) **el pelo** to dry one's hair, 5

secretario(a) secretary, 5

secreto secret

sed (*f.*) thirst; **tener** (*irreg.*) **~** to be thirsty, 7

seda silk, 8

seguido(a) continued

seguir (**i, i**) to continue, 6; **~ derecho** to go straight ahead

según according to

segundo(a) second, 10

seguro(a) sure, 4; safe, 7; **no es seguro** it's not sure, 11; **no estar ~ de** to not be sure, 11; **seguro médico** medical insurance, 13

seis six, P

seiscientos(as) six hundred, 8

selva: ~ amazónica Amazonian jungle, 14; **~ tropical** tropical jungle, 14

semana week, 3; **~ pasada** last week, 7; **fin** (*m.*) **de ~** weekend, 2; **todas las semanas** every week, 5

semejanza similarity

sencillo(a) simple; single (*room*)

sentarse (**ie**) to sit down, 5

sentir (**ie, i**) to feel, 4; to feel sorry, to regret, 11; **Lo siento.** I'm sorry. 4

señalar to point out

señor (*abbrev.* **Sr.**) Mr., Sir, 1

señora (*abbrev.* **Sra.**) Mrs., Ms., Madam, 1

señorita (*abbrev.* **Srta.**) Miss, Ms., 1

separarse to get separated, 5

septiembre September, 1

séptimo(a) seventh, 10

ser (*irreg.*) to be, 1

serio(a) serious, 2

servicio despertador wake-up call, 14

servilleta napkin, 9

servir (**i, i**) to serve, 4; **¿En qué puedo servirle?** How can I help you? 8

sesenta sixty, P

setecientos(as) seven hundred, 8

setenta seventy, P

sexto(a) sixth, 10

show (*m.*) show, 11

sí yes, 1

siempre always, 5

siete seven, P

siglo century

significar (**qu**): **Significa…** It means . . . , P

significado meaning

siguiente following, next

silla chair, P

sillón (*m.*) armchair, 10

símbolo symbol

simpático(a) nice, 2

sin without; **~ embargo** nevertheless; **~ que** without, 12

sincero(a) sincere, 2

sino but instead

síntoma (*m.*) symptom, 12

sistemático(a) systematic

sitio place; **~ web** website, 4

soberanía sovereignty

sobre on, above, 6

sobrepasar to surpass

sobresaliente outstanding

sobrevivir to survive, to overcome, 13

sobrino(a) nephew (niece), 5

sofá (*m.*) sofa, 10

software (*m.*) software, 4

sol (*m.*) sun; **Hace ~.** It's sunny. 7

solicitar empleo to apply for a job, 13

solicitud (*f.*) application, 13

soltero(a) single (unmarried)

sombrero hat, 8

sonar (**ue**) to ring, to go off (*phone, alarm clock, etc.*), 4

sonido sound

sonreír (*irreg.*) to smile, 8

sonrisa smile

soñar (**ue**) **con** to dream about, 4

sopa soup, 9; **~ de fideos** noodle soup, 9

sorprender to surprise, 11

sorpresa surprise
sorteo raffle; evasion
sortija ring
sótano basement, cellar, 10
su (*adj.*) your (*s. form., pl.*), his, her, their, 3
suave soft
subir to go up, to get on, 6
subtítulos: con ~ en inglés with subtitles in English, 11
suburbio suburb, 10
sucio(a) dirty
sudadera sweatsuit, 8
Sudamérica South America
suegro(a) father-in-law (mother-in-law), 5
sueño dream; **tener** (*irreg.*) ~ to be sleepy, 7
suéter (*m.*) sweater, 8
sufrir (las consecuencias) to suffer (the consequences), 13
sugerencia suggestion
sugerir (ie, i) to suggest, 8
superación (*f.*) overcoming
supermercado supermarket, 6
supervisar to supervise, 13
supuesto: por ~ of course, 10
sur (*m.*) south, 14
surfing: hacer/practicar (qu) ~ to surf, 7
sustantivo noun
sustituir (y) to substitute
suyo(a) (*adj.*) your (*form. s., pl.*), his, her, its, their, 10; (*pron.*) yours (*form. s., pl.*), his, hers, its, theirs, 10

T

tal vez perhaps
talla size, 8
también also, 2
tampoco neither, not either, 2
tan... como as . . . as, 8
tanto(a)(s)... como as much (many) . . . as, 8
tarde (*f.*) afternoon, 3; **de la ~** in the afternoon (*with precise time*), 3; **por la ~** during the afternoon, 3; (*adv.*) late, 3
tarea homework, P
tarjeta business card, 13; **~ de crédito** credit card, 8; **~ de débito** (bank) debit card, 8; **~ de embarque** boarding pass, 14; **~ postal** postcard, 14

taza cup, 9
te to/for you (*fam. s.*), 8
té hot tea, 9; **~ helado** iced tea, 9
teatro theater, 6
technología technology, 4
techo roof, 10
tecla key (*on a keyboard*), 4
teclado keyboard, 4
tejer to weave
tejido weaving
tela fabric, 8
telecomedia sitcom, 11
telecomunicaciones (*f. pl.*) telecommunications, 13
teledrama (*m.*) drama series, 11
teleguía TV guide, 11
telenovela soap opera, 11
teleserie (*f.*) TV series, 11
televidente (*m., f.*) TV viewer, 11
televisión (*f.*) television broadcasting, 11; **~ por cable** cable TV, 14
televisor (*m.*) television set, 10
temer to fear, 11
temperatura temperature, 7; **La ~ está a 20 grados centígrados (Fahrenheit).** It's 20 degrees Celsius (Fahrenheit). 7
temporada: ~ de lluvias rainy season; **~ de secas** dry season
temprano early, 3
tenedor (*m.*) fork, 9
tener (*irreg.*) to have, 1; **~ 128 MB de memoria** to have 128 MB of memory, 4; **~ ... años** to be . . . years old, 1; **~ algunos conocimientos de...** to have some knowledge of . . ., 13; **~ buena presencia** to have a good presence, 13; **~ calor** to be hot, 7; **~ cuidado** to be careful, 7; **~ frío** to be cold, 7; **~ ganas de** to have the urge to, to feel like, 7; **~ las habilidades necesarias** to have the necessary skills, 13; **~ hambre** to be hungry, 7; **~ miedo (a, de)** to be afraid (of), 7; **~ mucha experiencia en** to have a lot of experience in, 13; **~ prisa** to be in a hurry, 7; **~ que** (+ *inf.*) to have to (+ *verb*), 1; **~ razón** to be right, 7; **~ sed** to be thirsty, 7; **~ sueño** to be sleepy, 7; **~ vergüenza** to be embarrassed, ashamed, 7

tenis (*m.*) tennis, 7
teoría theory
tercer(o, a) third, 10
término term
terremoto earthquake, 13
terrible terrible, awful, 1
terrorismo terrorism, 13
tesoro treasure
texto text
tez (*f.*) skin, complexion
ti you (*fam. s.*), 8
tiburón (*m.*) shark
tiempo weather, 7; **a ~ completo** full-time (*work*), 13; **a ~ parcial** part-time (*work*), 13; **¿Qué ~ hace?** What's the weather like? 7
tienda store, 6; **~ de música (ropa, videos)** music (clothing, video) store, 6
tierra earth, ground
tímido(a) shy, 2
tinto: vino ~ red wine, 9
tío(a) uncle (aunt), 5
típico(a) typical, 9
tira cómica comic strip
tirita (small) bandaid, 12
tiroteo shooting
titular to title
título title, 1
tiza chalk, P
toalla towel, 5; **~ de mano** hand-towel, 5
tobillo ankle, 12; **~ torcido** twisted ankle, 12
tocador (*m.*) dresser, 10
tocar (qu) un instrumento musical to play a musical instrument, 2
todavía still
todo everything
todo(a) all, every; **todas las semanas** every week, 9; **todos los días (años)** every day (year), 9
tomar to take; **~ medidas** to take measures, 13; **~ la presión** to take blood pressure, 12; **~ una radiografía** to take an X-ray, 12; **~ un refresco** to have a soft drink, 2; **~ el sol** to sunbathe, 2; **~ la temperatura** to take the temperature, 12
tonto(a) silly, stupid, 2
tormenta thunderstorm
torpe awkward

tos (*f.*) cough, 12; **jarabe** (*m.*) **para la ~** cough syrup, 12
toser to cough, 12
tostadora toaster, 10
trabajador(a) (*adj.*) hard-working, 2; (*noun*) worker, 5
trabajar to work, 2; **~ a tiempo completo** to work full-time, 13; **~ a tiempo parcial** to work part-time, 13
traducir (zc) to translate, 5
traer (*irreg.*) to bring, 5
Trague. Swallow, 12
traje (*m.*) suit, 8; **~ de baño** bathing suit, 8
trama plot
transmitir to broadcast, 3
trapear el piso to mop the floor, 10
tratarse de to be a matter of; to be; **Se trata de...** It's about . . . , 11
través: a ~ de across, throughout
trece thirteen, P
trecho distance, period
treinta thirty, P
tren: en ~ by train, 6
tres three, P
trescientos(as) three hundred, 8
trigo wheat
tripulación (*f.*) crew
triste sad, 4
triunfar to triumph
trompeta trumpet, 2
trozo chunk, 9
trucha trout, 9
truco trick
tu your (*fam.*), 3
tú you (*fam.*), 1
tuyo(a) (*adj.*) your (*fam.*), 10; (*pron.*) yours (*fam.*), 10

U

ubicado(a) located
Ud. (*abbrev. of* **usted**) you (*form. s.*), 8
Uds. (*abbrev. of* **ustedes**) you (*fam. or form. pl.*), 8
último: lo ~ the latest (thing)
un(a) a, 1
único(a) only, unique
unido(a) united
unir to mix together, to incorporate, 9
universidad (*f.*) university, 6
uno one, P
unos(as) some, 1

uruguayo(a) Uruguayan, 2
usar to use, 2
usted you (*s. form.*), 1
ustedes you (*fam. or form. pl.*), 1
usuario(a) user, 4
útil useful
uva grape, 9

V

vacío(a) empty
vacuna vaccination, 12
valer (*irreg.*) **la pena** to be worthwhile
valioso(a) valuable
valle (*m.*) valley
valor (*m.*) value
vanidoso(a) vain
vapor: al ~ steamed, 9
vaquero cowboy
variedad (*f.*) variety
varios(as) various, several
varonil manly
vaso glass, 9
veces (*f. pl.*) times; **a ~** sometimes, 5; **(dos) ~ al día/por semana** (two) times a day/per week, 5
vecino(a) neighbor, 6
vegetal (*m.*) vegetable, 6
vegetariano(a) vegetarian
vehículo vehicle
veinte twenty, P
veintiuno twenty-one, P
venda de gasa gauze bandage, 12
vender to sell, 3
venezolano(a) Venezuelan, 2
venir (*irreg.*) to come, 5
venta: estar en ~ to be on sale, 8
ventaja advantage, 13
ventana window, P
ver (*irreg.*) to see, 5; **Nos vemos.** See you later. 1
verano summer, 7
veras: de ~ truly, really
verbo verb, 3
verdad true; **(no) es ~** it's (not) true, 11; **~** (*f.*) truth
verde green, 4
vergüenza: tener (*irreg.*) **~** to be embarrassed, ashamed, 7
verso libre blank verse
vestido dress, 8
vestir (i, i) to dress (*someone*), 5; **vestirse (i, i)** to get dressed, 5
veterinario(a) veterinarian, 5

vez (*f.*) time; **de ~ en cuando** sometimes; **en ~ de** instead of; **rara ~** hardly ever; **tal ~** perhaps; **una ~** once, 9
viajar to travel, 14; **~ al extranjero** to travel abroad, 14
vida life
videocámara videocamera, 4
videocasetera VCR, 4
viejo(a) old, 2
viento wind; **Hace ~.** It's windy. 7
viernes (*m.*) Friday, 2
vinagre (*m.*) vinegar, 9
vino: ~ blanco white wine, 9; **~ tinto** red wine, 9
violencia violence, 13
violín (*m.*) violin, 2
viraje (*m.*) turn
visitante (*m., f.*) visitor
visitar a amigos to visit friends, 2
visto (*p. p. of* **ver**) seen, 13
vitamina vitamin, 12
vivienda housing
vivir to live, 3
vivo: en ~ live, 11
volcán (*m.*) volcano, 14
volibol (*m.*) volleyball, 7
volver (ue) to return, 4
vomitar to throw up, 12
vosotros(as) you (*fam. pl.*), 1
votar to vote, 13
voz (*f.*) voice
vuelo flight, 14
vuelto (*p.p. of* **volver**) returned, 13
vuestro(a) (*adj.*) your (*fam. pl.*), 3; (*pron.*) yours (*fam. pl.*), 3

Y

yerno son-in-law, 5
yeso cast, 12
yo I, 1
yogur (*m.*) yogurt, 6

Z

zanahoria carrot, 9
zapato shoe, 8; **~ de tacón alto** high-heeled shoe, 8; **~ de tenis** tennis shoe, 8

ENGLISH-SPANISH GLOSSARY

A

a un(a), 1
à la carte a la carta, 9
above sobre, 6
abundance abundancia
academic académico(a)
accessory accesorio, 8
according to según
accountant contador(a), 5
accounting contabilidad (*f.*), 3
ache dolor (*m.*), 12
achieve alcanzar (c), lograr
acquisition adquisición (*f.*)
across a través de
action acción (*f.*), 5
active activo(a), 2
activity actividad (*f.*), P
actor actor (*m.*), 5
actress actriz (*f.*), 5
actually en realidad
ad: personal ~ anuncio personal
add agregar, añadir, 9
address dirección (*f.*)
advantage ventaja, 13
advertising (*adj.*) publicitario(a)
advice consejo, 12
advise aconsejar, 10
after después, 5; después (de) que, 12
afternoon tarde (*f.*), 3; **during the ~** por la tarde, 3; **Good ~.** Buenas tardes. 1; **in the ~** (*with precise time*) de la tarde, 3; **late ~** atardecer (*m.*)
age edad (*f.*)
agreement concordancia
agricultural agrícola (*m., f.*)
ahead adelante
air conditioning aire (*m.*) acondicionado, 14
airline línea aérea, 14
airplane avión (*m.*), 14
airport aeropuerto, 6
all todo(a)
allergy alergia, 12
alligator caimán (*m.*)
along por, 10
alphabet alfabeto

also también, 2
although aunque, 12
altitude altitud (*f.*)
always siempre, 5
ambassador embajador(a)
ambiguity ambigüedad (*f.*)
amusement diversión (*f.*)
ancestor antecesor(a), antepasado(a)
anger cólera
angry enojado(a), 4
animated film dibujos animados, 11
ankle tobillo, 12; **twisted ~** tobillo torcido, 12
announcer locutor(a), 11
anonymous anónimo(a)
answer contestar; **Answer.** Contesten. P
Antarctica Antártida
antibiotic antibiótico, 12
antiquated anticuado(a)
any algún, alguno(a) 6
apartment apartamento, 6
appear aparecer (zc)
apple manzana, 9
appliance electrodoméstico, 10
application aplicación (*f.*), 4; solicitud (*f.*), 13
apply for a job solicitar empleo, 13
appointment cita, 12
appreciate apreciar
appropriate apropiado(a)
April abril, 1
apt apto(a)
architect arquitecto(a), 5
architecture arquitectura, 3
Argentinian argentino(a), 2
arm brazo, 12
armchair sillón (*m.*), 10
armed forces fuerzas armadas, 13
army ejército, 13
around alrededor de
arrival llegada, 14
arrive llegar, 2
arrogant altivo(a)
art arte (*m.*), 3; **~ exhibit** exposición (*f.*) de arte, 11; **arts** arte y cultura, 11
article artículo, 1

artist artista (*m., f.*), 5
as como; **~ . . . ~** tan... como, 8; **~ many . . . ~** tantos(as)... como, 8; **~ much . . . ~** tanto(a)(s)... como, 8; **~ soon ~** en cuanto, tan pronto como, 12
ask: ~ questions hacer (*irreg.*) preguntas, 3; **~ for something** pedir (i, i), 1; **~ for the time** pedir (i, i) la hora, 3
asparagus espárragos (*m. pl.*), 9
aspirin aspirina, 12
at en; **~ least** por lo menos, 10; **~ low heat** a fuego suave/lento, 9
athletics track pista de atletismo, 6
atmosphere ambiente (*m.*)
attachment anexo
attack ataque (*m.*)
attempt intentar
attend acudir; asistir a, 3
attractive guapo(a), 2
audience audiencia; público, 11
audiotape cinta, P
auditorium auditorio, 6
August agosto, 1
aunt tía, 5
automated bank teller cajero automático, 6
autumn otoño, 7
availability disponibilidad (*f.*)
available disponible, 13
avenue avenida, 1
avoid evitar
awful fatal, terrible, 1
awkward torpe

B

baby-sitter niñero(a)
back espalda, 12
background fondo
backpack mochila, P
bad malo(a), 2; **it's ~** es malo, 11
badly mal, 4
baggage equipaje (*m.*), 14; **~ claim** sala de equipajes, 14
balance poner (*irreg.*) en equilibro
ball pelota, 7
ballpoint pen bolígrafo, P

banana plátano, 9
bandaid curita, tirita, 12
bank (commercial) banco, 6
barber peluquero(a), 5
barefooted descalzo(a)
baseball béisbol (*m.*), 7
basement sótano, 10
basket canasta
basketball básquetbol (*m.*), 7
bather bañador(a)
bathing suit traje (*m.*) de baño, 8
bathroom baño, 10
be estar (*irreg.*), ser (*irreg.*), 1; ~ . . . **years old** tener (*irreg.*)... años, 1; ~ **a matter of** tratarse de; ~ **able to** poder (*irreg.*), 4; ~ **afraid (of)** tener (*irreg.*) miedo (a, de), 7; ~ **ashamed** tener (*irreg.*) vergüenza, 7; ~ **born** nacer (zc); ~ **careful** tener (*irreg.*) cuidado, 7; ~ **certain of** contar (ue) con; ~ **cold** tener (*irreg.*) frío, 7; ~ **congested** estar (*irreg.*) congestionado(a), 12; ~ **embarrassed** tener (*irreg.*) vergüenza, 7; ~ **familiar with** conocer (zc), 5; ~ **going to** ir a, 3; ~ **happy about** alegrarse de, 11; ~ **hot** tener (*irreg.*) calor, 7; ~ **hungry** tener (*irreg.*) hambre, 7; ~ **important** importar, 4; ~ **in a hurry** tener (*irreg.*) prisa, 7; ~ **interesting** interesar, 4; ~ **jealous** tener (*irreg.*) celos; ~ **pleased about** estar (*irreg.*) contento(a) de 11; ~ **right** tener (*irreg.*) razón, 7; ~ **sleepy** tener (*irreg.*) sueño, 7; ~ **sure** estar (*irreg.*) seguro(a) de, 11; ~ **thirsty** tener (*irreg.*) sed, 7; ~ **worthwhile** valer (*irreg.*) la pena
beach playa, 14
bean haba (*f. but* el haba); **(green) ~** habichuela, 9; **refried beans** frijoles refritos, 9
beat batir
beautiful bello(a), hermoso(a)
beauty belleza
because porque, 3
bed cama, 10
bedroom cuarto, dormitorio, habitación (*f.*), recámara, 10
beef stew guisado, 9
beeper bíper (*m.*), buscapersonas (*m. s.*), 4
beer cerveza, 9
before antes, 5; antes (de) que, 12

begin comenzar (ie) (c), empezar (ie) (c), 4
beginner principiante
behave portarse
behavior comportamiento
behind detrás de, 6
believe (in) creer (en), 3; **not ~** no creer, 11
bellboy botones (*m. s.*), 14
below debajo de, 6
belt cinturón (*m.*), 8
benefit beneficio, 13
besides además
better mejor, 8; **it's ~** es mejor, 11
between entre, 6
beverage bebida, refresco, 9
bicycle: on ~ en bicicleta, 6
big grande, 2
bilingual bilingüe
bill cuenta, 9
biology biología, 3
bird pájaro
birthplace lugar (*m.*) de nacimiento
black negro(a), 4
blank verse verso libre
blender licuadora, 10
blind ciego(a); **~ date** cita a ciegas
block cuadra, 6
blond(e) rubio(a), 2
blood sangre (*f.*), 12
blouse blusa, 8
blue azul, 4
board abordar, 14
boarding pass tarjeta de embarque, 14
boat barco, bote (*m.*)
body cuerpo, 12
boil hervir (ie, i), 9
boiled hervido(a), 9
Bolivian boliviano(a), 2
book libro, P
bookstore librería, 3
boot bota, 8
border frontera
boredom aburrimiento
bored aburrido(a), 4
boring aburrido(a), 2
both ambos(as)
bother molestar, 4
bowl plato hondo, 9
box: large ~ cajón (*m.*)
boxing boxeo, 7
boy chico, P; muchacho, P; niño, P
boyfriend novio
bracelet brazalete (*m.*), pulsera, 8
bread pan (*m.*), 6

break (a record) batir
breakfast desayuno, 9; **~ included** desayuno incluido, 14
breathe respirar; **~ deeply.** Respire hondo. 12
brick ladrillo
brief breve
briefcase maletín (*m.*), 13
bring traer (*irreg.*), 5
broadcast transmitir, 3
broccoli brócoli (*m.*), 9
broken quebrado(a), 12; roto(a) (*p.p.*), 13; **~ leg** pierna quebrada/rota, 12
brother (younger, older) hermano (menor, mayor), 5
brother-in-law cuñado, 5
brown café, marrón, 4
brush cepillo, 5; **~ one's hair** cepillarse el pelo, peinarse, 5; **~ one's teeth** lavarse los dientes, 5
buddy cuate(a)
budget presupuesto, 13
building edificio, 6
bus ómnibus (*m.*), colectivo, guagua (*Cuba, Puerto Rico*), micro (*Chile*)
business negocio, 3; **~ administration** administración (*f.*) de empresas, 3; **~ card** tarjeta, 13; **~ district** centro comercial, 10
businessman hombre (*m.*) de negocios, 5; empresario, 13
businesswoman mujer (*f.*) de negocios, 5; empresaria, 13
busy ocupado(a), 4
but pero, 2; **~ instead** sino
butcher shop carnicería, 6
butter mantequilla, 9
buy comprar, 2
by por, 10; **~ bus** en autobús, 6; **~ car** en carro/coche/automóvil, 6; **~ check** con cheque, 8; **~ plane** por avión, 6; **~ satellite dish** por satélite, 11; **~ train** en tren, 6
Bye. Chau. 1

C

cable cable (*m.*), 4; **~ TV** cable (*m.*), 11; televisión (*f.*) por cable, 14
cafeteria cafetería, 3
cake pastel (*m.*), 9
calculator calculadora, P
calculus cálculo, 3

call llamar, 2
campaign campaña, 13
can opener (electric) abrelatas (*m.*) (eléctrico), 10
Canadian canadiense (*m., f.*), 2
candidate candidato(a), 13
candy dulce (*m.*), 11
cantaloupe melón (*m.*), 9
canyon cañón (*m.*), 14
cap gorra, 8
capital (letter) mayúsculo(a)
card tarjeta; **credit ~** tarjeta de crédito, 8; **debit ~** tarjeta de débito, 8
cardboard cartón (*m.*)
career carrera, 5
Careful! ¡Cuidado!
Caribbean (Sea) Caribe (*m., f.*)
carpenter carpintero(a), 5
carpet alfombra, 10
carrot zanahoria, 9
carry llevar
cartoons dibujos animados, 11
cash: in ~ en efectivo, al contado, 8
cashmere cachemira
cast yeso, 12
cat gato(a), 2
cattle ganado, ganadería
cattle-raising industry industria ganadera
cautious cuidadoso(a), 2
CD CD, P; **CD/DVD recorder** grabador (*m.*) de discos compactos/DVD, reproductor (*m.*) de discos compactos/DVD, 4
celebration celebración (*f.*)
cellar sótano, 10
Celsius degree grado centígrado, 7
census censo
cent centavo
center centro
Central America Centroamérica
century siglo
cereal cereal (*m.*), 9
certain cierto(a); **it's not ~** no es cierto, 11
chain cadena, 8
chair silla, P
chalk tiza, P
chalkboard pizarra, P
challenge reto
change cambio; convertir (ie, i); **~ the channel** cambiar el canal, 11
chapter capítulo, P
charity organización (*f.*) benéfica

chat chatear, 4; **~ room** grupo de conversación, 4
check cheque (*m.*); (*restaurant check*) cuenta, 9; **~ one's baggage** facturar el equipaje, 14
check-in desk mostrador (*m.*), 14
checkup chequeo médico, 12
cheek mejilla
cheese queso, 6
cheeseburger hamburguesa con queso, 9
chef cocinero(a), 5
chemistry química, 3
chess ajedrez (*m.*)
chest pecho, 12
chicken pollo, 6; **~ soup** caldo de pollo, 9; **~ with rice** arroz (*m.*) con pollo, 9; **fried ~** pollo frito, 9; **roasted ~** pollo asado, 9;
Chilean chileno(a), 2
Chinese chino(a), 2; **~ language** chino, 3
chocolate cacao; chocolate (*m.*), 11
choose escoger (j)
chronology cronología
chunk trozo, 9
church iglesia, 6
cinema cine (*m.*), 6
cinnamon canela
citizen ciudadano(a), 13
city ciudad (*f.*), 6
clam almeja, 9
clarity claridad (*f.*)
class clase (*f.*), P; **lower ~** clase baja
classroom salón (*m.*) de clase, P
clean the bathroom limpiar el baño, 10
clear the table quitar la mesa, 10
click hacer (*irreg.*) clic, 4; **double ~** hacer (*irreg.*) doble clic, 4
clinic clínica, 12
close cerrar (ie); **~ your books.** Cierren los libros. P
close to cerca de, 6
closet clóset (*m.*), 10
clothing ropa, 5; **article of ~** prenda de ropa, 8
cloudburst chaparrón (*m.*)
cloudy: It's ~. Está nublado. 7
coat abrigo, 8
code código
codfish bacalao, 9
coffee café (*m.*), 9
cold (*e.g., headcold*) catarro, resfriado, 12; (*adj.*) frío(a); **It's ~.** Hace frío. 7

Colombian colombiano(a), 2
color color (*m.*), 4; **solid ~** de un solo color, 8
comb peine (*m.*), 5; **~ one's hair** peinarse, 5
come venir (*irreg.*), 5
comedy comedia, 11; **romantic ~** comedia romántica, 11
comic strip tira cómica
comma coma
command mandato
compact disc CD, disco compacto (*m.*)
comparison comparación (*f.*), 8
compete competir (i, i)
competition competencia, 7
complain quejarse, 5
complexion tez (*f.*)
complicity complicidad (*f.*)
computer computadora, P; **~ center** centro de computación, 3; **~ functions** funciones (*f. pl.*) de la computadora, 4; **~ science** computación (*f.*), informática, 3
concierge conserje (*m., f.*), 14
conduct conducir (zc), 5
confection confección (*f.*)
connect conectar, 4
connection conexión (*f.*), 4
consider pensar (ie) en (de), 4
contest concurso
continue seguir (i, i), 6
continued seguido(a)
contract contrato, 13
contraction contracción (*f.*), 3
contrary: on the ~ al contrario
conversation conversación (*f.*)
cook cocinar, 2; cocer (-z) (ue), 9; cocinero(a), 5
cookie galleta, 9
cool: It's cool. Hace fresco. 7
copper cobre (*m.*)
corn maíz (*m.*)
corner esquina, 6
corporation: multinational ~ compañía multinacional, 13
correct corregir (i, i) (j)
cost costo, 13
Costa Rican costarricense (*m., f.*), 2
cotton algodón (*m.*), 8
cough toser, 12; tos (*f.*), 12; **~ syrup** jarabe (*m.*) para la tos, 12
counter mostrador (*m.*), 14
country país (*m.*)
courage coraje (*m.*)

course: basic ~ curso básico, 3
courtesy cortesía, 4
cousin primo(a), 5
cowboy vaquero
cradle cuna
cream crema, 12
create crear
creative creativo(a)
crew tripulación (*f.*)
crime crimen (*m.*), 13
critic crítico(a), 11
critical reaction reacción (*f.*) crítica, 11
criticism crítica, 11
crowd muchedumbre (*f.*)
cruise ship crucero
crushed molido(a), 9
crutch muleta, 12
Cuban cubano(a), 2
culinary culinario(a)
culture cultura
cumin comino, 9
cup taza, 9
current events noticias (*f. pl.*) del día, 13
curriculum vitae currículum vitae (*m.*), 13
curtain cortina, 10
custard flan (*m.*), 9
customer cliente (*m., f.*), 8
customs aduana, 14
cut (oneself) cortar(se), 12
cutting recorte (*m.*)
cyberspace ciberespacio, 4
cycling ciclismo, 7

D

daily cotidiano(a)
dam presa
dance bailar, 2; baile (*m.*), 3; danza, 11
danger peligro, 7
dangerous peligroso(a), 7
date fecha, 3; **blind ~** cita a ciegas
daughter hija, 5
daughter-in-law nuera, 5
dawn amanecer (zc)
day día (*m.*), 3; **~ before yesterday** anteayer, 7; **~ of the week** día de la semana, 3; **every ~** todos los días, 3
dead muerto(a), 13
December diciembre, 1
decoration decoración (*f.*), 10

definite definido(a), 1
degree grado
delay demora, retraso, 14
Delighted to meet you. Encantado(a). 1
demand exigir (j)
demonstrate demostrar (ue)
demonstration manifestación (*f.*), 13
demonstrative demostrativo(a), 6
denim mezclilla, 8
dentist dentista (*m., f.*), 5
deodorant desodorante (*m.*), 5
departure salida, 14
describe describir, 2
desert desierto, 14
deserve merecer (zc)
design diseño; **graphic ~** diseño gráfico, 3
designer: graphic ~ diseñador(a) gráfico(a), 5
desire afán (*m.*)
desk escritorio, P
dessert postre (*m.*), 9
destination: with ~ to con destino a, 14
detail detalle (*m.*)
detail-oriented detallista, 13
determined resuelto (*p.p. of* resolver)
develop desarrollar
development desarrollo, 13
dialect dialecto
dictionary diccionario, P
die morirse (ue, u), 8
difference diferencia
difficult difícil, 4
digital camera cámara digital, 4
dining room comedor (*m.*), 10
dinner cena
direct dirigir (j), 13
dirty sucio(a)
disadvantage desventaja, 13
disappointment desilusión (*f.*)
disaster desastre (*m.*); **natural ~** desastre natural, 13
discount descuento, 8
discover descubrir, 3
discrimination discriminación (*f.*), 13
disembark desembarcar (qu), 14
dish: main ~ plato principal, 9
dishonest mentiroso(a), 2
dishwasher lavaplatos (*m. s.*), 10
disillusionment desengaño
disk disquete (*m.*), P
dispatch despachar

disqualify descalificar (qu)
distance trecho
diversity diversidad (*f.*)
do hacer (*irreg.*), 5; **a lot to ~** mucho que hacer; **~ the homework for tomorrow.** Hagan la tarea para mañana. P; **~ the recycling** hacer el reciclaje, 10
doctor doctor(a); médico(a), 5
doctor's office consultorio del médico, 12
documentary documental (*m.*), 11
dog perro(a), 2
doll muñeca
dollar dólar (*m.*)
Dominican dominicano(a), 2
done hecho (*p.p. of* hacer), 13
door puerta, P
dorm residencia estudiantil, 3; dormitorio estudiantil, 6
doubt dudar, 11
doubtful dudoso(a), 11
downpour chaparrón (*m.*)
downtown centro de la ciudad, 10
dozen docena, 9
drama drama (*m.*), 11; **~ series** teledrama (*m.*), 11
drawing dibujo, P
dream sueño; **~ (about)** soñar (ue) con, 4
drenched empapado(a)
dress vestido, 8; **~ (someone)** vestir (i, i), 5; **get dressed** vestirse (i, i), 5
dresser cómoda, tocador (*m.*), 10
drink beber, 3
drive manejar, conducir (zc), 5
driver's license licencia de manejar
drops gotas, 12
dry (something) secar (qu), 5; **~ cleaning** lavado en seco, 14; **~ one's hair** secarse (qu) el pelo, 5
dryer secadora, 10
dubbed doblado(a), 11
during mientras, por, 10
dust polvo; **~ the furniture** sacudir los muebles, 10
DVD/CD-ROM drive lector (*m.*) de CD-ROM o DVD, 4

E

ear (inner) oído, 12; **(outer)** oreja, 12
early temprano, 3

earn (money) ganar
earphones audífonos (*m. pl.*), 4
earring arete (*m.*), pendiente (*m.*), 8
earth tierra
earthquake terremoto, 13
east este (*m.*), 14
easy fácil, 4
eat comer, 3; **~ dinner** cenar, 2;
~ **healthy foods** comer alimentos
nutritivos, 12
economy economía, 3
Ecuadoran ecuatoriano(a), 2
edit redactar
education educación (*f.*), 3
egg huevo, 6; **~ sunny-side up**
huevo estrellado, 9; **scrambled ~**
huevo revuelto, 9
egotistic egoísta, 2
eight ocho, P; **~ hundred**
ochocientos(as), 8
eighteen dieciocho, P
eighth octavo(a), 10
eighty ochenta, P
either . . . or o... o, 6
elbow codo, 12
election elección (*f.*), 13; **~ process**
proceso electoral, 13
electricity electricidad (*f.*)
electronic electrónico(a); **~ mailbox**
buzón (*m.*) electrónico, 4; **~ notebook** asistente (*m.*) electrónico,
4; **~ organizer** organizador (*m.*)
electrónico, 4; **~ product**
producto electrónico, 4
elephant elefante (*m.*)
elevator ascensor (*m.*), 14
eleven once, P
e-mail correo electrónico, e-mail
(*m.*), 4
embarrass avergonzar (ue) (c)
embarrassed avergonzado(a)
embroidered bordado(a), 8
emergency emergencia, 12; **~ room**
sala de emergencias, 12
emotion emoción (*f.*), 4
emphasize destacar (qu),
enfatizar (c)
employ emplear, 13
employee empleado(a), 13
empty vacío(a)
enchant encantar, 11
encounter encuentro
end cabo; fin (*m.*)

engineer ingeniero(a), 5
engineering ingeniería, 3
English inglés (inglesa), 2;
~ **language** inglés (*m.*), 3
enjoy gozar (c); **~ (life)** disfrutar
(la vida)
enroll alistar
enterprising emprendedor(a), 13
entertain entretener (*like* tener)
entertaining divertido(a), 2
environment medio ambiente (*m.*)
episode episodio, 11
equality igualdad (*f.*), 13
equator ecuador (*m.*)
essay ensayo
Europe Europa
evaluation calificación (*f.*)
evasion sorteo
even aun; **~ though** aunque, 12
evening noche (*f.*); **during the ~**
por la noche, 3; **Good ~.** Buenas
noches. 1; **in the ~** (*with precise
time*) de la noche, 3
everything todo
everywhere por dondequiera
example ejemplo, 10
exchange intercambiar; **~ money**
cambiar dinero, 14; **in ~ for** a
cambio de; **~ rate** cambio
Excuse me. Disculpe. Perdón. 4
exercise hacer (*irreg.*) ejercicio, 7
exhibit exhibir; **art ~** exposición
(*f.*) de arte, 11
exotic exótico(a)
expensive: It's (too) ~. Es
(demasiado) caro(a). 8
express preferences expresar
preferencias, 2
expression expresión (*f.*), 1
extroverted extrovertido(a), 2
eye ojo, 12
eyeglasses lentes (*m. pl.*), anteojos
(*m. pl.*)

F

fabric tela, 8
fact dato, hecho
factory fábrica, 13
Fahrenheit degree grado
Fahrenheit, 7
faint desmayarse, 12
fairy tale cuento de hadas

fall caer (*irreg.*); (*autumn*) otoño,
7; **~ asleep** dormirse (ue, u), 5;
~ **back on** recurrir; **~ in love**
enamorarse, 5
false falso(a)
family familia; **~ member** pariente
(*m., f.*), 5; **nuclear ~** familia
nuclear, 5; **~ tree** árbol (*m.*)
genealógico
fantastic fantástico(a), 11
fantasy fantasía
far from lejos de, 6
fascinate fascinar, 4
fashion moda, 8
fashionable: (not) to be ~ (no) estar
de moda, 8
fast rápido(a), 4
fat gordo(a), 2
father padre (*m.*), papá (*m.*), 5
father-in-law suegro, 5
fax: external/internal ~ fax (*m.*)
externo/interno, 4
fear temer, 11
February febrero, 1
feed the dog darle de comer al
perro, 10
feel sentir (ie, i), 4; **~ dizzy** estar
(*irreg.*) mareado(a), 12; **~ like**
tener (*irreg.*) ganas de, 7; **~ sorry**
sentir (ie, i), 11
feminine femenino(a)
fever fiebre (*f.*), 12
field of study campo de estudio, 3
fifteen quince, P
fifth quinto(a), 10
fifty cincuenta, P
fight (against) luchar (contra), 13
file archivar, 4; archivo, 4
film película, 11
final final
finally por fin, 9
financial financiero(a)
find out averiguar (gü)
Fine, thank you. Bien, gracias. 1
finger dedo, 12
fire (*from a job*) despedir (i, i), 13;
fuego; **~ fighter** bombero(a), 5
fired despedido(a)
fireplace chimenea, 10
first primer(o)(a), 10; **~ floor**
primer piso, 10
fish pescar (qu), 7; pez (*m.*) (*alive*);
pescado (*caught*), 9

fit apto(a); **It fits nicely/badly.** Me queda bien/mal. 8

five cinco, P; **~ hundred** quinientos(as), 8; **~ thousand** cinco mil, 8

flat llano(a)

flavor sabor (*m.*)

flight vuelo, 14; **~ attendant** asistente (*m., f.*) de vuelo, 14

floating flotador(a)

flood inundación (*f.*), 13

floor piso; **first ~** primer piso, 10

flour harina, 9

flourish florecer (zc)

flower florecer (zc); flor (*f.*)

flu gripe (*f.*), 12

fold doblar, 6

following siguiente

fondness cariño

food comida, 6

fool engañar

foot pie (*m.*), 12; **on ~** a pie, 6

football fútbol americano, 7

footprint huella

for para, por, 10; **~ example** por ejemplo, 10

forbid prohibir, 10

forest bosque (*m.*), 14; **~ fire** incendio forestal

fork tenedor (*m.*), 9

form formulario, 13

fortress fortaleza

forty cuarenta, P

founder fundador(a)

four cuatro, P; **~ hundred** cuatrocientos(as), 8

fourteen catorce, P

fourth cuarto(a), 10

fracture fractura, 12

French francés (francesa), 2; **~ fries** papas fritas, 9; **~ language** francés (*m.*), 3

frequently frecuentemente, 4

fresh fresco(a), 9

Friday viernes (*m.*), 2

fried frito(a), 9

friend amigo(a), P; cuate(a)

from the del (de + el), 3

front: in ~ of delante de, frente a, enfrente de, 6

frozen congelado(a), 9

fruit fruta, 6; **~ juice** jugo de fruta, 9; **~ salad** ensalada de fruta, 9; **~ shake** licuado de fruta

fry freír (i, i), 9

fun divertido(a), 2

function funcionar, 4

funny cómico(a), 2

furious furioso(a), 4

furniture muebles (*m. pl.*), 10

G

G (for general audiences) apto para toda la familia, 11

gallon galón (*m.*), 9

game partido, 7; **~ show** programa (*m.*) de concursos, 11; **interactive ~** juego interactivo, 4

gang pandilla

garage garaje (*m.*), 10

garbage basura, 10

garden jardín (*m.*), 10

garlic ajo, 9

gate: (departure) ~ puerta (de embarque), 14

gauze bandage venda de gasa, 12

generally por lo general, 9

generous generoso(a), 2

genre género

gentle apacible

geography geografía, 3

German alemán (alemana), 2; **~ language** alemán (*m.*), 3

get conseguir (i, i), 8; **~ ahead** adelantar; **~ along well with people** llevarse bien con la gente, 13; **~ chilled** resfriarse, 12; **~ cold** enfriarse, 9; **~ divorced** divorciarse, 5; **~ down from** bajar, 6; **~ dressed** vestirse (i, i), 5; **~ engaged** comprometerse, 5; **~ married** casarse, 5; **~ off of** (*a bus, etc.*) bajar, 6; **~ on** subir, 6; **~ ready** prepararse, 5; **~ separated** separarse, 5; **~ sick** enfermarse, 5; **~ together** reunirse, 5; **~ up** levantarse, 5

gift regalo

girl chica, P; muchacha, P; niña, P

girlfriend novia

give dar (*irreg.*), 5; **~ a blood/urine test** hacer (*irreg.*) un análisis de sangre/orina, 12; **~ a four-star rating** clasificar (qu) con cuatro estrellas, 11; **~ an injection** poner (*irreg.*) una inyección, 12; **~ directions** decir (*irreg.*) cómo llegar, 6; **~ personal information**

dar (*irreg.*) información personal, 1; **~ someone a bath** bañar, 5; **~ the time** dar (*irreg.*) la hora, 3

glass vaso, 9

globalization globalización (*f.*), 13

glove guante (*m.*), 8

go acudir; ir (*irreg.*), 3; **~ away** irse (*irreg.*), 5; **~ off** (*alarm clock, etc.*) sonar (ue), 4; **~ offline** cortar la conexión, 4; **~ online** hacer (*irreg.*) una conexión, 4; **~ out** salir (*irreg.*), 5; **~ shopping** hacer (*irreg.*) las compras, 6; ir de compras, 8; **~ straight** seguir (i, i) (g) derecho; **~ to bed** acostarse (ue), 5; **~ up** subir, 6

goal meta

gold oro, 8

golden dorado(a), 9

golf golf (*m.*), 7

good bueno(a), 2; bondadoso(a); **it's ~** es bueno, 11

good-bye adiós, 1

gossip chisme (*m.*)

gossiping chismoso(a)

government gobierno, 13

governor gobernador(a)

grade nota, P

granddaughter nieta, 5

grandfather abuelo, 5

grandmother abuela, 5

grandson nieto, 5

grape uva, 9

graph gráfica

gray gris, 4

great chévere (*Cuba, Puerto Rico*); grande, 2

greater mayor, 8

green verde, 4

greet saludar, 1

greeting saludo

grilled asado(a); a la parrilla, 9

ground molido(a), 9; tierra

group juntar

Guatemalan guatemalteco(a), 2

guess adivinar; **~.** Adivina. P

guinea pig cuy (*m.*)

guitar guitarra, 2

gymnasium gimnasio, 3

H

hair: blond ~ pelo rubio, 2; **brown ~** pelo castaño, 2

hairdresser peluquero(a), 5

hairdryer secador (*m.*) de pelo, 14
half mitad (*f.*)
half-brother medio hermano, 5
half-sister media hermana, 5
hallway pasillo, 10
ham jamón (*m.*), 6
hamburger hamburguesa, 9
hand mano (*f.*), 12
handicrafts artesanía
handkerchief pañuelo
handsome hermoso(a); guapo(a), 2
handtowel toalla de mano, 5
happiness dicha; felicidad (*f.*)
happy contento(a), 4
hard duro(a); ~ **drive** disco duro, 4
hardly ever rara vez
hardware hardware (*m.*), 4
hard-working trabajador(a), 2
haste prisa
hat sombrero, 8
hatred odio
have tener (*irreg.*), 1; ~ **128 MB of memory** tener (*irreg.*) 128 MB de memoria, 4; ~ **a fight** pelearse, 5; ~ **a good presence** tener (*irreg.*) buena presencia, 13; ~ **a lot of experience in** tener (*irreg.*) mucha experiencia en, 13; ~ **a soft drink** tomar un refresco, 2; ~ **fun** divertirse (ie, i), 5; ~ **some knowledge of** tener (*irreg.*) algunos conocimientos de, 13; ~ **the necessary skills** tener (*irreg.*) las habilidades necesarias, 13; ~ **the urge to** tener (*irreg.*) ganas de, 7; ~ **to** (+ *inf.*) tener (*irreg.*) que (+ *inf.*), 1
he él, 1
head cabeza, 12
headache dolor (*m.*) de cabeza, 12
health salud (*f.*), 3
healthy saludable
hear oír (*irreg.*), 5
heart corazón (*m.*), 12
heat calentar (ie), 9
heavy fuerte, 9
height altitud (*f.*), altura; (*of a person*) estatura
hello hola, 1
helmet casco
help ayudar; ayuda
her (*pron.*) ella, 8; (*adj.*) su, 3; suyo(a), 10; **to/for ~** le, 8
herb hierba, 12
here aquí, 6
heritage herencia

hers (*pron.*) suyo(a), 10
hide esconder
hike hacer (*irreg.*) alpinismo, practicar (qu) alpinismo, 7
him (*pron.*) él, 8; **to/for~** le, 8
hire contratar, 13
his (*adj.*) su, 3; (*adj., pron.*) suyo(a), 10
Hispanic hispano(a)
history historia, 3
hoax engaño
hockey: field ~ hockey (*m.*) sobre hierba, 7; **ice ~** hockey (*m.*) sobre hielo, 7
hole pozo
home hogar (*m.*)
homeless sin hogar
homemade casero(a)
homework tarea, P
Honduran hondureño(a), 2
honest honesto(a)
hope esperanza; esperar, 10; **I ~ (that)** ojalá (que), 11
Hopefully you'll get better soon! ¡Ojalá se mejore pronto! 12
horrible horrible, 11
hospital hospital (*m.*), 6
host anfitrión (*m.*); (*of a show*) presentador(a), 11
hot: be ~ tener (*irreg.*) calor, 7; ~ **dog** perro caliente, 9; **It's~.** Hace calor. 7
hotel hotel (*m.*), 14; ~ **guest** huésped(a), 14
hour hora
house casa, 6
housechore quehacer (*m.*) doméstico, 10
housing vivienda
how? ¿cómo? 3; ~ **are things going?** ¿Qué tal? 1; ~ **are you?** (*form. s.*) ¿Cómo está (usted)? / (*form. pl.*) ¿Cómo están (ustedes)? / (*s. fam.*) ¿Cómo estás (tú)? 1; ~ **can I help you?** ¿En qué puedo servirle? 8; ~ **do you say . . . ?** ¿Cómo se dice…? P; ~ **do you wish to pay?** ¿Cómo desea pagar?, 8; ~ **many?** ¿cuántos(as)? 3; ~ **much?** ¿cuánto(a)? 3; ~ **much does it cost?** ¿Cuánto cuesta? 8; **How's it going with you?** ¿Cómo te/le(s) va? 1
humanities humanidades (*f. pl.*), 3
humble humilde
humid húmedo(a)
hunger hambre (*f. but* el hambre)

hurricane huracán (*m.*), 13
hurry prisa; **be in a ~** tener (*irreg.*) prisa, 7
hurt doler (ue), 12; ~ **oneself** lastimarse, 12
husband esposo, 5
hymn himno

I

I yo, 1
ice: (vanilla/chocolate) ~ cream helado (de vainilla/de chocolate), 9; ~ **hockey** hockey (*m.*) sobre hielo, 7; ~ **skate** patinar sobre hielo, 7
identity identidad (*f.*)
illness enfermedad (*f.*), 12
immigration inmigración (*f.*)
impatient impaciente, 2
important importante, 11; **extremely ~** imprescindible, 11
impressive impresionante
improbable improbable, 11
impulsive impulsivo(a), 2
in en; por, 10; ~ **case** en caso de que, 12; ~ **order to** (+ *inf.*) para, 10; ~ **relation to** en cuanto a; ~ **short** en resumen; ~ **spite of** a pesar de; ~ **the direction of** para, 10
inch pulgada
increase acrecentar (ie), aumentar
incredible increíble
indefinite indefinido(a), 1
index índice (*m.*)
indigenous indígena
industry industria, 13
inequality desigualdad (*f.*), 13
infection infección (*f.*), 12
influence influir (y); influencia
ingredient ingrediente (*m.*), 9
inhabitant habitante (*m., f.*)
initiate iniciar, 13
injection inyección (*f.*), 12
injure oneself lastimarse, 12
injury herida, 12
in-laws familia política, 5
inline skate (rollerblade) patinar en línea, 7
inside of dentro de, 6; ~ **the house** dentro de la casa, 10
insist insistir, 10
install instalar, 4
instead of en vez de
instruction instrucción (*f.*), 12
instructor instructor(a), P

intelligent inteligente, 2
intention fin (*m.*)
interest interesar, 4
interesting interesante, 2
Internet Internet (*m. or f.*), red (*f.*); **~ connection** conexión (*f.*) a Internet, 14; **~ provider** proveedor (*m.*) de acceso, 4
interpreter intérprete (*m., f.*)
interview entrevista, 13
interviewer entrevistador(a), 11
intimate íntimo(a)
introduce someone presentar a alguien, 1
introverted introvertido(a), 2
investigate averiguar (gü), 13
iron planchar, 10; (*metal*) hierro; (*appliance*) plancha, 10
irresponsible irresponsable, 2
island isla, 14
Italian italiano(a), 2; **~ language** italiano, 3
itinerary itinerario, 14
its (*adj.*) su, 3; (*pron.*) suyo(a), 10

J

jacket (*suit jacket, blazer*) saco; (*outdoor, non-suit coat*) chaqueta 8
January enero, 1
Japanese japonés (japonesa), 2; **~ language** japonés (*m.*), 3
jealous celoso(a); **be ~** tener (*irreg.*) celos
jeans jeans (*m. pl.*), 8
jewelry store joyería, 6
jewelry joyas (*f. pl.*), 8
job puesto, 13
joke broma
journalism periodismo, 3
journalist periodista (*m., f.*), 5
July julio, 1
June junio, 1
jungle: Amazonian ~ selva amazónica, 14; **tropical ~** selva tropical, 14

K

key (*on a keyboard*) tecla, 4; (*to a lock*) llave (*f.*), 14
keyboard teclado, 4
kilo kilo, 9; **half a ~** medio kilo, 9
kind bondadoso(a)
king rey (*m.*)
kiss besar
kitchen cocina, 10
knapsack mochila, P

knife cuchillo, 9
know: ~ a person conocer (zc), 5; **~ a fact, ~ how to** saber (*irreg.*), 5

L

lake lago, 7
lamp lámpara, 10
language idioma (*m.*), lengua, 3
laptop computer computadora portátil, 4
late tarde, 3
later luego, 5
latest: the ~ lo último
laugh reírse (*irreg.*), 5
laundry room lavandería, 10
lawn césped (*m.*), 10; **mow the ~** cortar el césped, 10
lawyer abogado(a), 5
lazy perezoso(a), 2
lead a healthy life llevar una vida sana, 12
leader líder (*m., f.*), 13
learn aprender, 3
learning aprendizaje (*m.*)
leather piel (*f.*), cuero, 8
leave dejar, 2; salir (*irreg.*), irse (*irreg.*), 5
left: to the ~ a la izquierda, 6
leg pierna, 12; **broken ~** pierna quebrada/rota, 12
lemonade limonada, 9
less menor, 8; **~ than** menos que, 8
lesson lección (*f.*), P
level nivel (*m.*)
life vida
lifejacket salvavidas (*m. s.*)
lift levantar, 5; **~ weights** levantar pesas, 2
light luz (*f.*); (*adj.*) ligero(a), 9
like gustar, 11; **~ a lot** encantar, 4; **(They/You** [*pl.*]) **~ . . .** A... les gusta... 2; **He/She likes . . .** A... le gusta... 2; **I/You ~ . . .** A mí/ti me gusta... 2; **I'd ~** (+ *inf.*) quisiera (+ *inf.*), 6; Me gustaría (+ *inf.*)... 6
likely probable, 11
Likewise. Igualmente. 1
linen lino, 8
linguistic lingüístico(a)
link enlace (*m.*), 4
lip labio
listen escuchar; **~ to music** escuchar música, 2; **~ to the tape/ CD.** Escuchen la cinta/el CD. P

liter litro, 9
literature literatura, 3
little poco, 4
live vivir, 3; (*adj., e.g., a live show*) en vivo, 11
livestock ganadería
living room sala, 10
loan préstamo, 8
lobster langosta, 9
located ubicado(a)
logical lógico(a), 11
long for apetecer (zc)
look: ~ for buscar (qu), 2; **~ into** averiguar (gü), 13
lose perder (ie), 4; **~ oneself** perderse (ie)
loss pérdida, 13
love querer (*irreg.*), 4; amor, cariño
lover amante (*m., f.*)
lunch almuerzo, 9
lung pulmón (*m.*), 12
luxurious lujoso(a)
lying mentiroso(a), 2

M

made: It's ~ out of . . . Está hecho(a) de... 8; **They're ~ out of . . .** Están hechos(as) de... 8
magazine revista
mailbox buzón (*m.*)
majority mayoría
make hacer (*irreg.*), 5; **~ a reservation** hacer una reservación, 14; **~ a stopover in** hacer escala en, 14; **~ sure** asegurarse; **~ the bed** hacer la cama, 10
makeup maquillaje (*m.*), 5
mall centro comercial, 6
man hombre (*m.*), P
manager gerente (*m., f.*), 5
manly varonil
manners modales (*m. pl.*)
March marzo, 1
marital status estado civil
mark marcar (qu)
market mercado, 6
marketing mercadeo, 3
masculine masculino(a)
match emparejar; (*sports*) partido, 7
mathematics matemáticas (*f. pl.*), 3
matter importar, 4
May mayo, 1
mayonnaise mayonesa, 9
mayor alcalde (alcadesa)
me mí, 8; **to/for ~** me, 8; **with ~** conmigo, 8

mean: It means . . . Significa… P

meaning significado

means of transportation medios de transporte, 6

measure medir (i, i)

measurement medida, 9

meat carne (*f.*), 9

meatball albóndiga

mechanic mecánico(a), 5

media center centro de comunicaciones, 3

medical insurance seguro médico, 13

medicine medicina, 3

meditation meditación (*f.*)

meet conocer (zc), reunirse, 5

meeting encuentro, reunión (*f.*)

menu menú (*m.*), 9

messenger mensajero(a)

Mexican mexicano(a), 2

microphone micrófono, 4

microwave microondas (*m. s.*), 10

midnight medianoche (*f.*), 3

mild apacible

milk leche (*f.*), 6

mine (*pron.*) mío, 10

mirror espejo, 10

Miss señorita (*abbrev.* Srta.), 1

missionary misionero(a)

mix mezclar, 9; mezcla

mixed mixto(a)

modem: external/internal ~ módem (*m.*) externo/interno, 4

Monday lunes (*m.*), 3

money dinero

monitor monitor (*m.*), 4

monkey mono

month mes (*m.*), 3; **last ~** mes pasado, 7

mop the floor trapear el piso, 10

more más; **~ than** más que, 8

morning mañana, 3; **during the ~** por la mañana, 3; **Good ~.** Buenos días. 1; **in the ~** (*with precise time*) de la mañana, 3

mortality mortalidad (*f.*)

mother madre (*f.*), mamá, 5; **Mother's Day** día (*m.*) de las Madres, 3

mother-in-law suegra, 5

mountain monte (*m.*); **~ range** cordillera

mountainous montañoso(a)

mouse ratón (*m.*), 4

mouth boca, 12

move (*change residence*) mudarse

movie película, 11; **action ~** película de acción, 11; **horror ~** película de horror/terror, 11; **~ called . . .** película titulada…, 11; **~ genre** clase (*f.*) de película, 11; **~ star** estrella de cine, 11; **science fiction ~** película de ciencia ficción, 11

movies cine (*m.*), 11

mow the lawn cortar el césped, 10

Mr. señor (*abbrev.* Sr.), 1

Mrs. señora (*abbrev.* Sra.), 1

Ms. señorita (*abbrev.* Srta.), 1

much mucho, 4

museum museo, 6

music música, 3; **classical ~** música clásica, 11; **country ~** música country, 11; **modern ~** música moderna, 11; **world ~** música mundial, 11

musical musical, 11

mustard mostaza, 9

my (*adj.*) mi, 3; (*pron.*) mío(a), 10; **~ pleasure.** Mucho gusto. Un placer. 1

mystery misterio, 11

N

name llamar, 2; nombre (*m.*); **full ~** nombre (*m.*) completo; **My ~ is . . .** Me llamo…, Mi nombre es…, 1

napkin servilleta, 9

narrator narrador(a)

nationality nacionalidad (*f.*), 2

nature naturaleza

nausea náuseas (*f. pl.*), 12

navegation navegación (*f.*)

necessary necesario(a), 11

neck cuello, 12

necklace collar (*m.*), 8

need necesitar, 2

neighbor vecino(a), 6

neighborhood colonia, 1; barrio, 6

neither tampoco, 2; **~ . . . nor** ni… ni, 6

nephew sobrino, 5

nervous nervioso(a), 4

never nunca, 5; jamás, 6

nevertheless sin embargo

new novedoso(a)

news noticias (*f. pl.*), 11; **~ group** grupo de debate, 4

newspaper periódico

next próximo(a); **~ to** al lado de, 6; **~ to last** penúltimo(a)

Nicaraguan nicaragüense (*m., f.*), 2

nice simpático(a), 2

nickname apodo

niece sobrina, 5

night noche (*f.*), 3; **Good ~.** Buenas noches. 1; **last ~** anoche, 7

nine hundred novecientos(as), 8

nine nueve, P

nineteen diecinueve, P

ninety noventa, P

ninth noveno(a), 10

no one nadie, 6

nobody nadie, 6

none ningún, ninguno(a), 6

noodle soup sopa de fideos, 9

noon mediodía (*m.*), 3

normal normal, 4

North America Norteamérica

north norte (*m.*), 14; **~ America** Norteamérica

nose nariz (*f.*), 12

not: ~ any ningún, ninguno(a), 6; **~ either** tampoco, 2; **~ much** no mucho, 1

notebook cuaderno, P

notes apuntes (*m. pl.*), P

nothing nada, 1

noun sustantivo

novel novedoso(a)

novelist novelista (*m., f.*)

November noviembre, 1

novice novato(a)

number número, 8

nurse enfermero(a), 5

O

obey hacer (*irreg.*) caso

obtain conseguir (i, i), 8

obvious obvio(a), 11

ocean océano, 14

October octubre, 1

of: ~ course cómo no, 6; por supuesto, 10; **~ the** del (de + el), 3

offer: special ~ oferta especial, 8

office oficina, 6

old viejo(a), 2; old

old-fashioned anticuado(a)

olive oil aceite (*m.*) de oliva, 9

on en, sobre, encima de, 6; **~ behalf of** por, 10

once una vez, 9

one uno, P; **~ hundred** cien, P; **~ hundred and ~** ciento uno, 8; **~ hundred thousand** cien mil, 8; **~ million** millón (*m.*), un millón, 8; **~ thousand** mil (*m.*), 8

one-way ticket boleto de ida, billete (*m.*) de ida, 14

onion cebolla, 9

online en línea, 4

only único(a)

open abrir, 3; abierto (*p.p. of* abrir), 13; **~ your books.** Abran los libros. P

opera ópera, 11

opposite enfrente de, frente a, 6; opuesto(a)

orange (*color*) anaranjado(a), 4; (*fruit*) naranja, 9

order ordenar, 9; mandar, 10

ordinal number número ordinal, 10

originate originar

ought deber (+ *inf.*), 3

our (*adj.*) nuestro(a)(s), 3

ours (*pron.*) nuestro(a)(s), 10

outline bosquejo

outside of fuera de, 6; **~ the house** fuera de la casa, 10

outskirts afueras (*f. pl.*), 10

outstanding sobresaliente

oven horno

overcome sobrevivir, 13

overcoming superación (*f.*)

owner dueño(a), 5

P

package paquete (*m.*), 9

page página, P

pain dolor (*m.*), 12

paint pintar, 2

painting pintura, 3; cuadro, 10

palpitate palpitar, 12

Panamanian panameño(a), 2

pants pantalones (*m. pl.*), 8

paper papel (*m.*), P

parachute paracaídas (*m. s.*)

paragraph párrafo

Paraguayan paraguayo(a), 2

Pardon me. Con permiso. 4

parents padres (*m. pl.*), 5

park parque (*m.*), 6

parking lot estacionamiento, 6

parsley perejil (*m.*)

participant participante (*m., f.*), 11

participate in participar en, 13

pass (by) pasar, 2

passenger pasajero(a), 14; **coach ~** pasajero de clase turista, 14; **first class ~** pasajero de primera clase, 14

passport pasaporte (*m.*), 14

password contraseña, 4

patient paciente (*m., f.*), 2

patio patio, 10

paving stone baldosa

pay pagar (gu), 9; **~ attention** hacer (*irreg.*) caso

payment: form of ~ método de pago, 8

pea guisante (*m.*), 9

peace paz (*f.*); **world ~** paz mundial, 13

peel pelar, 9

pencil lápiz (*m.*), P

penguin pingüino

pepper pimienta, 9

percentage porcentaje (*m.*)

perhaps quizás, tal vez

period (*punctuation*) punto; trecho

permit permitir, 10

personality personalidad (*f.*); **~ trait** característica de la personalidad, 2

Peruvian peruano(a), 2

PG-13 (*parental discretion advised*) se recomienda discreción, 11

pharmacy farmacia, 6

philanthropic filantrópico(a)

philosophy filosofía, 3

photo foto (*f.*), P

physical chequeo médico, 12; físico(a), 5; **~ appearance** apariencia física; **~ trait** característica física, 2

physics física, 3

piano piano, 2

picturesque pintoresco(a)

piece pedazo, 9

pill píldora, 12

pillow almohada

pink rosado(a), 4

pirate pirata (*m.*)

pizzeria pizzería, 6

place lugar (*m.*), sitio

placed puesto(a), 13

plaid a cuadros, 8

plain llanura

plate plato, 9

play jugar (ue) (gu), 4; obra teatral, 11; **~ a musical instrument** tocar (qu) un

instrumento musical, 2; **~ sports** practicar (qu) deportes, 2; **~ tennis (baseball, etc.)** jugar tenis (béisbol, etc), 7

playful juguetón (juguetona)

plaza plaza, 6

please encantar, gustar, 11; por favor, 1

pleasure: A ~ to meet you. Mucho gusto en conocerte. 1

plot trama

plumber plomero(a), 5

poet poeta (poetisa)

poetry poesía

point: ~ out marcar (qu), señalar; **to the ~** al grano

policeman (policewoman) policía (*m., f.*), 5

political político(a); **~ science** ciencias políticas (*f. pl.*), 3

politics política, 13

polka-dotted de lunares, 8

pollution: air ~ contaminación (*f.*) (del aire), 13

poor pobre

pop songs música pop, 11

popcorn palomitas (*f. pl.*), 11

populate poblar (ue)

pork chop chuleta de puerco, 6

portable CD/MP3 player CD portátil/MP3, 4

position puesto, 13

post office oficina de correos, 6

postage stamp estampilla, 14

postcard tarjeta postal, 14

potato: ~ chips papitas fritas, 6; **~ salad** ensalada de papa

pound libra, 9

power poder (*m.*)

powerful poderoso(a)

practice practicar (qu)

prefer preferir (ie, i), 4

preference preferencia

prenuptual agreement contrato prenupcial

preparation preparación (*f.*), 9

prepare preparar, 2; **~ the food** preparar la comida, 10

preposition preposición (*f.*), 6

prescribe a medicine recetar una medicina, 12

prescription receta, 12

present (*gift*) regalo; **at the ~ time** en la actualidad

presenter presentador(a), 11

pretty bonito(a); lindo(a), 2
price: It's a very good ~. Está a muy buen precio. 8
priest sacerdote (*m.*)
prime rib lomo de res, 9
print imprimir, 3; (*patterned fabric*) estampado(a), 8; (*art*) cuadro, 10
printer impresora, 4
prize premio
probable probable, 11
profession profesión (*f.*), 5
professor profesor(a), P
profit ganancia, 13
program programa (*m.*); **anti-virus ~** programa antivirus, 4; **~ icon** ícono del programa, 4
programmer programador(a), 5
promote adelantar, promover (ue)
promotion ascenso, 13
pronoun pronombre (*m.*), 1
proud orgulloso(a)
provided that con tal (de) que, 12
provocative provocador(a)
psychology psicología, 3
public: ~ communications comunicación (*f.*) pública, 3; **~ relations** publicidad (*f.*), 3
Puerto Rican puertorriqueño(a), 2
punctual puntual, 13
purple morado(a), 4
purpose propósito
purse bolsa, 8
push oprimir
put poner (*irreg.*), 5; **~ away the clothes** guardar la ropa, 10; **~ my toys where they belong** poner mis juguetes en su lugar, 10; **~ on (clothing)** ponerse (la ropa), 5; **~ on makeup** maquillarse, 5

Q

quality calidad (*f.*); **of good (high) ~** de buena (alta) calidad, 8
queen reina
question pregunta, 12
questionnaire cuestionario
quotation cita

R

R (minors restricted) prohibido para menores, 11
raffle sorteo
railroad ferrocarril (*m.*)

rain llover (ue); **~ forest** bosque (*m.*) tropical, bosque (*m.*) pluvial; **It's raining.** Está lloviendo. (Llueve.), 7
raincoat impermeable (*m.*), 8
raise levantar, 5
ranch estancia
rank rango
rap rap (*m.*), 11
ratings índice (*m.*) de audencia, 11
raw crudo(a), 9
razor rasuradora, 5; **electric ~** máquina de afeitar, 5
read leer (y), 3; **~ Chapter 1.** Lean el Capítulo 1. P
really de veras
reason razón (*f.*)
receive recibir, 3
reception desk recepción (*f.*), 14
recipe receta, 9
recognize reconocer (zc)
recommend recomendar (ie), 10
record grabar, 4
recruit alistar
recycling reciclaje (*m.*), 10
red rojo(a), 4
redheaded pelirrojo(a), 2
reduced: It's ~. Está rebajado(a). 8
reflect reflejar
reflection reflexión (*f.*)
refrigerator refrigerador (*m.*), 10
register registrarse, 14
regret sentir (ie, i), 11
relate contar (ue), 4
relative pariente (*m., f.*), 5
relax relajarse
remain quedar(se)
remote control control (*m.*) remoto, 11
renovate renovar (ue)
renown renombre (*m.*)
rent alquiler (*m.*); **~ videos** alquilar videos, 2
repeat repetir (i, i), 4; **~.** Repitan. P
report informe (*m.*)
request pedir (i, i), 10
require requerir (ie, i), 10
requisite requisito, 13
reservation reservación (*f.*), 14
residential neighborhood barrio residencial, 10
resort to recurrir
respond responder, 1
responsible responsable, 2

rest descansar, 2
restaurant restaurante (*m.*), 6
résumé currículum vitae (*m.*), 13
retire jubilarse, 13
return regresar, 2; volver (ue), 4
returned vuelto (*p.p. of* volver), 13
revenue ingreso
review crítica, reseña, 11
rhyme rima
Rhythm and Blues R & B (*m.*), 11
rich adinerado(a)
ride montar; **~ a bike** montar en bicicleta, 7; **~ horseback** montar a caballo, 7
ridiculous ridículo(a), 11
right: to the ~ a la derecha, 6
ring sonar (ue), 4; anillo, 8; sortija
risk riesgo
river río, 7
roasted (in the oven) al horno, 9
rock (*music*) rock (*m.*), 11
role papel (*m.*)
roof techo, 10
room cuarto, P; **double ~** habitación (*f.*) doble (*f.*), 14; **single ~** habitación (*f.*) sencilla, 14; **smoking/non-smoking ~** habitación (*f.*) de fumar/de no fumar, 14; **~ with/without bath/shower** habitación (*f.*) con/sin baño/ducha, 14
roommate compañero(a) de cuarto, P
root raíz (*f.*)
rose rosa, 4
rough draft borrador (*m.*)
round-trip ticket boleto de ida y vuelta, billete (*m.*) de ida y vuelta, 14
route ruta
row remar, 7
rower remero(a)
rude descortés
rug alfombra, 10
ruin ruina, 14
rule regla
run correr, 3
rural campestre

S

sad triste, 4
safe seguro(a), 7
said dicho(a) (*p.p. of* decir), 13; **It's said . . .** Se dice…, P

salad ensalada, 9; **lettuce and tomato ~** ensalada de lechuga y tomate, 9; **tossed ~** ensalada mixta, 9

salary increase aumento de sueldo, 13

sale: It's on ~. Está en venta. 8

salesclerk dependiente (*m., f.*), 5

salmon salmón (*m.*), 9

salt sal (*f.*), 9

Salvadoran salvadoreño(a), 2

same mismo(a); **~ (thing)** lo mismo

sand arena, 14

sandal sandalia, 8

sandwich bocadillo, sandwich (*m.*), 9; **ham and cheese ~ with avocado** sandwich de jamón y queso con aguacate, 9

satisfied satisfecho(a), 13

satisfy satisfacer (like hacer), 13

Saturday sábado, 2

sausage salchicha, 6

say decir (*irreg.*), 5; **~ good-bye** despedirse (i, i), 1

saying dicho

scan ojear

scarcely apenas

scarf bufanda, 8

scenery paisaje (*m.*)

schedule horario

science ciencia, 3

scientific científico(a)

scream gritar; grito

screen pantalla, 4

script guión (*m.*); **~ writer** guionista (*m., f.*)

sculpture escultura, 11

sea mar (*m., f.*), 14

search engine buscador (*m.*), 4

seaside resort balneario

season estación (*f.*), 7; **dry ~** temporada de secas; **rainy ~** temporada de lluvias

seat asiento, 14; **aisle ~** asiento de pasillo, 14; **window ~** asiento de ventanilla, 14

second segundo(a), 10

secret secreto

secretary secretario(a), 5

see ver (*irreg.*), 5; **~ you later.** Hasta luego. Nos vemos. 1; **~ you soon.** Hasta pronto. 1; **~ you tomorrow.** Hasta mañana. 1

seem parecer (zc)

seen visto (*p.p. of* ver), 13

selfish egoísta, 2

sell vender, 3

send enviar, 4; mandar, 10

sentence oración (*f.*)

September septiembre, 1

serious serio(a), 2

serve servir (i, i), 4

set the table poner (*irreg.*) la mesa, 9

seven siete, P; **~ hundred** setecientos(as), 8

seventeen diecisiete, P

seventh séptimo(a), 10

seventy setenta, P

several varios(as)

shake hands darse (*irreg.*) la mano, 13

shame: it's a shame es una lástima, 11

shampoo champú (*m.*), 5

share compartir, 3

shark tiburón (*m.*)

shave oneself afeitarse, 5

she ella, 1

sheet of paper hoja de papel, P

shellfish marisco, 9

shelter albergar (gu)

shirt camisa, 8

shoe zapato, 8; **high-heeled ~** zapato de tacón alto, 8; **tennis ~** zapato de tenis, 8

shooting tiroteo

shore orilla

short (*in length*) corto(a); (*in height*) bajo(a), 2

shorts pantalones (*m. pl.*) cortos, 8

should deber (+ *inf.*), 3

shoulder hombro, 12

shout gritar

show demostrar (ue), mostrar (ue); espectáculo, show (*m.*), 11

shred picar (qu), 9

shrimp camarón (*m.*), 9

shy tímido(a), 2

sick enfermo(a), 4

sickness enfermedad (*f.*), 12

side lado; **on the ~ of** al lado de, 6

sign letrero

silk seda, 8

silly tonto(a), 2

silver plata, 8

similarity semejanza

simple sencillo(a)

sincere sincero(a), 2

sing cantar, 2

singer cantante (*m., f.*)

single soltero(a)

sister (younger, older) hermana (menor, mayor), 5

sister-in-law cuñada, 5

sit down sentarse (ie), 5

sitcom telecomedia, 11

six seis, P; **~ hundred** seiscientos(as), 8

sixteen dieciséis, P

sixth sexto(a), 10

sixty sesenta, P

size talla, 8

skate patinar, 2

ski esquiar, 7; esquí (*m.*)

skiing esquí (*m.*); **downhill ~** esquí alpino, 7; **water ~** esquí acuático, 7

skin tez (*f.*)

skirt falda, 8

sky cielo, 14

slave esclavo(a)

sleep dormir (ue, u), 4

slice pedazo, 9

slogan lema (*m.*)

slow lento(a), 4

slowly despacio

small pequeño(a), 2; **a ~ amount** un poco, 4

smile sonreír (*irreg.*), 8; sonrisa

snack merienda

sneeze estornudar, 12

snow nevar (ie); **It's snowing.** Está nevando. (Nieva.), 7

so por eso, 10; **~ that** para que, con tal (de) que, 12

soap jabón (*m.*), 5; **~ opera** telenovela, 11

soccer fútbol (*m.*), 7; **~ field** cancha, campo de fútbol, 6

sock calcetín (*m.*), 8

sofa sofá (*m.*), 10

soft suave; **~ drink** refresco, 6

software software (*m.*), 4

some unos(as), 1; algún, alguno(a), 6

someone alguien, 6

something algo, 6

sometimes de vez en cuando; a veces, 5

son hijo, 5

son-in-law yerno, 5

sore throat dolor de garganta, 12

sorry: I'm sorry. Lo siento. 4

So-so. Regular. 1

soul alma (*f.*) (*but* el alma)

sound sonido

soup sopa, 9; **cold ~** gazpacho (*Spain*), 9

source fuente (*f.*)

south sur (*m.*), 14; **~ America** Sudamérica

souvenir recuerdo

sovereignty soberanía

spa balneario

Spain España

Spanish español (española), 2; **~ language** español (*m.*), 3

Spanish-speaking hispanohablante

speaker conferencista (*m., f.*); altoparlante (*m., f.*), 4

species especie (*f.*)

spelling ortografía

spicy picante, 9

sponsor patrocinador(a)

spoon cuchara, 9

sport deporte (*m.*), 7; **~ activity** actividad (*f.*) deportiva, 7

sports coat saco, 8

spring primavera, 7

stadium estadio, 6

stairs escaleras (*f. pl.*), 10

state estado, 5

station estación (*f.*), 11; **bus ~** estación de autobús, 6; **train ~** estación de trenes, 6

stationery store papelería, 6

statistics estadística, 3

stay in bed guardar cama, 12

steak bistec (*m.*), 6

steamed al vapor, 9

steel acero

step on pisar

stepbrother hermanastro, 5

stepfather padrastro, 5

stepmother madrastra, 5

stepsister hermanastra, 5

Stick out your tongue. Saque la lengua. 12

still todavía; **~ life** naturaleza muerta

stock market bolsa de valores, 13

stomach estómago, 12

stomachache dolor (*m.*) de estómago, 12

stop (*e.g., bus stop*) parada ; **~ (doing something)** dejar de (+ *inf.*), 2; parar (de), 3

store guardar; almacén (*m.*), tienda, 6; **music (clothing, video) ~** tienda de música (ropa, videos), 6

stove estufa, 10

straight ahead todo derecho, 6

straighten out the bedroom arreglar el dormitorio, 10

strange exótico(a); extraño(a), 11

strategy estrategia

strawberry fresa, 9

street calle (*f.*), 1

strengthen acrecentar (ie)

strike huelga, 13

stringed al hilo, 9

striped rayado(a), a rayas, 8

strong fuerte

student estudiante (*m., f.*), P; **~ center** centro estudiantil, 6

studio estudio, 3

study estudiar; **~ at the library (at home)** estudiar en la biblioteca (en casa), 2; **~ pages . . . to . . .** Estudien las páginas… a…, P

stupid tonto(a), 2

style estilo; **in ~** en onda; **out of ~** pasado(a) de moda, 8

substitute sustituir (y)

subtitle: with subtitles in English con subtítulos en inglés, 11

suburb barrio residencial, suburbio, 10

subway: on the ~ en metro, 6

success éxito

suddenly de repente, 9

suffer (the consequences) sufrir (las consecuencias), 13

sugar azúcar (*m., f.*), 9; **~ cane** caña de azúcar

suggest sugerir (ie, i), 8

suggestion sugerencia

suit traje (*m.*), 8; **bathing ~** traje (*m.*) de baño, 8

suitcase maleta, 14

summer verano, 7

sun sol (*m.*)

sunbathe tomar el sol, 2

Sunday domingo, 2

sunglasses gafas (*f. pl.*) de sol, 8

sunlight luz (*f.*) solar

sunny: It's ~. Hace sol. 7

supermarket supermercado, 6

supervise supervisar, 13

support apoyar

sure seguro(a), 4; **it's not ~** no es seguro, 11

surf hacer (*irreg.*) surfing, practicar (qu) surfing, 7; **~ the Internet** navegar (gu) por Internet, 2

surpass sobrepasar

surprise sorprender, 11; sorpresa

surrounded rodeado(a)

survey encuesta

survive sobrevivir, 13

Swallow. Trague. 12

sweater suéter (*m.*), 8

sweatsuit sudadera, 8

sweep the floor barrer el suelo / el piso, 10

sweet dulce (*m.*); (*adj.*) dulce

swim bañar, 5; nadar, 7

swimming natación (*f.*), 7; **~ pool** piscina, 6

symbol símbolo

symptom síntoma (*m.*), 12

systematic sistemático(a)

T

table mesa, P; **night ~** mesita de noche, 10; **set the ~** poner (*irreg.*) la mesa, 9

tablecloth mantel (*m.*), 9

tablespoon cucharada, 9

tablet pastilla, 12

take tomar, llevar; **~ a bath** bañarse, 5; **~ a shower** ducharse, 5; **~ a tour** hacer (*irreg.*) un tour, 14; **~ an X-ray** tomar una radiografía, 12; **~ blood pressure** tomar la presión, 12; **~ measures** tomar medidas, 13; **~ off clothing** quitarse la ropa, 5; **~ out the garbage** sacar (qu) la basura, 10; **~ photos** sacar (qu) fotos, 2; **~ place** realizarse (c); **~ the temperature** tomar la temperatura, 12; **~ the dog for a walk** sacar (qu) a pasear al perro, 10

talk hablar; **~ on the telephone** hablar por teléfono, 1; **~ show** programa (*m.*) de entrevistas, 11

tall alto(a), 2

tamed domesticado(a)

taste gusto; **to individual ~** al gusto, 9

tavern bodegón (*m.*)

tea: hot ~ té (*m.*), 9; **iced ~** té (*m.*) helado, 9

teach enseñar

teacher maestro(a), 5

team equipo, 7

tear up rasgar (gu)

teaspoon cucharadita, 9

technology technología, 4

telecommunications telecomunicaciones (*f. pl.*), 13

television: ~ broadcasting televisión (*f.*), 11; **~ program** programa de televisión, 11; **~ set** televisor (*m.*), 10;

tell contar (ue), 4; decir (*irreg.*), 5; **~ the time** decir la hora, 3

temperature temperatura, 7

ten diez, P; **~ thousand** diez mil, 8

tennis tenis (*m.*), 7; **~ court** cancha de tenis, 6; **~ shoes** zapatos (*m. pl.*) de tenis, 8

tenth décimo(a), 10

term término

terrible fatal, terrible, 1

terrific chévere (*Cuba, Puerto Rico*)

terrorism terrorismo, 13

test: blood/urine ~ análisis (*m.*) de sangre/orina, 12

text texto

Thank you very much. Muchas gracias. 1

that (*adj.*) ese(a), 6; (*pron.*) ése(a), 6; **~ over there** (*adj.*) aquel (aquella), 6; (*pron.*) aquél (aquélla), 6

that's why por eso, 10

the el, la, los, las, 1

theater teatro, 6

their su, 3; suyo(a), 10

theirs (*pron.*) suyo(a), 10

them ellos(as), 8; **to/for ~** les, 8

then entonces

theory teoría

there allí, 6; **over ~** allá, 6; **~ is / ~ are** hay, 1

these (*adj.*) estos(as), 6; (*pron.*) éstos(as), 6

they ellos(as), 1

thin delgado(a), 2

think (about) pensar (ie) (en, de), 4

third tercer(o, a), 10

thirst sed (*f.*)

thirsty: be ~ tener (*irreg.*) sed, 7

thirteen trece, P

thirty treinta, P

this (*adj.*) este(a), 6; (*pron.*) éste(a), 6

those (*adj.*) esos, 6; (*pron.*) ésos(as), 6; **~ (over there)** (adj.) aquellos(as), 6; (*pron.*) aquéllos(as), 6

threat amenaza

three tres, P; **~ hundred** trescientos(as), 8

throat garganta, 12

through por, 10

throughout a través de

throw: ~ oneself lanzarse (c); **~ up** vomitar, 12

thunderstorm tormenta

Thursday jueves (*m.*), 3

ticket boleto, entrada, 11; billete (*m.*), pasaje (*m.*), 14; **one-way ~** boleto de ida, billete de ida, 14; **round-trip ~** boleto de ida y vuelta, billete de ida y vuelta, 14;

time hora; vez (*f.*)

times veces (*f. pl.*); **(two, three, etc.) ~ a day/per week** (dos, tres, etc.) veces al día/por semana, 5

tip propina, 9

tired cansado(a), 4

title titular; título, 1

to a; **to the** al (a + el), 3

toast pan (*m.*) tostado, 9

toaster tostadora, 10

today hoy, 3; **~ is Tuesday the 30th.** Hoy es martes treinta. 3

toe dedo, 12

tomorrow mañana, 3

tongue lengua, 12

too much demasiado, 4

toothbrush cepillo de dientes, 5

toothpaste pasta de dientes, 5

top: on ~ of encima de, 6

tourist guidebook guía turística, 14

toward para, 10

towel toalla, 5

town pueblo, 6

toy juguete (*m.*), 10

train (*for sports*) entrenarse, 7; tren, 6

trainer entrenador(a) (*m.*)

trait característica

translate traducir (zc), 5

travel (abroad) viajar (al extranjero), 14; **~ agency** agencia de viajes, 14

traveler's check cheque (*m.*) de viajero, 8

treasure tesoro

tree árbol (*m.*)

trick truco

triumph triunfar

trout trucha, 9

true verdad; **it's (not) ~** (no) es verdad, 11

truly de veras

trumpet trompeta, 2

try: I'm going to ~ it on. Voy a probármelo(la). 8

t-shirt camiseta, 8

Tuesday martes (*m.*), 3

tuna atún (*m.*), 9

turkey pavo, 6

turn cruzar (c), doblar, 6; viraje (*m.*); **~ in** entregar; **~ in your homework.** Entreguen la tarea. P; **~ off** apagar (gu), 2

TV (*see also* **television**): **~ guide** teleguía, 11; **~ series** teleserie (*f.*), 11; **~ viewer** televidente (*m., f.*), 11

twelve doce, P

twenty veinte, P

twenty-one veintiuno, P

twice dos veces, 9

two dos, P; **~ hundred** doscientos(as), 8; **~ million** dos millones, 8; **~ thousand** dos mil, 8

typical típico(a), 9

U

U. S. citizen estadounidense (*m., f.*), 2

ugly feo(a), 2

uncle tío, 5

underneath debajo de, 6

understand comprender, 3; entender (ie), 4

understanding comprensión (*f.*)

unique único(a)

unite unir, 9

united unido(a); **~ States** Estados Unidos

university universidad (*f.*), 6

unless a menos que, 12

unlikely dudoso(a), improbable, 11

unpleasant antipático(a), 2

untamed salvaje

until hasta (que), 12

Uruguayan uruguayo(a), 2

us nosotros(as), 8; **to/for ~** nos, 8

use usar, 2

useful útil

user usuario(a), 4

V

vaccinate poner (*irreg.*) una vacuna, 12

vaccination vacuna, 12

vacuum (*verb*) pasar la aspiradora, 10; **~ cleaner** aspiradora, 10

vain vanidoso(a)
valley valle (*m.*)
valuable valioso(a)
value valor (*m.*)
variety variedad (*f.*)
various varios(as)
VCR videocasetera, 4
vegetable vegetal (*m.*), 6
vegetarian vegetariano(a)
vehicle vehículo
Venetian blind persiana, 10
Venezuelan venezolano(a), 2
verb verbo, 3
very muy, 2
vest chaleco, 8
veterinarian veterinario(a), 5
videocamera videocámara, 4
videotape (*verb*) grabar, 11; (*noun*) video
viewpoint punto de vista
vinegar vinagre (*m.*), 9
violence violencia, 13
violin violín (*m.*), 2
visit friends visitar a amigos, 2
visitor visitante (*m., f.*)
vitamin vitamina, 12
voice voz (*f.*)
volcanic eruption erupción (*f.*) volcánica
volcano volcán (*m.*), 14
volleyball volibol (*m.*), 7
vote votar, 13

W

wait esperar, 11; **~ on** despachar
waiter camarero, 5
waiting: ~ list lista de espera, 14; **~ room** sala de espera, 12
waitress camarera, 5
wake up despertarse (ie), 5; **wake someone up** despertar (ie), 5
wake-up call servicio despertador, 14
walk caminar, 2; andar (*irreg.*), 8
walking a pie, 6
wall pared (*f.*), P
wallet cartera, 8
want desear, querer (*irreg.*), 10
war guerra, 13
warm caluroso(a)
warning aviso
wash lavar, 5; **~ one's hair** lavarse el pelo, 5; **~ oneself** lavarse, 5; **~ the dishes (the clothes)** lavar los platos (la ropa), 10
washer lavadora, 10

wastebasket basurero
watch reloj (*m.*), 8; **~ television** mirar televisión, 2
water agua (*f.*) (*but:* el agua); **fresh ~** agua dulce; **sparkling ~** agua mineral, 9; **~ skiing** esquí acuático, 7; **~ the plants** regar (ie) las plantas, 10
watercress berro
waterfall catarata
wave ola
we nosotros(as), 1
wealth riqueza
wealthy adinerado(a)
weather tiempo, 7; **It's nice/bad ~.** Hace buen/mal tiempo. 7
weave tejer
weaving tejido
web red (*f.*); **~ page** página web, 4
webcam cámara web, 4
website sitio web, 4
wedding boda
Wednesday miércoles (*m.*), 3
week semana, 3; **during the ~** entresemana, 3; **every ~** todas las semanas, 5; **last ~** semana pasada, 7
weekend fin (*m.*) de semana, 2
welcome bienvenido(a); **You're ~.** De nada. 1
well bien, 4; **(Not) Very ~.** (No) Muy bien. 1; **Quite ~.** Bastante bien. 1; (*for drawing water*) pozo
well-being bienestar (*m.*)
west oeste (*m.*), 14
what? ¿cuál(es)? ¿qué? 3; **~ are your symptoms?** ¿Qué síntomas tiene? 12; **~ day is today?** ¿Qué día es hoy? 3; **~ do you like to do?** ¿Qué te gusta hacer? 2; **What ~ does . . . mean?** ¿Qué significa…? P; **~ hurts?** ¿Qué le duele? 12; **~ is today's date?** ¿A qué fecha estamos? 3; **~ is your phone number?** ¿Cuál es tu/su número de teléfono? (*s. fam./form.*), 1; **~ time is it?** ¿Qué hora es? 3; **~'s he/she/it like?** ¿Cómo es? 2; **~'s the weather like?** ¿Qué tiempo hace? 7; **~'s your (e-mail) address?** ¿Cuál es tu/su dirección (electrónica)? (*s. fam./form.*), 1; **~'s your name?** ¿Cómo se llama (*s. form.*) / te llamas (*s. fam.*)? 1; **~ 's new?** ¿Qué hay de nuevo? 1

which? ¿qué? 3; **~ one(s)?** ¿cuál(es)? 3
wheat trigo
wheel rueda
when cuando, 12
when? ¿cuándo? 3; **~ is your birthday?** ¿Cuándo es tu cumpleaños? 1
where? ¿dónde? 3; **~ (to)?** ¿adónde?; **~ do you live?** ¿Dónde vives/vive? (*s. fam./form.*), 1; **~ does your . . . class meet?** ¿Dónde tienes la clase de… ? 3
while mientras
white blanco(a), 4
whitewater rafting: go ~ navegar en rápidos, 7
who? ¿quién(es)? 3
whose cuyo(a)(s); **~ are these?** ¿De quiénes son? 3; **~ is this?** ¿De quién es? 3
why? ¿por qué? 3
wife esposa, 5
wild salvaje
willing dispuesto(a)
win ganar
wind viento
window ventana, P; **~ seat** asiento de ventanilla, 14
windy: It's ~. Hace viento. 7
wine: red ~ vino tinto, 9; **white ~** vino blanco, 9
wineglass copa, 9
winter invierno, 7
wish desear, querer (*irreg.*), 10; esperanza
with con
without sin (que), 12
wolf lobo
woman mujer (*f.*), P
wonder maravilla
wood madera
wooden cart carreta
wool lana, 8
word-processing program programa (*m.*) de procesamiento de textos, 4
work trabajar, 2; **~ full-time** trabajar a tiempo completo, 13; **~ part-time** trabajar a tiempo parcial, 13
workday jornada laboral
worker trabajador(a), 5
world mundo; **~ Wide Web** red (*f.*) mundial, 4

worried   preocupado(a), 4
worry   preocuparse, 5
worse   peor, 8
wound   herida, 12
wrinkled   arrugado(a)
write   escribir, 3; **~ in your note-books.**   Escriban en sus cuadernos. P; **~ reports**   hacer (*irreg.*) informes, 13
written   escrito (*p.p. of* escríbir), 13

Y

year   año, 3; **every ~**   todos los años, 9; **last ~**   año pasado, 7
yellow   amarillo(a), 4

yes   sí, 1
yesterday   ayer, 3
yogurt   yogur (*m.*), 6
you   vosotros(as) (*fam. pl.*), tú (*fam. s.*), usted (Ud.) (*form. s.*), ustedes (Uds.) (*fam. or form. pl.*), 1; ti (*fam. s.*), Ud(s). (*form.*), 8; **to/for ~**   os (*fam. pl.*), te (*fam. s.*), le (*form. s.*), les (*form, pl.*), 8; **with ~**   contigo (*fam.*), 8
young   joven, 2
younger   menor, 8
your   (*adj.*) tu (*fam.*), su (*s. form. pl.*), vuestro(a) (*fam.*), 3; suyo(a) (*form. s., pl.*), tuyo(a) (*fam.*), 10

yours   (*pron.*) vuestro(a) (*fam. pl.*), suyo(a) (*form. s., pl.*), tuyo(a) (*fam. s.*), 10
youth   juventud (*f.*)

Z

zero   cero, P

INDEX

The authors and editors wish to thank the following persons and publishers for permission to include the works or excerpts mentioned.

Text

Chapter 1:
p. 25: From Almanaque Mundial 2000, p. L-9. Copyright © by Editorial Televisa.

Chapter 3:
p. 91: Adapted from, "Escuela Plena y bomba Rafael Cepeda," from Diálogo, Marzo 2000, Año 13, Num. 127, pg. 37.

Chapter 4:
p. 108: From Newsweek en Español, January 12, 2000, pg. 9. Reprinted with permission.

Chapter 5:
p. 161: Reprinted by permission of the Organization of American States.

Chapter 6:
p. 194: From El Universal online.

Chapter 7:
p. 227: From Aboard, In-Flight, January/February 1998, pp. 52–60. Reprinted with permission.

Chapter 8:
p. 262: Adapted from "El jean impone su encanto," from El Comercial, Familia Magazine, Numero 643, February 8 1998, Ano XII, pg. 27.

Chapter 9:
p. 272: From www.bolivian.com;
p. 292: Reprinted with permission from Tierra Lejana, from the column by Hernán Maldonado.

Chapter 10:
p. 310: Reprinted with permission of the publisher, Children's Book Press, San Francisco, CA, www.childrensbookpress.org. Poem copyright © 1997 by Francisco X. Alarcon. From the book, *Laughing Tomatoes and Other Spring Poems*; p. 329: *Dos Canciones de Amor Para El Otoño, I and II*, by José Coronel Urtecho. Reprinted with permission.

Chapter 13:
p. 417: Adapted from www.diariolarepublica.com/foro/netiquettes.html.

Chapter 14:
p. 447: © 1925 by Maria Kodama, reprinted with the permission of The Wylie Agency, Inc.

Photos, realia, and cartoons

PHOTOS:

Chapter 1:
p. 6, Royalty Free;
p. 16, Robert Frerck/Odyssey/Chicago.

Chapter 2:
p. 36, © Corbis/David Stoecklein;
p. 45, Courtesy of Isabel Valdés;
p. 60 left, © Schwartz Shaul/Sigma/Corbis;
p. 60 middle, © Ted Strenshinsky/Corbis;
p. 60 right, © Savino Tony/Corbis;
p. 63, © People en español, mayo de 1999 p. 114;
p. 63 top left, Luz Montero;
p. 63 top middle, Allsport/Getty;
p. 63 top right, Courtesy of Chef Pepin;
p. 63 bottom left, Brian Smith/Outline/Corbis;
p. 63 bottom right, Univision;
p. 65, © Christies Images/Corbis.

Chapter 3:
p. 68, Ulrike Welsch;
p. 76, Beryl Goldberg;
p. 79, Courtesy of Maria Carreira;
p. 92 right, © Daniel Laine/Corbis;
p. 92 left, © Tony Arruza/Corbis;
p. 93, © Tony Bean/Corbis;
p. 95, Dialogo/Fotos, Ricardo Alcaraz.

Chapter 4:
p. 100 top, © Jose Fusta Raza/Corbis;
p. 100 bottom, DRAWING Courtesy of Frank O'Gehry;
p. 111, Courtesy of Oxford University Press;
p. 127, Foto 1/© Jose Fusta Raza/Corbis, Foto 2/© Michael Busselle/Corbis, Foto 3/Robert Frerck/Odyssey/Chicago, Foto 4/Art Resource New York/Scala.

Chapter 5:
p. 134, Corey Langley;
p. 145, Graciela Kenig;
p. 158, Jim Whitmers;
p. 159 top, Suzanne Murphy;
p. 159 middle, Photo Researchers;
p. 159 bottom, AP/Wide World Photos;
p. 161, Byron Sletto.

Chapter 6:
p. 166, Robert Fried;
p. 176, Courtesy of Anna A. Álvarez;
p. 192, Foto 1/© Danny Lehman/Corbis; Foto 2/© Kevin Schafer/Corbis; Foto 3/© Natalie Forbes/Corbis; Foto 4/

illustration), 273, 291, 301, 303, 304 (all), 305 (top), 333 (all), 364 (all), 365, 369 (all), 396, 424 (all), 425 (all), 427.

Rick Morgan: pages 4 (top), 14, 64, 89, 137, 204, 212 (bottom), 246, 256, 334 (all), 335 (all), 337 (all).

Rossi Illustration & Design: pages 7, 29, 32, 37 (all), 69, 71 (all), 97, 101, 103, 104, 135 (both), 143 (bottom), 167 (all), 181 (all), 199, 207 (all), 212 (top), 223, 224, 225, 233 (all), 267 (all), 269 (El Menú box), 272 (Picadillo box), 279, 299, 324, 363, 383 (all), 384 (all), 385, 393 (all), 398 (all), 399 (all), 417, 418, 419, 423, 443.